Ella Shohat is Professor of Cultural Studies at New York University. Her books include *Taboo Memories, Diasporic Voices, Talking Visions*, and with Robert Stam *Unthinking Eurocentrism* and *Flagging Patriotism: Crises of Narcissism and Anti-Americanism*.

LIBRARY OF MODERN MIDDLE EAST STUDIES

Series ISBN: 978 1 84885 243 3

See www.ibtauris.com/LMMES for a full list of titles

Israeli Cinema

East/West and the Politics of Representation

Ella Shohat

I.B. TAURIS

LONDON · NEW YORK

Published in 2010 by I.B.Tauris & Co Ltd
6 Salem Road, London W2 4BU
175 Fifth Avenue, New York NY 10010
www.ibtauris.com

First printed in 1989 by University of Texas Press

Library of Modern Middle East Studies: 78

ISBN: 978 1 84511 312 4 (hb)
      978 1 84511 313 1 (pb)

A full CIP record for this book is available from the British Library
A full CIP record is available from the Library of Congress

Library of Congress Catalog Card Number: available

Contents

Acknowledgments

I thank the following journals for granting me permission to use previously published material: *Cineaste* for "The Return of the Repressed: The 'Palestinian Wave' in Recent Israeli Cinema" and "*Ricochets*" and *Film Quarterly* for "*Drifting.*" I also thank the following institutions and persons for lending me stills: Israel Film Archive; G"G (Golan-Globus); Israeli Film Institute; Nachshon Films; Museum of Modern Art/Film Stills Archive; Film Ventures International; IsraFest Foundation; InterPictures; Forum Film; Nathan Axelrod; Yossef Shiloach; Baruch Dienar, Yerach Gover; and Yehuda Ne'eman. I also thank the following institutions and persons for making my research on Israeli cinema possible—Jerusalem Film Center: Israel Film Archive/Jerusalem Cinematheque, its president, Lia Van Leer, for her encouragement and generosity which made possible this "voyage" into the history of Israeli cinema, and its workers, particularly Ilan de Fris, Shiba Skirball, Emanuel Chouraqi, and Deborah Seagal; the Israeli Film Institute, especially Dani Vert; the Film Division of the Histadrut, especially Arye Menahem; the Cinema Studies Department at New York University for its support in the form of scholarships; ISEF for the dissertation fellowships; and Nathan Axelrod, Baruch-Dienar, and Shimon Povsner for the interviews on the early days of filmmaking in Palestine/Israel.

I am deeply grateful to my colleagues and friends; to Robert Stam for his unfailing support and sincere enthusiasm for this project, which has benefited immensely from his careful and provocative reading, his methodological suggestions, and his superb sense of style as well as from his interdisciplinary and cross-cultural awareness; to Jay Leyda for his warm encouragement and extreme care in reading and commenting on the chapters, as well as for his invaluable commitment to young scholars and his contribution to the field of cinema studies, in which his extraordinary modesty and generosity will be long remembered by many; to William Simon for his dedicated teaching and concern for his students; to Ismail Xavier for his insightful comments; to Roberta Strauss Feuerlicht for her solidarity; to Robert Sklar for the many supportive gestures; to Richard Porton for his attentive reading of the manuscript and his stylistic suggestions, for the intellectually stimulating discussions, and for the warm concern he has always shown; to Ivone Margulies for her support, affection, and everyday generosities over the years; and to Lynne Jackson for her care and devotion. I would like to express my deep appreciation as well to Richard Peña, Susan Ryan, Yerach Gover, Bruce Robbins, Catherine Benamou, João Luiz Vieira, Luiz Antonio Coelho, Karen Backstein, William Boddy, Elia Suleiman, Carmel Eitan, Ido Zuckerman, Ayse Franco, Joel Kanoff, Randal Johnson, Amiel Alcalay, Patricia Erens, Annette Michelson, and Margaret Pennar, whose devotion for promoting Middle-Eastern culture will always be missed. And in Israel I thank Renen Schorr (Beit Tzvi Film School), Gabriel Ben-Simhon, Moshe Zimmerman, Yehuda Ne'eman, Nahman Ingber, Arnon Zuckerman, Ronnie Serr (Film Department, Tel Aviv University), and Yeshayahu Nir (Communication Institute, Hebrew University). Finally, I extend my gratitude to Carole Pipolo, who has been most helpful in the final stage of this work.

Date of Publication 1989

Acknowledgments for the New Edition

Revisiting the media and cultural practices in-and-around Israel and Palestine is in part an answer to the inquisitive readers, colleagues and students, who have expressed their desire, over the years, to see *Israeli Cinema: East/West and the Politics of Representation* republished and updated with a new postscript. It was Sheila Whitaker of I.B.Tauris, however, who initiated this new edition project. I truly appreciate her invitation, just as I value the efforts on behalf of the republication of the I.B.Tauris team, especially Philippa Brewster, Jayne Ansell, and Manish Sharma. I thank the filmmakers Michel Khleifi and Eyal Sivan, as well as Armelle Laborie at Momento-production for giving permission to use the still image from *Route 181* that appears on the cover. I am indebted to Ori Kleiner who was instrumental in designing the cover. The process of writing the postscript was closely correlated with my teaching of various seminars at New York University, notably "Imaging Palestine & Israel: Issues in the Politics of Representation," 'Representing the Middle East: Issues in the Politics of Culture,' "Performing Post/Colonial Memory," "The Media of Displacement: Postcolonial Culture," and "Arab-Jew and the Writing of Memory." I thank my students for making the revisiting process inspiring and meaningful. I especially would like to acknowledge TSOA Dean Mary Schmidt Campbell, Randy Martin, Anita Dwyer, and Emily Brown for their invaluable support. Finally, I am deeply grateful for the indispensable help and vital input at various stages of this project to: Jennifer Kelly, Benjamin Min Han, Richard Porton, Yigal Nizri, Shaista Husain, Yaron Shemer, Tikva Levi, Yvette Raby, Ivone Margulies, Evelyn Alsultany, and Yerach & Raquel Gover. And, as always, Robert Stam was closely engaged with the project. I thank him for his immense generosity.

Introduction

A veritable palimpsest of historical influences, Israel stands at the point of convergence of multiple cultures, languages, traditions, and political tendencies. Israeli
cinema, as the mediated expression of this multiplicity, is necessarily marked by
the struggle of competing class and ethnic discourses, of conflicting ideological im-
pulses and political visions, most obviously by the conflict with the Arabs generally
and the Palestinians in particular, as well as by tensions between Oriental Sephardi
Jews and European-origin Ashkenazi Jews, between religious and secular, between
"left" and "right." Israeli society and Israeli cinema are above all characterized
by contradiction and ambivalence. Geographically set in the East, the dominant
Israeli imaginary constantly inclines toward the West. On a political level, Israel
is at the same time an emerging nation, the product of a liberation struggle (that
of the Jewish people and particularly that of European Jews) in some ways not
unlike that of Third World peoples against colonialism, *and* a constituted state
allied with the West against the East, a state whose very creation was premised on
the denial of the Orient and of the legitimacy of another liberation struggle, that
of the Palestinians.

My purpose in this book is to offer a coherent theoretical and critical account,
within an East/West and Third World/First World perspective, of the development
of Israeli cinema. I trace the broad movement of Israeli cinema, from the first filmmaking attempts in Palestine at the turn of the century, when the Lumières' and
Edison's cameramen shot "exotic" footage of the "Holy Land," to the first Jewish
film pioneers (Nathan Axelrod and Baruch Agadati) making documentaries and
newsreels starting in the twenties and thirties, through to the emergence of a truly
national cinema after the inauguration of the Jewish state in 1948. I privilege the
feature-film production of the last four decades, making only occasional excur-
sions into the area of documentaries, during the prestate period, when feature
filmmaking was virtually nonexistent. I do not deal, however, with later documentaries, such as the significant works of Edna Politi and Amos Gitai. Occasionally I
venture into the area of coproductions and foreign productions made in or about

Israel (*Exodus*, 1960) and even relevant films and genres from other national traditions. Although the approach is largely diachronic, I occasionally flash forward or backward to draw a parallel, follow a theme, or trace an overall trajectory.

The corpus of Israeli films is not vast; feature production has hovered around the ten-film-per-year level over the past decades. The films nonetheless display a wide gamut of cinematic approaches, ranging from the Hollywood-style ambitions and "production values" of Menahem Golan to the low-budget austerity of the "Kayitz" group (from the Hebrew initials for "Young Israeli Cinema"). In generic terms, the films cover a spectrum from what I call "heroic-nationalist" films centering on the struggle for statehood and survival, through the commercially successful but critically disdained "bourekas" films—sentimental comedies and melodramas—to the personal and intimist, and at times socially and politically conscious, films of the "Kayitz" movement. I refer, in one connection or another, to virtually all of the fiction features produced in Israel up to the present (1986).

In addition to delineating the historical contours of Israeli cinema, my discussion is oriented by the larger thematic issue of the political and cultural encounter of East and West. My analysis is indebted to anti-colonialist discourse generally (Frantz Fanon, Aimé Césaire, Albert Memmi), and specifically to Edward Said's indispensable contribution to that discourse, his geneaological critique of "Orientalism" as the discursive formation by which European culture was able to manage—and even produce—the Orient during the post-Enlightenment period.[1] The Orientalist attitude posits the Orient as a constellation of traits, assigning generalized values to real or imaginary differences, largely to the advantage of the West and the disadvantage of the East, so as to justify the former's privileges and aggressions.[2] Orientalism tends to maintain what Said calls a "flexible positional superiority," which puts the Westerner in a whole series of possible relations with the Oriental, but without the Westerner ever losing the relative upper hand. This book concerns the process by which one pole of the East/West dichotomy is produced and reproduced as rational, developed, superior, and human, and the other as aberrant, underdeveloped, and inferior—in this case as it affects Palestinians and Oriental Jews.

The East/West dichotomy, however, is in some ways overly schematic and misleading. My approach, therefore, hopefully transcends this binarism to demonstrate flexibility and an eye to cultural syncretism. It is all too easy to fall into the temptation of limiting one's conception of the East to all that is Muslim, Arab, and Third World. But the Jewish people themselves can be seen as the product of East/West syncretism. As an ethnos with roots in Palestine, speaking (in Israel) a Semitic language, and with a religious idiom intimately linked with the topography, the seasonal rhythms, and even the vegetation of the Near East, Jews should be the last to endow the word "East" with exclusively negative associations. In the case of that oxymoronic entity, the "Arab Jews," or "Sephardim," the balance shifts even further to the Eastern side of the dichotomy, for here we have a people historically and culturally rooted, in most cases for millennia, in the societies of the East. The paradox of secular Zionism is that it ended a Diaspora, during which all Jews presumably had their hearts in the East—a feeling encapsulated in the almost daily repetition of the ritual phrase "next year in Jerusalem"—only to found a state whose ideological and geopolitical orientation has been almost exclusively toward the West. The Arabs, for their part, are hardly unalloyed representatives of a pristine East untouched by Occidental influence. The so-called "world of the Orient" has for centuries itself been syncretic, aware of the West and partially molded by it.

This book concerns, in a sense, the political uses of representation, which operates according to specific tendencies, within historical, cultural, and sociopolitical contexts. And while all representations embody intentions and have real reverberations in the world, filmic representations, given their technological, institutional and collaborative mode of production, and their public, mass mode of consumption, are even more consequential and especially well suited to accomplishing larger social tasks. The very word *representation*, of course, has political as well as aesthetic connotations. The Palestinians have been denied the right to "self-representation." Since Zionism undertakes to speak for Palestine and the Palestinians, the Palestinians have been largely unable to represent themselves on the world stage. The same "blocking" of representation takes place, in a different way and by different means, with regard to the Oriental Jewish population within Israel. The Zionist denial of the Arab Muslim and Palestinian East has as its corollary the denial of the Jewish "Mizrahim" (the Eastern ones) who, like the Palestinians, but by more subtle and less obviously brutal mechanisms, have been stripped of the right of self-representation. Within Israel, and on the stage of world opinion, the hegemonic voice of Israel has almost invariably been that of the European Jews, the Ashkenazim, while the Palestinian as well as the Sephardi voice has been largely muffled or silenced.

Superimposed on the East/West problematic is a corollary problematic, interrelated but hardly identical, namely that of the relation between the "First" and the "Third" Worlds. I take a "Third World" approach in a strangely double sense: first, in terms of the analogies between the struggle for Jewish liberation and Third World struggles against colonialism—Jews formed Europe's internal "other," Tzvetan Todorov points out, long before the nations in Latin America, Africa, and Asia became its external "other"[3]—as well as certain Third World characteristics of Israel itself; second, in terms of the negative consequences of this form of Jewish liberation for specific Third World peoples. Although Israel is not a Third World country by any simple or conventional definition, it does have affinities and structural analogies to the Third World, analogies which often go unrecognized even, and perhaps especially, within Israel itself. In what senses, then, can Israel be seen as partaking in "Third Worldness?" First, in purely demographic terms, a majority of the Israeli population can be seen as Third World or at least as originating in the Third World. The Palestinians make up about 20 percent of the population, while the Sephardim, the majority of whom come, within very recent memory, from countries such as Morocco, Algeria, Tunisia, Egypt, Iraq, Iran, and India, countries generally regarded as forming part of the Third World, constitute another 50 percent of the population, thus giving a total of about 70 percent of the population as Third World or Third World–derived (almost 90 percent if one includes the West Bank and Gaza). European hegemony in Israel, in this sense, is the product of a distinct numerical minority within the country, a minority in whose interest it is to deny Israel's "Easternness" as well as its "Third-Worldness."

At the same time, despite Israel's official First World orientation, Israel itself, as an emerging nation in the post–Second World War period, as the product of a liberation struggle (whatever the consequences of that struggle for others), offers certain structural analogies with emerging Third World nations. The situation of cinema in Israel is comparable to that of countries such as Algeria, not only in terms of the challenge of developing *ex nihilo* a cinematic infrastructure and wresting control of the domestic market from foreign domination, but also in terms of the overall historical evolution of the films themselves, moving from a somewhat idealizing nation-building "mythic" cinema into a more diversified "normal" kind of industry. Yet Israeli filmmakers and critics almost invariably speak, and make films, as if the natural points of reference were to countries with long-developed infrastructures, such as France or the United States. They rarely refer to Third World films or directors, or to the intense debates—practical, theoretical, political, aesthetic—that have animated Third World film discourse. While Israeli filmmakers have often referred their work to such movements as the French New Wave, British "Free Cinema," Italian Neo-Realism, and even Eastern European cinema, they have failed to perceive the relevance of movements such as Cinema Novo in Brazil or of the various liberation cinemas in Chile and Argentina, or of the attempt, by Algeria and Cuba, to create a cinematic infrastructure in a remarkably short period of time. Discussions of such alternative cinemas might have enriched debate in a country such as Israel, characterized by minimal infrastructure and low-budget films, with pressing political problems and a Third World population. Third World debates linking production strategies, aesthetics, and politics within the search for a dealienating, non-Hollywood mode of filmic discourse have unfortunately had little or no resonance in Israel.

An awareness of Israel's problematic situation as a volatile amalgam of East/West and First World/Third World is essential to analysis of such questions as how the Arab-Israeli conflict has been represented in film and how that representation has evolved over time. The early films, such as *Pillar of Fire* (*Amud haEsh*, 1959) and *Hill 24 Doesn't Answer* (*Giv'a 24 Eina Ona*, 1955), embody an unproblematized nationalistic spirit, pitting heroic Israelis against dehumanized Arabs, while later films, such as *Hamsin* (1982) and *Fellow Travelers* (*Magash haKessef*, literally *The Silver Platter*, 1983) eschew Manicheism, instead depicting a complex struggle between recognizably human adversaries. At the same time, the unvarnished military heroics of the early films give way, in some of the later films, such as *The Paratroopers* (*Massa Alunkot*, literally *Journey of Stretchers*, 1977), *The Wooden Gun* (*Rove Huliot*, 1979), and *The Night Soldier* (*Hayal haLaila*, 1984), to a more nuanced and even demystificatory portrayal of some of the negative consequences of militarization.

Corollary questions concern the role of Israeli cinema in the resurrection of Hebrew as a living quotidian language and the ways it has dealt with the challenge of a multilingual society in which Hebrew, Arabic, Yiddish, Russian, and English have all had their historical role to play; the extent to which classical Biblical stories (the Exodus, Abraham and Isaac, David and Goliath) resonate in the filmic fictions; the impact of specifically Western traumas, particularly the nightmare of the Holocaust; and the question of whether in some sense Israeli cinema, although physically situated in the Middle East, has repressed its "Easternness" by cultivating the image of an idealized West.

Another key issue orienting my analysis is the question of the filmic representation of the Oriental Jews, the Sephardim, the majority of the Jewish population in Israel, and the link between their representation and that of the "other East" of the Palestinians. In some films, such as *A Thousand Little Kisses* (*Elef Neshikot Ktanot*, 1982), partially filmed in a south Tel Aviv Sephardi neighborhood, Oriental Jews form a kind of "structuring absence" due to their conspicuous, even unnatural exclusion from the image. Other films, such as *Sallah Shabbati* (1964), promote a sentimental integrationism by having their Sephardi "noble savage" protagonists marry their children to the fair-haired offspring of a nearby kibbutz. *Casablan* (1973), a decade later, coming in the wake of the Sephardi revolt, follows a similar scenario, with the difference that the protagonist this time is more aware of the socially imposed nature of his "inferiority."

The terms of debate here presented are unabashedly political. For, while it can be argued that all films are political—or, more accurately, have a political dimension—Israeli films are necessarily and intensely political, including, and perhaps even especially, those films which claim not to be. Politics is of the essence in any discussion of Israeli cinema, for a number of reasons. First, the foundation of Israel as a state, unlike that of most countries, was the result of the enactment of an explicit political ideology, Zionism, rather than the product of a kind of aleatory historical accretion over centuries. The debates which attended the foundation of the state reverberate within the biographical and historical memory of the filmmakers. While the original debates concerning the Magna Carta or the Declaration of Independence are a distant memory for most English people or Americans, debates concerning the nature of Zionism and the Jewish state are not only fresh in the collective Israeli memory but continue to the present day. Second, the existence of the State of Israel as a political entity is the result of a problematical and much-debated—to put it euphemistically—exercise of power.

Jewish national liberation, as Said puts it, took place "upon the ruins" of *another* national existence. This problematic has a linguistic dimension as well, manifested in a kind of "war of nomenclatures." The process of writing is afflicted by a kind of lexical hesitation, since the very terms we use—"Israel?" "Eretz Israel?" "Palestine?" "Occupied Palestine?"—already implicate us in questions of point of view and political perspective. The act of textual interpretation, furthermore, has itself a political dimension; it is more than an autonomous hermeneutic enterprise designed to reveal immanent meanings. My intention, therefore, is to be deconstructive. Rather than submit to the textual discourse, I hope to provoke a rupture with the text, by unveiling, where necessary, its mythical tendencies. I hope to expose the text's other face, to make its silences speak.

Although this book is partially concerned with the question of the "image" of the Palestinians and of Sephardim within Israeli cinema, I have tried to transcend in its methodology some of the pitfalls and inadequacies of the "positive image" school of film criticism, a method which undialectically focuses on the positive or negative valence of characters within fiction films. Many of the existing studies of racism and colonialism in the cinema have been marred by theoretical and methodological naïvete, since they have too often been simplistically mimetic, assuming a one-to-one relation between the film text and the pro-textual reality, forgetting that films are inevitably constructs, fabrications, representations. Such studies have tended to privilege social portraiture in the conventional sense—i.e., "depiction of milieu"—and plot and character while slighting the specifically cinematic dimensions of films.[4] The emphasis on "positive images," meanwhile, has blinded some analysts to the fact that "positive images," if they are ill-informed, condescending, or stereotypical, can be as pernicious as overtly degrading images, as can be seen in the cases of the "good Arab" and the "warm Sephardi." "Negative" images, meanwhile, can form part of a critical dialectical perspective in which a negative character, even when a representative of an oppressed group, becomes, in Walter Benjamin's words, a "stage on which the contradictions of the age are played out."[5] Filmic signification, in other words, cannot be reduced to questions of character and image, excluding the full dynamic of ideological and cinematic contradictions. My approach, therefore, stresses what is excluded by the image as well as what is included in it, again in an attempt to articulate the "gaps" of the text. I also pay attention to questions of casting in relation to the issue of self-representation, exploring the implications of the fact, for example, that Ashkenazi Jews have often played Sephardi roles, while Sephardim have often played Arab roles. Rather than overly preoccupy myself with the question of "realism," I stress instead all the "mediations" which intervene between film and actual social life— mediations having to do with production methods and possibilities, with genre and with cultural codes. I am concerned with the generic conventions underlying the films; the "bourekas" films, for example, are frankly comic and often emphasize the grotesque, while the "high-art" personal films are absorbed in a quite different system of conventions. Rather than assume the possibility of a perfectly adequate representation, of fidelity to an originary "real," I emphasize intertextual analogies, i.e., the correspondence between cinematic and extracinematic discursive formations.

This book is not a study of auteurism or of authorial intention. It is not my purpose to establish or promote a "pantheon" of noteworthy Israeli directors, candidates for a universal gallery of film prestige, or to distribute praise and blame, bestowing adjectives and honorifics. Rather, I am proposing a theorized analytical history of Israeli cinema. It is a history, first of all, in its concern with the diachronic dimension, with providing a historical overview not only of Israeli cinema as a body of texts, but also of the intersection of film with historical process in the larger sense. When appropriate, I perform close textual readings, drawing on the methodologies of both film and literary analysis, bringing to bear all the relevant theoretical discourses available, discourses which concern not only the nature of Judaism, Zionism, colonialism, and so forth, but also film theory, text theory, and discourse theory.

To be more specific, my approach is, first of all, _textual._ Rather than consider the films merely as historical reflection or social symptom, I attempt to deal with them as films, seeing film texts, following Christian Metz, as the product of the interweaving of specifically cinematic codes (lighting, editing, camera movement) with more widely shared artistic codes (narrative structure, character, genre and point-of-view conventions), together with broadly disseminated cultural and ideological codes (the question of "Jewish identity," the myth of the "Sabra," the definition of the "terrorist"). In my discussion of individual films, I characterize their genre conventions and their particular style of narration, drawing on conceptual categories developed by Erich Auerbach, Mikhail Bakhtin, Roland Barthes, Fredric Jameson, and Gérard Gnette, among others. A political analysis, I am convinced, must also address the specific instances through which the film speaks. Questions of image-scale and duration, for example, are inextricably linked to questions of social representation, to the respect, or lack of it, accorded characters or groups, and to the potential for audience sympathy, solidarity, and identification. Which characters, representing which gender, ethnic groups, or nationalities, are afforded close-ups, and which are relegated to the background? Does a character look and act, or merely appear, to be looked at and acted upon? With what character or group is the audience permitted intimacy? In all such questions, politics and cinematics, text and context are intimately linked.

My approach, second, is _intertextual;_ that is, it deals with the relation between the film texts and all the other texts (filmic and non-filmic) that have preceded or influenced them. In the case of Israeli cinema, the intertext embraces a concentric set of progressively more inclusive categories: (1) the immediate play of allusion and citation within Israeli cinema itself; (2) the influence of specific non-Israeli films; (3) the more diffuse stylistic impact of broader movements such as Italian neo-realism, the French New Wave, or the American action film; (4) the presence of non-filmic texts in the films themselves, in the form of source-plays and novels adapted for the screen, along with the textual resonances of contemporary practices in the other arts (in this sense, I am concerned with "translations" from medium to medium, with what Metz calls "semiotic interference between languages");[6] and finally, (5) the larger textual practices or "discursive formations" (Michel Foucault) of a culture, within which each single text is situated. I discuss, for example, the ways in which the basic "discursive formations" of Zionism are mediated by film texts, and how they evolve over time along what Foucault would call "vectors of determination." I am concerned, with "lateral" relations between modes of discourse, the ways in which films might echo, in however distant or mediated a fashion, the "already said" and "prior speakings" (Bakhtin) of journalists, politicians, theologians, and propagandists. I am attentive to the inter-animation and inter-fecundation of texts. From time to time I leave the discussion of specific text, therefore, in order to see it as part of a larger discursive formation, or as parallel to other texts (for example, journalistic texts) by which it is inflected or whose underlying logic or "structure of feeling" (Raymond Williams) it shares.

I might add, here, that a textual and discursive approach is especially appropriate to the cultural products of a people which has enjoyed a kind of privileged relation to the very idea of textuality, which has cultivated a mystique and even erotics of the text in its physicality (the touch of the *tefillin* on arm and forehead, the kissing of the *muzuzah*, and the dance around the text in Simchat Torah), whose history has been deeply imprinted by texts. The messianic verses of the Sephardi poet Edmond Jabès describe Judaism as preeminently a passion for writing. For the homeless Jew, Jabès argues, the Book is fatherland and home is Holy Writ. Jabès anticipates, in this sense, not only George Steiner's "textual homeland," but also the glorification of text and writing in the work of another Sephardi—Jacques Derrida. In his essay on Jabès, Derrida speaks of the exchange between the Jew and writing as a "pure and founding exchange": the Jew chooses Scripture (writing-Ecriture) and Scripture chooses the Jew.[7] The Israeli state, meanwhile, is inextricably linked to texts, first as the long-term product of a historical memory stimulated by Judaic texts (the Bible, Tanach, the written "oral" Torah [Torah shebeAlpe]), and second, as partially the contemporary product of a body of Zionist writing. In this sense many of the films to be discussed can be seen as Zionist texts, which not only literalize specific Zionist tropes (for example, "making the desert bloom") but also translate the Zionist "master narrative" (Jameson) into the specific modalities of the film medium.

Textual and intertextual analysis do not, however, exhaust a film's significations, and for this reason my approach is also *contextual.* Films are informed by their ambient cultures, shaped by history, and inflected by events. The barrier between text and context, between "inside" and "outside," is, in this sense, an artificial one, for in fact there is an easy flow of permeability between the two. The context itself has passed through what Jameson calls "prior textualization,"[8] while the text is permeated at every point by shaping contextual elements (the temporal evolution of technology and cinematic practices, the historical stage of the language spoken by the characters, and so forth). It is important to see Israeli cinema, therefore, within multiple contexts—historical, economic, political, cultural. It is here that this project becomes necessarily interdisciplinary, exploring, for example, the evolving role of state regulations and government-sponsored financial incentives in relation to the film industry and the imprint on the films of contemporaneous events.

As a kind of bridge between text and context, Lucien Goldmann's notion of "homologies" between narrative structure and historical moment,[9] a notion developed with greater subtlety and density by Fredric Jameson in *The Political Unconscious*, is useful to this study, enabling me to draw parallels between filmic microcosm and social macrocosm. The tendency of the personal films of the seventies and eighties to portray outsider protagonists suffering from a claustrophobic sense of isolation, for example, might be metaphorically read as mirroring not only the directors' (largely illusory) sense of marginality, but also the political sensibility of a country under siege and diplomatically shunned by much of the world. The frequent recourse to the imagistic leitmotif of the sea as finale in such films as *Peeping Toms* (*Metzitzim*, 1972), *The Wooden Gun*, and *Transit* (1980), similarly, might be understood as an evocation of a watery escape route to a more "sympathetic" West.

Another category crucial to the bridging of text and context is the contemporary concept of allegory as a fragmentary utterance which solicits hermeneutic completion or deciphering. Building on the work of Erich Auerbach, Angus Fletcher, Walter Benjamin, and Paul de Man, both Fredric Jameson and Ismail Xavier have applied this conception of allegory to Third World cultural productions. Fredric Jameson generalizes somewhat precipitously, in his essay "Third World Literature in the Era of Multinational Capitalism," that all Third World texts are "necessarily allegorical," in that even those texts invested with an apparently private or libidinal dynamic "project a political dimension in the form of national allegory: the story of the private individual destiny is always an allegory of the embattled situation of the public third-world culture and society."[10] Ismail Xavier, meanwhile, in his "Allegories of Underdevelopment," traces two kinds of allegory within recent Brazilian cinema: the teleological Marxist-inflected meliorist allegories of early Cinema Novo, where history is shown as the unfolding of a purposeful historical design, and the modernist self-deconstructing allegories of the Brazilian Underground, where the focus shifts from the figural signification of the march of history to the discourse itself as fragmentary, and where allegory is deployed as a privileged instance of language-consciousness in the context of the total absence of teleology.[11]

Although both Jameson's hasty generalization about the necessarily allegorical character of Third World fictions and Xavier's application of the category to specific instances require modification and adjustment for the case of Israeli cinema, the category itself remains germane to this discussion. Indeed, the history of Israeli cinema demonstrates a striking penchant for projecting "national allegories" in the Jamesonian sense. The "heroic-nationalist" films of the early period constitute didactic allegories, in which an explicit Zionist-Socialist intention guides the staging of "sensible images," exemplary characters, and typical events calculated to inspire dedication and commitment to the Zionist cause. The Zionist didactic allegories remain, however, on the level of conscious intention. And indeed the classical definition of allegory has always privileged intention as well as the complementary activities of an author who hides and hints and a reader who discovers and completes. But it is possible to detach allegory from any originary intentionality in order to discern implicit, unconscious, and even inadvertent allegories. Here, the allegory lies less in the intention than in the reading, and also inheres in the context from which the films emerge. The comic "bourekas" films, for example, can be seen as submerged allegories of ethnic tension and reconciliation, in which mixed couples microcosmically unite conflicting communities. The apparently apolitical films of the self-designated "personal cinema," similarly, can be read as projecting allegories of solitude and displacement, in which anguished personal destinies, inadvertently and perhaps despite the intentions of the authors, come to "figure" the displacement of a milieu and the solitude of the nation state as a whole.

I am concerned, finally, with the *spectator-in-the-text*. The filmic experience is inevitably inflected by the cultural and political awareness of the audience itself, constituted outside the text and traversed by social realities such as nationality, ethnicity, class, and gender. The ideological "word" of a film, to use Bakhtinian terminology, is oriented toward an addressee, a spectator in this case, existing in clear social relation to the speaker or framer of the text, in this case, the cinematic institution, the filmmakers. The spectator is always specific, not an abstract human being but a woman or a man, an Ashkenazi, a Sephardi, a Palestinian, someone with more or less power, on intimate terms with the world portrayed in the film or more distant. One must take into account, therefore, not only the audience to which the film, explicitly or implicitly, is addressed, but also the possibility of "aberrant readings," the way films may be read differently by different audiences, the way that the particular knowledge or experience of a particular sector of the audience—for example, the Sephardi population in Israel—can generate a counter-pressure to oppressive representations. I see a film's significations, then, as negotiable, an object of struggle and dispute.

The struggle over filmic signification also takes place in the pages of newspapers, film journals, and books. The effort to analyze and contextualize Israeli cinema has scarcely begun to be engaged. There is but one published monograph on Israeli cinema: Ora Gloria Jacob-Arzooni's *The Israeli Film: Social and Cultural Influences, 1912–1973*, originally written as a dissertation for the Speech Department at the University of Michigan in 1975 and subsequently published by Garland Press in 1983. While the book does offer some plot synopses along with some basic contextual information, it is, unfortunately, methodologically flawed, offering little in the way of specifically cinematic, narrative, or ideological analysis. A discourse "of the object" rather than "on the object," it reproduces the same myths as the films, without any sense of rupture or provocation. The book betrays, furthermore, a severe lack of knowledge of Israel's Sephardi community, which is described repeatedly as "exotic" and which is said to have arrived in Israel plagued by "almost unknown tropical diseases" and "virtually destitute."[12] The putative "tropical" origin of the Sephardim is a bit of fanciful geography, and the description of their lives as "destitute" gives a misleading impression about the material conditions which the Sephardim left behind. The North African Jews, we are told in surprisingly prejudicial language, were hardly "racially pure," and among them one finds "witchcraft and other superstitions far removed from any Judaic law."[13] While Palestinians scarcely appear in the Jacob-Arzooni book, Guy Hennebelle and Janine Euvrard's *Israel Palestine: Que pent le cinéma?*, a special issue of *L'Afrique Littéraire et Artistique* (Summer 1978), is, as its title suggests, an attempt to promote an Israel-Palestinian dialogue. The book consists of interviews with Jewish and Arab filmmakers and historians (Ram Levi, Edna Politi, Moshe Mizrahi, Yigal Niddam, Monique Nizard-Florack, Tawfik Saleh, Maxime Rodinson), dialogues (Amos Kenan and Rachid Hussein), and articles (Mahmoud Hussein, Muhammad Ben-Salama, Walid Chmyat, Amnon Kapeliouk, Aly Choubachy). In sum, *Israel Palestine: Que peut le cinéma?* is a useful collection which provides a wealth of impressions from an alternative perspective.

Apart from these longer studies, there are a few memoirs by participants in the Israeli film industry, only two of which directly concern the cinema, Margot Klausner's *The Dream Industry* (*Ta'asiyat haKhalomot*), which was published by the studio she headed, Herzliya, in 1974, and Yaacov Davidon's *Fated Love* (*Ahava meOnes*, 1983). Generally, however, the commentary on Israeli cinema has been largely in the hands of journalistic critics, or part-time writers who also work in the film industry. Yehuda Har'el was the first Israeli to attempt a survey article about Israeli cinema, in his 1956 book *Cinema from Its Beginning to the present* (*HaKolnoa miReshito veAd Yamenu*).[14] Nathan Gross, Arye Agmon, and Renen Schorr have written useful overview articles for Israeli journals and newspapers.[15] Otherwise, film criticism is limited largely to the workaday "reviews" of newspaper journalists. Occasionally I cite such "reviews" in order to deconstruct the underlying premises of their discourse, performing, in certain instances, a kind of metacritique of what Metz calls the "third industry," the "linguistic appendage" of the film industry proper, i.e., the critical apparatus which mediates the relations between film and public. Israeli journalistic criticism, like film criticism in much of the world, has tended to be impressionistic and evaluative, conceived in conceptual categories that have been largely superseded by contemporary theory. At its most sophisticated, for example, in the film journals *Kolnoa, Close-Up*, and *Sratim* (which were published intermittently), it has been largely auteurist, generally untouched by the subsequent theoretical currents—Marxist, semiotic, and psychoanalytic—which have rendered auteurism somewhat obsolescent. Israeli film critics, furthermore, have tended to see Israeli films through the distorting lenses of high-art nostalgia and ethnocentric prejudice, often condemning them in the name of an internalized Western "ideal ego." While many contemporary film analysts, such as Richard Dyer and Jane Feuer, have usefully applied the category of the "utopian" to explore the dense significations of "low" popular genres like the musical comedy, Israeli critics have facilely dismissed the popular "bourekas" films as vulgar and unworthy of critical consideration. But Israeli cinema, in my view, merits a contemporary, politically informed methodology, one adequate to its cultural range and ideological complexity.

1.

Beginnings in the Yishuv: Promised Land and Civilizing Mission

The portrayal of Palestine in the cinema begins virtually with cinema itself, dating back to 1896 when Louis and Auguste Lumière shot "exotic" footage—much as they did in other Third World countries such as Mexico, India, and Egypt. At the turn of the century, Thomas Edison's cameramen also filmed local scenes, especially in Jerusalem. While the Lumière brothers' *Train Station in Jerusalem* echoes their *L'Arrivé du train en gare de la Ciotat*, Edison's *To Dance in Jerusalem* (1902) recalls his earlier *Fatima's Dance*. With very few exceptions, such as Sidney Olcott's Christian Biblical epic *From the Manger to the Cross* (1912), production in the silent period was limited to travelogues, newsreels, and documentaries largely by foreigners. Palestine was particularly attractive to Western filmmakers for its mythical locales. The Lumière brothers' crews shot scenes from Palestine to be shown on European screens, and *From the Manger to the Cross* was not only the story of Christ, but the story of Christ re-created in the land of his birth.

As in other parts of the world, film exhibition in Palestine began even before movie theaters were built. It was the Italian Collara Salvatore who first screened a number of films in various cities. In 1900, in Jerusalem's Europa Hotel, among the first films to be exhibited was *The Diary of the Dreyfus Trial*, an account of the September 1899 anti-Semitic trial of the French-Jewish officer. The subsequent establishment of new movie theaters was tangentially related to the major film industry in the Middle East, the Egyptian. The first movie theater, the Oracle, whose clientele was composed of the diverse ethnic-religious communities of Palestine, was inaugurated by Egyptian Jews in Jerusalem in 1908. In Tel Aviv, meanwhile, the first Yishuv (Hebrew for "settlement," referring to the Zionist Jewish settlement in Palestine) official to recognize the economic and cultural values of cinema was Tel Aviv's first mayor, Meir Dizingoff. In 1913, he traveled to Alexandria to study its urban administration, paying special attention to the management of the movie theaters, knowledge that contributed to the establishment of the first Tel Aviv movie theater, Eden Cinema, which opened in 1914. The actor and movie theater pioneer Yaacov Davidon, similarly, learned aspects of film techniques in

Egyptian studios. Egypt was also the center of distributing international (largely European and American) films in the Middle East; and it was via Egypt that these films were exhibited in Palestine. Even before the famous Yerushalyeem Segal's Tel Aviv film translation laboratory opened, moreover, movie theater owners ordered Hebrew film translations from Cairo—the major translation center in the area, whose services were used even by India—from the translator Piorilo.

There were also certain historical intersections between Egypt and Palestine on the level of production. Forties producer Yona Friedman, who produced one of the earliest Israeli films, *Faithful City* (*Kirya Ne'emana*, 1952), gained invaluable experience through his film company in Egypt, a company which produced films in Arabic with Egypt's great stars and musicians such as Muhammad Abdul Wahab and Farid al-Atrash.[1] In Palestine itself, an Arab from Jaffa approached Nathan Axelrod in 1944 about filming a newsreel in Arabic, resulting in a short film about an orphanage which was distributed in the major Palestinian cities. Axelrod was then invited by an Arab from Jerusalem (on behalf of himself and his Egyptian partners) to direct a narrative film in Arabic entitled *Oumniyati* or *My Wish*. (Axelrod, who did not know Arabic, worked with an Armenian translator.) The script, which employed the typical plot of the social melodramas, accompanied by songs and dances then produced largely in Egypt, concerned wealthy parents who oppose their daughter's marriage to a poor man, while urging her to marry a rich man of their choice. At the film's happy ending, the poor man manages to earn enough money to be able to marry his beloved. The film touched on some "delicate" matters, since one scene, set along the HaYarkon River (Tel Aviv area), featured Palestinians singing "our beautiful country," while another has a character, playing an important public figure, attend an Arab nationalist conference. Shot between the end of 1945 and the beginning of 1947, the film was screened in several Arab countries but, given increasing Jewish-Arab tensions, never reached the screens of Palestine. Following the United Nations vote in favor of partition of Palestine, the producers, frightened by the bad publicity that might arise were it known that the film had been made by Zionists, took the negatives to Beirut.[2]

The attention given to the first screenings in the Europa Hotel, particularly to *The Diary of the Dreyfus Trial*, led one of the major Hebrew-language revivers, Eliezer Ben-Yehuda, to Hebraize "cinematograph" to *re'inoa* ("moving images"). This gesture was especially striking in a period when respectable Hebrew journalism and Zionist institutions tended to completely neglect the cinema since it "did not suit the spiritual world of the Eretz Israeli [Hebrew 'Land of Israel,' Jewish and Zionist designation for Palestine that suggests its Biblical root] Jew and his labor ideology"[3]—an elitist attitude that has characterized the Israeli cultural establishment up to the present day. While Europe and America published magazines devoted to the "seventh art," writers and art critics in Palestine ignored cinema, obliging movie theater owners to translate segments of articles from abroad, or, at times, to write their own "criticism" for purposes of promotion. The first significant cultural figure to review cinema was the writer Avigdor Hameiri in his 1927 article on Charlie Chaplin.[4] It is only in the late fifties, however, that one can speak of the beginning of a film criticism industry, largely through David Greenberg's magazine *Omanut haKolnoa* (*The Art of Cinema*) which was active during 1957–1963.

Already in 1908, the establishment of the Oracle movie theater provoked anger in the ultra-orthodox Jewish-Ashkenazi religious community in Jerusalem. Three Yeshiva men broke into the movie theater and interrupted the screening with curses (among the films shown was *The Dreyfus Case*).[5] In 1913 the newspaper *HaAhdut* (*The Unity*) reported, similarly, on religious posters expressing rage against the "cinematograph" (in this case that of the Rumanian Eugin Jorilesh) with its promiscuous mingling of women and men in the movie theaters. Censorious voices of both religious leaders and puritanical laymen were also raised against theater plays and shows.[6] (This attitude still prevails in ultra-orthodox religious circles, which now demonstrate against Sabbath evening screenings.) Resentments of a different nature were voiced as well. Although cinema was considered a vulgar entertainment, it was nevertheless used by some Jews for charitable purposes. While the Jerusalem newspaper *HaOr* (*The Light*) praised such aid for the needy, the Jaffa newspaper *HaPoel haTzair* (*The Young Worker*) criticized this unworker-like habit of posting daily ads for "cinematographic shows for the benefit of the poor, sick, and helpless family, *hakhnasat kala* [dowry collected for a poor bride] and *pidion shvuyim* [redemption of prisoners; the terms used are those of religious Jewish duty] and in this way public charity is being utilized without any control or supervision."[7]

Much as in Europe and the United States, the distribution of sound films, furthermore, antagonized specific movie theater workers—the musicians. To their economically based resentment, there were added other more patriotic anxieties related to the putative negative effects talking cinema might have, for example, on the evolving Hebrew language:

> The growing importance of [sound] cinema endangers our independent, spiritual life-building in Eretz Israel; willy-nilly it infiltrates; foreign culture silences the Hebrew language, loudly proclaims visions and spectacles not our own. This diffusing poison might turn the hearts of the young generation from its people and culture, not to mention the amounts of money transferred to foreigners.[8]

The first sound film to be exhibited in Palestine, at the end of 1929, was *Sonny Boy* (1929)—which arrived even before *The Jazz Singer* (1927)—accompanied by a new lexical contribution to the Hebrew language, *kolnoa* ("moving sound"), suggested by the writer Yehuda Karni.

The origins and evolution of filmmaking in the Yishuv, meanwhile, closely paralleled the evolution of Zionist activity in Palestine, and on one level constituted an extension of that activity, thus establishing a basically harmonious interaction between film pioneers and Zionist pioneers. Moshe (Murray) Rosenberg, in all probability, authored the first Zionist film in Palestine, a short (twenty minutes) entitled *The First Film of Palestine* (*HaSeret haRishon shel Palestina*, 1911), which largely concentrates on Jewish locales and Zionist activities, and which was screened at the tenth Zionist Congress in Basel. In 1912, Akiva Arye Weiss, one of the founders of Tel Aviv, shot a film about Eretz Israel, subsequently distributed by the Jewish National Fund.[9] Later filmmakers such as Yaacov Ben-Dov, Nathan Axelrod, and Baruch Agadati filmically represented Jewish progress in Palestine from a Zionist perspective—Axelrod, for example, claimed to see himself first as a Zionist and only then as a cinematographer.[10] Zionist organizations, furthermore, formed a major financial source for such productions. Various Zionist institutions such as the Jewish National Fund (Keren Kayemet leIsrael), Jewish Agency (HaSokhnut haYehudit), United Jewish Appeal (Keren haYesod), and the General Federation of Laborers (Histadrut haOvdim haKlalit) were commissioning film production aimed not only at the local public, but also, and in fact primarily, abroad. At the same time, the financial problems faced by the first (Zionist) filmmakers engendered a dependency on Zionist institutions, trapping the filmmakers within the propaganda apparatus. As a consequence, very few narrative features were produced until the early sixties, while documentary practice in Palestine became virtually a synonym for Zionist propaganda films, some of which promoted specific enterprises and institutions.

Soon after his arrival from the Soviet Union in 1926, the foremost film pioneer, Nathan Axelrod, for example, was obliged to set aside his plans for narrative films, since he realized that it was impossible for the small Jewish Yishuv (with a population of around 200,000) to cover the expense of even low-budget films. Leaving the Soviet Union around the time when Sergei Eisenstein began shooting *Potemkin* (1925) and Vsevolod Pudovkin was working on *Mother* (1926), Axelrod arrived hoping to work in the Yishuv film industry but soon discovered that he would have to build that industry singlehandedly. Reportedly, Yaacov Ben-Dov, the only photo/cinematographer before Axelrod and Agadati, laughed at the newcomer's (Axelrod's) idea of a film industry, arguing that only in a country with a minimum of 40 million people would it be possible to build a film industry: "I shoot according to the invitations of the Jewish National Fund and make a living from my photo shop," Ben-Dov said, and added, "Cinema in Palestine is a fata morgana."[11] (In 1919 Ben-Dov had himself established a film company, Menorah, that survived only a year.)[12] A year and a half later Axelrod nevertheless made the first Eretz Israeli attempt at a narrative film, *The Pioneer* (*HeHalutz*, 1927), produced by that rare phenomenon, a film production cooperative, which included Axelrod, Yerushalayeem Segal, and the poet Alexander Penn. The film, never completed due to financial difficulties, was intended to deal with the dilemmas and ordeals of a Jewish pioneer. Its failure stands as an ironic testimony to the sufferings of the film pioneers themselves.

Nathan Axelrod in 1980 and photographed as a young filmmaker in Palestine, 1930.

Following this failure, Axelrod and some members of the cooperative established the Moledet (Homeland) company, which in its five years of existence produced a number of promotional films (for example, for the wine of Rishon leZion and Zikhron Yaacov in which a dozen bottles dance the hora à la Méliès), documentaries (e.g., concerning the establishment of the town Tel Mond), and the first Eretz Israeli newsreel ("Yoman Moledet"). The films of Moledet constituted a significant change in relation to earlier films produced in the Yishuv, since the Moledet projects were based on collective effort rather than individual initiative. It was primarily Axelrod, however, who built a celebratedly primitive laboratory in Tel Aviv. Due to lack of electricity, the filmmakers were forced to take creative advantage of sunlight focused with the help of a complicated series of mirrors and lenses.

Between 1931 and 1934 another major film pioneer, the artist and dancer Baruch Agadati, produced the second newsreel, "Yoman Aga," which appeared intermittently as well. In 1935 he produced the first sound documentary, *This is the Land* (*Zot Hi haAretz*), partially consisting of segments shot for newsreels, presenting early Zionist history in Palestine. Axelrod, meanwhile, expanded his operations after the success of his narrative *Oded the Wanderer* (*Oded haNoded*, 1933) and established Carmel Film Company, which began producing a weekly newsreel, "Yoman Carmel," in competition with Aga. From the fifties to the late sixties (when Israeli Television was established), two newsreels were appearing regularly—largely financed by advertisements—"Yoman Carmel-Herzliya" and "Hadshot Geva" "Geva News.") (In 1958 Carmel was incorporated into Herzliya Studios, which had been established in 1949 by Margot Klausner. Geva Studio was coestablished around the same time by Yitzhak Agadati, Baruch's brother, and Mordechai Navon.) The central role of news in Israeli daily life, then, already formed part of early Yishuv society, providing the basis for a far more promising industry than did local feature films.

While newsreels were largely financed by advertisements, the overwhelming majority of documentaries and docu-dramas were supported by Zionist organizations. These films were received enthusiastically abroad, especially in Jewish circles. Yaacov Davidon, for example, testifies in his memoirs that "tears of happiness gleamed in the eyes of Jewish audiences, thirsty for redemption," when they saw *The Life of the Jews in Eretz Israel* (*Hayei haYehudim beEretz Israel*, 1911) in Russia.[13] The popularity of the Zionist films—in particular, the earlier ones—seemed to derive not only from sympathy for the Zionist settlers in Palestine but also from the need to see images of the mythical holy land.

In the Arab World, particularly in Egypt where some of the documentaries and narrative films (e.g., Axelrod's *In the Times of,* or *VaYehi biYmay*, 1932, and *Oded the Wanderer*) were shown, meanwhile, there were angry reactions. Abu-el-Hassan, the Cairo correspondent for *Palestine* newspaper (published in Jaffa), sent several articles to the paper criticizing the "Zionist propaganda" in these films and demanded that the Arab Workers' Association respond with films of a similar nature:

> The Association must commission a cinematographic crew from Europe
> in order to film the sights of the country. And first of all, the two holy
> mosques, all of the Muslim ruins and buildings, and the sights of the cities
> of Palestine—and these images should be exhibited everywhere, especially in
> Egypt.[14]

Abu-el-Hassan's anger at the films—some of which, such as *The Life of the Jews in Eretz Israel*, were being successfully screened in the movie theaters—derived mainly from their ignoring the Arab majority population, a practice which gave the distinct impression that the country was solely Jewish.

British censor-bureaucrats based in Jerusalem, meanwhile, at times banned the Zionist films in the name of British colonial interests. An amateur cinematographer named Green, who arrived as an American tourist in the early twenties and shot throughout Palestine a film about the country's development, was the first to experience British censorship. Before each segment Green hoped to provide shots of the same location before the Jews had arrived, but since he could not find the requisite footage, he shot in nearby places which he assumed to resemble the sites prior to the establishment of the Jewish town. The British Board of Censorship banned the film out of fear that it would incite Arabs to riot. The film was nevertheless shown in Haifa, after its title had been changed from *The New Eretz*

A 1933 ad in Arabic for *Tel Avi Carnival* and *Oded the Wanderer* in the American Cosmograph Cinema, Cairo, defining the latter as a Palestinian film from Studio Palestine with HaBima actors.

1933 ad in Hebrew for *Oded the Wanderer* in Eden Cinema, Tel Aviv.

Israel (*Eretz Israel haHadasha*) to *The Legacy* (*HaYerusha*) and it had been provided with a new opening sequence. The film was screened unopposed for a week. According to Yaacov Davidon, Jewish spectators were enthusiastic about the film, even applauding certain segments, while the regular crowd of Arab movie-goers (Davidon's partner was an Arab too) voiced no objection to the film.[15] Although risking screening in relatively distant Haifa, Green did not show the film in Tel Aviv or Jerusalem, the seat of the censorship board. He left the country, screening the film successfully in the United States under its original title.

British censorship was also directed against the Hebrew newsreels which fostered the national interests of the Yishuv and therefore at times provoked Mandate sanctions. During World War II, however, the British Mandate employed the services of the local Yishuv filmmakers. Nathan Axelrod, for example, was invited by the Public Information Office to produce educational films in Arabic in order to

The British Censorship Board approving *Pai News*, 1933.

teach *fellahin* (peasants) new agricultural systems. One of the six films, according to Axelrod himself, concerned chicken-breeding, and featured kibbutzniks wearing the Arab headdress (*kaffiya*) in order to maintain a façade of Arab identity.[16]

Silent and sound documentaries became virtual prototypes for the later narrative films, at times made by the same filmmakers such as Nathan Axelrod and Helmer Lersky, and embracing similar world views, depicting Zionist themes in an idealized manner. The titles of the many propaganda films and documentaries, as well as those of the few narrative films, reflect the concerns, preoccupations, and Zionist point of view of the Yishuv. The very titles of the films, such as Axelrod's *The Pioneer*, Alexander Ford's *Sabra* (*Tzabar*, 1933), and Lersky's *Earth* (*Adama*, 1947), as well as of documentaries such as Ben-Dov's *Eretz Israel Awakening* (*Eretz Israel haMitoreret*, 1923) and *A Decade of Work and Building* (*Eser Shnot Avoda uVinian*, 1927) and Leo Herman's *New Life* (*Hayim Hadashim*, 1934), point to the collective enthusiasm of a national renaissance in the "*Altneuland*" (German for "Old-New Country," the original title of Theodor Herzl's major Zionist text).

Hoping to attract potential pioneers from the European Diaspora, as well as financial and political support, the documentaries and propaganda films, along with capturing landscapes and events, also emphasized the pioneers' achievements and the rapid pace of the country's development. Recurrent images of pioneers working the land, paving roads, and building towns show the Yishuv as symbolically "making the desert bloom" in agricultural, technological, and cultural terms. (In the post–World War II period and after the establishment of the state, the films acquired new themes: the underground, the rescue of refugees, the defense of the state, and mass immigration—the *kibbutz galuiot*, "ingathering of the exiles.") Written by William Topkis (an American Zionist leader then living in Palestine and doing pioneering work to promote Jewish tourism) and filmed by Ben-Dov, *Eretz Israel Awakening*, for example, was made at the invitation of the Jewish National Fund. The basic storyline of the documentary concerns a wealthy American Jewish cotton broker, Mr. Bloomberg, arriving in Jaffa for a twenty-four-hour stopover. Convinced by a guide that there is much to see in this "reborn land," he eventually spends a month touring the entire country. At the end of the film, after finding a cousin in Israel, he announces that his farewell will be a brief one since he is going only to wind up his business and then return to his "fathers' land."

A Zionist travelogue, *Eretz Israel Awakening* shows several towns and kibbutzim as well as famous figures from the Yishuv and provides vivid evidence of the successful revival of the Hebrew language. This documentary's narrative pioneered the device of employing a Western foreign agent whose role it was to bridge the distance between the Western spectator and the Oriental "reality" on the screen. This penchant for focalization became, as we shall see later, a dominant feature of the Zionist *Bildungsroman* fiction films. A Zionist celebratory reading was added, furthermore, by a journalist at the premiere, Jehuda Magnes (later to become president of Hebrew University), who concluded his review by linking the July 4 screening to the date of Herzl's death: "The fact that the film was exhibited in Jerusalem on the fourth of July, anniversary of the death of the greatest modern Messiah that Jewry has known, is in itself a significant omen. For Herzl himself would have said 'this is no fable.'"[17] Translated into thirteen languages, *Eretz Israel Awakening* was distributed worldwide to become a seminal classic of Zionist propaganda films. And even after Israel was established, documentaries and docudramas, produced by Zionist organizations and shown noncommercially in Israel for "educational purposes," were largely distributed abroad by Jewish institutions, especially in the United States.

The mechanism of Zionist idealization in documentaries as well as fiction texts, then, was subordinated both to producers (the commissioning Zionist institutions) and to receivers (Zionist journalists and public). This dependency, even when not involving actual censorship, encouraged a kind of self-censorship and a public-relations approach to questions of filmic fact and fiction. The first attempt at narrative film, Axelrod's *The Pioneer*, for example, was accompanied by public pressure against showing any "negative elements" from the life of the Yishuv. Conceived in the spirit of early Zionism, *The Pioneer* was supposed to show the dilemmas and sufferings of the Zionist pioneer in Palestine. The initial filming took place on a Tel Aviv street; the actor playing the pioneer role was to cross the street and collapse due to famine. While passersby gathered out of curiosity (and disturbed the filming), the newspapers the next day published a sensational report about the "anti-Semites" who had staged horrible scenes showing pioneers dying from hunger in the streets of Tel Aviv in order to denounce the pioneering enterprise. The protests created difficulties for Axelrod and the film's cooperative in obtaining money during the course of the production, and the film was never finished. But the thrust of the film, ironically, as Axelrod himself testified, clearly exemplifies the predilections of mainstream Zionism:

> I saw myself first as a Zionist and only then as a cinematographer. My purpose as a Zionist, therefore, was to show the good side in building the country. For example, I often shot streets in Tel Aviv and in other places, and always I took a lengthy and tiring walk in order to look for an angle or camera position from which the streets would look prettier. I made an effort so that vacant lots, unfinished streets, garbage, and dirt would not be seen. I wanted everything to make a good impression.[18]

Axelrod even refused a "scoop" by not shooting when the *Altalena* ship belonging to the Etzel underground (the National Military Organization under Menahem Begin's leadership) was bombed in 1948 under the order of the new prime minister, David Ben-Gurion.

Preconceived ideas about Zionist reality in Palestine/Israel came to provide a master code for filmmaking practice, and films became a highly sensitive barometer to the slightest digression from the Zionist consensus. The pressures aimed at fiction films such as *The Pioneer* were also directed at the documentary/propaganda films and continued into the post-state era, at times reaching absurd lengths. Nathan Gross, then a producer-director for the Histadrut (General Federation of Labor) during the fifties, testified, for example, that he worked on the script of *Thirteenth Kilometer* (*HaKilometer haShlosha Asar*, 1953), which deals with the paving of the road to Sodom, before he went to see how it actually looked, and even included a scene of workers dancing the hora after a day of work—an image in accord with the mythical figure of the Zionist pioneer. Gross, however, learned that in fact

> . . . after a hard day of work, the laborer had neither the energy nor the desire to dance the hora! Maybe in those days, but not today, especially as the workers who worked at the 13th Kilometer were mostly Druse and several elderly [Sephardi] Yemenites. The Histadrut was a little disappointed, but accepted reality as it was. However, Yossef Bornstein [the Histadrut guide and supervisor who accompanied over fifty of the first Histadrut films] paid attention and objected to the "neorealist" scene that I had included in which the workers return exhausted and broken after a day of work in the blazing sun of Sodom,

flopping powerlessly onto the beds in the huts. The camera panned over the shoes of the resting workers, among which there was a badly torn pair . . . here began the argument. Yossef and his advisors demanded that the pair of shoes be taken out: "It is impossible to show a worker in Israel with torn shoes. What will the Goyim say? What will the Jewish donors in America say?—And anyhow, a worker in Israel does not go around in torn shoes" . . . [19]

The Zionist mission in cinema at times even affected the exhibition of foreign films. In 1932 Yaacov Davidon screened his own edited version of Hollywood's *The Bible*, which recycled several Biblical stories, ending with passages from the Psalms. (The Hollywood film was shot silent in 1920 but added sound explanations for the Biblical events.) Davidon edited out the passages from Psalms, replacing them with glorious images of contemporary Zionist settlers ploughing the land, planting trees, and building houses. (Davidon quite often "improved" foreign films for local audiences, at times grafting more "appropriate" shots from other films.) During the screening Davidon superimposed on the English narration his own extemporaneous narration—through the movie theater speakers—alternating between the Biblical commentaries in English and the Zionist gloss in Hebrew. After the King Solomon episode the Hebrew voice said: "And the people of Israel were exiled from their land . . . but the day of redemption is near, and the sons will return to the land," followed by a short film lauding Zionist progress in the Promised Land. The lyrics of a pioneer song were added, encouraging the spectators to sing along, enthusiastically applauding the first sounds of Hebrew in a movie theater. Hollywood's version of the Bible, then, was also made to reinforce Zionist teleology.

In the mode of Socialist-realist films, most of the Zionist-realist films fostered a process of idealization, whether through pure and heroic protagonists, or through dramatically rousing commentative music, or, in documentaries (and at times even in fiction films), through bombastically confident male voice-over narration. Both fiction features and documentaries resolutely "improved," as it were, the reality they had undertaken to represent through the simultaneous elision of negative and enhancement of positive images. Reminiscent of the Soviet films, in particular those of the thirties and forties, the Yishuv period and early Israeli films reflect a consistent subordination of complex representation to the demands of ideology and edification.

Russian/Soviet ideological as well as artistic orientation of the Hebrew Yishuv, reflected in early features such as *Oded the Wanderer* and *Sabra,* must be understood within the specific context of the predominance of Russian Jewish settlers (especially in the first two decades of the twentieth-century) who along with their natural cultural affinities to their country of birth were also inspired by Mother Russia, hoping for a transformation toward a new (Jewish) society. The affinity with the motherland, the place of origin, as well as the strong desire for a Socialist (national) renaissance, made Soviet films extremely popular in the Yishuv (even more than Hollywood films), a tendency both reinforced and paralleled by an affinity with Russian songs, literature, and theater.

The two film pioneers, Nathan Axelrod and Baruch Agadati, furthermore, had witnessed the enthusiasm of October. Agadati, in particular, made it a habit to return for vacations to Russia and in 1914, due to the war, was forced to stay there until after the outbreak of the revolution. He took dance classes with Titoni and saw Eisenstein's and Pudovkin's early films. Having become familiar with the Russian avant-garde, Agadati returned to Palestine, sponsoring modern dance performances, inflected by Isadora Duncan, to the sounds of Béla Bartók and Arnold Schoenberg. The repertoire of Hebrew theaters such as Khovevei haBama haIvrit, HaTeatron haIvri beEretz Israel, Teatron Eretz Israeli, HaOhel, and HaBima tended toward Russian (e.g., Chekhov, Leonid N. Andreyev) and (Jewish) Eastern European (Y. L. Peretz, Abraham Goldfaden) plays, which were culturally closer to the actors and the audience than Western European fare (and certainly more familiar than that of the contemporary Oriental world).

Oded the Wanderer's actors, Menahem Genessin (in the role of the tourist) and Shimon Finkel (playing Oded's father), were part of a group of actors from Palestine (most of whom were of Russian origin) who in 1923 went for advanced study to Berlin, where they remained in contact through the "White Russian" club with Russian immigrants such as the actor Gregori Khmara, and the writers Victor Schklovsky and Vladimir Nabokov. Genessin imported Constantin Stanislavsky's method from Russia and later opened a studio in Palestine where Moshe Horgel (who played Oded's teacher) became one of his most famous students. But it is especially with the HaBima Theater—Alexander Ford's *Sabra* is cast almost uniquely with HaBima actors and actresses—that Stanislavsky's school of thought took on a crucial role in the formation both of Hebrew theater and of the cinema, especially since until the mid-60s most film actors and actresses were recruited from the theater. HaBima Theater, which came to be the national theater of Israel, was founded in 1917 in Moscow by Nahum Tzemach at the height of revolutionary euphoria and was initially affiliated with Stanislavsky's Moscow Art Theater, with the Armenian Yevgeni Vakhtangov as its first director.

The Stanislavskian method of identificatory fusion of actor with character was here allied with loud and exalted speaking and expressionist decor, all linguistically mediated by a secularized modern version of the Hebrew language. The spoken Hebrew in *Sabra* and even the Hebrew intertitles of *Oded the Wanderer* display, as we shall see, great pathos and an elevated style, paralleling the theatrical elevated manner of the Stanislavsky-style acting of the HaBima Theater. But while the Stanislavsky Hebrew was still "*drevni yebrisky yazik*" (the ancient Hebrew language), for HaBima's young Jewish actors it was a token of the realization of Zionist salvation.[20] The early messianic plays in HaBima's repertoire, in other words, were perceived differently by the director, who envisioned universal salvation through

Socialism, and by the HaBima actors, who saw their theater as a symbol of the Hebrew/Jewish renaissance. The success of plays such as David Pinski's *Der Eybiker Yid* (*The Eternal Jew*), S. An-ski's *Der Dybbuk*, and H. Leivik's *Der Golem* only increased anti-Hebrew harassment by the establishment, but at the same time, Stanislavsky, Maxim Gorki, and Anatoly Lunasharsky (the first Soviet commissar of education) supported HaBima's struggle.

One HaBima student, Moshe Halevi, immigrated in 1925 to Palestine, where he established the HaOhel Theater. Using a revolutionary method, he searched throughout the country for talent to take part in his studio/theater; in this way *Oded the Wanderer*'s main actor was found. Halevi also attempted to establish HaOhel on foundations typical of artistic activity in the Soviet Union in the twenties, i.e., a theater by the workers and for the workers in which the HaOhel members held jobs during the day and rehearsed and performed in the evenings. This arrangement did not survive for long; the performers soon became professional actors who, in addition to Biblical materials also included workers' themes in their repertoire. After a tour in 1928, HaBima, for its part, decided to move to Palestine in 1931, thus inaugurating a major cultural locus within the Yishuv.

"Making the Desert Bloom:" The Production of Emptiness

Although sound films had already been in distribution for several years, the first feature-length narrative film of the Yishuv, *Oded the Wanderer*, was produced as a silent film with a small budget of 400 Liras. Because it was made in completely local, technically primitive conditions, its preparations and shooting required two years. It was based on the Tzvi Lieberman story of the same title, with a director credit to Hayeem Halachmi, and shot and edited by Nathan Axelrod. Axelrod claims that in fact he directed the film as well.[21] Since Halachmi came from theater, it is plausible to assume that he worked with the actors, while Axelrod directed the cinematography. *Oded the Wanderer* tells the story of a Sabra (native-born Jew), Oded (Shimon Povsner), who goes on a brief outing organized by his school. During the trip he records his impressions in a diary. As his mind wanders toward his written reflections, he loses touch with his classmates. His teacher (Moshe Horgel from HaMatate Theater), with the help of a tourist, Milson (Menahem Genessin of HaBima), Oded's father (Shimon Finkel of HaBima), and some of his classmates, searches for him and finally brings him back home, but only after releasing Milson from the Bedouins, who have kidnapped him.

Oded's attempts to find his way back, as well as the complementary efforts to find him, become the pretext for the display of the country's landscapes in a travelogue of Palestine which the filmmakers hoped might lead to institutional support. When the film was screened before the national institutions in hope of distribution by the Jewish National Fund, the Fund's representatives complained about the lack of inspirational imagery: "The film is a film indeed, but there is too much desolation . . . Where is the renewed and constructive Eretz Israel, where is the pioneering spirit, the blossoming orchards, the sprinklers."[22]

FEI (Film Eretz Israel), the company which produced *Oded the Wanderer*, then filmed the requested images, but the Jewish National Fund still chose not to distribute the film. The film was received enthusiastically by Jewish journalists and the audience, however, when it was shown for eight weeks to a packed house in Tel Aviv's Eden Cinema—a distinguished achievement considering the small Jewish population in Palestine. (Its success even stimulated the establishment of several ephemeral film companies.)

According to Hayeem Halachmi, the filmmakers contacted an Egyptian distributor for foreign distribution,[23] but after a few days and subsequent to payment for the prints, the Egyptian notified the filmmakers that he had lost the negative. Fortunately they had kept a work-print from which the Israeli Film Archive managed to reconstruct the film in 1963. (The actual work was done by Hayeem Halachmi's son, Yossef Halachmi.) The extant copy was in terrible shape, with sequences spliced incorrectly and some sequences missing. Other sequences not in the original, meanwhile, had been added over the years, when the film was shown by different organizations, in accord with specific political agendas. While in the original, for example, Nahalal (a village in the Jezreel Valley) farmers ploughed the land with horses, the Zionist institution preferred more "modern" images of tractors, and so the desired images of tractors were added, while other institutions requested other favored images, of cows and ships, for example, to show the development of the country—often without the least concern for plausibility or for the overall coherence of the film's plot.

Like documentaries of the same period, *Oded the Wanderer*—the first fiction feature to speak of Sabras and the Yishuv—also documents the country's landscapes. As Shimon Povsner, who played Oded, testifies, "There were trips to different places in the country, because the main purpose of the film was to show Eretz Israel and its people. The director made efforts to reveal the most beautiful corners, those that city people rarely have a chance to see."[24] *Oded the Wanderer* also gratifies the Diaspora Jewish desire to see and know both the old Biblical land and the modern Hebrew Yishuv. (The qualifier "Hebrew" in this period entered the Zionist lexicon as referring to the Jews in Palestine, thus implying a break with Diaspora Jewry, and indicating both a connection to the historical past in Eretz Israel and to the renewed nationality with the old/new language. "Hebrew man" is the predecessor of "Israeli.") In this sense, the film implies the continuity of an indissoluble Jewish bond with the land of Israel. The literalization of knowledge through a bodily connection to the land is conveyed first by the very theme of the film—the Hebrew school trip around Eretz Israel. Collective trips were a norm in Hebrew and later in Israeli schools, as well as in the various Zionist youth movements and in organizations such as the Association for the Protection of

The Sabra masters the land: *Oded the Wanderer*.

Nature. The desire to know the country, to master its topography, became virtually institutionalized in the educational system as an academic field, Yedi'at haAretz (Knowledge of the Country/Land) suggesting a broader and deeper unveiling of the country than that of mere surface geography.

The emphasis on images of the Land and Nature in the film are intrinsic to Oded's and his classmates' "Sabraness" and are intended as an antithesis to two thousand years of lack of knowledge of the land of Israel. The land here forms the contrary of "Egyptian" bondage, just as free farming constitutes the opposite of slave labor. Oded—the name is typically Sabra—wanders in the open space of the land of the Fathers (Abraham, Isaac, and Jacob), unlike the Wandering Jew of the narrow shtetl of the Diaspora. Two thousand years of living a vicarious textual geography through the scriptural nostalgia for the Promised Land and of being forced into non-agricultural work is transformed by the Zionist into a concrete touching of a palpable land. The territorialist tendency advances in its religious formulation the idea of the Land as quasi-magical transformer and guarantor of blessings. Already the titles literalize this process of concretization. Tzvi Goldyn's drawings in the background of the credits show the title, *Oded the Wanderer* moving from the left to the right side of the screen over the image of a dry land, while "FEI production" appears against the background of a drawing of a gazelle, plants, and a cluster of grapes—images associated with the Biblical land (clusters of grapes—one of the seven fruits a Jew has to bless as the fruits of Eretz Israel—tend to ornament Jewish texts such as the Passover Haggadah). *Oded the Wanderer* externalizes the Zionist desire for a physical Eretz Israel and turns literal what was before, in George Steiner's phrase, a purely "textual homeland."

Oded the Wanderer explicitly fuses history with geography. The teacher explains to the children during the trip, for example, that "Until just a few years ago the Valley of Jezreel was desolate and neglected until your fathers came and with their work and energy, revived the valley and turned it into a source of life and work." The images documenting agricultural work following his speech provide visual verification for what is presented as extra-fictive, enjoying the status of "documented truth." A Soviet-style montage series summarizes the collective life of work and progress, of ploughing, sowing, harvesting, sinking wells, and operating progressively more modernized machines—a summary that celebrates the fruitful results of *avoda ivrit* (Hebrew work) and *avoda atzmit* (self work).

Avoda ivrit and *avoda atzmit* have formed orienting principles (although with different emphases) within the Zionist movement, suggesting that one should earn from one's own and not from hired labor, an idea whose origins trace back to the Haskalah, or eighteenth-century Hebrew Enlightenment. Many Jewish thinkers, writers, and poets such as Avraham Mapu, Yossef H. Brener, Dov Ber Borochov, Aharon D. Gordon, and Berl Katzenelson highlighted the necessity of transforming Jews by "productive labor," especially agricultural labor. Relatively leftist movements such as Poalei Zion (The Workers of Zion) and HaPoel haTzair (The Young Worker)—movements that aspired to synthesize two prevailing revolutionary conceptions concerning European Jews, one which saw the only solution as a national one in Eretz Israel and another conception whereby a solution for Jews necessarily formed part of a wider Socialist-internationalist solution for the world as a whole—supported the "non-exploitation" of Arab work. They advanced *avoda ivrit* as a necessary condition for Jewish recuperation, whereby Jews would be returned to Eretz Israel and life would be organized on a more just social basis. Foregrounding its Socialist-Zionist ideology, the Second Aliya (Jewish immigration to Palestine/Israel, 1904–1914, largely from Russia), in particular, viewed *avoda ivrit* as an absolute value (its famous slogan was *"kibbush haavoda"* ["conquering of the work"]), since every people's right to a land is conditioned not on exploitation of the other, but on its own cultivation of the land. The Third Aliya (1919–1923, largely from the Soviet Union), which took place following the Russian revolution, brought further Socialist-Zionist hopes for a new society based on justice and equality, and was a major force in establishing the collective settlements. The policy and practice of *avoda ivrit* deeply affected the historical positive self-image of the Hebrew pioneers and later of Israelis as involved in a noncolonial enterprise, which unlike colonialist Europe did not exploit the "natives" and was, therefore, perceived as morally superior in its aspirations.

In its actual historical implication, however, *avoda ivrit* had tragic consequences engendering political tensions not simply between Arabs and Jews, but also secondarily between Sephardi Jews and Ashkenazi Jews as well as between Sephardi Jews and Arabs. The Jewish newcomers needed a place to work in order to survive.[25] For Arab *fellahin*, in contrast, *avoda ivrit* meant the loss of employment, especially after the *effendis* (land owners) sold their lands to the newcomers.[26] "Hebrew work" for them meant the boycotting of Arab labor. And for the Yemenite Jews who were imported in order to substitute for cheap Arab labor, and who were viewed through the same lens of superiority as were the Arab *fellahin*, it meant harsh conditions (contrary to the Zionist myth, the material life of Jews in Yemen was superior to what they encountered in Palestine/Eretz Israel) as well as exclusion from the Socialist benefits and camaraderie enjoyed by Ashkenazi workers.[27] This skewed version of *avoda ivrit* generated a long-term structural competition between Arab workers and the majoritarian group of Jewish workers, i.e., Sephardi workers. At the same time, the fact that the dominant ideology within Zionism was Socialist provided no guarantee against ethnocentrism. Even Marxism itself was profoundly imbued with Eurocentric assumptions and prejudices. Marx himself, in his writings on India, showed that he shared this colonial vision, calling for "the annihilation of the Asiatic society, and the laying of the material foundations of Western society in Asia,"[28] while Engels supported the French conquest of Algeria as a progressive step for the advancement of culture. In regarding Palestine as a kind of vacuum, an empty land to be transformed by *avoda ivrit*, and in eliding the Arab presence there, Socialist-Zionist thinking was thus closely attuned to dominant nineteenth-century European modes of thought.

Oded the Wanderer's montage-celebration of work, then, must be seen within a precise ideological and historical context. Later narrative films portraying similar achievements, such as Baruch Dienar's *They Were Ten* (*Hem Hayu Asara*, 1961), produced decades after early pioneering activities, tend toward a more anthropocentric representation foregrounding the *workers* themselves. *Oded the Wanderer*, being closer to the period of the conceiving ideas of "Hebrew work" and a product of the same generation of newcomers who realized the "*kibbush haavoda*," emphasizes *work* itself. The abstract notion of "Hebrew work" is rendered first through the absence of the close-ups which might have fostered identification with individual settlers. Instead, we see a farmer harvesting in a long shot while the dissolve to a close shot shows only his legs and hands operating the scythe. Thus work itself is fetishized, evoking A. D. Gordon's notion of "*dat haavoda*" ("religion of work"). This writer—an important figure for the Hebrew Labor movement, although not a Socialist—viewed work, especially agricultural work, as a means of spiritual-existential salvation for the person as well as the key to Zionist redemption in Eretz Israel.[29] *Oded the Wanderer*'s montage series also highlights the natural progression from sowing to blossoms and trees, as well as the technological progression of a machine sinking into the earth and bringing up water. Work and water, two essential sources of life, energize the film's enthusiastic montage.

After the teacher (and the film) offers a history lesson to the children (and spectator) he redundantly asks them to look at the desolate mountains before them, intoning: "The Valley of Jezreel was also desolated like these mountains before your fathers' hand touched them. And what they have begun you must continue." The modern history of the Promised Land begins, therefore, with the return of the Hebrew pioneers; such is the Zionist myth of Origin. The Zionist call for normalization of the situation of the Jewish people implied that two millennia of wandering had constituted a deviation from a normative teleological history. Only with the return—thanks to the active role of Zionism—will the Jewish people be redeemed, and thus enter history again, becoming a "normal nation" with a crystallized geography and history. Not only will the Jewish people be redeemed from extrahistorical status, it was argued, but the land itself will be made fruitful. The structural contrast between former desolation and current cultivation serves, as in the documentary films of the period, as an encomium to Hebrew labor, reinforcing the didactic call of the teacher to the younger generation.

The renewed contact of the Jewish people with Eretz Israel led to a certain revival within (secular) Zionism of Biblical themes and epic stories, presented as relevant to the modern history being carried out on the self-same land. The working of the land lauded in *Oded the Wanderer* not only forms an implicit contrast with the historical image of Diaspora peddlers and merchants, but also represents the coming into touch with the past of the people of Israel (Am Israel) who worked the land of Israel (Eretz Israel) and who also fought against conquerers within a political-military framework. It is no accident that it was in the Zionist period that the anti-Roman rebel Bar Kokhba (whose rebellion brought disaster and exile) was exalted and mythified as a hero after two thousand years of neglect by the Jewish historical imagination (and, at times, even, of defamation, for instance, by Maimonides as not being *Bar Kokhba*—Hebrew for "Son of a Star"—but rather *Ben Kozibah*—Arabic for "Son of a Liar"). This symbolic fusion with the dignified pre-exile past took academic expression in the form of research into historical wars in Palestine, those mentioned in the Bible and elsewhere, now retrospectively analyzed from a strategic point of view emphasizing the politics of topography.

Oded's teacher points to the pioneers' revival of the desolate Valley of Jezreel. Images of this valley reinforce the connotative link to the Biblical past, since the textual memory of the spectator is informed by the knowledge that many Biblical events took place in the Valley of Jezreel. The desolation, by implication, is a consequence of a "land without its people;" when the Israelites return to cultivate it, the valley is re-dynamized. The name of the Valley of Jezreel, Emek Yizrael in Hebrew, is especially interesting in this context for its etymology; *yizra'* signifies the male third person future for "to sow," i.e., "he will sow," and *El* means "God." The juxtaposition of agriculture and religion so central in Jewish texts—where holidays are linked to the Middle Eastern seasons, and prayers allude to local fruits and flora—becomes transmuted in secular Zionism into a celebration of the agricultural aspects of Jewish holidays, which come to be practiced (especially in the kibbutzim) as an homage to (the God of) Nature. Zionism deploys, in this sense, what Walter Benjamin terms "revolutionary nostalgia," whereby a retrospective look toward an idealized past historical moment becomes the trampoline for the projection of a future utopia.

The historical fusion with the ancient Israelites—and the dramatic rupture with the Diaspora Jew—are made explicit in another sequence as well. The young Sabra protagonist, Oded, dressed in typical short trousers and *tembel* hat, is seen against a bucolic backdrop writing in his diary—in a romantic image fusing Text and World: "Walking, setting up the camp, and the camp itself evoke in me historical memories. I see our compatriots, how they wandered in the desert before entering Eretz Israel; time and again they set up the camp, wander, and thus approach Eretz Israel." Wandering, the desire for the Land, and the entry into the Promised Land are viewed then as a recapitulation and a prolongation of ancient events. The exodus from Egypt, paralleled with the Diaspora and crossing into the "land of milk and honey" (meanwhile receiving the sacred texts and the Ten Commandments) figures forth the advent of modern-day Israel. We see here a Zionist version of what Auerbach calls the "figural method," common to both Judaic and Christian exegesis, whereby, within the overall teleology of Jewish destiny, earlier moments of the trajectory are seen as prefiguring later moments.

(One can detect a similar figural undercurrent in certain Hollywood spectaculars such as *Samson and Delilah* [1952] and *The Ten Commandments* [1955], in which the narrative opposition of ancient Israelites and pharaonic Egyptians are strangely more evocative of the contemporary Middle East than of the Biblical past.) The close shot of Oded's handwriting in modern Hebrew, meanwhile, emphasizes the contemporary linguistic renewal and the rootedness of the "people of the Book" in the palpable Biblical landscape. The etymology of the word *Hebrew*, as referring both to the people and to the language, it should be noted, derives from the root *EVR*, which signifies as a noun "land/region across-beyond" and as a verb "to travel," "to cross." Both Oded's *écriture* in the language celebrated by the Zionist film, Hebrew, and the theme of his writing, the crossing of the Israelites to the Promised Land, are evoked, then, by the resonances of the very word *Hebrew*.

The interaction of the Sabra with the landscape reveals still another dimension, one carrying with it a certain ambivalence. *Oded the Wanderer*, in accord with Zionist thought, typifies a Romantic image of the Sabra. The rootedness of the healthy, happy, proud Sabra, a member of the "generation of the future," forms an implicit binary contrast with the image of the presumably unhealthy, self-tormenting, and cowed Diaspora Jew lacking all concrete attachment to a land. This concept is also conveyed through the portrayal of the American tourist, who, unlike the simply dressed, energetic, and free-spirited, playful Sabras, dresses with inappropriate elegance and interacts awkwardly with nature. He rides a donkey with difficulty and is afraid of innocent spurs and thorns. A stereotypical image of the sympathetic urban Westerner visiting the countryside, he becomes a ludicrous figure for the tough but sweet Sabras. In *Oded the Wanderer*, the American plays a role occasionally given to the stereotypically urban Jew in Hollywood films, especially in Westerns, where the Jew is shown to be out of his normal habitat. But if Jews in the classical Western introduce a note of parodic out-of-placeness (for example, in *The Frisco Kid*, 1979), the Hebrew/Israeli, in Zionist-nationalist films, becomes himself the Western hero, in relation to whom the others are out-of-place. The depiction of the Sabra along the lines of a collectively desired renewed Jewish image—as will be seen in the discussion of *Sabra*—accounts, in many ways, for the success of *Oded the Wanderer*. Even the advertisement/review of Eden Cinema emphasized: "Reality and art go hand in hand to highlight the image of the Hebrew child who grows up in the motherland, healthy in body and soul, the fresh, dreamy, and tough Hebrew Man."

At the same time, however, the Sabra's naturalness, associated with the reborn land, the modern villages, and the "civilized world" of the Hebrew Yishuv, is set in contrast to the East, to the desolation and the "wild mountains" described by Oded in his diary. In the story *Oded the Wanderer*, this interaction of the "civilized" Sabra with the nature of the "underdeveloped" world is further emphasized when Oded, after washing his clothes, writes: "How strange it is! Do I dare sit naked next to our house or school? And here I sit completely naked like the savages in Africa, who walk naked without shame. Will I return home soon or will I grow savagely and become a savage? What a horrible thought."[30] Although this specific scene was excised from a film directed at the puritanical Yishuv, the underlying, colonialist attitude dominates the film as well. Even though Oded is a villager himself, his attitude toward nature is that of a "modern" man trapped in a dangerous and "primitive" world. The wilderness from which he feels estranged includes the local inhabitants, to whom the camera grants no autonomy or individuality beyond being an extension of the landscape. The teacher's history lesson, for example, ignores the Arab presence, denuding them of all history and geography, in homological continuity with a Zionist discourse that consistently played down Arab Palestine as of secondary, even negligible importance.

The Zionist enterprise was premised on the assumption of the right to access to what was, temporarily at least, the other's land, an assumption integral to the Western view of the East as "available" for its interests. Yet, although Zionism generally denied or ignored the Arab presence in Palestine, specific Zionists, at times, posited negative characteristics for the presumably nonexistent Arabs. One finds a tension between these two attitudes, for instance, in Chaim Weizmann's remarks to Arthur Balfour on May 30, 1918:

> The Arabs, who are superficially clever and quick witted, worship one thing, and one thing only—power and success . . . The British author- ities . . . knowing as they do the treacherous nature of the Arabs . . . have to watch carefully and constantly. . . . The fairer the English regime tries to be, the more arrogant the Arab becomes. . . . The present state of af- fairs would necessarily tend toward the creation of an Arab Palestine, *if there were an Arab people in Palestine* [emphasis added]. It will not in fact produce that result because the fellah is at least four centuries behind the times, and the effendi . . . is dishonest, uneducated, greedy, and as unpatriotic as he is inefficient.[31]

The implications of this self-contradictory attitude are revealed on some levels in *Oded the Wanderer.* Axelrod's and Halachmi's camera, which imagistically sustains the teacher's speech concerning an "empty" and abandoned Palestine prior to the arrival of the pioneers, ironically reproduces through location shooting two Arab women carrying baskets on their heads, walking in a direction opposite to Oded's class. Along with regarding a Third World area as devoid of people, largely by sublimating the "natives" into part of the wilderness, the film also denigrates the Arab presence through the hierarchy of casting and representation; while some of the fictitious Bedouins are played by actual Bedouins, the major Bedouin role is given to Dvora Halachmi, the director's wife, who enacts the "exotic woman."

In comparison to the source story, the film reduces the contact of the Sabras with the Bedouins. In the story, the "exotic natives" show hospitality to the lost Oded; indeed, he spends a few days recuperating in their tents. The description of the evolving relationship is focalized through Oded, in contrast to the omniscient narrator's earlier description of the Hebrew village and the class's trip. The form of presentation shifts, upon the entry of the Bedouins into the story, to the particular point of view of the protagonist, and thus to the binarism of observer/observed, subject/object. As in European humanist-colonialist literature, the Bedouins are presented as "natives" who have never before seen Western clothing and who are bedazzled by Oded's stories about the world of modern technology and education. The poor Bedouin children, astonished by the happy life of Hebrew children, yearn for enlightenment. Oded's impressions of his voyage into the depths of the Orient are written in the exemplary genre of the European expeditionary/travelogue diary.

> Here not only is nature savage, but the people as well. One of them once saw a train, and he tells wonders about it; a second went to Tiberias and was amazed by the big city, with its many houses, stores, and wealth. None of them knows how to read and write. Except for what happens to their flocks, their tents, and the neighboring villages, they know nothing but savagery, savagery.[32]

One of the Bedouins, furthermore, proffers self-incriminatory testimony: "You the Jews are learned, educated, you know everything. And we are savages."[33] Oded takes on a missionary role of teaching them to read and write Arabic, rescuing Homo Arabicus from his own obscurantism, reconstructing his lost script and thus restoring his "real" language. Oded takes back to the Hebrew village his excellent student, Khalil, to acquire disciplined knowledge "in order to spread it" among the Arabs, thus instructing the Orient in the ways of the modern West. The story ends with the superficial harmony of non-equals: Oded and Khalil shake hands, promising to be friends forever. Although the role of enlightening the "primitives," part of a Zionist "mission civilisatrice," is minimized in the film, compared with the story, the conception of redemption by Zionist progenitors lies at the core of both texts, but realized in the film, as we have seen, more through the reconstruction of the land than through the denigration of its inhabitants.

Imaging Palestine: Pioneer Sabras and Exotic Arabs

While *Oded the Wanderer* was still in the production phase, the impresario Ze'ev Markovitz invited the young Polish filmmaker Alexander Ford to direct a film about the pioneers, after seeing Ford's earlier film, *The Street Legion* (*Legion Ulicy*, 1932), about abandoned street children. Although Ford arrived in Palestine without a prepared script, he was clear about choosing a style of "dramatic reportage," combining documentary elements with staged scenes along the lines of *The Street*

Legion.[34] Over a period of six months, Ford, together with his wife, Olga, and the German cinematographer Frank Weinmar, toured the country shooting documentary footage—at times employing hidden cameras—of diverse events such as the World Makabiya (international Jewish sport competition), Jewish-Arab clashes, and Nabby Mussa (Prophet Moses) Muslim celebrations. While most of the authentic material was later edited in Poland into a series of newsreels and a short film titled *Eretz Israeli Chronicled*,[35] other parts, such as the Nabby Mussa celebrations, were included in *Sabra*. Through direct contact with the country, the original invitation to produce a film about the pioneers metamorphosed gradually into a film about Jewish-Arab tensions and the struggle over land and water.

The cinema followed the same trajectory as the modern Hebrew literature of Palestine (written since the late nineteenth-century), which at first revolved around pioneer characters resuscitating a desolate land, while only decades later the Arab presence erupted into stories in the form of violence, precipitating dramatic catharsis in which the Jewish hero reaches virtual martyr status. In cinema, the first phase of primary focus on the pioneer took place in the early documentaries, while the Arab presence made itself felt only in the thirties. Beginning in the thirties, then, fiction films form part of an evolving context of nationalist conflict that penetrates all Hebrew fictions. Even when not foregrounding the nationalist theme, as in *Oded the Wanderer*, the films allude to it by highlighting the cultural tensions of Occident and Orient, invariably ending with the peaceful and "logical" triumph of the former over the latter. The original invitation to Alexander Ford, in other words, to direct a film along more traditional documentary lines, with little concern with the Arab "element," was transformed through the filmmaker's experience in Palestine, with the result that he registered, from a specific perspective, the central Zionist issue, not the pioneer in a vacuum, but rather the pioneer in a specific Arab context. In this sense, the production story of *Sabra* reflects the evolving preoccupations of Zionism, whose early texts, especially those written prior to actual travels in Palestine, ignored or minimized the Arab issue; it was to require decades of ongoing tensions to force the issue to center stage.

Sabra, the first sound feature film, revolves around a group of Jewish immigrants who, after buying a desolate piece of land from an Arab Sheik, settle close to an Arab village. Although initially welcomed, the enthusiastic young pioneers soon find themselves the victims of Arab irrationality, being blamed for a drought presumably caused by their pioneer witchcraft. The objective hardships of the idealistic newcomers on a waterless soil are now exacerbated by Arab hostility. Misled by the exploitative Sheik, the Arabs attack the Zionist settlers just when the latter find water. The bloodthirsty Arabs cease their destruction, however, when it is revealed that it was the Sheik himself who had closed the Arab well. This discovery about the true nature of the greedy Arab leader as opposed to the generous Zionists is "blessed" by a happy downrush of water, leading to acceptance by the Arabs, and to peace and harmony.

Sabra was made with a relatively high budget (5,000 Liras), and the lab work, synchronization, and editing were performed in Poland, in contrast with *Oded the Wanderer*, which was completely made in Palestine on a very low budget (400 Liras). Despite the happy ending, British censorship objected to *Sabra* because it showed clashes between Arabs and Jews. The film, it should be added, was originally intended to have a tragic ending in which a young Jewish shepherd and a young Arab woman would be killed during the clashes. Due to the producer's pressures and in the hopes of persuading British censors, the ending was changed: the Arab woman bandages the wounds of the shepherd, following a sequence of images intimating a future of harmonious progress and modernization spearheaded by the pioneers. The British censored the film, nevertheless, for a potpourri of offenses, calling it "propagandist, anti-Arab, leftist, and dangerous."[36] Pressures from Zionist institutions did not change the decision. Yaacov Davidon testified that he exhibited *Sabra* in the thirties and forties after changing its title to *The Pioneers* (*HeHalutzim*) and excising all the combat sequences, thus minimizing the Arab presence in the film. In 1954 the excised sequences were reinstated and shown in the first film festival in Haifa.

Sabra was dubbed in both Polish and Hebrew versions and premiered successfully in Poland in 1933. Warsaw critics received the film with mixed feelings (e.g., praising the script but denouncing the film's technical inadequacies).[37] While in Poland there were arguments about whether the film was pro-Zionist or pro-Arab (the Polish critic Stanislav Yanitski, for example, claimed that the film was anti-Zionist, since it showed Arabs defending their rights), the Hebrew Yishuv in Palestine received it as supportive of Zionism.[38] Ford, as one of the leading actors in *Sabra*, Shimon Finkel, recalls, was skeptical about the Zionist enterprise,[39] and although he was offered a job in Palestine, he returned to Poland, later becoming an important figure in the Polish film industry.[40]

A close reading of *Sabra* may help to clarify the patterns of representation of Arabs within Israeli fiction, patterns set long before the establishment of the state. The sounds and images of *Sabra* form a kind of aesthetic tributary to mainstream Zionist ideology; they typify the films of the period, even those not directly funded or assigned by Zionist institutions. The title "Sabra" already epitomizes the stance taken by a film which can be regarded as an example of "didactic allegory." In Hebrew "Sabra" literally refers to the cactus plant, common in the area ("prickly pear" in English), thorny on the outside but sweet on the inside. While it denotes the native-born Jews, it also came to metaphorize the Zionist concept of the prototype of the newly emerging Jew in Eretz Israel, whose characteristics constitute the antithesis of the image of the Diaspora Jew. The mythological Sabra was created by the immigrant generation of pioneers who raised the native-born children as the hope of Jewish salvation and universal values, thus endowing this first generation with the proud status of a kind of moral aristocracy. The Sabra, as pointed out by the legal scholar-politician Amnon Rubinstein,[41] was born into a vacuum in which the ideal figure of education is not the father but a collective, abstract "I." The mythological Sabra literature, therefore, was premised on the absent Diaspora parent. The heroes were celebrated as eternal children devoid of parents, as though born by spontaneous generation of nature, as, for example, in Moshe Shamir's novel *In His Own Hands* (*Bemo Yadav*) which introduces the protagonist as follows: "Elik was born from the sea." In this paradoxical and idiosyncratic version of the Freudian *Familien-roman*, Zionist parents raised their own children to see themselves as historical foundlings, worthy of more dignified, romantic, and powerful progenitors.

The process of the Sabra's mythification condensed various Zionist ideals. The myth involved, for example, a multi-leveled mystique of physicality. The Sabra has been portrayed as healthy looking, tanned, with European features. (Short stories, novels, plays, and films quite often even attributed blond hair and blue eyes to their heroes.) In terms of personality, the Sabra is cleansed of all "Jewish" inferiority complexes, a kind of child of nature (a conception partially influenced by Gustav Wyneken and the Jugendkultur [Youth Culture] fashionable in Germany at the turn of the century, especially in the German youth movement, Wandervogel), confident, proud, and brave, with a mask of cynical toughness in language and manner, which, as with the *sabra* plant, conceals great sensitivity and tenderness. In terms of profession, Sabras are workers of the land, forming part of the collective effort to be "normal." Collectively, they negate what one of the Marxist-Zionist founding fathers, Dov Ber Borochov, termed the "inverted pyramid," i.e., the situation in which "exterritorial Jews" were forced into nonproductive secondary economic areas (commerce, middlemen).[42] In Palestine, the "inverted pyramid," it was hoped, would give way to an egalitarian Hebrew society. As opposed to the Jewish "loftiness" both in profession and in relation of Zion, the Sabras were perceived as cultivating the land, and enjoying the fruits of their own labor—and therefore, at long last, fully rooted in the Biblical landscape.

Within the reality of conflict with Arabs, and later in the post-Holocaust context, furthermore, the very physicality of the Sabra came to evoke the notion of the strong, robust Hebrew/Israeli who fights back and resists victimization, who refuses to go like a "sheep to the slaughter." The superior Sabra, in other words, avenges the historical inferiority of the Diaspora father. Yossef Trumpeldor, the turn-of-the-century immigrant from Russia, for example, whose single hand (the other was lost in the Russian-Japanese war) ploughed during the day and wielded a guard-rifle at night, and who said, after being fatally wounded by the Arabs, "*Tov lamut be'ad artzenu*" ("It is good to die for our country"), became a kind of mythic figure incarnating the proud new Jew. Expression of fear, weakness, and humiliation came to be despised as "*galutyeem*" (belonging to the Diaspora), while courage and "standing tall" came to be regarded as constitutive Sabra/Israeli traits which ultimately penetrated political discourse, constituting a kind of characterological paradigm for the young nation.

The very title of *Sabra*, then, intimates the perspective through which the narrative is focalized. The credit sequence literalizes the titular motif through images of a *sabra* plant against a background of clouds, evoking the positive stereotype of the native-born pioneer whose thorny exterior hides an inner visionary, dreamy, and idealistic quality, a theme carried over into the language by such phrases as "*holmim velohamim*" ("dreamers and fighters"). The credit-sequence image of *sabra* plants then dissolves to images of stormy seas, ominous clouds accompanied by claps of thunder, superimposed with titles over a shot of crashing waves, cutting into the first sequence of camel-borne pioneers on their way to the settlement. *Sturm-und-Drang* commentative music, making instrumental allusion to pioneer song motifs, here sets the ponderously didactic tone of the film as a whole. The sequencing of the images, proceeding from sea to land, also recapitulates the perspective of the Europeans who arrive in the East from the sea, from the West, geographically (Mediterranean), metaphorically (identifying with Europe), and even linguistically (since *yam* in Hebrew signifies both "sea" and "west").

An intertitle:—"It is not a very long time since an enthusiastic group of young people, sick of the 'advantages' of civilization, arrived in the Promised Land in order to begin a life full of efforts and trouble but new and free"—reveals, meanwhile, an ambivalence toward Europe which was to characterize many Zionist films. Zionism, after all, was born against the illuminated backdrop, as it were, of the incendiary fires of the Russian pogroms of the 1880s and the seismological shock of the Dreyfus Affair. On the one hand, then, Europe represents the locus of pogroms, persecution, and anti-Semitism—a place a Jew must abandon in order to be free—on the other, it represents civilization, knowledge, and enlightenment. The film places the advantages of Europe in quotation marks, therefore, not because Europe does not possess advantages but because Jews had never been free to enjoy them. Jews could only enjoy the enlightenment of the "civilized world" in a new territory, which became—by consensus—the Middle Eastern Promised Land after the "Uganda crisis" in the Zionist Congress. There, Jews would, ironically, reconstruct the very "civilized world" they left behind.

This ambivalent relation to Europe also has implications for the attitude toward Palestine and its inhabitants, discernible both in the Jewish characters and in the ideology underlying the film. As in many First World films about the Third World, the vantage point is that of the Westerner arriving in a new place, passing through the open space, and gradually stripping the land of its mystery. The motif of European newcomers' first perspective on the land and its inhabitants, seen in the film's initial juxtaposition of sea and land, carries with it a certain historical burden, sensed, for example, in innumerable Hollywood films concerning First World/Third World encounters. In the following sequence, furthermore, the spectator discovers the existence of Arab villages quite literally through the point of view of the European immigrants, and then is introduced to Arab "manners" and "customs" through the European settlers' gaze, all accompanied by Hollywood, Ali

Baba–like "exotic" musical themes. A panning camera, for example, follows the responses of the newcomers to Arab cuisine, which they are obliged by politeness to eat with their hands. One of the newcomers hiccoughs and is unable to eat the alien food. The Arabs are hospitable, the sequence suggests, but what they have to offer is scarcely worth accepting. (Albert Memmi in *The Colonizer and the Colonized* discusses this snobbish attitude of Europeans toward Arab hospitality, whereby a virtue, generosity, was turned into a vice, stupidity.)

In a film made thirty years later, Baruch Dienar's *They Were Ten* (*Hem Hayu Asara*, 1961), which revolves around the same theme—the valiant struggle of ten Russian Jews to found a colony in Palestine in the late nineteenth-century, focusing on their attempt to develop the barren land in the face of Arab resentment and Turkish obstructionism—we encounter a similar structuring of imagery. The Arab village is seen in the distance and from the point of view of the newcomers. Later in the film, when one of the settlers takes an adventurous walk to the neighboring Arab village, the exploration is focalized through him: the movements of the hand-held camera in the narrow lanes of the village subjectivize his impressions, not merely as being from his point of view, but also as relaying his dynamic movement across a passive, static place, gradually unveiling its mystery. And in the house of the Mukhtar (head of the village), the spectator wins visual access to Oriental treasures through the eyes of the European discoverer. The pioneer films, in other words, claim to initiate the Western spectator into Oriental culture. The spectator, along with the pioneers, comes to master, in a remarkably telescoped period of time (in terms of both "story" and "discourse" time) the codes of a foreign culture, shown as simple, stable, unselfconscious, and susceptible to facile apprehension. Any possibility of dialogic interaction and of a dialectical representation of the East/West relation is excluded from the outset. The films thus reproduce the colonialist mechanism by which the Orient, rendered as devoid of any active historical or narrative role, becomes the passive object of study and spectacle.

In *Sabra*, in particular, the early ambiguous portrayal of legendary Arab hospitality soon gives way to a more frankly negative portrait of Arab rituals: the tribe people clap rhythmically as an Arab dances with a sword. The film intercuts to close-ups of the smiling Sheik informing the pioneers: "Our people always dance; at birthdays, weddings, funerals, or at the approach of the enemy." The sudden intrusion of aggressivity, in other words, is first associated with the Arabs through the sword dance on the image track, as well as through the Sheik's disturbing reference to enemies on the dialogue level. A close-up shows the Sheik curling his lips and casting an evil look. After he bears witness against himself and his group—"We are poor savage people"—the film cuts to a shot of desert land, while we still hear the voice-over of the Sheik accusing the pioneers: "And you are entering a beautiful and fertile land." The contradiction between the arid "reality" on the image track undercutting the "unreal" accusation of the Sheik is further underlined by a rhetorical panning of the camera along the desert sands following the Sheik's monologue. The land the pioneers are about to enter, the film further suggests, was legally purchased. The characterization of the Arab leader as irrational in terms of his unjustified need for aggression and as a prevaricator in his blind arguments, as we shall see later, has important ideological implications.

The origins and mentality of Zionism, as pointed out by scholars like Maxime Rodinson,[43] can be traced to the conditions of nineteenth- and early twentieth-century Europe, not only in terms of anti-Semitism but also in terms of the rapid expansion of capitalism and the empire building which led finally to the first imperialist world war. Zionism cannot, of course, be simplistically equated with colonialism or imperialism. Unlike colonialism, Zionism constituted a response to millennial oppression and, in counter-distinction to the classical colonial paradigm, in this case metropolis and colony were ideologically located in the self-same place. There was no France or Great Britain to which one might repatriate profits or to which one might return after colonial expeditions. Palestine/Eretz Israel, furthermore, had always been the symbolic seat of Jewish cultural identity. At the same time Zionism was clearly allied to Western colonial interests, was ideologically inflected by colonialist discourse, and often behaved in a colonialist manner, especially in its deprecatory attitude toward what we would now call Third World lands and peoples and their rights. Written during the period of European colonialism in the Orient, Zionist texts perform a kind of topographical reductionism, whereby Palestine is ultimately rendered as little more than a desert or a swamp, an unproductive land awaiting Western penetration and fecundation. (Viewing a region as originally barren or neglected, we might remember, was a rather standard justification for colonial conquest.) The settlers with their advanced mentality and technology were presumed to have only beneficial effects on this "underdeveloped land." It is only within this context, of viewing one's deeds as manifesting a higher morality, that we can understand the naïvely idealistic thrust of films like *Sabra* with its literalization of the phrase "to make the desert bloom," presented without a trace of self-doubt, as a heroic image of the pioneers and their political practice in Palestine.

The pioneers in *Sabra* embody the humanitarian and liberationist project of Zionism. They carry with them, in many ways, the same banner of the "universal" "civilizing mission" that European powers proclaimed during their surge into the "underdeveloped" world. Alternating sequences between the Hebrew settlement and the Arab village, the film imagistically compares the structure of the two societies, directing the sympathies of the spectator to the young enthusiasts. A series of iterative shots, to use Gérard Genette's terminology, show primitive *fellahin* at work, children laboring as the Sheik looks on with indolence, thus revealing the backwardly hierarchical structure of the Arab community, here contrasted with the innovating egalitarianism of the settlement, in which the (collective) landowners and the workers are one and the same. The inconsequential and unreflective work of Arab peasants is foiled by the pioneers' glowing productivity and conscious solidarity. As revolutionary idealists, they, unlike the Arabs, are clearly illuminated by a goal and a vision. Despite their past naïve anticipations of an already forested new land—the visualization of which is accompanied by music evoking certain leitmotifs of what was to become the national anthem "HaTikva" ("The Hope")—they continue their struggle within the present desert. As in *They Were Ten*, the film emphasizes the Europeanized intellectual formation of the pioneers. In *Sabra*, a flashback conveys a settler's memories of past work with a printing machine connotatively associated with revolutionary activity, much as, in *They Were Ten*, the pioneers show their mastery of Pushkin and Chekhov. Thus, the films reinforce the image of the pioneers as possessors of knowledge, implicitly suggesting their potential power to enlighten an Orient presumed to be living in the Dark Ages. Their spiritual superiority is further emphasized in both *Sabra* and *They Were Ten*, since despite their formation as intellectuals they are largely shown in physical contact with the earth, culminating in images of a productive revivification of a once wasted soil.

The early contrast between the two societies is sharpened throughout *Sabra*, forming part of the evolving conflict. The already exploited *fellahin* are forced by the Sheik to pay exorbitant prices for water—a price far beyond their means. The drought forces one of the older Arabs to implore the Sheik to provide water from his large well. (Both roles are enacted by Jews.)[44] Portrayed as a cruel feudal lord, the Sheik dangles his feet pleasurably in the water as he responds: "No money, no water." And the older Arab answers: "You have stones instead of a heart. But your rule is not for long; the new immigrants will give everybody water without payment." Not only is the Arab character himself made, by Zionist ventriloquism, to expose the exploitative attitude of his leader; he is also made to laud the humane generosity of the Zionists' Socialist attitudes. In *They Were Ten*, similarly, the Arabs impede settler access to the well, legally supposed to be shared by both Arabs and Jews. When the settlers forcefully realize their rights to the well, however, the film emphasizes their moral superiority and a generosity which surprises even the Arabs. *Sabra*, meanwhile, suggests that the Sheik exploits the drought in order to provoke the Arab *fellahin* against the pioneers by blaming them for the drought, since otherwise, as the Sheik himself confesses: "I will lose my reputation and my water income." (Karl Wittfogel claims, interestingly, that Oriental despotism has its origins in control of the water supply.)[45]

The characterization of the Sheik points to one of the Zionist (especially the Socialist-Zionist) arguments also used by the European left (especially before 1967) in support of the Zionist struggle. The presumed Socialist nature of Zionism becomes a justification for land acquisition. Jewish liberation is seen as also liberating Oriental peasants oppressed by pleasure-loving feudal lords. This Socialist outlook animated much of the Yishuv—at least in its earliest waves, precisely those waves that exercised the greatest influence on the collective ideology. Yet, as Rodinson points out, this Socialist outlook is not incompatible with the simultaneous colonial character of the Yishuv: "A society that internally ranks among the most democratic or the most Socialist can quite easily have relations with the outside world in which they deny the rights of other societies."[46]

The theoreticians of Jewish nationalism paid very little attention to the societies their project threatened to hurt or destroy, believing that Jewish political renewal could have only a benign effect on these societies and consequently it was pointless to determine in advance the nature of the relations to be established with them. In this sense, Rodinson continues:

> The analogy with the mental attitude of the French colonizers . . . imbued with the democratic ideology of the French Revolution, is obvious. It was for their own good that the Algerians and the Tonkinese were subjugated. In this way they would be prepared little by little for the day when later— much later—they would understand the Declaration of the Rights of Man and when, still later, it could be applied to them too.[47]

The conflict between the humanist ideology of Socialist Zionism and the real praxis of Jewish domination in Palestine found "resolution" in the inviting thesis that the Arab masses, subjected to "feudalism" and exploited by their fellow countrymen, stood only to benefit from the Jewish conquest, at least in the long run. The epilogue of *Sabra*, which celebrates the flourishing of technology and the blossoming of agriculture in Palestine, implicitly celebrates the success of Jewish-European settlers in hewing a civilization out of a godforsaken wilderness. Within this humanist ideology, the Arabs are thought to be made, or prepared to be made, happy in spite of themselves.

The superiority of pioneer over Arab society in *Sabra* is also suggested through the portrayal of the status of women in the two communities. As equal members of the collective, women pioneers work alongside the men, and even betray—in accordance with a positive female stereotype—an enhanced mental capacity to continue the struggle in times of crisis. Images of women working the land and, in later films, wielding weapons further strengthen this egalitarian mystique.[48] (In fact, even in the communes women were still largely limited to traditional roles.) *Sabra*, furthermore, directly correlates female equality with conformity to Zionist pioneering ideals. In contrast to the hard-working pioneer-woman who sacrifices her beauty and comfortable life in Europe, the provocatively dressed Jezebel-like woman figure refuses to abandon the hedonistic life of drinking, dancing, and listening to the "gramophone" in the pioneers' tent. The film enforces identification with her boyfriend's puritanical censure, culminating in his final expression of contempt: "You only know how to drink, while we go hungry. You would have danced all your life, but here dancing is death."

In *They Were Ten*, produced at a distance of decades from the early pioneer practices, the concept of the pioneer woman as a madonna is further exalted, and

Testimony to modernity: The female pioneer in *Sabra*.

even mythologized into the status of a veritable Great Mother. The film portrays Manya (Ninet Dienar), the only woman among nine men living in over-crowded conditions, as unable to find the privacy even to fulfill her promise as a wife to her pioneer husband (Oded Teomi). An exemplum of self-abnegation, she is characterized as a substitute mother who takes care of all the pioneers' needs. When one of the pioneers desires her, however, she rebuffs him, leading to his embarrassed confession of moral weakness. The only lovemaking between Manya and her husband during the film takes place outdoors, and leads to her pregnancy. Fulfilling her ultimate woman-mother role of giving fruitful birth, she dies shortly thereafter, suffering the fate of the frontier woman in many Western films.

While pioneer women in *Sabra* are granted few roles and little dialogue, no dialogue whatsoever is accorded the Arab women, who appear but briefly in the film. The few shots of Arab women reduce their image to the exotic Orientals familiar to the Western imagination. A rather improbable mélange features a belly dancer with a ring in her nose, a dot on her forehead, and a jar on her head, thus condensing several Third World female stereotypes. The dot on the forehead is usually associated with women from India, and specifically Hindu women, while

The self-sacrificing frontier mother: *They Were Ten*.

the ring in the nose is more common in Africa, and a jar is usually carried on the head for practical rather than exotic-artistic purposes. This Hollywood-style "mark of the plural," to use Albert Memmi's terminology, flattens a diversity of Third World cultures in an unlikely synthesis, much like Hollywood films such as *The Sheik* (1921), which superimposes an Indian-style dance onto a presumably Arab dancer, and *The Thief of Bagdad* (1924), which melds the visual traces of civilizations as diverse as Arab, Persian, Chinese, and Indian into a single figure of the exotic Orient. While the belly dancer in *Sabra* leaves the screen when an Arab man signals for her to go, the equally brief appearance of a noble Arab woman is associated with one of the pioneers. She exchanges with him shyly affectionate glances early in the film and later succors his wound and gives him water as in the classical-Biblical figure of the worthy woman.

Presented as ignorant of the potential salvation being offered them, however, the Arab masses are preparing to attack while the pioneers, struggling against relentless sun and frequent injuries, dig for water. Images of Arabs gathering during Nabby Mussa celebrations (some of the footage shot by Ford is authentic), plant in the spectatorial mind the subtle expectation of subsequent Arab violence. Under British colonialism in Palestine, it must be pointed out, the Nabby Mussa religious ritual also became a nationalist platform, for example, in 1919 and 1920, for attacking the Hebrew Yishuv. *Sabra*'s juxtaposition of Islamic tradition with preparations to destroy the Jewish settlement, in the absence of all reference to a general nationalist Arab upsurge, however, becomes a mere reproduction of the Eurocentric view of Islamic fanaticism. (Indeed, although Zionism was a product of the same historical forces that produced Arab nationalism, it has tended to minimize and denigrate such affinities and analogies.)

Floating into irrational ecstasy, the Arabs, like the Indians of Hollywood Westerns, dance around the fire, clapping their hands for water. They pray to God and to "Mohammad, His Only Prophet," while one of them tears his clothes and exclaims: "O righteous Allah, curse those who caused our misfortune!" With swords in the air, the crowd screams for revenge: "Death to the infidel!" Lurking behind these images of Muslim Arab irrationality and bloodthirstiness lies the perennial European fear of *jihad*. (The equivalent Western/Christian term "crusade," frequently used in Occidental political discourse, meanwhile, has never been seen as similarly reflecting religious irrationalism, even though it too, historically evokes religious fanaticism, intolerance, and implicitly the use of force.) In still another dimension, the segment of ritualistic preparation for violence can be seen as projecting onto Arabs, as the new Goyim, the experience of Jews in Europe with the old Goyim (Christians). The Arab accusation against the Jewish immigrants, unjustifiably blamed for bewitching the water, is reminiscent of similar accusations in Europe, as during the "black plague." Thus Jewish anxiety about Goyische (Christian) violence is here combined with the Western view of the Muslim, to quote H. A. R. Gibb, as having an aversion to "the thought-processes of rationalism."[49]

Immediately preceding the actual attack by the Arabs, the film celebrates the pioneers' spirit and brings spectatorial identification to a kind of paroxysm; after their long and painful sacrifice, the pioneers, at the edge of despair, locate a source of water. They celebrate by singing: "We will all become crazy and create miracles." The utopian moment of celebration, consecrating a major step toward creating a civilization, is interrupted, however, in a pattern which we will encounter in other films, by Arab bloodthirstiness. Together with the pioneers, the spectator perceives the Arabs, in long shot, approaching the small band of settlers. The construction of a mass of Arabs (quantity) attacking a handful of Jews (quality) comes to form, over the years, a kind of David/Goliath leitmotif in the representation of the Israeli/Arab conflict, frequent through the early 1970s. When the Arabs are about to stab the settlers with knives, an Arab child reveals the truth that it was the Sheik who closed the well. This mythical moment of Arab *prise de conscience* of the corruption of their leadership generates, within the Zionist logic of the film, the non sequitur that the settlers must, therefore, be welcomed (rather than the logic of independence and Socialism for the Arab peasants). The cognitive break, with its clear didactic thrust, follows with a deus-ex-machina solution of the conflict in the form of a providential fall of water. The elderly Arab who earlier criticized the Sheik sheaths his knife and walks away from the camera, i.e., from the settlement. In a long shot he turns his head and makes a gesture of blessing toward the settlement, while a young Arab woman cures the injured pioneer who first discovered the water. The film then cuts to a close shot of gushing water in a classical narrative closure evoking the restoration of a fruitful harmony.

They Were Ten, based on the diaries and intimate letters of the *Bilus* (Hebrew initials for "Beit Yaacov Lekhu veNelekha," the first Zionist settlers in the late nineteenth-century), to whose perspective the film is faithful, offers a similar narrative pattern. A period of fruitful labor and the birth of the first baby are followed by a drought. Some hostile young Arabs steal from the settlers, and one of the thieves is caught. The conclusion swells to a crescendo in which an enraged army of Arabs descend upon the tiny settlement, demanding the return of the thief, who had made them believe he was being tortured. Only when the Mukhtar realizes that his own young men were stealing and lying does he promise to return the stolen goods. The renewed peace is blessed with the clear symbolism of falling rain, simultaneous with the death by malaria of the woman who has just given birth, followed by her burial in the rain. The implied future progress from that point on is obvious for the Israeli and Western spectator (in 1961). Unlike *Oded the Wanderer* and *Sabra*, the film does not feel obliged to employ a redundant montage-summary of pioneering development.

The temporal setting of *They Were Ten* in the later nineteenth-century, as if in an attempt to go back to the roots of the Israeli-Arab conflict, however, does not suggest at its core a different vision from that of Zionist texts in the late nineteenth-century or of *Sabra* in the thirties. In both *Sabra* and *They Were Ten* the notion of an "inexplicable" Arab refusal is projected as the root explanation of the conflict, while natural afflictions are given the dramatic role of exacerbating the presumed irrational tendencies of the Arab mind. The source of refusal, in other words, is not narratively or cinematically structured as a consequence of the material practices of *Realpolitik*, but rather as an innate and inexplicable hostility, against which the settlers have no other choice but to fight, much as they fight against the plagues, here malaria, typical of an underdeveloped area. These films are, in other words, informed by the familiar West/East binarism: one group, from the West, incarnates all that is progressive, rational, peace-loving, and logical; the other embodies the contrary of these qualities.

Also symptomatic of East/West binarism in *Sabra* is the implied association of the pioneers with technological advancement and the reduction of the East to its absence. The film's brief epilogue, for example, begins with an image of ploughed fields superimposed with intertitles:

Years passed by and in the place of a barren desert fertilized by the blood and sweat of these first pioneers, blossoming fields, gardens, and spacious towns emerged and the harmonious rhythm of the implements and machinery produced a powerful symphony of work upon that blessed soil.

The ensuing flux of images illustrates the progress of agricultural development. The montage alternates close shots of single machines or fruits with long shots of progressively increasing numbers of trees and machines, communicating a feeling of flourishing agricultural production, culminating in a superimposed image of etherealized pioneers walking through thriving orchards. (The filmic celebration of agricultural revolution and its concomitant benefits for the people recalls, as in *Oded the Wanderer*, a less sophisticated version of Eisenstein, especially of *The Old and the New*.) This superimposition evokes a pioneering spirit engendering immense achievements, realizing Herzl's slogan: "If you wish, it is not just a legend."

The antagonism between a dynamic West and an inchoate East at times takes on the dimensions of a veritable *psychomachia*, the narrative mode in which protagonists become mere pawns in an ongoing process of ideological warfare. Both *Sabra* and *Oded the Wanderer* combine images of Zionist fecundation of the desert with emblems of Arab "primitivism" and "backwardness," and thus share certain features with the dominant outlook of European chauvinism. The visible prosperity serves as a kind of retroactive validation of the Zionist vision, defined by one of its leading publicists, Israel Zangwill, as "A land without people for a people without land." In its early conceptualization, Zionism tended to consider a territory empty and available if its indigenous population had not yet achieved national independence and recognized statehood. *Sabra*'s close shots of the land and of the pioneers' literal, constant touching of the soil suggests a passive land, sterile for centuries, a land under what from a Zionist perspective is "foreign" domination, redeemable only by the penetrating dynamism of the settlers.

The theme of finding water, typical also of commissioned documentaries, is hardly an aleatory one within this context of the Hebrew/Israeli nation-building process. While in the past the land was barren, the theme of finding water points to the future, suggesting the establishment of a new settlement as one more step toward the goal of Jewish independence, a concept foregrounded by one of the Zionist currents, Tzionut Ma'asit (Practical Zionism), according to which the infrastructure was to be created by acquisition and cultivation of *dunam ahar dunam*. (one acre after another). (The theme of searching for water continued after the establishment of the state not only in documentaries, but also in narrative films, as in Sacha Alexander's *The Golden Key* [*Mafteah haZahav*, 1954].) *Sabra*'s "metaphysical" solution for political conflict between European Jews and Palestinian Arabs, furthermore, plays down the political significance of Arab resentment toward Zionism, reinforcing the notion of fanatic hostility on the part of Arabs. The Arabs' fight against the Hebrew pioneers is presented as reflecting a primitive belief in witchcraft, or as a desire for an Islamic *jihad*, or as the result of a kind of bloodlust, or, at the very best, as the result of manipulation by corrupt leaders who use the Zionist enemy to control their people.[50]

The War of Languages

Sabra must also be seen as existing at the point of conjuncture of an embryonic Hebrew Yishuv film industry and the beginnings of the revival of Hebrew as a (secular) spoken language. The film refers in an intertitle to the pioneers' decision to speak "exclusively the eternal language of their fathers," suggesting a reflexive dimension, for *Sabra* is itself a kind of pioneer as the first Hebrew-speaking narrative.[51] During the first three decades, plays, operas, and films were often discussed in terms of their contribution to the reinforcement and dissemination of Hebrew. The eagerness in the Yishuv to see *Sabra* derived, at least partially, from its Hebrew soundtrack. And when the first Hebrew-talking documentary, Agadati's *This is the Land*, was exhibited, it was enthusiastically welcomed as "a celebration of the Hebrew language" and advertised as "a film of *beReshit* [signifies both "in the beginning" and Genesis] with energies of *beReshit* about the way of life of people who began from *beReshit*." Thus advertisers-critics linked the film's theme of the modern beginnings of the Hebrew Yishuv and the theme of the modern secular renewal of the Biblical language.

Since the revival of Hebrew was perceived as playing a pivotal role in the national renaissance, deviations were strongly opposed by various organizations such as the association Only Hebrew (Rak Ivrit) and the Battalion for Defense of the Hebrew Language (Gdud Maginei haSafa haIvrit), protesting against the "Babel of tongues and foreign-language singing that swallow the sounds of our language in the streets of the first Hebrew city [Tel Aviv]."[52] The Battalion for Defense of the Hebrew Language used the strategy of singing Hebrew songs in Tel Aviv streets, and especially the song "Jew, speak Hebrew." Non-Hebrew-speaking theater and cinema became an object of attack. When Goldfaden's operetta *Shulamith* was performed in its original language, Yiddish, the Hebrew-language fanatics threw stink bombs. And when the film *My Jewish Mother* (*Mayne Yid-dishe Mame*, 1930)—the first American-Yiddish sound film to be distributed in Palestine—was premiered, they threw ink at the screen and stink bombs. Outside of the movie theater members of the Yishuv demonstrated, leading to the film's removal from the screen till a compromise was achieved. The compromise entailed the editing out of the Yiddish talking and singing parts, exhibiting the film without sound.[53] The shortlived use of dubbing during the late thirties and early forties is indebted to the unofficial banning of Yiddish in the Yishuv. Yaacov Davidon, for example, dubbed to Hebrew several imported Yiddish films. (Only in the sixties were Yiddish films shown again in the original language, when Israel was confident that Hebrew became its established language. And in 1983, the first Yiddish film, *When They Give, Take*, or *Az Men Git, Nemt Men*, was produced in Israel.) The "war of languages" played a role also in the resistance against other foreign talking cinemas. It was feared that such cinemas, predominant in terms of exhibition, would slow the spread of Hebrew as a spoken language—a concern also expressed in support of the musicians' protest against (foreign) talking cinema.[54]

The Hebrew language as spoken in Israel, however, has also not been exempt from the traces of Orientalist oppression. Through European-Jewish settlers, European languages penetrated Hebrew vocabulary, syntax, and pronunciation, forcing Hebrew Semitic phonetic patterns into a more European mold, one which took into account the language-learning difficulties of European Jews. (Yiddish and German were also considered as possible national tongues.) The new European Hebrew speakers preferred not to draw on the original Semitic and historically more "correct" pronunciation practiced by Sephardi speakers, one which more closely resembled Arabic. In the spirit of the nineteenth-century philological tradition, which censured defects ("barbarisms," "rigidity," "vagueness") in Arabic, thus implying the inferiority of its speakers and their civilization, the "pioneers of modern Hebrew" borrowed their methods from European comparative linguistics. Referring Hebrew to their native European tongues, the Ashkenazim imperiously assigned a negative value to everything specific to the Hebrew language. The practice of de-Semitization of Hebrew received, furthermore, institutional legitimation. Although the Committee on the Hebrew Language approved in 1913 the Sephardi accent as the correct one, Eurocentric linguistic criteria led some linguists to request the official elimination of certain consonants described as "barbarian," "clumsy," and "ugly."[55] Without the slightest scientific basis, Semitic phonemes came to be the object of derision; the Middle East was tuned out even as part of a linguistic paradigm.

The academic discourse concerning the Hebrew language bore serious consequences for performance on stage and screen. During the twenties, for example, some actors and actresses came under the influence of Ze'ev Jabotinsky, who taught them the Hebrew accent. In Jabotinsky's pseudo-geographical view, Hebrew was a Mediterranean language whose sounds more closely resembled Italian and Spanish than the languages of the Orient. Continuous and inseparable from his political views, such as his proposed "Iron Wall" in relation to the Arabs, his 1930 essay "The Hebrew Accent" displays the linguistic dimension of anti-Arabism:

> There are experts who think that we ought to bring our accent closer to the Arabic accent. But this is a mistake. Although Hebrew and Arabic are Semitic languages, it does not mean that our Fathers spoke in "Arabic accent" . . . We are European and our musical taste is European, the taste of Rubinstein, Mendelssohn, and Bizet.[56]

In the face of the most obvious linguistic and historical evidence, some scholars, along with the Yishuv's European practitioners of Hebrew, insisted on putative links of Hebrew to languages other than Arabic. The actors'/actresses' choice of

Jabotinsky's approved accent was of crucial importance in the more flexible accent-shaping period. Embodying the renaissance of the Hebrew language, the national HaBima Theater, for example, legitimized the assimilated version of modern Hebrew through its performances in the Jewish Yishuv and in Europe.

The pretext of rendering Hebrew pronounceable for Europeans becomes especially ironic when we recall that Sephardi Jews (and to some extent Israeli Palestinians) form the overwhelming majority of Hebrew speakers. Yet the Hebrew based on European linguistic habits came to be considered "Sabra Hebrew" or the "Israeli accent" and, in sociological terms, the accent of upward mobility, while the Semitic pronunciation of Hebrew, that of the Sephardim and Palestinians, became that of the marginal. The Hebrew (later Israeli) theater and cinema, meanwhile, as well as other institutions such as the educational system, radio, and television, also remained under the linguistic dominance of European Jews, further reinforcing a Eurocentric orientation. Casting in the theater and the cinema thus became inflected by countries of origin, as Israeli theatrical establishments denied roles to actors with Oriental accents. Arye Elias, who had played scores of classical roles on the Iraqi stage, for example, was rejected by government-subsidized repertory theaters on the grounds that his Oriental accent disqualified him for playing "classic" and "universal roles."[57] (Cultural prestige, as Pierre Bourdieu demonstrates, is inextricably linked to questions of class.)[58] When Elias at one point suggested himself for the role of Shylock, he was told that the audience would find his accent unduly "comic,"[59] an unfortunate refusal since a knowing director might have used the "marginal" accent as a way of underlining Shylock's own marginality within Christian Venice.[60] In this way most Sephardi actors were obliged to work largely in commercial theaters and popular cinema ("bourekas" films), where they often achieved impressive successes.

This ideologically motivated rejection of all Hebrew-Arabic cultural links implied the denial of a problematic Arab-Jewish entity. This denial seems especially strange when we recall that major Jewish texts in philosophy (Rav Saadia Gaon's *Hebrew Grammar*), poetry (Yehuda AlHarizi's and Ibn Gabirol's poems), and medicine (Maimonides' medical texts) were written in Arabic, and that both Hebrew and Arabic were at times together the "bad object" for anti-Semitic European philology, which posited a binary opposition, flattering to Europe's self-image, between the "organic" and "dynamic" Indo-European languages and the "inorganic" Semitic languages, "arrested, totally ossified, incapable of self-regeneration."[61]

Emphasized already in Yishuv cinema, as in *Sabra*'s celebration of the pioneers' return to the "eternal language of their fathers," the Zionist renewal of the Hebrew language reveals the paradox of resurrecting an Eastern tongue while simultaneously uprooting its Easternness. The Hebrew revival within the Zionist discourse of early Israeli cinema also entails the schism of a basically secular political movement whose nationalist linguistic paradigm is modern Hebrew, a movement whose superstructure had at the same time to be supported by a religious-ideological sub-stratum implicit in the notions of the Return of the "People of the Book" to the "Promised Land," and implicitly to the Edenic language.[62] In the following years, the ideal of a redemptive language unsullied by human intervention will be eclipsed by the "profane" concerns of a state in the process of consolidation, just as the residue of messianic fervor discernible in the pioneer film will give way to the secular concerns of an emerging nation.

2.

Post-1948: The Heroic-Nationalist Genre

Virtually no narrative films were produced between *Oded the Wanderer* and *Sabra* and the establishment of the state,[1] since most of the cinematic machinery was oriented toward the immediate practicality of newsreels and propaganda films. The year 1948, however, is significant in terms of both the establishment of the state and the development of the cinema. Film activity begins to be more organized and takes on a greater role not only in propagandizing for Zionism abroad but also in "socializing" new immigrants at home. Although roughly three decades separate pre-state films such as *Oded the Wanderer* and *Sabra* from post-state films such as *Hill 24 Doesn't Answer* (*Giv'a 24 Eina Ona*, 1955), *Pillar of Fire* (*Amud haEsh*, 1959), *They Were Ten* (*Hem Hayu Asara*, 1961), *Rebels Against the Light* (*Mordei Or*, 1964; distributed abroad as *Sands of Beer Sheba*), *Target Tiran* (*HaMatara Tiran*, 1968; distributed abroad as *Sinai Commando*), and *The Great Escape* (*HaPritza haGdola*, 1970; distributed abroad as *Eagles Attack at Dawn*), and although the political situation has evolved, in these films we still encounter a fundamentally similar structuring of images shaped by rudimentary Zionist ideology.

Until the mid- to late sixties most Israeli films focused on the virtually mythic Israeli heroes: Sabras, kibbutzniks, and soldiers, often within the context of the Israeli-Arab conflict, either as a backdrop, as in *Dan Quixote and Saadia Panza* (*Dan Quixote veSa'adia Panza*, 1956), *The Hero's Wife* (*Eshet haGibor*, 1963), *What a Gang* (*Havura sheKazot*, 1962), and *Give Me Ten Desperate Men* (*Havu Li Asara Anashim Meyuashim*, 1964), or at the center of the plot, as in *Hill 24 Doesn't Answer*, *Sinaia* (1962; distributed abroad as *Clouds over Israel*), *Rebels Against the Light*, and *Five Days in Sinai* (*Hamisha Yamim beSinai*, 1969). When not in the background, the conflict was presented within the confines of the war genre. I will examine several films that foreground the nationalist encounter between the two camps, scrutinizing their cinematic, narrative, and ideological codes, pointing out their patterns of self-representation and the representation of the Other, patterns which recur in the Zionist-nationalist films.

State of Siege and Didactic Allegories

During the fifties and early sixties, many of the producers, directors, and techni-
cians were foreign or recent immigrants such as the British filmmaker Thorold
Dickinson (*Hill 24 Doesn't Answer*),[2] the Jewish-American Larry Frisch (*Pillar
of Fire*), and the Iraqi-Jew Nouri Habib (*Without a Homeland* [*BeEin Moledet*,
1952]), all of whom contributed to an embryonic feature film industry. Initially
invited by the army film unit (established in 1948 by the Israeli Defense Forces
to commission instructional films for the army), Thorold Dickinson, for example, directed *The Red Background* (*Hareka haAdom*, 1953), a documentary on the
infantry. Dickinson, who had worked primarily on documentaries in Britain, was
influenced by the Grierson school, an influence partially seen in his feature, *Hill
24 Doesn't Answer*.

A relatively high-budget film ($400,000), *Hill 24 Doesn't Answer* was to a certain
extent commercially successful both in Israel and abroad and won two honorable
mentions at the Cannes Film Festival. Set during the 1948 war, the film revolves
around the personal stories of four fighters—an Irishman (Edward Mulhare), an
American-Jew (Michael Wager), a Sabra (Arik Lavi) and a Sephardi (Margalit
Oved)—assigned to defend a strategic hill outside Jerusalem and thus guarantee
Israel access to the city. On the way to their last mission they tell about the roots
of their Zionist conviction and of their previous battle experiences. The episodic
narrative structure attempts to present the Israeli struggle for independence from an
"objective" perspective, from several points of view—a practice quite uncommon
in the heroic-nationalist films.

Rather like the documentary procedures of Roberto Rossellini's *Paisan* (1946),
Hill 24 Doesn't Answer opens with an image of a strategic map of Israel and a
male voice-over which explains the movement of forces. The style of the opening
sequence already implies the status of "truth-telling" and documentation of "facts,"
while simultaneously assuming a specific Israeli perspective. The arrows which
designate the several directions of Arab attack on Israel point to the Israeli topos of
a nation-under-siege—a motif that will be expanded upon later in the film. *Hill 24
Doesn't Answer* then moves into its presentation of the four major characters, first
seen in close-up/medium shots identifying them as dead, while an offscreen voice
recites their names and provides a transition to the time when they were still alive,
before their mission. Their tragic dénouement is revealed at the very beginning of
the film, thus partially undercutting the dramatic tension of the story. Within this
general flashback, three additional flashbacks structure the film as three distinct
episodes, the stories of the fighters whose different histories converge on Hill 24.
Once their stories have been completed, and we now identify with their struggle,
they arrive by night at the hill, whose actual defense is not presented. We only hear
gunfire, after which the film cuts to the morning after and the arrival of a U.N.
jeep carrying a French U.N. official with an Israeli and an Arab, each claiming the

hill. The Arab argues that the defenders did not survive to claim the hill, but the official discovers the Israeli flag in the hands of the woman fighter, who obviously died when they were about to claim it. The Frenchman declares, therefore, that Hill 24 belongs to Israel.

Completing the narrative circle, the film returns at the end to the images of the dead protagonists, bringing to a climax the spectator's full identification, in contrast to the earlier, relatively distanced emotions towards the unknown dead soldiers of the opening sequence. The death of the protagonists, as in many non-Israeli nationalist films such as *Open City* (*Roma Città aperta*, 1945) or *The Battle of Algiers* (*La Battaglia di Algeri*, 1966), is allegorically compensated for by the rebirth of the country—the ultimate protagonist of the film. Within the Israeli context this narrative framework is intimately linked to the concept of self-sacrifice for the homeland expressed in such phrases as "*Bemotam tzivu lanu et hahayim*" ("In their death they granted life to us"). Death and Independence are strongly fused in the collective mind, a link rendered explicit in the close temporal neighboring of Yom haZikaron (Memorial Day) and Yom haAtzmaut (Independence Day). Marked by a symbolic transfer, the celebration of independence begins immediately following the end of the day of national mourning. The collective triumph concluding *Hill 24 Doesn't Answer*, by the same logic, is shown to be the result of an aggregate of numerous heroic acts of individuals whose death was necessary for the birth of the nation.

The didactic preoccupation with familiarizing the spectator with the story/ history of the Zionist fighters exists in flagrant contrast with the lack of concern for providing any substantial information about the Arabs. *Hill 24 Doesn't Answer*, like Larry Frisch's *Pillar of Fire*, perpetuates the classic cinematic dichotomy in war or Western genres by which the enemy's very anonymity is an integral necessity to the construction of his abstract evil character. As a kind of structuring absent-presence within the specific Middle Eastern context, the Arabs' nonexistent history implies as well a lack of solidified national identity. In other films set during the 1948 war, such as *Pillar of Fire*, Ze'ev Havatzelet's *What a Gang*, and Yossef Millo's *He Walked through the Fields* (*Hu Halakh baSadot*, 1967), Arab characters, similarly, do not appear, and particularly in *Pillar of Fire*, which focuses on the war itself, Arab soldiers, seen at a literal distance, are merely agents of violence. In *Give Me Ten Desperate Men*, furthermore, the Arabs do not appear in the film but perform the narrative role of abstract agent of death, since it is an Arab mine that kills the hero's beloved.

The brief appearance of two Arab officials in *Hill 24 Doesn't Answer* only reinforces the impression of a violent siege of Israel. At the same time, although there are no significant Arab characters in *Hill 24 Doesn't Answer*, the Arabs' existence is constantly referred to by the dialogue or implied by the actions of the protagonists. Their exclusive and fetishized narrative function is to attack, a mechanism that reinforces spectatorial identification with the Israeli forces. Seen

Triumph and martyrdom in *Hill 24 Doesn't Answer*.

largely within combat circumstances, the Arabs are almost always presented in long shot. When the battles take place at night, the spectator is completely distanced from their humanity. Their great numbers, in soldiers and tanks, contrast with their minimal impact on the spectator. They are not privileged with close-ups and are often identified as the enemy through the synecdochic *kaffiya* on the head and gun in the hands. During the battles, the camera is usually literally "on the side" of the Israeli soldiers, virtually suturing the spectator into a pro-Israeli position.

Although set during the British Mandate over Palestine (the earliest chronological point in *Hill 24 Doesn't Answer*), and more specifically during the post-Holocaust period of illegal Jewish immigration, when the British were seen as enemies by the Yishuv and violently resisted by Jewish underground movements, the film has the British soldiers exert more presence than the Arabs and treats them more sympathetically. This appointing of sympathy and interest reflects a broader attention given to European history and culture, while completely marginalizing that of the Arabs, an orientation continuous with policies outside of the cinema, for example, in terms of educational policy.[3] The British in *Hill 24 Doesn't Answer* are privileged in relation to the Arabs in terms of the narrative time devoted to them, in terms of the right to dialogue and close-ups, and even in terms of the cinematic eliciting of identification. In an early sequence in the film, for example, a Jewish child is crying when a British jeep stops and a soldier expresses great concern. After a woman explains that the child wants to go home, the film cuts to a medium/close-up shot of the British soldier staring pensively in the distance and saying, "So do I. So do I." The sequence then suggests both the good-heartedness of the British soldier and the fact that his presence in Palestine is reluctant. Unlike the Jordanian and Egyptian soldiers in the later episodes, he is there against his will. The portrayal of the British Mandate reflects not only the fact that the film was made by a British filmmaker, but also the warm relations between Israel and Britain at the period in which the film was made. (In 1956 Israel, Britain, and France fought together against Egypt in still another expression of geopolitical affinity with the colonizing West.)

The vacuum in relation to the Arabs also forms a striking contrast with the portrayal of the Druse. As we see images of a Druse village, a male voice-over narration informs us that despite certain similarities with the Arabs, the Druse are nevertheless religiously distinct. A Druse woman who sings in Hebrew and Arabic is played by a popular Israeli (a Yemenite Jew) singer, Shoshana Damari. The casting of a well-known singer here reinforces the categorization of the Druse as the "good natives." The sympathy projected toward the Druse also directly reflects official Israeli policies, which treat the Druse as trusted allies who are even allowed to serve in the Israeli army.

While the Arabs are anonymous both as individual characters and as a collective, the Israeli soldiers (or allies) are presented as individual subjects whose evolving consciousness forms part of a national collective history. The Israeli position is summarized several times through various cinematic and narrative means. On the dialogue level, in the second episode, for example, when the American Jew—still in the role of the objective observer who has not yet taken sides—asks an Israeli, following an Arab attack, how the Israelis could possibly win against the Arabs' superior numbers, the Israeli responds: "No choice. This is our secret." The answer prepares for the next, more visual explanation. In the swimming pool sequence, forming part of the same episode, the American, while still in the first stages of his education, is initiated into the realities of the Jewish experience and the nature of Zionism; the experience and views of the Arabs, meanwhile, remain unexplained. Arguing with an Englishman and an Arab representative, the American complains that the British help the Arabs because of oil interests while the Jewish refugees, returning to their homeland and with no other place to go, are expelled. The selfless concern of the American with Jewish suffering is contrasted with the superficiality of the Arab enjoying himself at the pool, with no ennobling political cause to defend. The sequence ends with the Arab character demonstrating exactly how Jewish existence in Palestine will come to an end; he pushes the Jewish-American into the pool.

While echoing the rhetorical excesses of Arab propaganda, this image also plays to the fears of Israel as a state under siege between the literal sea and the metaphorical sea of Arabs. The "no-choice" structure of feelings is thus correlated with a precise topographical situation, reproduced in Israeli propaganda as well. Feature films, in this context, must be seen in homological terms as part of a continuum of "discourses" which includes political speeches, journalistic editorials, song lyrics and cartoons. Commissioned documentaries, official speeches, and propaganda booklets designed for Israeli tourists abroad, for example, all emphasized the Arab desire to throw the Jews into the sea, and at times featured the caricature of a huge Arab with a *kaffiya* kicking a tiny Sabra with a *tembel* hat. In the face of Arab aggression, Israeli tourists, primed with the "knowledge to answer," were perceived by the state as potential ambassadors of good will, representatives of a collective entity, expected to suppress all potential criticism in the face of the West- ern "Goyim," presented somewhat schizophrenically as both "natural" allies and anti-Semites *in potentia.* The proportions in the caricature as well as the need for an image of unanimity partially stem from a state-of-siege mentality whose collective origins can be traced not only to the disproportionate numbers of Arab soldiers available for combat, but also to the Europe of the pogroms and to the justified ghetto paranoia of a few defenseless Jews under attack from crazed anti-Semitic mobs.

Although Israel viewed itself as the antithesis of the ghetto mentality, its official discourse inevitably transposed certain elements from the shtetl past, especially the notion of the few under siege by the many, now within the anguished heroism of the "no-choice" situation. It is in this context that we must understand the Israeli man's statement to the Jewish-American in *Hill 24 Doesn't Answer*, as well as the cut from the end of the swimming pool sequence—in which the American figuratively experiences what might happen to Jews in Palestine if the Arabs win— to a close shot of a newspaper headline: "Israel is born." The juxtaposition of images comes to illustrate what has been already expressed by the Israeli character, namely that the lack of choice, the lack of an alternative refuge, is the secret fount of heroism and of Israel's moral right to exist. The rationale reflects Zionist hermetic debate; its main flaw is the exclusion of the Arabs of Palestine. The films relay, in this sense, an official Israeli political discourse which has consistently elided the reality of the Palestinian people, whether explicitly (Golda Meir's affirmation that there is no such thing as the Palestinian people) or implicitly (in the current denial of the Palestinian right for self-representation and even the denial of the legal right of Jewish Israelis to conduct a dialogue with the Palestine Liberation Organization).

This historical elision, then, is reproduced in films such as *Hill 24 Doesn't Answer* through their nonrecognition of Arab-Palestinian history and culture. The Arab attack is decontextualized, rendered as irrational and malignant, while the spectator is prepared psychologically and historically to take the Israeli side, as, for example, in the sequence preceding the battle over the old city of Jerusalem. The commander (played by Yossef Yadin, a brother of the famous archeologist Yigael Yadin) makes a speech about the Jewish return to the Holy Land (presented ethno-centrically as unproblematic). While he speaks offscreen about the walls of Jerusalem waiting expectantly for Israeli soldiers for two thousand years, the camera performs a lengthy pan along the walls, followed by a parallel lengthy pan along the line of Israeli soldiers standing at silent attention like the walls. The Hebrew expression denoting the military "stand at attention" (la'amod dom), likewise, signifies both nonmovement and silence, setting also the metaphorical parallel between the "waiting" walls and the soldiers waiting to break in and reach them. The standing still, of both Israeli soldiers and the walls that surrounded the Jewish Temple, before the crucial act of reunification, encodes the idealist view of the Jewish people as excluded from world history since the rebellion of Bar Kokhba and the subsequent exile, and with the rise of modern Zionism finally melting two millennia of frozen history. The visual and linguistic metaphors point, then, to a didactic allegory of renewal: the need of the Israeli Defense Forces to regenerate, via the ancient walls, the links of the present, of the young reborn Jew, i.e., Israeli, with the past, with the Kingdom of Israel.

The role of archeology in Israeli culture, it should be pointed out, has been crucial in the disinterring of remnants of the Biblical past, at times enlisted in the political effort to demonstrate a historical right to Eretz Israel. In dramatic contrast to the Jewish "archeology of the text," this idea of physical archeology as demonstration carries with it the obverse notion of the physical homeland as text, to be allegorically read, within Zionist hermeneutics, as a "deed to the land." And corollary to this is the notion of historical "strata" within a political geology. The deep stratum, in the literal and figurative sense, is associated with the Israeli-Jews, while the surface level is associated with the Arabs, as a recent "superficial" historical element without millennial "roots." Since the Arabs are seen as "guests" in the land, their presence must be downplayed, much as the surface of the land has at times been "remodeled" to hide or bury remnants of Arab life and Arab villages, which, in certain instances, have been replaced with Jewish ones. The linguistic, lexical expression of this digging into the land to reach the substratum is the archeology of place-names. Some Arabic names of villages, it was discovered, were close to or based on the Biblical Hebrew names of the pre-Arab period; in some cases, therefore, Arabic names were replaced with old-new Hebrew ones.

In *Hill 24 Doesn't Answer*, the protagonists themselves invariably explain and justify Zionist logic and acts. The Western connections of the protagonists— an Irishman, a Jewish-American, and a Sabra of European origin—is a device partially designed to make the film's didactic thrust palatable to Western audiences through the assumed intimacy and sympathy of "us" versus "them." Such a device is especially important since Zionism, being conceived in the colonialist Europe, could only hope for essential support in the area that remained (at least partially) its spiritual motherland. Through the Western characters, the film prods its spectators toward specific positions and conclusions. The Western spectatorial consciousness is deemed inseparable from the world view of the protagonists; the spectator is assumed to begin the viewing at a specific cognitive stage as the non-Israeli characters begin the story, either as an ideological tabula rasa like the Irish character, or as objectively skeptical like the American.

The Zionist rhetoric of the film is further emphasized by the ordering of the episodes, of which the first is devoted to the Irishman, the second to the American, and the last and briefest to the Sabra, who is a priori convinced of his role and his country's role within history. The three episodes, forming a kind of tripartite *Bildungsroman*, all point to the same conclusion. They chronicle the evolving Zionist consciousness of the protagonists and, through them, of the spectator. The device of focalizing the narrative through various characters who are historically and ethnically diverse enables the film to maintain a façade of democratic distribution of points of view despite its didactic agenda. Informed by Zionist teleology, the stories, told on the way to Hill 24, realize the full potential of their telos only upon arrival. The merging of the three stories into the brief final episode on Hill 24 reflects the final unification of points of view within a heroic-nationalist mold.

In the first episode, devoted to the Irishman, the flashback begins in the pre-state days of illegal seaborne transport of Holocaust survivors. The Irishman works for the British Mandate police. In the course of preventing Jewish immigration and following suspected members of the underground, he becomes enamored of the Zionist Sabra played by Haya Hararit (who later became famous through *Ben Hur*) and through her gradually comes to identify with the Zionist cause. Haya Hararit is privileged by many close-ups which not only emphasize her beauty and warmth but also encourage spectatorial identification with her passionate declarations. Close shots, for example, accompany the dialogue in which she rhetorically asks the British police: "We only want home and peace. Is that too much to ask?" The Irish-Sabra love affair, made impossible by conflict between Jews and the British, is in the end facilitated by the British departure from Palestine and the Israeli declaration of independence. The Irishman returns, joining not only the Israeli woman he loves (now a soldier in the Israeli army), but also the struggle of her country. The Israeli woman fully accepts him when he is about to go and fight on Hill 24, when he, the Christian, takes an active role in the Israeli struggle. The transformation of a British officer into a pro-Zionist soldier, then, allegorically evokes the recruitment of the West for the Israeli struggle. The real enemies of Zionism, it is implied, are not the British but the Arabs. At the same time, the Irishness of the character calls subtle attention to possible analogies between Ireland under British rule and Jews under colonial rule in Palestine. The Irishman sacrifices his life for Israel, and his death ultimately links the Western spectator to the Israeli cause. And for the Israeli spectator of the fifties, when immigrants were arriving from different parts of the world, the fact that even a non-Jew was willing to die for Israel heightened the sense of pride, unity, and collective responsibility. At the same time, the Irishman's death conveniently ends the mixed romance between Jewish woman and Christian man, still a problematic issue within Jewish Israel.

Beginning an "Israeli phase" in 1949 with *Sword in the Desert* through such films as *The Juggler* (1953; the first to be shot entirely on location in Israel), *Exodus* (1960), *Judith* (1965), and *Cast a Giant Shadow* (1966), Hollywood films about Israel tended to present mixed romances quite differently. Celebrating not only the literal exodus from Europe to Israel, and the spiritual one, from the plight of being passive Diaspora victims to becoming courageous Israelis, *Exodus*, to take one example, also celebrates the cognitive transformation and the recruitment of the Wasp American woman (Eva Marie Saint). Due to her particular circumstances, she happens to come to the area without prior commitment to any side, but through witnessing the struggle for survival and being forced to make choices, as well as through her romance with a Sabra officer (Paul Newman), she becomes an enthusiastic supporter of Zionism, joining the country and her lover. The same Waspish-looking woman who at the inception of the film confessed to the British officer, "I feel strange among them" (referring to Jewish refugees), appears dressed like a Sabra in the final sequence where she is struggling alongside the Israelis. The sincerity of the tough Sabra, the burden of war, and the murder of both a young Holocaust survivor and a peace-loving Arab make possible her spiritual exodus from alienation. Now she is an immigrant within a Jewish majority, suggesting for the mainstream American spectator that Jews are not a wandering minority, but a normal nation with a country of their own.

The narrative closure formulaically seals the classical constitution of the couple and its integration into a harmonious world of order. This topos of unification comes to signify, in the context of such films as *Exodus* and *Sword in the Desert*,[4] a quasi-total harmony of interests between Israel and the West (and the United States in particular). This mythical Hollywood identity of interests can be seen on another level as well. The casting of a virtually archetypical Anglo-American star in the role of the Sabra undoes the largely negative connotations of the stereotypes of the Jew within the Western-Christian popular mind and equates him with the desired hero of American dreams. Paul Newman embodies the virility of both the Sabra soldier and the American fighter, merging both into one myth, reinforced and paralleled by the close political and cultural Israeli-American links since the sixties. Israel, in conjunction with Hollywood, in other words, made possible the filmic transformation of the passive Diaspora victim into the heroic Jew. Not only is he not afraid of anti-Semites; he has the courage and chutzpah to mock them. Believing the young officer, Paul Newman, is not a Jew, the British officer makes anti-Semitic slurs. When the officer claims that "They look funny; you can spot them right away," Ari Ben Canan (Newman) tricks him into checking his eyes. The film thus establishes a kind of complicity between the spectator, who knows the young officer is Israeli, and Ari Ben Canan, who charmingly demonstrates the blind inanity of anti-Semitic prejudice. The film hints, in a sense, that Israeli experience has "normalized" the Jew, so that now even the anti-Semite cannot spot him. The Sabra-Wasp link is reinforced, finally, on a linguistic level. While the weak Jewish immigrants to Israel generally speak Yiddish-accented English, the Sabra hero and his heroine sister speak with the hegemoic American accent.

Hill 24 Doesn't Answer's second episode chronicles the conversion of the American Jew to Zionism, a theme foregrounded later in Hollywood's *Cast a Giant Shadow*, which tells the story of the actual Colonel Marcus (Kirk Douglas). (In *Pillar of Fire*, in contrast, the American Jew is assumed to be Zionist from the very beginning of the film.) The education of the American Jew in *Hill 24 Doesn't Answer* evolves through several phases within the flashback. First, during his visit to Jerusalem (before the establishment of the state), he witnesses a surprise attack by Arabs who throw stones at the travel agency office he happens to be visiting. When his cheek is slightly injured, he experiences in his own body, for the first time, Arab aggressivity, provoking him to ask skeptically how so few could fight so many. He receives, we recall, the determined answer that the "no-choice" situation engenders the audacity of survival. In the later swimming pool sequence, the Jewish-American already takes a less aloof position, posing the British and Arab representatives a Jewish-Israeli question: "What will happen with the Jewish refugees?" In this second phase of his education, he is forced to experience at first hand the future of Jews in Palestine if Arabs attain power, i.e., the Jews will be thrown into the water/sea. Twice the victim of cruel and irrational Arab aggression, he comes to appreciate the "no-choice" situation of Jews in Palestine. With the birth of the State of Israel he joins its army to fight in one of the landmark battles of the 1948 war—the struggle for the old city of Jerusalem. Indeed, it is in the fabled old city of Jerusalem that he is initiated into the last phase of his Zionist apprenticeship, not simply joining the righteous, but also shedding his assimilated past and returning to his Jewish origins.

The final transition occurs when the Jewish-American is injured in battle during the siege. In an atmosphere of Jewish solidarity, in which nurses take care of the wounded, the Jewish-American still refuses the (Ashkenazi) Rabbi's religious proddings: "I hate your God . . . he has no mercy . . . Anyway where is he? Where was he everytime we needed him?"—a rhetorical question often asked by nonreligious Jews to justify their anti-religious feelings in the post-Holocaust period. The Rabbi is seen largely from the point of view of the American lying on the bed; yet the subjective medium shots from low angles emphasize the Rabbi's authority. His abstract religious speech—"The forces of evil are bigger, seeking destruction"—lends a metaphysical aura to the political struggle over Jerusalem. While in *Sabra* "metaphysics" provided a solution for political conflict in the form of a deus-ex-machina finale, in *Hill 24 Doesn't Answer*—the latter made twenty years after the former, years during which the historical chasm of the Holocaust and the establishment of the State of Israel took place—metaphysics are integrated into Zionist apologetics. Within the context of Jordanian siege, the Rabbi's words gain the specific implication that the many Arabs are the "forces of evil seeking destruction." In the post-Holocaust period, the Rabbi's words, furthermore, implicitly link what are seen as two parallel forces of evil for Jews: Nazis and Arabs. This link, as we shall see, will be clearly stated in the following Sabra-soldier episode. Another wounded Israeli soldier, meanwhile, quotes an appropriate verse from Psalms (in English), ". . . Though I walk in the shadow of the valley of death, I shall fear no evil, for thou art with me. . . . ," emphasizing trust in God and hope even in moments of despair. This quotation reminds the Jewish-American of his religious upbringing, and while Jews are forced to evacuate Jerusalem we witness a climactic and final moment in his education, that of absolute acceptance: the wounded Jewish-American on the stretcher and the Rabbi hold hands as they are evacuated from the holy city of Jewish dreams.

Mourning the fall of the old city to the Jordanians, the Jews are forced to be refugees from Jerusalem—a sequence characterized by heightened drama, even in relation to other sequences in the film. The symphonic music of Paul Ben-Haim and the long takes showing Jews (some carrying the Torah) walking between smoke and fire expressionistically draw attention to this tragic moment in Jewish history. The evacuation is largely seen in long shot with scarcely any close-ups of individuals; the long shots (long in both focal length and duration) of the stream of Jewish refugees give a collective-national dimension and evoke a figural series of disastrous departures and painful exiles within Jewish history. Within this emotionally elevated moment of conflagration the holding of hands—also one of the concluding shots of the episode—by the Rabbi and the American Jew, a climactic moment of Jewish unity reflects the solidarity of Jews from different places as well as the unity of secular and religious Jews.

The enlistment of religious Judaism into the Zionist struggle reflects the incorporation of religious persuasion into the apologia of what is basically a secular, political Zionism (although one might argue that Zionism itself is characterized by a constant sliding between the two, in which subliminally religious ideas transmute themselves into political discourse). The appearance of a Rabbi in the Jerusalem sequences is essential to the Zionist claim on Jerusalem. The evacuation sequence also features an Arab looting a religious object while the camera tilts up to the Jews walking on the walls looking down (as if looking down at him)—thus evoking a certain moral and religious superiority. Although the Arabs have won this battle, the image suggests, the Jews remain on a spiritually superior plane. The Jerusalem episode, in other words, posits two claims over Palestine: one historical, emphasized by the inception of this section through the commander's speech about the ancient walls, preceding the battle over Jerusalem, and the other religious, expressed through the Rabbi's evocation of the Biblical claim on the Promised Land.

Staging partition: Jewish refugees evacuate the Old City in *Hill 24 Doesn't Answer.*

Focusing on the Sabra, the third episode takes place largely in the southern zone, during the battle with Egypt, and therefore summons up again the siege situation of simultaneous attack by several Arab countries, a theme graphically initiated by the menacing arrows of the opening map sequence. The Sabra is portrayed as a humanistic soldier who takes pity on his enemy, whom he assumes to be a wounded Egyptian soldier, only to discover that he is in fact a German-speaking Nazi. Carried on the Sabra's shoulders, the wounded "Egyptian" does not appreciate the help and tries to release the trigger of the hand grenade literally behind the Sabra's back. The Israeli manages to control him and does not even lose his sense of humor. "Things like that cost money," he says in an obvious reference to the scarcity of means that characterized Israel in its early years and especially to the idea that despite the lack of weapons Israelis managed to fight the Arabs thanks to improvisation and the recycling of captured Arab weapons. The Sabra takes care of the wounded enemy even when he discovers he is a Nazi. A close-up reflects his internal conflict, followed by the Nazi's monologue. Afraid of being killed, the Nazi "explains" his acts, portraying Nazis like himself as bloodthirsty animals: "We are born to fight. If there are no wars we'll have to invent them." A quick pan from the Nazi to the Sabra shows the Sabra from the point of view of the Nazi as a humiliated Jew from the ghetto. The Nazi is not killed by the Israeli; rather he talks himself to death. The Sabra asks rhetorically: "He is one. How many more of them are there?" suggesting that there are more Nazis fighting along with the Arabs against Israel. Appearing toward the end *of Hill 24 Doesn't Answer*, the Nazi sequence offers the final clinching "argument" within the didactic allegorical thrust of the film. The defense of the hill immediately following the Nazi sequence suggests that Israel fights the Arabs in the spirit of "never again." In keeping with the feeling of the post-Holocaust era, the film then cultivates the new Jewish hero in the East, rising phoenix-like from the ashes of Western catastrophes, to confront a similar enemy in another place.

The Arab-Nazi link is made explicitly or implicitly in other films as well. Also set during the 1948 war, Larry Frisch's *Pillar of Fire*, for example, tells the story of the defense of a small pioneering southern kibbutz against superior numbers of Egyptian tanks. The image expressed in the film's title evokes the Auschwitz death apparatus, a point confirmed by one of the film's central characters, a Holocaust survivor, who is reminded of Auschwitz' smoke chimneys when he sees a pillar of smoke rising from a burned tank. His anguished reminiscences about the extermination camps are delivered simultaneously with a threatened Arab attack. In Menahem Golan's James Bondian *Cairo Operation (Mivtza Cahir*, 1965), German scientists, old and young, work for the Egyptians in the effort to develop atomic missiles against Israel, showing a narrative contrast between the scientifically advanced Germans and the backward Arabs—in accord with stereotypes of stupid Arabs reflected in popular culture, especially in sketches and jokes—here united in their evil acts. In Golan's children's film *Eight Trail One* (*Shmona beIkvot Ehad*, 1964; based on Yemima Chernewitch's children's book of the same title), a German, disguised as a respectable university science professor, spies on the Israeli air force (an elite unit within the Israeli army) in the service of the Arabs. (German, it is worth mentioning, is virtually a synonym for Nazi in the Israel of the late forties through the early seventies.) The film pays homage to certain literary trends, especially in youth literature, that evoke the Nazi-Arab analogy as in Ze'ev Vardi's *Who Runs in the Lanes (Mi Ze Ratz baSimta'ot)* and On Sarig's *Danideen in the Hijacked Airplane (Danideen baMatos heHatuf*).[5]

In addition to Israeli coproductions that focused on Holocaust survivors—*The Glass Cage (Kluv haZkhukhit*, 1964)—and on Nazis in Israel—*Hour of Truth* (*Sh'at haEmet*, 1964)—films that were made immediately following the furor surrounding the Eichmann trial—other films also explicitly posited an Arab-Nazi link. *Judith*, for example, revolves around the Jewish ex-wife (Sophia Loren) of a Nazi officer smuggled into Israel by the Haganah (Defense) underground to help identify her former husband, who is advising the Arabs in their war against the new state. Based on Leon Uris' novel and shot largely in Israel, *Exodus* also directly associates Arabs and Nazis as conniving in the destruction of Israel. Murderous Arabs, trained by an expert sadistic Nazi, hang a peace-loving Arab and slaughter a young woman Holocaust survivor. The Nazi-Arab connection even penetrates Hollywood films which do not involve Israel, as suggested indirectly in *Ship of Fools* by having a former German Nazi praise the Arabs as "my kind of people."

These films wildly stretch the limits of historical verisimilitude, suggesting that we are dealing with a misplaced political paradigm. Although never victimized by Nazism the way Jews were, Arabs were also despised as a Semitic sub-Aryan race (witness German propaganda films denouncing the Allies for using Blacks, Berbers, and Arabs from the colonies as part of their army). It is true that during World War II certain currents of Egyptian nationalism did consider Germany as a potential ally, but the tactic was largely motivated by hostility to British domination and colonialism in Egypt.[6] (The pro-Axis temptation was later criticized by Egypt's president, Abdul Gamal Nasser, in *The Philosophy of the Revolution*.) It is also true that the Grand Mufti of Jerusalem was in contact with Hitler about a possible alliance, but some Zionist leaders in Palestine also were not above making alliances of convenience with the Nazis in pursuit of their own nationalist goals.[7]

It is a historical irony that both Semitic groups, the Israeli Zionists and the Arab anti-Zionists, have ended up relying, whether explicitly or implicitly, on traditional anti-Semitic imagery in relation to their "ethnic cousins." Arab books on the Israeli-Arab conflict such as one published by the Jordanian Educational Ministry included, for example, nine pages of the classic European anti-Semitic literature "Protocols of the Elders of Zion" with the additional explanations, for instance, that the "Jews regard themselves as the chosen people and want to take over the world."[8] In Arab folklore stories and fiction, as pointed out by Shmuel Moreh and Shimon Ballas,[9] the Jew (the Israeli is frequently regarded as the Jew) is portrayed in a manner reminiscent of European anti-Semitic folklore, as tight-fisted and cowardly, part of a conspiratorial group accumulating capital through high-interest loans, an aggressive pariah whose hand is against every man and against whom every man's hand is raised, a crook who exploited the good-heartedness of the Arab and, therefore, won in 1948. (The first novel to introduce anti-Semitic elements to the Palestinian novel and to the Arab one was, according to Shimon Ballas,[10] Halil Baidas—considered the pioneer of the Palestinian story— in his novel of the thirties, *The Inheritor*.) If Israeli fiction structured the syntagm of Arab and Nazi united against Israel, Arab fiction employed a contemporary process of shaping the negative image of the Israeli, developing a quite similar chain of association by which the Jew practiced the Nazi extermination methods toward the Arabs.[11]

In Israeli fiction, it is especially in youth literature that we find clearly anti-Semitic imagery supporting the negative portrayal of the Arab, metonymically linking supposed Arab cruelty and violence with Semitic features. The stereotypical characteristics include the hooked nose, scar, dark terrorizing eyes, face of a bird of prey, yellow rotten teeth, and dark complexion, all correlated with the internal properties of the Arab as hot-blooded, cruel, mendacious, avaricious, and cowardly.[12] Israeli heroic-nationalist cinema proliferates similarly negative characterizations, at times offering, as in *Dynamite at Night* (*Pitzutz baHatzot*, 1965; an Israeli-French coproduction), the European medieval anti-Semitic portrayal of the Jew transposed onto the Arab; a satanic image of the Arabs as potential thieves of children is here filtered through the story of the presumed kidnapping of the daughter of a French engineer in Israel. The Franco-Israeli alliance after the 1956 war was reflected on a cinematic level by Israeli-French coproductions on Jewish themes, such as *The Glass Cage* (*Kluv haZkhukhit*) and *Only Not on Saturday* (*Rak Lo beShabbat*). As often, official ideology and cinematic practice show themselves to be intimately linked.

More common than the traditional anti-Semitic imagery, however, is the ritualized use of references to recent modern anti-Semitism (whose basis is not simply religious, but also racial). Associating Nazis with Arabs and juxtaposing the Holocaust and Nazism with the Israeli-Arab conflict became not merely a staple of Zionist rhetoric—but also a symptom of a Jewish European nightmare projected onto the structurally distinct political dynamics of the Middle East. The process involves, on one level, a mechanism of displacement, the product of a kind of ideological desire, a wish for an equation, which, while historically false, has the value of rationalizing present behavior and eliminating ethical and political ambiguities. In a context of Jews experiencing an utterly different history within the Arab world than that which haunted the memories of European Jews, and in a context of Palestinians' dispossession of their national rights by European Jews, the conflation of Arabs with the archetypal oppressor of Jews grotesquely oversimplifies an ideologically complex question and equates the present-day oppressed with the past oppressor. The Arab-Nazi conflation, in other words, serves as a mechanism by which it is possible to censor any skepticism with regard to a self-image of moral superiority and of sincere faith in a just cause. Such images are calculated to appeal to the stock responses of uninformed spectators, while also catalyzing for the post–World War II spectator the release of negative emotions toward the Arab image as a corollary of the Nazi, the grand antagonist within the twentieth-century Western imagination. At the same time, for the Jewish spectator especially, the depiction of a militant Israel punishing its enemies could provide a kind of cathartic feeling of vicarious vengeance for centuries of humiliation now exorcised on the backs not of the Nazis but of the Arabs.

Arab antagonism to Jewish Israel can in no way be equated with European anti-Semitism, even if European anti-Semitism has occasionally penetrated Arab culture. An essential difference separates the failure of the nineteenth-century and early-twentieth-century Jewish attempt at assimilation in Europe and the Arab refusal to accept Israel. European anti-Semitism had only the "testimony" of its own myths about the crucifixion of Christ and the imagined conspiratory power of the elders of Zion to incriminate the Jews. Arab antagonism toward Jews, meanwhile, derives from an actual process of Arab victimization. While assimilation was not at the expense of Europe, and was not directed at creating a separate and different identity, the establishment of the State of Israel was directed at creating a separate Jewish-European entity in a territory already inhabited by the Arabs and occurred at the expense of the Palestinian people, who paid the price for Europe's overwhelming oppression of its Jews. The irony of representing the historical processes in Palestine through the interpretative frame of an anxiety borne of specifically European history, as done in relation to the 1948 war in *Hill 24 Doesn't Answer*, *Pillar of Fire*, and *Exodus*, is obvious when one considers that the Israeli war of independence is perceived by the Arabs as *elNakba* (the catastrophe).

Hill 24 Doesn't Answer's reductionist view of the Arab as a synecdoche for negativity and violence is accompanied by European paternalism toward the "friendly East," the Druse and especially Oriental Jews epitomized in the Esther Hadassi character. The only detail she provides about herself concerns her place of birth—Jerusalem—but her accent and appearance make it clear that her family's country of origin is Yemen. She appears briefly in the background in the Jerusalem episode as a nurse, subordinated to the Jewish-American story. Yet, although she is one of the four protagonists assigned to defend Hill 24, she is granted no episode of her own, as if she had no particular story to tell. It is up to us, therefore, to make the text's silences, and her silences, speak.

As a corollary to Zionist Eurocentricism, the history of Jews from the Middle East is also eliminated/subordinated to the Jewish-European memory. (In Israeli schools, the numerous Jewish-history classes feature very little reference to the history of Jews in the Arab and Muslim world.) The Arab historical memory of the Jewish-Yemenite woman is elided, an absence forming an integral part of her definition as one of the four Zionist heroes. The Arab-inflected culture of Oriental Jews was seen as fated for extinction, in accord with general colonialist assumptions with regard to the East, as expressed by various Zionist leaders, whether on the right (Ze'ev Jabotinsky and the Revisionist movement) or on the left (David Ben-Gurion and the Labor movement). In the context of the mid-fifties (when the film was made), following the mass immigration of Arab-Jews, the creation of Jewish national unity came to imply the melting down of Orientals into the hegemonic Ashkenazi culture and ideology based on the assumption of a single official Jewish history, that of Europe. In this sense, it is scarcely surprising that the film has the (Ashkenazi) Sabra reencounter his European history, condensed into the image of the Nazi, the oppressor of his ancestors, but never shows an encounter of the Oriental "Sabra" (the term does not normally include Israeli-born Orientals but does include European and American-born Israelis raised in Israel)[13] with her historical roots in the East, or with those with whom her ancestors shared, basically, a life of coexistence, i.e., the Arabs, even though the film, like Israel, is "set" in the Middle East. While European Jewish history is referred to in all three episodes—through Holocaust refugees in the Irishman episode, through the Jewish-American arguments, and through the Nazi character in the Sabra episode—Oriental Jewish history is totally excluded from representation. Through a process of elimination of the East and privileging of the West, the heroic-nationalist films thus structure the dominant Zionist historiography of all Jews as that of European pogroms and persecutions.

Filtered out by a Eurocentric grid, the Orient lacks all history and its inhabitants remain anonymous. But while the "bad East," the Arabs, is spuriously linked to the evils of European-Nazism, the "good East," the Arab-Jews, is absorbed into the history of European Jews. This image of the civilization of the Other—seen as a vacuous space onto which the European projects progress and enlightenment—fosters the paternalist attitudes seen in the heroic-nationalist films directed toward Arabs. The presence of the Oriental Jewish character in *Hill 24 Doesn't Answer* is in fact somewhat anomalous in the heroic-nationalist films, which tend to focus exclusively on Occidental Jewish history and on the pioneering work and defensive war of the Sabras. It is through the Sephardi woman character, furthermore, that the film structures the intersection of sexuality and Orientalism as inferiority. She asks the Irishman, for example, with her Yemenite accent (associated with "cuteness," "naïveté," and sincerity), a rather ignorant question: "Where is Ireland, in England?" a question that reflects negative stereotypes of Orientals as being "primitive," "illiterate," and having lower I.Q.s. The Sabra man answers ironically: "And where is Israel, in Egypt?" Although she has a "natural" religious ability to quote the Hebrew Bible, she lacks a "universal" knowledge (held as more significant than the Biblical by predominantly secular official Israel). "Real" knowledge is monopolized by the Sabra man, who thus serves as translator and cultural mediator between her and the Irishman, between the "underdeveloped" and the "civilized" world, paralleling the Zionist view of its role as bridging the gap between East and West.

Casting in *Hill 24 Doesn't Answer* also has certain ideological implications. In many films of the heroic-nationalist genre, Sephardim tend to perform Arab roles, while in the "bourekas" films of the sixties and seventies—to be discussed in Chapter 3—Ashkenazim tend to play Sephardi characters. In *They Were Ten*, for example, the Arab thief is played by Yossef Bashi, in Ilan Eldad's *Sinaia* the Egyptian soldier is played by Shaike Levi, while in Menahem Golan's *The Great Escape*, the cruel head of a Syrian jail for war prisoners is performed by Yossef Shiloach, and the Druse by Yossef Levi. "Arab masses" for crowd scenes were usually recruited from Sephardi towns, as in *Five Days in Sinai*, which employed the inhabitants of the "development towns" Dimona and Yeruham. In *Hill 24 Doesn't Answer*, the Sephardi singer Shoshana Damari enacts the role of a Druse woman, while nonprofessionals, all Oriental Jews, appear as Arab soldiers. The schizophrenic complexity of the Jewish-Arab identity in Israel is signaled, to a certain extent, by this phenomenon of exploiting the Sephardim's Middle Eastern body language and Semitic physiognomy, thus casting them as an integral part of the Arab Middle East. Their Jewishness, however, categorizes them, as in *Hill 24 Doesn't Answer*, as knowing the Hebrew Bible, but as otherwise lacking all specific Jewish-Arab history. This hegemonic, artificial Arab/Jewish dichotomy, reproduced in *Hill 24 Doesn't Answer*, reifies the oppression (and implied repression) of the Arabness of Jews in the name of integrating them into a monolithic European-Jewish society, to "give" them the pseudo-equality of top-down integration. Despite massive pressure for assimilation the Sephardi resemblance to the "Other" could still cast them as the enemy.[14] In most Israeli films of the eighties, this kind of ethnic casting has changed dramatically, but some foreign productions about the Middle East, such as Golan's *Delta Force* (1985), which casts David Menahem as terrorist, still continue the traditional Israeli casting of Oriental Jews as the Arab enemy.

Hill 24 Doesn't Answer intimates, then, the ironic means of "redemption" of Orientals from their "primal sin" of fully belonging to the Orient—war against the Arabs. It is significant, in this sense, that the U.N. decision that Hill 24 belongs to Israel—even though the fighters did not survive to claim it—is a consequence of the Israeli flag found in the hand of the Sephardi woman. The sequence inadvertently suggests the ironic nature of her "equality" and "redemption;" she is accepted (as a martyr) even though, as the film implies, she has no story to tell. Her (hi)story begins here, with the Zionist founding gesture, not before it, and will only be told through the agency of male Western (Jewish and non-Jewish) narrators.

The Orient and the Promethean Narrative

A few films within the heroic-nationalist genre such as *Hill 24 Doesn't Answer* and *Pillar of Fire* feature virtually no Arab characters, although Arabs do appear en masse as incarnations of violence. The majority of films, however, reflect what can be termed the humanist-Zionist trend within the genre, and feature Arab characters in minor, largely "positive" roles. The narrative time devoted to individualized "good Arabs" distinguishes them from the anonymous Arab aggressors who are nonetheless not eliminated from the humanist trend. This mechanism serves less to humanize the Arabs than to point up the "objective" stance taken by the film, apparently eschewing a Manicheism which would reduce all Arabs to one-dimensional enemies. The imagistic symptoms of the classically unequal First World/Third World encounter, in other words, are clearly in evidence in the construction of Arab characters and of their role within the narrative, not only when they are depicted negatively but even when they are characterized positively.

Films like Baruch Dienar's *They Were Ten*, Ilan Eldad's *Sinaia*, and Alexander Ramati's *Rebels Against the Light* structure the Arab image in dualistic terms, as already presented in embryo in *Sabra*, purely in function of the acceptance or the rejection of the authority and generosity of Israel. The mythological pioneer, Sabra kibbutznik, and/or Israeli soldier, meanwhile, has, as is typical of the war and Western genres, a stable ethical character, that of the ideal hero. The embodiment of humanity and sympathy, he enacts the missionary role of converting the Eastern "natives" to Western values. While the cultivated Israeli is celebrated as a successful bearer of Western achievements into an "underdeveloped" area, the Arab who opposes the Sabra is presented negatively. The "philistine" who welcomes European enlightenment, meanwhile, is granted a "human face." Such a "meeting" between Occident and Orient betrays the Zionist assimilation of certain nineteenth-century European pro-Zionist attitudes, for example those of George Eliot, who in *Daniel Deronda*, as Edward Said points out,[15] cannot sustain her admiration of Zionism except by seeing it as a method for transforming the East into the West.

This Zionist version of East/West interaction is incorporated into other genres where the Israeli-Arab conflict is quite peripheral to the central plot, for example, in the psychological drama of Peter Frey's *The Hero's Wife* and in the light comedy of Frey's *I Like Mike* (1961). In these films too the brief and apparently aleatory appearance of Arab characters serves as a support for the idealized image of the central Sabra characters. In *The Hero's Wife*, one of the central characters charitably offers a water flask to a simple Arab shepherd even though his friend was killed by Arabs, and even though his kibbutz is under constant Arab bombing. In *I Like Mike*, the kibbutz members harmonize around the fire with a Bedouin tribe singing traditional Israeli songs and even cite an American country lyric, "Wyoming will be your new home," but, undialogically, never singing Arabic songs. The image of a presumed ideal coexistence between Arabs and Jews is mediated, in this case, through the "exotic" attachment of both groups to nature. Narratively and cinematically the encounters, as in the heroic-nationalist genre, are focalized through Israelis. In *I Like Mike*, we gain a supplementary external look at the Arabs through the point-of-view of the Jewish-American character whose vision "exotically" foregrounds camels and desert rather than the Bedouins themselves. The harmony with specific Arabs within different genres in the fifties and sixties, then, is typically a harmony of non-equals.

Written, directed, and produced by Alexander Ramati, *Rebels Against the Light* revolves around the Jewish-Arab skirmishes of 1949. It features a tale of conflict between a pacifist Sheik and his rebellious-terrorist son as well as the tale of a Christian-American woman on a pilgrimage to visit the grave of her Jewish-American lover. Set within the temporal framework of a single day, the film has terrorists, headed by the Sheik's son, mine the roads and harass Jewish outposts while also robbing and killing their own people in the name of their need for guns, food, and money. The mine that causes the death of an Israeli forces the Israeli protagonist, Dan (Tom Bell), and Susan (Diane Baker), on her way to the airport, to seek help in the Arab village. They are given refuge by the Sheik, Daoud (David Opatoshu), while his son, Salim (Paul Stassino), leads an attack against them. During the fight Dan is wounded; under siege he and Susan experience a *coup de foudre* and fall in love. Salim is killed by a friend of his father and Susan drives Dan back to the Israeli settlement, deciding to stay in Israel.

The title *Rebels Against the Light* already conveys the axiomatic vision of the West as the originator of light and the East as shrouded in darkness. This leitmotif of the heroic-nationalist films manifests a structural irony since the etymology of the words "west" and "east" in Semitic Hebrew imply an opposite concept: *ma'arav* (Hebrew for "west") derives from the root ERV, whose noun signifies "evening," "twilight," and the verb signifies "to be dark," "to grow dark," "becoming evening," "be obscured," "become gloomy." *Mizrah* ("east") meanwhile derives from the root ZRH, signifying the opposite: as a noun, "sunrise," "shining," "glowing," and as a verb, "to rise," "to shine," "to glow." In Arabic, similarly, the geographical directions also point to periods of light and darkness within the day embedded with culturally rooted metaphors playing with the antonyms *sharq*, which signifies both "east" and "sunrise," and *gharb*, which signifies "west" and "sunset." It is here that the Zionist Western missionary role of enlightening the East becomes paradoxical, especially when one recalls that Zionism was also preoccupied with the revival of Hebrew, and with returning to the sources of the Jewish past, to the East. A synonym for *mizrah* ("east") in Hebrew is *kedem*, which also refers to "ancient times," "antiquity," and evokes the traditional Jewish yearning, expressed in the Biblical verse (from Lamentations 5:21): "*Hadesh yamenu keqedem*," i.e., "Renew (restore) our days as of old!" The Jewish textual and popular oral cult of the past in Zion, was, in other words, transformed by Zionism and its concomitant fictions into a cult of the West, of renewing European thinking and life patterns in the Orient.

The film's narrative is framed by Biblical quotations partially suggesting a modern parable, as well as the specific position taken by the film. The initial quotation is taken from Job (24:13): "They are of those that rebel against the light; they know not the ways thereof, nor abide in the paths thereof." The citation forms part of Job's homily about injustice in human life whereby the powerful violently rob the poor, as well as of his description of the various modalities of oppression and exploitation. "Light" metaphorizes the paths of righteousness refused by the wicked, who know only the regime of the darkness that literally covers their acts. The intertitle is superimposed on a long shot of Arabs sitting next to their tent, while the ensuing credit sequence is superimposed on an extreme long shot of armed Arabs riding in the desert as the commentative music features hackneyed Oriental motifs. The "rebels against the light" of the title and intertitle, then, are linked to the simultaneous image of the Arabs. The association of Arabs with violence is further reinforced in the following sequence, where they are observed in long shot and from a low angle, overlooking the valley where an Israeli bus is passing, carrying a sympathetic American woman. Although the point of view is literally theirs, the cinematic angles render them as threatening. On the hill they enjoy a privileged observation post, affording a comprehensive look at Israeli movements. In order to kill as many Jews as possible, they decide to place the mine in the evening. Their sadistic delight in killing is accentuated through the obese terrorist who smirks as he says, "I can hardly wait." (In Melville Shavellson's *Cast a Giant Shadow* [1966], interestingly, a similar depiction of Arab violence is interwoven with certain sexual undercurrents; the Arab men leer and laugh as they shoot an Israeli woman trapped in a truck at the bottom of a valley.) In *Rebels Against the Light*, the commander, Salim, even links this personal bloodthirstiness to a putative Arab tradition: "Be patient. Remember the old Arab proverb: 'Patience, and they will carry your enemy's body in front of your home.'" Later in the film, the narrative device of placing the Israeli man, Dan, the American woman, Susan, and the "good Arabs," Daoud and his daughter, Naima, "under siege" (in a kind of microcosm of a saintly alliance), enlists the mechanisms of identification against the besiegers, whose instinctual sadism is underscored by their diabolical look. The obese terrorist fires his gun, for example, despite his commander's order, confessing, "I could not help myself; the Jew was right at the window." Here, again, we discern the rhetorical device of self-incriminatory actions and dialogue, which has the Arab characters testify "objectively" to their own evil nature. The apparent alternation of point-of-view, in other words, merely constructs a façade of objectivity that further essentializes the notion of Arab violence.

Rebels Against the Light, before presenting "exotic" images of Arabs, first perpetuates the stereotypical image of the Third World as it haunts the colonial Western mind. First World traditional discourse often offers a reductionist view of the violence involved in national struggles for independence as involving perverse pleasure in gratuitous killing, as irrational rituals deriving from fanatical nationalism or religious zealotry. The anti-Arab imagery which pervades the media and the culture ultimately traces its origins to early European attempts to represent the Orient. European colonialism in the Orient was similar in structure to that in Africa, America, and Asia, but unlike the encounters with Black Africans and Native Americans, Europe encountered the Arabs long before the advent of colonialism. Muslim Arabs had always been seen as a provocation to Christian Europe: geographically close, their religion drew on the Judaic tradition and also borrowed creatively from Christianity. Linguistically, Semitic Arabic was of interest because of Greek philosophy (Semitic Hebrew, because of the Bible), and politically and militarily Arabs at times held sway over Europe in Iberia and during the Crusades. These encounters, as Edward Said discusses them in *Orientalism*, had epistemological consequences for the European attempt to know the Orient, to represent it, and make it comprehensible. The Europeans, ultimately, defined themselves in opposition to the constructed otherness of the Orient. With colonialism, already-distorted images were systematized to legitimize Europe's right to domination. The orientalization of the Orient, to borrow Said's term, confirmed European superiority, glorifying the West's "philanthropic" role of bringing Reason to a world of disorder. Even after the end of classical colonialism in the Arab world, the most blatant distortions are regularly reproduced by the Western cultural industry, in songs, jokes, political cartoons, comics, television movies, and feature films.[16]

Apart from "exotic" images of the "erotic" Orient favored by Hollywood from *The Sheik* (1921) through a series of remakes of *Kismet* (1920, 1930, 1944, 1955) to the Hollywood-style *Lawrence of Arabia* (1962) and even the recent *Sahara* (1983), Arabs have tended to constitute "bad objects" within the Hollywood narrative, culminating, especially since the late sixties, in the image of the terrorist. In *Black Sunday* (1971), for example, Palestinians are portrayed as psychotic, bloodthirsty fanatics. The distortion, furthermore, forms part not only of the film industry but also of the film criticism industry. Assuming the validity of the negative stereotypes, Vincent Canby, for instance, goes a step beyond the film's discourse: "Marthe Keller has some difficulty portraying a Palestinian terrorist, looking as she does, as beautiful and healthy and uncomplicated as a Californian surfer."[17] Within Canby's fairytale logic, conventional beauty cannot be allied to evil, and Palestinian terrorists cannot be physically beautiful. As metonyms of anti-European violence, Arab and Muslim terrorists appear briefly even in films whose subjects have nothing to do with the Middle East, as in the case of the nightmarish Iranian terrorists chasing the "all-American boy" through a Midwestern town in Steven Spielberg's *Back to the Future* (1985). And in a recent novel, *The Haj*, Leon Uris (author of *Exodus*) presents the traditional colonialist vision of the "inferior" Third World people. Arab characters are explicitly qualified as "lazy," "boastful," "murderous," and "rapists," while the manipulation of point of view has Arab characters incriminate themselves as people living in "hate," "despair," and "darkness." Perceiving Jews as the Arabs' "bridge out of darkness," an Arab doctor elaborates his self-denigration:

> Islam is unable to live at peace with anyone. We Arabs are the worst. We can't live with the world, and even more terrible, we can't live with each other. In the end it will not be Arab against Jew but Arab against Arab. One day our oil will be gone, along with our ability to blackmail. We have contributed nothing to human betterment in centuries, unless you consider the assassin and the terrorist as human gifts.[18]

Compared with the Hollywood images of the Arab, Zionist-Israeli fiction on the Israeli-Arab conflict is somewhat more nuanced. Negative characters appear, at times, within a humanist framework of psychologizing the terrorists' motives, whether in the form of the Oedipal inflection of *Rebels Against the Light* or male jealousy and weakness at times of crisis in *They Were Ten*. Unlike the dominant American representation of Arabs, Israeli heroic-nationalist films supplement the image of the evil Arab with that of the "positive" Arab character, as in *Rebels Against the Light*. The Israeli dualism of heroes and villains, thus, is slightly less monolithic, endeavoring to propose also "positive" Arabs who struggle along with the Israeli protagonists against backward Arab antagonists.

After introducing the terrorists, *Rebels Against the Light* cuts to the Arab village, cloaking its inhabitants in "exotic" images. As in *Sabra*, the Arabs, as if by way of self-introduction, dance suddenly and without any explanation. Fearing Salim's terrorism, they escape to their homes, hoping that the Israeli police will arrive in time to defend them, and leaving Daoud, Salim's father, to confront the terrorists alone. Courageous, Daoud demands that the band stop its repeated thefts from the village, but his son insists they are collecting the tax they deserve instead of the Israelis. The dialogue between the father and son, just when the terrorists are about to rob and kill, is strangely reminiscent of a dialogue between a Zionist (the pacifist Arab) and an anti-Zionist (the terrorist Arab), all presented from a Zionist perspective:

> DAOUD: Since you left the village you have been poisoned; you learned to hate.
> SALIM: And you learned to love your enemy. You are an old man, Father, too old to understand.
> DAOUD: What is there to understand? We want to live in peace. You want to steal and kill.
> SALIM: We want our country back. And we are ready to get it back. We'll keep on killing until there are no Jews in Palestine.

The dialogue begins in long shot, shifts to medium shot, and culminates in a shot-counter-shot (as Salim says, "We'll keep on killing"), underlining the inevitable conflict between two generations, between two positions, between father and son. The cinematic-political confrontation immediately gives way to brutality directed against the village: the kidnapping of men from their homes, the setting on fire of a field, and the murder of an Israeli-Arab policeman, despite Daoud's noble cry to the terrorists that he himself is the only one responsible for the rebellion.

This early confrontation between the "good" Arab, Daoud, and the "evil," Salim, already sets in motion the Manichean scheme on which the film is built. In the dialogue between the two, Daoud speaks with naïve pacifism of his longing for peace, blaming his son and his followers for simply "hating." He is thus a mouthpiece for the Zionist myth that opposes those who want to live in peace, i.e., Zionists and Arabs who welcome Israel, to those who—as Daoud testifies about his own people and his own son—only want "to steal and kill." And those who steal from and kill their own people in the film also happen to be those who totally refuse Israel, those who will go on "killing until there are no Jews in Palestine." Such statements, accompanied by scenes of terror against Salim's own people (as well as against Israelis), undermine his potentially more politically serious claim: "We want our country back." Similarly, in an earlier sequence, *Rebels Against the Light* offers its "objective" acknowledgment of the Other through Salim's invocation of Palestinian exile: "Every Arab in Palestine has a relative among the refugees in Egypt and Syria." Compared with the hermetic nationalist discourse of virtually all films of the period, the mere reference to Palestinian refugees on the screen in 1964 provides an ephemeral progressive touch. But this brief conjuring up of Zionism from the perspective of its victims is unquestionably undermined by the violent connotations of Salim's immediate next statement: "There is no such country as Israel. There is Palestine!" as well as by his subsequent criminal acts. The rejection of Israel, furthermore, is made simultaneous with the plans to murder an Arab policeman with whom the spectator has already come to sympathize. The framing of complex political questions such as Palestinian rights and claims within the essentialist characterization of Arab bloodthirstiness and relentless hostility to Jews and Israel virtually compels a simplistic identification with Israel. Zionism is grasped only in a celebratory dimension, as a Jewish liberation movement.

The sequences of the Arab village and its terrorization run parallel to sequences involving another potential victim, the "all-American woman," Susan, on the bus from Be'er Sheva to Sodom. The bus is seen from the Arab-terrorist perspective, as the selected target to be exploded on its return trip in the evening. The spectator's knowledge of Susan's plan to return on the evening bus heightens suspense in the Hitchcock manner. It is within this story-time framework that the film constructs the first phase of its didactic message through neutral, Christian Susan, presumably tabula rasa in terms of Zionism and even Judaism. The chronicle of her coming to consciousness constitutes a kind of Zionist *Bildungsroman*. Susan originally makes her voyage in an attempt to determine why her dead lover, Mark, volunteered for Israel's war of independence—was it for idealist motives, or in order to escape their difficulties as a mixed couple?

Once in Israel, Susan's voyage becomes a Zionist pilgrimage. Susan embodies a character typical of Zionist-nationalist films, whether Israeli productions or co-productions, or foreign productions largely directed toward the American market. She represents the figure of the "objective observer," the traveler whose narrative function as ideological mediator is to make Zionism palatable to the Western spectator. Whether an American-Jew (*Hill 24 Doesn't Answer, Pillar of Fire, The Hero's Wife* [Mexican-Jew], *Neither at Day Nor at Night* [*Lo baYom velo baLaila*, 1972], *Cast a Giant Shadow*, and *The Great Escape*) or Christian (*Sword in the Desert, Hill 24 Doesn't Answer* [Irishman], *Exodus, Rebels Against the Light*, and *60 Hours to Suez* [*Shishim Shaot leSuetz*, 1967; distributed abroad as *Is Tel Aviv Burning?*]), the outsider is recruited to the Israeli cause, often through a gradual process of progressive enlightenments, and at times with the erotic stimulus of a romance with a Sabra.

Like other nationalist films, then, *Rebels Against the Light* employs an outsider Western character. The chronicle of the visitor's journey from ignorance to "awareness" is intrinsically connected to the stable, virtually perfect nature of the Sabra character, whose integrity becomes a kind of final post or telos in the gradations of self-improvement offered the outsider. He/she is subsequently transformed into a quasi-insider within a narrative structure that resembles a secular grail story, a quest accompanied by the archetypical tropes of redemption and moral edification.

Theodicy in its secular-Zionist version is, therefore, superimposed on the story of the Christian—once an oppressor and still a dormant enemy within the Jewish mind—who subliminally atones by expressing enthusiasm for the modern Jewish destiny.

Susan's process of Zionist education is roughly divided into two stages, beginning with her portrayal as a spoiled, naïve, and uninvolved Mid-westerner and ending with her transformation into a virtual sister of mercy in the Mid-East through her dialogue with Dan. She is progressively initiated into basic Jewish and Israeli historical information, as well as into nationalist myths and the Zionist idealist discourse. Susan finds it difficult, for example, to comprehend Mark's idealist gesture of moving into the desert, into a place she "never even knew existed except from the Bible," as well as his valiant solitary battle against numerous Arabs to defend an old rickety bridge in a place without women and children. Answering her questions, Dan advances the idea that death is sometimes necessary for others to live; the bridge Mark defended gave access to the Mifal haAshlag (mine project) that the Arabs were planning to bomb; without it "our desert would have stayed a desert and we would not have been able to settle the survivors." This link of Israel and Holocaust survivors leads her to invoke Mark's recurrent lament: "One-third of my people were killed by the Nazis. I must help the rest live in peace." Her naïveté, similarly, is accentuated when she asks for flowers to place on Mark's grave, unaware that Sodom has no flowers, "not yet anyway," as Dan states. The shot of Susan facing Mark's desert grave, unable to perform a simple gesture— placing flowers—illustrates her realization of the importance of his sacrifice. With such ideologically informed details, the film constructs several tropes: that of the visionary pioneer who makes the desert bloom (*hafrahat hashmama*) subsequent to Arab neglect, as well as the salvation of the Diaspora (*migola legeula*) and the life-and-death trope of the devoted soldier who gives his life so the rest might live (*bemotam tzivu lanu et hahayim*).

Guided by the highest kind of idealism, the dialogue propagates a narcissistic self-image flattering to the Israeli, and even more to the distant and often unin- formed Zionist sympathizer. Although Dan, for example, has painterly talents, he has abandoned his profession, since "in Israel there are already too many doctors and painters but not enough workers." Israeli soldiers and workers, then, are not "simply" soldiers and workers but "high-quality," "cultured" people. Dan's desire to return to painting when peace comes reflects the Sabra image (and self-image) as a soldier who, despite war, never loses either humanity or artistic sensitivity, an image also evoked by the writer Amos Kenan when he discerns the violinist behind the army uniforms, the violinist who momentarily hangs up his violin while he picks up the gun.[19]

The encounter between the American, Susan, and the Israeli, Dan, establishes the narrative dualism focalized, to a certain extent, through Susan; the potential victim of Arab terrorists is now exposed to the Sabra who, despite his innate peace-loving nature, is condemned to war and consequently to heroism. The Sabra in Israeli films is forced to shoot by Arab hostility, but in his heart of hearts he would rather work the land, or create his art, and bring light to the East, whether through educating the Arabs to modernity, as in *Oded the Wanderer*, or working the land, as in *Rebels Against the Light*, or curing the wounds of a Bedouin woman, like the Israeli pilot in *Sinaia*. The martyr-like mentality of "shoot-and-cry" humanism was satirized in the Israeli-Palestinian Emile Habiby's novel *The Secret Life of Saeed: The Pessoptimist*.[20] Through the perspective of a Good Soldier Schweik–like protagonist the reader learns the actual repercussions of humanist Israel for the Palestinians. And like Voltaire's *Candide*, which mocks the Leibnizean idealism of "All is for the best in the best of all possible worlds," *The Pessoptimist* comically demystifies the idealist discourse of Zionism.

While adopting the Sabra anti-heroic style with its avoidance of flowery language, the film also exalts the ethos of the heroic Sabra. Dan, for example, criticizes Susan, as the representative of Europe and the United States, for loving heroes. Mark, according to Dan, did not want her to think that he was better than others: "He defended that bridge because he had no choice. None of the people here ever had," he says angrily as he walks out of the frame, while she remains, thinking and lowering her look. Presumably rebelling against the myth of the "heroic Sabra," Dan only redoubles mystification by emphasizing the "no-choice" situation forced on Israel. His tough manner, his concentration on his country's goals, his scorn for the "spoiled" American, his willingness to sacrifice his talent and life contribute to his portrayal as a hero, despite his apparent endorsement of "anti-heroism." Twice the film shows Susan lowering her head (first when Dan accuses her of non-involvement), as if in embarrassment, shame or guilt—an expression rhetorically underlined by a close-up, inducing the spectator to share the moment of reflection together with Susan. (A similar encounter is suggested between the still neutral Kitty Freemont [Eva Marie Saint] and Ari Ben Canan [Paul Newman] on board the ship in *Exodus*. When she tries to convince him to surrender the ship and its refugees to the British in order to prevent a tragedy, Ari Ben Canan responds in righteous wrath: "Each person on board this ship is a soldier. The only weapon we have is our willingness to die.")

Rebels Against the Light cuts from Susan's reflective look to the Arab planting a mine in order to sabotage the bus on which she is planning to leave. This juxtaposition provides the proof, as it were, of the Arabs' violent propensities. The gap between Susan's knowledge and the spectator's knowledge is now brought to the foreground. The same gap was evoked earlier, when the spectator was conscious that Salim's gang was planning to target her bus, just as the spectator is aware of the Arab "evil" gang that robs and murders its own people under the pretense of nationalism—all of which remain hidden from her. But the moment of Dan's anger at her lack of any general empathy which might transcend her individual

Geopolitical *Bildungsroman*: The Sabra and the American in *Rebels Against the Light*.

loss, juxtaposed with the placing of the mine, prepares the spectators for still another pivotal phase in her apprenticeship—that of actual personal experience rather than abstract speeches.

In the next sequence the second stage of education within Zionist theodicy begins. Due to a state of emergency (the Egyptians are concentrating forces on the border), the evening bus does not leave (the driver explains to Susan that "Arab savages might be in the desert and it would be dangerous to drive"). She insists on leaving, however, and a volunteer drives her. They ride over the mine and he is injured. Approaching them, Dan carries the wounded man to the nearby Arab village. At this point the two parallel plots merge; from now on the terrorists, the "good" Arabs, and the Israeli will all share a single space where choices will have to be made, not only by the Arabs but also by the American visitor. Fearing reprisals by the terrorists, an Arab refuses to help Dan. Daoud and his graceful daughter, Naima (Didi Ramati), nevertheless volunteer to assist, but the wounded driver dies, as funereal commentative music accompanies the long shot of Daoud's peace-loving monologue: "Killing, killing, all the time killing. My wife was killed by a Jewish mine and a Jew is killed by an Arab mine." The wounded Israeli is buried next to Daoud's wife, suggesting that in death they will find a peaceful coexistence. (A similar scene appears in *Exodus*: the burial which ends the film with the tough but emotional mourning of Ari Ben Canan, with the difference that Hollywood portrayed the two victims—a young woman Holocaust survivor and a peace-oriented Arab—as two victims of Nazi-connected Arab aggressors.) Dan, meanwhile, gives his peace-speech in the form of a Jewish mourning prayer, ending with "*Ose shalom bimeromav*" ("He makes peace in heaven"). As we hear the peace blessing offscreen, we see Susan before her second grave, containing the Israeli victim of an Arab attack. This time she has herself witnessed Arab violence, and indeed might have been a victim herself. This directly personal threat ends, in a sense, her period of detached noninvolvement.

Susan encounters two peace-loving groups: Israelis (peace-loving by definition) and some Arabs, suggesting that harmony will prevail only in the absence of Arab terrorists. The film emphasizes this point in the sequence following the burial in which Dan and Daoud engage in friendly, almost "utopian" dialogue. The exclusion of the terrorists from the peace interlude (even avoiding any reference to them on the dialogue track) offers the spectator a glimpse of a possible shared future between Arab and Jew. Hospitable Daoud, sitting in Oriental fashion, drinking coffee with Dan, begins their conversation by expressing admiration for Dan's truck. Accustomed to the idea of technological advancement, Dan replies that the truck is an old one. Daoud then describes the poverty and backwardness to which he has been accustomed; he has no horse, only a few animals and a piece of land inherited from his father, his grandfather, and his great-grandfather who could hardly make a living. The Israeli then expresses his desire to work the land as well and in his free time to paint rivers and forests—the Israeli's imaginary also revolves around land. The characters thus express complementary desires to exchange places with each other; the Arab, without even a horse, admires Dan's old truck, while Dan, with his Romantic nostalgia for agrarian simplicity, desires to work the land. The pride of the pioneering heritage, of working the land, with its connotations of a salutary rootedness, constitute the ideological bedrock of the nationalist films. Thus, even when not dealing directly with the achievements of Dor haMeyasdim (Founding Fathers Generation), the nationalist films assume their ideology or allude to their dreams—at times even within war circumstances—but now carried by Dor haBanim (Sons Generation).

Dan's desire to reincarnate the pioneer myth characterizes other nationalist films as well. Larry Frisch's *Pillar of Fire*, for example, although it focuses on the 1948 battle with Egypt, in certain sequences evokes the pioneering spirit as a pacific foil to the violence of war, and as part of a characterological dichotomy between Egyptian aggressors and peace-loving Israelis. This opposition manifests itself in the narrative's schism between the female protagonist's longing for agrarian pastoralism and the tangible reality of the Egyptian military threat. The pioneer idyll is marred by the rude onslaught of an Egyptian bomb, destroying Israeli achievements. In *He Walked through the Fields*, the hero is a kibbutznik who also studies in an agricultural school. (Israeli official discourse had tended to implicitly contrast Israeli agricultural expertise, i.e., the science of knowledge of the land, with the "natural," quasi-instinctual labor of the *fellahin* who emerge from the land, as it were, rather than dominate it in the Western sense.) While fighting in the Palmach, he also works the land. The pioneer myth, then, simultaneously posits a liberation from oppressive Jewish-European history while channeling the European rescue fantasy of liberating the Orient from the parabola of its inevitable decline. That the light-bringers are the traditional victims of Europe constitutes just one more irony in an interminable chain of historical inversions.

Daoud's final admission then recognizes not merely that Arabs spent centuries in darkness but also that Western Israel brought light. We see here evidence of the Western "Prospero complex," of the colonizer who will redeem Caliban's isle with technological magic.[21] In a frontal shot, seated next to Dan, Daoud expresses gratitude to the Israeli for the fertilizer that enables him to grow tomatoes from the desert, a feat "unavailable to his father, grandfather, and great-grandfather." Daoud, dressed in traditional Arab clothes, ends the sentence drinking the *ahwa* (Turkish/Arab coffee) so typical of the area. The stereotypical Oriental thus lends credibility to the vision of Western-Zionist enlightenment as an altruistic endeavor. The "making-the-desert-bloom" leitmotif, here mouthed by the Arab character, as well as his testimony that Arabs (can) actually benefit from Israel and his implied acceptance of the authority and generosity of the state apparatus, determine his cinematic status as the "noble Arab."

The modernizing rescue fantasy of the Orient conveyed by the film relays a similar attitude to that advanced in Hebrew-Israeli fiction. An Arab teacher in Eliezer Smoli's *The Sons of the First Rain* (*Yaldei haGeshem haRishon*) takes his class on a visit to a Jewish school, and is so impressed that he delivers the following encomium:

> By God, we have very much to learn from you, the Jews. This place was abandoned and desolate—and then you came along with all your energy and transformed it into a veritable Garden of Eden. . . . Every day I read diatribes in the newspapers against the Jews, and there are a lot of agitators who stir up trouble between us and you! But as I walk through your streets and as I see the tremendous labor you have invested in these desolate abandoned sand-dunes, which you've turned into such flourishing land, I have to say to myself that it was God who sent you here to serve as an example to us, so that we could look at what you do and do likewise ourselves. . . . It's to you that we owe the prosperity, to your capital, your energy, to all the good things you've given us.[22]

Zionism's providential melioristic design, then, is here blessed by its putative beneficiaries, the Arabs. Thus, when not a terrorist, the Arab is a passive entity—at best "exotic"—awaiting Sabra redemption. The good Arab is a grateful Arab. The active agent, the Israeli, grants the Arab identity and purpose, saving him from his own destructive weaknesses. The dualistic representation of Arabs as either terrorists or noble savages, in other words, is a subsidiary reflection of a more comprehensive dualism, the Manichean allegory of the heroic-nationalist genre, that of Israel versus the Arabs. Thus the fictive construction of the "good primitive" concatenates the positive adjectives "good," "noble," with Arab obeisance as a means of transcending the negative Oriental essence. In this sense, the film positions the Western/Israeli spectator, along with the Sabra man and the American woman, as superior in their liberal sympathy toward the Arab, thus reaffirming a humane and democratic self-image.

Placing Zionist arguments in the mouth of an Arab character (who is willing even to defend Israelis against his own terrorist son) functions, in other words, as a rhetorical device that lends institutional apologetics a higher status of truth. Just as *Hill 24 Doesn't Answer* employed a façade of democratic distribution of points of view, *Rebels Against the Light* has its monolithic Zionist view masquerade as a mission desired by three synecdochic representatives: Israel (Dan), peace-loving Arabs (Daoud, Naima), and the West (Susan). The harmonious interchange between the Arab and the Israeli reflects the ersatz dialogism of the Zionist-heroic films. The last shot of Dan and Daoud, seen in a frontal shot, sitting together drinking the "exotic" coffee of the Orient, is interrupted by a cut to the next sequence in which the "other kind" of Arabs, the terrorists, try to hijack the Israeli truck. The "utopian" sequence ends, then, with a rhetorical "but" conveyed by the montage juxtaposition; the condition for harmony is the elimination of the bloodthirsty Arabs who inflict violence not only on peace-loving Israelis but on peace-loving Arabs as well. The harmonious moment, however well-intentioned, ultimately rings false because it is constructed on a patronizing view of the culture and history of the Other with whom one claims to hope to dialogue. Set in 1949, this "utopian dialogue," for example, ignores the dystopian reality that Palestinians since the foundation of Israel have been relegated to a literal "utopia," etymologically, "no place." Zionism undertook to speak for Palestine and Palestinians, thus blocking Palestinian self-representation. The heroic-nationalist films provided audiovisual legitimation for Zionist historiographical doxa, and contributed—especially in the United States, where they were widely distributed— not only to the clear disproportion between the media presence of Israeli versus Palestinian causes, but also to a qualitative gap, an asymmetrical circulation of self-representative texts, on the one hand, versus delegated, suspectly mediated representation on the other.

The dualistic representation of Arabs in *Rebels Against the Light* plays on the tradition of Arab hospitality. While Daoud and Naima follow the code of hospitality, Salim's bandits violate that code. Their dramatic intrusion into the peaceful world of Dan and Daoud triggers the inevitable confrontation between Daoud and his son, Salim. The father urges his son to respect a law of hospitality that embraces all human beings (Christians and Jews alike and not only Muslims), but his son insists that the code does not include Jews. Salim's response to his father's question—as to whether he is not tired of killing—reveals Salim's fanaticism: "When the battle is over I will take the body of the Jew out of the grave and leave it for the dogs; for no Jew will contaminate the land where my mother was buried." And Salim's anti-Jewish fanaticism prompts him to refuse to release even the "neutral" American, under the pretext that she came with the Jew; thus the film wins Western spectatorial sympathy for a victimized American woman whose fate is now inseparable from that of the Israeli. The confrontation between father and son on the dialogue level ends with a war in which the diverse forces of good are finally united against the forces of evil: Generous Daoud and his beautiful daughter, Naima, are united with the quasi-perfect Israeli, Dan, and the innocent American, Susan, against the terrorists who besiege them. This human and ideological unity is cinematically rendered by the spatial separation of "good" and "evil" territory within the mise-en-scène, and by the point-of-view shots shared by Dan and Daoud. The cinematic, narrative, and ideological codes link the "good-natured," "backward" Arab (usually elderly) with the humane, sensitive pioneer or soldier, set structurally in opposition to forces of disorder and terror, i.e., bloodthirsty Arabs (usually young) whose elimination is required to restore harmony.

The schism of good versus evil within the Manichean allegory intensifies when Dan goes to his truck for ammunition. Originally intended for the Israeli border settlement for defense against Egyptian attacks on "women and children," the arms now gain a double, even triple dramatic role—not only to defend Israeli settlements against the well-equipped Egyptian army but also for defense against the terrorists, whose possible control of the truck would entail the surrender of the besieged protagonists as well as the future terrorizing of the peaceful Arab village. In this triple mission, Dan is injured, again strengthening the Israeli-American connection through the love-death nexus. The sequence prior to his injury when all are besieged and under fire features the classical cinematic topos of the amorous exchange of looks rendered in formulaic shot-counter-shot. When he is injured, Susan saves his life through artificial respiration. From this point on, the American woman, now irrevocably integrated into the travails of Israeli existence, helps load the guns. And when the battle ends in triumph, she drives the truck (with her wounded beloved beside her) to the border settlements and reassures him that she will not return to the United States. The triple mission thus ends happily for Israel and the West.

Whereas the romance in *Exodus* between a Christian woman and a Jewish man is celebrated by the narrative closure, and while *Hill 24 Doesn't Answer*'s romance between a Christian man and a Jewish woman is tragically cut off by the heroic death of the Zionist Christian, in *Rebels against the Light* it is only after Susan's first Jewish-American lover is killed by the Arabs, when she becomes a Zionist, that her romance with a Jewish Israeli becomes a reality, making possible harmonious narrative closure. The *Bildungsroman* structure, then, is marshaled to tell an exemplary tale of Western or Christian conversion to Zionism. Susan's moral stance, meanwhile, suggests for the Western spectator a subliminal analogy with early American settlers, evoking nostalgia for their mythical idealistic spirit, set in implicit contrast to the present prosperous, spoiled life. Symptomatically, the dialogue between Susan and Dan sounds rather like a conversation between the idealist European settler explaining the land's potentialities to a visitor from the motherland and initiating her/him into the codes of the new frontier. Although the heroic-nationalist films present the Westerner joining Zionism, however, a hidden set of codes point in an opposite direction, to Jewish assimilation to Western Orientalist discourse embodied, in many ways, by Zionism. By a concatenation of events and circumstances the European Semitic myth, as Edward Said points out, bifurcated in the Zionist movement: "one Semite went the way of Orientalism, the other, the Arab, was forced to go the way of the Oriental."[23] (Jews from Arab countries, as shown in the next chapter, also went the way of the Oriental.) *Rebels Against the Light*, in this sense, reflects the literal recruitment of the West to Zionism. Internalizing the West, the Sabra and his progenitor, Zionism, regard the East through a prejudicial grid shaped by European culture. Zionist historiography and its cinematic prolongations and mediations has remained faithful, generally, to the ideological habits of the European colonial mind. The cinematic, narrative, and ideological fusion of the Israeli and American characters, in this sense, externalizes the ongoing Israeli desire to form an appendage of the West. The liberation of oppressed European Jews from the ghetto, from pogroms, and from genocide, unfortunately, did not guarantee a liberation from Eurocentrism.

The American woman's ideological Zionization is characterized in a manner reminiscent of the mythological Sabra woman of some of the nationalist films. From a spoiled and naïve American she is transformed by her Israeli experience into a valiant fighter, nursing the wounds of the Sabra man and assisting in his war against Arab terrorists. The Sabra woman herself, meanwhile, in *Pillar of Fire*, for example, is shown in the inadvertently comic image of a superwoman who simultaneously chauffeurs her wounded Jewish-American lover and throws hand grenades at Egyptian jeeps. In *Target Tiran* (1968) the daring military exploits of the Israeli army are accompanied by the prowess of a charming Sabra who ferries soldiers in her boat to their destination. About to be discovered by an Egyptian, she resourcefully crashes the boat and swims to the Israeli shore. (Such mythologized images of tough Israeli women, when disseminated in the United States, provoked some parodic re-elaborations, for example, in the Philip Roth novel *Portnoy's Complaint* and in its film adaptation.) The very same Sabra woman who can fight the Arabs, however, becomes in the company of Sabra soldiers a defenseless little girl needing protection.

The exalted heroic image of the Sabra woman, it should be pointed out, circulated more widely in the United States, penetrating Israeli war films as part of a commercial appeal aimed at American spectators. Hebrew novels, much less dependent on these financial underpinnings, displayed a more passive Sabra woman character more in accord with Israeli popular culture. Rendered larger-than-life by Palmach-generation literature (of the forties and fifties), the epic Sabra heroes of such writers as S. Yizhar and Moshe Shamir are manly in both sex and manner. Women, even those playing central roles in the lives of the heroes, appear as mere background shadows, lacking any autonomous existence. The narratives of such novels tend to be focalized through a single Sabra male who subsumes all other political and sexual views. Based on Moshe Shamir's play of the same title, Yossef Milo's film *He Walked through the Fields*, for example, suggestively juxtaposes the hero's conquest of a woman, from courtship to pregnancy, with his immediately following conquest of a military target. The Hebrew words *gibor* ("hero"), *gever* ("man"), *gvura* ("bravery"), *ligbor* ("to conquer," "to overpower"), and *ligbor 'al* ("to win") all derive from the same etymological root (G.B.R), reflecting concepts of mastery, masculinity, and bravery as closely linked—all interwoven within the Palmach-generation literature and its cinematic analogue, the heroic-nationalist films.

The paradigmatic filmic encounters between Israelis and Arabs in the heroic-nationalist films typically involve situations of siege. In *Rebels against the Light*, most of the story time and narrative time devoted to Susan's and Dan's sojourn in the Arab village is spent under siege. Similarly, much of *Pillar of Fire* takes place in the small besieged settlement under constant Egyptian attack, while virtually all of the Jerusalem episode in *Hill 24 Doesn't Answer* occurs during the Jordanian siege of the old city. The siege situation functions to intensify and dramatize the protagonists' emotions, which crystallize in climactic episodes, offering mythic (Barthes) situations as well as narrative closure: in *Hill 24 Doesn't Answer* the rediscovery of Judaism by the American, and in *Rebels Against the Light* the unification of the three forces of good (led by the Israeli), as well as the coupling of the Israeli man and the American woman.

The battle between the Israeli heroes and their Arab enemies is filtered through images of encirclement which focus the spectator's attention and empathy on familiar protagonists defending themselves against incomprehensibly violent Arabs. As occurs with the Indians in Westerns,[24] the attitude toward the hostile Arab is premised on his literal and metaphorical exteriority. The terrorists in *Rebels Against the Light* are seen largely from the point of view of the besieged. The terrorists are seen, as it were, through the sights of the Israeli guns. The point-of-view conventions suture the spectator into a Zionist perspective, instituting a broader metaphorical meaning of a state under siege that must repel the surrounding invaders in order to survive. The image of sallying out from an encircled center, a paradigm inherited from American Westerns—although in fact it was of course the First World that moved upon the Third World and not vice versa—perfectly serves the dominant Israeli ideology of offensive defense, of fighting back forcefully against aggressors. These Zionist films prolong as well what might be called the frontier analogy, which opposes Western pioneers, Americans/Israelis, with

The Israeli David against the Arab Goliath: *Pillar of Fire*.

The anxiety of siege: *They Were Ten.*

"savages," Indians/Arabs, the former being the agents of a manifest destiny and the latter having no historical destiny beyond marginality and silence.

Within specifically Jewish history, images of siege play into a syndrome of traumatic memories originating in the ghetto experience. This latent anxiety, typical of the heroic-nationalist genre, is directly manifested in *They Were Ten.* Although the pioneers initially try to avoid open struggle with Arab aggressors by getting water from the legally shared well at night, some, impatient with persecution in Palestine after having fled European pogroms, goad the others to take the water openly, arguing that "we did not leave Russia for another ghetto." The argument reflects deeply ambivalent feelings toward Russia specifically and toward Europe generally. The situation of victimization without any provocation recalls the European ghetto (but here they strive to establish a rupture with shtetl history), while at the same time their nostalgic sense of superiority derives from belonging to the "civilized world." The heroic-nationalist films, in this sense, celebrate the liberation from the past by demonstrating the aggressive defense of Jewish rights. That this liberation is not achieved against past oppressors but rather at the expense of the oppressed Palestinians is simply ignored by Zionist fictions, which blur the distinction by conveniently appealing to the more inclusive category of the gentiles, the "Goyim."

The triumphant breaking of the siege and the concomitant celebration of Israel/West unity coincides with tragedy for the Arabs, a self-inflicted tragedy, it is suggested by *Rebels Against the Light*, largely due to their vindictive mentality. Angered by the terrorists' brutality, some villagers join Daoud's fight. It is Daoud's best friend (with whom he fought against the Turks in World War I, presumably with T. E. Lawrence—a reference implying a previous commitment to the West) who shoots Salim on his horse. Salim tries to hold onto a tree, but falls dead. The image is clearly Biblical, a visual paraphrase of the story of King David's son, Absalom, who rebelled against his father and was killed by Joab as he was escaping on muleback and whose long hair became entangled in the branches of a tree. Absalom fought against his father, the king, in order to usurp his father's throne. The film names the father "Daoud"—Arabic for David—and his soil Salim, a name phonetically reminiscent of Absalom. The noble Daoud mourns his son and the film ends with a quotation from II Samuel 18:33: "And the king was much moved, and went up to the chamber over the gate and wept; and as he went, thus he said, 'O my son Absalom, my son, my son Absalom! Would God I had died for thee, O Absalom, my son, my son!'" The long shot of the mourning father kneeling over his dead son with the village and the tree in the background together with the concluding Biblical quotation suggest a modern parable based on the Biblical tale.

The film, then, allegorically refers the Islamic present to ancient Biblical times, while associating Jewish Israel and the Christian West with modernity. The Arab who rebels against the light is punished, leaving the obedient Arab to mourn him. This mythical resolution suggests that the eradication of the "negative element" will bring peace. As in the classical narrative, order is restored when the forces of evil are defeated. Dedicated to the "absolute good" of his community, Daoud welcomes Israel's Promethean mission in the Orient, and he is rewarded with knowledge and material for growing tomatoes even at the price of sacrificing his own terrorist son. Thus the ideology of Enlightenment pervades the Humanist thinking of (European) Zionism and here dovetails with the modernizing rescue fantasy whereby Zionism saves the Orient from darkness and obscurantism. The heroism and the triumph of Israel in these films (even at the price of Israeli loss of life) is not merely the triumph of Israel over the Arabs but also that of modern civilization over the barbarism of Dark Age fanatics. This leitmotif must also be seen within a specifically Jewish context, to wit, the story of the ancient Jewish Maccabees' wars against Greek conquerers. The Hanukah celebrations commemorate the literal light miraculously made available to the Maccabees, symbolizing the struggle of the "sons of light against the sons of darkness." (The rituals themselves involve the lighting of candles.) In its selective rereading of Jewish history, Zionist culture has privileged this episode and its symbolism, using the past to "illuminate" the present. Hanukah children's rhymes in Israel, for example, are constructed around the light/darkness trope: "Banu hoshekh legaresh"—"We came to drive away the darkness/In our hands, light and fire/Everyone is a little light/And together we are the forceful light/Depart darkness/Depart, the light has

The Arab through a Biblical lens: *Rebels Against the Light*.

come." *Rebels Against the Light*, in this case, incorporates the fund of traditional imagery and marshals it in a pro-Zionist cause.

Framing the Israeli/Arab conflict both within Jewish-Biblical tradition and within a psychologizing Oedipal interpretation obviates, on another level, the possibility of understanding Arab resentment toward Israel in political terms. In the wake of early Zionist and Hebrew literary texts, which projected the legitimate paranoia of the European Jewish experience onto the new Middle East encounter, with the Arab cast as the "new Gentile" persecutor and the Jew in the traditional role of the persecuted, Israeli cinema, decades later, contributed its more contemporary texts, inflected with the additional ingredient of the "positive" stereotype of Arabs as "authentic" and "genuine." Similarly, in the thirties film *Sabra*, the prevailing image of Cossack-like Arab mob violence was also accompanied by "positive" images, that of the "noble savage" who blesses the pioneers at the end of the film as well as that of the noble Arab woman who takes care of the wounded pioneer. The "exotic" elements which add spice to the Zionist films—the myth of tribe and tent, sand and camel, and "noble savage"—are, in many ways, the product of the poetic imaginary of a late-Romantic fascination with the Other.

The representation of the Arab woman is, in many ways, subordinated to Romantic fascination with the Other. Arab women, as pointed out by the Israeli literary critic Gershon Shaked with regard to Hebrew literature of the twenties and the thirties,[25] tend to assimilate with Jews, as though their origin were in the East but their heart in the West (i.e., as represented by Israelis). The casting of a nonprofessional actress, and specifically the director's wife, in the role of the "pure exotic" in *Oded the Wanderer* (Dvora Halachmi), *Rebels Against the Light* (Didi Ramati), and *Sinaia* (Dina Doron) accentuates the Western Romantic association between the Orient and femininity. The epistemological challenge of opening up the Orient to knowledge, by which the Orient is exposed to the penetrating gaze of the Westerner, is accompanied by the harmonious "knowledge" in the Biblical sense—an intimacy of conquest. The Orient is regarded as mute and powerless, available for European plunder despite the desires and resistance of the indigenous population. The traditional Western male fetishization of Oriental women—for example, Flaubert's imperious desire to omnisciently unveil all of Salammbô's thoughts and emotions—in the Israeli Zionist films, takes the form of the image of the virtually silent Arab woman behind whose melancholy eyes seems to lurk a desire for rescue by the Western male. The minor Arab woman character in *Sabra* is granted no dialogue, and Naima in *Rebels Against the Light* mouths only a few sorrowful words of mourning.

In *Sinaia*, the noble Bedouin mother who hides an Israeli pilot (who has bandaged her wounds) from Egyptian soldiers—even though it was his crashing airplane that caused the destruction—is marginalized within the film's narrative. (The Hebrew title *Sinaia* is taken from the actual Hebrew name given to a Bedouin baby girl rescued by an Israeli pilot during the 1956 war—the case which inspired the film.) Set during the 1956 war, the film has the Bedouin become an object of ethical debate between the Israeli pilot and the infantry. Although there is no room on the helicopter, the pilot insists on not leaving behind the Bedouin mother and her two small children. The infantryman argues that during war soldiers must have first priority. His mean-spiritedness is explained in the film as a product of traumatic memories of Arab terror (a massacred sister) as well as the recent loss of his best friend in the war. He gradually, however, adopts the pilot's morally superior stance, and even saves the life of the woman's son from the threatening Egyptian soldier. Unlike the Egyptian soldiers who torture her to extract information about the Israeli pilot, the Israeli soldiers rescue her. The infantryman agrees to stay behind to facilitate the rescue. When the helicopter crashes, only the baby girl survives. The depiction of the Bedouin woman as mostly silent, expressing through gesture primal emotions of motherhood and fear, forms a striking contrast with the portrayal of the Israelis' free stream of expression. Close shots emphasize the beautiful (light) eyes of the Bedouin woman (the actress' credit is superimposed on a close shot of her eyes), but otherwise she forms part of the desert scenery, embodying nature. The actress, painted dark with makeup, literalizes the notion of a Western soul below the Oriental surface, allowing the film to construct her as "positive," as the "exotic" woman on whom an expansive and eroticized "generosity" can be projected. Arab women, in other words, can be seen as analogizing the settlers' relation to "alien" land and culture via a subtending

Femininity and the exotic Oriental: *Sinaia*.

metaphor which links the Orient and sexuality. The Middle East is subliminally conceived as fallow land awaiting ploughing, as a resistant virgin coyly eager to be conquered.

The Romantically suffused presentation of "positive" Arab characters, alongside the unequivocally negative Arab image, must be seen not only within the European Orientalist tradition but also within the specific Jewish-European context of the first-stage projection of the Arab as merely a "new Gentile." The subsequent accretion of Arab as "noble savage" is tributary to the Zionist-Hebrew effort to construct a new Jewish identity. The obsessive negation of the Diaspora which began with the Haskalah (Jewish Enlightenment) and the return to the Middle-Eastern Homeland led, at times, to the affirmation of Arab "primitivism" as a desirable antithesis to what Polish anti-Semites called the "Zid" ("Jew"). The Arab was perceived in this perspective as the incarnation of "the ancient, the pre-exiled Jew," "the Semite not yet corrupted by wanderings in exile," and therefore, to a certain extent, an authentic Jew. The perception of the Arab as preserving archaic ways, and Arab rootedness in the land of the Bible—in contrast with the landlessness of the ghetto Jew—provoked a qualified identification with the Arab as a desired object of imitation for Zionist youth in Palestine, and as a reunification with the remnant of the free and proud ancient Hebrew.[26]

This Romantic search for origins, disseminated in writing, especially from the teens to the thirties, attributed the same ancestral forefathers to both Arabs and Jews, usually with the explanation that some of the local Arabs were remnants of the ancient Hebrews who converted to Islam and Christianity after the destruction of the temple. This ideology was not entirely without basis in historical research. Colonel Conder of the Palestine Research Fund, for example, found Aramaic and Hebraic traces in the language of the *fellah*, and found that a quarter of the Arab villages retained their Hebrew-Biblical names.[27] While nineteenth-century writers such as George Eliot used, to quote Edward Said, "the plight of the Jews to make a universal statement about the nineteenth-century's need for a home,"[28] Zionists used the rootedness of the local Arabs to project their own desire for a legitimate place and origin. (The Arab was also seen as more intrinsic not only to the land but also to the more circuitous, Casbah-like ways of the Middle East.) And as Amos Elon points out in *The Israelis*, if the Israeli founding fathers expected the Arabs to welcome the returning Jews for economic and cultural reasons, then they expected to be welcomed even more if they were seen as relative-remnants, as the long-lost cousins of the Arabs.[29]

This somewhat sentimental idea of a link between Arabs and Jews provides the context for the nostalgia for primitivism expressed in *Rebels Against the Light*, for its Biblical parable, and for its ambivalent stance toward Arabs. The schizophrenic Zionist attitude of viewing Arabs simultaneously as the enemy and as the ongoing incarnation of Semiticness penetrated the humanist-nationalist films in the split Manichean image of Arabs: one representing the archetype of the "good Orient" (obedient, hospitable, Biblically primitive), in support of Israel, and the other, the archetype of the "evil Orient" (irrational, corrupt, bloodthirsty), opposed to the new state. Dan's desire for Arab simplicity is a luxury premised on Western power and "sophistication"—the advanced industry of Ashlag built in the desert, for example, contrasts sharply with the "backwardness" of the Arab village—and explicitly acknowledges the benefits brought to the Arabs by Promethean Israel. On this level, the Zionist presence denotes the Arab absence. The Biblical story superimposed on the Arab characters and the Zionist reunification with ancient remnants mummified by the "natives" thus also reinforces the idea of Jewish rootedness in the "Land of the Fathers." The Arabs' "positive presence," in this sense, paradoxically calls attention to their absence, their subordination to the Jewish collective memory.

Even on a fictive level, the Arabs lack independence and all capacity for self-representation. They can be understood only if their history and feelings are transposed into the history and feelings of the film's creators, the constructors of their image. Just as, for the French poet Lamartine, "un voyage en Orient [était] comme un grand acte de ma vie intérieure" ("a journey to the Orient [was] like a grand act of my interior life"), so for the Israeli liberal filmmaker a voyage into Arabness becomes a grand tour through the collective Jewish archival memory. In the personal filmmaking of the seventies (Dan Wolman's *My Michael* [*Michael Shell*, 1974]), this liberalism frees itself from a collective Jewishness, and the Arab becomes the mere object, as in Romantic poetry, of individual fantasy. *Rebels Against the Light*, for its part, offers a textual interaction with the Arabs through its Biblical quotations. Susan mentions that she did not "know this place existed except for the Bible," thus evoking the Western system of knowledge about the Orient, whereby "the Orient is less a place than a topos, a set of references, a congeries of characteristics, that seems to have its origin in quotations, or a fragment of a text."[30] The scriptural topos becomes a real place for Susan not simply in her literal voyage to Israel, but also through her moral-ideological pilgrimage; only then does the Orient turn into an experiential site with its own laws and codes—not the codes of a lived Arab historical consciousness, but rather of a Jewish-Israeli ideological grid.

Despite the evocation of a certain nostalgia for the "rooted natives," in other words, the film itself uproots the Arabs from their ambient social and cultural ecology, presenting them as historically barren, like the barren topography which is their natural habitat. The zigzag dialectics of Arab rootedness and unrootedness within the humanist-Zionist filmic discourse is further revealed in the recurrent fetishized images of picturesque tents and camels, as well as through the tendency to choose Bedouins as the positive Arabs. This latter tendency extends to other genres not focusing on the Israeli-Arab conflict. In the comedy *I Like Mike*, the Bedouin tribe and its camels add "Oriental" spice, evoking an affective, almost Wordsworthian link between the Arabs and kibbutzniks in their closeness to nature versus the rising Israeli bourgeoisie who at the mythical conclusion happily return to their pioneering origins. Bedouin tribes are rooted in the traditional Orient, yet—unlike other Arabs—they are also themselves uprooted in that they are nomads, and are thus less threatening to Israeli claims on the land.

A cognate Zionist fondness, for the figure of the simple Arab shepherd (*Oded the Wanderer, The Hero's Wife*), is also overdetermined, fusing a number of motifs; first the pastoral image of the shepherd, as in Romantic poetry, as eternal and somehow beyond politics; second, the shepherd as connoting a relatively primitive stage of economic development; and, third, the shepherd as embodying a specific relation to the land. Unlike the Bedouin, he is not a wandering nomad, but his flock does wander and thus he is connotatively less connected to a specific plot of land. The Bedouin characters (and even the traditional tribal Sheik characters) condense, in other words, the paradoxical nature of Zionism with regard to the East, on the one hand expressing the desire of the European-Jewish return to the Eastern origins, away from oppressive Europe, on the other hand, reflecting the colonial view of the Third World and its inhabitants as inconsequential nomads possessing no valid claim on the land and therefore devoid of real cultural or national legitimacy.

Spectacle of War in the Wake of 1967

Israel's victory over the Arab states in June 1967 had crucial consequences not only for the collective psychology of the Arab world but also for Israel itself. The military triumph created an atmosphere of national arrogance and a feeling that military dynamism might provide the solution for political problems, a feeling intensified following the courageous operations of the Israeli army during the war of attrition that took place in the late sixties, as well as the (temporary) success of the army in repressing Palestinian resistance. At the same time, the constant war with the Arabs and the Palestinian attacks increased the hostility toward the Arabs in general and the Palestinians in particular. The right-wing tendencies of the ruling Labor Party were fully consolidated, manifesting its lack of real difference from the right opposition, Gakhal Party (Likud), especially with regard to the Palestinians, a right-ward drift that brought with it the contraction and virtual collapse of an already marginalized left.[31] The war brought economic prosperity through various capital investments and support from the United States (the major Western power behind Israel after the deterioration of the Israeli-French relationship), along with the availability of cheap labor power from the occupied territories, resulting in an increase in the standard of living, which in fact largely benefited the upper and middle classes. Capitalist values of consumerism became dominant in all classes. Paralleling the political and military spheres, the American orientation of Israeli society was evident in the style of advertisements, in the interior design of stores and boutiques, and in the burgeoning importation of American cultural products (for example, in commercial theater shows à la Broadway), replacing the earlier more European cultural orientation, Russian-Soviet, Polish, German, and French.

The 1967 war furnished a renovated arsenal of themes and intrigues, such as Koby Jaeger's *60 Hours to Suez* (1967), Raphael Neussbaum's *Target Tiran* (1968), and Maoricio Lucidi's *Five Days in Sinai* (1969), which along with successful documentaries and newsreels celebrated the victory and the Israeli army, creating the cinematic equivalent of the popular feeling expressed in the widespread billboards and poster of "*kol hakavod letzahal*" ("bravo to IDF," the Israeli Defense Forces). The 1967 war and the Israeli army itself became objects of popular fascination, capturing the imagination of the Western world, leading producers, both Israeli and foreign, to attempt to reproduce the "splendid war" on the screen. The commercial potential and popular appeal of the topic at times led even to the inclusion of archival footage, as in *60 Hours to Suez*, which incorporates some documentary action shots provided by the Israeli army, as well as television segments shot during the war by Arab states. Israeli productions about the war also lured foreign capital investment. Along with its Israeli investors, *60 Hours to Suez* had Swiss backing, and it was sold in advance to German-speaking countries and to Australia.[32] *Five Days in Sinai*, which employed the Italian Western director Maoricio Lucidi, was an Israeli-Italian coproduction, while the Israeli *Target Tiran* was produced by a German film company. Even exhibition became connected to the victory euphoria; the profits of the premieres of *60 Hours to Suez* and *The Great Escape*, for example, were donated to the Israeli army.

Heroic-nationalist films which did not focus on the 1967 war were nevertheless related to it through heroic stories inspired by the war. Propagating the same pride in the fighting spirit as the films that deal explicitly with the 1967 war, Menahem Golan's *The Great Escape* (nominated for an Oscar as "Best Foreign Film"), although not based on an actual case, not only depicts the heroic acts of the Israeli army but also touches on the collective trauma of circulating stories and the witness of Israeli soldiers who suffered in Syrian prisons during the war. (The film *The Death of a Jew* [*Moto shel Yehudi*, 1971] shows torture to death by Arabs.) Whereas *The Great Escape* revolves around the successful rescue of Israeli war prisoners from a hellish Syrian prison, Al Muzir (a name phonetically reminiscent of the infamous Syrian prison Al Mazar), the film's intertitles state that the "events and characters are fictive." Menahem Golan's 1971 filmic fantasy became historical actuality in the Entebbe rescue, the basis of his subsequent *Operation Thunderbolt* (*Mivtza Yehonatan*, literally *Jonathan Operation*, 1976), whose glowing presentation of the prowess of an Israeli elite force during the Entebbe hijacking had become, by the mid- to late seventies, somewhat anachronistic within the generic evolution of Israeli cinema. Although the film *Operation Thunderbolt* was made within a quite different political context, it employs the discourse of the post-1967 heroic-nationalist films. While the post-1973 war was characterized by a collective hangover, a disenchantment with post-1967 euphoria, the Entebbe operation victory engendered a "structure of feeling" similar to that of 1967, quickly becoming a celebrated, almost mythical military action. (Israelis chose to call the 1967 war "the Six Days War," emphasizing a victory achieved in a brief period, while the Entebbe operation is named "Jonathan Operation" after the commander, Jonathan Netanyahu, who was killed during the operation.) Both films, interestingly, cast the Israeli star Yehoram Gaon in the leading role.

Children's films, such as Boaz Davidson's *Azit of the Paratroopers* (*Azit shel haTzanhanim*, 1972), also celebrated battle operations, evoking the grandeur of 1967. Based on the heroic children's story, *Azit the Paratrooper Dog* (*Azit haKalba haTzanhanit*) by ex-chief-of-staff Mordechai Gur, the film adds to elite units a courageous (the Hebrew root of *azit* signifies courage) "Sabra" she-dog who assists the Israeli army against Arab terrorists. Even a film whose major theme concerned the 1948 war, *He Walked through the Fields*, added the frame story of the contemporary (1967) soldier to whom the heroic story of his father's generation is presumably being told—a framing device added to the Moshe Shamir (1948) play on which the film is based, an addition clearly motivated by the 1967 war. Joseph Leits' *Faithful City* (1952), which focused on a children's dormitory in the besieged Jerusalem of 1948 and the attempts of the freshly created Israeli army to help the Jewish citizenry, was supplemented in 1967 by a new segment celebrating liberated Jerusalem within a teleological fulfillment of Zionist dreams. There is a kind of isomorphism between the historical Israeli incorporation of Jerusalem and the filmic incorporation of 1967 footage of Jerusalem—this in a film set in 1948 and modified in 1967 to illustrate the realization of Zionist hopes with images desired but unavailable before 1967. Some films which revolved around the theme of class-ethnic tensions, such as *My Margo* (*Margo Shell*, 1969), were partially set and shot in the old city of Jerusalem, demonstrating national pride in the full control of the "City of Peace," subliminally compensating for the ethnic dissonances. Other films, notably Uri Zohar's *Every Bastard a King* (*Kol Mamzer Melekh*, 1968) and Gilberto Toffani's *Siege* (*Matzor*, 1969), although focusing on the 1967 period and its aftermath, did not employ the war genre, but used the war and its consequences as mere background for psychological drama.

The Americanization of Israeli culture also affected the heroic-nationalist films, which acquired the epic style and "larger-than-life" heroes of Hollywood war films. The epic scale can be seen as the cinematic rendering of the sensation of spatial liberation when a physically small country overcomes the siege situation and expands, a fact of immense psychological import for the Israeli collective unconscious, generating a feeling of liberation from the terror of encirclement. The budgets of the post-1967 heroic-nationalist films were relatively high, reflecting the post-war economic prosperity, and they allowed for the adoption of the more "appropriate" sophisticated "look," a refusal of the austerity and "neglect" manifested in both the content and the inexpensive "look" of earlier films that suited a young country with Socialist aspirations. The new films were mostly shot in color (Nouri Habib was the first to introduce color filmmaking in 1952 with his *Without a Homeland*, but only after Golan's *Cairo Operation* of 1965 and particularly after the 1967 war, did color film become standard); and *Five Days in Sinai*, for instance, was shot in Cinemascope as well.

The pre-1967 films' modest mise-en-scène, for example that of those set in simple settlements, in a barren locale (*Pillar of Fire, They Were Ten, Rebels Against the Light*), combined a tendency toward unostentatious camera style with a relatively slow rhythm. These films also tended to present the Israeli-Arab battles with minimal props such as revolvers and guns (*They Were Ten, Rebels Against the Light*), at times adding a few tanks (*Hill 24 Doesn't Answer, Pillar of Fire*), or a shabby airplane (*Sinaia*)—in the pre-state pioneers' films the central characters lacked even these minimal props—as well as usually relying on a small number of actors (*Pillar of Fire, They Were Ten, Rebels Against the Light, Sinaia*).

Post-1967 films, in contrast, employed a faster rhythm of editing and placed more emphasis on production values. Hollywood-oriented films such as *60 Hours to Suez, Five Days in Sinai*, and *Target Tiran* (whose script was written by Hollywood screenwriter Jack Jacobs), included larger numbers of extras, more special effects, and the evocation of battle atmosphere through pyrotechnical means, tending to pay attention to (expensive) verisimilitude in the mise-en-scène. Golan's *The Great Escape*, for example, is precise about military details, a precision achieved with the aid of the IDF, which lent some of its spoils, in the form of Syrian arms and transport, to the filmmaker. Virtually all war-genre films, it should be noted, were obliged, at least partially, to depend on the army for military equipment, and *60 Hours to Suez* even staged battle sequences reconstituted by the Israeli infantry and armored troops especially for the film. At the same time, however, the post-1967 films continued the practice of earlier heroic-nationalist films—and of Israeli cinema generally—of shooting on location due to a limited budget. While sea battle scenes in Hollywood's *The Guns of Navarone* (1961) were shot in a special swimming pool built in the studios, *Target Tiran*, for example, was shot on location in the Red Sea.

Casting in this period often involved relatively prestigious names, either "Hollywood"-identified Americans like Robert Fuller in *Target Tiran* and Rick Jayson and Peter Brown in *The Great Escape*, or Israeli stars like Yehoram Gaon in *Five Days in Sinai, 60 Hours to Suez*, and *The Great Escape* (cast again in a similar role later in Golan's *Operation Thunderbolt*)—as well as in *Every Bastard a King* and *Siege*—and Assaf Dayan in *He Walked through the Fields* and *Five Days in Sinai*. Quite apart from his artistic talents, Assaf Dayan (son of the then celebrated Minister of Defense, Moshe Dayan) was also attractive to producers for his name, especially in the case of *Five Days in Sinai*. The Italian producers placed exaggerated

Mobilized spectatorship: Assaf Dayan in *Five Days in Sinai*.

hopes on the Dayan name (for instance, assuming the probability of full military backing), leading to serious financial miscalculations and disasters throughout the shooting—and the production was saved largely through the efforts of Menahem Golan, who was called to assist without benefit for himself.[33]

In his recent Hollywood work (with Cannon Production Company) Golan has showed continued interest in the heroic-nationalist genre, but this time transposed into North American superpatriotic films such as *Delta Force* and *Cobra*, gratifying the desire for an American heroic image suitable to the Age of Reagan. In *Delta Force*, produced, written, and directed by Golan, an American elite unit releases a hijacked airplane, much as in Golan's earlier *Operation Thunderbolt*, thus granting Americans an "Entebbe" of their own. The anti-Arab thrust of the Israeli films is transferred and even magnified in the Hollywood films, resulting in a stereotypical treatment quite unthinkable within current Israeli cinema, in accord with the general, at times hysterical, anti-Arabism of the American mass media.

Post-1967 heroic-nationalist films maintained, in many ways, the same Zionist ideological line as their predecessors (for example, the decontextualization of the Arab anti-Israeli stance) and employed fundamentally similar narrative, cinematic, and characterological codes: the dichotomy of "good" Israeli protagonists versus "evil" Arab antagonists, focalization through Sabra heroes, the suturing of the spectator into a pro-Israeli perspective through point-of-view shots, and non-diegetic celebratory epic music. These films reflect, nevertheless, a clear drift to the political right, in accord with the dominant political situation. The theme of qualified few versus Arab many continues to constitute a major element in the representation of the Israeli/Arab confrontation, yet, within the context of victory euphoria, it suggests less an apology for the violence practiced by peace-loving Israel than sheer celebration of the brilliant military performance of the Israeli army. A spirit of anti-Arab mockery at times comes to be allied to the general self-celebratory tone, for example, in the tendency to characterize the Arab enemy not simply as cruel but also as inept, a portrayal widely disseminated in the post-war popular culture of jokes, sketches, and cartoons.

The new titles celebrate army heroism, avoiding the liberal undertones of such pre-1967 titles as, for example, *Rebels Against the Light*. Titles highlight military prowess, for example (*60 Hours to Suez*, the short amount of time required for the Israeli army to reach Suez), or grant a laudatory adjective to a military exploit (*The Great Escape*). Here the mockery is more subdued, existing only by negation, implying the inability of Arabs to cope with the Israelis. *The Great Escape* was distributed abroad under the title *Eagles Attack at Dawn*, maintaining the focal attention given to the hero's mission, and "architextually" (Genette's term for the genres invoked by a title) associating the film with American war and Western films. *Sixty Hours to Suez* was distributed as *Is Tel Aviv Burning?*, evoking the famous blockbuster *Is Paris Burning?* The sensational Israeli title also alludes to the film's Nasser character, serving as a sarcastic paraphrase of the Egyptian president's promise to his army that they would reach Tel Aviv before their cigarettes had burnt to the end. (As proof of fulfilling the promise, the Egyptians had shown an old documentary about the burning of the Zim building, an event which had taken place two years before the war.)[34] An attitude of ridicule also characterizes *The Great Escape*, where Syrian soldiers are presented as lazy, stupid, cowardly, and almost exclusively preoccupied with playing the Oriental game of backgammon. The single shrewd Syrian, the commander, is extremely cruel and, toward the end, with the Israeli victory, reveals himself to be a coward, like the others. In the style of American war films of the forties and fifties, *The Great Escape* also employs comic relief through a charming (Sabra) character who manages to joke confidently as he shoots at the Syrians. (His recklessness leads to his narrative punishment by death.)

Within films where the war was magnified so as to become a virtual protagonist, there was little room for the venerable character of the positive and obedient Arab, nor for the corollary theme, the idealism of enlightening the East. In the new phase, the narrative structure is premised from the outset on the impossibility of any common language—beyond the language of power—between the forces of light and the forces of darkness. If films from the thirties to the mid-sixties emphasized the protagonists' "universal humanism" with regard to the Orient, showing them teaching Arabs the alphabet, implementing technological advances, and manifesting good will for unselfish peaceful coexistence, post-1967 heroic-nationalist films stress, especially through narrative time, the fraternal loyalty of the soldiers and the details of military operations. Israelis in this period have lost the "naïveté," the "utopia" of an Arab pro-Zionist prise de conscience (even if such a utopia is maintained in the diplomatic endorsement of "responsible" and "moderate" Palestinians); ergo we find a modulation into a new discourse, that of "The only language they understand is power." The centrality of war is, at times, clearly manifested through the narrative structure, as in *60 Hours to Suez*, whose different stories of four Israelis in different war zones who never meet suggest the war as a common factor in the characters' life and as a unifying narrative element.

The pre-1967 emphasis on Zionist apologetics and on the didactic moralism of the *Bildungsroman* subplot is also minimized in the post-1967 films. The objective-witness character, usually an American, now tends to be committed to Israel from the inception of the film. Rather than have the hero explain his nation's history and justify its stance, the new films present the Sabra warrior in his now clearly defined historical role as a kind of military engineer fighting for his homeland. The positive nature of Zionism and Israel is simply assumed, and we therefore seldom encounter the kind of virtuoso rhetorical display exercised in the films of the thirties through the sixties. In the face of Arab hostility, the soldiers are presented as simply fighting with conviction, defending themselves, and winning. The pragmatic stance of the films and their Sabra protagonists has directed the heroic-nationalist films into a clearly classic war-film genre with more emphasis on "action" and "larger-than-life" heroics, devoting more narrative and story time to the actual war. Post-1967 films also no longer prod their spectators toward specific positions and conclusions concerning the nature of Zionism and Israel; rather, all the narrative energy is channeled into the evolving drama as to whether the forces of light (i.e., the Israelis) will win. It is already taken for granted that they are "good" and that their political cause is just in the establishment sequences that construct the obvious dualism. Here, the spectator is assumed to be beyond the tabula-rasa cognitive stage. From the very inception of the film, the spectator is fully integrated into the "obvious" and taken-for-granted authoritative ideology of the text and into the perspective of the privileged (Israeli) narrator-focalizers, from which perspective all other ideologies are evaluated.

The full process of Israeli bourgeoisification after 1967 (the main precedent occurred in the fifties thanks to the cheap labor provided by the mass immigration of Jews from Arab and Muslim countries) involved a manifest neglect of Socialist values. Already in the early sixties the Zionist-Socialist idealist spirit of films like *They Were Ten* and *Rebels Against the Light* came to be regarded by both critics and audience as anachronistic both thematically and in terms of the histrionic pathos-oriented style of representation. The decreasing Israeli interest in the familiar images and ideology of the heroic-nationalist genre—which were, in any event, directed more toward foreign audiences—paved the way for the rise of genres other than the heroic-nationalist films, such as the social comedy. Employing a different representational set of codes than those of Zionist pioneering, the comedies of the early to mid-sixties nevertheless basically continued the heroic-nationalist films' system of beliefs. Peter Frey's *I Like Mike*, for example, accentuated the ideological conflict between bourgeois Zionist values of the city and the Socialist-Zionist ideals of the kibbutz, concluding with a happy-ending consecration of the latter, while Ephraim Kishon's *Sallah Shabbati* (1964; distributed abroad as *Sallah*) celebrated the integration of the "primitive" Arab-Jew into Israeli society—here directing the Orientalist paternalism of the heroic-nationalist films toward Oriental Jews rather than Arabs. The diminution of Zionist pathos in Israeli culture is seen in the cinema, then, through the very rise of another genre, the comedy.

The heroic-nationalist films of the post-1967 period, meanwhile, diverted the pathos of the idealistic spirit into a different direction, displaying it within the military sphere per se. Whereas in the earlier heroic-nationalist films the protagonists' Zionist idealism was often presented on the dialogue level through pioneer-like speeches and, in terms of staging and setting, largely in modest settlements, post-1967 films incorporated urban topography, as well as the relatively high standard of living of the main Sabra characters, who are no longer "blessed" with the older generation's idealistic monologues. Images of solidarity in battle (*Target Tiran, 60 Hours to Suez*), of an officer's total commitment to his soldiers (*The Great Escape*), or of enthusiastic service in the army, at times presented as standing in opposition to quotidian superficiality (as in Assaf Dayan's character in *Five Days in Sinai*, who immediately quits his decadent city life when the army calls him), constituted the only legitimacy granted to pathos, i.e., the pathos of war. The films, in this sense, prolonged a pervasive sentimentality in Sabra popular culture shown, for example, in the many songs that tell of wartime solidarity, self-sacrifice, and the immortality of slain heroes.

The same mythological Sabra characteristics were delineated by the post-1967 heroic-nationalist films, but with greater emphasis on the "negative" quality of toughness, here explained as a product of a harsh reality in a fanatically hostile region, and thus ultimately positive within a context of a war of self-defense. While pre-1967 films divided their narrative time equally between the Israeli fighter (*lohem*) and the dreamer/visionary (*holem*), as in *Hill 24 Doesn't Answer* and *Pillar of Fire*, or within the humanist trend devoted more time to the visionary, as in *They Were Ten, Rebels Against the Light*, and *Sinaia*, post-1967 Sabras were presented mainly within the war context as fighting with a high level of morale and courage, with little inclination for "intellectual" pursuits, as tough in action and sparse in speech, as twentieth-century exemplars of the *fortitudine et sapientia* of the classical epic hero. The evolution of the characterization of Israeli protagonists from pre- to post-1967 films parallels the stereotypical images of the fathers' generation and the sons' generation as drawn in Amos Elon's depiction of the two first Israeli generations in *The Israelis*. In the later films the Sabra image is condensed to a manly, courageous warrior, idealistically devoted to and responsible for his comrades. The national consensus, then, is expressed microcosmically and characterologically through the protagonists' actions and demeanor rather than through lofty dialogue.

Assuming as a starting point the status quo of incessant conflict, these films, in comparison with the fiction films from the thirties through the early sixties, make relatively little reference to the origins of war. Their Zionist message is centered on the military aspects, focusing not on the dramatic outcome of winning or losing (since the generic codes promise Israeli triumph) but rather on the degree of loss or the magnitude of victory for the Israeli side. (As in many pre-1967 films, the Arabs tend to be killed en masse, unregretted, while the few Israeli losses are mourned intensely.) In *The Great Escape*, for example, the main questions do not revolve around former concerns (the Sabra Israeli as a negation of the Jewish Diaspora experience, the enlightenment of the East), but rather on whether the crucial operation will succeed. Military success or failure is thus presented as the exclusive concern eliding all the ideological-reflective issues so crucial to the pioneering films and the early phase of heroic-nationalist films. The rescue of friends left in the enemy's hellish prison (years before *Rambo*) shows the solidarity between Israeli soldiers and demonstrates the willingness to risk one's own life to save a comrade, a quality especially exemplified in the character of the officer played by the Israeli star Yehoram Gaon. The Sabra toughness is directed at the cruel, sadistic enemy, while his sweetness is expressed toward his own small group of friends, a microcosm of the nation. The sense of celebration, however, is also accompanied with melancholy at the loss of friends in the battle, a feeling which takes on the dimensions of a national myth.

Israeli solidarity is constructed in opposition to Arab officers' lack of concern with their soldiers, betraying as well their indifference to loss of life, even on their own side. Post-1967 films continue and even exacerbate the earlier-traditional representation of the cruel Arab tyrant. Close-ups of Arab characters laughing sadistically at the suffering of the tortured Israelis here become an emblem of Arab sadism and cruelty. The commander of the Syrian jail (Yossef Shiloach) in *The Great Escape* and the Arab terrorist (Shmuel Omni) in *Azit of the Paratroopers* act out the anxiety of the collective Israeli unconscious concerning what might happen if the Arabs ever achieved victory. The post-1967 films present momentary nightmare-situations of Arab takeover, and thus exorcise a latent fear, through an imaginary that ends the nightmare through the restoration of Israeli order.

Although post-1967 films such as *The Great Escape* do not revolve around any putative Israeli humanist mission with regard to the Orient, they also never show cruelty toward the Arab characters who have previously tortured the Israelis' friends. In this sense, the films structure humanism by negation, forming part of the representation of the Israeli as morally superior. In *60 Hours to Suez*, for example, a bereaved father whose son was killed in the war offers a routed Egyptian soldier water. In the post-1967 films, humanism takes a more physical form since the Israeli-Arab contact now takes place through the "physical" form of war, and not,

The rescue of Israeli prisoners from Syrian torture in *The Great Escape*.

as in the earlier films, within a more intellectual-ideological sphere. On another level, Arab tyranny, both among Arabs themselves and toward Israeli prisoners (*The Great Escape*), and potentially toward an occupied Israel—a latent anxiety underlying these films—projects despotism as an Oriental monopoly. Here Israeli filmmakers, the survivors and descendants of European tyrannies such as Fascism and Nazism, elide Western oppressions by attributing these negative qualities to an exclusively Oriental essence. This fictive construction extends the frequent Western tendency to downplay the West's own despotic tendencies or its own implication in despotism. Here again we see the flexible positional superiority of which Said speaks, the need to formulate issues in such a way as to maintain a self-flattering image.

Some of the heroic-nationalist films both before and after 1967 were shot in English (*Hill 24 Doesn't Answer, Pillar of Fire, Rebels Against the Light,* and *Five Days in Sinai*) not only because some were coproductions or had foreign backing, or because of aspirations for distribution facilities, but also, at times, because their directors barely spoke Hebrew. In the coproduction *Five Days in Sinai*, Israelis speak English while the Arab characters speak Arabic, so that English masquerades as "Hebrew." (This use of the Anglo-Saxon lingua franca recalls the linguistic cannibalism by which Hollywood made English "stand in" for a whole series of national tongues.)[35] The unequal and artificial dichotomy of Israelis speaking English and Arabs, Arabic, reinforces the identification of Israel with the West and particularly with the United States, while simultaneously betraying a linguistic neocolonialism ironically extending to the United States' staunchest ally, Israel.[36] Other films in the genre, *They Were Ten, Sinaia, Target Tiran,* and *The Great Escape,* meanwhile, were shot in Hebrew, maintaining a linguistic "realism," whereby Israelis speak Hebrew, Arabs, Arabic, and Americans, English. *They Were Ten* also presents a linguistic encounter between Russian-Jewish-Hebrew pioneers and an Arab Sheik groping toward communication; they discover French as a common language, but move throughout the film toward a dialogue in Arabic, symbolizing the pioneers' openness and flexibility. For his performance in *The Great Escape,* Yossef Shiloach, who plays the main Syrian character, studied the Syrian dialect. *The Great Escape* and *Target Tiran,* however, were also shot in an English version (for distribution in the United States), which minimizes the language difference and relies on the Hollywood tradition of accented English, especially accentuated with the Arab characters.

In the early sixties the heroic-nationalist films were already suffering from declining popularity in Israel, although winning basically positive responses in the United States, less for their cinematic quality than for the curiosity and enthusiasm Israel tended to elicit in the United States. In Israel both the ideology and the cinematic and generic codes of the films were almost annoyingly familiar. The Israeli public was looking for cultural products that would reflect not the "obvious" Zionist themes, but rather daily, social, individual concerns. The post-1967 heroic-nationalist films which reflected the release of pathos only on the battlefield were closer to the Israeli mood, and the public, at least in the period of the "Six Days War" euphoria, was eager to view them; but their quality was quite often unsatisfying. Golan's *The Great Escape* and *Operation Thunderbolt,* in contrast, with their effective, fast-paced storytelling, were quite successful. In a country where, ultimately, the state had created the nation, it was symptomatic that the heroic-nationalist films with their edifying and moralizing tone had been the dominant genre for almost two decades after the establishment of the state, but with the sixties we find a move away from the dominant heroic-nationalist genre, reflecting a need for relief from the constant barrage of news items and small-country concerns.

Beginning with Ephraim Kishon's *Sallah Shabbatti* (1964), the archetypal "bourekas film," and with Uri Zohar's *Hole in the Moon* (*hor baLevana,* 1965), the first fiction film that opened the way for less conventional cinematic and narrative codes, Israeli cinema points toward new "social" as well as "individual" themes. Yet, as we shall see, these genres do not suggest any radical move away from Zionist concerns or from Israel's Western orientation.

3.

The Representation of Sephardim/Mizrahim

Up to this point, I have merely touched intermittently on a topic which I will now develop more fully—the filmic representation, within Israeli cinema, of Oriental Jews. Despite occasional attempts, in such films as *Light out of Nowhere* (*Or min haHefker*, 1973), *The House on Chlouch Street* (*HaBait biRhov Chlouch*, 1973), and Haim Shiran's *Pillar of Salt* (*Ntziv haMelah* 1979), to offer an alternative to the undisputed stereotypes of Oriental Jews, Israeli cinema has clung, for the most part, to myths widespread in Israel and often disseminated by the media outside of Israel. According to that mythic discourse, European Zionism "saved" Sephardi Jews from the harsh rule of their Arab "captors." It took them out of "primitive conditions" of poverty and superstition and ushered them gently into a modern Western society characterized by "humane values," values with which they were but vaguely and erratically familiar due to the "Levantine environments" from which they came. Within Israel, of course, they have suffered from the problem of "the gap;" not simply that between their standard of living and that of European Jews, but also that due to their "incomplete integration" into Israeli liberalism and prosperity, handicapped as they have been by their Oriental, illiterate, despotic, sexist, and generally pre-modern formation in their lands of origin, as well as by their propensity for generating large families. The political establishment, the welfare institutions, and the educational system, according to this discourse, have done all in their power to "reduce the gap" by initiating the Oriental Jew into the ways of a "civilized, modern society." At the same time, intermarriage is proceeding apace and the Sephardim have won new appreciation for their "traditional cultural values," for their folkloric music, rich cuisine, and warm hospitality. A serious problem persists, however. Due to their inadequate education and "lack of experience with democracy," the Jews of Asia and Africa tend to be extremely conservative, even reactionary, and religiously fanatic, in contrast to the liberal, secular, and educated European Jews. Anti-Socialist, they form the base of support for the right-wing parties. Given their "cruel experience in Arab lands," furthermore, they tend to be "Arab-haters," and in this sense they have been an "obstacle to peace," preventing the efforts of the "Peace Camp" to make a "reasonable settlement" with the Arabs.

It is not my purpose here to address the fundamental falsity of this discourse on virtually every point.[1] I wish, rather, to call attention to the wide dissemination of this discourse which is shared by "right" and left," and which has its early and late versions as well as its religious and secular variants. An ideology which blames the Sephardim (and their Third World countries of origin) has been elaborated by the Israeli elite and expressed by politicians, social scientists, educators, writers, and, obviously, filmmakers. This ideology orchestrates an interlocking series of prejudicial discourses betraying clear colonialist overtones, fruit of what Anouar Abdel-Malek calls the "hegemonism of possessing minorities."[2] First World attitudes toward the Third World are reproduced in their Ashkenazi/Sephardi variants, at times quite explicitly in comparisons of Oriental Jews to Arabs and Blacks. Speaking of the Sephardim, Arye Gelblum wrote in *HaAretz* in 1949 of the "immigration of a race we have not yet known in the country," whose "primitivism is at a peak," and "whose level of knowledge is one of virtually absolute ignorance, and, worse, who have little talent for understanding anything intellectual." These immigrants are, Gelblum continues, "only slightly better than the general level of the Arabs, Negroes, and Berbers in the same regions. In any case, they are at an even lower level than what we knew with regard to the former Arabs of Eretz Israel." "These Jews," he goes on, "also lack roots in Judaism, as they are totally subordinated to the play of savage and primitive instincts." They also display "chronic laziness and hatred for work," and "there is nothing safe about this asocial element.... Aliyat HaNoar [organization for immigration of youth], which is the official institution, refuses to receive Moroccan children and the kibbutzim will not hear of their absorption among them."[3]

Ben-Gurion, similarly, described Oriental immigrants as lacking even "the most elementary knowledge" and "without a trace of Jewish or human education,"[4] and repeatedly expressed contempt for the culture of the Oriental Jews: "We do not want Israelis to become Arabs. We are duty bound to fight against the spirit of the Levant, which corrupts individuals and societies, and preserve the authentic Jewish values as they crystallized in the Diaspora."[5] Over the years Israeli leaders constantly reinforced and legitimized these prejudices, which encompassed both Arabs and Oriental Jews. For Abba Eban, the "object should be to infuse [the Sephardim] with an Occidental spirit, rather than allow them to drag us into an unnatural Orientalism." Or again: "One of the great apprehensions which afflict us . . . is the danger lest the predominance of immigrants of Oriental origin force Israel to equalize its cultural level with that of the neighboring world."[6] Golda Meir projected the Sephardim, in typical colonialist fashion, as coming from another, less developed time—for her, the sixteenth-century (and for others, a vaguely defined "Middle Ages"). "Shall we be able," she asked, "to elevate these immigrants to a suitable level of civilization?"[7] Ben-Gurion, who called the

Moroccan Jews "savages" at a session of a Knesset committee, and who compared Sephardim, pejoratively (and revealingly), to the Blacks brought to the United States as slaves, at times went so far as to question the spiritual capacity and even the Jewishness of the Sephardim.[8] (Indeed, one might invert the thrust of the comparison to point out certain structural analogies between the oppression of Blacks in the New World and the situation of Sephardim in Israel. If the Palestinians can be seen as the aboriginal "Indians" of the dominant discourse, the Sephardim constitute its "Blacks.") Zionist writings and speeches, furthermore, frequently advance the historiographically suspect idea that Jews of the Orient, prior to their "in-gathering" into Israel, were somehow "outside of" history, thus ironically echoing nineteenth-century assessments, such as those of Hegel, that Jews, like Blacks, lived outside of the progress of Western Civilization. European Zionists in this sense resemble Fanon's colonizer who always "makes history;" whose life is "an epoch," "an Odyssey" against which the natives form an "almost inorganic background." One would like to think that such attitudes disappeared with the fifties, but as recently as 1983, *HaAretz*, a liberal daily favored by Ashkenazi academics and known for its presumably high journalistic standards, published an article by "leftist" Amnon Dankner comparing Sephardim to "baboons."[9] And "liberal" Shulamit Aloni, head of the Citizen's Rights Party and a member of the Knesset, in 1983 denounced Sephardi demonstrators as "barbarous tribal forces" that were "driven like a flock with tomtoms" and chanting like "a savage tribe."[10] The implicit trope comparing Sephardim to Black Africans recalls, ironically, one of the favored topoi of European anti-Semitism, that of the "Black Jew."

The racist discourse concerning Oriental Jews is not always overwrought or violent, however; elsewhere it takes a "humane" and relatively "benign" form. Read, for example, Dr. Dvora and Rabbi Menachem Hacohen's *One People: The Story of the Eastern Jews*, an "affectionate" text thoroughly imbued with Eurocentric prejudice. In his introduction, Abba Eban speaks of the "exotic quality" of Jewish communities "on the outer margins of the Jewish world."[11] The text proper and its accompanying photographs convey a clear ideological agenda. The stress throughout is on "traditional garb," "charming folkways," pre-modern "craftsmanship," cobblers and coppersmiths, and women "weaving on primitive looms." Repeatedly, we are reminded that some North African Jews inhabited caves (intellectuals such as Albert Memmi and Jacques Derrida apparently escaped this condition), and an entire chapter is devoted to "The Jewish Cave-Dwellers." The actual historical record, however, shows that Oriental Jews were overwhelmingly urban. What is striking, on the part of the commentator, is a kind of "desire for primitivism," a miserabilism which feels compelled to paint the Sephardi Jews as innocent of technology and modernity. The pictures of Oriental misery are then contrasted with the luminous faces of the Orientals in Israel, learning to read and mastering the modern technology of tractors and combines. The book forms part of a broader national export industry of Sephardi "folklore," an industry which circulates (the often expropriated) goods—dresses, jewelry, liturgical objects, books, photos, and films—among Western Jewish institutions eager for Jewish exoticism.

The dominant sociological accounts of Israel's "ethnic problem," similarly, attribute the inferior status of Oriental Jews not to the class nature of Israeli society but rather to their origins in "pre-modern," "culturally backward" societies. Borrowing heavily from the intellectual arsenal of American "functionalist" studies of development and modernization, Shmuel Eisenstadt and his many social-scientist disciples gave ideological subterfuge the aura of scientific rationality. The influential role of this "modernization" theory derives from its perfect match with the needs of the Establishment. Eisenstadt borrows from the American "structural functionalism" of Talcott Parsons its teleological view of a "progress" from "traditional" societies, with their less complex social structures, to "modernization" and "development." Since the Israeli social formation was seen as that entity collectively created during the Yishuv period, the immigrants were perceived as integrating themselves into the pre-existing dynamic whole of a modern society patterned on the Western model. The "absorption" (*klita*) of Sephardi immigrants into Israeli society entailed their acceptance of the established consensus of the "host" society and the abandonment of "pre-modern" traditions. But while European immigrants required only "absorption," the immigrants from Africa and Asia required "absorption through modernization." For the Eisenstadt tradition, the Oriental Jews had to undergo a process of "desocialization"—that is, erasure of their cultural heritage—and "resocialization"—that is, assimilation to the Ashkenazi way of life. Thus cultural difference was posited as the cause of maladjustment.[12] (The theory would have trouble explaining why other Sephardim, coming from the same "premodern" countries, at times from the very same families, suffered no particular maladjustment in such "post-modern" metropolises as Paris, London, New York, and Montreal.)

On whatever level—immigration policy, urban development, labor policy, government subsidies—a pattern of discrimination touches even the details of daily life. These discriminatory processes, shaped in the earliest period of Zionism, are reproduced every day and on every level, reaching into the very interstices of the Israeli social system. As a result, the Sephardim, despite their majority status, are underrepresented in the national centers of power—in the Government, in the Knesset, in the higher echelons of the military, in the diplomatic corps, in the media, and in academic work; and they are overrepresented in the marginal, stigmatized regions of professional and social life. The Ashkenazim, however, have hidden behind the flattening term "Israeli society," an entity presumed to embody the values of modernity, industry, science, and democracy. As Shlomo Swirski points out, this presentation camouflaged the actual historical processes by obscuring a number of facts: first, that the Ashkenazim, not unlike the Sephardim, had also come from countries on the periphery of the world capitalist system, countries which entered the process of industrialization and technological-scientific development roughly at the same time as the Sephardi countries of origin; second, that a peripheral Yishuv society had *also* not reached a level of development comparable to that of the societies of the "center"; and third, that Ashkenazi "modernity" was made possible thanks to the labor force provided by Oriental mass immigration.[13] The ethnic basis of this process is often elided even by most Marxist analysts, who speak generically of "Jewish workers," a simplification roughly parallel to speaking of the exploitation of "American" workers on Southern cotton plantations.

Orientalism and its Discontents

Israeli films on Sephardi subjects, then, must be seen as part of this larger circulation of images and ideology. Although the discussion of the images of Oriental Jews in Israeli cinema is often limited to their appearance in the "bourekas"—the name derives from a popular Sephardi pastry—films of the sixties and seventies, it should be remembered that the image of the Oriental Jew already appeared in the children's movies of the fifties and sixties, films such as Nathan Axelrod's *Dan Quixote and Saadia Panza* (1956) and Menahem Golan's *Eight Trail One* (1964). The ethnic/class division is presented, in these films, as natural and inevitable. The detectives and investigators, "the intellectual minds," are defined as Sabras (Ashkenazim) while the Yemenite children play the role of servant boys. *Dan Quixote and Saadia Panza*, for instance, retains little from Cervantes' *Don Quixote* beyond the master-servant relationship of the two central characters. While Dan is associated with school and a well-kept respectable home—the camera's pan over his books emphasizes his status as "a man of letters"—Saadia is shorn of all familial and educational context and is portrayed as a shoe-shine boy, a neglected street urchin. His world is presented as a given, scarcely deserving narrative attention, much in contrast with Dan's world. The latter is privileged both by superior position in the plot and by the stylistic design of the film, which provides authenticating details concerning his background. As in Axelrod's earlier film, *Oded the Wanderer*, Axelrod has his young Sabra protagonist undertake intellectual activities as well as physical tasks. In one of the first agricultural-boarding-school sequences, Dan tries to read while he ploughs, but he soon forgets ploughing and continues only with his reading. The film then cuts to Saadia, who immediately and enthusiastically adjusts to his new job as a shepherd, happy in the position generously offered him by the institution. In another sequence, Dan sketches the targets while Saadia digs in the ground. Dan, attached to Saadia only through their common fondness for fantasy, acts as the "great detective," authoritatively commanding Saadia, while the camera and editing emphasize the clear-cut division of roles.

This division continues in a seventies children's film, *Hasamba* (1971), based on the popular book series by Yigal Mossinzon. Inspired by adult elite-unit heroism, the young Sabras are not only courageous, but also able to creatively employ sophisticated technology, using it fairly against the paradigm of Oriental evil, the underworld Sephardi antagonist (played by Ze'ev Revah), who, despite his relatively older age, is more primitive in his methods. In these children's films (and literature), the ethnic stereotypes are obvious. The narratives' schematic opposition—for example Dan the intellectual versus Saadia the laborer in *Dan Quixote and Saadia Panza*—reproduces the ethnic division of labor as daily produced by the educational apparatus. Largely segregated and unequal, the system of education consistently orients Ashkenazim toward prestigious white-collar positions requiring a strong academic preparation while pointing Sephardi pupils toward low-status blue-collar jobs. The educational system functions, as Swirski puts it, as "a huge labeling mechanism that has, among other things, the effect of lowering the achievement and expectations of Oriental children and their parents."[14]

In *Dan Quixote and Saadia Panza* it is war, furthermore, that brings the children "down to earth," and now they use their detective-like skills in support of the adult war against the Arabs. (The American reader might be reminded of Tom Sawyer and Huck Finn plotting against the "A-rabs.") Dan Quixote grants Saadia Panza permission to join the private war (in support of the adults) because his knowledge of Arabic might be useful. As a secondary character, the Yemenite boy—Saadia in *Dan Quixote and Saadia Panza* or Yehya in *Eight Trail One*—is forced to prove to the heroes of the "First Israel" that he is entitled to the name "Israeli." In *Eight Trail One*, the kibbutz Sabras doubt Yehya's inarticulate messages about the German spy (for the Arabs) and dismiss them as a mere irrational fantasy. This dismissal provokes his individual action aimed at proving that he tells the truth and is worthy of being integrated with the Sabras. The kibbutz Sabra society embodies from the beginning the hegemonic codes, expressed in the theme song of the film: "... *Kulanu Yahad/Hey, ein lanu pahad/Kadima uveometz lev/Navis taoyev* ... " "... All together/ Hey, we know no fear/ Bravely forward/ We'll defeat the enemy ... "). The (narrative) process of initiation for the Sephardi and his final happy acceptance into Sabra society (the city in *Dan Quixote and Saadia Panza* or the kibbutz in *Eight Trail One*) are contingent on heroic action against Arabs (*Dan Quixote and Saadia Panza*) or spies (*Eight Trail One*). Only with participation in the burden of war, according to the myth dominating these films, can equality be granted to the Sephardi, the Arab-Jew.

The homology between the marginal presence of Orientals in the narrative and the marginality of the Israeli Sephardi majority in relation to the centers of power continues to characterize films produced in recent years. In the "gefilte-fish" films ("the Ashkenazi bourekas"), which largely deal with Ashkenazi ghetto folklore, such as *Lupo in New York* (*Lupo beNew York*, 1976), *Kuni Lemel in Tel Aviv* (*Kuni Lemel beTel Aviv*, 1976), and *Kuni Lemel in Cairo* (*Kuni Lemel beCahir*, 1983), we encounter the character type of the Yemenite servant. In *Kuni Lemel in Cairo*, the Hassidic village employs Ovadia, a religious Yemenite, as a janitor. Ovadia's character fulfills the stereotype of the "good-natured Yemenite" as well as that of the irrational Oriental. Asked to explain the way to Rabbi Kuni Lemel, Ovadia offers nonsensical instructions in a Yemenite singsong accent accompanied by extravagant gestures. He repeats himself several times, and when the Israeli woman, dressed as an American Hassid, and the spectator cannot understand, he tells her, "O.K., then just go straight ahead and you'll get there." The "good," religious Ovadia, as in the structural division between "good/bad" Arabs in the humanist-Zionist films, is foiled by the secular Oriental "bad guys," the underworld, that the heroes, the Ashkenazi Hassids (along with their secular relative, Muni Lemel), ultimately overcome. The Hassidim manage to retrieve the stolen present given to them by the Jewish community in Cairo (old coins from the Second Temple worth a million dollars), and they celebrate their triumph with the song "This is the Torah and this is its reward," in a manner reminiscent of the link, frequent in bourgeois ideology, of divine blessing and financial reward. This link is especially relevant in the context of a film which also parodies Israeli-U.S. relations. In an English/Hebrew musical review show, Muni Lemel, dressed as Uncle Sam (played by the American Yiddish actor Mike Burstein), flirts with his partner, Miss Israel (Hanna Laslo), here presented as a prostitute available for his pleasure.

In contrast with the underworld, the faithful servant wins the paternalistic love of Rabbi Kuni Lemel, summed up in affectionately stereotypical sentences such as: "If there's anything more stubborn than a stubborn donkey, it's a stubborn Yemenite." When the village elders secretly confer in the inner chambers, the Great Elder, Rabbi Shlomo, approaches the door and opens it. In long shot, we see the eavesdropping servant fall straight into the room. We view him through the eyes of the young Jewish scholars, and he is again compared to an animal by Rabbi Shlomo: "A wise man knows the soul of his animal." This constructed gap in intellect generates throughout the film a feeling of comedic superiority in relation to the "simple laborer." (Shot partially on location in Cairo, the film also provoked Egyptian anger against the portrayal of Arabs, depicted, like the Yemenite character, as lacking intelligence.)

The stereotype of the Sephardi man as a member of the "underworld" at times carries over into the more recent "quality films," or personal cinema. Although these films tend to focus on "First Israel," Sephardim do appear occasionally as marginal characters, often associated with violence. In Yehuda Ne'eman's *The Paratroopers* (*Massa Alunkot*, literally *Journey of Stretchers*, 1977), it is the Sephardi Macho (Motty Shirin) who abuses the more sensitive soldier Weisman (Moni Mushonov). Even though on another level the film offers an eloquent indictment of the dehumanizing processes of military life, on the level of Sephardi representation, the film prolongs the image of the violent Sephardi. His aggressions, whether intended as fun (in the shower sequence) or revenge (in the violent sequence after the soldiers are collectively punished), aggravate the pressures already placed on

Weisman by the commander (Gidi Gov), and thus form a contributing cause to Weisman's suicide. That the first half of the film is focalized through Weisman, with whom we have been led to feel a strong identification, and the second part through the guilt-ridden Sabra commander, strengthens the image of the Sephardi man as exempt from humane feelings; vulture-like, he tries to appropriate the gift package sent by Weisman's mother.

In a recent film, Eitan Green's *Till the End of the Night* (*Ad Sof haLaila*, 1986), Sephardi men invade the collapsing world of the Sabra protagonist (Assaf Dayan) and act as the catalysts for violence. The (Sephardi) underworld characters burst into the protagonist's bar demanding "protection money." The protagonist, a re-serve officer in the army (who by implication belongs to the elite formation), arranges a surprise for the "underworld" (and for the spectator): when a Sephardi threatens the protagonist with a knife, his army comrades draw their guns, gratify-ing the spectator with their quick-witted solidarity with the protagonist. Military camaraderie functions this time against the "enemy" in civilian life. Furthermore, the Sephardi character also embodies the recent stereotype, fostered by Israeli liberals, of the Sephardi as "Arab-hater," since the Sephardi beats the bar's Arab worker as a "message" to his boss. *Till the End of the Night*, while taking the image of the Sephardi underworld as a social "given," also takes the image of the Arab worker for granted, foregrounding the protagonist, the bar owner, in the bar's kitchen (where the Arab works) and strictly panning with the protagonist as he walks away from the mute Arab worker. Finally, it is the honest and gracious Austrian-Christian doctor (converted to Judaism), the father of the protagonist, who charitably treats the Arab beaten by the Sephardi; and it is he who becomes, at the end of the film, the unfortunate sacrificial victim of Oriental violence originally directed at his decadent son. His murder triggers the protagonist's tears and the film's quasi-catharsis. The East here allegorically moves upon the West, coming from "nowhere" and threatening the latter's existence. Here the film betrays a latent anxiety about the penetration of an "alien" Oriental into a self-enclosed universe.

In Oded Kotler's *Romance Resumed* (*Roman beHemshekhim*, 1985; distributed in English as *Again Forever*), set in 1977 prior to the Likud rise to power, the Sabra protagonist (played by Topol) is a successful lawyer intimately linked to the Labor Party. The film focalizes the lawyers' quotidian experience of Sephardi aggressivity (rooted in politics as well as ethnicity), an experience which even provokes nightmares in which knife-wielding Sephardi thugs threaten him in dark alleys. These oneiric incarnations of anti-Sephardi paranoia imagistically translate the latent Ashkenazi fear of a Sephardi takeover, phantasized as the violent victimization of those who in fact retain control of the reins of power. Although the film thematizes the corruption of Sabra Labor leaders, it nevertheless fosters clear sympathy with them, idealizing their past "purity," while completely demonizing Sephardim as the symbol of the country's fall from innocence. The Sephardi issue, it might be argued, is ultimately more threatening to the elite's status and self-image than the Palestinian issue, for whereas the Israeli/Palestinian conflict can be presented as the inevitable clash of two nationalities, any acknowledgment of the exploitation and deculturalization of the Sephardim, in a putatively egalitarian Jewish state, implies an indictment of the social-political system of Israel itself as oppressive toward all Oriental peoples, whether Arab or Jewish.

Other personal films feature Sephardi women, who, as in Israeli/Hebrew literature, are presented as housemaids. *A Thousand Little Kisses* (*Elef Neshikot Ktanot*, 1982), for example, fosters identification with the elegant and sophisticated bourgeois Ashkenazi widow facing a crisis in her life. Through the visually "precious" and sophisticated mise-en-scène and complex camera movements, we are made to identify with the "complex" world of the widow against that of the petty, intrusive, and materialistic maid who is merely interested in taking food and clothing from her employer and who totally lacks sensitivity to the widow's emotional state. Due to their conspicuous and unnatural exclusion from a film shot in a well-known Sephardi neighborhood, Orientals (other than the maid) form a "structuring absence" in *A Thousand Little Kisses*. The film, which consistently maintains a hygienic and self-conscious atmosphere of artistic beauty, exploits the old local architecture of the neighborhood but eliminates almost all traces of its inhabitants.

The Bourekas and the Carnivalesque

The discussion of Sephardi/Ashkenazi tension in Israeli cinema has import especially because it pervades most of the "bourekas" films which have formed a dominant genre within the Israeli film industry. Since their first successes in the early sixties, "bourekas" films have contributed significantly to the development of the Israeli film industry, with Menahem Golan and Ephraim Kishon as major initiatory figures. The term "bourekas" films gained currency among film crit-;ics around 1972 and gradually spread to the general public. Boaz Davidson, one of the major "bourekas" directors, with such films as *Charlie and a Half* (*Charlie vaHetzi*, 1974), *Billiards* (*Hagiga BaSnuker*, 1975), and *Tzan'ani Family* (*Mishpahat Tzan'ani*, 1976), claims to have coined the term.[15] From around 1967 to 1977 the "bourekas" films were absolutely dominant in the film industry. In the late seventies, the genre underwent a kind of mutation, moving from folkloric ethnic cinema into a kind of soft-core porn, especially in what came to be known as the *"Lemon Popsicle* series"[16] of Davidson (director) and Golan-Globus (producers)—a series sometimes also dismissed as "bourekas," in this case a synonym for "bad."

But "bourekas" films with ethnic, rich/poor themes did not completely vanish; some filmmakers, such as Ze'ev Revah, continued to produce them, and there were also rescreenings of older films. In the seventies, films of the sixties such as Kishon's *Sallah Shabbati* (1964), Golan's *Fortuna* (1966), Uri Zohar's *Moishe Vintelator* (1966), Golan's *999 Aliza Mizrahi* (1967), Uri Zohar's *Our Neighborhood* (*HaShkhuna Shelanu*, 1968), Golan's *My Margo* (1969), and Golan's *Queen of the Road* (*Malkat haKvish*, 1971) retroactively came to be seen as "bourekas" as well. A more marginal group of "bourekas" films featuring Ashkenazi protagonists and ghetto folklore, meanwhile, came to be called "bourekas for Ashkenazim" and "gefilte-fish" films. The films in this group include Israel Bekers' *Kuni Lemel* (1968) and Golan's *Lupo* (1970), but especially the more recent Yoel Zilberg's *Kuni Lemel in Tel Aviv* (1976), Davidson's *Lupo in New York* (1976), Zilberg's *Hershele* (1977), Zilberg's *Marriage Tel Aviv Style* (*Nisuin Nosah Tel Aviv*, 1980), and even Avraham Hefner's *Aunt Klara* (*HaDoda Klara*, 1977).[17] "Gefilte-fish" films were produced and directed by those who also made "bourekas" for Sephardim.

It is especially since the early seventies that the "bourekas" became largely the industrial enterprise of producers/distributors such as Menahem Golan, Simha Zvuluni, and Baruch Ella (these last two coming originally from distribution and exhibition and movie-theater ownership). "Bourekas" filmmakers and producers have praised the genre. In interviews Boaz Davidson, for example, defended the genre against film critics and the filmmakers of "quality films:"[18]

> "Bourekas films" are a film genre. A genre from which there was no escape. In this country, the potential audience that comes to see films constitutes an intersection of people coming from different countries . . . so many kinds and types of people . . . in order to reach such a public . . . you must have some common denominator . . . The films I made dealt with these people and spoke to this audience. These films are entirely local, although they partially succeeded abroad. . . . "Bourekas films" deal with our local folklore in its different colorings. Then came journalists and . . . wise and beautiful souls who said that "ethnic" is "bad." Why is it bad? Why is it bad to deal with ethnic groups and ethnicity? After all, this is our situation. There are Ashkenazim and Frenks [colloquial pejorative for Sephardim] and they don't like each other. Period. This is a fact and there is nothing we can do about it.[19]

The main criterion for the success of "bourekas," according to filmmakers and producers such as Davidson, Golan, and Yoram Globus, is popularity with the audience rather than prestige with the critics.

Film critics such as Ze'ev Rav-Nof (*Davar*), Yossef Sharik (*HaAretz*), Shlomo Shamgar (*Yedioth Ahronoth*), Aharon Dolav and Moshe Nathan (*Maariv* and *BaMahane*), who basically supported "quality films," as well as the personal filmmakers such as Yigal Bursztyn (in interview in *Kolnoa*), Yehuda Ne'eman (in his article "Zero Degree in Cinema" in *Kolnoa*), and Nissim Dayan ("From Bourekas to the Ghetto Culture" in *Kolnoa*) attacked both the "bourekas" themselves and the governmental "subsidies" they were given. Although the term "subsidies" has been frequently used, it should be pointed out that "bourekas" films were never literally subsidized by government money; rather, they were granted a partial tax return on each ticket purchased (as were all Israeli films made at the time).[20] The audiences that saw the films, in effect, helped pay for them. (The only real governmental subsidy, in the conventional sense, is currently given through the Fund for the Encouragement of Original Quality Films.) Mainstream critics used the term "bourekas" as a pejorative noun (and later adjective) while also expressing moral and aesthetic outrage in evaluative and judgmental language, condemning the films as "commercial," "vulgar," "cheap," "dumb," "Eastern," "Levantine," and even "anti-cinema." The "bourekas" melodramas and comedies (the vast majority were comedies) were also disdained for their "stereotypical characters" with whom it was almost too "easy to identify" (Ne'eman), for their "lack of depth," "vulgar jokes," and "predictable plots" (Dayan) in "comedies and melodrama, classic forms of cinema" (Ne'eman), as if stereotypical characters and predictable narratives in comedies and melodramas were necessarily and irrevocably negative qualities.

With the distribution of "gefilte-fish" films such as *Lupo in New York* and *Kuni Lemel in Tel Aviv*, Nissim Dayan supplemented his attack on "bourekas" with a significant metacritique concerning the exclusive attribution by critics of the films' negative qualities to the Orient (specifically to Egyptian, Turkish, Persian, Indian, and Greek films), pointing out the Yiddish-European cultural origins of this "evil." But after having correctly identified an important intertext of the "bourekas" films in Yiddish culture, Dayan went on to subject such "low" traditions to elitist censure:

> The vociferous style and vulgar jokes, the heavy, theatrical gestures, the silly popular characters, and the empty and predictable plots, all these are proofs for this argument, especially when the actors are trained to speak in a strong Oriental accent. We forgot that the creators of the films are Menahem Golan, [Fred] Steinhardt, Davidson, Zilberg (pay attention to the names), and therefore we kept on cursing the Eastern wall. And then we have this year [1976] two pure Ashkenazi types—Lupo and Kuni Lemel—who confidently and nostalgically lean on the culture of the Jewish ghetto in Eastern Europe, while their plot is sewn to the measure of the Yiddish vaudeville plays that you can still see here and there in Israel. And then it becomes clear to you, beyond any doubt, that the primary causes of injury of Israeli cinema are not the descendants of Juha [a clownish character from the Arabian tales] but the grandsons of Hershele [clownish character in Yiddish tales].[21]

"Those who supply Bourekas and Haminados [Sephardi-style cooking] for the masses," Dayan added, "secretly eat 'gefilte fish' at home."[22]

In their general refusal of the genre, however, critics ignored the playful, carnivalesque aspects of "bourekas" films and, at times, even their parodic and self-parodic reflexive quality, to which the audience in some ways was attracted. The intertext of the "bourekas" films was, in fact, much more complex than the high-cultured critique implied. That intertext includes, for example, the Hollywood musical (*West Side Story* [1961] clearly influenced Golan's *Casablan*[23] [1973]; the Italian melofarce (Pietro Germi's *Seduced and Abandoned* [*Sedotta e abbandonata*, 1963] inflects Golan's *Fortuna* [1966]; and, more generally, the tradition of the "comedy of errors," of comic identity confusions clearly discerned in such films as Ze'ev Revah's *Hairstylist for Women* (*Sapar Nashim*, 1983) and *He Who Steals from a Thief Is Not Guilty* (*Gonev miGanav Patur*, 1977), Yoel Zilberg's *Kuni Lemel in Tel Aviv* and *A Millionaire in Trouble* (*Millionaire beTzarot*, 1978), and George Ovadia's *Ariana* (1971), *Midnight Entertainer* (*Badrarit baHatzot*, 1978), and *The Aunt from Argentina* (*HaDoda meArgentina*, 1983). These influences are mingled with the more familiar borrowings from Yiddish cinema and theater, as well as from Middle Eastern cinema. In Yiddish cinema and theater, we also find family melodramas focusing on the destruction of the warm familial world by the new, secular world, usually associated with the idea of "Americanization," a process accompanied by intense pathos and grand gestures, all within the framework of a teleological structure leading to a grande finale in which marriage and family unity come to symbolize the continuity of the Jewish people. To these basic melodramatic and comic structures are added the thematic leitmotifs common in Egyptian, Iranian, Turkish, and Indian popular cinema, such as socially marginalized protagonists, the contrast between the rich and the poor, and the topos of love's triumph over social obstacles, all at times against a backdrop of "exotic" criminality or folklore.

The connection of the "bourekas" to this Oriental cinema derives not only from immigration from these same film-producing countries but also from the frequent screening of such films on Israeli television (as well as on Jordanian television, accessible in much of Israel), for example, through the Friday-night screenings of Egyptian films, precisely for the same public which appreciates the "bourekas" films. In the films of George Ovadia, who had himself worked in the Iraqi and Iranian film industries, the rich/poor motif predominates, while Ashkenazi/Sephardi tensions are barely mentioned (becoming an explicit theme only in his *Midnight Entertainer*)—generally remaining present, however, in the collective consciousness of the spectators.

Davidson's *Charlie and a Half* began as an enterprise by Iranian immigrants, all former film producers in Iran. Owners of film studios in Iran, they began to import foreign films after coming to Israel. They later decided to produce an Israeli film based on a story written for them by an Iranian author-scriptwriter. The narrative concerned a local neighborhood protagonist connected to the criminal underworld, always accompanied by a child (the "Half" of the title), who falls in love with a daughter of a wealthy family. The scriptwriter of *Charlie and a Half,* Eli Tavor, was asked to write a script based on this plot outline and adapt it to

Israeli reality.[24] And since the paradigm of rich and poor in Israel coincides, by definition, with that of Ashkenazim and Sephardim, Charlie (Yehuda Barkan) is incarnated as a Sephardi from a poor neighborhood while the rich woman is a beautiful Ashkenazi (played by Haya Kazir, a beauty queen and model at the time the film was made). At the same time the theme of assimilation to the "new world," a commonplace in the "modern" Yiddish cultural tradition, is here transferred to the new context of Ashkenization in which the poor Sephardi neighborhood is projected as parallel to the ghetto and the "new world," to a certain extent, is that of Ashkenazi society. The Yiddish immigrant accent here becomes Oriental, while Yiddish, in its turn, metamorphoses into the oppressor-language, a motif repeated in many "bourekas" films. (In *Casablan*, for example, the Sephardi protagonist angrily tells the Yiddish-speaking bureaucrat about to raze the neighborhood: "Here no one speaks Yiddish.")

In a few "bourekas" films (especially in the wake of the Sephardi Black Panther movement and the 1973 war crisis), integration by marriage is no longer seen as sufficient, and emigration from Israel becomes the solution. The United States is presented as the source of a "real" hope. In *Charlie and a Half*, for example, Charlie himself marries the rich Ashkenazi, but his "half," the child Miko, flies to the United States with his sister. The separation between Charlie and Miko is bittersweet rather than purely sad, because now both marginals join the center, through marriage to an Ashkenazi for one and a marvelous future in the United States for the other. Such a device plays to the collective feeling—especially among marginalized Sephardim—that a fair chance can only be found in the United States and not in Israel. Having the child fly to the United States represents the ultimate dream of the Sephardi, to flee from the local oppressive reality and take flight into the more promising future of a new generation.

Originally, Davidson had imagined and even filmed a different ending. Miko was to get on the airplane, leaving a desperate Charlie behind. As Charlie was getting into the car to leave the airport, an airplane was to be seen taking off on the horizon. Suddenly the child shouts, "Charlie!" Charlie turns and sees the child, who did not, after all, get on the plane. They run toward each other while sentimental music consecrates their reunion. Davidson ultimately abandoned this ending in favor of another kind of happy end, partially due to the comments of a studio janitor. Davidson relates that the janitor came to him and said, "Look, I like the film very much, but why does the child come back? He could have already gone to America to become a human being . . . Why do you bring him back? I was so happy he was going and suddenly he comes back . . . "[25] As a result, Davidson changed the ending of the film to a "happier" ending which meant not assimilation to Ashkenazi codes but rather assimilation to something quite new. The janitor's comment reflects a collective desire. Progress for the Sephardi individual—after the repression of collective struggles—is seen as available only in the New World. Return to Israel has come to signify a regression.

Other popular trends could be added to the "bourekas" intertext, especially that of the popular commercial theater particularly in vogue between 1967 and 1973, a period characterized by economic acceleration. The post–1967 war period brought a degree of economic mobility for Sephardim (partially facilitated by the availability of cheap Arab labor from Gaza and the West Bank), but it also deepened the social and economic gap between the two major Jewish ethnic groups. At the same time, the relative lack of apparent external threat—a threat which had historically served, and been exploited, as a unifying factor—allowed *internal* tensions to surface with more vigor. It is in this period, for example, that we find a strong political expression of Sephardi militancy in the form of the emergence of the Black Panthers, led by the children of the immigrants, as well as a flourishing of popular theater and "bourekas" films dealing with this topical issue. The "bourekas" tended to draw on the same elements as commercial theater, on ethnic stereotypes and heavy ethnic accents in scenes reminiscent of popular theater sketches (also played on the radio) largely based on verbal humor. Indeed, the stock characters and archetypal situations of the "bourekas" films have a kinship with the commedia dell'arte tradition, which began as a popular art form before being subsequently domesticated for bourgeois consumption. Many popular actors from commercial theater (along with popular singers) played in "bourekas" films. At times these films were constructed as popular sketch-entertainments, as in the case of Zohar's *Our Neighborhood* and Assaf Dayan's *Smash-Hit* (*Shlager*, 1979), employing the famous trio HaGashash haHiver. In the case of *My Mother the General* (*Imi haGeneralit*, 1979), the whole successful theater show was adapted to the screen. Celebrated performers were cast for major roles in these films (for example, Yehuda Barkan and Sassi Keshet for male roles and Efrat Lavi and Yona Elian for female roles) while the same secondary actors were employed in most of the films (for example, Jacques Cohen and Gabi Amrani for the Sephardi roles and Yehuda Efroni and Lia Kenig for the Ashkenazi roles).

Many of the "bourekas" films also feature elements from the popular tradition of the photo-novel, read largely by women, with its rapid pacing and high density of incident, made possible by the target audience's familiarity with the conventions. As in the photo-novel, love in the "bourekas" films is never an evolutionary process, but germinates spontaneously, "at first sight." Cinematic devices such as commentative music and expansive body gestures externalize emotions and render them redundantly explicit. "Bourekas" films, which employ broad types rather than rounded characters, are non-psychologized, in this sense, unconcerned with the psychic nuances of the protagonist's internal world. Close-ups tend not to pinpoint a psychological dynamic but rather to reveal perceptible signs, such as tears. The manifestation of emotions through expression and gesture often borders on the caricatural, and at times (in Revah's films, in particular) becomes consciously parodic. As in the photo-novel, the interaction between the individual characters effaces the personal dimension and is congruent with the social paradigm.

Most "bourekas" films combine some studio shooting with authentic locations, often in actual poor neighborhoods, especially in the south of Tel Aviv and Jaffa. Nevertheless, they tend to minimize the engagement of nonprofessionals, as well as the use of background action, both of which are usually reserved for market sequences, as in *The Advocate* (*HaMeshakhnea*, 1973) and *Midnight Entertainer.* Neighborhood streets also provide the backdrop for car chases as in *The Policeman Azulay* (*HaShoter Azulay*, 1971). Interior shooting of the houses of Sephardi characters emphasizes poverty as well as communality: many people are crowded into a single room and disorder pervades both the image and the sound track. The colors, however, are warm and bright, appropriate to the characterization of Sephardim as warm, familial, lively, trustworthy, and affectionate. The shooting of the houses of wealthy Ashkenazim, in contrast, calls attention to enormous spaces inhabited by few people, quiet, with colder colors and more restrained acting—all suggesting an alienated, cold world, often in conjunction with Ashkenazi characters who are snobbish and hypocritical egotists. (These contrasting images largely correspond to the Ashkenazi and Sephardi stereotypes in Israel.)[26] By marrying the Ashkenazi at the end of these films, it is implied, the Sephardi gains material luxuries and social status without losing his/her Sephardi essence. Since the early seventies, the filmmakers have emphasized a more "positive" image of Sephardim. Sallah's characteristics of warmth and honesty, shown in the archetypal "bourekas" film from the mid-sixties, *Sallah Shabbati*, have since become central features of Sephardim characters, often in binary contrast with the image of Ashkenazi hypocrisy and coldness.

The "bourekas" films offer escapism for the lumpenproletariat and the (Jewish) working class and, less frequently, for the Oriental petty bourgeoisie. "Bourekas" escapism derives from the almost utopian desire to bridge the gaps of Israeli society and thus promote an image of ethnic/class equality, pluralistic tolerance, and solidarity. Since the target audience is the Oriental public, the films are necessarily permeated by social and ethnic tensions. In the world of the oppressed, the oppressor is a constant (historical) presence in relation to whom the repressed must either assimilate or rebel. The "bourekas," in this sense, are characterized by what Bakhtin would call "carnivalesque" humor; the people on the margins laugh irreverently at the powerful, at characters who for the Oriental collective consciousness represent the oppressive center. These films frequently feature situations, consequently, in which a Sephardi protagonist—often a crude brute concealing a heart of gold (*Casablan, Let's Blow a Million* [*Bo Nefotzetz Million*, 1977]) or a schlemiel with self-deprecating humor and joie-de-vivre (*Today Only*, [*Rak haYom*, 1976], *Half a Million Black* [*Hamesh Meot Elef Shahor*, 1977])—deceives, with the aid of his friends, the Ashkenazi antagonist. The Sephardi tricks the Ashkenazi, whether the individual (the humorless municipal inspector and the doctor in *Today Only*), or the institution (the Bank of Israel in *Let's Blow a Million* and the police in *Arvinka* [1967] and *The Policeman Azulay*), or in a more roundabout manner the whole

The brute with the heart of gold in *Casablan*.

The carnivalesque marketplace in *Today Only*.

system, as through the Ashkenization of the family name in order to succeed in business (*Half a Million Black*).

In Ze'ev Revah's film, *Today Only*, for example, Sasson (Ze'ev Revah), a tomato vendor in Mahane Yehuda (an open-air market in Jerusalem) is virtually raped by a bourgeois woman from Rehavia (a luxurious Jerusalem neighborhood). Welcoming her advances, he cries out "Today only!," the common vendors' shout at the market, meaning the produce is cheap today only, but here taking on the signification of unexpected sexual/social opportunity. He thus satisfies two hungers, for tomatoes and for sex. (The film also implies another pun since in Hebrew the words *'agvania*, "tomato," and *'agavim*, "flirtation," share the same etymological root, AGV.) When the woman's doctor husband inconveniently returns for lunch, unenthusiastic about the tomato diet which has been forced on him, she hides Sasson, through whom we witness the events and with whose point of view we identify. With one blow the man of the margins tricks the man of the center several times over; he wins an enthusiastic female customer for his tomatoes, he is desired by the woman he serves (a synecdoche for the elite with whom the market vendor has no social intercourse), and he gains free medical treatment for his sick friend (Jacques Cohen) from her husband.[27] In this provisional reversal of the power structure, a comic politicization of the erotic is created when oedipalized sexuality—in the sense that libidinal energy is turned against the symbolic representative of a superior social position—together with financial profit and brotherly solidarity are all achieved under the nose of the Ashkenazi, who although portrayed here as a harmless individual is nevertheless linked through social position to the Establishment. The politically impotent marginal manages, not without self-parody, to vanquish in bed and, in the carnivalesque "logic" of the "turnabout," to acquire power and symbolic potency. Viewing these films becomes, then, a therapeutic process in which the periphery laughs not only at its own weakness, but also at the limits of the strength of the center—a liberating collective laughter.

In most "bourekas" films, the ethnic/class tensions and conflicts are solved by a happy ending in which equality and unity are achieved by means of the unification of the mixed couple. Social integration is dreamed via eroticism, and the wedding, which presumably "bridges the gaps," celebrates familial harmony, well expressed in the *Casablan* song, "Kulanu Yehudim" ("We are all Jews") or the *Salomonico* (1973) song "LeHayei ha'Am haZe" ("To the Life of This Nation/People"). The sentiment of nationality in some "bourekas" films, then, "mythically" transcends ethnic and class discriminations. Indeed, most "bourekas" films give expression to the dominant attitude that cultural differences and class distinctions will be eliminated by the younger generation, especially through marriage, as, for example, in the marriage of the children of wealthy insurance agents in *Katz and Carassu* (*Katz veCarassu*, 1971) or between the daughter of the Jaffa porter and the son of the northern Tel Aviv doctor in *Salomonico*.

In *Katz and Carassu*, the few post-1967 nouveaux riches Sephardim become representative of all Sephardim. Carassu's two sons marry Katz' two daughters. All are Sabras with minimal cultural differences (unlike their parents). There is, however, an implicit celebration of Sephardi continuity, through the sons, who will carry the Sephardi name.[28] All they have at the finale is the symbolic pride of name, while in fact they have already assimilated to the dominant Sabra-Ashkenazi codes. The Sephardim are ultimately accepted by the Ashkenazim, who learn to recognize their merits, while the Sephardim are Ashkenized, their complex historicity reduced to exotic folklore. Based on Yigal Mossinzon's fifties play, turned into a musical show in the sixties, *Casablan* has the hero of the title (Yehoram Gaon) prove himself worthy of the love of the Polish/Sabra woman (Efrat Lavi), and show despite everything that he is not a "*schwartze khaye*" ("black animal," a common Yiddish slur toward Sephardim, also expressed in the film toward Casablan and his friends); rather he is an honest man with "*Kavod*" ("dignity" in Hebrew, and the title of a famous song from the musical) as testified by his neighborhood compatriot (Arye Elias). The charming gangleader, Casablan, the film slowly reveals, is a hero of the 1967 war who risked his life for his upper-class commander. When the Polish/Sabra woman and her family become aware of his benevolent heart and patriotic nature, his ascendance on the social ladder is legitimized, as is the celebration of the long-desired couple's "(in)gathering."

The Oriental, after the Black Panther rebellion, is authorized to voice a cautious protest, as in Salomonico's anger over prejudice against Sephardim, and about the resources given to recent Ashkenazi immigrants instead of to old and poor Oriental immigrants from thirty years before. (In the Likud era, the Oriental already demonstrates a certain pride in his refusal to Ashkenize his family name in order to ascend, as in Ze'ev Revah's *Shraga Katan* [1978], as well as, in opposition to the "bourekas" tradition, in his preference for a Sephardi girl from the development town Kiryat Shmona over the wealthy Ashkenazi woman from Tel Aviv.) The protest in films such as *Salomonico* and *Casablan* tends to find only superficial expression, however, and toward the end the somewhat inarticulate critique is rendered irrelevant by the ideology of integration, presumed to resolve the conflicts, as if mixed marriage and the Westernization of the Orient were sufficient to modify the political and economic structures of domination. Like Israeli politicians and social scientists who hail the trend (now about 18 percent) toward mixed marriage as a sign that the ethnic problem is disappearing, so the happy endings of "bourekas" films foster a "mythical" solution which in fact buttresses the status quo. Social inequality is, in fact, more glaring between second-generation Ashkenazim and Sephardim, i.e., among those born and raised in Israel, than among the immigrant generation. The very process that created the ethnic division of labor in the fifties and early sixties also installed the mechanisms of reproduction to perpetuate that division of labor.[29]

Despite these general tendencies, "bourekas" films are not of one homogeneous mold. While Ze'ev Revah's films emphasize parody and the play of carnivalesque inversions, and George Ovadia's films create the atmosphere of an Israeli "Thousand and One Nights," filmmakers such as Ephraim Kishon, particularly in his comedies *Sallah Shabbati* and *Arvinka*, and Menahem Golan, especially in his melodramas *Fortuna* and *Queen of the Road*, might be said to "orientalize the Orient." The (Ashkenazi) filmmaker, in other words, tends not only to project the Orient as he imagines it, but also to reproduce the Establishment explanations for Oriental "backwardness." Most of the "bourekas" films are made by Ashkenazi filmmakers such as Menahem Golan, Ephraim Kishon, Yoel Zilberg, Fred Steinhardt, and Boaz Davidson (Ovadia and Revah are the exceptions). This ethnic imbalance is especially true for the sixties "bourekas," in which the overwhelming majority of the producers, writers, directors, actors, and musicians were Ashkenazi. *Sallah Shabbati*, for example, was produced by Golan and scripted and directed by Kishon and starred Topol in the leading role, while Sallah's wife was played by Esther Greenberg. The leading roles in Golan's *Fortuna* were given to Ahuva Goren and Gila Almagor, while the father was played by the French actor Pierre Brasseur; in *Eldorado* (1963), *My Margo*, and *Queen of the Road* the leading woman

Sephardi role was played by Gila Almagor. At the same time, Arab roles, in this period, tended to be assigned to Sephardim. We thus encounter a kind of ethnic displacement down the social ladder, with both Arabs and Sephardim denied the right of "self-representation." In film, as in other realms, the Establishment undertook to speak for Sephardim, so that Sephardim were denied the right to represent themselves directly on the national (and world) stage. Much like the colonizing experts who believed that only they could speak, in loco parentis, as it were, for the "primitives" and the "natives" of the societies they had studied, so too the Ashkenazi politicians, social scientists, writers, and filmmakers undertook to speak "on behalf" of Sephardim.

These films had an impact on the general image of Sephardim far beyond the cinematic framework. The expression "Sallah Shabbati," for example, became part of the everyday language, used to denote the Sephardi immigrant of the fifties who had lived through the *ma'abara* (transient camps hastily constructed of corregated tin), as well as evoke the sum of "essential" characteristics associated with the common Sephardi. The Sephardi characters and their characteristics tended to be received as "real." The dominant ideology that marked these films even penetrated the ranks of Oriental Jews themselves, many of whom came to absorb the prejudices embodied in the films, for example, that Ashkenazim are in fact intellectually superior and, therefore, merit their higher social positions. Thus, not only did the "West" come to represent the "East," but also, in a classic colonialist play of specularity, the East came to see itself through the West's distorting mirror.

This is not to minimize the positive importance of films dealing with Sephardim, especially in the context of the sixties, when the state apparatus tended to regard Oriental Jews as absent or, in the best of cases, as existing in a vacuum. In schools, for example, the history and literature of Jews from Arab and Muslim countries has scarcely been studied. The print media and the government-owned radio stations reinforce the impression of Sephardi absence and the implicit need for their "resocialization" and assimilation into Ashkenazi codes. Even today, Oriental music, despite its wide popularity among the majority Oriental population (and even among Palestinian Arabs), is ghettoized as "folkloric" as opposed to "universal" music, with the national stations devoting approximately one-tenth of the available music hours to Oriental music.

In this context, Sephardi eagerness for *any* filmic representation—even if not self-representation—is more comprehensible, and it became a major factor in the success of the early "bourekas" films. It is often assumed that only comedies on the subject were popular, but, in fact, even before *Sallah Shabbati*, Golan's dramatic *Eldorado* was also quite profitable (265,000 Israeli Lira and 618,000 spectators). The films' success catalyzed a trend in the industry toward depicting Sephardim in the context of ethnic tensions, but the critics, as we have seen, disdained the films as "low-brow" and "vulgar." It is scarcely surprising that the audience for "bourekas" declined in the late seventies with the Likud rise to power. The Likud, although it did not improve the real situation of the Sephardim, did at least make some symbolic nods toward Sephardi culture. The Likud victory had a significant collective psychological effect, since it managed to remove from power the Labor Party, an oppressive regime installed since the establishment of the state (and embryonically even during the Yishuv period), an elitist regime which pursued discriminatory policies and demonstrated arrogant attitudes toward Sephardim. The Likud, whatever its faults, gave a certain legitimacy to Sephardi cultural expression, resulting in a reduced need for the psychic satisfactions provided by the escapist and idealist "bourekas" films.

Although Jewish National Fund documentaries and docu-dramas had featured Sephardi characters in a patronizing manner, as models of adjustment to modernity, the decision of commercial cinema in the sixties to also deploy Sephardi protagonists has important implications. First, the legitimation of the depiction of the Oriental Jews on the screen and the dissemination of that image in major movie theaters were especially meaningful in a young country with a small industry in which the release of each Israeli film became a cause for national celebration and was thus judged by less demanding criteria, especially prior to the seventies. Second, the inclusion of Sephardi protagonists implied film-industry recognition of the economic power of Sephardim as the majority population of Israel, a sector whose film-audience potential was even larger because of its youthfulness. This economic power, whatever its limits, was meaningful in a country where the Ministry of Commerce and Industry encouraged the film industry through giving tax returns on tickets purchased. Third, the recognition of this commercial reality meant that the filmmakers had to make some concessions to the Sephardi audience not merely by making a film about Sephardim but also by manifesting sympathy for their problems. And in some cases—especially in Ephraim Kishon's films—this sympathy came accompanied by criticism of the Establishment. In these terms the features were different from the official docu-dramas such as Baruch Dienar and Leopold Lahola's *Tent City* (*Ir haOhalim*, 1957). Dienar as producer and scriptwriter and Lahola as director made the film for the Zionist organization Keren HaYesod—whose humanist-paternalist representation of Oriental Jews is complemented by an ideal image of Ashkenazi immigrants and of the Establishment. The traditional "moral" of the story, as recounted in the style of Socialist realism, was to appreciate institutional generosity for promoting the "melting pot;" the Sephardim are praised for their successful upgrading, and the Ashkenazim for their patience with their less-developed fellow citizens.

Despite the a priori inclination toward the Sephardi audience in the private film industry, the commercial features not assigned by institutions also "Orientalized the Orient" and parroted hegemonic explanations for the "underdevelopment" of the Sephardim. Whether in the generic framework of comedy, as in *Sallah Shabbati* or in the melodramatic framework of *Fortuna*, these explanations were largely presented within a "humanist" perspective of patronizing pity, thus producing what might be called the optical illusion of a pro-Sephardi attitude. In Kishon's films, especially, the anti-Establishment satire buttresses this illusion. Close textual analysis of the comedy *Sallah Shabbati* and the melodrama *Fortuna*, films which together laid the foundations for the representation of the Orient, will reveal the core set of formulaic images reworked and reelaborated in subsequent films.

Narrating Nation and Modernization

Sallah Shabbati, although not the first film to fully concentrate on the subject (it was preceded by Golan's first dramatic feature, *Eldorado*), is important because it achieved unprecedented success. Stimulating the production of a series of films on the Ashkenazi/Sephardi tension, *Sallah Shabbati* was also thought, retroactively, to be the archetypical "bourekas." It is therefore illuminating to examine not only the film itself but also how the Establishment, as well as film critics, responded to the film's partial satire and to the image of the Orient.

Sallah Shabbati not only won unprecedented success in Israel in 1964 (1,184,000 spectators saw it, roughly twice the audience of other films considered successful; its budget was relatively low, 330,000 Israeli Liras);[30] it also had unprecedented impact abroad. Running six months in New York's Little Carnegie Theater, *Sallah Shabbati* was nominated for an Oscar and won the Hollywood Foreign Press Association's award as outstanding foreign film. It opened and closed the Berlin Film Festival, and its creators won numerous awards, such as the Best Actor and Screenplay awards at the 1964 San Francisco Film Festival. In association with the 1966 Vienna Film Festival, the film was screened along with a literary evening devoted to its author-director, Ephraim Kishon. An emigré from Hungary, Kishon had a brand of humor and satire derived from the Central European tradition; his works have a wide readership in many languages, especially in Europe. *Sallah Shabbati*'s script is based on five Kishon sketches, particularly "Zigi and Habooba." All of the sketches were performed during the fifties by the military troupe HaNahal and later by the theatrical group Green Onion, both times with Topol in the leading role. The sketches were broadcast successfully on the radio, and also shown on many European television channels.

The story of the film takes place during the period of mass immigration in the fifties. The new immigrant, Sallah, lives with his large family in the *ma'abara* (transient camps characterized by harsh conditions, overwhelmingly populated by Orientals, who were supposed to stay for a "short period" but who, in fact, remained for many years). Lazy, amiable Sallah—his Arabic name points to his Arab-Jewish origins—whose major competence is in the Oriental dice game backgammon, demands *shikkun* (permanent housing) as he was promised. In his attempt to obtain *shikkun*, he tries his luck at varied trades ranging from hunting Jeremiah, a gigantic black bulldog from the kibbutz, and selling him to a bourgeois couple who have lost their white poodle, through selling himself during parliamentary elections to rival political parties, to selling his beautiful daughter to the man offering the highest marriage price.

Around the basic plot of Sallah's demand for *shikkun*, Kishon builds an incisive satire of the Israeli Establishment. This anti-Establishment satire must be appreciated in the context of the late fifties and sixties when *Sallah Shabbati* played on stage as well as screen. During this period the consensus on such myths as the "Sabra" and the "kibbutz"—the core of Israeli identity as conceived by the major ideologists of Zionism—remained unquestioned and was still reflected in idealized images in films. The film-criticism industry that shared the established consensus was deeply shocked, therefore, by the irreverent depiction of sacred-cow institutions such as the kibbutz and the Jewish National Fund.

The demystificatory portrayal in *Sallah Shabbati* is seen first on the level of characterization and acting. All the characters in the film, Ashkenazi and Sephardi, are ridiculous and portrayed as grotesque. Sallah, for example, walks with heavy movements while the soundtrack exaggerates the noise of his footsteps; the kibbutznik woman social worker is a silly schlemiel, whose laughter sounds like hiccoughs; the two kibbutz bureaucrats are totally humorless; the woman in particular is a cartoonish repressed tough "feminist;" the bourgeois couple have exaggerated upper-class mannerisms and become grotesque when they display parental solicitude toward their "doggy."

Sallah Shabbati's success prodded the commercial industry to imitate its style of characterization and acting, which subsequently came to permeate "bourekas" comedies. The use of grotesque acting and parodic characterization was virtually a subversive gesture on Kishon's part, a cinematic as well as political "carnivalization" of the idealist, sanctimonious, and self-congratulatory nature of Israeli official discourse; *Sallah Shabbati* thus subverted the ideal image of "beautiful Israel" with aesthetic forms deriving from lower-class popular festivities. *Sallah Shabbati* shattered the consensus on the depiction of Israelis, not merely by showing them in daily life rather than on the battlefield, but also by showing them in a manner opposed to the traditionally flattering self-image.

On a content level, *Sallah Shabbati* provoked strong reactions by demystifying the pretensions of the Labor apparatus. The kibbutzniks in the film resemble bureaucrats and are clearly divided into veterans with managing roles and "simple" workers, a division which contradicts the myth of Socialist solidarity and collectivist idealism. The kibbutzniks betray total indifference, furthermore, to the miserable conditions of the poor *ma'abara* next to them. In a meeting where the kibbutz' secretary (Zaharira Harifai) suggests the adoption of the *ma'abara*, they all raise their hands in mechanical consensus while continuing their games of checkers, their knitting, their nibbling, and their flirting. They do not volunteer, however, to do the actual work necessary for helping the *ma'abara*. The two "volunteers" are selected accidentally because they are so deeply engaged in flirting that they forget to put their hands down when the second vote is called. The secretary, however, puts events in the best possible light, summing up the meeting in a confident voice typifying the self-pride of the kibbutz: "I see that the kibbutz has once again proven its ideological maturity." The kibbutznik social worker (Gila Almagor) then goes, reluctantly, to the *ma'abara*. Her problems of communication begin with her attempts to pose the standard bureaucratic questions. While Sallah seeks concrete economic help, she attempts to unearth the childhood traumas, such as a snakebite, which might have brought him to his present condition. In a carnivalesque inversion of roles, it is poor, illiterate Sallah who becomes the "therapist," the one to whom she complains about her harsh fate in the kibbutz: having to share a room with two roommates, as if Sallah, whose huge family lives in a single room with a leaky roof, were in a position to sympathize with her "plight."

In contrast with the kibbutz' Socialist ideology of egalitarian labor, the kibbutzim in reality have often employed cheap labor from the neighboring *ma'abara*. (While in the early sixties such a portrayal was considered shocking it has recently become a major issue in terms of criticism of the kibbutz as an institution.) Sallah, for instance, is hired to carry a wooden wardrobe, but since the kibbutz has no official budget for outside hired labor, it is decided that he will be paid from the cattle budget. When their tight-fisted bureaucrat-leader asks them to help carry the wardrobe, since Sallah is demanding a raise, the kibbutzniks respond with indifference. Since no one volunteers to carry the wardrobe, quite in contrast to the dedicated image of the kibbutz, it remains on a hilltop, a low-angled shot emphasizing its silhouetted form against the sunset. Much later, toward the end of the film, we discover the same wardrobe, now transformed into a chicken coop. At that point it undergoes still another functional transformation within the narrative, into a site of commercial exchange. It is in the wardrobe that Sallah, presumably in the Sephardi tradition, accepts, and carefully counts, the kibbutz' payment for the hand of his daughter. To his chagrin, however, he is immediately forced to return the payment when his son arrives with a kibbutznik fiancée. This situation had earlier been the cue for a highly comic ideological debate. The "feminist" bureaucrat, objecting to any kibbutz complicity in the oppressive "Oriental" tradition of wife-selling, warns that soon the *ma'abara* inhabitants will be abandoning all productive labor in order to sell their daughters en masse at exorbitant black-market prices. Another kibbutznik points out that communally bought property should also be communally shared, and that there is no budget for purchasing women. The kibbutznik groom responds, however, that there is indeed a precedent for purchase on behalf of an individual member, citing the time that the kibbutz budget was used to buy a mattress for a member with back problems, and "he was the only one who slept on it." The unintentional analogy between bride and bed provokes general hilarity.

The political parties, for their part, are also depicted satirically. After Sallah dramatically pleads for God's help, the camera tilts from him kneeling to a notice concerning the upcoming elections for the Knesset. The film cuts to motorized party members arriving in the *ma'abara* (a car in the *ma'abara*, we must remember, was a rare thing). Based on the experience of previous corrupt elections, the two well-dressed politicians seek out the *ma'abara* "leader." The film emphasizes the efficiency of their corruption; they immediately nod in agreement as to who is the "leader" when they see Sallah singing (in Oriental style, the film song "Old Mashiha") and dancing in the *ma'abara* café (the sequence recalls the famous Piraeus café scene in Jules Dassin's *Never on Sunday* [1960]). The sequence ends with a close shot of Sallah's chest and then cuts to a close shot of his back, walking away from the camera, arm in arm with the two politicians. They promise him *shikkun* in exchange for votes, after which the other parties make an identical arrangement with Sallah. (Their dress and manner—one sports the Israeli kibbutz-style simple clothes and the *tembel* hat and another wears a more formal European bourgeois suit and hat—evoke specific political groups/parties in Israel.) Sallah and his wife naïvely wish God's blessing on all the parties of Israel for their generosity in giving them *shikkun*, only to discover later that the issue is considerably more complicated. During the voting each party member brazenly bribes Sallah with little presents, while Sallah mischievously stands in the line repeatedly in order to receive multiple bribes. When he is about to enter the polling booth to vote, the camera pans, from Shabbati's point of view, as the diverse party bureaucrats each signal, by gesture or facial expression, their clear expectation of his support. The last bureaucrat, with the Israeli flag in the background, winks knowingly to Sallah, but the clumsy protagonist, after almost causing the polling booth to collapse, is inconveniently honest and delivers on his promise to all parties, voting many times for all of them, to the point that the overstuffed envelope cannot enter the slot. His vote is, of course, canceled. Finally, Sallah obtains *shikkun* after being advised by an Ashkenazi cab driver that "you always get what you *don't* want." Sallah consequently organizes a demonstration *against* the *shikkun* and in favor of the *ma'abara*, leading the governmental housing office to use the police to force Sallah's clan to accept the *shikkun*.

Sallah Shabbati's mordant satire of the diverse branches of the Labor establishment's economic-political empire provoked the reaction not only of Labor-oriented journalists but also of politicians normally indifferent or even scornful toward the cinema. Golda Meir opposed sending the film to Hollywood and was especially angry at a sequence in which the Jewish National Fund official switches the signs naming the Jewish-American contributors[31]—after the Detroit visitor and before the New Yorker—announcing that "This is the tourist season; everyone wants his own sign." In the offending sequence, each American visitor is made to believe that the (same) forest is being planted from his donation, marked with his name. (Sallah, with his thick-skulled honesty, takes out the plants to plant them elsewhere, since "for Mr. Barrenbaum you should make a new forest.")

Newspapers announced[32] that the producers of *Sallah Shabbati* would follow the Foreign Minister's appeal not to distribute the film in Eastern European countries. As a result, one producer claimed they would suffer a financial loss of

$100,000. Abba Eban, then Foreign Minister, in reply to a parliamentary question by Knesset member Tawfiq Toubi (of the Communist Party), denied that the Foreign Ministry had intervened to prevent the distribution of the film in Eastern European countries; rather, Eban argued, he had only expressed his opinion that "in countries in which it was generally impossible to exhibit films which gave a factual and full version of real life in Israel, it was inadvisable to exhibit the image of Israel and her society in a manner likely to be wrongly interpreted."[33]

The myths purveyed about Israel abroad were also those that the press cultivated within the framework of consensus on the "Oriental problem." The "official" journalistic film critics, with their talk of "refined taste" and "artistic quality" and their high-brow scorn for the "bourekas" films, showed themselves to be increasingly out of touch with the audience that rushed to *Sallah Shabbati*. Most critics deplored the vulgar taste of the public that flocked to the film and in so doing inadvertently revealed that they saw themselves as part of the ruling elite. In this context, it is worth pointing out that in Israel artistic criticism is in part a function of politics, in that most major daily newspapers were established by or have been intimately linked to political parties. The critics from the daily *Al haMishmar*, the organ of Mapam (representing the left wing of Labor), Y. H. Biltzki[34] and Nehama Ganoth[35] were shocked by the anti-Establishment satire and voiced misgivings about screening the film abroad. The ironic title of Nehama Ganoth's review—"The People Chose—an Elite Film"—already betrays a condescending attitude toward the audience for the film. In a censorious tone, Ganoth wrote:

> Even in caricature, not everything is allowed. There is caricature in which the long nose of a Jew is made very prominent and there is a caricature in which the State of Israel is portrayed in the image of a little "Palmahnik" ["Palmach" member, also metaphorizing good-quality Sabra] and as a dreamer among the giants of the world. And in this film, there are some too long noses— and that is its major flaw. How is the Jewish National Fund presented? As an organization that makes its fortune through deceit, planting forests named af- ter the beloved of Jews? (and this film is going to be shown abroad, so they say . . .). And the parties?—*all of them*—in the same bag of cheating and treachery . . . And the kibbutz—a group of fine young people lorded over by antipathetic and humorless veterans. And the [Jewish] Agency bureau- crats . . . all of them speak endlessly of "back when we came."[36]

The critic went on to contrast the stage version of *Sallah Shabbati*, by the Nahal troupe and Green Onion, with the filmic adaptation:

> It [the stage version] had an educational line. The educational values of a progressive society were emphasized, . . . and it seemed that Sallah [the protag- onist's name is here used as a synecdoche for all Sephardim] had then begun

to understand it. . . . The film, on the other hand, has no educational orientation . . . when he [Sallah] hates to work and plays backgammon—this is very
funny. In the film one laughs at *everything* and in our reality—that of receiving immigrants—one should not laugh at *everything* . . . The film *strengthens*
the feelings of deprivation. This is *Sallah Shabbati*'s main flaw.[37]

In the *Jerusalem Post* (an English-language daily, read by the diplomatic and foreign
community as well as by English-speaking immigrants, with a substantial clientele
abroad, especially in Great Britain and the United States), the film critic also
expressed doubts about showing *Sallah Shabbati* abroad:

> Viewed as an industrial product, one can only describe *Sallah* as being strictly
> for local consumption and not for export. This comment is not meant as a
> reflection on the acting, and even less on the photography [the film was shot
> by Floyd Crosby]. It is merely to suggest that the film would scarcely provide
> added value to the Israeli image abroad.[38]

The same critic takes the "ethnic problem" as presented in the film at face value,
perceiving Sallah's transition from the *ma'abara* to the *shikkun* as the solution,
and seeing the problems exposed by the film, therefore, as belonging only to the
past: "As the *ma'abara* era is fortunately so many years in the past, Kishon can
make us look back with laughter and not with anger—especially those of us who
never had to endure *ma'abara* existence." Fixated on a particular stance, the critic
fails to perceive that although the *ma'abara* era officially ended in the sixties, the
same problems persisted and were even becoming exacerbated, and that the same
class/ethnic tensions were carried over into the "permanent housing."

In another case, shock at the sardonic representation of the Establishment is
accompanied by condescending pity and misplaced empathy for Sephardim. Here
is Biltzki again in *Al hoMishmar*:

> I followed the protagonist and everything surrounding him and my heart
> was bitter. Bitter—because the State of Israel in its first salvation stages is so
> corrupt, so inhuman and ugly . . . Because the . . . kibbutz is presented in such
> a distorted mirror, that only a skillful enemy could present it in such a way;
> because the immigrant-receiving bureaucrats list brothers returning to the
> homeland, they are unconcerned and show not the slightest interest in those
> who came from darkened ghettos and from world conflagrations . . . because
> the Israeli bourgeoisie is presented in the light of a lost little dog. . . . Because
> parties in Israel are presented not only in the distorted mirror of a distorted
> humor but also in the ugly mirror of the image of public and organizational
> life. . . . One has to think twice if such a film should represent us abroad.[39]

The Jewish historical memory of the writer—like that of Zionism generally—is
limited to the Jewish-European experience, and the film-criticism industry, like

the film industry, conceives the Jewish Middle Eastern experience along the lines of Eastern European traumas. Biltzki, for example, does not argue with Kishon about the "fact" of the backward life of Jews in Arab and Muslim countries, but rather about the means Kishon employed to portray backward Sallah. Comparing Kishon's work to that of the Yiddish fiction writer Sholom Aleichem, the humanist chronicler of Jewish life in the Eastern European ghetto, the journalist points out that Sholom Aleichem's greatness derives from presenting his protagonists of the Eastern European ghetto with compassion and love:

> Also Sholom Aleichem heroes, set in the *ma'abara*, in the suffocated ghetto, wanted to get out of it and looked for ways. And the great writer softened the way of those who left the ghetto. . . . Kishon does not—even for a moment— hear his protagonist. . . . His protagonist does not grow in the *ma'abara;* he does not grow in love or in compassion. . . . He lacks the tragic element. Therefore, he has a major lack . . . the primitive in him lacks the nuanced lyrical tone, that pours love and mercy.[40]

Biltzki's review, then, not only shows a structural misapprehension of the Sephardi situation, but also commits a "genre mistake" by applying the lofty standards of tragedy to a comic carnivalesque film. Comparisons between the miserable Middle Easterner Sallah and East European Jewish characters, however, were more frequent in the United States, largely because of a receptive Jewish-American audience eager to perceive Oriental Jewish history through the grid of their grandparents' shtetl stories. But more important, the success of *Fiddler on the Roof* (1971), with Topol in the leading role of Tevye (based on Sholom Aleichem's *Tevye and His Seven Daughters*),[41] brought *Sallah Shabbati* back to the screens with publicity that explicitly evoked *Fiddler on the Roof.*[42]

The Israeli critics, for their part, excoriated the "rightist" Kishon for ridiculing an Establishment with which they instinctively identified, but had no quarrel with his condescending portrayal of the Oriental Jew. Here they reflected a consensus which embraced not only the film's producers and its critics, but also "left" and right. In a re-evaluation of the film at the time of its 1970 re-release, during a period of accelerating Sephardi rebellion, the reviewer Yossef Sharik refers to *Sallah Shabbati* as if it were a documentation of Orientalism:

> Kishon did not shed tears and sentimentalism about the discrimination against the poor and helpless Oriental immigrant. Sallah . . . is a lazy para- site who refuses to work, but takes the money his children earn to get drunk in the café. Sallah wants favors for nothing and exploits the argument that "Blacks are screwed" [a phrase more common in the period in which Sharik writes than in the period when *Sallah Shabbati* was made]. As you see, Kishon's comedy is better when it is serious than when it is funny.[43]

Sharik concludes his article as follows: "The strength of this film is that it will continue to exist primarily as a social document and only secondarily as a comedy." *Sallah Shabbati* was received by critics, in sum, as if it were authentic anthropological testimony concerning Sephardim.

A close scrutiny of the narrative structure and cinematic techniques of *Sallah Shabbati* reveals a powerful demystification of the Establishment, marred by an implicit acceptance of Establishment explanations concerning what is euphemistically called "the problem of the gap." The film, in this sense, and Topol's charming portrayal of a "noble savage"[44] exploit Oriental stereotypes in order to excoriate the Establishment. As an anti-Establishment satire, *Sallah Shabbati* lampoons various branches of the power elite: (1) governmental bureaucracy; (2) party corruption; (3) the Socialist/capitalist kibbutz; (4) Jewish National Fund hypocrisy; and (5) the upwardly mobile urban bourgeoisie. The exploitation of Sephardi oppression as a platform for attacking the "left" Establishment was in many ways politically prophetic on Kishon's part. For the partial and highly ambiguous alliance between Sephardim and Likud, effected in 1977, derived more than anything else from Likud's ability to take advantage of Sephardi resentment against thirty years of Labor government.

While the protagonist of *Sallah Shabbati* is Sephardi, the perspective of the film is decidedly *not* Sephardi. Sallah is on one level a *naïf*, an exemplum of a perennial tradition in which the figure of the uninitiated outsider is deployed as an instrument of social/cultural critique or distanciation. But in contrast with the naïveté of literary protagonists like Candide, Schweik, or Saeed Abi alNakhs alMutasha'il (in Emile Habiby's *Pessoptimist*), which is used primarily as a narrative device by which the author strips bare the received wisdom and introduces a new perspective, Sallah's naïveté functions less as a means of attacking the mythifications of "Working Eretz Israel" ("Eretz Israel haOvedet")[45] than as a vehicle for mocking Sallah himself and what he supposedly represents—i.e., the Orientalism of the Sephardim. In other words, in opposition to Jaroslav Hašek, who exploits the constructed naïveté of his character in order to attack European militarism, and not as a satire of Schweik's backwardness, Kishon molds Sallah in conformity with socially derived stereotypes, here deployed in a caricatural mockery of the Sephardi majority (minority) itself.

Sallah was not designed, and was not received by critics, as a satire of an individual but rather as a summation of the Oriental-Jewish "essence." As with the portrayal of Arabs, we find again a Manichean splitting of affectivity typical of colonialist discourse. The putative "essence" is separated out into positive—the Sephardim are warm, sincere, direct, shrewd—and negative poles—they are also lazy, irrational, unpredictable, primitive, illiterate, and sexist. Accordingly, Sallah (and the film) speaks in the plural, "we," while the Ashkenazi characters address him in the second-person plural, "you all." Kishon's anti-Establishment satire places on the same level the members of the Establishment and those outside it and distant from all real power. In this sense, the satire is reactionary in that it fails to satirize the Establishment view of the Oriental and unthinkingly perpetuates pre-existing prejudices.

Already at the beginning of the film, during the credit sequence, Sallah descends from a plane and "lands" in Israel shorn of a personal or collective past. Since the country from which he has emigrated remains unspecified, he is a man without a country or positive culture. His first steps in the Holy Land are not presented from his point of view, for the camera is placed in the abstract perspective of the old-timers, the "veterans" in the country. In this sense, the film endorses the hegemonic historiography according to which the Jews from Arab and Muslim countries appear on the world stage only when they are seen on the map of the Hebrew state, just as the modern history of Palestine is seen as beginning with its "discovery" by European Jews. Modern Sephardi history, in this perspective, is seen as beginning with the "Magic Carpet" and "Ali Baba" operations (the latter is also known as the "Ezra and Nehemiah" operation, and refers to the bringing to Israel of the Jews of Iraq in 1950–1951, while the former refers to that of Yemenite Jews in 1949–1950). The names themselves, borrowed from *A Thousand and One Nights*, evoke Orientalist attitudes by foregrounding the naïve religiosity and technological backwardness of the Sephardim, for whom modern airplanes were supposedly "magic carpets" transporting them to the Promised Land. The lack of specificity in relation to the country of origin continues in the character of Sallah, who represents an amalgam of Oriental Jewish stereotypes: his pajama evokes the Iraqi, his Bible and synagogue-attendance the devout Yemenite; his violence and penchant for *kriza* (frenzy) call up the image of the Moroccan, while his arak (Oriental liquor), backgammon, and indolence are presumed to be common to all Orientals. The lack of national specificity carries over even into the accent of the new immigrant, which is clearly intended, by both director Kishon and actor Topol, to be a kind of "pan-Oriental." This flattening of heterogeneity recalls Hollywood's monologic vision of the Orient where Baghdad, for example, is transformed into an amalgam of Persians, Indians, and even Chinese, all grouped under the sign of "the Orient." In *Sallah Shabbati*, these generalizations about Oriental Jews, in a clear context of ethnic oppression, evoke what Albert Memmi calls "the mark of the plural," by which subjected classes or entire nations under the rule of European colonialism are reduced to a homogeneous essence: "They are all the same," a forced ideological unity which functions as an alibi for domination.

While the Ashkenazim in the film present a wide spectrum of types from different backgrounds with varied occupations—kibbutzniks, a "Freudian" social worker, a romantic Sabra, the Ashkenazi of the *ma'abara*, a cab driver with a good income, a wealthy urban couple quarreling, representatives from a number of parties, Jewish contributors from New York and Detroit—the Sephardim appear as a uniform and homogeneous mass whose identity derives from Sallah and is identical to his. Only Sallah's two "exotic" children (Shaike Levi and Geula Nuni), who in the end marry Sabras, are granted a certain individualized presentation, but not insofar as they are Sephardim, but rather as young people forging a new identity—a privilege especially granted them in the shots shared with their Ashkenazi lovers (Arik Einstein and Gila Almagor). (The critic Yossef Sharik even complained that Kishon did not sufficiently emphasize "the conflict between the Oriental Jewish father and the son and daughter who *see themselves as Sabras*"[46] [emphasis added]—as if for the younger Oriental Jews the need for assimilation into Sabra society were a simple and unproblematic issue, as if "seeing oneself as Sabra" were for the Oriental Jews a matter of free and spontaneous will.)

The sparse references to Sallah's past, interestingly, operate a topographical reduction to the Orientalist topos of the East as "desert," a reduction to which the Sephardi characters seemingly acquiesce by their silence. Habuba, Sallah's sweet daughter, complains gently and moralistically when her kibbutznik boyfriend accuses her father of living in the desert, telling him that "It's not nice to talk that way," but she never refutes him. This desert reductionism must be regarded as part of the tradition of the topographical representation of the Third World in First World filmic fiction, whereby Africa, in Tarzan films for example, is reduced to an immense jungle, and its inhabitants to savages, while no distinctions are made between diverse languages, cultures, and peoples. Hollywood's portrayal of Arab countries, similarly, tends to reveal nothing more than a vast desert. Even the sequences showing urban civilization in the Middle East in *Lawrence of Arabia* (1962), for instance—a film superficially sympathetic toward Arabs—are associated with British colonialism and not with the Arabs. In this context, unsurprisingly, the Arab-Muslim countries of origin in *Sallah Shabbati* are imagined as an empty and desolate terrain, as countries bereft of civilization.

According to the dominant ideology which pervades *Sallah Shabbati*, the "underdeveloped" countries of origin and the Levantine traits which were imported from those countries are responsible for Oriental backwardness in the State of Israel. When Sallah arrives at the *ma'abara*, his first act is to play backgammon. In a long take/long shot, we see him playing (with the "Ashkenazi of the *ma'abara*") in the foreground, as his wife and children organize and clean in the background. The Sephardi's problems of making a living, it is implied, stem from his "natural" enjoyment of and daily addiction to dice and arak. The background music, which accompanies the long shot, features the characteristic motifs and keyless quarter-tones of Arabic music (emphasized by the sounds of the oud and the flute) and thus reinforces the association between Orientalism and idleness. Sentimental European music (also written by Yohanan Zarai), meanwhile, is employed in the romantic flirtation sequence between Habuba and Ziggi, her kibbutznik boyfriend.

The Oriental essence is presented in contrast to the Ashkenazi; the first sequence of backgammon—a game which tends to be associated with a parasitic life style and low intelligence—is followed by a fadeout to the first sequence of the kibbutz and two kibbutzniks playing chess—a game associated with high I.Q. and creativity (despite the irony that the game's origin is Oriental). In its progression, the film obsessively repeats the leitmotif of Sallah's chronic laziness. In the forestation sequence, for example, Sallah blames the seedling for being a "wild tree which does not want to become a forest." The close shot emphasizes his marking the potential hole but without digging, while the long shot emphasizes the difference between the industrious workers and Sallah, who tries to avoid work by circling around the pitchfork with a pronounced lack of interest. When the American Jew tries to photograph him, he claims that the man is disturbing his work, and when he finally digs his first and only hole, the close shot emphasizes that he actually buries the seedling. When Sallah is fired from his relief job, he thanks God.[47] And in Topol's opinion, Kishon called the character "Shabbati" because for Sallah Shabbati every day is the day of the Shabbath.[48] (In Hebrew the word *Shabbath*—Saturday—derives from the root SBT, to rest, to stop doing work.)

With the ambivalence that characterizes ethnic stereotypes, idleness forms part of Sallah's anti-Establishment charm, but it also "explains" his backwardness and, even more, his children's backwardness. Sallah refuses to bear the burden of family support for his many children, whose numbers and names he can barely remember; in the words of the film's quasi-Oriental song, "Old Mashiah" (meaning "Messiah" but also a typical Sephardi family name), sung by Sallah at the café when seen by corrupt party politicians, "How many children did he give birth to? Allah knows. Maybe thirteen. Maybe a hundred times . . . Allah will bring him good luck." The motif of "infinite children" functions as a comic element in diverse situations in the film. At the beginning of the film, for example, in contrast with the American Jew who counts his suitcases, Sallah counts his children, one of whom arrives with the airplane freight. To his unborn baby he gives the name Ben-Gurion, but when the baby is born as a girl he calls her Pola (the name of Ben-Gurion's wife). The film also exploits the children motif in order to satirize the Establishment in general as well as Ben-Gurion's propaganda for increasing the birth rate (a grant of 100 Liras was given for each ten children), propaganda which formed part of the campaign to increase the Jewish population of Israel.[49]

Since Middle Eastern history is elided in *Sallah Shabbati*, there is no mention of the fact that large families in the countries of origin of Sephardim never seemed to present a significant financial problem as they now do in Israel. Sallah continues in his irresponsible ways even when his son (Pupik Arnon) is forced to quit school. He even takes the wages of his two Ashkenized children in order to get drunk and play backgammon. According to the belief of his creators, Sallah the Patriarch (patriarchy is portrayed as an Eastern monopoly) sells his daughter as a means of subsistence (minimal research would reveal that the traditional tendency of most Oriental-Jewish communities is actually toward the bride's parents giving a dowry to the bridegroom).[50] Sallah also states, in a style more befitting Ashkenazi orthodoxy than Sephardi customs, that he refuses to talk to women. The speaking privileges that the film itself grants Sallah's wife (Esther Greenberg) are limited to a dialogue in which she blames her husband for their predicament. The image-track serves as witness for her complaints about him: "Sitting like a king, all day long, doing nothing but backgammon and arak." As she cleans the rice in the foreground, Sallah sits in the background, doing precisely nothing. While she takes responsibility, performing her woman's role, cooking—here literally foregrounded by her closeness to the camera—Sallah does not. This filmic accusation against Sallah recalls the common and even at times the official ideas about the "backwardness" of Sephardim in Israel:

> SALLAH'S WIFE: The young children are crawling in the dirt, and the older ones walk around like criminals.
> SALLAH: Is it my fault, is it?
> WIFE: Maybe the government got me pregnant?
> SALLAH: What to do? They said they'll give us *shikkun*. They don't give. Why would I go to work?

This dialogue reinforces the view of Sephardi men as parasites who expect to be supported by government welfare, who expect to be given housing yet make no effort toward that end, even at the price of exploiting both wife and (hard-working) children who are themselves on the way to acceptance by Sabra society. The sequence ends with Sallah forcefully taking the money from his daughter Habuba, money which she earned in forestation (and after he has already taken the money of Shimon, his Ashkenized son) in order to get drunk. Thus, the ending lends credence to his wife's accusations. In a dramatic monologue (before God), as he lies in the mud in the rain, Sallah admits the truth of her accusations, an example, once again, of the rhetorical technique of having the victims blame themselves.

This representation, then, reproduces the official ideology by which the low economic and sociopolitical standing of Sephardim is held to result from the pre-modern "backward" countries of origins of Sephardi and from their "backward" mentality, rather than from the class nature of Israeli society. In the happy ending that celebrates not only the marriage of Habuba and Shimon to the kibbutz romantic Sabra and "Freudian" social worker, but also the Shabbatis' move, "against their will" to the *shikkun*, we see Sallah and all his clan in the truck, taken to the *shikkun*. In the last shots Sallah, even in the truck on the way to permanent housing, continues to play backgammon. The official institutions, then, generally offer their help, but he refuses to abandon his Oriental addictions. This portrait of Oriental laziness and parasitism fits well within the framework of colonialist Western culture, whose texts repeatedly present those who in fact worked the hardest as "lazy."[51] In Israel, the Sephardi, whose entrance into the work force was usually at the level of unskilled labor—whatever the wide range of skills with

The Mizrahim as lack: Sallah and daughter at the employment bureau in *Sallah Shabbati.*

which they arrived—labor involving hard physical work for low wages, labor which made possible huge profits for advantaged groups such as the veteran Ashkenazi population—this same Sephardi is presented as irresponsible and lazy.

Sallah is projected as a superimposed series of lacks; he comes from nowhere, i.e., presumably from a noncivilized world without language and culture, and he exercises no profession. The Ashkenazi waiting in line in the employment office, in contrast with Sallah, is a dental technician. The implicit claim that the different immigrants were all treated equitably is reinforced when the educated European is sent to do forestry work together with the illiterate Sephardi. The real injustice, it is implied, is to the Ashkenazi, presumably the victim of "reverse discrimination." Sallah's ignorance is metaphorically underlined when he is unable to distinguish between a wardrobe and a bookcase in the scene in which he works as a porter for the kibbutz. Even his shrewd ideas for tricking the Establishment come, ultimately, from the Ashkenazi characters. It is Goldstein (the *ma'abara* Ashkenazi who keeps losing to Sallah in backgammon) who informs him about the possibility of making money during elections. Sallah finds this good "job" somewhat problematic since he is only partially familiar with the alphabet (each party in Israel is given different Hebrew letters). Then the Ashkenazi parties choose him, as one with great potential, to be bribed. But Sallah's ignorance, as we have seen, makes him stuff all the votes in the same polling box. In his final successful act of anti-Establishment trickery, whereby he gets the *shikkun*, Sallah is again inspired by an Ashkenazi, the cab driver who tells him, "you always get what you *don't* want." Applying this aphorism to his particular need to move to a *shikkun*, Sallah takes his family to "demonstrate" against their (desired) transference to the *shikkun*—a demonstration which is disastrously successful.

Sallah Shabbati also purveys the misinformed Zionist account which projects Oriental Jews as coming from rural societies lacking all contact with techno-logical civilization, as if metropolises such as Alexandria, Casablanca, Baghdad, Istanbul, and Teheran were nothing but desolate backwaters without electricity or automobiles. We detect this misapprehension in the *shikkun* sequence, where Sallah's naïveté lacks even the narrative and satiric function of lampooning the Establishment. The Shabbati family members are presented by a mise-en-scène which isolates them from all Ashkenazi presence, and therefore gives the viewer the "objective" opportunity to watch them "as they are." We witness their first attempts to master "Israeli" technologies like electrical switches, water faucets, and sliding doors—"like a train," the Shabbatis say excitedly—as well as to Sallah's naïve fear of a cuckoo clock which obliges the "Ashkenazi of the *ma'abara*" to explain that "it's only a clock." Oriental primitiveness is contrasted with European technological expertise.

This binary contrast of Ashkenazi technological finesse and Sephardi ineptitude also operates in another of Kishon's comedies, *Arvinka*, where the charming, confident, and boisterous Sabra, Arvinka (Topol), has a Yemenite neighbor (Yossef Banai) who believes that radios have souls. A pan from one apartment to the next shows that the strange voices emitted from the radio are actually a trick by Arvinka. The zoom-in to the horseshoe and garlic (fetishes against the "evil eye") hanging from the radio emphasizes the presumed incompatibility of technology and the Oriental mind. *Sallah Shabbati* and *Arvinka*, then, dictate, through their portrayal of Oriental characters, the safe and comedic superiority of the "enlightened" Israeli/Western spectator, who plays Prospero to the Oriental Caliban.[52]

The Oriental's encounter with the "twentieth-century" is made possible, in other words, thanks to the State of Israel. The Shabbatis' visit to a modern building—presumably the fruit of Ashkenazi invention—reveals, to anyone who had doubts, that the *ma'abara* is the Sephardi's natural environment. If not for the Zionism which redeemed the Shabbatis, it is suggested, these Jews would have remained immersed in oppressive exile among the nations of darkness. A quick glance away from the dominant-Zionist historiography, however, reveals that the opposite is true. For many of the Sephardi immigrants, *aliya* (immigration to Israel; literally "ascent") entailed a significant *yerida* ("descent, decline;" metaphorically, emigra-tion out of Israel) in standard of living, housing conditions, occupational level, and even nutrition.[53] "Bourekas" films like *Sallah Shabbati* are based on the mythical double illusion in relation to both the countries of origins and the social/ethnic division in Israel that turned the tables. The representation of the Sephardi Sallah is focused on his Levantine characteristics, thus helping conceal the fact that the "modernity" of the Ashkenazim is not part of their historical legacy, but rather a system of privilege which is achieved, for the most part, thanks to the Oriental Jews' positioning in the process of economic development—a place that was attributed to their "traditionalism."[54]

Sallah Shabbati inadvertently provides a kind of apologia for discrimination. When Sallah's son asks, "Why do they cheat us?" his father answers, "Because we are new here, and the new ones are always cheated. But one day I'll be the old one, and then I'll cheat the new ones." Here again, Sallah, the victim of the system, uses the logic of the system, thus legitimizing it by the dream that he will one day be part of it, thanks to a kind of "pyramid scheme" of oppression. This apologia ignores key facts, however, since not all newcomers are received in the same way. Veteran Sephardim are still severely discriminated against in comparison, for example, with recent immigrants from the Soviet Union.[55] Thus the situation of oppression, overall, is not eased. In *Sallah Shabbati*, as in the overwhelming majority of Israeli films, the ethnic division of labor is reproduced by an ideological apparatus that presents the low economic and social standing of Sephardim as due not to the class nature of the Israeli society but rather to their origins in "nonmodern" and culturally "backward" societies. This ideology forms part of the general European colonial feeling of superiority over the people of the Third World which Ashkenazim share (as Europeans). The feeling of superiority also stems (especially for the "veteran" Ashkenazim) from being the creators of the Zionist movement.

In the framework of film comedy, Sallah's Levantine characteristics are laughable, eliciting paternalistic "forgiveness" on the part of the "progressive" spectator, since the Establishment eventually tames him and gets his children to assimilate in the happy ending of the double mixed marriage. His children are "redeemed" from their dark past in "remote countries" and from their present in the *ma'abara* (or development-town) by the "enlightened" Sabras of the kibbutz. By marrying off the children of the "Black" Jew, Sallah, to proper White kibbutzniks, Kishon resolves the contradictions of plot and social reality. While Habuba and Shimon move to the kibbutz, Sallah himself and the rest of the clan are transferred to permanent housing for domestication. The classic comedy celebrates Israeli continuity, the death of the Oriental-Jewish *dor hamidbar* ("desert generation," generation of wilderness) and the (mixed) birth of "beautiful Israel."

Rescue Fantasies and the Libidinal South

These same traditional Middle Eastern qualities lead to different, more bitter endings, predictably, within the framework of the melodramatic genre of films such as *Fortuna*, where the structuring of spectatorial identification arouses contempt and disdain toward what is presented as typical Sephardi family and pity toward its victims. The Algerian Bousaglo family from Dimona, a development town in the south of Israel, force their submissive daughter Fortuna (Ahuva Goren)—in accordance with the stereotypes of Oriental marriage—to wed Shimon (Saro Orzy), a rich old man from their community, to whom she was promised at an early age and through whom they will be able to emigrate to the city of their dreams—Paris. At the same time they aggressively sabotage her love for the gentile French engineer (Mike Marshall), a guest factory consultant in Sodom. Within the *liebestod* tradition of impossible love, the obstacles lead, ultimately, to the death of the heroine.

Fortuna, like *Sallah Shabbati*, was neither designed nor received as a specific story of a specific family, but rather as a generalized "allegorical" portrait of the Sephardim in general, and of the North African Jews in particular. In the response to the film, we find again a kind of specular reflection between the ideological assumptions of the filmmakers and those of the critics, who regard the world portrayed on the screen as "real," ignoring the nature of cinema as a fictive construct. One leading critic, Ze'ev Rav-Nof, wrote in the Histadrut daily *Davar*:[56]

> The film revolves around a "second Israel" milieu, where the petrified values of tradition and superstition often destroy noble emotions . . . in a tragicomic melodrama, the plight of good people . . . foreigners in a culture of opposite and differing values, is presented while one of them stands up . . . proud against the defective yesterday.[57]

Another journalist, Immanuel Bar-Kadma of the mass-circulation daily *Yedioth Ahronoth*, parrots the official view of the pre-modern origins of the Sephardim: "The encounter of the Bousaglos with the twentieth-century began quite late . . . Golan chose as a social and plot background . . . a world making its first steps beyond the confines of the Middle Ages."[58] In Shidurei Israel Radio (radio and television in Israel are governmental) we encounter the same symptomatic interpretations:

> Golan chose a typical problem, a problem of the "second Israel" . . . a conflict typical of an immigrant country like ours. There are here prejudiced immigrants from backward countries, who happen to be in a progressive country. They cannot accept the new world; they display irrational conservatism, especially with regard to women. And things end in disaster. . . . Golan presents very well this kind of clan terror. Terror on the job . . . terror with regard to the election of the mayor . . . also terror in the family, since in such a family no one has a right to personal happiness or personal choice.[59]

The Western rescue fantasy: "Sephardi despotism" in *Fortuna*.

The Galei Tzahal Radio Station (the army radio), for its part, emphasized the role of the army with its salutary effects on the "good Bousaglos":

> There is one son in the Bousaglo family, angry, selfish and stubborn. But in contrast there is another son, Yossef, played by Yossef Banai, a son who points to a new youth, to development, thanks to the influence of the army; he is the revolutionary son fighting the prejudices of the other son. There is a struggle in the family... and the good proves it is righteous.[60]

Other critics, meanwhile, remarked on what they saw as the "absurd" juxtaposition of Oriental artifacts and Western technology: "In the house there is an electric refrigerator, a transistor, and also... a *narghileh* [hookah, or Oriental tobacco pipe]."[61]

While most critics emphasized the "love and respect" Golan showed for his characters, *Fortuna* nevertheless provoked some anger among Oriental Jews, anger which found public expression only in some irate letters to newspapers and a protest committee against the screening of the film. The promised official screening in Dimona, where the film was shot, was postponed, in fear of public reactions.[62] The mayor of Dimona protested the "distorted image of the town and its community," and a protest committee was formed to struggle against a film which "distorts the image of North Africans in Israel."[63] The fact that *Sallah Shabbati* did not provoke similar reactions in terms of the image of Orientals has a good deal to do with its genre. Apart from the significant difference that the Establishment was satirized in the film, there was also the notion of comedy as somehow "less serious" and, therefore, "less harmful" and more "forgivable," as the *Fortuna* protest committee put it, than a "drama with knives, fights and murder."[64]

A close textual reading of *Fortuna* helps to comprehend the negative ramifications of the Sephardi image. The film forces identification, first of all, with a passionate, boundless love that can be realized only despite an Oriental tyranny which ultimately brings destruction to the heroine. The unbridled violence of the father (Pierre Brasseur) and his son (Shmuel Kraus) is structured by the narrative as in permanent opposition to the virginal lovers, a conflict reaching its paroxysm at the end of the film. The camera set-ups and the juxtaposition of the shots, especially in the violent scenes, suggest a perspective supporting the victims of this familial despotism. In one sequence, for example, the French engineer is nearly killed by the Bousaglos but is saved by the good (i.e., Ashkenized) Bousaglo (Yossef Banai), through whose eyes we witness the dramatic events. In the sequence where Fortuna is punished for her forbidden love, when her hair is cut (off screen) while her screams fill the void, a pan over to her father and brothers visually designates the guilty parties. In another sequence, we see, from Fortuna's point of view, the old, obese fiancé, Shimon, snoring on the night before the forced marriage, thus strengthening our feelings of empathy and pity for the heroine. When her brother, Yossef, asks her why she doesn't run away, the film answers his question (and ours) by having the father immediately appear and place his restraining hand on Fortuna's shoulder. In the wedding sequence, Shimon forces Fortuna to dance and tries to kiss her, while she tries to free herself—the camera moves quickly in circular movement (to the rhythm of the music of the Greek singer Arisan), and the rapid circular movements emphasize the subjective feeling of Fortuna's dizziness. Everything conspires to legitimize her next act: fleeing from this oppressive world.

This criticism of the "inferior culture" imported from the Arab countries, according to the prevailing ideology which underlies the film, is supported and reinforced, as in *Sallah Shabbati*, by the topographical reduction of the Orient to a desert (*shmama*) and metaphorically, of Orientalness to dreariness (*shimamon*). The desert, with the traditionalism and backwardness it supposedly represents, is referred to in the dialogue—particularly in the criticism of the "objective witness," the "cultured" Bousaglo. It also appears as a visual leitmotif throughout the film, which begins and ends with shots of the desert. Both on the implied, associative level and in explicit utterances, the desert is presented as essential to the Orientals and their Arabized history and, of course, has no place in the "new era." The Sephardi, in other words, is associated with images of underdevelopment, poverty, and backwardness, in contrast with the Sabra, who is portrayed, in Israeli discourse in general, and in the cinema in particular, as an antithesis to the (Oriental) desert, as an active, productive, and creative pioneer, as a redeemer who "makes the desert bloom." It is interesting to note in this context, that Alexander Ramati, who (along with Vladia Smitiov and Yossef Gross) participated in the writing of the script (based on Menahem Talmi's book), wrote and directed *Rebels Against the Light*, which also includes the motif of desert. There the desert, as in *Fortuna*, is connected with the Oriental, while the "enlightened" Westernized Sabra, who brings the advance of technology, wins the gratitude of the "good" and "noble" Arab, who thanks Israel for redeeming him from the Dark Ages.

The Orient becomes, therefore, a world immersed in death. In *Fortuna* this "morbidity" is emphasized by shots of circling birds of prey, and by the association of the Bousaglo family with Sodom, the Biblical "city of evils." This connection is explicitly expressed by the potential local council head (Avner Hizkiyahu): "This Hell; as if the angel of death has made his home here since the days of Sodom and Gomorrah." The conflictual dichotomy of Orient/death and West/life structures the film. The Orient appears as the enemy of Eros (life) and the partisan of Thanatos in various respects, in the attempts to kill the French suitor and the forced marriage to an elderly groom which leads Fortuna to escape to her death. The West, on the other hand, is embodied both in the image of the handsome Frenchman, who brings technological advancement to the (under) developed town and tries to save the oppressed daughter with whom he has fallen in love, and in the character of the son, educated for modernity by the military "melting pot,"[65] who rises against the family to help the lovers. The same dichotomy also pervades the design of the scenes themselves. Like Elia Kazan's *Splendor in the Grass* (1961), *Fortuna*'s famous Ein Gedi waterfall sequence stages sensual lovemaking[66] against a beautiful natural backdrop, underlined by melodramatic Western music. The cut to the oppressive "reality" and the fear of the future of Fortuna and her sister-in-law Margo (Gila Almagor), who warns Fortuna that she is being pursued as they run through a desolate landscape, is emphasized on the soundtrack via the superimposed sounds of birds of prey and Oriental music.[67] Spring water, in other words, is metaphorically associated with the West and the desert with the East.

The victimization of the Sephardi woman by Sephardi men and her implicit salvation by the Western world, and particularly by a Western man, is seen in other Israeli films and also finds antecedents in Hebrew literature. In Golan's *Queen of the Road*, for example, the narrative promotes an opposition between the gentle kibbutznik (Yehuda Barkan), who gives the protagonist, a Moroccan prostitute in Tel Aviv (Gila Almagor), warmth and affection, and the rough Sephardi men, especially those of the development town in the south who brutally rape her during her first months of pregnancy. Her involvement with the kibbutznik, her pregnancy by him, and her visit to the kibbutz, where she sees his well-ordered family life, make her decide to give up prostitution and raise the child herself. While visiting her mother in the south of Israel, she is raped. The rape, filmed in a style influenced by the hallucinatory violence of American cinema in the late sixties and early seventies,[68] leads to the birth of a retarded child.

The rape, retardation, and even death, all caused by Sephardi male mistreatment of Sephardi women in these films, stimulate a kind of rescue fantasy in the "progressive" male spectator. The films carry on the masculine colonialist tradition, for example, of René Clair's *Les Belles de nuit* (1952), where Gérard Philippe, serving in the French Legion, fantasizes the rescue of an Algerian woman trapped in an Algerian harem.[69] Israeli melodramas such as *Fortuna* and *Queen of the Road* emphasize the victimization of the woman protagonist, while in comedies such as *I Like Mike* and *Sallah Shabbati*, the minor roles of the Sephardi women (played by Geula Nuni) go hand in hand with an "exoticism" which captures the heart of both producers and spectators. The "exotic" young woman is often a Sephardi who assimilates to the Sabra codes. In *I Like Mike* she is a kibbutz member, and in *Sallah Shabbati* she is about to become one. The schematic dichotomy between Sephardi men and women perfectly fits the Ashkenazi clichés about Sephardim, as in the common Yiddish expression "A frenk es a chaie, a frenkina a mechaie," i.e., "The frenk [nickname for Sephardim] man is an animal, the frenk woman brings one back to life."

A similar representation of sexual tensions between Sephardi men and women is extended to the present day in Nadav Levitan's comedy, *You're in the Army, Girls* (*Banot*, literally *Girls*, 1985). The film recounts four weeks of boot-camp training for women soldiers in the Israeli army, the locus of ethnic encounters which generate dramatic and comic situations. From the very beginning, the film develops a structural contrast between its major characters, an upper-class Sabra woman, Niva (Helly Goldberg), and a development-town Sephardi woman, Shula (Hanny Azoulay). Already in the credit sequence, the film cuts from Niva's separation from her father to Shula's separation from her family, underlining their opposing class and ethnic backgrounds. Within this representation of similar moments, however, the film betrays a differential attitude toward the characters' respective backgrounds, an attitude anticipating that which permeates the film as a whole. Whereas the camera foregrounds Niva and her handsome, protective father, revealed to be an "insider" in relation to the Establishment, implied to have power to assist his daughter—he asks her if she would prefer to join a military entertainment troupe (a prestigious position in the army)—Shula's large family remains anonymous as the camera pans over their shoulders to record the daughter kissing them goodbye, while she censures their overly emotional (i.e., non-Israeli) reaction to her departure. Shula the Sephardi is dressed in colorful but cheap clothing, while Niva is dressed in expensive and fashionable clothing acquired in the boutiques of Paris and New York. (The contrast in their appearance and manner, translated into a North American context, would correspond, grosso modo, to the stereotypes of the refined, perhaps repressed, Wasp and the sexy Latina—in Hebrew "Sephardi" literally signifies "Spanish," so the comparison is not entirely fortuitous.)

Acknowledging that her situation at home is unbearable and rebelling against the (presumably Sephardi) prospect of "ending" her "life at the age of thirty with fifty children," alternating "between the grocery store and the laundry," Shula joins the army. But once in the army, she becomes the object of prejudice not only on the part of Niva but also of the Sabra woman commander, Talia (Anat Topol), who at a climactic point in the film challenges her to fight because "violence is the only language she understands." (A voyeuristic camera highlights the submerged eroticism of women wrestling.) Perhaps in reaction to the treatment accorded her, Shula escapes from the army and encounters her Sephardi boyfriend, depicted as good-hearted but also stuttering and unintelligent. But out in the brutal Oriental world, she finds herself forced to take drugs and about to be raped by three Sephardi men. Unable to save her, the weak and pitiful boyfriend calls Shula's military unit for help. Despite earlier misunderstandings, the members of the Sabra women's unit collectively perform a kind of private military mission to save their comrade from the Sephardi sexual vultures, thus compensating for their previous lack of sensitivity. In a heroic action, they release Shula and humiliate the surprised and frightened Oriental machos. The unit's patriotism, finally, is expressed by an additional act of generosity toward the "culturally deprived" Sephardi woman. With the help of her father, Niva gets the musically talented Shula into the prestigious army entertainment troupe, while she herself gets another (prestigious) position in military radio. The army, metonymic of Israel itself, and the Ashkenazi elite, then, together save the Sephardi woman from her backward, violent world, giving her the opportunity to develop her talents and resolve the sexual conflicts presumably endemic in Oriental society in a way that intimates a peaceful transcendence of the class-ethnic tensions of Israeli society.

Although Sephardim have been a minor topic in Hebrew literature, such images can be found there as well. In short stories since the beginning of the century, such as those of Levin Kipnis, Moshe Smilansky, and Nehama Bohachevsky, we find the contrast between the Yemenite woman of the immigrant generation, a victim of her husband and culture, and the woman of the younger generation, virtually a Sabra, a free liberated girl and woman saved by Sabra culture. In Haim Hazaz' story "Salima," the heroine's husband beats her and spends his money on drinking, cards, and women. Salima, a housemaid, receives some support from her employer, Mrs. Lehman. In the same story the negative image of the Sephardi man is accompanied by the favorable image of the Ashkenazi elite even though it was that elite, and not Sephardi men, which exploited Sephardi women by granting them the lowest salaries in Jewish-Israeli society. In Hazaz' "Extended Horizon" ("Ofek Natui"), similarly, husbands beat their wives and act cruelly toward them in public. In Hemda Ben-Yehuda's "Lulu," the husband brutally and irrationally beats his wife and even bites off her finger. After her divorce, Lulu finally finds work as a maid in an Ashkenazi *moshava* (agricultural settlement) and ultimately marries an Ashkenazi and finds happiness. When an Ashkenazi husband

The IDF saving Mizrahi women from Mizrahi men in *You're in the Army, Girls.*

beats his wife, as Lev Hakak points out,[70] it is portrayed as the result of mental breakdown, a consequence of the 1967 war, as in Yitzhak Gluska's "Wounded Olives" ("Zeitim Ptzuim"), rather than as an example of cultural atavism. When the wife manages to cure him he returns to his loving relation to her. As in the films *Sallah Shabbati* and *Fortuna*, Sephardim in literature are depicted as abusing their children as well. In Mila Ohel's "To the Right Path" ("LaMutav"), Yaacov Horgin's "Eliyahu the Butcher" (Eliyahu haKatzav") and "At Uncle Raful's" ("Etzel haDod Raful"), and Yitzhak Shinhar's "The Soul of Esther Ma'adani" ("Nishmata shel Ester Ma'adani"), the Sephardi men, as well as the wives, act violently toward their children without any justification. Sephardi men are also drunk, lacking in emotional depth, lazy, and exploitative parasites, in contrast with Ashkenazi men, as in Haim Hazaz' "And My Father Is Enlightened" ("VeAvi Naor") and in Yitzhak Shinhar's "Street of Zion Lovers" ("Rehov Hovevei Zion").

In *Fortuna*, salvation for the victims of coercion and (Sephardic) orthodoxy[71] must come from without, from the open and modern Sabra world. Although Sabraness is concealed in *Fortuna*, it is present as a tacit antithesis in the consciousness of the Israeli spectator. The film's moral confirms the shallow view of the sociologists, that only desocialization of the "traditionalism" and resocialization into "Israeli modernity" will solve the "gap problem." The development town, in other words, is portrayed as cut off from the overall Israeli system, as a product of Arab-Algerian values, and not as a marginal entity controlled and exploited by the economic, political, and cultural institutions of the center. In line with the view of Orientals as "marginals," we should add, it was official Israeli policy to settle Sephardim in the literal margins of the country, in Israel's outermost areas in settlements which were less well defended than the kibbutzim, thus making the Sephardi settlers the easiest targets available to Arab attack (and engendering an, in some ways, artificial enmity between the two groups).[72]

The images of the final sequence in *Fortuna* support this conclusion. Defending her French lover against her brother, Fortuna is killed. The whole town arrives, and the father and his son weep over Fortuna's body. The Frenchman drives north by jeep. In extreme long shot, the jeep progresses toward the camera, leaving the (under) developed town to mourn its victim in the far background. When the jeep goes out of frame, the film ends. Together with the Frenchman, the enlightened and now relieved spectators end the voyeuristic voyage into the threatening world of the other, carrying with them a moral concerning the dangers of Levantinity. The producers of the Sephardi images in films such as *Fortuna* express what the author Haim Hazaz (who among his other stories also wrote on Sephardim) was publishing in the same period:

> An abyss separates us in terms of Levantism! We should try and bring Euro-pean culture to the Oriental communities. We cannot become an Oriental nation. I have a strong reaction against it. We passed through two thousand years till we became a Jewish-European cultural unit; we cannot now turn the wheel back and receive the culture of Yemen, Morocco, Iraq.[73]

The film explicitly regards "Sabraness," furthermore, as an alternative to old-fashioned Oriental expressivity, in the character of the company director (Yitzhak Shilo). (The actor Shilo, during the fifties and early sixties, significantly, tended to be cast in the role of the model Sabra, for example, as the officer in *Hill 24 Doesn't Answer*.) The director is depicted as rational and educated, and from the beginning he warns the Frenchman that he is not in France but in Sodom. His warning operates as a proleptic clue to the accelerating clash of cultural codes. Forward-looking, progressive Israel is mainly represented, however, by the "objective" Bousaglo, who, unlike his illiterate family, is devoted to reading, who has had the privilege of knowing advanced Israel thanks to the military "melting pot," and who is therefore authorized to speak for the nation. The voice of this Israel is heard in his peroration to the Frenchman, with phrases like: "In a modern country, in a modern state, they behave like primitives," or in the revulsion he expresses toward his family: "We are not in Algiers. Here everyone is free to do what he wants." The blond engineer, furthermore, who incarnates the Israeli ego ideal, is categorized together with the "modern Israel," within *Fortuna*'s Eurocentric schematism, both by his association with the company director, who protects him from the "Bousaglo knife" (the term "Moroccan knife," it should be pointed out, has become a kind of epithet to denote North Africans as violent people), as well as by his friendship with the "Sabra" Bousaglo Yossef, who saves his life. The Frenchman expresses a similar disgust toward the family. When they cut Fortuna's hair, he angrily protests: "Do you think you live in the jungle?"[74] The Frenchman, in friendly reciprocity with Yossef, advises him to go north, to Tel Aviv, expressing the concept that "out of the north good shall break forth" (an inversion of Jeremiah 1:14).

In this respect, *Fortuna* reflects a culturally overdetermined geographical-symbolic polarity: a double axis of East/West and North/South which also informs other films such as Golan's *Eldorado* and *Queen of the Road*. As if in a reversion to deterministic climatic theories (such as those of Madame de Staël or Hippolyte Taine), the films present the south[75]—whether of Tel Aviv, or of Israel generally—as the locus of backwardness, of uncontrollable instincts and irrational passion, in short, as the world of the out-of-control Id. (The film was even called a "Southern" by analogy with "Western.") The concept of the south is especially interesting, since Golan initially wanted the Italian Saro Orzy, who plays the role of the old groom, to play the role of the father, following a similar role in Germi's *Seduced and Abandoned* (1963). Operating within the moralist-paternalist framework of the film, some critics compared the plot development and the social background to those of Sicily, in order to illustrate the backwardness of the milieu[76] (the more appropriate analogy, ironically, may be that of the two souths as internal colonies). The geographical mind with its double axis reaches its climax in *Fortuna*'s final sequences, at the wedding. The festivity gathers a grotesque collection of obese old people and a dwarf together with Greek Sirtaki music and dancing[77]—Greek music, in many ways, became for Sephardim in Israel a kind of substitute for the pariah, excommunicated Arabic music. The popular trio HaGashash haKhiver performs at the wedding and sings: "The heat/of the sun that rises and blazes/the storms will come/Because the way to Sodom/Slowly descends/There on Dimona road/Don't go there/There blazes the south/Don't go there/Because it's burning/burning there in Sodom . . . "

To the sound of this tune, Fortuna escapes from the horrific wedding, to her lover awaiting her in the jeep to travel northward together, to be saved from the fires of hell, but the wickedness of Sodom prevents her. Orientalist essentialism, in other words, creates an identification between the north, Tel Aviv, and "progressive" European France, as well as between the south, Dimona, and "backward," Arabic Algeria, a geographical conceptualization strongly reminiscent of European colonialist formulations. Indeed, the film translates some of the colonialist *topoi* circulating in the Israeli media. Throughout such discourse, European culture is seen as the norm, while Orientalized culture is seen as lack and aberration. One, the European, is seen as inherited wealth to be preserved, while the other is seen as a "problem" to be "solved."

Fortuna is not only the victim of Algerian tyranny, but also the sexual object of Golan's fetishistic camera. Already in the credit sequence, for example, Fortuna runs barefoot in the sand to catch a truck home. While she sensually eats an apple, the driver gazes at her, and from his point of view the film cuts to a close shot of her breasts jiggling up and down in accord with the bumps of the rough road. On the level of narrative, meanwhile, Fortuna, who has lost her virginity, is punished with her final death, and her sacrifice helps free the Frenchman from the pitiless town and thus end the film. Fetishization and objectification of women, one might add parenthetically, are frequent in Golan's films. Close shots of bodily fragments as well as languorous pans over the body can be found, for example, in *999 Aliza Mizrahi*, especially with regard to the rich young wife, Mrs. Grinboim (Ziva Rodan), or in *Cairo Operation* with regard to the Egyptian singer (Gila Almagor), images carried into Golan's recent American productions such as *Over the Brooklyn Bridge* (1984) with regard to the Margaux Hemingway character. In *Cairo Operation*, the Egyptian woman takes risks to spy for Israel against her Egyptian officer lover (Yossef Yadin), but she too is punished for her infidelity by death. Masochistic sacrifice on the part of women is also seen in Golan's *Eldorado*, where Margo, the Sephardi prostitute, is willing to sacrifice her love for the Sephardi protagonist (Topol) and go to prison, so as to enable him to continue an honest life with the "madonna" (Tikva Mor) of north Tel Aviv.

Arab-Jews, Dislocation and Nostalgia

Some of Moshe Mizrahi's films—which have not received due credit from Israeli film critics—demonstrate sensitivity to the status of women in general and Sephardi women in particular without ever descending into the formulaic dualism of "enlightened West" versus "oppressive East." Set in the late nineteenth-century, *I Love You, Rosa* (*Ani Ohev Otakh Rosa*, 1972) presents the religious laws of Judaism in a somewhat critical fashion by emphasizing the humiliation associated with the Law of Levirate (forced marriage to the deceased husband's brother, if the deceased has no children to carry on his name). Structured as a flashback, the film begins with the recently widowed Rosa (Michal Bat Adam) waiting, in accordance with Judaic law, for her husband's younger brother, Nissim, to attain maturity and either marry her or offer her *haliza*, the freedom to marry someone else. As Nissim enters adolescence, he begins to desire Rosa, but Rosa, who is portrayed as a strikingly independent woman, demands *haliza* even though she loves him in return. Her demand is motivated, it turns out, by a desire to be chosen not solely because of Judaic law but also by Nissim's personal choice. After telling her story to her grandson, Nissim, named after her husband, Rosa expires peacefully. Mizrahi sets this love story within an authentically reconstructed Sephardic culture, within an imagery and atmosphere imbued with Middle Eastern sensuous elements, suggesting the deep-rootedness of this community in the area.

The Sephardi community in nineteenth-century Palestine: *I Love You, Rosa.*

Although hardly a feminist in the Western sense, Rosa is also not a weak, sub-missive creature or a victim of Sephardi fatalism. In unequivocal opposition to the Orient/death connection in *Fortuna*, *I Love You, Rosa* reflects, through intimate acquaintance, a flexible Sephardi world encapsulated by the character of the gentle Jerusalem *hakham* (rabbi) (Avner Hizkiyahu) who searches for solutions through a sensitivity to the historical dimension of time and place—solutions that will en-able one to live Halacha (Jewish Law) in harmony, without oppressing the human being. He explains to Nissim (Gabi Onterman), who has told of his (forbidden) love for Rosa, "Love is never a sin," and before the Levirate ceremony, he declares: "Man is more important than law; His love of Man is greater than law." His interpretations do not derive from the pious commandments of a rabbinical hier-archy, or from clerical study in abstract law, but rather from a concrete encounter with his community in their homes and in alleys, from a Buberian "I-Thou" dialogue.

The autobiographical *House on Chlouch Street*, set in the 1947–1948 period, reconstructs, like *I Love You, Rosa*, fragments of the Sephardi experience, this time from the perspective of the protagonist Sami (Ofer Shalhin). The film presents a world of neighborhood cooperation and familiarity, with all its advantages and disadvantages. The dialogue in the family sequences is handled by a kind of "plurilogue," that is, the editing eschews the binary shot-counter-shot structure of alternating faces—a style more appropriate to Western individualism—in favor of a collective familial intimacy. The mise-en-scène emphasizes the inner courtyard—an indispensable element in the architecture of an Oriental tableau—where people are in constant contact and life takes place exposed to all eyes in a kind of maskless theater. In this theater of daily life, the roles of actor and specta-tor are constantly intermingled.[78] The neighbor Nissim (Yossef Shiloach) courts Klara (Gila Almagor) openly in front of her family. His amorous declarations, rich in verbal evocations of colors and smells and uttered in a wide diversity of languages,[79] as well as the warm repartee of Klara, are not hidden behind re-spectable curtains. When the Sephardized Ashkenazi (Shaike Ofir) first appears in the courtyard to be tested as a suitor, Nissim takes the role of observer, and, with the others, he is surprised at this character who knows their ways of ex-pression and thus breaks down the cultural partition between them. (The casting of Shaike Ofir, an Arabic-speaking Ashkenazi, in this role, here has a reflexive element.) *The House on Chlouch Street* conveys the impression that it is impossible to separate the Middle Eastern way of speaking—rich in imagery, proverbs, and aphorisms—from body language, gestures, subtle movements of the head, hand, and finger. The film (aided by Adam Greenberg's sensual photography) gives ex-pression to the Sephardi verbal and physical codes in which all five senses play a role, including the sense of smell. When Sami buys a pita with grilled meat, for example, the smoke is evocatively carried by the wind toward the camera/ spectator.

In Mizrahi's films, Sephardi characters are designed through their (essential) connection to Arab culture. In *I Love You, Rosa*, intimate friendship with Arabs is shown to be common among the Jerusalem Jews of the end of the last century: we have, for example, Rosa's friendship with the Arab woman Jamilla (Levana Finkelstein), who encourages Rosa to free herself from the burden of her widowhood, and Nissim's friendship with the Arab adolescent who prepares him for sexual initiation. The first dialogue in *The House on Chlouch Street* is spoken in Arabic (the topic: politics in Mandate Palestine), and as the film progresses, the characters repeatedly feel the need to return to Arabic. We also hear Arabic music and the voice of the famous Egyptian singer Umm Kulthum, much beloved not only in the Arab world but also by Oriental Jews, forming more than a merely decorative acoustic background. But this Jewish entity, which is at the same time Arab, is regarded with contempt by the Ashkenazi shop manager. As Sami is eating, the manager derides him: "Olives and onions, like an Arab!" The manager is seen from the point of view of Sami—whose economic dependence forces him to keep quiet—and therefore from a perspective critical of such prejudice. Toward the end of the film, with the foundation of the Israeli state, Sami's brother is killed by an Arab bomb, and the major first steps toward Sephardi identity crisis are implicitly created; the two poles of Oriental Jewish identity—Arab and Jewish—are pressured to pull apart.

Whereas the twelfth-century Spanish Sephardi poet Yehuda Halevi wrote of his nostalgia for the East, i.e., for Zion ("My heart is in the East/And I am at the end of the West"),[80] the contemporary Sephardi Jews, now located in a Westernized Zion, paradoxically, feel nostalgia for an Eastern elsewhere, which, at the same time, is associated with the new enemy, the Arab. This schizophrenia of the Arab Jew in Israel, pressured by the Zionist dichotomy of Arab-versus-Jew to choose a single identity, is the subject of Yigal Niddam's documentary film *We Are Arab Jews in Israel* (*Anahnu Yehudim Arvim beIsrael*, 1977) and implicitly of Haim Shiran's *Pillar of Salt*, based on Memmi's novel.

Serge Ankri, in *Burning Land* (*Adama Hama*, 1982), attempts to structure a certain analogy between the uprooting of the Palestinians and the uprooting of Jews from Arab countries following the establishment of Israel by cutting from a sequence of the uprooting of a Palestinian family's olive trees to the uprooting of those belonging to a Jewish family in Tunisia. This conception differs sharply from that guiding Uri Barabash's *Beyond the Walls* (*MeAhorei haSoragim*, literally *Behind the Bars*, 1984) in which the sympathetic portrait of the Sephardi prisoner is compromised by the dominant Israeli stigma of "Arab-hater." In this context, the *Bildungsroman* of *Beyond the Walls* is one-sided, especially with regard to the Sephardi, who in the microcosm of the prison eventually reaches a feeling of brotherhood with the Palestinian against the prison management. The Palestinian's consciousness remains static throughout, without undergoing the equivalent educational process in relation to the Sephardi, even though the history of the Arab

Jew and his positioning with regard to the Palestinian question, is different, at its core, from the dominant Israeli experience, that of European Jews.

The films of Mizrahi cannot be reduced to a nostalgia for "roots." They must be seen in relation to the period in which they were produced, and specifically to the protest movements of the early seventies. To quote Mizrahi (whose very name in Hebrew means "Eastern"):

> What is taking place in this country [Israel] is cultural genocide. The very existence of the State of Israel brought the ideological dictatorship of Jews from Eastern Europe over another Judaism with its rich and deep culture. . . . There began a process by which the Oriental Jews lost the ingredient spices of their culture and began to mimic the other culture. Thus they lost their souls, they lost the strength to be themselves. The Oriental Jews turned into *halturot* [Hebrew for sloppy unprofessional work and kitsch showmanship]; they became folkloric caricatures on small stages.[81]

The Sephardi family in *The House on Chlouch Street* is not cut off from the sociopolitical context of 1947–1948, and the film reflects the beginning of the emergence of the ethnic/class divisions in Israel which generated the strong protests of the past decade. The members of the wealthy Egyptian family are turned into workers in the "State on the Way."[82] Klara works as a housemaid, and this is a rare case in Israeli cinema where the Sephardi female laborer receives understanding treatment, largely through mechanisms of identification. She is portrayed in a way that contrasts with many other films, in which the maid is depicted as a symbolic ornament for the upper class and presented from the vantage point of her employers (and her producers), whether as a marginal character in such films as *I Like Mike*, *Two Heart Beats* (*Shtei Dfikot Lev*, 1972), and *A Thousand Little Kisses* (as already discussed), or as a central character in *999 Aliza Mizrahi*. The protagonist (Edna Flidel) of *999 Aliza Mizrahi* is a department-store cleaning woman depicted in the *Sallah Shabbati* manner, a contradictory figure at once naïve and somehow also shrewd. The acting, as in *Sallah Shabbati*, emphasizes almost caricaturally heavy body movements. As in Hebrew literature, the filmic Sephardi woman character is usually assigned the role of the maid, and is presented, even when she is granted a central role, in a patronizing manner.

I Like Mike and *Two Heart Beats* employ the marginal housemaid character to especially emphasize the high status of the foregrounded bourgeois characters with whom she lives (live-in maids are, in fact, quite uncommon in Israel). The maid herself lacks personality and autonomy in a manner reminiscent of the traditional Hollywood depiction of the devoted black servant. In *I Like Mike*, for example, the maid character becomes so depressed in empathetic identification with her saddened employers that they must calm *her* down. This pattern of marginalization of the Sephardi maid character, granted little narrative time and at times even no dialogue whatsoever, has been reproduced even in foreign productions in Israel.

The Arab bomb and the identity crisis of the Arab-Jew.

In *Hanna K.* (1983), the first Hollywood feature to deal sympathetically with the Palestinian question, Constantin Costa-Gavras, by almost completely excluding Oriental Jews from the narrative and mise-en-scène, perpetuates the hegemonic patterns of representing Israeli social life. The very film that attempts to offer an alternative for the Israeli/Palestinian problem, ironically, ignores the schism between East and West that exists also among Jews in Israel by portraying Israel as an exclusively Western entity. The minimal presence of the Jewish "East" consists in the presence of Hanna's maid.

In more alternative fiction, maids have often served as symbolic or synecdochic figures in artistic representations, for example, in Jean Genet's play *Les Bonnes* or Ousmane Sembène's film *La Noire de . . .* (1966), precisely because they exist at the point of convergence of multiple oppressions—as women, as maids, and, often, as in *The House on Chlouch Street*, as members of oppressed ethnic groups. Flaubert's "Un Coeur simple," meanwhile, can be seen as a story which treats a socially degraded maid-character with great stylistic dignity, an exemplum of Auerbach's ideas of a democratization of Western literature deriving, ultimately, from the dissemination of the progressive Judaic principle of "all souls equal before God." While other Israeli films show the maid only in her "professional" function within Ashkenazi "territory," *The House on Chlouch Street* devotes most of Klara's narrative time to events in her home, showing her on her own terrain, where she is independent and even a "boss" herself to her children. In contrast to most Israeli fiction, *The House on Chlouch Street*'s portrayal of the maid's emotionally deep character not only eschews all condescension, but also reinforces spectatorial identification with her struggle as a widowed working mother. When Klara (Gila Almagor) is first seen scrubbing the floor, the act is not presented from the employers' point of view. She is seen from the point of view of her son, the protagonist, who intensely identifies with her feelings of intense shame and hurt, an identification underlined by close shots of his face. His humiliation is exacerbated when Klara's employer, Mrs. Goldstein, enters the house, for her remarks call attention to a painful situation of dependency.

Sami himself is forced to go to work in Mr. Goldstein's metal shop, and there is thus created a homological and familial network of masters and servants: the Ashkenazi woman has a Sephardi maid, and her husband has a Sephardi worker. In contrast to the Sephardi anti-intellectual stereotype, the film depicts Sami as a true bibliophile. When he steals, it is a book he steals (ironically, Gorki's *Earning My Bread*), and his first love is for a librarian. On his first day of work he is humiliated by the authoritarian shop manager, who is racist toward both Arabs and Sephardim. The sequence concludes with a close-up of Sami, with tears slowly streaming from his eyes. An ironic disjunction is created between the image-track and the celebratory music-track, which features a famous singer of independence songs, Yaffa Yarkoni, singing the patriotic classic: "Our little country, after 2,000 years of exile, you're mine alone."

The allusion to the protest movements of the seventies, meanwhile, is strengthened through the sympathetic character of Max (Yossi Pollak), the Ashkenazi Communist, who in a dialogue with Sami, after the strike, predicts that the metal shop workers will continue drilling all their lives and that the current struggle will probably not change things very much. The film emphasizes solidarity between the Sephardi worker and the Ashkenazi leftist. When Max encourages Sami to leave the metal shop for a better future, the conversation is interrupted by two thugs, presumably defending the interests of Mr. Goldstein, who attack Max, the organizer of the workers' strike. The film cuts from the stricken Max, breathing heavily, to Sami, also breathing heavily in the librarian's apartment, while on the soundtrack the cut is virtually "inaudible" since their breathing is completely melded. When Max organizes the workers' strike, another nostalgic old song from the same period, "Kalaniot" ("Anemones"), sung by Shoshana Damari, is heard, provoking a disjunction between its festive good cheer and the quite unidyllic image of the workers' struggle, thus providing a critical perspective toward a historical period generally represented only by tales of Sabra heroics and idealism.

The Imaginary of Inside/Outside

A qualifiedly progressive representation of the Orient is also seen in the films of Nissim Dayan, *Light out of Nowhere* (1973) and *The End of Milton Levi* (*Soffo shel Milton Levi*, 1981). (Dayan also directed for Israeli television *Michel Ezra Safra and His Sons* [*Michel Ezra Safra uVanav*, 1983], based on Amnonn Shamush's novel concerning Syrian Jews before the establishment of Israel.) A quasi-neorealist film, *Light out of Nowhere* was made in black and white and employs location shooting in authentic poor neighborhood locales, using largely nonprofessional actors drawn from a social world not dissimilar to that depicted on the screen. Most of the actors in the film are Sephardi, a rare practice in the early seventies. (Mizrahi, in contrast, employed a mixed cast.)[83] Most of the scenes are shot outdoors—at times with images reminiscent of Pier Paolo Pasolini's *Accattone!* (1961), of people sitting in the sun with sand and gravelstone—and often shot with a handheld camera, which, along with the authentic "street language" spoken in the film, strengthens the impression of documentary veracity.

Light out of Nowhere presents Israeli-born Sephardim in the context of the 1970s, at a time when their world, like the family's culture, is already disintegrating. The protagonist, Shaul (Nissim Levi), is caught between two oppressed family members: on one side, a criminal brother (Abie Zelzberg) who scorns everything belonging to any Establishment framework, and, on the other, a worker-father (Shlomo Basan) who drifts in the grip of poverty, from which it is unlikely he will ever be extricated. Crime, as the brother, Baruch, sees it, is an active way to break out of the social trap, but as the film presents it through Shaul's perspective, this option is also dangerous and could lead to other traps. Shaul, who according to the director, Dayan, has a "healthy moral instinct, a kind of natural immunity against a certain type of fateful mistake,"[84] does not join Baruch's world, but is still not willing to bow his head in hopeless subservience like his father, Avraham. The father encourages Shaul to continue in his way; and the rift between them is not—as in films like *Fortuna*—between the "primitive" country of origin and "modern" Israel. It is rather a rift between the Sephardi laborer in Israel, consigned to unimaginative jobs and whose salary will not extricate his son from the periphery, and the young Shaul, who is quite understandably less than enthusiastic about his future possibilities. In contrast to *Sallah Shabbati*, the lack of motivation for work is not presented as a problem of Oriental mentality but rather as a symptom of the political structure. Within a social system where work implies little future, low work motivation becomes a kind of passive, sullen protest on the part of the exploited. Shaul and his friends refuse to cooperate by performing the roles designated for them and their parents by the Establishment.

Beyond this relatively innocuous gesture of refusal, however, Shaul and his friends ultimately dream of "another place." (In Baruch's case, the dream of "another place" takes on ironic connotations; he dreams of Germany because "there they don't suffocate a man, as they do here.") A Scandinavian woman, because she is from an inaccessible world, provides sexual reassurance in implicit compensation for rejection by Jewish-White society. The Scandinavian prostitute, ironically, contaminates them with disease. The fetishistic longing for "another place" is symptomatic of their dead-end situation. They suffer from the anomie typical of a historical phase prior to the transition to some collective action which would turn them from objects into subjects of the sociopolitical process.

Light out of Nowhere concludes open-endedly, when Shaul, who has no common language either with his family or with his friends, is seen sitting on the sidewalk with his head in his hands. Although his future is left a question mark, the film hints at his sensitive personality and inner strength, as the light out of nowhere within the world embodied by Baruch. (Dayan himself pointed to Shaul's potential as an artist.)[85] Like that of *The House on Chlouch Street*, whose final sequence shows a matured Sami, separating from his past, joining the Israeli army and heading toward a future of his own, the ending of *Light out of Nowhere* suggests an individualistic solution to the collective problem raised. In this sense, the texts undermine their subversive potential, although in the context of the early seventies, and in some ways even today, the films represent a relatively progressive gesture. *Light out of Nowhere*'s falling back on the "inner strength" and sensitivity of a protagonist within an open-ended narrative is typical of the personal cinema (see Chapter 4) with its tendency to foreground "unique" and solitary individuals. The separation of the Sephardi protagonist from his own community—not unlike that of the Ashkenazi protagonists of personal cinema—depoliticizes *Light out of Nowhere*. For here it is not a question of an individual's alienation from his bourgeois milieu but rather from his oppressed people. (Interestingly, the few personal films which focus on Sephardi characters, such as *Dead End Street* [*Kvish lelo Motza*, 1982], *Coco at 19* [*Coco ben 19*, 1985], and the television dramas *Koby and Maly* [*Koby veMaly*, 1977] and to a certain extent Ram Levi's *Bread* (*Lehem*, 1986), carry this theme to an extreme by projecting individualized tragedies of their sensitive, isolated, and politically quiescent protagonists, ending the films with the death of the Sephardi.)

The real politicization in *Light out of Nowhere*, however, is found not so much in the delineation of the central character and his ultimate isolation as in the film's contextual references. The Establishment is consistently presented from the perspective of its victims. The film highlights the dependency relationship between the "nobodies" and the world of power, as well as the pervasive sense of alienation, features also present in Nissim Dayan's later film, *The End of Milton Levi*. In one scene in *Light out of Nowhere*, for example, the street gang members enjoy mocking Israeli sacred cows such as Herzl, Golda Meir, and Abba Eban, deriving their sense of belonging from the camaraderie of sardonic laughter and their common feeling of revolt, their refusal to be "well-behaved kids." (It was in the early seventies that Golda Meir maternalistically chastised the Black Panthers for not being "nice kids.") In another sequence they ridicule a neighborhood type who has enlisted in the army; they grab his army hat, use it for handball and soccer, and tell mocking stories about the army and heroism. Making fun of the army constitutes, in many ways, an indirect expression of rebellious feelings against the Ashkenazi Establishment, for whom high achievement in the army tends to imply a heightened social status. (This same attitude is expressed in *Coco at 19*, another attempt at progressive images.)

In *Light out of Nowhere*, in the Histadrut[86] club sequence, as well, the instructor teaches folk dances—part of the Sabra youth movement tradition[87]—to youth not at all enthusiastic about this foreign culture. They comically transpose words with provocative vulgarity. The innocuous song/dance entitled "The Pomegranate Tree," which describes pastoral nature "from the Dead Sea to Jericho," metamorphoses into a song about farts—an expression of carnivalesque protest against the cultural coercion which imports Israeli-Ashkenazi folklore into Sephardi neighborhoods, instead of encouraging independent creation according to the desires and tastes of the local residents. When a Yiddish-style song is played on the radio, they reject a music which belongs to the world of the Establishment which broadcasts and receives it. The song on the radio stands in opposition to the film's jazzy and Oriental music, more appropriate to the social background. On the soundtrack itself, the musical score at times suggests a possible associative link between Blacks in America and those in Israel, a connection definitely relevant in the era of the Israeli Black Panthers, who took their name from the American movement.

Inside/outside as metaphor: *Light out of Nowhere.*

While institutions like the Histadrut (labor federation) club and the Working Youth are mainly presented in interiors, the neighborhood youths are usually seen in exteriors, in their gathering place, the street. The opposition between indoor/outdoor shots can be seen as metaphorizing, on a homological plane, the relation between "insiders," at the center of action, and the "outsiders," on the margins, outside the official building where their fate is being decided, and where they can never be more than guests. In the Working Youth sequence, for instance, Shaul (along with other Sephardi youths) awaits his turn, shuffling his feet with annoyance. The cut to the Ashkenazi clerk's office emphasizes that he, in contrast to Shaul, is sitting relaxed, eating yogurt. Without even giving Shaul a glance he reads off a list of bureaucratic questions and decides which type of work will suit him.

Establishment representatives are also seen in outdoor shots, in the neighborhood; in these cases they break into the underclass world only in the roles of policemen and municipal inspectors (also Sephardi, as *Light out of Nowhere* shows) securing the implementation of social policy. The sequence in which the inspectors and the police execute the destruction order literalizes the notion of a life being lived on the street, since there is no shelter and when an attempt is made to build one, it is destroyed. Shaul's neighbor (a woman) rebels by shouting: "Our children fight against the Arabs, but that there should be a place for a child to live—that is impossible! Since when has this government cared? Go on, bring those *vuzvuzim* [a nickname for Ashkenazim] from Russia. . . . [88] We won't let you destroy them. ["Them" could refer to both the houses and the children.] Blood will be spilled here." (This shout is heard from the film ten years before the murder of Shimon Yehoshua, the Tel Aviv Sephardi killed by the police while trying to prevent the destruction of his house.) The protesting neighbor is also seen in the distance, in long shot, when she burns the instructor's van and is arrested by the police. The distance of the long shot diminishes identification with the individual incident in favor of a quasi-Brechtian abstraction. From her arrest, there is a cut to a long shot in which two instructors—protected by the police officer—destroy the building in the background, while two family members, one with head in hands and the other embracing him, sit before the building in the middle of the image as the building is being destroyed. An identification, then, is formed with the Sephardi perspective of the neighborhood against the Establishment's violent invasion. The scene concludes with a shot of the burned car, the product of Shaul's neighbor's violence.

In *Light out of Nowhere*, as in *The House on Chlouch Street*, and in contrast to such "bourekas" films as *Fortuna*, the Sephardi woman is not passive. On the contrary, she fights within the limited framework of her possibilities. Her oppressor, furthermore, does not take the form of a monstrous Sephardi man, but rather that of an oppressive Establishment. *Light out of Nowhere* does not ignore the macho behavior of the street youths toward women, but at the same time it demonstrates that the Sephardi woman and man, whatever their differences, are nonetheless victims of the same policy. The woman's violence is presented within the context of a violent policy and, as a consequence, takes on a different signification, in opposition to the stereotypes of *kriza* ("frenzies") and "Oriental irrationality." Here she expresses the anger and violence of a subjugated group which, as Fanon points out, is first and foremost a reaction and rebellion *against* violence, the violence rooted in the asymmetries of power.

4.

Personal Cinema and the Politics of Allegory

Israeli cinema constitutes fertile ground both for allegory and for allegorical inter-pretation. This penchant derives not only from the fact that Israel participates in "Third Worldness" and therefore in the "necessarily allegorical" (Jameson) charac-ter of Third World texts, but also from cultural and historical specificities having to do with Jewish culture and the nature of the Israeli state. The allegorical tradi-tion, at least within the West, is itself deeply rooted in the purposiveness of Jewish conceptions of temporality as expressed in the Hebrew Bible, and in the Judaic emphasis on the ultimate meaningfulness of history. In the Jewish tradition, even food carries a charge of allegorical-historical meaning: the *matzah*, in the Passover Seder, symbolizes the hasty departure from Egypt, and the hard egg, the harshness of slavery, just as the pomegranate, in Rosh Hashana, figures forth the seeds of wisdom.[1] Allegorical expression and interpretation are also linked to the idea of a special or sacred language involving various degrees of concealment; the Torah, as a fragmentary discourse, virtually solicits the hermeneutic deciphering which typifies, for example, the Talmudic commentaries. And the Zionist hermeneutic offers a teleological reading of the ruins and fragments of Jewish history as autho-rizing a return to the Biblical land, suggesting, if only subliminally, a move from cosmic design into political history, from worldly tyranny (the Babylon of exile) to messianic Kingdom.

There are more immediate reasons, however, for the relevance of the category of allegory to Israeli cultural production, reasons having to do with the nature of the Israeli nation/state and the relations between individual and national destiny which obtain there: Israel's status as a nation still in the stage of self-formulation; the shifting borders of the state itself; the constant questioning of the nature of Israeli identity (not only by those displaced by its creation but also by Israelis themselves); the feelings of uncertainty concerning Israel's future; the awareness of collective responsibility for Jewish survival in the wake of the Holocaust; the impact of the various exoduses *from* Israel and the new waves of immigration *to* Israel (in what amounts to a mobile palimpsest of crisscrossing diasporas); the continual debates about "Who is a Jew?"; the incessant pressure for commitment; and the fact that the individual Jewish Israeli, whether he/she wishes or not, is taken outside of Israel as an exemplum of the nation; in sum, all the ways in which the individual is implicated in the collective destiny—all this leads almost inevitably to a kind of national self-consciousness quite likely to generate allegorical forms of expression. Everything militates to create a situation in which the micro-individual is doubled, as it were, by the macro-nation, where the personal and the political, the private and the historical, are inextricably linked, a situation easily engendering implicit or explicit allegories of heroism, isolation, or claustrophobia, in which individual dramas tend to be "writ large" on a national scale.

The Context of Production

Before exploring the allegorical dimension of recent Israeli cinema, however, it is necessary to sketch out the historical and production context of the most recent films. The dominant genres of the previous period—the heroic-nationalist and the "bourekas" films—provoked a first counter-response around the mid- to late sixties; resulting in a harvest of films by a new generation of filmmakers: Uri Zohar's *Hole in the Moon* (*Hor baLevana*, 1965), *Three Days and a Child* (*Shlosha Yamim veYeled*, 1967), and *Take Off* (*Hitromemut*, 1970); Yitzhak Yeshurun's *A Woman in the Next Room* (*Isha baHeder haSheni*, 1967); Micha Shagrir's *The Patrollers* (*HaSayarim*, 1967); Jacques Katmor's *A Woman's Case* (*Mikre Isha*, 1969); Yehuda Ne'eman's *The Dress* (*HaSimla*, 1969); Avraham Hefner's short films *Slower* (*Le'at Yoter*, 1967 [based on a story by Simone de Beauvoir]) and *Sians* (1967); and the films of David Perlov, who after creating lyrical government-assigned documentaries[2] made the fiction feature *The Pill* (*HaGlula*, 1972).[3]

While the earliest genre, the pioneer/heroic-nationalist film, was already losing its preeminence during the sixties, and while "bourekas" films, especially those of Ephraim Kishon and Menahem Golan, were commercially dominant, a new current of personal filmmaking was being formed, a current which viewed itself as the polar opposite of commercial cinema. These filmmakers first formulated their cinematic ideas during the late fifties and early sixties, often while studying abroad (mainly in Paris). Their films betrayed, to various degrees, the influence of the French New Wave as well as of the films of Michelangelo Antonioni and Federico Fellini. Uri Zohar, meanwhile, came to cinema from the theater and from variety shows (a more common path to directing in that period, followed as well by Menahem Golan, Peter Frey, and Yossef Millo). Indeed, some of Zohar's films were marked by a distinct stylistic orientation in some ways close to that of the "bourekas." Zohar was also the first to provide the foundations for a different kind of filmmaking. His first full-length film *Hole in the Moon*, was the first narrative film to use a handheld camera, to work with a new generation of actors (and non-actors), and to subvert classical narrative and traditional psychologism. The thematic orientation of this new trend no longer revolved around collective Zionist/Israeli political and social questions, but rather focused on individual quandaries and "universal" protagonists, as part of an aspiration to create a "quality" cinema free of all sociopolitical obligations. These filmmakers generated a kind of thematic and stylistic paradigm for the personal films of the seventies and eighties, gradually forming a major movement within Israeli cinema, one generally supported by a sympathetic film-critical apparatus.

This movement's contribution must be understood against the backdrop of the Israeli industry during the fifties and sixties. Although there existed, over a decade after the establishment of the state, the requisite technical infrastructure, Israeli cinema remained caught in a kind of historical time-warp, in the sense that it was still at the stage of proving its status as an art form. Whereas Woodrow Wilson could praise D. W. Griffith's *The Birth of a Nation* (1915) as "history written with lightning" and Lenin could insist that "for us, cinema is the most important of all the arts," Israeli Establishment leaders such as Ben-Gurion dismissed cinema as "subculture" and a "waste of time." While the theater profited from governmental subsidies granted by the Ministry of Education and Culture, allowing for nonprofit ventures, films were largely under the auspices of the Ministry of Commerce and Industry. After the Knesset passage of the Encouragement of Israeli Film Law in 1954, the Minister of Commerce and Industry laid the basis for a tax-return policy in 1960. The measure paved the way for the establishment of production companies and the entrance of private entrepreneurs into the industry. Coping with the problem of a small domestic market and the lack of systematic distribution abroad, the tax return helped, during the sixties and especially following the post-1967 economic development, to accelerate the rhythm of production, which now could be aimed at profits from the local market.

At the same time, this system of encouragement left little room for the development of a noncommercial cinema. Awards, such as those granted for completed scripts by the Council for Culture and Arts under the auspices of the Ministry of Education and Culture—annual awards for "quality films" had been given since the early seventies—were not sufficient to finance the actual production of a film and were unable to foster an infrastructure for noncommercial cinema. The box-office failure of the filmmakers' first personal films, meanwhile, tended to jeopardize producers' subsequent support. As a result, relatively long periods separate the first from the second productions of many of these filmmakers. Eight years elapsed, for example, between Yehuda Ne'eman's first film, *The Dress*, and his second, *The Paratroopers*, while nine years separate Yitzhak Yeshurun's first feature, *A Woman in the Next Room*, and his second, *Jocker* (1976). Financial difficulties also tended to lengthen the time between the writing of a script and film's actual production; five years passed, for example, between the writing of Yigal Bursztyn's script for *Belfer* and its production in 1978.

Personal filmmaking during the second half of the sixties through the late seventies remained, therefore, a somewhat infrequent practice. Gradually, however, there evolved an alternative production schema in which small crews, directors, camerapersons, actors, and actresses participated in each other's films. In the sixties, for Micha Shagrir's *The Patrollers*, Avraham Hefner wrote the script and Yehuda Ne'eman was the production manager, while Micha Shagrir helped Yitzhak Yeshurun in the post-production phase of *A Woman in the Next Room*. In the seventies, Gedalia Besser, who played the leading role in Daniel Waxman's *Transit* (1980), also had an important role in Yaki Yosha's *Rocking Horse* (*Susetz*, 1977); the cameraman for both films was Ilan Rosenberg, and the *Transit* filmmaker, Daniel Waxman, played the role of a cameraman in *Rocking Horse*. Various strategies have been employed to finance the films and lower their budgets: 16mm shooting followed by blowing up to 35mm; paid subliminal advertisements; and personal and official loans (for example, from the Ministry of Commerce and Industry). Apart from small private investors or personal financial means, the filmmakers since *Hole in the Moon* have gradually set the pattern of working for a percentage, according to which the cast and crew, rather than being paid a precise amount upon completion of the film, agree to receive a certain share of the film's future profits. The commercial nonviability of the films, however, has had the retroactive effect of making this kind of film work a "labor of love."

The financial difficulties of noncommercial cinema, along with the government's discriminatory preference for other artistic forms and media, led to a struggle by the filmmakers and film critics—and not infrequently the filmmakers were also film critics—for national assistance in producing personal cinema. As part of that effort, a filmmakers' consortium was formed in 1977, a consortium whose participants included Nissim Dayan, Renen Schorr, Yehuda Ne'eman, Nadav Levitan, Rachel Ne'eman, and Uzi Peres. They called themselves the "Kayitz" group—the Hebrew initials standing for "Young Israeli Cinema" but also signifying "Summer"—and they worked to support the project within political circles. In a manifesto published in the magazine *Kolnoa*, they emphasized their shared aspiration for an innovative film language but insisted that they shared no single ideology or uniform aesthetic taste. They shared, rather, a production strategy, the belief that Israeli films must be produced for low budgets and with small crews; in short, they must be produced in a manner appropriate to actual conditions in Israel. A change in government policy toward Israeli cinema, it was hoped, "will enable a director and producer to make a film at least once a year without depending on the box office; the failure of a film will not hinder the future possibility of a filmmaker's continuing to direct films."[4]

The filmmakers' lobbying resulted in the establishment of the Fund for the Encouragement of Original Quality Films in 1978. Establishment of this fund helped to accelerate the production of noncommercial cinema, which also helped young filmmakers in the production of their first feature films. Whereas earlier films had been made thanks to awards and scholarships (which during the early seventies assisted such films as Avraham Hefner's *Where is Daniel Wax?* [*Le'an Ne'elam Daniel Wax?*, 1974], Dan Wolman's *My Michael*, and Yehuda Ne'eman's *The Paratroopers*), the new method assisted a film's production through partial financing (about $70,000)—a system inspired by Western European models such as those of France, Germany, Holland, Belgium, and Sweden. Daniel Waxman's *Transit*, Avi Cohen's *The Real Game* (*HaMishak haAmiti*, 1980), Yeod Levanon's *Not for Broadcast* (*Lo leShidur*, 1981), Shimon Dotan's *Repeat Dive* (*Tzlila Hozeret*, 1982), and Eitan Green's *Lena* (1982), for example, were all first features supported by the Fund for the Encouragement of Original Quality Films. During the eighties, as a result, noncommercial personal cinema has achieved relative dominance, amounting, at times, to almost half of film production (Menahem Golan's departure for Hollywood reduced the number of non-personal productions in Israel, at least until recently when he began producing foreign films in Israel).

At the same time, the encouragement of "quality films" was accompanied by new obstacles for commercial cinema. One of the measures taken by the Ministry of Commerce and Industry to encourage the Israeli film industry consisted of a 2.5 percent tax on each ticket sold for a foreign film—a sum which was then given to the Public Fund for Encouraging the Israeli Film under the ministry's auspices. The fund board consists of representatives of movie-theater owners, distributors, producers, filmmakers, and members of the Center for the Israeli Film—an organ of the Ministry of Commerce and Industry. The Public Fund for Encouraging the Israeli Film gave a tax rebate of 8.3 New Shekels[5] on each ticket sold for Israeli films, meaning that the more successful the film the more "returns." The return was not restricted until recent years, when it was limited to 300,000 spectators, and later to 100,000. Filmmakers were fighting, in other words, for an additional bonus based not on quantity but rather on quality. The changed policy and the limitation on the returns discouraged investors; this policy was partially responsible for the virtual disappearance of "bourekas" films in this period.[6]

Although the original goal of the Fund for Encouragement of Original Quality Films was to assist ten film projects per year by providing half of the production costs, in fact the fund could only provide about a third of the costs and managed to support no more than six films per year. As many film critics have pointed out, the crux of the problem lies in governmental discrimination against the cinema and favoritism toward other arts. The Council for Culture and Arts gives only 2.7 percent of its budget ($13 million) to films, while theater, for example, receives 21.3 percent of this budget, museums 24.5 percent, and symphony orchestras 19.4 percent. Furthermore, a fifth of the cinema budget goes for the Israeli Film Institute, thus draining support from the production of films. The hope that the funded "quality films" would be profitable, thus fostering future funding activities, proved to be vain, as did the more general hopes for international distribution. In this sense, it remains difficult to speak of a well-established state apparatus for Israeli cinema.

Compared with the late sixties, when personal filmmaking began, however, one does notice a certain progress. The early filmmakers of the "Israeli New Wave" (another honorific granted by critics) were operating in a context deprived of cinematheques, film societies, and academic departments. Apart from making films, they were preoccupied with gaining intellectual recognition and cultural prestige for film art, hoping to create an Israeli cinema which would be a means for intellectual expression and a springboard for discussion. In the early seventies the Israeli Film Institute, the municipal cinematheque, and the film departments in Tel Aviv University and Beit Tzvi School were established, contributing to a new generation of filmmaking and to a broader dissemination of film culture; film magazines such as *Kolnoa* and *Close-Up* contributed their share; and in the eighties, the inauguration of the Jerusalem Film Archives, the success of the Jerusalem Film Festival, and the International Student Film Festival, initiated by Tel Aviv University students, all contributed to the prestige and divulgation of a film culture virtually nonexistent in the late sixties and early seventies.

Reflexivity, Parody and the Zionist Epic

Unlike the French New Wave, the personal filmmakers were the heirs neither of a well-established visual culture nor of a more experimentally oriented cinematic tradition. Despite the lack of a national avant-garde filmic intertext, Uri Zohar's work, and specifically his *Hole in the Moon*, managed to create a nonconventional cinema fully imbricated in the Israeli imaginary. Zohar's oeuvre of eleven feature films is deeply rooted in popular entertainment. Apart from his non-mainstream films such as *Hole in the Moon*, *Three Days and a Child*, *Take Off*, and the trilogy *Peeping Toms* (*Metzitzim*, 1972), *Big Eyes* (*Einayeem Gdolot*, 1974), and *Save the Lifeguard* (*Hatzilu et haMatzil*, 1967), he also directed more conventional films, largely comedies, such as *Moishe Vintelator* (1966) and *Our Neighborhood*. Zohar played leading roles in most of his films. (He had begun his career alongside Topol in the military entertainment troupe HaNahal and continued with Green Onion.) He also acted in the films of others: in the heroic-nationalist films, such as *Pillar of Fire* and Raphael Neussbaum's *Blazing Sands* (*Holot Lohatim*, 1960) (and even a brief appearance in *Exodus*), in the role of the archetypical Israeli Sabra, as well as in the popular "bourekas" films such as Golan's *999 Aliza Mizrahi* and George Ovadia's *They Call Me Shmil* (*Kor'im Shmil*, 1973). Zohar's deep involvement in Israeli popular entertainment sets him apart from most of the personal filmmakers, making him a somewhat atypical figure. In interviews, Zohar, unlike the film critics and "quality filmmakers," did not attack commercial cinema as "bad" cinema. Playing leading roles in most of his films—partially because he himself was the "lowest-paid actor he could get"[7]—Zohar managed to work intensively like Menahem Golan and Ephraim Kishon, two major figures in the Israeli film industry. Although Zohar was ultimately more interested in making maverick films like *Hole in the Moon*, that film's commercial failure forced him into a more conventional, narrative direction. Yet, in many ways, he carried his unconventional style into some of his narrative films, and even into the dozens of short promotional films and his famous early seventies television series, *Lul*.[8]

The experimental film *Hole in the Moon* was produced with a relatively low budget of $100,000—an amount made available through the producer Mordechai Navon (Geva Studio)—initiating the "percentage method" by which the crew and cast were paid a minimal amount along with a percentage of the film's future profits. The film, which was received enthusiastically at various film festivals (Cannes, Lucarno) and in film reviews (in *Sight and Sound*, *Variety*, *New York Times*, *Le Monde*, *Positif*, *Cinema 65*), is based on an idea by Zohar himself, who also directed, cast the actors, played the major role, and supervised the editing, while collaborating as well with writer Amos Kenan (script),[9] artist Yigal Tumarki (decor), Michel Columbieu (music), and Ana Gurit (editing), as well as with leading Israeli actors-entertainers.

Hole in the Moon was inspired by Adolfas Mekas' *Hallelujah the Hills* (1963), which Uri Zohar saw during a visit to Paris, an inspiration especially reflected in the parodic-reflexive mode of the film. *Hole in the Moon* allegorizes both filmmaking itself and the Zionist master-narrative. Its anti-illusionistic strategies raise questions not simply with regard to the coherence of the fictive world it creates, but also, as we shall see, with regard to the coherence of Zionist-realist fiction. Zohar's Cervantic strategy makes of the critique of cinematic fictions the point of departure for the interrogation of a socially constituted world.

The fractured "story" of the film centers on Tzelnick (Uri Zohar), who after arriving by raft in the port of Jaffa, goes south and opens a kiosk in the Negev desert. Upon waking the next morning he discovers that another kiosk has been established across from his by Mizrahi (Avraham Hefner), who also came "straight from nowhere—but from another nowhere."[10] In the absence of customers in the middle of the desert, the newcomers sell each other their merchandise. They imagine a fata morgana in the form of a beautiful woman (the French actress Christiane Dancourt)—a vision which subsequently transmutes into reality and multiplies into many beautiful women. While they stand bedazzled, a guest (Topol, very much associated with *Sallah Shabbati* at that time) arrives and tells them, "You want to be somebody?—make films. Take me as an example." Following his advice, Tzelnick and Mizrahi take a camera from Uri Zohar and his crew, who are shooting *Hole in the Moon*. Novices in filmmaking, the two create ex nihilo a "chaos" of clashing generic worlds in which cowboys shoot Arabs, a Samurai fights against Tarzan, and Charlie Chaplin does his famous cakewalk across a typical Western landscape. When Mizrahi shouts for them to stop, Indians attack him with an axe. When he shouts "cut," the Indians are freeze-framed in their own act of "cutting." But soon someone shouts again and the previous freeze frames "melt" and movement resumes, including the axing of Mizrahi. Mizrahi's spirit advises Tzelnick to avoid disaster, to follow a system: "Bring a specialist for humor, for psychoanalysis, for love, and for violence. These are the four elements on which the system of cinema is built. And bring many beautiful women."

Screen tests for young women begin, and experts discourse on the "theory" of the "four elements" as well as their various juxtapositions and permutations. This parodic initiation into the codes of filmmaking structures *Hole in the Moon* and furnishes, in a classical *mise-en-abîme*, the basis for the construction of the cinematic-fictive world of the film-within-the-film, in an atmosphere of surreal nonsensicality reminiscent at once of Gabriel García Márquez and Mel Brooks. A gorilla hostile to its own role angrily razes the cardboard film-town, a razing followed by Zionist-style speeches about construction, creation, fruitfulness, and the establishment of a "real" place to live in. The workers now build a city of concrete rather than cardboard, and the women get pregnant, but since Tzelnick and Mizrahi's script (Mizrahi meanwhile having been "resurrected") does not specify the date of birth, the women stay pregnant for eleven months. Although the filmmakers have the powers to decide on an ending, they seem impotent in a world that has by now taken on its own "reality," with its own codes and laws. In this hallucinated city where the villains are tired of their role as villains and the good guys are bored with being good, and where the gangsters, cowboys, and Indians have no energy left for fighting, where women feel cheated out of their right to give birth, the people organize and rebel against their creators—a protest which culminates in the filmmakers being put to death by the enraged mob.

Hole in the Moon was the first, and remains the most radical, Israeli film to experiment with cinematic language and subvert the classical narrative codes typifying the heroic-nationalist films of the period. The conventional decorum of the fiction film is here completely subverted. The modernist narrative of *Hole in the Moon* foregrounds the cinematic construction and demands active-playful engagement on the part of the spectator. In a manner reminiscent of alternative cinema, especially in the sixties (the works of Bruce Connor, Kenneth Anger, and Adolfas Mekas), the film's reflexivity is also anti-illusionistic. The film calls attention to its own status as a fictive construct and, more generally, to the status of all films as artifacts. The arbitrary nature of film form is first evoked by the very title "hole in the moon," a phrase with no clear indexical relationship to the film (the original title—"Let's Make a Movie"—pointed even more flagrantly to the film's reflexivity). The film never shows the promised moon of the title, nor its hole, much as Luis Buñuel never gives us the announced Andalusian dog. In both cases, the refusal itself evokes the fantastic possibilities of film. As Zohar himself said of the title:

In the moon there is no hole. Any normal person knows that the moon is complete and has no hole. But *Hole in the Moon* is a film. And if *Hole in the Moon* is a film then it could show a hole in the moon; and this is the reason

Constructing film/constructing the nation: Parodic analogies in *Hole in the Moon*.

for the film's title. *If Hole in the Moon* were not a film, it would not have been given this name, since then the moon would not have a hole.[11]

The absurdity of the title, then, points to the film's subversion of the concept of realism; images, rather than reveal the world, reveal themselves.

Freeing itself from the illusionist idiom, *Hole in the Moon* demonstrates narrative filmmaking to be a process of mediation, a process embedded in every genre, be it the Western or the melodrama, and permeating every cinematic code from montage to mise-en-scène. Although the film is largely based on the generic conventions of the thirties' crazy-chase comedy, its intertext is much broader. The parodic "double-voiced" discourse of the film revives virtually all the classical genres, initially as part of Tzelnick and Mizrahi's imaginary "film-town" but soon gaining independent status "outside" of the filmmakers' subjectivity. The film alludes to various archetypes within film history, both individual personae such as Charlie Chaplin, Tarzan, and King Kong, and larger generic entities such as cowboys, Indians, cabaret hookers, gangsters, and private eyes, as well as specific types from Israeli film history: pioneers, the Palmach, the Arabs. In addition, *Hole in the Moon* deploys a variety of generic codes, often especially foregrounded within specific segments: the Western duel, the hara-kiri of Samurai films, the bank robbery of the gangster film, the happy ending of the melodrama (a handicapped woman suddenly stands up, crying, "I can walk"), the physical play of slapstick comedy, the absurd interweaving of imagination and "reality," typical of Surrealist cinema and cinéma-vérité-style interviews (Uri Zohar actually conducted interviews with women who responded to ads for *Hole in the Moon*'s screen tests). *Hole in the Moon* also refers to literary figures such as Don Quixote, Hamlet, and Tom Jones, and indulges in frequent filmic homages. In a Godardian distanciated "love scene," for example, the actors' faces show not a trace of emotion and the repeated kisses are performed in a monotonous rhythm, while the voice-over expatiates on the lack of relation between marriage and love. (Written material in French here reinforces the allusion to the New Wave.) The film also refers to Hollywood type-casting; the actors play multiple roles, but within the same type: Shoshick Shani, for instance, is cast as the "vamp" or "femme fatale," Arik Lavi as the "good guy," Shmuel Kraus as the "bad guy," and Ze'ev Berlinski as the "intellectual." Another sequence especially lampoons the Hollywood star system. An actress (Shoshick Shani) descends regally from a plane and performs the requisite star gestures and poses for the assembled admirers and cameras. A Hollywood-style "director's chair" serves as throne for a dog, fitted out with a Hollywood-style cap for protection from the sun.

Hole in the Moon also deploys specifically cinematic codes to deconstruct the traditional illusion of reality fostered by classical narrative cinema. Zohar uses the freeze frame in a quasi-Cervantic fashion to congeal crucial actions such as the Indian's attempt to rape an eager blonde woman or his attempt to kill a somewhat less eager Mizrahi, thus extending the discursive time devoted to especially dramatic moments. The editing, meanwhile, lampoons the classical Western duel: the two combatants are seen to fall over each other several times, each time from a different angle. A similarly whimsical approach to causality occurs in another example of "variorum" editing: Tzelnick's morning jog is rendered by showing him running in different directions with rapid cuts on each shot. In another instance, the Hamlet character, after his "to be or not to be" soliloquy, jumps into an empty swimming pool. We expect the next shot to show him crashing into the pool floor, but instead we see a man falling from a high building onto a donkey. The movement, as in Bruce Connor's compilation films, is continuous but carried across a completely discontinuous space. In other instances, the montage calls attention to the film medium as mediating other arts. One of the screen tests features a woman dancing in a single space, but the editing makes her fly in quantum leaps around the stage. Then, in a kind of cinematic "commutation test," we see the same dance filmed in static long shot; this time, the woman's grace and agility vanish and her clumsiness becomes visible.

Hole in the Moon exercises a kind of filmic pedagogy; it initiates the spectator into the cinematic codes. The hyperbolic virtuoso display of fast motion, slow motion, reverse movement, shots in negative, and exacerbatedly high and low angles disrupts the "natural" harmony and coherence of the images. Rather than foster homogeneity, the film catalyzes the clash of codes: Tarzan's violence is accompanied by gentle classical music, and television reportage techniques are used to relay fairy-tale-like stories. We are made to witness the preparation for shooting—for example, the sheriff applying make-up for his role—as well as the post-synchronization techniques by which image and sound are melded into a factitious unity. As an airplane lands, for example, we see a sound technician dubbing the appropriate whooshing sound into a microphone. The devices are laid bare, at times quite literally, as when the unusual spectacle of a love scene between gorilla and blonde is interrupted when the ape's mask begins to fall, thus exposing the actor's face.

The specialist lectures within the film playfully deconstruct filmic schemas and academic categorizations. The psychoanalyst "works on" the neuroses of women who hope to participate in *Hole in the Moon*. As he gobbles down enormous quantities of food, he offers paternalistic advice, largely having to do with sexuality. (The psychoanalyst is played by Dan Ben-Amotz, a bohemian writer-celebrity known for his sexual escapades, thus adding another level of irony for the Israeli spectator.) He tells one woman, for example, that she will never go far unless she learns to "give"—a word which in the sexist conventions of Hebrew slang also refers to the woman lending her body to the man, who "takes." Zohar thus lampoons both psychoanalysis and filmmaking as two realms obsessed with sex. The other putative "experts"—on humor, violence, and love—purvey nothing more than cinematic clichés. While the examples proposed by the lecturers are obviously derived from filmic convention—slapstick pies in the face offered as examples of "humor"—the conventions are named and designated rather than actually used for spectatorial gratification. The humor does not provoke laughter, just as the reconstructions of violent and romantic scenes do not promote either tension or eroticism, since the scenes are decontextualized, fragmented, and performed in a mechanical manner. The standard analytical categorizations are also ridiculed as gratuitous and artificial segregations: the teacher on "humor," for example, refuses to explain the "violence"—which has resulted from his demonstrations of slapstick—on the grounds that violence does not form part of his area of specialization.

Hole in the Moon calls attention, furthermore, to its own process of production. During the screen-test sequences, the clapboard is inscribed with the words "Hole in the Moon," marked with the actual dates of production. These sequences form part of *Hole in the Moon*'s story, i.e., of Tzelnick and Mizrahi's attempt to create a film, and thus refer both to the film itself and to the film-within-the-film. During the interviews and screen tests for *Hole in the Moon*, Uri Zohar appears as himself, thus luring the women to believe it is an actual test, the "chance of a lifetime" to work with the famous entertainer, Uri Zohar. (The film's reflexivity, however, has little place for any reflection or interrogation of the phallocratic processes of film production.) Authentic sound from the actual shooting is incorporated—for instance, the dialogue of crew members asking for Uri Zohar's opinion—thus blurring the boundaries between *Hole in the Moon* and the film-within-the-film. *Hole in the Moon* at times reveals its own filming. During a dialogue, the camera moves back to a long shot which discloses the crew of *Hole in the Moon* as they accompany the shooting of the dialogue (about the nature of the characters in Tzelnick and Mizrahi's film). At several points, Tzelnick and Mizrahi's camera moves directly to face the camera of *Hole in the Moon*, i.e., the spectator, thus (as with the actors' direct address to the camera) breaking the inviolability of the fictional space. In calling attention to its own making, *Hole in the Moon* adopts what one might call the *8 1/2* principle, i.e., a strategy by which the chaotic attempt at filmmaking depicted by the film is compensated for and redeemed, as it were, by the alternative order of the film itself (*8 1/2*, *Hole in the Moon*) in which the chaos is depicted. The filmmakers in *Hole in the Moon*, despite their great effort and despite the specialists' lectures, are unable to construct an orderly, decorous filmic world; yet the spectator is left, nonetheless, with the ordered disorder of *Hole in the Moon* itself. The filmic palimpsest, the dialogue of textual citations in the middle of the Negev, finally constructs itself on the deconstruction of its own codes, creating the syncretic ideolect which is *Hole in the Moon* itself.

What sets *Hole in the Moon* apart from the overwhelming majority of the "Israeli New Wave" films is its adaptation of alternative-cinema strategies to a specifically Israeli context. The film's subversion of classical narrative and of ossified generic conventions is interwoven with parodic references to Zionist cinema. The basic narrative of *Hole in the Moon* relays the Zionist "master narrative," but this time in a comic register. Pursuing their vision of a vibrant new world, the immigrants arrive in the desert. Despite obstacles, their dream becomes a reality: the desert is made to bloom. The Zionist construction, posited as ex nihilo, suggests a parallel hope for the construction of a viable film industry which could transcend the obstacles and become an energetic, blossoming cinema, which would be another "miracle" of construction. *Hole in the Moon* is itself a pioneering film, making way for innovative cinematic strategies, production methods, and thematic orientations. This fantastic voyage is located in the classical site of Zionist myth: the desert. The Zionist vision of making-the-desert-bloom and the masculinist fantasy of beautiful women in *Hole in the Moon* become "reality" at the power of will; the fata morgana turns into "reality" when the visionaires take the initiative and move into the world of "action." As in Herzl's slogan: "If you wish, it is not just a legend," Mizrahi says, "If I wish, here, in this place, a whole city will be established." Paralleling Tzelnick and Mizrahi's foundation of a desert civilization, *Hole in the Moon* offers, in this black-and-white film, a dominant white tone that captures the feeling of a relentless local sun, thus suggesting the potentiality of a cinema that does not repress its topographical context.

From another point of view, the filmmakers' struggle in *Hole in the Moon* can be seen as analogizing the Zionist struggle. Yet the appropriation of Zionist teleology, fictionally concretized in the heroic-nationalist genre, is presented without the usual clear-cut beginning, middle, and end, in an episodic structure that allows for various trajectories, thus opening up to the imagination the myriad directions in which Zionist projects might have evolved. From the film's perspective, as also expressed by Uri Zohar, the success of the pioneering vision, the existence of the country itself, was "an ongoing miracle,"[12] not unlike that of the art work, one involving the conceptualization and the concretization of a fantasized desired world. The analogy suggests Zionist astonishment at the success of its own enterprise. Here the success is not attributed solely to the metaphysical value of the Jewish resurrection and renaissance, however; rather, the film adopts a more humorous and playful perspective toward a "miracle" associated with the artistic process and, by analogy, with the magic of film itself. The unproblematized religious or at least idealist view of Zionist "miracles" is here associated with a quasimystical view of art.

The "miracle" of Zionism allegorized in the film also takes place, according to Uri Zohar, on a daily basis:

> The difference between *Hole in the Moon* and other fiction films has to do with the fact that these miracles take place here in the country everyday and each day and each hour; these miracles verify and reaffirm that what is most unreal, the thing that transcends the wildest imagination, can also become real. We do not refer to that historical miracle of the actual Renaissance and resurrection of our people, rather to the "little" miracles, daily ones, such as an official ceremony in a desolate place resulting in the building of a city in the middle of the Negev desert.[13]

Tzelnick and Mizrahi, in this sense, recapitulate what Zohar sees as the experience of Ben-Gurion, who "looked at the map, put his finger on an empty spot, and thus, where there had been nothing, the town of Arad was established. For what kind of a mad dreamer would come to such an empty, distant, and dangerous place?"[14] Zohar's vision of these events, it goes without saying, is somewhat naïve and romantic, for the historical prototype of their filmic "development town" in fact was the product of a well-considered policy, one which was imposed on the newcomers rather than their spontaneous creation.

Hole in the Moon's protagonists are not always able to dominate the world they have dreamed. When their world takes on autonomous life, with its own laws, the two visionaries begin to lose control. Conflict becomes inevitable, and the created world brings about the end of its creators. In the world of action, it is suggested, little room is left for the dreamers; the pragmatists, therefore, take control. In this sense, the film elegiacally laments the passing of the vanished original dreamer-poets of a Zionism now handed over to a generation of unimaginative bureaucrats.

That the schlemiel poets are led to their own death by the Golem they themselves created implies, ultimately, a Romantic nostalgic view of early Zionist leaders. Like Tzelnick and Mizrahi, the early Zionists are presumed to have been sympathetic dreamers, rather like magicians surprised by the efficacy of their own magic. Despite its local formal subversions, then, *Hole in the Moon* ultimately reproduces the liberal myth, first promulgated in the late fifties, of lost Zionist "innocence"—a myth pervading personal cinema.

Within its basically Zionist orientation, the film does, nevertheless, offer a parodic representation of the Zionist epic. The first sequence already plays off the mythical relation of the Jew to the Holy Land. Within an anachronistic mise-en-scène, dressed in a modern suit, but arriving on an old raft, Tzelnick's arrival encapsulates the older generation's Jewish dream of Aliya. Tzelnick's disembarking gives way to an image typical of Zionist propaganda films, that of kissing the ground of the Holy Land. We see Tzelnick in long shot kissing the ground, underlined by the dubbed "smack" of a kiss. The following close shot shows his face marked with mud in the shape of lips; the land, it is implied, has kissed him back. Like the pioneers in the heroic-nationalist films, Tzelnick arrives in the desert to found a settlement. On his T-shirt is written "HaPoel Tzelnick" ("The Worker Tzelnick"). "HaPoel" evokes the Histadrut sporting association established in 1924. The allusion, then, associates the individual Tzelnick doing his morning jogging in the desert with the socializing infrastructure established in the first decades.

In its parody of Zionist fiction, the film also presents an oxymoronic figure surrounded by Israeli associations—the prostitute pioneer (Zaharira Harifai)—whose gestures are reminiscent of silent film and whose style of singing is more appropriate to the teens and twenties than the sixties. The opening lyrics present a patriotic attitude toward the land, but the image contradicts her words: the place where she walks is desolate, and attached to her heart is not the daffodil of the lyrics but rather a thorn. The lyrics about justice and equality soon turn into a brazen call for sexual nondiscrimination. Since she has slept with all the pioneers and is now pregnant, "all the pioneers will be the proud father." A Zionist demagogue, meanwhile, delivers a pathos-filled speech—in a manner and accent associated with the founding fathers—encouraging the "brothers" not to despair because the enemy has destroyed their homes, but to proudly and unitedly rebuild their homes, while the workers build the town. The speech clearly parodies the Zionist style and exaggerates the hope of "resurrection from the ashes." The practical Zionism of one-acre-after-another is also ridiculed, not only in the speech but also in a sequence where the camera follows a series of workers with each handing a brick to the next in line until the last one throws it away.

The construction and progress are accompanied by propaganda exhorting Israelis to "be fruitful and multiply," an important issue within the politicized demographics of Israel. The film here cuts to tents specially constructed as part of a projected child-production industry. The screen tests, meanwhile, parody the style of Zionist pathos, a style pervading a wide range of Zionist discourses: newspaper editorials, travel literature, children's textbooks, theatrical productions, newsreels, and propaganda films. The film reveals the implementation of Zionist education in Israel, here in the ridiculous form of aspiring actresses reciting Zionist texts in the declamatory style taught in Israeli schools. Uri Zohar, directing their performances, accentuates the incongruous and grotesque. One woman is asked to recite the Zionist lyrics of "Stronger Will Be Our Brothers' Hands" in a sexy voice, while another, dressed as a cowgirl and riding a horse, is made to read the manifesto of the First Zionist Congress. When she has difficulty recalling the test, the film cuts to a portrait of Herzl, who initiated the First Congress, hanging in the Knesset and being dusted off by a janitor. The primordial dreamer of Zionism is now a mere decorative object in the central Zionist institution.

The film also does not completely neglect the pioneer/Arab conflict. By developing the imagery of Westerns, of gun-toting cowboys on horseback and evil Indians emitting bone-chilling yelps, *Hole in the Moon* hints at a structural analogy between the pioneer and the Western genres. The pioneer man and woman work the land, and the woman recites, in the emotive Russian style, the famous pioneer song "God Will Build the Galilee" ("El Yivhen haGalilah"). The song is interrupted by muffled sounds in Arabic, and the pioneers realize that they are about to be attacked. This formulaic Arabs-attack-settlers scene is suddenly interrupted, however, when the film freezes the Arab attack. Later, the Arab characters make an impassioned appeal to the filmmakers: "Why must we always play the bad guys?" they complain, "Why can't we, just once, play the good guys?" (One of the three "Arabs" is painted black, alluding to the Hollywood practice of having White actors play in blackface.) Mizrahi and Tzelnick, astonished at the unusual question, look at each other in amazement, and Mizrahi answers with a question: "Are you abnormal? Good guys? But aren't you Arabs?" The "Arabs" repeat their plea in childlike unison, forcing the two filmmakers into an argument:

MIZRAHI: But they are Arabs, Tzelnick.
TZELNICK: This is cinema!
MIZRAHI: But that's why . . .
TZELNICK: This-is-cinema!
TZELNICK AND MIZRAHI TO THE ARAB CHARACTERS: It's all right.
THE "ARABS": Thank you.
TZELNICK: But only one little scene!

The "Arabs" accept the deal and make a gesture suggesting that this unusual scene will also be unusually brief. Tzelnick's rationale for changing the traditional distribution of hero and villain roles inherited from Zionist Manicheism derives from the view of the artistic imagination as shattering the social consensus. On the

From the Far West to the Near East: The "Arabs" in the saloon in *Hole in the Moon*.

screen, the impossible becomes possible—a view which somewhat anticipates the cinema of the eighties in which Arabs no longer constitute "bad objects" within the narrative, and where Arab actors represent Arab characters and even exert an influence on the production process.

The next sequence parodies the canonized imagery of the heroic-nationalist films, largely by inverting typical patterns of narrative structure and characterization. This time three Arab characters carry the hoes as they dance and sing in an Arabic accent, "God will build the Galilee, *wallak*" (a common Arabic expression). Suddenly they realize along with the spectator—in a parodic recasting of the identification mechanisms of the heroic-nationalist genre—that three Jewish pioneers in Russian dress are aiming guns at them. The peaceful Arab-pioneers wave a white flag, and the Russian-Jewish pioneers throw away their guns and shout, "Our dear cousins," as the two groups embrace. Freeze frames and accelerated motion call attention to the purely cinematic nature of a utopia made possible only by the filmic imaginary.

Hole in the Moon subverts the traditional imagery only up to a certain point, however. The Arabs, now cast as "good," are made to sing in Hebrew a Jewish pioneer song, thus still associating pioneer ideology with the heroes, and only transferring certain formal elements (Russian dress) to the antagonists. Eliding a possible Arab perspective, the inversion, in sum, is more formal than real. In fact, the film allegorically laments the deterioration of early pioneering culture. While building the city, and realizing the visionaries' hopes, the new world acquires codes quite distant from the intentions of the visionaries, a situation where pragmatic demagogues have taken over from the creative idealists. This view is prophetic in many ways of the nostalgia for early Zionism that will characterize the seventies and eighties.[15] Following the death of Tzelnick and Mizrahi, the last shot of the film shows the Messiah, in extreme long shot, walking on the water, and then almost immediately sinking—clearly an allegory of vanished charisma. At the same time, perennial Jewish irreverence combines with Sabra culture's ironic attitude toward the outward expression of idealism to produce a carnivalesque look at the end of a mythical figure like the Messiah. Even the death of Tzelnick and Mizrahi is not final, however; after their demise, they place flowers on their own tombs.

Personal Cinema and the Diverse New Waves

In Israel, as in much of the world, the various new wave movements—Italian neorealism, the French New Wave, the New German Cinema—had immense importance in gaining prestige for the art film and for the director-auteur and in opening up film culture worldwide. The influence of the French New Wave, especially on many of the young personal filmmakers such as Yitzhak Yeshurun, Yehuda Ne'eman, and Jacques Katmor, results in a slightly different orientation from the parodic strategies of *Hole in the Moon* and several other films in a similar parodic-reflexive mode, namely Uri Zohar's *Take Off*,[16] Boaz Davidson's *Snail* (*Shablul*, 1970), and Benjamin Hayeem's *The Black Banana* (*HaBanana haSh'hora*, 1977). These later films fuse the subversion of classical narrative with the parody of certain myths and, at times, subvert certain institutions such as puritanical bourgeois sexual codes in *Take Off* or the religious establishment in *Snail* and *The Black Banana*—all within typically Israeli imagery, scenery, and dialogue. Films like *A Woman in the Next Room*, *The Dress*, and *A Woman's Case*, meanwhile, repress such references, aspiring instead toward a rarefied Gallic look and atmosphere. While Zohar's *Hole in the Moon* represents, in many ways, a reaction against the heroic-nationalist films, most personal films reflect a strong reaction against "bourekas" films by choosing to be hermetically introspective within an intimist, understated style. Zohar's films, in contrast, even when dealing with personal themes such as marginality, incorporate certain features associated with the "bourekas" such as "vulgar" scenes and externalized, expressive dialogues.

The somewhat acritical valorization of the French New Wave in the personal filmmaking of the late sixties is evident everywhere: in thematic emphases, in the imitation or quotations of specific segments, in the "Frenchification" of the protagonists, and in the deployment of narrative and cinematic codes. Most of the films develop a serious tone, however, developing neither the ironic, subversive charm that typified the early films of Jean-Luc Godard and François Truffaut nor the intellectualized hieratic poeticism of Alain Resnais and Marguerite Duras. The themes of *A Woman in the Next Room* (the original title of the script, which was written in Paris in French, was "Variations sur une thème d'amour"), *The Dress* (its English title was "Boys and Girls"), and *A Woman's Case* concern the world of the individual filtered through the relationship between a man and a woman. The bohemian characters live in a solipsistic world, out of touch with ambient reality, with souls seemingly more French than Israeli. The films do not end in conventional forms of closure; indeed, a refusal of closure and a fondness for open endings and indeterminacy form an important mark of personal filmmaking.

In *A Woman in the Next Room*, a middle-aged couple's deteriorating relationship, taking place in the house of a younger couple, leads to the middle-aged man sleeping with the younger woman; yet the film ends with him looking at his sleeping wife. The three episodes that constitute *The Dress*—"The Dress," "The Letter," and "The Return of Thomas"—revolve around attempts at communicating. The reconstitution of a couple, however, leaves the protagonist alone. "The Return of Thomas," in particular, is reminiscent of Truffaut's *Jules and Jim* in its triangular love affair of two men and a woman. In *A Woman's Case*, the one-day affair between a woman, a sculptor's model, and an advertiser ends with her death. The themes of love, individuality, and marginality, in these films, are not enlisted in the construction of an emotional world of character and action. Eschewing psychologism, the films tend not to foster identification. They minimize dialogue, as if the mere presence of words would necessarily detract from the visual. Emotions, when expressed, are rarely expressed directly, while the acting style is subdued, employing restrained gestural codes and reserved facial expressions. The camera avoids the psychologism of close-ups in favor of an impassive look, while the montage avoids analytical editing in favor of a more experimental juxtaposition of shots that blocks spectatorial empathy with engaging characters and sweeping emotions.

In *A Woman in the Next Room*, for example, the distant look at the characters' melancholy and alienation is largely achieved through the refusal of dramatization in the acting as well as by the frequent use of long shots. In *The Dress*, in the episode "The Return of Thomas," the declarations of love are proffered in long shot and in an understated manner. In "The Letter" episode, the manly Sabra unemotional style is evoked by the Ray Ban sun glasses the protagonist wears virtually throughout the episode. The characters' manner, in other words, is synchronous with the film's understated style that masks the emotional dynamics not only within the characters but also within the narrative itself. In *A Woman's Case*, the intimation of the death of the woman protagonist in the first sequence minimizes dramatic tension. The highly understated end of the film devotes minimal narrative time to her death: As part of a play, the man stretches a cloth on her face, she says, "Stop," and the film cuts to the final shot—her lifeless form pushed down the hospital corridor.

The Dress and *A Woman's Case*, in particular, proliferate self-referential gestures à la Godard. The flirtation set in a library in *The Dress* provides the pretext for innumerable image and soundtrack allusions to books. The young librarian recommends to an old man a number of *série noir*–style novels: *Murder on the West Coast, Fu Manchu, The Deadly Hitch, Phone after Six, The Gorilla in the Secret Service*, and *The Murder in the Library*. When a child asks for the second part of *The Little Prince*, she tells him that the book has no end, in an obvious reference to the film's own refusal of narrative closure. The bookish references serve, at times, to comment on the characters and situations; when a man asks for *The Problems of Education in Their Historical Development*, a child barges in for *Fanny Hill*. When the librarian tells the main male character that *The Idiot* is about an epileptic, he asks what the word means. When she laments that the library has no copy of *Quo Vadis*, he responds, "What are you doing tonight?"

The films also make specific reference to New Wave films. Certain scenes in *A Woman's Case* are strongly reminiscent of Godard's films, especially *Breathless* (*A bout de souffle*, 1959). One sequence, for example, stages a dialogue between the two main characters (in fact more a monologue of the woman about herself) using close-ups and jump cuts in a manner clearly evoking the café scene involving Patricia (Jean Seberg) and a journalist. The film also employs the existentialist style paradoxes common in early New Wave films. The woman tells the lover: "If you will fall in love with me there is only one way to prove it—to sleep with me; which in fact proves nothing." The dialogue sequence, which avoids the conventional "ping-pong" editing, is presented, as in sequences from *Breathless* and *Masculine-Feminine* (*Masculin-féminin*, 1966), as a direct-to-camera interview. As in *The Married Woman* (*Une Femme mariée*, 1964), the potential eroticism of the image of the woman is abstracted through fragmentation as well as through a critique of the mass media and their role in fostering female consumerism, for example, in the form of bra advertisements. Another sequence features intertitles in French, where wordplay is developed through formal positioning and fragmentation. One intertitle shows three related crisscrossing words: "*violation/violateur/violeur*"— words which anticipate a later sequence in which a woman, as part of an aesthetic game, is suffocated to death, victim of a sterile fascination with beauty.

Unlike other alternative film movements such as the convocation of "young German" cinema which produced the Oberhausen statement or the Latin American agitation for a viable "third cinema," the Israeli filmmakers lacked a clear-cut political orientation: the principle of individualism reigned supreme. While these other movements tended to allude not only to a specifically cinematic intertext, but also to the contemporaneous cultural milieu in which characters were rooted, Israeli personal filmmakers went to great length to eliminate any references to the Israeli context, preferring always to develop an aesthetic of transcendence, abstraction, and "airy nothing." The films' hermetic discourse tends to foreground the subjective world of individual experience. All that is "provincial," i.e., Israeli, is repressed as part of a process of complete assimilation to the "universal," i.e.,

Tel Aviv and the French New Wave: *A Woman's Case.*

the West, without demonstrating awareness of the exclusionary mechanisms and discursive formations which determine what is to be regarded as "provincial" and "local" and what is "universal."

Diverse strategies of inclusion and exclusion are engaged to create this "effect of universality" in the personal films. Often the main characters remain unnamed (for example, we never learn the woman's name in *A Woman in the Next Room*, or the man's in *A Woman's Case*), thus avoiding specific associations with Israeli milieus, locales, or ethnic origins. Elsewhere, the names are "excentric" or defiantly non-Semitic, as with the name Thomas in "The Return of Thomas" or the protagonist's playful reference to his friend as "François." Linguistic markers also play a part in this flight from the Middle East, from local habitations and local names. French and English repeatedly slip into the dialogue, are inserted into the intertitles, or are voiced in the lyrics featured on the music track. While the late sixties' personal films alluded more often to Europe, however, the personal films of the seventies and eighties are predominantly English (American) oriented, and tend to refer more to places in the United States (and especially New York). The characters often speak of life "abroad," a term which in Israel almost invariably refers to the Western world, not simply as more accessible than the East for geopolitical reasons but also as a locus of desire for those with the means to travel. Location shooting, finally, tends to exclude the more typical Israeli imagery of streets and people, a device which contributes to the anonymity of locales. At times, the location shooting focuses on interiors, and in *A Woman in the Next Room* on a single interior location, which subliminally metaphorizes the closed world in which the protagonists dwell.

While Rossellini and the neorealists took their cameras outdoors to document Italian working-class people and their environment, and while Godard and the New Wave playfully interwove fiction and documentary as part of a broader concern with making sense of the human figure within the immediate French milieu, the Israeli New Wave's use of similar strategies operated in a kind of social and historical vacuum. The hand-held camera with its sense of immediacy and the location shooting with its implicit sense of documenting fragments of actuality are here applied to an identityless world. The hand-held camera here evokes a presumably modern-Western character and world "beyond" the provincial Israeli "here and now"; location shooting is not used to capture the people and ambiance of Tel Aviv but rather to frame "extraterritorial" and "classless" protagonists. Whereas the New Wave filmed a pre-existing Parisian milieu, its Israeli epigones had to artificially construct an ersatz left-bank Paris-sur-la-Méditerranée, an ambiance actually quite out of synch with the social reality of Tel Aviv. In this sense, the films inherit the "atemporality" and "placelessness" of romance as defined by literary critics such as Arnold Kettle and George Lukács, a world whose ethereal nowhere-ness is counterposed to the temporal specificity and social rootedness of the novel. They inherit, to put it differently, the Baudelairean love for *ailleurs* (elsewhere), the anywhere-out-of-the-world spirit of latter-day romanticism. The apparent modernism of the style of the personal films is somewhat misleading. Brechtian/Godardian artistic strategies questioned not simply "dramatic theater" or classical narrative cinema per se but sociopolitical structures, exposing, for example, the relationship between realism and bourgeois ideology or between illusionism and capitalist culture. The Israeli New Wave, in contrast, borrowed certain cinematic distancing strategies, but left unclear precisely from what the spectator was being distanced. The devices derive from anti-illusionistic cinema, but the world portrayed on the screen remains illusionistic since the films hardly confront or dismantle the assumptions undergirding their own practice.

The films' mythical discourse conceals its own origins. However unwittingly, they betray the characters' social status through elements in the mise-en-scène (the spacious house with piano in *A Woman in the Next Room*) or through dialogue (the references to globetrotting friends in *A Woman in the Next Room* and in "The Return of Thomas" in *The Dress*)—elements which in the Israel of the sixties ultimately connote a specific milieu, that of the Ashkenazi upper middle class. The films' universalized milieus paradoxically reveal the social origins of their non-mainstream protagonists, since young actors like Liora Rivlin and Assaf Dayan ("The Dress" in *The Dress*), Motty Barkan and Rina Ganur ("The Letter" in *The Dress*), Gabi Eldor, Amir Orian, and Ya'eer Rubin ("The Return of Thomas" in *The Dress*), or Helit Katmor-Yeshurun and Yossef Spector (*A Woman's Case*) embody, by their appearance and through their gestural codes, Sabra figures, and represent, therefore, young people of the upper middle class. Rivlin, Dayan, and Katmor-Yeshurun are actually from famous families in the history of Israel and inevitably carry those familial connotations with them and the characters they play.

The Seeds of Disillusionment

The shift toward existentialist individualism had already begun in novels, poetry, theater, visual arts, radio, and press, involving a movement in the late fifties and sixties from the consensus of the earlier decades when cultural figures of diverse Zionist positions, for example, the poets Uri Tzvi Greenberg, Avraham Shlonsky, Nathan Alterman, and Haim Guri, or the writers and playwriters Moshe Shamir, Aharon Meged, and S. Yizhar, shared nevertheless a readiness and even eagerness to give expression to collective Zionist aspirations. The "Palmach generation" (or 1948 generation) view of the role of literature as educating for Zionist values and dealing with national concerns such as Aliya, the struggle against the enemy, and the pioneering settlements, was followed by the "state generation" downplaying of such ideals. Poets and writers such as Nathan Zach, David Avidan, Yehuda Amichai, Dalia Rabikowitz, Amalia Cahana-Carmon, Amos Oz, and A. B. Yehoshua were beginning to dominate the literary scene especially through the magazines *Keshet* and *Achshav*. The critical essays as well as the poems and stories published in the sixties were calling for and practicing a literature that bypassed Zionist collective ideals, arguing in contrast to the "Palmach generation" that literature's only role was aesthetic, and that just as art's *raison d'être* was nothing more than beauty, so literature's "reason" was itself. The role of art, according to the "state generation," was to give the reader aesthetic pleasure rather than social insight. The "Palmach generation" in literature—the literary branch of a discursive formation which also included the heroic-nationalist films—was partially inspired by Soviet-style Socialist realism with its fondness for positive, active, upright heroes whose stance epitomized collective goals. That generation preferred conventional linear narratives characterized by common-sense causality and verisimilar authenticating procedures, often accompanied by omniscient narrators who clarify the perspective of the text. The perspectival shift of the "state generation" with regard to literature's role, in contrast, was correlated with a kind of "opting out" from national goals and a creeping loss of confidence in Zionist and Socialist-Zionist ideology. The literary journals *Keshet* and *Achshav* argued for a literature of ambivalence and complexity infused with an ironic attitude expressed in sophisticated *écriture*.

Certain "state generation" writers such as Amos Oz and A. B. Yehoshua favored symbolism, with actions set in imaginary space. But even when set in more defined locales, the description of Israeli "reality" tended to be subordinated to a more universal symbolism. The imprisoning situation was seen as deriving from "the human condition" and not from sociopolitical structures. The protagonists of fiction since the sixties have been individualists, concentrating on their private world, and their actions within the social realm tend not to form the major focus on the narrative but rather their inner states and personal experiences presented from a subjectivized point of view. They remain, to invoke George Orwell's memorable phrase, "inside the whale," largely impervious to social concerns and preoccupied with private minutiae. Writer after writer has explored the bourgeois topos of "the failure of communication," foregrounding themes of loneliness, despair, and ennui, inspired less by Ecclesiastes than by the existentialist and absurdist writing, but generally lacking the philosophical-reflective base of those movements. As often occurs, the conscious striving for "universality" boomerangs, resulting in an even more obvious (and this time extraterritorial) provinciality.

The personal films emerged from this cultural ethos. The transition from heroic-nationalist films to personal cinema formed part of a general Sabra fatigue with explicit ideology. The need for an art of ambivalence and ambiguities reflected, in many ways, positions of artists who had no clear idea in whose name it was possible to speak and struggle. The partisans of "quality cinema," like the "state generation" writers, did not subvert the Establishment myths or refer to alternative visions of their heritage; they mainly saw themselves as rebelling against the burden of commitment and collective reflexion. When Micha Shagrir dared to touch on a more topical subject in his film, *The Patrollers* (albeit in a subjectivized, individualized manner), he was criticized for dealing with a topic more appropriate to newspapers.[17] Such a critique manifests the full disdain toward "actuality" as well as a willed (but ultimately unreal) marginality in relation to the political concerns of the founding generations. In this period, the word *ideology* acquired negative connotations and became virtually a "put-down" word; political actuality and contemporary relevance were perceived by these filmmakers as provincial and somehow antithetical to "universality," i.e., Western culture, whose status and imbrication with Western power has never been questioned.

In a recent evaluation of these films, Yigal Bursztyn expressed the cultural necessity of personal cinema: "It was a political act to be apolitical. . . because you did not manifest bombastic Zionism and therefore you did the right thing."[18] The importance of personal cinema, at the same time, consisted in its resistance against pressure to make propagandist cinema along with its desire to experiment with film language. As with the contemporaneous Hebrew poets, the romanticism of individual experience formed an act of rupture with the filmmakers' history and culture. This rupture was welcomed enthusiastically by young Sabras, for whom it connoted "modernism" and opening to the "wide world." Whereas existentialism and the French New Wave developed within a certain cultural ethos, Israeli personal poetry and cinema constituted a kind of blind refusal of one's own history and culture. The openness to the modern West, accompanied by the reductionist and even distorted view of existentialism as merely "non-involvement," easily transmuted into a process of flight from confrontation with the problems of identity for a secular (Zionist) Jew in the State of Israel.

The filmmakers and writers thus practiced the high modernist segregation of art and politics—an attitude dominant up to recent years. (Even when some writers such as Amos Oz and A. B. Yehoshua later became more involved in political questions, they still strove to keep their art as immune as possible from "digressions" from the apolitical individual imaginary.) This apolitical *parti pris*, at times, applies even when the fiction revolves around characters whose sociological being necessarily implies the problematics of the political scene. The Arab twins in Amos Oz's *My Michael*, and in Dan Wolman's filmic adaptation, presented within the woman protagonist's stream of consciousness, serve little narrative function beyond mirroring and metaphorizing the repressed Dionysian inner self of the Madame Bovary–like protagonist and her romantic frustration with her humdrum and unimaginative existence. In this sense, the Arab presence penetrates the hallucinatory space of Jewish-Israeli subjectivity, but is silenced as a political voice. (A. B. Yehoshua's short story "In Front of the Forests" similarly features an elderly Arab speech-impaired character, literally voiceless, and although the story hints at the previous, now-buried existence of his village under the forest, it is the Sabra who must speak for him—or, more accurately, it is the Sabra's existential nausea that speaks and in function of which the Arab exists.)

The personal cinema's ideology-of-having-no-ideology must be linked to a more general withdrawal from Zionist concerns. This withdrawal must itself be seen within the context of the establishment of the state, at a point after the Zionist project had achieved its major goal. In this period, Sabra culture underwent a crisis in values. The Sabra entity, which had always conceived itself as antithetical to that of the Diaspora Jew and as disconnected from Diaspora history, had to confront its Jewishness with the arrival of Holocaust survivors. Ilan Mossinzon's *The Wooden Gun* (*Rove Huliot*, 1979) and Dan Wolman's *Hide and Seek* (*Mahboim*, 1980) give expression to the Sabra children protagonists' estrangement from the European Jews and to their hard time comprehending the survivors' nightmare. In both films the children's violent games constitute a psychic residue of the Sabra/Survivor encounter, as if the children were eager to demonstrate that to the Sabra breed the Holocaust could not have happened. The immigration of survivors, then, posed a question mark over the Sabra repression of Jewish identity.

Before the establishment of the state, the "fathers' generation" and the "sons' generation" saw themselves as realizing Socialist-Zionist dreams. During World War II, the belief in this ideology was further strengthened, since the fight of Jews defending Palestine was interwoven with the fight as Socialists against Fascism; Socialism and Zionism were viewed, therefore, as complementary entities. During the early fifties, with the Soviet execution of a group of Yiddish writers and the "Jewish Doctors' Trials," events which pointed to institutionalized anti-Semitism

Orientalist hallucinations: The fantasy twins in *My Michael.*

in the Soviet Union, the two presumably linked ideologies, Zionism and Socialism, came to be seen as in potential conflict. The disenchantment with the Soviet Union—the backdrop of Yitzhak Yeshurun's *Noa at Seventeen* (*Noa Bat Shva-Esre*, 1981)—was further intensified after the death of Stalin, with the Khrushchev-era revelations about the Stalinist reign of terror, provoking the younger Israeli generation to refuse all ideologies and political commitments of whatever stripe. The pioneering ideals of volunteer agricultural work and economic equality came to be seen as so much cant, since they were unaccompanied by any real attempt to achieve Socialist goals and actually masked movement in the opposite direction. Over the years security rather than equality or justice came to form the overriding value of Zionism. It was in the name of economic and political security, for example, that the government signed the reparations agreement deal with West Germany, a deal which caused a kind of crisis of values in some intellectual circles.

In the fifties, the capitalist nature of the Israeli economy had also become clear, despite the loudly proclaimed Socialist ideology of the ruling Labor Party and the Histadrut. In any case, the ideology of an independent economy was meaningless given the reality of an unstable balance of payments and increasing dependency on American aid. The centralization of power in the hands of Prime Minister (who also served at times as Minister of Defense) David Ben-Gurion also came to be seen more clearly in such cases as the repression of the "sailors' rebellion" and in the "Lavon case" which exposed hidden manipulation, rivalries, and corruption in a system revealed to be somewhat less ideally democratic, egalitarian, and Socialist than had been thought. The chasm between Labor's Socialist credo and its actual machinations recalls the literary theorist Peter Sloterdijk's definition of cynicism: false consciousness masquerading as enlightenment.

Once the principal goal of Zionism was achieved with the certainty of a topographically defined collective existence, i.e., the State of Israel, it was possible for the younger generation to adopt a less idealistic view of the political leadership. The younger generation refused to cope with what turned out to be an immensely complex and conflictual collective identity. The immigrants from the Third World, and especially from Arab-Muslim countries, furthermore, provoked even more "anti-Jewish" feelings in the secularly oriented Sabra culture, not simply through the implicitly threatening idea of the heterogeneity of Jewish cultures, but also through the discomfiting amalgam of "Jewishness" and what was seen as "backwardness." This latter combination was seen as something to be annihilated—an ideological impulse manifested in the measures taken to strip Arab Jews of their heritage: religious Yemenites shorn of their *peot* (side-locks), children virtually forced into Euro-Zionist schools, and so forth.

The Oriental Jews have clearly represented a problematic entity for European hegemony in Israel. Although Zionism collapses the Sephardim and the Ashkenazim into the single category of "one people," at the same time the Sephardi's Oriental "difference" threatens the European ideal-ego which phantasizes Israel as the prolongation of Europe "in" the Middle East, but not "of" it. Ben-Gurion, we may recall, formulated his visionary Utopia for Israel as that of a "Switzerland of the Middle East." The leitmotif of Zionist texts is the cry to form a "normal civilized nation," without the myriad "distortions" and forms of pariahdom typical of the Diaspora. (Zionist revulsion for shtetl "abnormalities," as some commentators have pointed out, is often strangely reminiscent of the very anti-Semitism it presumably so abhors.) The Ostjuden, perennially marginalized by Europe, realized their desire of becoming Europe, ironically, in the Middle East, this time on the back of their own "Ostjuden," the Eastern Jews. Having passed through their own "ordeal of civility," as the "Blacks" of Europe, they now imposed their civilizing standards on their own "Blacks."

It is within this "relational" context of a menacing heteroglossia that we must understand the openness toward Western European culture, not only as correlated with a newly dominant pro-Western political orientation, but also as a reaction both against the vestiges of Eastern European shtetl culture and, even more, against the Oriental Jews, now insistently and embarrassingly present in the form of thousands of Oriental newcomers officially recognized as Israeli citizens. The tendency on the part of the elite artists to distance their fictions from the native Middle Eastern environment, then, found a corollary in the cinema in the form of hostility to the "bourekas" as a "Levantine" genre. The question of "taste," as Pierre Bourdieu argues in *Distinction: A Social Critique of the Judgment of Taste*, is intimately tied up with class prestige and differentiations. Bourgeois taste requires its artists, writers, and composers to "provide emblems of distinction which are at the same time means of denying reality," and the Israeli artists' affection for the aura of high art can be viewed as a ploy to insulate themselves from the discomforting consequences of societal reality. The antipathy for the popular, not so much in the box-office sense of the word, but rather in the sense of "representative of the marginalized masses" is emblematic of a hierarchical mind set. The "quality films" supplant the defiant orality—the emphasis on "banquet imagery," "marketplace speech," cooking, sexuality, and the "lower bodily stratum"—of the "bourekas," an orality explicitly designated by the gastronomic rubric of the genre, named after a cheap, oily, "vulgar" Oriental food. The high-art refinement and "civility" of much of personal cinema, thus, was also a refusal—of the lower-class vulgarity of the "bourekas" and the Sephardi audience that frequented them, and even of the traditional earthiness and irreverence of lower-class shtetl culture.

It was also during the fifties that the mass immigration from Arab and Muslim countries provided Israel with cheap labor, thus allowing the Ashkenazi veterans, and Ashkenazi newcomers, to transform themselves into an emergent upper middle class. The hegemonic Israeli intellectuals, overwhelmingly Ashkenazi in origin, also benefited from this process of bourgeoisification, made possible through rapid and unequal economic development. The world portrayed in their fictions reflects the preoccupations of a specific milieu, that of the Sabra elite. The frequent focalization through eccentric, outsider protagonists suggests, on certain levels, a pseudo-binary structure in which the young anti-hero favored by the narrative is posited as opposing the mainstream bourgeoisie. In the venerable tradition of bourgeois thought, the individual is projected as being against society rather than thoroughly immersed in society. The negation of the bourgeois is seen not as the proletarian, à la Marx, nor as the oppressed ethnic, à la Fanon, but rather as the "bohemian" floating on the surface of social life.

The Foregrounding of Marginality

The marginalization of the protagonists, a theme at the very center of the overwhelming majority of the personal films of the seventies and early eighties, is, in many ways, illusory. The artists project themselves onto characters conceived as marginal—an artistic device by which the authorial "I" can be isolated and explored. The identification with the marginal, then, in contrast with that of many Third World films, does not represent a form of mediated solidarity with the oppressed but rather a pretext for narcissistic self-contemplation. Virtually all of the protagonists of personal cinema, like those of the heroic-nationalist films, come from "First Israel." Unlike the heroes of the earlier films, however, the new anti-heroes do not embody the Zionist mission and they do not usually belong to any defined collectivity or organization such as Palmach, the kibbutz, or the Israeli Defense Forces. And even when they do, as in Yehuda Ne'eman's *The Paratroopers* (the army), in Akiva Tevet's *Atalia* (1985)[19] (the kibbutz), and in Yitzhak Yeshurun's *Noa at Seventeen* (the youth movement), it is in order to assume their individuality in the face of collective expectations and group pressures.

The film which best embodies the spirit of new individualism versus Zionist-Socialist collectivity is *Noa at Seventeen*. Set just a few years after the foundations of the state (1951), the film revolves around an adolescent, the seventeen-year-old Noa. A member of a Socialist-Zionist youth movement, Noa fights for her right to question received wisdom. With the Korean War at its peak, the Israeli Labor movement is undergoing an ideological crisis, confronted with the dilemma of whether to follow Soviet-style Socialism or the Social Democracy of certain Western countries. The film portrays the ideological stresses that tore families apart, splitting the kibbutz movement and even triggering outbursts of violence. This conflict is focalized through Noa as part of her process of maturation. As a rebel, Noa fights her way through a world of shattered values. The simple sets and minimal camerawork of the film appropriately mirror a fictional world prizing simplicity and modesty of appearance. Chronicling the assertion of individuality in the face of "pressure-cooker" collectivism, the film traces the early origins of the decline of the Socialist-Zionist ethos. The interest in the subject of individualism partially derives, of course, from the period of the film's production. The mimetic reflection on a First-Israel microcosm (the city and the kibbutz), however, hinders a broader analysis of individualism within the context of the general embourgeoisement of Ashkenazi society, made possible by the availability in the fifties of a massive (largely Sephardi) working class. The individual-versus-society topos is discussed in idealistic terms which ignore the internal dynamic of Israeli society seen as a totality. The force of the film lies in its capacity to present both individualist and collectivist polarities without caricature; its weakness lies in not dialectically thinking through the full relational dynamics of the dichotomy in a precise historical context.

The more dominant tendency in personal films was to privilege the individual side of the individual/society polarity. The tension between the two, and the protagonist's deviation from societal norms, comes to metaphorize the personal cinema's own struggle to create an alternative to mainstream filmmaking. The new filmmakers soon became the object of "great expectations" on the part of film critics. The concern with the "personal signature of the author," which began with the filmmakers themselves in the late sixties, became a veritable obsession in film critical discourse only in the seventies, especially in the film magazine *Close-Up* (associated with Tel Aviv University). This auteurist preoccupation still plays a disproportionate role in the discussion of films in Israel, where the term *auteur* has often operated as a kind of incantatory chant of praise. At times the concept was abused to justify mediocre films perceived as "good objects" uniquely for being marked by the personal traits of a filmmaker. This search for the "personality" behind the film resulted from the confluence of individualist Sabra culture with the specific influence of the auteur theory imported from France and the United States. The concept tended to refer less to "*la politique des auteurs*," i.e., the filmmaker's struggle for expression against the oppressive production hierarchies of an established system—in any case, no such established system existed in Israel—than to a kind of "*culte de la personnalité*," i.e., a relentless search, with the advent of a second or third film by a director, for the imprint, the personal monogram, as it were, of an originary personality as the source of all signification.

The personal cinema of the seventies and eighties, despite its professed fondness for the New Wave, was not especially attached to the specific texts or the textual strategies of the New Wave. It was particularly uninterested in certain New Wave attempts to interrogate and subvert filmic illusionism. The attempts at formal subversion, in personal cinema, are limited to the films of the late sixties. The spatio-temporal discontinuities of the early films (for example, *The Dress* and *A Woman's Case*) in the seventies tend to be masked by a generally "plausible" representation, one which does not oblige the spectator to take consciousness of the cinematic gesture being performed. The episodic fragmentation characteristic of the narratives of some sixties films (for example, *Take Off* and *Snail*), is in the seventies subsumed within an anthropocentric overall schema. (Benjamin Hayeem's *The Black Banana* of 1977 stands out as an exception.) Basically, in fact, the films of the seventies and eighties carry on the production methods and cinematic strategies molded by the first Israeli personal films. Although the personal filmmakers tend to emphasize, both in interviews[20] and in their manifesto (the "Kayitz" manifesto), their heterogeneity and diversity and their lack of a single artistic orientation or political predisposition, in fact the films do share a common stylistic and ideological perspective.

I will examine the recurrent thematic and stylistic orientation of their films, therefore, notably of Dan Wolman's *Floch* (1972), Avraham Hefner's *Where is Daniel Wax?*, Yaki Yosha's *Rocking Horse*, Daniel Waxman's *Transit*, and Michal Bat Adam's *On a Thin Line* (*Al Hevel Dack*, 1980). I will attempt to contextualize the films within the seventies, especially within the Israel of the post-1973 war period and the change of power, from the thirty-year reign of Ma'arach (Labor Party alignment) to Likud (Unity). The "individualism" process that began in the fifties, and was then shared only by few intellectuals, became a widespread posture in the seventies, and was fully realized in the personal films of the seventies and eighties. The films of this period prolong the thematic concerns of existential-psychological quandaries, of the individual alienation and (pseudo) marginalization, only this time with a clearer emphasis on the world of the protagonist, usually a sensitive eccentric—preferably an artist—as implicitly, or explicitly, opposed to mainstream Israel society. Here we might distinguish roughly between two groups. Films such as Dan Wolman's *The Dreamer* (*HaTimhoni*, 1970) and *Floch*, Yaki Yosha's

Rocking Horse, Michal Bat Adam's *Moments* (*Rega'im*, 1979; distributed abroad as *Each Other*) and *On a Thin Line*, Mira Rekanati's *A Thousand Little Kisses*, Amos Guttman's *Drifting* (*Nagoo'a*, 1983) and *Bar 51* (1986), and Eitan Green's *Till the End of the Night* focus on intimist *angst* and on basically introspective, isolated protagonists on the margins, treated through the grid of generally human issues, "beyond time and place," such as love, aging, and the crisis of creativity. Films such as Uri Zohar's *Big Eyes*, Yehuda Ne'eman's *The Paratroopers*, Avraham Hefner's *Weinchel Affair* (*Parashat Weinchel*, 1979), Ilan Mossinzon's *The Wooden Gun*, Dan Wolman's *Hide and Seek* and *The Night Soldier* (*Hayal HaLayla*, 1984), Yaki Yosha's *The Vulture* (*HaAyit*, 1981), and Yitzhak Yeshurun's *Noa at Seventeen*, meanwhile, deal with psychic marginality within a precise social orientation, projected onto a specific Israeli milieu such as the army or the kibbutz, or onto a specific historical moment such as the British Mandate period or the time of the split in the kibbutz movement.

Whereas the first group of films tends to focus on rootless outsiders, usually closed within that world, the second group tends to focus on the confrontational tension between the individual and the social formation. A review of a few representative films of each group will give an idea of their thematic orientation, and more specifically, of their ways of projecting marginality. In this discussion we will see personal cinema as allegorical, in Jameson's sense, as a fragmentary discourse often unwittingly projecting, even where the apparent topic is private or libidinal, a larger political or national dimension, projecting in this case a kind of Sabra "structure of feelings," a First-Israel "take" on the world.

Dan Wolman's two early films, *The Dreamer* and *Floch*, portray a world of solitude linked to the question of aging. In the former film, a young painter, Elimelech (Tuvia Tabi), working in an institution for the elderly, alternates between an involvement in this milieu and specifically with an elderly woman, and the world of his young girlfriend. While the elderly woman shares with him a sensitivity to beauty and a sense of nuance and subtlety, the young woman—who together with her family incarnates the vulgar, acquisitive, and anti-poetic bourgeoisie—fails to understand the depth of his presumably reflective looks. In the end, he prefers the dreamy and eccentric world of the elderly, a choice metaphorized by the location of the old people's home in the old city of Saffad, a city associated with deep archeological strata as well as with mysticism. (The city has also, in recent years, become a favored place of residence for visual artists.)

Floch tells the story of an aging man (Avraham Halfi) who, after losing his only son and his son's family in a car accident, becomes obsessed with the idea of divorcing his wife to begin a futile search for a younger woman who might provide him with a son and heir. The film was coscripted by the director with Hanoch Levine, one of Israel's most sardonic playwrights, known for gloomy surrealist plays in which Everyman is a hapless and lonely creature unworthy of any compassion. *Floch* elaborates absurd situations in which the protagonist's attempts at compassionate communication invariably result in disaster. (A predilection for the absurd was already visible in *The Dreamer*, for which Hanoch Levine served as literary consultant: an aging waiter in a hotel enters the room of a bourgeois family, hoping for love and community, only to be thrown out.) In the final sequence of *Floch*, the protagonist arrives by night at a bus station where a bizarre bagel vendor pretends that the bagel is a steering wheel. In the final shot, Floch walks after the vendor and both vanish into the darkness. After suffering alienation from his own family and being rejected elsewhere, Floch is accepted, then, only by another outsider, just as in *The Dreamer* it is only the eccentric old lady who shows the protagonist any sympathy. Floch, the anti-hero, is accepted by a person who lives in fantasy and fiction, and whose "art" is not institutionalized by the bourgeoisie—in clear opposition to the pianist and the cellist whose art is directed at a wealthy audience. Real life, in sum, is the scene of alienation, where the strong reject the weak, where even the lonely Floch divorces his wife because she cannot bear children and rejects another woman seeking marriage. Floch's typically Jewish obsession with continuity becomes especially understandable in the post-Holocaust era. Despite his absurd irascibility, Floch elicits a certain sympathy when seen within this historical context. Rejected, Floch finds room for himself in the world of fiction—in the world of the lunatic and, allegorically, in the world of film.

Set in the Jerusalem of the fifties, Dan Wolman's later film *My Michael* explores the internal world of Hanna (Efrat Lavi), a former literature student who has become the Bovary-like wife of a geology professor (Oded Kotler). Filtered through the claustrophobic existence and private hallucinations of the introverted female protagonist, the film recounts her progressive disenchantment with her reliable but unimaginative husband. The film faithfully follows the events and atmosphere of the Amos Oz novel, interweaving the political symbolism of Hanna's childhood memories of Arab twin friends with the mundane realities of the Israeli sector of Jerusalem. Here again we encounter the self-imposed marginality of a First-Israel protagonist, this time a woman, inextricably connected widi yet irremediably alienated from the pragmatic and utilitarian milieu of which she forms a part.

Personal cinema largely foregrounds male perspective, legitimized, as it were, by male concrete sacrifice in a society at war. But the decline of the mythic heroic Sabra and the new emphasis on sensitive, vulnerable male characters had the indirect effect of opening up some space for women characters. This same period witnessed the emergence of women filmmakers such as Michal Bat Adam and Edit Shchory, who, like their male colleagues, tend to highlight the quest for self through intimate relationships, a quest set, once again, in the artistic milieu. (The focus on women, as with the male filmmakers, is not an explicitly feminist one.) Michal Bat Adam, one of the major filmmakers, began her career as an actress, playing the female lead in Mizrahi's *I Love You, Rosa*. Her first feature, *Moments*, an Israeli-French coproduction, revolves around a chance meeting between two young women—an Israeli writer (Michal Bat Adam) and a French photographer on holiday—in a train from Tel Aviv to Jerusalem. Structured around a flashback to an earlier meeting between the pair, the film progressively zooms in on their relationship, so that the film becomes a review of past memories, of feelings sensed but never defined. Bat Adam's oblique refusal to offer the audience decisive confirmation of the protagonists' presumed lesbian interlude recalls Diane Kurys' similar stratagem in her art house hit, *Entre Nous* (1983). Bat Adam made three more films—*On a Thin Line, First Loves* (*Ben Lokeah Bat*, 1982), and *The Lover* (*HaMe'ahev*, 1986), which is based on A. B. Yehoshua's novel—in this same intimist psychological spirit.

Another woman filmmaker, Mira Rekanati, sets her *A Thousand Little Kisses* in an artistic milieu as well, a milieu reflected in the visual style of the film, with its self-conscious preoccupation with painterly devices and compositional sophistication. The story of Alma (Rivka Noyman), the protagonist, is told through her relationship with her mother following the death of her painter-father. The discovery of her father's secret affair draws her to his ex-lover's son, and as a result she becomes torn between loyalty to her mother and her father's passionate past. Her mother, tormented by jealousy and feeling doubly betrayed, goes on a rampage of self-destruction. Despite the mother's attempts to provoke guilt, Alma fights for her independence and right to self-realization. We find again, then, the struggle for self *against* society (here incarnated by the upper-middle-class mother) but this time with a woman taking the "actantial slot" (Julien Greimas) usually occupied by a man.

Amos Guttman's *Drifting*, a reflexive film about a filmmaker, presents an isolated, introspective world focalized through its homosexual cinéaste protagonist, Robby (Jonathon Segal). The film begins with Robby's direct-address monologue to the camera in which he speaks of his need to make a film. *Drifting*'s thematic prolongs the late romantic tradition of the lament concerning creative block and artistic paralysis. Robby also recounts the financial obstacles confronting a would-be filmmaker living on the margins of a society hostile to all deviation. The anti-hero's alienation from Israeli mainstream society is reflected in his relationships to his family and especially to the disdainful grandmother with whom he lives. Most of the film takes place in the apartment, a visual strategy that reinforces the sense of isolation.

Although Robby finds Israeli political and cultural struggles irrelevant, he is nevertheless caught up in the country's power structures. Certain men he brings home are on the margins for reasons that go beyond homosexuality: the Oriental Jew, Ezri, a high-school dropout, is a male prostitute, and the two Palestinian "terrorists" who find refuge in his apartment are at the very limits of social inequality. The film's narrative leaves ambiguous the Palestinian's rationale for having sex with Robby, although the film intimates the possibility of prostitution for survival.

(The unusual display of a certain sympathy for the Oriental Jew and the Palestinian men is undermined, however, by the misogynistic portrayal of women.) At the same time, the narcissism of *Drifting* is not unaccompanied by self-mockery. Early in the film, for example, Robby recounts his daydream: living in Beverly Hills with his lover, Ilan, and receiving the Oscar for the first Jewish gay film. Guttman's own non-Hollywoodian film, however, ends with Robby's voice-over explaining what the film is about: "it is about what still has to be done and about the need to make this film." In *Drifting* (as in *8 1/2*), Robby's failure to complete the film-within-the-film coincides with the conclusion of the film itself.

The rootless alienation of the Sabra protagonist is even more total in another reflexive film, Yaki Yosha's *Rocking Horse*. Here the alienation applies to friends, country, family, and even to his own relation to his art. Based on a novel by Yoram Kaniuk (who collaborated on the script), the film deals with an unsuccessful young painter, Aminadav Susetz (Shmuel Kraus), who goes back to Israel after spending ten years in the United States. Frustrated, he returns, hoping for self-revelation, only to find himself a stranger in his own land. In order to understand his roots and to find answers to his many questions, he tries to retrace his origins by registering his findings, feelings, and reflections on film. The film-within-the-film, concerning the past (beginning with his parents' first relations in Vienna before immigrating to Israel) is in black and white, a choice which, although originally motivated by financial necessity, nevertheless serves to emphasize the gap between the generations. Just as he reaches the moment of his birth, when he has traveled back to his mother's womb in order to set himself free, he burns the film.

The open-ended narrative structure, shared by many films of the Kayitz (Young Israeli Cinema), reflects the collapse of the confident value-systems dominant during the two first decades of Israeli existence. The protagonist himself, who had fought in the early wars, now finds himself without any strong emotional or intellectual involvement in the activities of mainstream society. The Hebrew title, *Susetz*, is both the protagonist's family name and a pun. The family name of the author of the novel, Kaniuk, means "small horse" or "pony" in Russian. By giving his hero such a striking name, Kaniuk not only hints at autobiographical elements, but also suggests the thematic leitmotif of both novel and film: constant movement without real change. The protagonist, despite his eternal wanderings, never finds peace or fulfillment. In *Rocking Horse*, as in his earlier work, *Shalom, Prayer for the Road* (*Shalom, Tfilat haDerekh*, 1973), Yosha links a concern with personal discovery to the imprisonment of characters within the closed frame of a suffocating world.

Personal cinema inscribes, at times, not only the rootlessness of Sabra protagonists, but also that of the European immigrant. In *Rocking Horse*, Aminadav's father, an Austrian musician, is completely disconnected from present-day Israel, just as father and son are completely unconnected with each other. In Daniel Waxman's *Transit*, the European outsider and his lack of interaction with Israel, and even with his Sabra wife and son, form the focal point of interest of the film. *Transit* is a slow-paced portrayal of an aging German-Jew, Erich Neusbaum (Gedalia Besser), who decides after twenty years in Israel to return to Berlin, where he had worked in museums. The film depicts roughly a week during the winter of 1968 as Neusbaum bids farewell to his unmarried sisters (who never learned Hebrew), his Sabra ex-wife, and their twelve-year-old son. Despite his many years in Israel, Neusbaum cannot adjust. His German cultural formation contradicts the norms of Israeli life; his compulsively neat and modest "Yekke" (German-Jewish) mentality ill suits the freewheeling conventions of a post–Six Day War Israel heady with confidence. In this atmosphere, he pines for his old Berlin, even while he recognizes that the Berlin of his youth no longer exists. Thus he belongs nowhere; the old has vanished (and as a Jew, it is suggested, he never really belonged to it) and the new remains foreign. In this sense, the film resurrects the archetype of the wandering Jew, unable to find roots or solace, even, paradoxically, in the land of Zion. While the heroic-nationalist films deployed the Holocaust in a somewhat abstract fashion, as a kind of "move" in Zionist polemics, personal films such as *Rocking Horse*, *Transit*, and *The Wooden Gun* offer concrete and sympathetic portrayals of the survivors themselves, while simultaneously questioning the notion of Israel as the final resting point of solace and redemption.

The Hidden Face of Militarism

Films which diverge from the introspective mode feature personal alienation and artistic themes only to illuminate broader confrontations between protagonist and societal codes. Based on Kaniuk's novel *The Last Jew*, Yaki Yosha's *The Vulture* offers an antiheroic protagonist, Boaz (the vulture of the title), a disenchanted reserve officer who has lost his childhood friend Menahem in a pointless skirmish on the Egyptian front, moments after the cease-fire that ended the 1973 war. (It took almost a decade for Israeli cinema to register the after effects of that war in terms of both a certain disillusionment within Israeli society and a sharply changed attitude toward the Arab-Israeli conflict.) In a hapless attempt to comfort the dead man's parents, Boaz informs them that Menahem (evidently something of a lout) had taken to expressing himself in poetry in his final days. Under the rather hysterical pressure of Menahem's schoolteacher father, Boaz feels obliged to actually produce some of the putative poems—which he then cynically plagiarizes from a book. When the poems deeply impress the parents, Boaz becomes the reluctant "editor" of an entire memorial volume. Despite his apparent self-assurance, Boaz is a man adrift, scarred by the memories and pains of war and displaying the typical stigmata of survivor-guilt. His sexual adventures only exacerbate his confusion, as he first sleeps with Menahem's girlfriend and then seduces a librarian employed by an organization dedicated to memorializing the young casualties of the war. For

Boaz, what began as a sincere attempt to console the parents of a fallen comrade soon becomes a business enterprise creating memorial booklets for other bereaved parents. Without any real effort, Boaz finds himself at the head of a small but lucrative industry devoted to the dead. The Israeli IRS finally puts an end to this necrophilic enterprise by arresting Boaz, the vulture, the bird of prey living off carrion. Not surprisingly, *The Vulture* stirred up considerable controversy in Israel and was ultimately shown only in a censored version. Probing the open war wounds of the Israeli national psyche, the film sheds a less than idealized light on the military heroism that had sustained the cinema in earlier decades. The film also exposes an unforeseen side effect of war: the felt need of many parents to idealize, through art, the sacrifice of their children, as a way of immortalizing the dead and thus coping with otherwise unbearable grief.

Other films such as Ilan Mossinzon's *The Wooden Gun* (and his recent *The Night Soldier*) and Dan Wolman's *Hide and Seek* explore the psychological impact of militarization on pre-adolescent children, in films set in past historical periods which also serve to allegorize the present. Set in Jerusalem in 1946, *Hide and Seek* focuses on the relationship between a twelve-year-old boy, his mother, and his tutor. His crisis of self-discovery is engendered by his discovery of the homosexual relationship between the gentle tutor and an Arab, pointing to the sensitive issue of forbidden love between Arab and Jew. The film's subdued drama reflects the conformism of a society living in a state of crisis and siege, permeated by a kind of muffled everyday political violence. By returning to a scene in some ways less complicated than the anguished present, *Hide and Seek*, as well as other personal films, communicates a sense of lost possibilities on both a human and a political level. Made with the collaboration of his immediate family, Wolman's film, like some of the Kayitz films, adopts a low-budget approach, eschewing the well-made Hollywood formula in favor of a modest strategy more in keeping with the resources available to Israeli filmmakers.

Like *Hide and Seek*, *The Wooden Gun* is also set in the past, in this case in the tense atmosphere of Tel Aviv in 1950, just after Israel had become an independent state. The struggles and the anxieties of the grownups are reflected in the war between two rival gangs of children who play "war games." Instilled at home and in school with the values of toughness and heroism, their behavior and their interpretation of honor, nationalism, and friendship show the problematic aspect of values that had been taken for granted prior to the Yom Kippur War, and certainly within the majority of films throughout the sixties, by presenting an ironic and demystificatory look at the nationalist pathos. The protagonists' final estrangement from violence in both *The Wooden Gun* and *Hide and Seek* translates a desire on the part of the filmmakers for a nonviolent national trajectory. *The Wooden Gun*'s irreverence toward the older generation's ethos, heroes, and style of pathos (which in itself evokes the heroic-nationalist films) serves to demystify the macho-heroic mentality which animates the earlier war films. The critical stance

The Sabra and the Holocaust: Palestina nursing Yoni's wounds in *The Wooden Gun*.

of the film is encapsulated in a sequence where the protagonist, Yoni, slightly wounded in the war games and believing that he has killed another child, wanders into the beachside hut of a disturbed woman named Palestina (Ophelia Stral), who had lost all her children in the Holocaust and who, perhaps in compensation for her trauma, savors the company of children. On Palestina's wall, Yoni sees a photo of Jewish children threatened by armed Nazis. The cinematic handling conveys his perspective on the photo, one mingling recognition and a certain distance. The juxtaposition of Yoni with the Nazi of the photo implies the boy's realization of some of the possible ramifications of his own violent games. The confident Sabra who mocked the survivors and, in line with the dominant Sabra perspective, looked down on them as cringing and cowardly victims, discovers through Palestina both the anguished reality of victimization and his own potential for violence. As Palestina takes care of his wounds, he is seemingly rendered more mature by this ephemeral encounter with the human cost of violence. The final shots, of Yoni climbing a hill as he observes his playmates down below and refuses their invitation to join them, intimate his new alienation toward war games.

The Holocaust, significantly, is deployed in these films in a manner diametrically opposed to that of the heroic-nationalist genre. The earlier films merely paid lip service to the Holocaust, usually in the form of Sabras speaking for the victims or former-victims-now-become-soldiers fighting for Israel and articulating its *raison d'être*. The survivor-soldiers, symptomatically, displayed almost no physical or psychological traces of their trauma, traces presumably eradicated by contact with the Jewish-nationalist struggle in the Promised Land. The personal films, in contrast, probe the wounds of the survivors, making them concrete and palpable. Not only do films such as *The Wooden Gun*, *Transit*, and *Hide and Seek* thematize the psychological after-effects of the Holocaust—whether in the foreground or the background—they also deploy the idea of the Holocaust in an innovative manner. In *The Wooden Gun*, the encounter with the Holocaust survivor, rather than becoming a platform for justifying military action, as in the heroic-nationalist films, serves to crystallize the perception of the human toll of violence. And while the heroic-nationalist films imply that the proud existence of Israel is itself an answer to the Holocaust, as well as a solution for the survivors—a view which elides the continuing psychological torment of Holocaust survivors in Israel—the personal films cast doubt on such a simplistic teleology, suggesting that the abstract category of nationhood is not always an adequate solution for personal woes.

The social and psychological impact of constant military preparedness and the demystification of heroic-national myths surrounding the Sabra are further explored in such films as Yehuda Ne'eman's *The Paratroopers* and Shimon Dotan's *Repeat Dive*. Unlike the idealizing attitude typical of the heroic-nationalist films of the fifties, both films undercut the myth of the brave Israeli warrior. Rather than being set in combat situations, a more likely locus for heroism, the films emphasize the more mundane reality of military training (*The Paratroopers*) and the mental pressures deriving from combat (*Repeat Dive*). The revisionist view of the military is especially striking in that it centers on two elite groups within the Israeli Defense Forces—paratroopers and frogmen. Such a disabused view of the military is a sensitive matter in a country where every male Jewish citizen is obliged not only to serve three years in the armed forces, but also to spend roughly thirty years in the reserves. The military experience is an integral part of Israeli life: for many Israelis, having served as a soldier forms part of one's self-definition as a man and as a citizen. Until the war in Lebanon, the consensus view was that failure to fulfill one's military duty was tantamount to a kind of primordial taint.

The Paratroopers portrays the plight of Weissman (Moni Mushonov), a recruit who volunteers for an elite corps of paratroopers but finds himself unable to bear the physical and mental strain. He tries to repress his own doubts, and his desire for self-respect prevents him from requesting a transfer. Eventually, intense peer pressure and a conflict with the company commander (Gidi Gov) make him break under the stress and commit suicide. The film does not end with his death, however, but rather with the cutting off, by the high command, of an investigation into its causes.

Shimon Dotan's *Repeat Dive*, meanwhile, focuses on the contradictory aspects of the lives of volunteer frogmen. After the death of his diving comrade, the commando Yoav (Doron Nesher) tries to console the comrade's widow, Mira (Liron Nirgad), and to overcome his own trauma. Unlike Weissman in *The Paratroopers*,

The dehumanization of the soldier in *The Paratroopers*.

Militarism and its discontents in *Repeat Dive*.

Yoav is an efficient professional, whose bravery borders on the heroic. But the film contrasts this bravery and efficiency in battle with the ineptitude and even cowardice that characterize his private life. The challenge of combat, paradoxically, provides Yoav and his peers with a kind of refuge from the more banal, but equally real, "dangers" of everyday emotional encounters.

Even when dealing with broader Israeli concerns such as the army (*The Para-troopers* and *Repeat Dive*) or the militarization in Israel (*The Wooden Gun, Hide and Seek*, and *The Night Soldier*), the films tend to couch their discourse in psycholog-ical terms, focalizing the effects of the Israeli political situation and militarization through the Sabra Protagonists. In *The Paratroopers*, for example, the Israeli situ-ation of incessant war is simply assumed as the basis for the events of the story. The critical stance and the doubts in the films are focused, therefore, on the psy-chological level, on the dubious morality of harassing soldiers. (The film's release in Israel provoked animated discussion about specific abuses within military train-ing.) Although the films do not fundamentally question the national consensus, they do demystify the traditional idealist representation of Sabra ideology, at least insofar as it negatively affects the individual. In *Hide and Seek*, the delicate, un-aggressive tutor, who does not join the Haganah (Defense) underground and has an affair with a Palestinian man, is violently threatened by Haganah members who falsely accuse him of being a spy—a presentation which demystifies the Haganah as intolerant. Although the main interest of the film is the ambiant violence and its effect on children and outsiders, the conflict between sensitive tutor/intolerant Haganah offers a displaced allegorical intimation of the relationship between the sensitive filmmaker and the Israeli Establishment, intolerant of sexual, political, and cinematic "deviations."

The Signification of Style

In personal films, the thematic interest in inner processes and the psychological states of the protagonists does not necessarily entail the use of the classical pscyhol-ogizing style of analytic editing. The art of "personal cinema" is one of reticence and pudeur, an art of litotes. Emotions are hinted at, obliquely suggested, left to be inferred by the spectator. The theme of loneliness is rendered by an intimist style, minimal dialogue, and the indirect expression of emotions. The refusal of dialogue betrays, at times, an allegiance to the "hegemony of the visible," the per-ception of the cinema as a "primarily visual" medium, in which dialogue forms an "acinematic" element. Long silences, unfinished sentences, and pauses pervade these films, contributing to a feeling of existential suspension. Unconventional angles underline the unsteadiness of the phenomenal world. An emphasis on interiors creates a sentiment of suffocation and claustrophobia, while even the occasional location shooting in the streets emphasizes emptiness and the lack of life. Largely shot in the older sections of Tel Aviv, *Transit*, for example, privileges decaying houses, dirty streets, and aging, antipathetic people. At times, the protagonists visit the Tel Aviv beach area—for example, in *Rocking Horse, Transit, The Wooden Gun,* and *A Thousand Little Kisses*—emphasizing their closeness to more classically defined marginals such as pimps and prostitutes. Both beach and street are imbued with a melancholy and gloom achieved not only through the isolation of the outsiders but also through a predilection for a "wintry" look which suggests a locale closer to the North Sea than to the Mediterranean. (Often these films are shot in the early morning, using filters to block the bright light.) Most of the films feature non-diegetic chamber music, usually scored for single instruments such as piano or flute, a choice well suited to the lugubrious atmosphere and slow pace of the films. The acting tends to be understated, a clear antithesis to the overt emotionalism of the "bourekas," but implying as well a rejection of the theatrical acting which had long characterized Israeli cinema due to the theatrical origins of many of its actors and actresses. Even the most dramatic moments, as a result, are played in a sober and restrained manner.

Although dealing with similar themes, Uri Zohar's films demonstrate a different stylistic approach. His sixties New Wavish film *Three Days and a Child* tells the story of a student (Oded Kotler)[21] asked by his ex-girlfriend and her husband to babysit their child, entailing three days in which he implicitly manifests a love-hate relationship to the child. In this film Zohar fuses a certain distancing with a more phenomenological approach, managing to extrapolate a New Wave ideology to the Israeli student milieu in the sixties. The symbolism of A. B. Yehoshua's short story, on which the film is based, is abolished, a refusal reflected particularly in the portrayal of Jerusalem not as the mystical city of God but rather as a human city daily lived, a mundane city of down-to-earth sensuality.

The films of Zohar's trilogy, *Peeping Toms, Big Eyes,* and *Save the Lifeguard*, together form a poignant and humorous portrait of the "never-grown-up" instability of restless Sabras. *Peeping Toms*, for example, is set mainly on a Tel Aviv beach. The film focuses on Israel's post–1967 war "lost generation," those Sabras who lost interest in the larger struggles of their country and retreated into a life of bohemian escapism. The rootless beach bums of the film, the partial products of the economic prosperity of the period, superficially mimic the life-style aspects of American counterculture, without in any way incorporating the political impetus of that movement. The lives of the characters, seen by the director with a kind of bemused sympathy, revolve around phallocentric sex, pop music, and a pronounced aversion to responsibility and family life. An old Ashkenazi man, a veteran of the pioneering idealism of another generation, scolds them: "That's the problem. You never accomplished anything, and you never will accomplish anything!" The literal voyeurism of the characters—they peek at women in the dressing rooms—comes to metaphorize the passivity and scopophilic non-involvement of the protagonists. As the generality of the title already suggests, their voyeurism goes beyond the sexual. As uncommitted observers, the film's marginal characters have a voyeuristic relation not only to mainstream Israeli society but also to Western post-sixties counterculture. The location shooting on the beach, unlike that of many of the personal films, reveals not a place for the introspection of an isolated protagonist, but rather a Mediterranean scene of summer festivity crowded with people. Within the shots there is constant movement, and dialogue plays an important role; the protagonists are prolix, they speak with expressive gestures in dialogues and monologues which in fact conceal their inner emotions, for they themselves are not terribly aware of the implications of their actions or life style.[22] Melancholy in the film is only implied, rather than stated, since the foreground of the film is taken up with humorous situations, a tone that sets Zohar's films like *Peeping Toms* apart from the earnest, high-serious tone of personal cinema.

Personal films tend toward subjectivized focalization of the protagonists, who often serve as the filmmaker's delegates expressing his/her point of view and the implicit "norms of the text." The subjectivization reflects a univocal perspective, since the films monologically restrict themselves to a single point of view, in both characterological and authorial terms. The films' closed discourse prevents the possibility of a polyphonic mode that might give voice to the multiplicity of voices within the entire culture. Narrative structure in personal cinema tends, at times, towards unconventionality, obvious, for example, in Yehuda Ne'eman's *The Paratroopers*, where the protagonist soldier is killed (or commits suicide) in the middle of the film, while the second part is focalized through the commander partially responsible for his death. Most of the personal films display an open-ended narrative structure reflecting a world of uncertainty and vagueness as well as the collapse of the value systems regnant during the first two decades of Israeli existence. In Avraham Hefner's *Where is Daniel Wax?* the middle-aged protagonist's quest for his youthful hero, the titular character, continues throughout most of the film. In the final sequences he discovers Daniel Wax, the ironic and anticlimactic embodiment of his idealized image. The problematic aspects of the protagonist's existence tend not to find resolution; it is left to the spectator to anticipate possible future developments. In the wake of the 1973 "Yom Kippur" War many films discard the conventional narrative closure typical of the earlier "heroic-nationalist" and "bourekas" films in favor of ambiguous, open-ended structures, as if classical narrative forms were incapable of "containing" the explosive ideological complexities of the altered perception of Israeli reality.

Personal cinema, as part of a general trend in world cinema, tends toward reflexivity (although rarely as part of a politicized Brechtian approach), whether by foregrounding the desire to make films (*Drifting*) or presenting the actual filming of a film (*Rocking Horse* and *Dead End Street*). The reflexivity consists as well in featuring surrogate artist-protagonists (a painter in *The Dreamer*, a singer in *Where is Daniel Wax?*, a painter-filmmaker in *Rocking Horse*, a writer in *Moments*, and a windowshop designer *in A Thousand Little Kisses*). When the characters are not artists they at least have a past connected to the arts (*Transit*) or show artistic sensitivity (to music in *Floch*, to poetry in *My Michael*). In other instances, the introspective protagonists are outsiders whose sensitive personalities clash with the ambiant conformism (the soldier in relation to the army in *The Paratroopers*, the member of a youth movement with regard to the kibbutz's Socialism in *Noa at Seventeen*, and a widow and the kibbutz in *Atalia*). Personal cinema's reflexivity operates, finally, on the level of introspective characters who serve as delegates of the filmmakers reflecting on themselves, symptomatically related to the autobiographical trope Paul de Man conceives as a "specular mode of cognition."[23]

These filmmakers at times literalize the notion of personal filmmaking by making personal appearances in their own films, whether playing major roles (for example, Uri Zohar in *Peeping Toms*, *Big Eyes*, and *Save the Lifeguard*) or making quick cameo appearances (for example, Yaki Yosha in *Rocking Horse* and *Dead End Street*). In *Dead End Street*, Yaki Yosha appears briefly as an actor in a television documentary, where he plays a prostitute's John. (The Godardian leitmotif of prostitution as metaphor is omnipresent in the film; the prostitute compares the television director to a pimp: "He sold me for money, and you are selling me for a film.") In *Rocking Horse*, Yosha appears as the conductor of a choir who asks the filmmaker-within-the-film to make less noise as he directs. Later, as the cameraman for the film-within-the-film (played by filmmaker Daniel Waxman) tells the filmmaker-protagonist that he's "not a real filmmaker," Yaki Yosha, in a self-ironic device, is shown standing behind his protagonist, as if the comment also applied to Yosha himself.

Rocking Horse also evokes the source novel's censure of the generally low level of Israeli cinema by obliquely criticizing the commercial films of Menahem Golan. The portrayal of the protagonist Aminadav's friend, a veteran from the Palmach period now become a prestigious producer whose thinking and personal style are reminiscent of Golan, intimates a critique of a once-idealistic generation which has now become obsessed with status and material success. At one point in *Rocking Horse* we see a poster of Yehuda Ne'eman's *The Paratroopers*, a film which demystifies military heroism as well as the heroic cinematic presentation of the army. The self-destructiveness of the protagonist of *The Paratroopers* mirrors that of the protagonist of *Rocking Horse*. When the filmmaker-protagonist asks the producer for help in making a personal film about his own past, the fast-talking producer responds with blustery talk about Hollywood and Oscars (at that point five of Golan's productions—*Sallah Shabbati*, *The Great Escape*, *I Love You, Rosa*, *The House on Chlouch Street*, and *Operation Thunderbolt*—had been nominated for Oscars). The producer also dictates memos concerning his new film called "the Parashooting of Arik," an obvious allusion to Golan's penchant for spectacular heroic films such as *The Great Escape* and *Operation Thunderbolt*. (Arik Lavi, who plays the producer, had acted in the latter film.) Here, *Rocking Horse* is ironic toward the heroic-idealistic image inscribed in Golan's films, echoes of a generation which has long since forgotten its ideals and now can do little more than profit from its past glory.

While the producer represents the Hollywood-style ambition of Golan, Aminadav as personal filmmaker serves as a delegate both for the state-generation writers and for the Kayitz filmmakers interested in quality films. Aminadav's production strategies also suggest an alternative to those of Golan. Indeed, the production methods of the film-within-the-film mirror those of *Rocking Horse* itself. The crew is minimal, the cast includes friends, i.e., nonprofessional actors, and the general approach is improvisational. The film-within-the-film also shows the actual filming of Aminadav's "father," shown as part of an attempt, quite typical of the personal filmmakers, to construct their own identity via filmmaking. Like Anthony Newley's *Can Hieronymus Merkin Ever Forget Mercy Humppe and Find True Happiness?* (1969), Fellini's *8 1/2* (1962), and Woody Allen's *Stardust Memories* (1980), *Rocking Horse* makes ironic references to film criticism. When Aminadev tells his cameraman that the shot has to be "authentic with soul as if everything is alive taking place now," the cameraman responds angrily: "Tell me close-up, and I'll shoot a close-up. Tell me zoom-out, and I'll understand. I am a technician, and the cinema is a dirty job. As for the matter of soul, leave it to those newspaper film critics. Soul is their profession." With the completion of the film-within-the-film, *Rocking Horse* as well comes to an end. After recuperating his past via the cinema, Aminadav burns his film. The final shot of the burning is accompanied by the film's theme song about "rocking horses all running in a circle," an image appropriate to his treadmill-like struggle. Just as he had earlier burned his paintings before leaving New York, now he burns his film back in his own land. The attempt to find his roots by filmically reconstructing his past from the day he was born seems only to have brought him back to the same zero point at which he began. Thus the film is hermetically sealed in the manner of "narcissistic narrative." Here personal cinema has reached its apogee in a totally specular structure which ends, like the Narcissus myth, in self-destruction.[24]

Marginality Revisited

If in *Rocking Horse* the filmmaker is figuratively present in the form of a Sabra outsider, in *Transit* the delegate of the feeling of marginality is a cultivated European immigrant in Israel. Waxman's reflexive-introspective film has numerous autobiographical elements. Born in Shanghai to a German refugee who never adjusted to Israel, Waxman sees in the story of Erich Neusbaum the preoccupation of two generations, both of which live in Israel but do not feel at home there and aspire to leave. The voice-over narration of the Sabra son, in this sense, adds the Sabra generation's perspective to a film largely focalized through the European immigrant. Feelings of rootlessness are reflected throughout the film not only as part of the story but also in terms of imagery. Erich's life in Israel has all the marks of transience; he has not established any lasting relationships, he does not speak Hebrew fluently, and his apartment is set for demolition. Erich Neusbaum's life is falling apart. Whereas in Germany he gained respect and recognition as an expert in antiquities in an important museum, in Tel Aviv he is the owner of an antique shop. "Is this what I dreamed about?" he asks Willi, his childhood friend. He forgets that he was fired from work and expelled from his house only because he was a Jew (although he always considered himself German). Willi reminds him: "We thought we were Germans, but one day they told us we were Jews."

Erich remembers an idealized Berlin. His attempts to adjust, his marriage to a Sabra, Yael, and the presence of their son, Michael, do not help him overcome his yearning for a mythical "back there." He prefers to speak German with his friend and sisters, reads newspapers in German, listens only to classical music on the radio, and dreams about his glamorous period in Berlin when he was surrounded by "culture," concerts, museums, pretty gardens, and good manners. His marriage now has disintegrated since his wife cannot handle the pressures of bridging the cultural differences. His relationship with his son is alienated as well: Michael cannot adjust to a father who speaks Hebrew with a heavy German accent and walks in the streets of Tel Aviv with a hat, scarf, and heavy coat brought from "there." The landlord forces him out of his apartment, his last refuge, and makes him pack his clothes in the leather suitcase which has accompanied him ever since his escape from Germany. His wanderings now are restricted to Tel Aviv. For a transitional period he lives in a motel near the beach, in a place frequented by drug dealers and prostitutes. While walking the streets of the alien city, Neusbaum ends his life in slow decay. The film ends with the voice-over of his son, who narrates, saying: "Sometimes I would run into him, but he would ignore me, until he altogether vanished."

Waxman's film deals with a protagonist, then, whose life in Israel is a kind of transit, a station on the way to somewhere else; a person who lives neither here nor there. The final shot of the film, an image of the sea, condenses the meaning of living in transit, of dwelling in the Levant but dreaming and hoping for the "there" beyond the sea, the West. His last station, the motel, encapsulates the marginality and feeling of non-belonging. Its location, not far from the sea, calls attention to his feeling of exclusion from the "real world"—Berlin, or Europe. The longing for another world, partially as a memory and partially as a response toward the present Levant, are emphasized through the physical closeness to the *yam* ("sea" as well as "west" in Hebrew), a recurrent image in the personal cinema. The East, then, is a place of transit, while the sea connotes the West and the route back to the "civilized" world.

These feelings of poetic alienation in Israeli cinema tend to be restricted to Israelis of European origin. Alienation, here, has nothing to do with a lack of

Without solace: The Holocaust survivor and son in *Transit*.

access to power; it derives, rather, from a feeling of a displacement of a European entity now forced to adapt to another climate. Although the Israeli welfare state supplies people like Neusbaum with the physical and economic means for their well-being—Neusbaum also owns an antique store and presumably receives German reparation money—he does not feel at home. The memories of European victimization have been repressed in favor of an obsessive daydream, reflecting deeply ambivalent and contradictory dynamics; on the one hand, he is a refugee expelled from his country simply for being a Jew; on the other, he not only misses the country of his youth but also despises everything Israeli as vulgar and underdeveloped. The European Jew has found physical and economic safety in Israel, Waxman implies, but he has not found emotional refuge there.

In the same vein, film critic Yossef Sharik writes: "Daniel Waxman thinks that many of Neusbaum's countrymen share his tragedy—whether their origin is Hungary, Poland, Russia, whether they are veterans or newcomers."[25] In this sense, both film and film critic share an idealist view of alienation and marginality. In this view, it is not those from the Middle East (Palestinians and Sephardim) who are the marginals and lack power, but rather the rootless European in the Levant, even though it is not he who is denied social mobility, and even though it is his beloved musical culture of Beethoven and Bach which is broadcast daily by the official radio, and even though European high culture forms the ideal ego of the national Establishment. This paradox of felt marginality and real power is revealed in the film itself. Neusbaum is annoyed by the ill-mannered aggressivity associated in the film with "natural" outsiders, i.e., pimps and prostitutes, the Sephardi underworld. (Neusbaum's detachment from Israeli reality and thinly veiled racial hostility strongly resemble the prejudices of the title character of Saul Bellow's *Mr. Sammler's Planet*, a European emigré who yearns for Old World gentility and feels menaced by black street crime.) He detests the loud Greek-Oriental music he is forced to hear in the streets. Alone in his room, he turns to classical music for solace. It is here that the superficiality of the film's view of marginality is exposed. The music heard in the streets is precisely that which is *not* broadcast on the radio; it is the popular expression regarded by the Establishment as dubious legitimacy. In *Rocking Horse*, similarly, Aminadav, although psychically an outsider, nevertheless enjoys access to power; he asks for support for his introspective films from his well-placed producer friend. In both *Transit* and *Rocking Horse*, the background of pimps and prostitutes merely accentuates the status of the protagonists as unconventional people marginalized by their sensibilities or cultural orientation; their marginalism is, as a matter of choice, a luxury.

The feelings of alienation depicted in personal films are shared by European immigrants and even by their Sabra offspring. The feelings are those of the ethnic elite which nevertheless feels it does not belong, for reasons that are almost never political or economic but always artistic and cultural. The constant flight from "here" to an internal space of an imaginary revolving around the United States and Europe suggests a feeling of being on the periphery, a feeling not without analogies to that of many Europeanized Third World intellectuals. This feeling of living at the margins of the "real world" is doubled, in the Israeli context, by a sentiment of superiority on the part of the elite as the internal representatives of what the Israeli media still like to term "the civilized world."

If in the early films pioneers arrived from the sea to make the desert bloom, in personal films—presumably decades after the desert has bloomed—the protagonists still dream of elsewhere. Even when the films do not involve flight in the literal sense, the feeling of flight still structures the films, since the protagonists, who are never at home, are continually searching. If the Palestinian has been displaced, and the Sephardi is misplaced, the European immigrant and the Sabra, ironically, feel out of place, still longing like any extraterritorial for an imaginary home. Although the West does form part of the protagonists' world in these films—they have returned from there (*Rocking Horse*), or dream of traveling there (*Drifting*), or develop relationships with those who arrive from there (*Moments*, *A Thousand Little Kisses*, and *The Lover*), or the presence of an "alien" Holocaust survivor impinges on their consciousness (*The Wooden Gun* and *Hide and Seek*) or forms part of their spiritual world—it also corresponds to a broader Israeli obsession with "being elsewhere," deriving partly from the lived paradox of physical closeness to Eastern neighbors combined with a feeling of being "closed" off from them and by them.

Whereas the "bourekas" references to the West tend to focus on the United States as a symbol of the material possibilities it offers the Sephardi working class and lumpenproletariat, in personal cinema the West also includes Europe and has a more idealized role in the narrative, implying a world of quality and sensibility with which the characters feel a strong affinity. And whereas in the heroic-nationalist films the Western character was gradually incorporated into the unshakable Sabra world and into the unshakable Zionist-moralist values, in personal cinema the Sabra protagonists, who no longer embody rootedness in the old/new land, tend to find identificatory solace in an implied West. In this sense, Vitek Tracz' *Fantasia on a Romantic Theme* (*Fantasia al Nosse Romanti*, 1978), scripted by Hanoch Levine, implies a certain historical irony. Tracz' oneiric film deals with provincial "little people" who spend their days eagerly preparing for the arrival of the Queen of Sweden. The adoration of the quintessentially Nordic glamor of the queen comes implicitly to symbolize the inferiority complex of a small Middle Eastern country which dreams of sharing the faraway romance of the Occident. In personal cinema, the *nostalgie d'Europe*, the passivity, the impotence, the introspection, and the marginalization from a mainstream orderly world—all stand in opposition to the cinematic inscription of the Sabra in the heroic-nationalist films. The existential vision of beleaguered individuality must be viewed, in allegorical terms, as homologizing a collective unconscious feeling of the State of Israel as itself isolated in the Levant and whose mental affinity is with the West.

The themes of alienation and the search for identity, the open-ended narrative structures, and the often claustrophobic atmosphere of the personal films reflect a kind of political and emotional impasse, a dead-end structure of feeling. The negativity of most of the films, in which the spectator is offered a series of lacks, absences, and deteriorations, with few clues as to the possible transcendence of ambiguities, must be understood within the broader seventies context. Although the narratives of such films are structured around the intimate tales of sensitive outsider protagonists, such protagonists embody the relatively new culture of Sabras, whose mystique can no longer base itself on the pioneering myth of making the desert bloom and establishing the state, since those goals have been achieved, or around the Socialist ideals of an egalitarian society, since the Black Panther revolt revealed that there is an angry "Second Israel" which threatens the economic, political, and cultural hegemony of the Ashkenazi Sabras. The ongoing occupation of Palestinians in Gaza and the West Bank since the 1967 war, meanwhile, has contradicted the humanist image of "beautiful Israel."

The rootlessness and the quest for identity of the Ashkenazi Sabra protagonists in the unresolved narratives and the pessimistic tone of these films can be seen as allegorizing, even if inadvertently, the political scene, especially in the wake of the 1973 war. The Labor Party, then headed by Golda Meir, lost a good deal of its mystique and was forced to transfer leadership to a younger generation, that of the Sabras Yitzhak Rabin and Shimon Peres, untainted by the *mehdal yom haKippurim* (the common term referring to the political failure to foresee and successfully carry out the war). At the same time, "dovish" Sabras established the Shinui (Change) movement to protest government ineptitude. A few months before the 1977 Knesset election, a new political party, the Democratic Movement for Change (DMC) (HaTnua haDemocratit leShinui) was established, drawing members from the whole spectrum of nonreligious Zionist parties from Labor to Likud. The common theme uniting this coalition of hawks and doves, conservatives and liberals, extreme and moderate nationalists was their resentment against Labor mismanagement and against the corruption, nepotism, and cronyism which had characterized the previous Labor-led coalitions. The establishment of the new party, in other words, revealed the extent of Ashkenazi-Sabra disenchantment with Labor without revealing a strong ideological shift away from the ideological assumptions of Labor. Just as personal cinema did not question fundamental ideology, preferring to deal with symptoms, so the new movement did not question underlying political doxa and entrenched structures. It was this situation that led to the loss of prestige of "politics," a word that came to be synonymous with corruption and petty power-seeking. The world of art and the imagination, in contrast, came to form a kind of antithesis, a Kantian realm of pure and disinterested ideas, far from the trivial, mundane and inevitably disappointing world of political action.

The rise of Likud in 1977, meanwhile, led to concrete feelings of marginality and threatened hegemony on the part of young Sabras. This feeling too was somewhat artificial, however, in the sense that the surface political change—after thirty years in power Labor was forced into opposition—masked the deep structural control still exercised by Labor through its tentacular economic institutions. The illusion of marginality in personal cinema, and in Sabra culture generally, is thus quite ironic, in the sense that it is precisely those who feel marginalized who in fact continue to exercise political, economic, and cultural hegemony. The symptomatic martyrdom and projected exclusion of their narrative delegates has to be seen, therefore, as a kind of romanticized fantasy of victimization, or as a melodramatic allegory of a bitter, and largely imaginary, marginality.

The emphasis on interiority and introspection reflects, then, not only an attempt at psychological self-insight but also a Sabra refusal to confront the deterioration of the Sabra ethos. This flight from deep-structural reassessments helps explain, perhaps, certain thematic and stylistic features of the films, for example, the fondness for fantasy and daydream, on a content level, in *My Michael*, *Floch*, and *Fantasia on a Romantic Theme*, as well as a certain preference for soft focus and abstraction of time and place. The historical period in *Transit* is never specified, while the references to the 1967 war in the source novel for *Rocking Horse* were changed in the film to an abstract notion of "future wars," a rendering which translates the feeling, in the seventies, of a general anxiety which, together with the rise of Likud, generated the Peace Now movement (Tnuat Shalom Achshav), characterized by vague hopes for an "end to wars" rather than by any clear ideological perspective.

The high hopes for the Democratic Movement for Change as an alternative to the decaying Labor Party which would bring "new blood" to the political scene were soon disappointed when in 1977 the DMC joined the Begin coalition, thus contradicting the convictions of many of its voters. The gap between the "idealism" of the pioneers and the "materialism" of the society of the seventies, where corruption had become commonplace, created in the young Sabra generation what is commonly referred to in Israel as the "crisis of values." It is no accident, perhaps, that for the first time in the history of Israeli cinema, the films begin to feature narrative instances of mental breakdown—the case with *On a Thin Line, Mark of Cain* (*Ot Cayin*, 1982; distributed abroad as *Stigma), Romance Resumed* and *Rocking Horse*—as if Israelis were beginning to collapse under the strain of disillusionment within a "no-exit situation." The personal cinema of this period narrates the Sabra's shattered consensus and can be seen as allegorizing on another register the Sabra mood of disenchantment and loss of faith in collective ideals. Art, in this context, came to be seen as protected from the insidious effects of the political. In this period, we often find artists defining themselves as "apolitical" or "uninterested in politics." Such affirmations were made, ironically, even when the subject matter of the films was charged with social and political themes. Yitzhak Yeshurun said of his television social drama *Koby and Maly* (*Koby veMaly*, 1977) that the film was "not meant to be relevant to today's social reality" and that he made the film because of his own problems of "confrontations with the Establishment."[26]

The ideological vertigo of this Sabra generation resulted in a pronounced nostalgia for the easy certitudes associated with earlier stages of Zionism, especially that of the pioneers and to a certain extent that of the Palmach. This nostalgia manifested itself in diverse cultural areas in the late seventies. The celebrated singer Arik Einstein (who played major roles in Zohar's *Peeping Toms* and *Big Eyes* and in Boaz Davidson's *Snail*) recorded many "Shirei Eretz Israel haYeshana vehaTova" (Songs of Old and Good Israel) updated with modern orchestration and arrangements. The very term "Old and Good Israel" (or "Old and Beautiful Israel") came to connote the idealist spirit of early Zionism, sometimes seen as predominating up to the foundation of the state, and sometimes seen as extending to later periods (the early fifties, as in *Noa at Seventeen* and Yehuda Ne'eman's documentary *Crush* [*Ya Brechen*, 1985], or to the 1967 war, or to the 1973 war.) Many of the pioneering songs, usually Russian songs translated into Hebrew, or Russian-influenced songs evoking the Socialist-Zionist enthusiasm of the Second Aliya, represented for Sabras a sentimental memory of a past utopia capable of nourishing them in the present confusion. This nostalgia was implicit already in Zohar's *Hole in the Moon*, and in more recent texts we find any number of allusions to this lost paradise: the old lifeguard in *Peeping Toms*, who criticizes the present-day Sabras for their listless life; the elderly Max in *Atalia*, who criticizes the bourgeois tendencies of the kibbutz (he protests the exploitation of Arab labor in the kibbutz and calls for *avoda ivrit*). *Romance Resumed* foregrounds this nostalgia through its middle-aged Sabra protagonist, resuming his love for his ex-wife, his first love, who represents the idealistic purity and virgin outlook of his younger self and of his generation. Crushed by the corruption of his Labor Party friends, the ambitious lawyer yearns for his/their youth and attempts unsuccessfully to resuscitate past moments, places, and symbols. Produced in 1985 but set in 1977, the historical moment immediately preceding Labor's partial loss of power, the film elegizes the disappointed hopes of the Sabra generation.[27] The casting of Topol for the role of the protagonist (with his wife Galia as the divorcée and his real-life daughter as the daughter) adds a further layer of meaning, since he incarnates the early idealism as well as the later embourgeoisement of his generation.[28]

The romanticized portrayal of the Tel Aviv of the thirties in Ran Adar's recent film *Gloves* (*Kfafot*, 1986), similarly, suggests a nostalgia for the cultivated European spirit of the early immigrants.[29] (The high production values of the film translate this nostalgia by depicting a standard of living considerably higher than that actually enjoyed.) The sensitive, educated boxer protagonist of the film, associated with haPoel, the workers' sporting association, fights the supposedly unbeatable Italian-American boxer only to prove that he is not afraid, and he rejects the offers to become a corrupt boxing "star" in the United States. The films' narrative dynamic is not unlike what Harold Clurman[30] termed the opposition of "fist and fiddle" in Clifford Odets' depression drama *Golden Boy* (filmed by Rouben Mamoulian in 1939), a play in which the hero renounces the unlucrative vocation of concert violinist for the lucre of professional boxing. At the high point of his success, he abandons championship boxing for the love of a woman and the cultivated life. The implied contrast between the Americanization of present-day Israeli society and the vanished idealism of a projected past has as its corollary a nostalgia for the idealistic Zionism of the founding fathers. The nostalgic focus, ultimately, constitutes a form of displaced narcissism. There is no critique in *Atalia*, for example, of the theory and practice of *avoda ivrit;* rather, the film purveys an idealized view of the purity of the pioneer stage. The mystique of "beautiful Israel" treats the founding fathers as if they operated in a vacuum, rather than as power figures presiding over three distinct groups: Ashkenazim, Sephardim, and Palestinians. Personal films separate the present-day Sabra world from these relations of interdependency, as if the history of these other groups were not imbricated with their own history. The more recent political phase of personal cinema, as discussed in Chapter 5, attempts to draw out such implications, yet remains marked by an idealized self-image combined with great difficulty in truly dealing with the "other"—the Palestinian, the Sephardi—in his/her complexity.

Whatever the social and ideological limitations of personal cinema, there can be no underestimating of the long distance traveled since the time of the heroic-nationalist films. While the 1967 war generated a euphoric expectation of long-term political stability and military security, the 1973 war only revealed the intractable nature of the conflict. The extension of Israeli territory, it turned out, had merely expanded the dimensions without changing the nature of Israel's fundamental dilemmas. The grandiose sentiment of an end-to-war slowly gave way to a sinking feeling of "inevitable" and interminable conflict. (This feeling was presciently anticipated in the late-sixties plays of Hanoch Levine: *You and I and the Next War* [*At veAni vehaMilhama haBa'a*, 1968], *Ketchup* [1969], and *The Queen of the Bathtub* [*Malkat haAmbatia*, 1970].) This larger trajectory of disenchantment is reflected in the evolution of Israeli cinema from the heroic-nationalist to the personal phase. The political optimism of the earlier films turns into the pervasive pessimism of the later films; triumphant closure gives way to unresolved non-endings. Heroes, dynamic agents taking control of the land and of their collective destiny, metamorphose into anti-heroes, passive playthings of a situation beyond their control. The collective thrust of the heroic-nationalist films gives way, with the personal films, to a focus on isolated, monadic protagonists. Confident speeches give way to anxious reticence, and the old pride gives way to vulnerability. War itself, treated as ultimately salutary, a school for valor and ethnic self-pride in the heroic-nationalist films, becomes in the personal films a training ground in disillusionment; now the soldiers appear weary, cynical, and even resentful, but, never, finally, rebellious. No longer enthusiastic participants in a glorious struggle for liberation, they now see themselves as performing the drudge work of military duty. The clearly delineated external conflicts of the earlier films now give way to internalized psychic battles without easy solutions or "victories." The feeling of national unity, achieved in the heroic-nationalist films by military victory against the Arabs and in the "bourekas" by interethnic marriage, gives way to a generalized feeling of anomie, atomization, deviation, and marginality.

This overall evolution from confidence and unity to dispersion and nagging self-doubt is reflected even in the stylistic traits of personal films. In contrast with the grand-scale exterior shooting and epic spatiality of the heroic-nationalist films, the personal films, precisely in a period when Israel has expanded its territory, are shot in claustrophobic interiors, developing a suffocating atmosphere of confinement hemming in lost and disoriented Sabra protagonists. The "opening up of the borders," far from definitively pushing the Palestinians off the stage of history, meanwhile, left Israel as haunted as ever by the Palestinian presence, revealing in clearer outlines what had always been at the root of the Israeli-Arab conflict. The personal films, however, rarely dealt directly with the conflict; they expressed only the feeling of a general malaise which could be read as generated by an ongoing state of war and the shattering of Zionist hopes for a "new man" and a new society. Personal cinema articulated little serious dissent from the Zionist consensus, and it was only with the 1982 invasion of Lebanon that it began even to address the perennially explosive issue: the Palestinians.

5.

The Return of the Repressed: The Palestinian Wave in Recent Israeli Cinema

Most Israeli artists and intellectuals belong, in a general sense, to the social stratum whose basic values have been expressed within the Labor movement. Since the late fifties, this group had chosen to turn "inward," implicitly expressing reservations toward Ben-Gurionism, reservations which at times took on the overtones of an Oedipal revolt. With the 1977 rise of Likud to political power, artist-intellectuals began to express vigorous discontent, largely channeled through the Peace Now movement. The policies of Likud, which ultimately have differed but slightly from those of Labor, provoked reactions not simply against the policies themselves but also against the very idea of Likud, considered by this milieu as virtually a "foreign" government, being in power at all. Despite their dissatisfaction with Labor, the liberal (in Israeli discourse "left") Sabra artists supported the Labor oppositional party by establishing Peace Now in 1978.

The incursion into Lebanon in 1982, which lasted far longer than originally planned, generated not only political movement but also oppositional artistic practices in the form of poems, plays, photographs, and films thematizing the political situation. This transition is clearly seen in the works of former self-designated "apolitical" personal filmmakers such as Yehuda Ne'eman and Daniel Waxman, or poets such as Nathan Zach and Dalia Rabikowitz. Student films, which before the Lebanon war tended to betray indifference to political issues, began focusing on aspects of the Israeli-Arab conflict. (Some of these films, such as Gur Heller's *Night Film* [*Seret Laila* 1986], won various awards abroad. Even feature films whose themes do not involve the Israeli-Arab conflict, such as Eitan Green's *Till the End of the Night*, Michal Bat Adam's *The Lover*, Yitzhak Yeshurun's *Queen of the Class* [*Malkat haKitta* 1986], and Amnon Rubinstein's *Nadia* [1986], have begun including Palestinian characters, mostly in minor worker or student roles.) Although this political wave has been far from revolutionary and shares the psychologizing tendency of personal cinema, it marks, through its references to a Palestinian entity, a new phase within Israeli culture.

The "Palestinian Wave" must first be examined in relational terms. Since the decline of the heroic-nationalist films, Israeli cinema had tended to repress the Arab issue on the screen. Israel's isolation from its neighbors, its political rejection by many states, and the facts of military duty and constant wars gradually came to be assumed as axiomatic to the country's existence. The Israeli-Arab conflict and the siege mentality remained latent, however, an unspoken presence in "bourekas" as well as personal cinema. The mythical celebration of ethnic/class and Ashkenazi/Sephardi unity in the "bourekas" participates in and forms part of this un-uttered context of Jewish unity in the face of Arab animosity. The implicit presence of an "Arab" figure functions as an unconscious catalyst of a desire for a narrative closure that celebrates "familial" solidarity against a presumed common enemy. The integrationist ideology is, at least partially, premised on the "Arab" figure as equally threatening to both Ashkenazim and Sephardim, a view that ultimately legitimizes Ashkenazi hegemony, in the sense that the pressures of security and burdens of defense do not allow, as officials point out, for the "betterment" of the Sephardi situation or for "ethnic division" in the form of Oriental political self-assertion.

In personal films, meanwhile, the escape into existential-psychological inwardness can be seen as a symptom of fatigue with a condition of constant political tension, where the grinding daily barrage of news items, followed avidly by the general populace, simply feeds into a general anxiety. Individuality represents, in this sense, the site of solace from the constant ideological pressure to "take a position." The elision of the Israeli-Arab conflict, in other words, allows for a "broader" discourse of universality beyond the annoyingly limited "here and now." The repression of specific markers of Israeli quotidian reality and the abstraction of time and place in many personal films suggest, to quote what literary critic Nurit Gertz wrote of Amos Oz (particularly of his early writings), an underlying conception that "reality in itself is not worthy of description and is presented only as an empty sign for the (threatening) phenomena that lie beyond it."[1] While implying a desire to escape from a dead-end situation to "another place" (the title of one of Amos Oz' novels), the structuring of introverted solitude, alienation, and the search for identity comes to allegorize Israel itself as a nation shunned by many countries, alienated from the Middle East, closed within its geographical and mental borders, and borrowing much of its political and cultural identity from the West.

At times, personal films interweave an intimate story with the conjuring up of the Israeli-Arab conflict. Dan Wolman's *My Michael* has the woman protagonist's imaginary revolve around Arab twins with whom she used to play before Jerusalem was divided in 1948. Living in the Western part of Jerusalem, the world of science and rationality represented by her husband, she is unconsciously lured to the sexually and politically unattainable "Other." The twins, in other words, form part of a binary structure—typical of Amos Oz' writing—which unveils a quasi-metaphysical collision of forces. In this sense, evocations of historical, political context are transcended to symbolize universal, metaphysical phenomena. Films such as *The Paratroopers, The Wooden Gun, Hide and Seek, The Vulture, Repeat Dive, The Last Winter* (*HaHoref haAharon*, 1982), and *Atalia*, meanwhile, assume the Israeli-Arab conflict as a given. The narrative is developed on the axiom of the concrete Israeli experience of wars and militarization, examining, within a psychological discourse, the Israeli protagonists and, by implication, the Israeli mental state.

The Focalization of Politics

Refusing its taken-for-granted status, the recent political films foreground the Israeli-Arab conflict. The first attempt at a relatively critical representation of the conflict was seen in 1978 in Ram Levi's *Khirbet Khizeh*,[2] produced by Israeli Television, the single, government-owned station. Based on S. Yizhar's 1949 story of the same title, the film, which revolves around a detachment of Israeli soldiers sent to evacuate the Arab inhabitants of Khirbet Khizeh (a fictional Arab village), provoked public anger, even in liberal circles, and was even denounced as PLO propaganda.[3] (This claim was further "supported" by the fact that the film was taped from Israel and broadcast by Jordanian Television.) After the Lebanon war, however, the reception of political films such as Daniel Waxman's *Hamsin* (1982), Yehuda Ne'eman's *Fellow Travelers* (*Magash haKessef*, literally *The Silver Platter*, 1983), Uri Barabash's *Beyond the Walls*, Nissim Dayan's *A Very Narrow Bridge* (*Gesher Tzar Me'od*, 1985), Shimon Dotan's *The Smile of the Lamb* (*Hiukh haGdi*, 1986), Amos Gitai's *Esther* (1986), and Raffi Bukai's *Avanti-Popolo* (1986) was generally more positive. The few angry rightist reviews were more than offset by the predominantly liberal media, and, at times, as in the case of *Beyond the Walls*, antagonist Meir Kahane demonstrations were met by enthusiastic counterdemonstrations. Most of the "Palestinian Wave" films, furthermore, have been partially funded by the government through the Fund for the Encouragement of Original Quality Films. Some of the films have won prizes offered by official institutions and have officially represented Israel in international film festivals, where some have again won prizes. *Hamsin*, for example, was awarded the Israeli Oscar for Best Israeli Film for 1982, an award granted by the Ministry of Commerce and Industry and the Ministry of Education and Culture. *Beyond the Walls* won the same award for 1984 and was selected as Israel's official representative for Hollywood's Academy Awards (where it was nominated for Best Foreign Film) as well as for the Venice Film Festival (where it won First Critic's Prize). *The Smile of the Lamb* also won the Israeli Oscar (handed over by the Minister of Commerce and

Industry, Ariel Sharon) and represented Israel at the Berlin Film Festival for 1986 (where it won Best Actor Award), while *Avanti-Popolo* represented Israel at the Lucarno Film Festival for 1986 (where it won First Prize).

The official recognition and partial support has been reductively seen by Palestinian newspapers (particularly in East Jerusalem) and Egyptian journals (renaming, for instance, *The Smile of the Lamb* as "The Smile of the Wolf") as proof of a sophisticated Israeli propaganda ploy, whereas, in fact, the mechanisms have been much subtler, and often have gone unrecognized by the filmmakers themselves. Although the films offer progressive images within the history of the Israeli representation of the conflict, they operate within the general framework and assumptions of Zionism. Rather than expressing any clear ideological perspective, they translate Sabra confusion and bewilderment at the realization of the existence of the Other, the Palestinian, as victim. This dynamic, ultimately full of ambiguity, ambivalence, and vagueness, muffles the critical thrust of the films and allows for official support. The filmmakers tend to be from the same milieu, class, and ethnic origins as the members of the governmental fund committees, furthermore, and are therefore not perceived as a threat. (It is hard to imagine at the present any equivalent support for a militant Palestinian-Israeli film on the same subject. In Gaza, a Palestinian painter was arrested simply for using the colors of the Palestinian flag in one of his paintings. Israel in this sense is democratic only for Sabras.)

The question of self-image, furthermore, plays an important role for the Israeli Establishment which partially draws its Western support on the basis of the topos "only democracy in the Middle East." The preoccupation with projecting the liberal image of a country with free speech that exposes critical views constitutes an important factor in the government's tolerance of such films. Sabra liberal culture, meanwhile, shares this general concern with its self-image and that of Israel as a whole, a concern pervading speeches, manifestos, articles, and books. (This emphasis derives partially from the liberal-Socialist education of the Labor movement and its belief in its own moral qualities and spirit.) Many filmmakers, upon arriving from political screenings abroad, report on the important service the films have rendered in disseminating a democratic image of Israel. In the wake of the Lebanon war, the non-Israeli Zionist need for reassurance concerning Israel's moral credibility also meant a more receptive attitude toward critical Israeli films on the part of Jewish distributors who previously displayed hesitation toward such "deviations." The producers of *Hamsin*, for example, found to their surprise that Jewish distributors abroad accepted the film, arguing that "such a film proves that there is a democracy in Israel, and a free stage to express opinions."[4] Government support, based at least partially on the idea of exporting a liberal image, was given also to foreign productions such as Costa-Gavras' pro-Palestinian *Hanna K.* As a government official remarked: "We got favorable publicity for being liberals. Had we made problems for Costa-Gavras, the left-wing press would have had a field day."[5] The very exhibition of an Israeli film on a Palestinian issue certifies, as it were, the reality of democracy and reassures the liberal conscience of both the producers and the receivers of the images.

The refusal to censor or prohibit the films did not, however, exempt them from semiofficial obstacles, at times, engendered by the self-same preoccupation with images, this time from a more rightist concern with the negative impact of projecting a critical picture of Israel. An unproblematic film within the country can become controversial when distributed abroad. When *Hamsin* was shown at the Israeli Film Festival in New York, for example, the General Consul of Israel in New York decided not to lend official backing to the festival and not to take part as a major speaker because the "film might hurt the image of Israel."[6] (The Israeli economic representative in New York and the Center for the Israeli Film in Jerusalem, however, gave support to the screening of *Hamsin* in New York.) In the case of *Israel 83*, a compilation of six short films made by various filmmakers, whose common theme is the Israeli occupation of the West Bank, and more precisely the effect of the occupation on the occupiers, classical censorship was applied. Yehuda Ne'eman's episode, *The Night the King was Born* (*HaLaila bo Nolad haMelech*), was originally censored by the Council of Criticism of Films and Plays because the film defamed the Israeli Defense Forces (IDF) and would provoke storms among the Arab population,[7] as if "storms" on the West Bank depended on the reproduction of abuses on celluloid. The censorship order was canceled only after a protest from the producer (Tzavta Theater). Whereas most of the episodes tended toward absurdist symbolic tales such as Yigal Bursztyn *The Anguish of Dr. Vider* (*Yisurav shel Dr. Vider*) and Ram Levi's *Survival* (*Hisardut*) or toward psychological drama as in Shimon Dotan's *Souvenirs from Hebron* (*Mazkarot meHevron*), *The Night the King Was Born* focuses directly and in a realistic style on the violent expropriation of land carried out on the West Bank with the support of the army. This directness provoked the ire of the censors, who, although formally prohibited from censoring on purely political grounds, could nevertheless, according to the enabling 1928 law (inherited from British colonialism), refuse or allow permission to a film "according to its view." The producers' legal defense was obliged to contest the censors' argument about the distortion of the IDF's image by citing cases in which the army actually used its power to force Arabs to sign papers. Thus the censors were obliged to permit the film's screening, managing only to excise some footage showing the army's physical abuses, on the grounds, ironically, of "morality."[8]

The films at times face obstacles at the production stage. In the case of Nissim Dayan's *A Very Narrow Bridge*, the filming suffered from the very pressures and barriers discussed in the film. *A Very Narrow Bridge*, which revolves around a tortured love story between a reserve military prosecutor in Ramallah (West Bank) and a Christian Palestinian woman school librarian, was the first feature to be shot on the West Bank. The location shooting in occupied territory and the necessity of shuttling between actual groups rather than completely restaging events triggered political reactions that quite often hampered the production. Even a few days before filming, the crew was not entirely sure that the filming would take place. Army authorities originally refused to permit the production on the West Bank and only at the last minute did Haim Hefer, the co-scriptwriter, convince some old friends from Palmach days, presently in power, that despite "the script, however problematic, it was still fair to reality."[9] And since connections (*protektzia*) are an indispensable lubricant within the Israeli social system, the permission was granted. The film crew had permission from the army spokesman to film outdoors in the West Bank, though not in the offices of the civilian administration there. The support, however, was minimal. The production company was obliged to buy uniforms and guns from the same source that supplies the IDF, even though American film productions were usually given the equipment (and often more sophisticated equipment, such as tanks)[10] by the army. Menahem Golan's *Delta Force*, based on the TWA hijacked airplane and shot the same year as *A Very Narrow Bridge*, was produced with the full support of the Ministry of Defense, with Yitzhak Rabin's and Ariel Sharon's assistance."[11] Although the Cannon Production Company paid about $175,000 for the services and even contributed the money from the premiere to the Association for the Soldier,[12] one can also notice the Establishment enthusiasm for films like *Delta Force* in contrast to its hesitation with regard to more critical films like *A Very Narrow Bridge*.

The production company of *A Very Narrow Bridge* also had to pay for the services of two border patrol soldiers to guard their camp, and when filming in the city of Ramallah had to rely on their own resources. To guarantee security, the crew dressed up some extras as border patrolmen, which did little to diminish the stones and even Molotov cocktails thrown at them by angry Palestinians. And when the crew staged a curfew scene, some Ramallah residents, believing it to be an actual military curfew, ran to their homes, in a literal crossover between fictive microcosm and social macrocosm. On another occasion there was a clash between military people and the Israeli-Palestinian actor Yussuf Abu-Warda.[13] The producer, Micha Sharfshtein, spent much of his time asking for army authorizations for filming, authorizations that were promised and then canceled as the film's political drift became clear. On the Israeli right, the film, like all the "Palestinian Wave" films, provoked anger, not only for its "leftist" stance but also for its foregrounding a mixed couple, an explosive issue given paranoid emphasis by the Kahane forces.

The reactions against the film on the Palestinian side were even stronger. Although the film was declaredly sympathetic toward the occupied people, suspicion was inevitable in the case of a film made by Israelis about Palestinians, especially one with governmental support. The antagonism derived not only from political motives but also from sexual ones: the Palestinians objected to the proposed love affair between an Arab woman (played by the Israeli-Palestinian actress Salwa Nakara-Haddad) and an Israeli officer (Aharon Ipale).[14] (Most films tended to feature the converse, i.e., sexual interaction between an Israeli woman and a Palestinian man, as in *Hamsin, The Lover*, and *Hanna K.*, a filmic emphasis reflecting a real social tendency, by which most mixed couples consist of Jewish women and Arab men.) The Greek Orthodox Patriarch of Ramallah placed a ban on all contact with the film crew, obliging the caravan of twenty vehicles to travel to Kuffur Yassif in the Galilee (the village of the Israeli-Palestinian actor Makram Khoury) to film church interiors. The West Bank Teachers' Association published a statement denouncing "coexistence" as expressed in a film where a Palestinian teacher educates her students to the struggle, but then succumbs to the wiles of an Israeli officer. *Al Fajr*, the East Jerusalem newspaper, published two articles criticizing the film. Published after clarifications from Nissim Dayan, the second article was more fervent than the first and even offered a list of all those who had agreed to allow filming on their property. As a consequence, some of those who had promised access to locales withdrew their permission.

The Arab members of the crew, and particularly Salwa Nakara-Haddad, received threats, and even the East Jerusalem Palestinian theater, Al Hakawati, which generally objects to any form of censorship, denounced and pressured her. Salwa Nakara-Haddad was placed in a paradoxical situation in which Israeli soldiers, whom she as a Palestinian resents, had to protect her from her own people, a situation revealing the anguished ambivalences of the encounter between Israeli-Palestinians and the Palestinians of the West Bank and Gaza Strip since the occupation began in 1967. The reactions against the "negative" image of an Arab woman had the paradoxical effect of convincing Salwa Nakara-Haddad of the progressive (feminist) import of her cinematic role (even though she did not agree with all the points made by the film and thought that a Palestinian writer could have shaped a more authentic Arab image), thus creating a certain feminist parallelism between her cinematic role as a Palestinian woman and her actual role in life as a daring Palestinian actress. The hostility the Israeli/Palestinian couple face from both the occupiers and the occupied, within the film, was, in other words, mirrored by the production, a parallelism registered by Dina Tzvi Riklis' documentary on the making of the Dayan film, *View from a Very Narrow Bridge* (*Mar'e miGesher Tzar Meod*, 1985).

The political films of the eighties deviate dramatically from the traditional representation of the Israeli/Arab conflict by focusing more on the Palestinian (as opposed to the Arab) dimension of that conflict—a change in emphasis that parallels the emergence of the "Palestinian entity" within left-wing discourse as a whole. The war-genre schema that mediated most of the heroic-nationalist films, and which was intrinsic to the David/Goliath ideological perspective, is no longer suitable at a time when the Jewish side wields disproportionate power in relation to the Palestinian, as opposed to the venerable tiny-Israel/mighty-Arabs trope. The new generic locus for the Arab/Jewish encounter is no longer the battlefield; the

"Palestinian Wave" includes a fairly wide range of narrative and generic patterns that depart from the traditional Manichean representation.

Fellow Travelers, for example, combines a thriller format with aspects of film noir, while *Beyond the Walls* forms part of the generic tradition of prison films; *The Smile of the Lamb* unfolds its narrative enigmas within the general framework of fantasy and particularly of the thousand-and-one-nights folk tale. *Avanti-Popolo* is a Surrealist farce about war, while *Esther* borrows modernist avant-garde codes reminiscent of the work of Jean Marie Straub/Danièle Huillet. Most of the films, however, share a melodramatic orientation (*A Very Narrow Bridge* explicitly uses conventional melodramatic codes of larger-than-life heroes and a narrative permeated with passion and death), developing an intimate and even "familial" attitude toward the Palestinian issue. The Arab here is no longer an anonymous enemy but rather a Palestinian (often noble) fighting for his/her national rights and, simultaneously, the object of desire within the love story. At least half of the films foreground, or use as a subplot, a love story which not only signifies the individual case of a mixed couple within a hostile environment but also allegorizes the Israeli/Palestinian attempts at dialogue. Although presumably the fictive couple tries to transcend the ambient conflict, in fact, as the films show, they simply live the conflict, as it were, at close range, in their own flesh. In the tradition of die open-ended narratives of personal cinema, Laila (Salwa Nakara-Haddad) in *A Very Narrow Bridge*, for example, is forced to cross the Allenby Bridge to Jordan, but promises to return, leaving the future dialogue, here allegorical of the larger Israeli/Palestinian dialogue, under a question mark.

Reflecting the recent changes taking place in what is termed in Israel the Peace Camp, the political films acknowledge a Palestinian entity and thus create a certain rupture with the long history of the denial of such representation. The Israeli filmmakers, in the process of cinematically representing the Israeli/Palestinian question, not only sympathetically acknowledge Palestinian victimization, but also grant the major characters dialogue expressing legitimate national anger and struggle. The films also grant Palestinian characters close-ups and point-of-view shots which foster emotional identification with them. In contrast to the Zionist humanism of the heroic-nationalist films, which constructed a classically Orientalist image of the Arab, and thus elided the question of political rights in Palestine, the political films of the eighties root the Palestinian characters in their own terrain, thus implying the possibility of a legitimate claim on the land. This stance does not simply form part of the story of the films but also penetrates the narrative and cinematic codes deployed to tell the story.

A Very Narrow Bridge offers a symbolic image of the Palestinian fighter, Toni Hilo (Yussuf Abu-Warda), first seen in extreme long shot in the pastoral open space (as he crosses from Jordan to Ramallah), filmed as if emerging from the land. His knowing exchange of looks with some Palestinians in tents along the road underlines his status as a people's fighter. This rootedness in the land and the

Love story as allegory of peace: *A Very Narrow Bridge.*

connectedness with its inhabitants is reinforced through the location shooting in Ramallah, documenting its Oriental-Byzantine architecture. The Byzantine link is further invoked through the Greek Orthodox Palestinian woman protagonist who does volunteer work restoring church icons and who confides in the Orthodox priest, Gregorious (Victor Atar), who is sympathetic to her love (unlike the real-life West Bank Patriarch, who banned the film). *A Very Narrow Bridge* consciously develops a Byzantine aesthetic, emphasizing arches and frames, and composes shots to resemble icon-like portraits, as with the slant of Laila's head in close-up, or backlighting to produce a golden aura behind her father-in-law (Toncel Kurtiz) when he throws open the doors to announce her expulsion from his house. The golden-reddish lighting too is strongly reminiscent of Byzantine painting. Such references evoke an archeology of the Middle East as a historical palimpsest involving complex layers of cultures, suggesting that the rootedness of the inhabitants of Palestine in the area goes even further back than the Muslim conquest.

Based on David Grossman's novel, *The Smile of the Lamb* revolves around the friendship between an Israeli military doctor, Uri Laniado (Rami Danon), and Hilmi (Toncel Kurtiz), an eccentric Arab who lives in a cave in the mountains near a village on the West Bank, a friendship born when the military governor, Katzman (Makram Khoury), places a donkey carcass at the center of the village so the smell will "convince" the villagers to hand over the "terrorists" hiding there. After his

The emergence of the Palestinian character: *The Smile of the Lamb*.

terrorist adopted son is killed by the Israelis, Hilmi kidnaps Uri and threatens to kill him if the Israeli forces do not withdraw from the occupied territories. This evocation of present-day politics is combined, in the film, with more fantastic elements, such as a narrator's voice-over in the Arab tradition of the local storyteller ("*al hakawati*") and the framing of the story by the classic beginning of folk tales of "*Kan yamakan*" (Arabic equivalent to "Once upon a time"), which invoke a multi-layered culture. Fantastic stories from Hilmi's past, such as the hunting of lions in Mandate Palestine, suggest a long historical presence prior to the establishment of Israel and the present state of occupation. One of his past stories, concerning pregnant women who were sent to him by their families to give birth in order not to disgrace the families, further accentuates the multigenerational attachment to this place. The mythical figure of Hilmi, a latter-day incarnation of the Arab-as-primeval-Semite, is implied to be a lamb, as an occupied Palestinian, but also a lion, whose force, underlined by the actor's mesmerizing physicality, is ultimately stronger than that of the occupier, since his organic attachment to the land is implied to be deeply rooted, perennial. That he stems from the motherland is emphasized by the clear and full sunlit cinematography and by music employing traditional Arab rhythms and percussion instruments.

While *A Very Narrow Bridge* and *The Smile of the Lamb* situate the acknowledgment of the Palestinian entity within the less ideologically disquieting framework of the occupied territories, the setting of *Hamsin* in the Galilee touches on a more taboo issue for the Peace Camp in Israel, that of nationalist feelings within Arab Israel and Palestinian rootedness in the land of Palestine. The title *Hamsin* (left untranslated in the English version) refers to the hot desert wind which blows through the Middle East. Set in an old farming village in Galilee, the film focuses on the Birman family—Malka, the mother, Gedalia, her son, and Hava, her daughter—descendants of the Jewish European immigration of the turn of the century, those pioneers who devoted themselves to the ideology of *avoda ivrit.* Some of the current farm employees, ironically, are now Israeli Palestinians. One employee, Halled (Yasin Shawap), works for the Birman family. When Gedalia (Shlomo Tarshish) hears that the Israeli government plans to confiscate the Abass land, he attempts to buy it, hoping to construct a dream ranch on land conjoining his family's ancestral land with that of the Abass family. The head of the Abass family, who had been on friendly terms with Gedalia's father, is willing to sell, but he changes his mind under pressure from young Arab nationalists. For the Palestinian nationalists, an imposed Israeli nationalization is more honorable than the apparent "choice" of selling the land. An erotic relationship between Halled and Hava (Hemda Levi), meanwhile, breaks a taboo in segregated Israeli society. Tensions escalate between Arabs and Jews, leading inexorably to the film's violent climax in which a wild bull, impulsively set free by Gedalia, gores Halled to death. Whereas Waxman's first feature, *Transit*, portrays rootless European immigrants, *Hamsin* examines people, both Palestinian and Israeli, deeply attached to ancestral land. The conflict over land, while on one level material and economic, also takes on strong emotional and symbolic connotations within an atmosphere heavy and suffocating like the *hamsin* of the title.

In contrast to the heroic-nationalist hierarchical casting, whereby Oriental Jews, although outcast from the narrative between heroic (Ashkenazi) Israel and villainous Arabs, were yet cast, and therefore present, for the "degraded" roles of Arabs, in virtually all the recent political films Palestinian (mostly Israeli-Palestinian) actors and Palestinian nonprofessionals play the Arab roles. Such casting, at times for major roles, allows, to a limited extent, for literal "self-representation." In this sense, the Palestinian presence is felt not only in content but also in the form of actors "representing" their national identity. In *Hamsin*, for example, the Palestinian worker Halled is played by the Israeli-Palestinian nonprofessional actor Yasin Shawap, and in *Fellow Travelers* the head of the Palestinian militant group is played by the student Suhir Hani (who was herself once arrested for illegal political activity). The films also feature such leading Israeli-Palestinian actors as Muhammad Bakri (*Hanna K., Fellow Travelers, On a Clear Day You Can See Damascus* [*Be-Yom Bahir Ro'eem et Damesek*, 1984], and *Beyond the Walls*), Yussuf Abu-Warda (*Fellow Travelers, A Very Narrow Bridge*, and *Nadia*), and Salwa Nakara-Haddad (*A Very Narrow Bridge* and *Nadia*). Playing similar roles in the theater, the actors have contributed to the construction of a more self-determined Palestinian image.

War and the absurd: Imagining the Arab in *Avanti-Popolo*.

At times, the casting of Palestinian actors in the political films is not strictly limited to Palestinian roles. In *Avanti-Popolo*, which recounts, in a style verging on Surrealism, the attempts of two schlemiel Egyptian soldiers in 1967 to reach the Egyptian border after the cease-fire, the casting of Israeli-Palestinian actors Suhil Haddad and Salim Daw in the roles of Egyptians implies an opposite perception of the Israeli-Arab conflict to that offered in the heroic-nationalist films. Not only does the film present the war from an Egyptian perspective, and thus demonstrate empathy with the "other," it also, by featuring recognizably Palestinian actors, indirectly evokes a Palestinian framework of feelings. Paradoxically, then, the Palestinians are more present in *Avanti-Popolo*, set far from Palestine, than they ever were in the heroic-nationalist films which consistently pushed them offstage. The film further plays with self/other polarities by positing the Egyptian/Palestinian soldier as a professional actor who had always wanted to play Shylock on the Egyptian stage and who declaims to the Israeli soldiers Shylock's famous "Hath not a Jew eyes?" (The casting of Israeli-Palestinian actor for Egyptian roles had a precedent in Assaf Dayan's ["bourekas"] comedy *Hill Halfon Doesn't Answer* [*Giv'at Halfon Eina Ona*, 1976], set during the war of attrition, which partially parodies the idealized image of the Israeli heroic soldier, embodied now in the clumsy Sephardi Halfon [Shaike Levi], who while being imprisoned by the Egyptians offers the hospitable Egyptian officer [Makram Khoury] a lesson in Orientalness

Subverting chromatic symbolism in *Beyond the Walls:* Issam (Muhammad Bakri, right) and Uri (Arnon Tzadok, Left).

by criticizing the Egyptian's "Ashkenazi" way of preparing coffee and teaching him the correct way.)

In both *A Very Narrow Bridge* and *The Smile of the Lamb*, Makram Khoury plays a military governor. (He also plays a similar role in Michel Khleifi's *Wedding in Galilee* [*Urs bil Galil*, 1987].) In *A Very Narrow Bridge*, he even wears the knitted *kippa*, usually connotative of religious nationalism, while the young stone-thrower from Ramallah is played by Shahar Cohen (son of religious Jews from Jerusalem), and the Palestinian Greek Orthodox priest is played by Jewish Israeli Victor Atar. This inversion of casting, whereby a Palestinian plays the role of an Israeli occupier, distances the spectator and shrewdly intimates the non-essentiality of power structures. In *Beyond the Walls*, the figure of the Jew-criminal prisoner also perturbs essentializing representation by inverting (at least insofar as the traditional imagery is concerned) the representation of Arabs and Israeli Jews. The counterposing of a blond Palestinian and a dark Israeli Jew subverts the standard chromatic symbolism. Given this reversal of physical types, it is not surprising that European critics, at the time of the Venice Film Festival, misperceived the blond Arab as the Israeli Jew, and the dark Sephardi Jew as the Arab. Most Italian newspapers, as a result of the switching of racial conventions, identified the photo of Arnon Tzadok (the Jew) as Muhammad Bakri (the Arab) and vice versa, a reaction which simply calls attention to the efficacity of the original calculated inversion of roles.[15]

The Israeli-Palestinian actors and nonprofessional participants have shown deep concern and involvement in the process of production with regard to their images and, at times, have forced radicalization of certain scenes. Salwa Nakara-Haddad and Yussuf Abu-Warda, for example, influenced one of the crucial scenes in *A Very Narrow Bridge* in which Toni is supposed to infiltrate Israel from Jordan to kill his sister on orders from the PLO. In the completed film, he infiltrates the country after being called by a relative. But he does not kill her to maintain family honor; instead, they embrace. To quote Salwa Nakara-Haddad's explanation of the ideological change:

> It seemed to me stupid. Why would a PLO militant kill a woman just because she falls in love with a Jew? For me it was to present the PLO in a ridiculous light. Already without such accusations, the PLO is now at the nadir, so to come and say that the PLO now finishes off love stories? Nissim [Dayan] understood me and he changed it.[16]

In *Beyond the Walls*, Muhammad Bakri also affected a radicalization of a crucial point in the film. Toward the end of the film, the head of the prison attempts to break the prisoners' strike, which is directed against management violence and manipulation, by breaking the Palestinian leader, Issam (Bakri). The head of the jail brings Issam's wife, whom he has not seen for years, and his son, whom he has never even met. In the original script Issam, with the encouragement of his fellow-inmates, goes out to his wife and child. The filmmaker, Uri Barabash, expressed the following perception of the sequence:

> To me it was clear that Issam must go out with the wife and child, and that was how it was written in the script. I said that in such a human moment everyone must forget the political, social statement—there is here a human interest that stands above everything. You are a man, you have not seen your wife for ten years, you do not know your son, you must go out; even at the price of breaking the strike.[17]

The Palestinian actors perceived this moment differently, in a more political fashion. After tense arguments, Bakri suggested that the director film two takes. Barabash shot first Bakri's version in which Issam steps out only to tell his wife and son to go back home, a scene whose authenticity led Barabash to completely give up his original idea. And to quote Muhammad Bakri's explanation for the import of the alteration:

> Throughout all the rehearsals I told Uri and Beni Barabash and Eran Prize [the director and the scriptwriters] that it would not work . . . If I were a leader like Sirtawi [the first name of Bakri's character in the film, Issam, is a reference to PLO figure Issam Sirtawi, who was murdered], I would not

have been broken, because I am a symbol. I told them that they would kill the utopia; that if I do something I do not believe in I would be a shit. I sat with my head between my hands and I could not do it. Here it was not a matter of being the fucker of the management. Here there appears a PLO leader, which in my eyes is the only representative organization of Palestinians; and I am for PLO leadership that argues for coexistence and dialogue with Israel and the shattering of prejudices. I am indeed not a politician but an actor, but the message is important to me. The real Issam Sirtawi was killed because he believed in dialogue.... Issam would not break and meet with his wife and son.... [When] the cameras worked, I began walking toward my wife and son in the film. All the prisoners began to cry ... Uri [Barabash] cried, the cameraperson cried. I finished the scene and walked crying to the dressing room, because that was the story of my life that was focused in one moment.[18]

A corollary to the more self-representational casting is the incorporation of the Arabic language in the films. The few Arabic "dialogues" in the heroic-nationalist films tended to be restricted to nouns and adjectives for exotic Oriental objects (usually associated with the "positive" Arab character) as well as to despotic commands, and, at times, to paralinguistic war cries (projected onto the "negative" Arab mass)—reflecting the intersection of language and power as operating within asymmetrical political arrangements. The political films, in contrast, have the Palestinian characters express themselves, forcefully, in their own idiom. Such a mechanism obliges the spectator—the films are largely aimed at Israeli and Western spectators—to meet the Palestinian characters on the latter's linguistic turf (of course, with the assistance of subtitles). Palestinian characters speak Arabic among themselves, especially when making political decisions. For example, in *Hamsin*, the Arab workers discuss how to cope with the accelerating tensions between them and the Jewish villagers, and in *Beyond the Walls*, the Arab prisoners debate the steps to be taken against their humiliation by a Jewish prisoner. The Palestinian characters, furthermore, tend to be fluent in Hebrew, in contrast to the Israeli characters, who tend not to speak Arabic. Here the films do not simply imply the bilingual and even bicultural dimension of Palestinian existence in Israel, but also evoke the linguistic and social dynamics of a classical encounter between dominated people and colonizing society.

The Politics of Focalization

The limited space opened up for Palestinian self-representation in recent Israeli political films tends to be subordinated ultimately to the Peace Camp ideological perspective. Rather than deal in depth with the Palestinian question, the films focus on the situation and dilemmas of the Israeli "doves." The real protagonists of the films, as a result, are virtually always the Sabras, through whom the political and/or erotic interaction with Palestinians is focalized. The films of Palestinian filmmakers, such as Ahmed Masri's *Airplane* or *Kite* (*Teyara*, 1980) and Michel Khleifi's *Fertile Memories* (*La Mémoire fertile*, 1980) and *Wedding in Galilee*, as well as that of the Egyptian Tawfik Saleh, *The Dupes* (*Al-Makhdu'un*, 1972), in contrast, foreground the Palestinian question and present Israel from a Palestinian perspective. One scene in *Wedding in Galilee*, for example, shows a young Arab woman inviting a baffled Israeli soldier to dance but also asking him to take off his uniform, a scene that allegorizes, according to Michel Khleifi, the feeling that it is possible to forgive the Israelis, but only if they "take off their uniforms," and "if they cease the military oppression of the Palestinians."[19] In a kind of complementarity, Israeli political films, meanwhile, see the Arab characters and the Palestinian question through the eyes of the soldiers, or ex-soldiers, who are presented as being ready, as it were, to take off their uniforms, with all participants forming part of a historical *rendezvous manqué*.

The "dovish" Israeli protagonists in the Palestinian Wave of films inevitably betray some of the vestiges of personal cinema, vestiges which often undermine a more structural-political reflection. The Sabra protagonists in the political films tend to be introverted, "artistic" figures, outsiders, shown to be morally superior in their compassion toward the plight of others, in this case, the Palestinians. In *On a Clear Day You Can See Damascus*, for example, it is the kibbutznik musician protagonist who attempts to rescue Palestinian political prisoners. In *Hamsin*, Gedalia is friendly with his Arab worker, Hallad (they work together and even take a playful improvised shower together in the field), protecting the worker against the nationalist mood of the Jewish *moshava*.[20] (His "open-minded" sister [a pianist], meanwhile, has an affair with Hallad.) In *A Very Narrow Bridge*, the military prosecutor gradually abandons his hard-line attitude because of his love for a Palestinian woman and, at the end, is completely rejected and isolated from both societies. And in *The Smile of the Lamb*, the doctor protagonist becomes an exemplar of tolerance and humanity. It is the poetic sensibility of the protagonist Uri that makes possible his friendship with the eccentric Palestinian Hilmi. The "marginality" of Uri, who professes faith in liberal humanism and in an oxymoronic "enlightened occupation" (in contrast to most hard-liners in the military government) is romantically allied with that of a simple land-born Palestinian.

Just as the heroic-nationalist films and Hollywood films set in Palestine/Israel incorporated the Western character, at times as a protagonist, as a messenger in the service of Zionist pedagogy—a way of making Zionism palatable for a Western audience—the recent political films employ an updated version of the same device, lending "humanity" to the Palestinian through focalizing a basically pro-Palestinian, Jewish Israeli protagonist. This strategy, which filters all points of view through a single dominant perspective, raises questions concerning what the Russian literary critic Boris Uspensky terms "the norms of the text." All ideological points of view, both Palestinian and Israeli, are subsumed by that of the Sabra protagonist. (Even in the cases of *A Very Narrow Bridge* and *The Smile of the Lamb*, where Sephardi origins are alluded to, the ideological perspective conforms to that of the Sabra.) The ideology of the narrator-focalizer, as Uspensky remarks, is usually understood as authoritative, and all other ideologies in the text are evaluated from this privileged position. Or, to use Bakhtinian terminology, social heteroglossia is flattened into a kind of ventriloqual monologism. The protagonists' dilemmas—Yoni caught between the Israeli Shin Bet (Secret Service roughly equivalent to the FBI) and Palestinian extremists, as well as his romantic involvement with a nurse in a mental institution (in *Fellow Travelers*), Uri's struggle against the harsh policies of his friend, the military governor, who also has an affair with Uri's wife (in *The Smile of the Lamb*), or Benni's struggle to fulfill his duty as a military prosecutor while sustaining his romantic relationship with a Palestinian woman in the face of Israeli and Palestinian opposition (in *A Very Narrow Bridge*)—are collapsed into a privileged position. *A Very Narrow Bridge* and *The Smile of the Lamb* follow the occupation not from the perspective of the occupied but rather from that of the "enlightened" occupier. Both on the narrative level and on the image track, it is the occupier-protagonist who forms the dynamic force, who generates and focalizes the narrative, and it is he whom the camera obediently follows, even when he walks through Palestinian towns. In the sequences in which Uri (*The Smile of the Lamb*) and Benni (*A Very Narrow Bridge*) defend the occupied Palestinians before the military authorities, for example, not only are the protagonists foregrounded but they literally *speak for* the Palestinians. The dialogue and mise-en-scène essentially relay their narrative dominance, perpetually orienting the spectator to the protagonists' peace-loving humanism and to their status as persecuted rescuers.

In the episode *Souvenirs from Hebron* in *Israel 83*, similarly, the daily work of occupation performed by two handsome young Sabra soldiers is focalized through their patrol in the casbah of Hebron. The dramatic tension is structured through the subjectivization of the shots, that is, through the limitation of spectatorial knowledge to the situation as seen by the soldiers. The spectator is drawn into their fear and anxiety about sudden attacks by the people of the casbah; everyone they encounter—a child causing a watermelon to explode next to the soldiers, or a butcher sharpening his knife—is a source of terror, and every corner, alley, and upper floor is a potential place of danger. Focalizing the films through the occupier's fears—even of children—in an episode forming part of a self-declared pro-Palestinian series, also displaces the Palestinian-Israeli question onto a psychological register which evades the central political issues. In this sense, the film prolongs the identificatory mechanisms and even the ideology of personal cinema, this time with the occupation as a backdrop for "universal" human concerns. Furthermore, such a film is ultimately not so different ideologically from the IDF-produced and commercially distributed *Ricochets* (*Shtei Etzbaot miTzidon*, literally *Two Fingers from Sidon*, 1986), which focuses on the human face of the soldiers—although in contrast to *Souvenirs from Hebron*, it also demonizes the Arab side and, in the manner of heroic-nationalist films, adds the "good Arab," the Druse. Both films mask the origins of the policies by foregrounding only those who carry them out, the soldiers.

Produced by the Film Unit of the Israeli Defense Forces and shot on location during the last month of Israel's invasion of Lebanon, Eli Cohen's *Ricochets* is a war film that blurs the boundaries between fiction and documentary. While employing professional actors, classical narrative strategies, and dramatic-heroic music, the film also deploys the shaky camera associated with television reportage, vividly capturing the language, gestures, emotions, and stories of Israeli infantry fighting in Lebanon—all based on extensive research. In the background actual soldiers play their real-life roles, as do the occupied, for example as in the case of the South Lebanese village Al Hiyam, whose inhabitants play themselves and reenact for the film their real-life reactions to Israeli soldiers breaking into their houses. *Ricochets'* relative austerity in terms of production values is largely a result of the limitations of filming during war, a context that forced the actors to go through basic paratrooper training and to carry guns even during the breaks in filming. Within the history of the war genre, very few films have been shot on actual battlefield locations, and even fewer have risked filming dramatic events under actual fire. Much of the authenticity of *Ricochets* derives from narrating the experience of Israeli soldiers at the very moment events took place, during the historical process itself. The film, which was well-received by both soldiers and civilians in Israel, came to function as a kind of collective story-teller for the traumatized young soldiers, mediating between them and their families and friends.

The authentic depiction of the physical, psychological, and moral dimension of what has often been referred to as the "Lebanese swamp," however, led to the self-deluding claim that, to quote the filmmaker himself, *Ricochets* is "not an army propaganda film." The fact that "the military is not always shown in the best light," furthermore, was perceived by spectators and by a large number of film critics, especially outside of Israel, as evidence for a "critical" film. The Israeli army was praised for producing, to cite Thomas L. Friedman,[21] a "highly critical" film about a "war it conducted," generating an implicit pride in the democratic nature of Israeli institutions. The subtext of such a reception assumes a comparison to more traditional propaganda films premised on an absolute Manichean division between good and evil forces, a structure that foregrounds not moral dilemmas but rather a glamorized heroism embodied in the actions of individuals who personify the "true" spirit of their nation. *Ricochets* is obviously not the ideological twin of the reactionary *Rambo;* it is more like the Israeli ideological counterpart to the liberal-humanist *Platoon* (but generally without that film's demystification of its soldiers). *Ricochets* must be seen as a latter-day heir of the Israeli heroic-nationalist films which tended to privilege Zionist apologetics rather than action. Coming almost

"Enlightened occupation": *Ricochets*.

forty years after Israel's foundation as a state, *Ricochets* bypasses such apologetics, but it does imply a certain legitimization through its framing of the question in terms of the narrowly defined issue of "the war for Peace in Galilee."

An important motif in the heroic-nationalist films, carried on by *Ricochets*, is the moral superiority of the Israeli soldier, a presentation which displaces central political issues. The film foregrounds the human aspects of war—hysterical collapse, weeping, and hatred as well as the ability to laugh, love, and show softness even in the presence of death: Efi conducts a platonic exchange of loving glances with a young Shiite woman—he leaves her chocolates while patrolling and she returns with cherries—and Bambino becomes attached to a little boy to whom he repeatedly hands sweets; Rauf the Druse hopes to marry a Lebanese Druse he loves; Gadi becomes intimate with an Israeli woman soldier; and Georgie suffers battle fatigue. The human face of the soldier—and more precisely of the Israeli soldier—can be sustained, the film suggests, even during a war which poses ambiguous moral choices. This is embodied largely in the character of the officer Gadi, through whom most of the narrative is focalized. Freshly arrived in Lebanon, he gradually learns the bitter truth of life and death through the crushed bodies of his comrades; but as an archetypical Peace Now soldier he wants to excel as a soldier and at the same time maintain civilized behavior and moral principles. This conflict is heightened in the final sequence. Gadi and his men have managed to track the Shiite guerrilla leader Abu Nabil (the name obviously echoes Abu Nidal) through a banana grove to the home of a Lebanese villager. Hiding in the brush the soldiers argue about whether they should storm the house or just blow it away, thus probably killing Lebanese civilians but protecting Israeli soldiers. Gadi's choice is virtually that of a martyr: he storms the house alone, risking neither his men nor the Lebanese civilians.

Although the film's ideal-ego is the Peace Now soldier, it elicits, at the same time, the spectator's sympathy toward the hard-bitten veteran company commander, Tuvia. His tough attitude is explained by the film, attributed to his long and harsh experience in Lebanon—and particularly to his having had to face his own friend's death, killed, it is implied, because he confused the humane norms of Tel Aviv with the tricky Shiite realities of Lebanon. A suspicious attitude is portrayed as an understandable survival mechanism in a place where, to cite Tuvia, "black is white and white is black." The evolution of the narrative supports his disenchanted attitude by having the oasis of human exchange during war revealed to be a fantasy engendered by the naïve goodwill of the Israeli soldier. The Lebanese young woman, it turns out, is in fact an informer for Shiite terrorists, and the Israeli Druse engaged to the Lebanese Druse woman ends up with his throat slit. Tuvia's position, then, is understandable in the Lebanese context, which could be summed up in Georgie's explanation to Gadi:

> They brought us some Ph.D.—an Orientalist—and he gave us a lecture about the lay of the land. Now I see the light. Well, this is the way it goes. The Christians hate the Druse, and the Shiites—the Sunnis and the Palestinians, too. The Druse hate the Christians. No . . . Yes . . . O.K., the Druse hate the Christians, the Shiites, and the Syrians. Why? The Shiites, they've been shafted for ages, so they hate them all. The Sunnis hate whoever their boss tells them to hate, and the Palestinians hate one another in addition to all the other factions. . . . Now, there's one common denominator. All of them to- gether hate—and, oh boy, how they hate—us, the Israelis. They would like to smash our faces—if only they could.

Such a caricatured presentation of the post-colonial sociopolitical dynamics of Lebanon leads to identification with the "rational" Israelis whose presence there is implied, in obedience to official discourse, as uniquely serving to maintain order. The reasons for hating the Israelis are dehistoricized, and the spectator inevitably identifies with the nice young Israelis who wish no one any harm. Since all other paths of spectatorial identification are closed off, attempts to comprehend why the soldiers are hated can lead in only one direction: Arabs are fanatical and irrational.

The image of the Israeli is contrasted with that of the Lebanese. *Ricochets* does not schematically portray all Arabs as fanatical terrorists, but it does schematically divide up Arabs into "good" ones and "evil" ones. As in the heroic-nationalist films, the obedient civilian-Arabs are portrayed positively, while the rebellious ones operate as narrative devils who endanger not only the Israeli protagonists but also their own people. The Lebanese child who accompanies Bambino on his patrol, for example, is killed accidentally by the Israelis because of the cruelty of his own people—it is of course the Israelis, through whose eyes the spectators see, who mourn the Lebanese child's death. In another case, Gadi does not risk his soldiers' and civilians' lives, but the Shiite guerrilla, in contrast, imposes his presence on a family who might have been killed were it not for Gadi's courageous act of conscience. The Shiites, it is suggested, do not care about their own people's lives, in contrast to the Israelis, who risk even their own lives in order not to hurt innocent Lebanese civilians.

Ricochets' narrative thus privileges the tormented shoot-and-cry soldiers who supposedly suffer from the very fact of being conquerors, who do not hate those they occupy, and who, despite the death ready to surprise them at every corner, are still capable of expressing affection toward the Lebanese. Despite the hardship of war, in other words, they maintain a civilized ethos. The happy moment of withdrawal in the film's final sequence reassures the spectator that the soldiers never desired the role of the occupier in the first place. The symbolic ending of the military vehicle stuck in the mud on the way out from Lebanon and the collaborative delirium of the Israeli soldiers who succeed in releasing it from the mud is hardly critical; rather it sums up the happiness of returning back home, of the return to sanity. The moments of soldierly discontent about fighting in Lebanon, furthermore, generate nothing more than diffuse feelings of depression in the face of death and uncertainty about the end of the war, feelings expressed in their song: "Sitting here depressed/looking toward the city Sidon/thinking maybe everything was just a dream." But even here the film offers only a softened paraphrase of an actual song sung by some Israeli soldiers in Lebanon: "We'll fight for Sharon/and we'll come back in a coffin."

The film should not be perceived simply as propaganda promoting the idea that Israeli policies are not so bad after all; it must be perceived even more as symptomatic of a sincere belief in the ethical and conscientious Israeli fighter. The humanist-Socialist education of the dominant elite perpetuated such myths, encapsulated in such tropes as *tohar haneshek* ("purity of arms"), implying the killing of only necessary targets, never touching civilians, *musar halehima* ("moral of fighting"), and *kibush na'or* ("enlightened occupation"). The theme of universal moral dilemmas during war is in itself legitimate. The problem raised, however, is the uses of such representation, i.e., the implicit alibi for brutal policies dictated by governments as the narrative foregrounds the ambivalences of those who carry out the policies, eliding those who determine them. The Israeli invasion of Lebanon is never questioned. By focusing on the narrow question of the humanity or inhumanity of Israeli soldiers rather than on the larger political context,

Ricochets becomes a kind of promotional brochure for official Israeli policies and perspectives.

Whether the space is Lebanon, the West Bank, or Israel, the politics of narrative and cinematic strategies remain similar. In *Hamsin*, the Gedalia character demonstrates liberalism, treating his Arab worker humanely, while "naturally" letting him sleep in a shed in the backyard and "accidentally" murdering him after the Arab has slept with his sister. This concatenation of events undermines potential critique precisely because the film is focalized through Gedalia, and even the murder is narrated from his perspective. This device sublimates the melodramatic emotionalism of this moment in the film and thus represses the cathartic release of spectatorial anger at the liberal protagonist. The rain that falls and breaks the *hamsin*, in the final shot, washing away the blood, leaves the narrative open-ended. The film in this sense merely reflects the current political stalemate as a kind of ongoing tragedy for both sides, ultimately caused by individual prejudices, thus displacing the political issues onto a psychologized, anthropocentric plane. The Jewish and Arab lovers who epitomize the romantic option (love, not war) are ultimately victims of circumstances. Those who taste the forbidden fruit are punished by the narrative. The privileging of the apolitical Halled over the nationalist Palestinian workers to whom the film briefly alludes, furthermore, undermines all discussion of power structures, transferring such discussion onto the realm of libidinal anxieties. The film also projects a past Zionist utopia, evoked through constant allusions to Gedalia's dead father and his friendship with the elderly Arab Abbas, a relationship now implied to be deteriorating with Gedalia's generation because of government policies and nationalist extremism. The projection of a past utopia is not performed in the spirit of "revolutionary nostalgia" (Benjamin) but rather in the spirit of nostalgia alone.

As in the apolitical personal films, the protagonists of the films remain delegates of the filmmakers, who attempt to ruminate on their situation as Israelis caught between their core Zionism and their sympathies for Palestinians as tragic victims. It is not surprising in such a context that Udi Adiv, a real-life kibbutznik officer imprisoned for giving military information to Palestinians/Syrians, became a source of artistic inspiration, not so much because of the filmmakers' support of his action or even identification with his group's leftist perspective, but rather because Adiv represented a version *in extremis* of their own dilemmas and ambiguities. The Sabra/kibbutznik/officer, a combination forming a kind of Israeli aristocracy, as the locus of patriotism, morality, and heroism, which once served as human exemplum in the Zionist didactic allegories, in the Adiv case came to exemplify national trauma for the Sabra establishment.

A number of films clearly evoke the Udi Adiv phenomenon. Eran Riklis' *On a Clear Day You Can See Damascus*, for example, revolves around two kibbutznik friends, Uri Sharon (played by Daniel Waxman, director of that other political film, *Hamsin*), who quite early in the film is imprisoned for giving military information to the Syrian authorities, and Ron (Eli Danker), the apolitical musician, the real protagonist. While Ron at one point tells the Palestinian Naim Bakri (Muhammad Bakri) that art has nothing to do with politics, he later becomes politicized when he learns that Uri's friend, a fellow-activist, Joseph, a Jewish-British volunteer in Israel, is a Shin Bet agent who helped arrange Uri's imprisonment. The chronicle of the musician's coming to political consciousness metaphorizes the shift of personal filmmakers themselves from apolitical to political themes. Neglecting his stage experiments in combining Western and Arabic music—experiments analogizing the filmmakers' attempts to get closer to the Palestinian theme—Ron becomes involved in a dangerous game of East/West political encounter. He contacts and later tries to kidnap Joseph, the Shin Bet agent, in order to hand him over to the Palestinian organization, which would then demand the release of Uri along with Palestinian political prisoners. Driving to the northern border, Ron and Joseph are fired upon by two cars, one driven by Palestinians and the other by the Shin Bet. The pincer movement by extremists on both sides encapsulates the victimization of the Israeli peace activist.

A similar renegade figure is the political prisoner Assaf (Assaf Dayan) in *Beyond the Walls*, an activist who has taken the initiative in contacting Arab militant groups. While the Jewish inmates consider him a traitor responsible for promoting terror, the Palestinian prisoners are suspicious of him for staying in the Jewish cell. In this sense, the film evokes another political prisoner, Rami Livne, who preferred to stay in Jewish cells and not to be included in the prisoner exchange list when Palestinians took over a school in the seventies and demanded in return the release of their prisoners, including Livne, who refused to be released. When the Israelis won the battle and Livne went back to his cell, he was received with suspicion by both sides, by the Jews for being included on the list and by the Palestinians for refusing their offer. Rami Livne himself appears in *Beyond the Walls*, ironically playing a role quite opposite to his real-life role; he appears as a criminal prisoner who refuses to collaborate with the Arabs against the management. Like other real-life prisoners cast in the film, he contributed inside information about the details of prison life and relationships.[22] Yehuda Ne'eman's *Fellow Travelers* is also loosely based on the case of Adiv. The film tells the story of an ex-kibbutznik intellectual and army officer who wants to help Arabs in Israel achieve a measure of cultural autonomy. The protagonist, Yoni, whose name derives from the word "dove," participates in a leftist Palestinian group, raising money in Germany to support the founding of an Arab university in Israel, but protests when he discovers that the members of the group have abandoned the original project and intend to use the money for violent purposes. Consequently, he becomes hunted both by the Palestinian group and by the Shin Bet, leading to his murder.

Although the "Palestinian Wave" of films criticizes the Israeli Establishment, its critical look tends to be directed more at the Establishment's victimization of the Israeli protagonists than at oppression of the Palestinians, in the name of whom the protagonists are presumably fighting. In *Fellow Travelers*, for example, the lyrics critical of the political structure of Israel sung by Yoni's friend (the singer Nurit Galron)—"Ahmed will harvest/Muhammad will guard/Abed will clean/and Ibrahim will build/What then will beautiful Uri do?/Beautiful Uri will count the money"—find no parallel within the film itself. Although Yoni does not count money, and in fact raises money for Palestinians, the film nevertheless plays off his victimization against that of the Palestinian characters. The militant group appears several times and is associated with violence, as opposed to Yoni, who seems to be the "real" object of the Shin Bet hunt rather than the Palestinians. Meanwhile, the Palestinian intellectual (Yussuf Abu-Warda), who, like Yoni, detests violence and hopes to use the money to found a university—through which they will fight against the Israeli Establishment—is granted little narrative time. His function within the narrative is a subsidiary one, subordinated to Yoni's presence in the scene even though his plight, as a Palestinian who prefers nonviolent to violent means, forms the thematic focus of the film. (In *A Very Narrow Bridge*, furthermore, Yussuf Abu-Warda, playing a PLO man, is made to struggle with the Israeli officer not on political grounds, but rather on familial ones.)

A hierarchical representation which ultimately comes to project the Sabra peace activist as the real martyr caught between two violent worlds finds some echoes in the Hebrew title of the film, *Magash haKessef, The Silver Platter*, distributed in English as *Fellow Travelers*, the name of a club in the film that serves for shadowy and claustrophobic noir-style encounters. "Silver Platter" alludes to the nationally celebrated Nathan Alterman poem whose central motif is the idea that Israel was not handed to the Jews on a "silver platter," but only at the cost of the sacrifice of the youth for the nation. *Fellow Travelers* lends some subversive connotations to the poem, for in the film the "sacrifice" is not for the young nation and against the Arabs, but rather for the Arabs against the Israeli state. At the same time, the exclusive focus on Yoni's victimization, caught between two extremist forces, culminating in the crucifix-like image of the assassinated hero, is symptomatic of a rather narrow perspective on historical process.[23]

Similarly, the characterization of Uri, the doctor in *The Smile of the Lamb*, as a reluctant occupier, who at the same time is frightened by the prospect of a Palestinian state animated by hatred for Israel, applies to many of the protagonists of the "Palestinian Wave" films. While in David Grossman's novel the military governor, Katzman, is shot by the Palestinian Hilmi, and thus the Israeli occupation is punished, in Shimon Dotan's filmic version it is the peace activist Uri who is killed mistakenly as Katzman and Hilmi are fighting over a gun. As in *Fellow Travelers*, it is the passive, tormented, and conflicted hero who pays with his life, who is crucified for his peace nostalgia. Like the Palestinian, Uri is oppressed by the military government, but on an individual scale, since the governor sleeps with his wife; he too is thus rendered as victim. Grossman in the novel refers to the protagonist's "lamb's smile," a synecdoche for the young, harmless person who

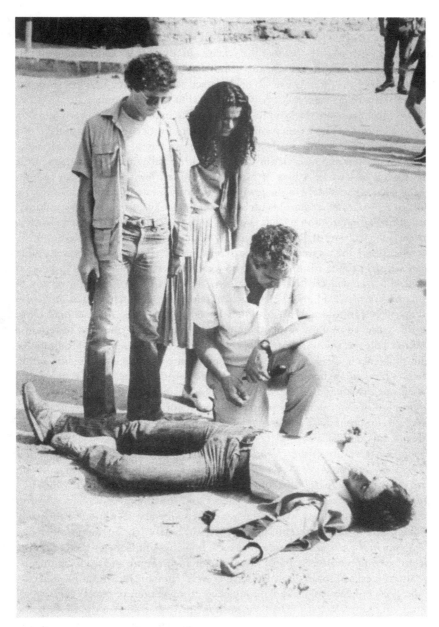

Sacrificed on the alter of peace: Sabra vicitimhood in *Fellow Travelers*.

dreams of practicing "enlightened occupation" and is thus trapped between the Palestinian struggle for liberation and Israeli military rule. In the film his death, caused by both of them, evokes the fatalism of a sacrificial lamb taking all sins upon himself. The protagonist, the believer in nonviolence, is himself sacrificed on the altar of violence. The death of the Israeli activist is foregrounded, while the plight of the Palestinian collectivity is relegated to the background.

We encounter here the symptoms of acute discomfort with the very idea of a Jewish victimizer. The Jewish people, after all, are historically unaccustomed to the role of oppressor. Jewish rituals relay the collective lore of an interminable series of victimizations and near-victimizations. Jewish holidays recount the tales of the oppression of Jews by a host of historical enemies. Jewish history can recount the collective backsliding of the Jewish community under the influence of diverse golden calves. It can recount Jewish acts of vengeance against gentile oppression. It has difficulty in recounting a tale showing Jews as a collective oppressor. Nothing in the long culture of Judaism prepares its artists for such a role. After 1967 Israelis found themselves in the clear position of an occupying power. What were artists, primed historically to know themselves only as victims in relation to neighboring collectivities, to do? How were they to deal with the inversion of the imagery of David and Goliath when Palestinian children, armed only with slings, were confronting Israeli soldiers armed to the teeth? The personal films, in this sense, convey the diverse compromise solutions encountered in response to this challenge, solutions involving halfway confrontations, partial focalizations, and problematic displacements. A predisposition to a discourse of victimization leads to films whose narrative and cinematic codes present the Sabras as the central victims of the situation. The lament, therefore, is not primarily for the national oppression of the Palestinian people but rather for the Sabras' own torment, as passively innocent Isaacs to be sacrificed in fear and trembling, on the altar of Abrahamic (nationalist) faith.

The sense of suffocation (*Hamsin*), paranoia (*Fellow Travelers*), and alienation (*The Smile of the Lamb, A Very Narrow Bridge*) from both Israeli mainstream and Palestinian activists, the construction of overpowering forces in which the protagonist's efforts are doomed to failure, and, finally, the dead-end situation reflect the feelings of paralysis of the filmmakers' liberal milieu more than a truly politicized cinema. The recent Sabra discovery of Israel's ugly face in the mirror (*An Ugly Face in the Mirror* is the title of a recent book by Adir Cohen which traces the dehumanization of the Arab in Hebrew children's literature and from a humanist perspective calls for more "positive" images) was traumatic for "beautiful Israel"— a discovery made possible also through the disintegration of Israel's high moral image on the world stage. The fight to show the "other side" of the country, the self-designated "sane Israel" (as opposed to Kahane and Likud), has, therefore, the implicit corollary of nostalgia for an older, presumably saner Israel. Furthermore, the films' acknowledgment of the Palestinian entity never ventures beyond the basic

Zionist consensus and, in this sense, very much reflects the Peace Now ideology of "realistic Zionism," a position acknowledging Palestinian national existence (along with Israel's need for secure borders), but leaving everything else rather vague.

The films' foregrounding of the tormented Sabra hero, in other words, takes place at the expense of stripping bare the real societal power mechanisms. The problematic aspect of the films does not lie in the fact that some of the Shin Betniks are portrayed as nice people (some Israeli film critics[24] criticized the sympathetic portrayal of the Shin Betnick Jacques Cohen in *A Very Narrow Bridge*), but rather in the lack of real critique of the political system of occupation within which Shin Betniks are merely the executors. Unlike Gillo Pontecorvo's *The Battle of Algiers* (*La Battaglia deAlgeri*, 1966), which showed the French colonel Mathieu as individually sympathetic yet the instrument of an oppressive colonial system, the "Palestinian Wave" films tend to limit their analysis to individuals. There is little collective struggle in these films: collectivity, in whatever form, as in the personal film, is presented as oppressive, violent, and "insane." (In *Fellow Travelers* this statement takes a direct expression: hunted by Israelis and Palestinians, Yoni hides in a mental hospital, where his story is taken by the psychiatrists as symptomatic of paranoia.) The terror of the group is applicable to both Israelis and Palestinians. The traditional personal-cinema theme of individual-versus-society, in other words, is now interwoven with the Israeli-Palestinian conflict.

The limitations of the Israeli liberal/leftist discourse are reflected on still another level, with regard to the Oriental Jews. Most of the protagonists of the films, the delegates of the filmmakers, are Sabra, i.e., Ashkenazi. This is true even for *The Smile of the Lamb*, which casts the Oriental Jewish actor Rami Danon (who in *Beyond the Walls* and the television drama [*Bread, Lehem*, 1986] played the more typical Sephardi roles of a criminal prisoner and a development-town unemployed man) in a "dovish" role that contrasts with the Sephardi "right-wing" stereotype; in other words, the Oriental Jew character simply inherits the ideological position of the Sabra. The same point applies to *A Very Narrow Bridge*, whose Sephardi protagonist, Benni Tagar (an Ashkenazation of his original Sephardi name, Binyameen Turgeman), is a product of assimilation to Ashkenazi society in his military and class ascendancy. This film, furthermore, despite the non-idealized image of Benni's wife, a Peace Now activist who simultaneously designs buildings for the West Bank, does not offer any non-hegemonic view of the dynamics between Oriental Jews and Palestinians. In *A Very Narrow Bridge* and *The Smile of the Lamb*, as in Israeli cinema generally, the Sephardi character is simply cut off from any sense of his/her collective history in the Middle East, and thus his/her relation to and attitude toward the Palestinian question begin, as is the case with official historiography, at the point of European Jewish history. And the films, even when their protagonists are Sephardi, make no reference to the collective Sephardi class positioning and its important relation to the Palestinian labor force in Israel.

The films, in continuity with the general liberal discourse, now make a step toward recognizing a Palestinian entity, but in fact focus on Sabra ambivalence in relation to that question while hermetically shutting off the Sephardi issue as an "internal social problem" to be solved after peace is achieved. The intrinsic relations between the Palestinian and the Sephardi questions form, in the "Palestinian Wave" of films, a "structuring absence." Just as the hegemonic discourse elides the historical origins of the Palestinian struggle and thus nostalgically looks back to an Edenic prelapsarian past, so does it elide the historical origins of Oriental-Jewish resentment and thus constructs the myth of "reactionaries." This discourse compartmentalizes one problem as "political" and "foreign" and the other as "social" and "internal"; that the two issues are implicated in each other is rarely acknowledged, since it is assumed and disseminated that Oriental Jews are "Arab-haters."

Peace Now leaders such as General Mordechai Bar-On attribute the lack of Sephardi enthusiasm for Peace Now to "strong rightist tendencies" and "excited loyalty to the personal leadership of Menachem Begin," symptomatic of a Sephardi "natural and traditional tendency . . . to follow a charismatic leader" all compounded with a "deep-rooted distrust of the Arabs."[25] The Sephardi Other is portrayed as uncritical, instinctual, and, in accord with Oriental-despotic traditions, easily manipulated by patriarchal demagogues. Sephardi hostility toward Peace Now, rather than being discussed in class and ethnic terms, is conveniently displaced by the films of Ashkenazi liberals onto the decoy-issue of a presumed general Sephardi animosity toward Arabs. In fact, however, the relatively high Sephardi vote for Likud has almost nothing to do with the latter's policies toward the Arabs; it is, rather, a minimal and even misplaced expression of Sephardi revolt against decades of Labor oppression (especially since within the present system the Sephardim cannot represent themselves). The hegemonic view, this mythical discourse that masks its own origins, refuses to see that the same historical process that dispossessed Palestinians of their property, lands, and national-political rights was linked to the process that dispossessed Sephardim of their property, lands, and rootedness in Arab countries (and, within Israel itself, of their history and culture). This overall process has been cynically idealized in Israel's diplomatic pronouncements as a kind of "spontaneous population exchange" and a justification for expelling Palestinians, but the symmetry is factitious, for the so-called "return from exile" of the Arab Jews was far from spontaneous and in any case cannot be equated with the condition of the Palestinians, who have been exiled from their homeland and wish to return there. These First World/Third World encounters typify, as we have seen, both the relations between European Jews and Arabs and those between European Jews and Oriental Jews. This pattern of domination and manipulation is exemplified in the "divide and conquer" approach to "Hebrew work," as well as by other power mechanisms in Israeli society fostering economic fears and political antagonism between Sephardim and Palestinians (and not "natural hostility"). The rise of the Sephardi petite bourgeoisie, for example, was made possible only after 1967, after Israel began using new sources of cheap labor, allowing certain beneficial side effects for Sephardim. Presently, among most of the Sephardi working class, it is cheap Palestinian labor that affects the competition over places of work and over salaries. The fact that most border settlements, under thirty-five years of attacks and bombing by Arabs, were populated by Sephardim also created antagonism, as well as the constant psychological pressures to be Israeli (i.e., repress Arabness). Presently class ascendancy for Sephardim, furthermore, is very much made possible through achievements in the army, implicitly against the Arabs. Because of segregation in Israel, finally, both groups tend to be informed about each other through the media, with little direct contact, thus leaving each group the victim of the stereotypes projected by the media. Thus the Sephardim learn to see the Palestinians as "terrorists," while the Palestinians learn to see the Sephardim as Arab-hating fanatics, a situation hardly facilitating mutual understanding and recognition.

Beyond the Walls, in some ways, would seem to be pointing to such truths, since the Oriental Jew, Uri Mizrahi (Arnon Tzadok), and the Palestinian, Issam Jabarin (Muhammad Bakri), manipulated into artificial conflict by the Ashkenazi prison management in order to control both groups, end up striking together and symbolically triumph over their oppressors. The pride and courage expressed through the emotionalism of Arnon Tzadok, and the quieter, almost saintly, presence projected by Muhammad Bakri, as well as the film's cinematic structuring of identification with the Palestinian and the Oriental Jew, forge a powerful image of the alliance between two oppressed groups. The Sabra "leftist," Assaf (Assaf Dayan), in contrast to most of the political films, furthermore, is apparently marginalized within the narrative, as if having a less important historical role to play, while the Sephardi character evolves from anti-Palestinian positions (and disdain for the "leftist") to recognition of Palestinian victimization and the justice of the Palestinian cause, and thus solidarity with the "leftist."

This utopian collaboration masks, however, a certain monologism concerning the relational structures of Ashkenazi/Sephardi/Palestinians in Israel. As a didactic allegory, the film projects a pedagogic telos for the Sephardi, assumed a priori to be "rightist." The fact that there have been Sephardi pro-Palestinian activists imprisoned for long periods is never evoked by the film, which unthinkingly conveys the received wisdom of the Israeli media in its construction of the superior morality of the Sabra "leftist." In this battle over imagery, Oriental Jews are simply taken for granted as "Arab-haters," a presentation which indirectly implies that those who denounce the (supposed) Sephardi hostility are themselves pro-Arab (a recent study of the Institute for Middle East Peace and Development at the City University of New York showed that Sephardic attitudes run very much counter

Cross-national utopia in *Beyond the Walls*.

to the stereotypes),[26] thus implying that "fanatic" and "backward" Oriental Jews form the major obstacle to peace. The assumptions behind these films, then, allow only for a Sabra "leftist."

In *Beyond the Walls*, after several incidents, Uri Mizrahi becomes politicized and reaches the phase of comprehending the basic political mechanisms. His consciousness evolves to the level of the Palestinian and Ashkenazi characters, whose consciousness remains static. It is their level of consciousness as constructed in the fiction which constitutes the telos of the film. The film that began with Uri ends with Issam's heroic act of not breaking the strike even though he is encouraged by all prisoners to do so. (The collaborative rebellion then celebrates the existentialist idea that it is possible to be a prisoner and still remain free.) In other words, although the Sabra's character is in the background, it is precisely his delegated views which represent the film's ideological horizon, the final positive stop in the political trajectory.

Metaphorically, *Beyond the Walls* links the Establishment oppression of the Palestinian, the Oriental Jew, and the Sabra peace activist. Within the allegory of the prison as microcosm, the film then points to the camaraderie of the oppressed. Yet, since the film alludes to Palestinian contextual reality but elides that of the Sephardi, its didactic allegory lacks reciprocity. The film refers, however superficially, to the experiential reality of the Palestinian—Issam speaks, for example, of the bombing of refugee camps by Israeli phantom jets as a violence equal to

Palestinian bombs in one thousand buses—thus offering a condensed apologia for Palestinian counter-violence in a war, to paraphrase Issam, whose rules were not invented by the Palestinians. The Sephardi Uri is convinced, and as an Israeli following the Peace Camp line he does not take the additional pedagogical step which would manifest awareness of his situation as an Oriental Jew. He does not reach the recognition that the very same historical process that created the "Palestinian problem" also created the "Oriental Jewish problem." Because of his lack of awareness, he never presents his problem as a collective one; he interacts with Issam as an Israeli-Jew, not as a Sephardi.

Although the filmmaker Uri Barabash himself has pointed out in interviews that Sephardim are also political prisoners[27] (over 90 percent of Israeli-Jewish prisoners are Sephardi), the film makes no references to such a view. The film also downplays the reality of class. *Beyond the Walls* presents Uri's antagonism to Assaf as having to do with the Palestinian question; when that problem is solved, the problems between Assaf and Uri disappear. This false issue implies that the struggle between the upper-middle-class Sabra and the lower-class Sephardi is over the Palestinian question, a presentation which perfectly suits the Peace Camp refusal to recognize that it itself forms part of the oppression of the Oriental Jews.

Barabash's presumed inversion of the stereotypes of dark Arab and blond Israeli, meanwhile, is also limited, for the blond Israelis in the stereotypical Arab/Jewish filmic encounter were Sabras and not Sephardim. In this sense only the stereotype of the dark Arab is inverted into "positive" blond, while the Sephardi conforms to the traditional stereotype in both look and manner. Thus, there is no real inversion of earlier imagery, since the darkness and criminality are applied not to the protagonists of the heroic-nationalist films, i.e., the Sabras, but rather to the "realistic" notion of the dark Sephardim who form the majority of prisoners.

The positive, saintly image of the Palestinian, meanwhile, points to a new iconography of the Arab, whose image, as the Israeli-Palestinian writer Anton Shammas has pointed out,[28] has undergone a gradual de-Semitization, finally becoming Western, and "dressed" with blond hair and blue eyes, not unlike the Christ figure in European portraiture. The positive, saint-like image of the Palestinian, which, in some ways, balances within Israeli culture the Kahane demonization of the Arab, enacts at the same time a kind of compensation mechanism. The films in this sense focus on the construction of a positive image of the Palestinian, a presentation whose import lies not in the filmic text but in the context of relativizing the colonialist negative imagery of the Arab that exists in the West. Within the textual strategies, however, such a presentation falls back into the irrelevant Romantic idealism which masks the central issue of the Israeli/Palestinian question—that of the dynamics of asymmetrical relations of power.

Israeli cinema has come an impressive distance since the days of *Oded the Wanderer* and *Sabra*. From a fragile, fledgling, artisanal filmmaking movement which saw itself largely as a means to political and even propagandist ends, it has become an enduring and productive film industry responsible for a significant corpus of films. Against substantial obstacles, Israeli filmmakers have collectively forged an instrument of personal and national expression, in films which treat a coherent set of themes, in a recognizable style, offering a gallery of character types within a wide diversity of genres. The industry now has a large number of practicing directors, a substantial pool of technical talent, and an audience accustomed to seeing Israeli films along with foreign productions. Israeli cinema, furthermore, has achieved a certain presence, a volume and weight, on the world film scene.

But much remains to be done. I have tried to highlight the achievements of Israeli cinema as well as to stress its ideological limitations, limitations quite inseparable from those of the ambient political culture. Israeli cinema, like Israeli official society generally, has shown ambivalence toward its status as a country "in" the East but determined not to be "of" it. Israeli cinema, like Israeli society, remains haunted by the East in the form of the Palestinian question. Elided, distorted, or idealized by the early films of the heroic-nationalist phase, the Palestinian issue has been confronted, albeit timidly, only in the eighties. Even the eighties "political" films, as we have seen, tend to merely translate the identity dilemmas of Sabra protagonists rather than purvey a truly oppositional voice. Too often the films betray a kind of failure of intellectual nerve, a paralysis of the political imagination, a refusal to radically supersede the exhausted paradigms supplied by the Zionist master-narrative.

In cultural terms, Israeli cinema has been relentlessly "Eurotropic" in the main, spurning any authentic dialogue with the East. Even when critical, it has tended to focalize Western-oriented characters from a Western-oriented perspective. Whereas the heroic-nationalist films glorified the Zionist New Man, the personal films lament his decline and disappearance; neither genre imagines a more dialectically historical or even a more deeply "anthropological" view of Jewishness as lived in Israel. The filmmakers take for granted the Zionist rejection of the Diaspora without offering any deeper analysis of the Israeli Jew as a multidimensional precipitate of millennia of rich, labyrinthian syncretic history lived in scores of countries. One is struck by a kind of cultural superficiality in Israeli cinema, a lack of reflection concerning issues that have preoccupied Jews over the centuries, issues which often have cinematic resonances. What might be the cinematic implications, for example, of the fabled Hebraic fondness for hearing as opposed to the Greek predilection for sight, as manifested in the deployment of image versus sound in an audiovisual medium? Although Hebrew *kolnoa* signifies "moving sounds," Israeli filmmakers and critics have tended to regard cinema as a primarily visual medium. What is the relation, one might ask similarly, between what Derrida terms the Jewish "passion for writing" and the specific modalities of cinematic *écriture?* How might Jewish "textophilia" be inscribed via the deployment of written materials in the cinema, and how could perennial Jewish modes of textuality and exegesis be "translated" into cinematic modes of expression?

Israeli cinema has also yet to become "polyphonic," not only in cinematic terms (the contrapuntal play of track against track and genre against genre), but also in cultural terms, of the interplay of socially generated voices. Israeli cinema has yet to articulate the desire of the marginalized minority-majorities of the area, not only those dispossessed because of national origins, but also those stigmatized by their appartenance to overlapping sets of differences of class, gender, and ethnicity. The overall trajectory of Israeli cinema does point, thankfully, to the progressive incorporation of more social and cultural perspectives, even if that process has been slower and less thoroughgoing than one might have hoped. The personal films have managed to significantly broaden and enrich the portraiture of Ashkenazi Jews in Israel (particularly of Ashkenazi-Jewish men), as well as to introduce more complexly human Palestinian characters. (In the case of the Sephardim, Israeli cinema generally has failed to make even that liberal step.) The challenge now is to go beyond positive portraits of individual representatives of the diverse groups, to go beyond even a concern with positive and negative images in order to present diverse community perspectives, to stage, as it were, the polyphonic clash of what Bakhtin would call "socio-ideological languages and discourses." In a situation of conflict, it is the responsibility of the cinema to orchestrate the war of competing discourses, while intimating the long-term possibilities of change. True cinematic polyphony will emerge, most probably, only with the advent of political equality and cultural reciprocity among the three major groups within Israel—European Jews, Oriental Jews, and Palestinian Arabs. But until the advent of such a utopian moment, cultural and political polyphony might be filmically evoked, at least, through the proleptic procedures of "anticipatory" texts, texts at once militantly imaginative and resonantly multivoiced.

Postscript

Reflecting on *Israeli Cinema: East/West and the Politics of Representation*, some two decades after its first publication, calls for some remarks about the context in which it was written. The manuscript was completed as a doctoral dissertation at New York University toward the end of 1986 and published virtually unaltered in 1989 by the University of Texas Press.[1] The historical scope of the text, beginning with the emergence of the Zionist movement in the late nineteenth-century and ending in the mid-1980s, reflected its date of completion. To be more precise, the book was written prior to the first Intifada, in the pre-Oslo era, at a time when Israeli officials were still engaged in the mental acrobatics of denying the existence of anything called "the Palestinian people." At that time, merely enunciating the word "Palestine," or displaying images of the Israeli and Palestinian flags side-by-side, was considered unpatriotic and even treasonous by the mainstream. Meetings between Israeli citizens and Palestinian representatives were banned, and Israelis who dared cross the lines risked imprisonment. The dominant Israeli media and academia resisted any Palestinian counternarrative, while also silencing a Sephardi/Mizrahi/Arab-Jewish perspective dissonant with the premises of the Zionist masternarrative. The only "legitimate" Sephardi/Mizrahi position was to parrot the standard rhetoric of a "population exchange" between Palestinians and Jews of Arab/Muslim countries. Articulating the concept of "Arab-Jew" apart from any triumphant nationalist teleology, as my work tried to do, was basically taboo.

That discursive landscape changed dramatically in the wake of the Oslo Accords, even while the violence on the ground continued to worsen. At the same time, beginning in the mid 1990s, the Anglo-American academic debates swirling around "multiculturalism," "postnationalism" and "postcolonial theory" began to enter the academic scene in Israel. Some more critical strains of scholarly writing, notably the work that has come to be called "Post-Zionism," emerged into view. The late 1990s brought an increased receptiveness toward transgressive readings of precisely the kind that had earlier made *Israeli Cinema* such a controversial book. Collaborative intellectual projects between Israeli and Palestinian scholars became less anomalous. Some of the texts with which *Israeli Cinema* dialogued have been translated into Hebrew, notably, Edward Said's *Orientalism* (in 2000); Frantz Fanon's *Black Skin, White Masks* (2003), and *The Wretched of the Earth* (2006); and Albert Memmi's *The Colonizer and the Colonized* (2005). The current reprint of *Israeli Cinema* thus appears within a somewhat transformed intellectual environment with regards to the question of Palestine in Israel as well as in the United States.

At the same time, the fundamental questions—the historical and legal rights to the land, the nature of Zionism and the Palestinian struggle, the Israeli Law of Return and the Palestinian Right of Return, and the political and historical status of dislocated Arab-Jews in the wake of the partition of Palestine—remain unresolved and passionately contested. Current critical perspectives, furthermore, have also been caught up in the right-wing backlash in the wake of the second Intifada in Israel and of 9/11 in the United States. All these contradictions haunt contemporary work on the cultural politics of Israel and Palestine. Like the original book, this postscript too appears against a poignant landscape of political impasse. Yet unlike then, this postscript is written at a time when cinematic productions about and around Israel and Palestine are being disseminated globally.

This postscript is not intended as a survey of the evolution of Israeli cinema or as a summary of major trends since 1986, which would be an impossible task given the quantity and complexity of the films over the past two decades. Any such overview, moreover, would be redundant at this point since a good number of publications have already performed such work.[2] This postscript is also not intended as an in-depth survey of the emergence of a multidisciplinary critical scholarship in Israel. Instead, this postscript will focus on the mutations in the themes addressed in the original book, incorporating arguments elaborated in my subsequent publications. The postscript will also reflect on cultural practices and filmic examples pertinent to the issues raised in the book as well as throughout my writing, issues having to do with the critique of Eurocentrism, Orientalism, and colonial discourse.

Writing Between "the National" and "the Colonial"

Israeli Cinema attempted to examine the shaping of national imaginary, and cultural memory within a movement—Zionism—that emerged simultaneous with the cinema, and which was well aware of film's visual force and consciousness-shaping power. Zionism invented, as it were, the Israeli nation partly through its literary and cinematic narrative. Rather than see filmic fiction as a passive reflection of dominant discourse, *Israeli Cinema* analyzed the agency of cinema in narrating the nation, especially in a context where people(s) had to be brought from "the four corners of the world" in order to create the new nation-state. The cinema went beyond mirroring ambient reality to help produce a new Jewish identity. It mobilized spectators to identify with modernization projects such as "making the desert bloom" through settlement practices, all wrapped in Messianic terminology that stressed the redemptive return of the Diaspora to the Biblical "land of milk and honey." The book traced the contours of this shaping of the nationalist historical memory through the cinema, reading films not as documents of fact but as registers of perceptions and perspectives on "reality" and, simultaneously, as a means to actively shape that reality through a celebratory narrative of Jewish revival. The corpus of cinema in Palestine/Israel thus constitutes an audio-visual archive that can be read within a broader contested history, one traversed by manifold discursive contradictions. Exploring the uneasy relation between "the national" and "the colonial" within the contested terrain of Palestine and, later, Israel, the book suggested that cinema formed a vital arena for the representation of history and nation.

At the time I wrote *Israeli Cinema*, the interdisciplinary field of cultural studies was gaining momentum in the U.S. academy. While conceiving my project as part of this field, I attempted to facilitate a dialogue, as it were, between cultural studies and Middle Eastern studies. At that time, cultural studies "traveled" largely along a British-American axis, while "culture" within Middle Eastern studies was viewed mostly through the lens of positivist or Marxist approaches. (The endorsement of Said's *Orientalism* within anti-Orientalist Middle Eastern studies has tended to reflect a shared ideological critique, but usually not a methodological one.) Moving beyond the base/superstructure approach and deploying poststructuralist methods, *Israeli Cinema* viewed culture and politics as intimately linked and highly contested. Rather than seeing "culture" as an afterthought of Zionist practices, I suggested that from the very early days of the Yishuv in Palestine, the diverse cultural practices of the emerging Israeli nation—language, music, dress, cuisine, landscaping, and urban planning—were shaped by a discourse at once colonialist and nationalist.

The tension between "the national" and "the colonial" was to my mind central to any discussion of Hebrew fiction and Israeli culture. While *Israeli Cinema* on the one hand offered archival research into the history of Hebrew/Israeli film, it also invited readers to analyze Zionist discourse through the prism of national and colonial discourse theory. My text was also engaged in probing the implications of "Third World" debates for the politics of culture of Israel/Palestine. At the time, I opted to publish the manuscript with the University of Texas Press partially because of its substantial list of books devoted to what used to be called "Third World Literature and Cinema." The academic space available to such perspectives was still rather limited in a period when multiculturalism and postcolonial theory had not yet emerged as consolidated fields of inquiry in the Anglo-American university. The quite plausible cataloguing of the book only within the fields of "Jewish/Middle Eastern studies," on the one hand, and within "cinema/media studies," on the other, would not have guaranteed an engagement with another "interpretative community," i.e., readers for whom a central frame of reference was the corpus of anti-colonial Third Worldist—a field that later morphed into "postcolonial studies." Indeed, the book in a sense belonged to a historical moment characterized by a search for an analytical language appropriate for cultural production within the ambivalently twinned spaces of the national and the colonial. More specifically, the text was written at a time when Third Worldist discussions were often split around the question of Israel/Palestine, when American academics, with the notable exceptions of a few Third Worldist leftists, were ignorant of or hostile to the Palestinian counternarrative and completely unaware of Sephardi/Mizrahi/Arab-Jewish perspectives. Given the ideological, political, and institutional constraints within and in relation to Israel/Palestine, this search for a new language turned out not to be a simple task.

As part of the then emerging field of "Third World Literature and Cinema," *Israeli Cinema* tried to draw the limits of the analogies to more paradigmatic cases of both "colonial discourse" and "national culture." Throughout, the book was developing an anti-colonial critique but in relation to a national space that had rarely been seen as "Third World" in any conventional sense, but which viewed itself in terms of national liberation. Within a comparative framework, the text highlighted the tensions and anomalies of "the colonial" and "the national" in the case of Zionist discourse. While the book was about "the national" and "national cinema," its reading was not nationalist; rather, it was concerned with dissecting the nationalist imaginary. Indeed, the text was written at a time when "nationalism" itself was beginning to be interrogated by what would later come to be called "postnationalism."

While, as we know, all nations are invented, I suggested that some nations are more invented than others, especially since, in the case of Israel, the state can be said to have invented the nation. Engineering the transplantation of Jewish populations from extremely diverse cultural geographies, the Zionist movement managed to found a nation-state in 1948, but did so on the ruins of another potential state project—the Palestinian state—with grave consequences for the lives of the people in the region, including for Jews themselves. The (already problematic) link often made between the Holocaust and the establishment of the state of Israel, for example, does not "work" for the Jews from the Muslim world, whose historical experience did not include any genocidal Final Solution. Revisionist Israeli historians who focus on the partition and its aftermath, meanwhile, have rightly called attention to the tragic human costs of 1948 and thus come much closer to the Palestinian narrative of *al-nakba* (the catastrophe). But even that work tends to ignore the story-within-the-story, i.e., the historical and political links between the dispossession of Palestinians and the dislocation of Arab-Jews. My work, in contrast, has tried to articulate the political, social, and cultural ruptures that the partition generated for Arab-Jews, and its reverberations within the cultural sphere.

Carrying the same banner of the "civilizing mission" that the European powers proclaimed during their thrust into "found lands," Zionist texts viewed Palestine as *terra nullius* and indigenous Palestinian culture as *cultura nullius*. At the same time, that land was also a *terra santa* and a multiply promised land, and Palestinians superfluously "happened" to reside in the place designed as the Jewish homeland. The concealment of Palestine took place within two parallel narratives that put forth two opposite time-lines; Palestine was in excess of the march of Progress but it was also in excess of the disinterring of remnants of the Biblical past. As a modern science, archeology's role was to provide evidence for the historical right to the ancient "Land of Israel." Jewish "archeology of the text" (George Steiner), I argued, was transmuted into Zionist archeology of the land, invested in the reading of territorial homeland as a document of possession. Excavation, as a hermeneutic, didactically demonstrated Jewish genealogy and teleology through its uncovered traces in *terra firma*. While Jewish fragments dug up from the belly of the earth were indexical of millennial depth, Arab presence was merely its surface dust. The iconography of Biblical vistas and scenes of archeological excavations have entered Israeli popular culture in the form of coffee table albums, tourist pilgrimages, or cinematic narratives (see especially the section of *Hill 24 Doesn't Answer*).[3] Discourses of colonial discovery, in other words, were intermingled with discourses of return to the land of origins. In contradistinction to the classical colonial paradigm, the metropole and the colony, in this case, I suggested, were conceived as located in the self-same place. The syncretic palimpsest of both Hebrew and Arabic histories in the Land of Israel/Palestine makes any discourse of linear genealogies, schematic origins, and nationalist DNA seem too violently exclusionary to account for intersecting multilayered histories.

Zionism, I suggested, forms an anomalous project—at once a liberation movement for Jews and a colonial imposition on Palestinians. The book examined the repercussions within the cinema of these anomalies of the national for the representation of Palestine as well as of Jewish history, or more precisely, of a plurality of Jewish *histories*. The in some ways schizophrenic Zionist narrative combined a redemptive nationalist narrative *vis-à-vis* European anti-Semitism, with a colonialist narrative *vis-à-vis* Arab Palestine, in this sense recapitulating the schizophrenia of the U.S. exceptionalist narrative, anti-colonial *vis-à-vis* Great Britain, yet colonial *vis-à-vis* indigenous Americans and enslaved Africans. The "East," in the Israeli case, is simultaneously the place of Judaic origins and the locus for implementing the "West." Associated with backwardness, "the East" is also associated with the solace of a return to origins and reunification with the Biblical past. The "West," meanwhile, is also viewed ambivalently, both as the historic crime scene of anti-Semitism and as an object of desire, an authoritative norm to be emulated in the "East." My decision to end the book with a call for a heteroglossic art that relays a polyphonic diasporic perspective went against the grain of the thoroughly Zionist notion of the "negation of Exile" (see especially the discussion of the Sabra in relation to the rejection of the ancestral Diaspora Jew in the first two chapters.)

Through a relational approach, I sought to link a number of issues, arguing that certain segregationist approaches entail an uncritical replication of the doxa and analytical frameworks of Zionist discourse. While the questions of Palestine and Arab-Jews/Mizrahim have been studied as completely separate issues, one seen as "internal" and the other as "external," I tried to offer a cross-border analysis that demonstrated their close connections. *Israeli Cinema* also examined the colonial/national discourses as gendered allegories advancing pioneer-settlement and war narratives. In a sense, I was concerned with searching for narrative moments in the films themselves that either forged or erased the links of the internal and external. While the book focused on Zionist narratives, images, and discourses, it also looked at their subterranean affinities with discourses elsewhere. Tropes of the "Promised Land," "virgin land," and "civilization-versus-savagery," for example, clearly resonated with the American pioneer imaginary of settling the empty land and taming the frontier. Images of the Hebrew pioneer, the masculinized new Jew, the desert redeemer Sabra, mimicked the American Adam and his creation of order out of a wilderness chaos.

At the same time, a narrative of national liberation—with Zionism seen as the national liberation movement of the Jews—resonated with anti-racist nationalist discourse. It is not a coincidence that black liberationist movements such as Rastafarian Pan-Africanism dialogued with Zionism, drawing parallels between their turn to Africa and the Jewish return to Zion. The Zionist movement offered a philosophical and organizational model for widely different activists and writers, such as the American W.E.B. Du Bois, author of *The Souls of Black Folk,* and the Jamaican Marcus Garvey, leader of "Black Zionism," who coined the slogan "Back to Africa." It is also not a coincidence that Fanon himself, especially in his *Black Skin, White Masks*, dissected the pathologies of anti-black racism in relation to the phobias of anti-Semitism.[4] These analogies and disanalogies between the (diasporic) Jew and the black in the context of Europe and the West, however, shift their valence once the Jew is reterritorialized and positioned as the new hegemon, The Fanonian analogy, wherein the analysis of racism was in some ways modeled on the analysis of anti-Semitism, slowly turned into what seems more like an opposition between "the Jew" and "the black," especially after 1967. No longer a signifier of victimized minority, "the Jew" in its Israeli incarnation came to be associated with colonialism and racism, leading to splits even among leading anti-colonial thinkers (e.g., Albert Memmi and Jean Paul Sartre, on the one hand, and Josie Fanon and Jean Genet, on the other.) It is against this intellectual backdrop that I tried to explore the anomalies of the Israel/Palestine case, including its often obscured story of the Arab-Jews/Mizrahim. Rethinking the question of Sephardim/Mizrahim outside the ready-made notion of "the Jewish Nation," has formed part of a larger effort to view identity formations within multiple comparabilities and relationalities.

My discussion of Zionism and the cinema thus attempted to locate the political within artistic realms conventionally regarded as apolitical. At the time, the

Bourekas genre, for example, was viewed merely as popular comic entertainment about ethnic tensions. *Israeli Cinema,* in contrast, portrays nationalist ideology as permeating a genre that resolves the Mizrahi/Ashkenazi conflicts under the celebratory sign of "we're all Jews." The so-called "personal cinema," meanwhile, was usually viewed as apolitical, but *Israeli Cinema* proposed to read that genre as a political allegory that projected a feeling of alienation, siege, and claustrophobia—at least on the part of Euro-Israel—in the wake of a political landscape changed both by post-1967 expansionism and the post-1977 Likkud rise to power. The political *parti pris* of personal fiction, I suggested, was not completely untouched by nationalist discourse and by an Orientalist imaginary. In Dan Wolman's filmic adaptation of Amos Oz's novel, *My Michael* (1975), for example, the male Arab twins occupy the female protagonist's stream of consciousness, metaphorizing the repressed Dionysian inner self of the protagonist and her romantic frustration with her humdrum and unimaginative existence. Within this reading, the Arab presence infiltrated the eroticized hallucinatory space of Jewish-Israeli subjectivity but was silenced as a national, political voice. Similarly, A.B. Yehoshua's story, "Facing the Forests" (1962) normalized the silence assigned to the speech-impaired Arab (i.e., Palestinian) character who becomes a vehicle for the Sabra's existential nausea. (See the chapter entitled "Personal Cinema and the Politics of Allegory.") Echoing fiction written by the Algerian-born *Pied Noir* Albert Camus, where Algerians form an extension of the landscape, Israeli fiction literally denied its Arab characters any significant speaking role. Around the same time, interestingly, Sami Michael's novel *All Men are Equal—But Some Are More* (1974) has the alienated Iraqi-Israeli protagonist fight on the 1967 Egyptian front, but also has him bond with a Palestinian during a moment of despair over his separation from his Euro-Israeli wife.

Addressing Eurocentrism as a shaping-force of culture and epistemology, my text placed Zionism on the couch, as it were, dissecting the (self)rejection of the Diaspora *Ostjuden* as intimately linked to the disdain for Jews from another East, the Mizrahim.[5] Zionist discourse not only internalized anti-Semitic tropes toward the *shtetl ostjuden*, I suggested, but also projected that internalized image onto the newly discovered other *Ostjuden*—the Eastern non-Ashkenazi Jews. Dismembering Jews from their Arab-Islamic historical and cultural context, Zionist discourse turned the concept of "Arab-Jew," into an antonym, an oxymoronic identity. My work argued for a conceptual space where one could read not only the question of Palestine but also the question of Arab-Jews/Mizrahi beyond the taken-for-granted masternarrative of Arab versus Jew, while also attesting to the split fashion in which the two questions were articulated—the Sephardi/Mizrahi as the good (Jewish) orient and the Palestinian as the bad (Arab) orient.

Israeli Cinema contained, in embryonic form, a number of ideas about Arab-Jews, developed in my subsequent essays, including: "Sephardim in Israel: Zionism from the Standpoint of its Jewish Victims," "Rethinking Jews and Muslims," "The Narrative of the Nation and the Discourse of Modernization," "Taboo

Memories, Diasporic Visions: Columbus, Palestine and Arab-Jews," "The Invention of the Mizrahim," and "Rupture and Return: Zionist Discourse and the Study of Arab-Jews."[6] My aim was to question the received paradigms about Arab-Jews by interrogating the historical and geographical boundaries characteristic of Eurocentrism. Zionist discourse regarded the "return" of Middle Eastern Jews to historical time and a reterritorialized space, on the one hand, and the "rupture" from their Eastern Diaspora on the other, as two parts of a single equation—the denial of the relevance of a Judeo-Islamic cultural formation. Indeed, this ambivalence, which combines fear of the "Arab" within the Arab-Jew with a vested interest in the "Jew" within the Arab-Jew, resulting in inconsistencies and contradictions in hegemonic scholarship in the various disciplines. While for decades Jewish/Israeli history and cultural criticism marginalized the study of Middle Eastern Jews, for example, sociology and criminology did precisely the opposite, by studying within a modernization narrative that treated them as a severe "problem" accompanied by maladjustment and underdevelopment. This fissured approach removed Mizrahim from their Arab and/or Muslim history as a civilizational space, yet that repressed history returned as an explanatory principle for their social pathologies. In the recent episode of this saga of disavowal, the figure of the Arab-Jew has come into the limelight. Despised for their Arabness, Mizrahim were once rejected, but now that a younger generation has reclaimed their Arabness, a public mobilization has emerged to "reject the Arab-Jew."[7] Among Arab intellectuals, meanwhile, the nostalgia and desire for an alternative Arab-Jew calls attention to an ongoing anxious debate, where the Arab-Jew in not merely a historical figure but a trope embedded in conflicting nationalist imaginaries.

While it has sometimes mistakenly been read as offering an unduly rosy portrayal of Jewish history in Muslim/Arab spaces, my work on Arab-Jews has actually tried to demystify the ethnocentric self-idealization of the Zionist narrative, without necessarily glorifying Arab nationalism, or, for that matter, Arab-Jews/Mizrahim themselves, some of whom have played an alienated and ambiguous role in this convoluted story. I tried to analyze the question of Arab-Jews by going beyond the limiting nation-state framing, moving toward a relational and palimpsestically diasporic story, located in between diverse geographies, nations, ideologies, and discourses.[8] My interrogation of the premises in the popular representations and scholarly texts on Arab-Jews/Mizrahim, whether in *Israeli Cinema* or subsequent publications, was in many ways a call for an interdisciplinary cross-border project that would further explore such tensions.[9]

The Politics of Representation Revisited

Films about the Arab/Israeli conflict were usually assigned to the generic space of epic. The Bourekas genre, meanwhile, was assigned to the comic category. But its relegation to the supposedly "lower" genre of comedy did not prevent it from also articulating Ashkenazi/Mizrahi tensions, so that it became a celluloid reflection of the nationalist splitting of the question of Palestine from that of Arab-Jews. Yet a close examination of the narratives revealed the subterranean links between the two "segregated" genres, within a co-entangled habitus. Although usually absent in the heroic-nationalist genre, the latent presence of the Arab-Jew could be read throughout, at times even through the narrative's negations and denials. By making the silences speak, my project called attention to the paradoxical presence-absence of the Arab-Jew.

The politics of casting, for example, offered a dense site for exploring the schizophrenic existence of the Arab-Jew within a partitioned land.[10] Often cast to play the enemy in the war film—the Arab—the Arab-Jew's corporeal presence on the Jewish-Israeli screen staged another, unspoken, clash. The Jewishness of the Arab-Jew made it possible to safely enlist him or her in the Israeli re-enactment of the Israeli-Arab war; but the Arabness of the Arab-Jew relegated him or her to re-enact the very same denigrated role—the Arab—he or she was asked *not* to perform as a citizen. In the 1950s film *Hill 24 Doesn't Answer*, an Arab-Jew extra, cast to play a Jordanian soldier, forgot, perhaps symptomatically, his enemy role, and ran to kiss the Torah during the filming of the 1948 Jewish withdrawal from the old city of Jerusalem. The entire scene, employing some six hundred extras had to be shot over again. On the battlefield, the hyphen between "the Arab" and "the Jew" was bound to exist within an anxious zone of remembrance and forgetfulness. While the Arab-Jew was to be cleansed of Arab traces, his or her Jewishness was guaranteed an entry permit into the national family. Arab/Muslim spaces were gradually emptied of their Jewish members, while Palestine was dismembered of its indigenous Jews, as it was subjected to the Middle East's version of Manifest Destiny. In the re-enactment of settlement and war, the cinema narrated the "vanishing" of the Arab/Palestinian, but through the linguistic acoustics and corporeal visibility, ironically, of the Arab-Jews who "stood in" for them as their body doubles.

Hollywood and American TV have continued to cast Mizrahim to play the equally dubious Middle Eastern roles of either fanatic terrorists or of noble savages (for example, in *Rambo III* [1988], *Steal the Sky* [1988], *True Lies* [1994], and *Not Without My Daughter* [1991]). Israeli filmmakers, meanwhile, have gradually become concerned with corrective self-representation through casting. Already in the 1980s, one of the early critical films, Uri Barabash's *Beyond the Walls* (1984), set out to subvert the chromatic hierarchy of the Israeli/Arab stereotypes, casting a blue-eyed Palestinian actor (Muhammad Bakri) and a dark Jew (Arnon Tzadok). This visual inversion nevertheless persisted in the casting of Mizrahim in the "dark" roles. At screenings in diverse festivals, audiences and critics sometimes assumed on chromatic grounds that Bakri's character was actually "the Israeli" and Tzadok's character was actually "the Palestinian."[11] With the growing debates over multicultural identity, postcoloniality, and post-Zionism during the 1990s, the trend of experimenting with fixed and ossified identities became more visible in Israeli cultural practices. The generic walls separating "ethnic tension" and "national conflict" narratives began to gradually crumble. As a result, different cinematic encounters became possible, creating new hybrid generic spaces, where the war film, the Bourekas, and personal cinema have begun to meet and interface in fascinating ways.

Bypassing earlier rigid ethnic and national categories, the emerging tendency to break with paradigmatic generic spaces has been at times performed through a refusal of an explicitly labeled ethnicity altogether. Jewish characters have come to bear a more ambiguous and diffuse marker—"the Israeli"—no longer imagined as either the Euro-Israeli Sabra or the Sephardi/Mizrahi immigrant, and no longer fixed within nationalist-war or ethnic tension genres. The character's blurred ethnicity sometimes contrasts with the actor's own visible Ashkenaziness or Mizrahiness, however, not merely in terms of the biographical origins of the actor, but also in looks, accent, body language, cultural allusions, and so forth; thus, throwing off balance the conventional genre/ethnic equations, especially since the films do not revolve around ethnic tensions.

Eran Riklis's *Cup Final* (1991), a farcical film set on the Lebanese/Israeli border, shows Israeli soldiers and their Palestinian kidnappers united in their desire to watch the soccer World Cup Final. The film cast Moshe Ivgy, a Moroccan-Israeli actor—and by implication in the role of a Mizrahi character—to play the Israeli soldier. Such films fashion Mizrahi characters as somehow *above* Mizrahiness, incarnations of a new refashioned universal Israeliness situated between East and West. While moving beyond Mizrahi stereotypes into a post-ethnicity Israel, such representational practices also end up bracketing, as it were, the Arab or Middle Eastern past of the Mizrahi actor/character. In *Cup Final*, Ivgy's character shares with the Palestinian the masculine space of soccer spectatorship, but is narratively barred from an engagement with shared Arabness.[12] By framing the narrative around Palestinian kidnappers and besieged Israelis, furthermore, the film, despite the humanization of the Palestinian characters, evokes the earlier heroic-nationalist genre in its penchant for images of siege and encirclement. Conforming to the usual Palestinian aggression/Israeli retaliation sequencing of events, the conflict begins with "their" (the Arabs) hostile actions, which renders the film's Israeli "us" innocent, the micro-narrative allegorizing the macro-narrative of the conflict's genealogy. The humanized noble Palestinian actor/character nonetheless thus continues to carry the burden of the conflict's original sin, while the ethnically elusive Mizrahi actor/screen body remains under the shield of "the Israeli." The newly trans-ethnic Israeli characters persist to signify ambivalently around the traces of Arabness of the Mizrahi body. No longer fixed to the "negativities" of a cultural Arab geography, Mizrahi identity over the past decade has expanded yet remains tethered to an exclusivist vision.

Some recent films stage such encounters between the Mizrahi and the Palestinian or the Arab, even when that encounter does not form the film's explicit theme. Eran Kolirin's *The Band's Visit* (2007), for example, revolves around a tour to Israel by an Egyptian orchestra, which accidentally ends up in an isolated Southern development town, where Mizrahi characters interact, rather than with the Palestinians, with Egyptian Arabs. The Mizrahiness of the actors/characters and their impoverished social circumstances against the backdrop of the Negev recall the 1950s and 1960s settlement policies of newly arrived North African and Middle Eastern Jews. In contrast to earlier Israeli films, such as Menahem Golan's *Fortuna* (1966), where the South (i.e., Algeria in relation to both France and Israel) signified fatal backwardness, in *The Band's Visit*, underdevelopment and provinciality come to play a sympathetic role in a cross-cultural theatre of the absurd. But here again one wonders about the flaunting of a Mizrahiness ultimately devoid of its own Arabness, even of any search for its Arabness. While such narratives have moved beyond the limits of previous generic spaces and of ready-made nationalist paradigms, they also betray a certain anxiety about the staging of the Arab-Jew in relation to his or her Arabness. Despite a few references to Arab culture, Mizrahi identity is addressed in the present-tense as though always-already confined to an Israeli-Sabra national zone, as though this unusual encounter with the Egyptian Arab did not carry dense significance for a collective that had been dislocated overnight from its Arab cultural geography. Wrapped in the safe embrace of universal absurdity, the specificity of the encounter seems to be narratively aborted, aligned with some invisible walls that render such a historical rendezvous out-of-bounds. This diegesis raises the question of whether, and to what extent, recent cinema echoes, albeit in a lighter postmodern fashion, the same amnesia critiqued earlier in *Israeli Cinema* in relation to both the nationalist-heroic genre in films such as *Hill 24 Doesn't Answer*, on the one hand, and the Palestinian Wave in films such as *Beyond the Walls*, on the other.

At times, casting has also become a creative site generating multiple layers of significance. Within a Boalian theatre of the oppressed, Palestinian actors could enact their Israeli oppressor. Palestinian (from Israel) actors, such as Makram Khoury, were cast to play Israeli military roles, already in the 1980s films *A Very Narrow Bridge* (1985), *The Smile of the Lamb* (1986), and *Wedding in Galilee* (1987), directed by Michel Khleifi, a Palestinian from Nazareth. Within anti-occupation cinema, such provocative, virtually anti-illusionistic casting had the effect of non-essentializing violence, placing the blame on the system of military occupation itself. As one Palestinian female character in *Wedding in the Galilee* puts it provocatively to the Israeli soldier: "You will have to take off your uniform if you want to dance." In contrast to Egyptian or Syrian films where Arab actors have played Israelis, Elia Suleiman (also a Palestinian from Nazareth) casts Israeli actors to play the soldiers, yet the aesthetic aggression lies elsewhere. *Divine Intervention* (2002) has the Israeli star Menashe Noy play the role of the villain, a soldier who sadistically abuses Palestinians at the checkpoints, stopping all cars and using the microphone to order the drivers out of their cars to sing and dance "Am Israel Hai" (Long Live the People of Israel.) For the role of Santa Klaus killed by Palestinian children, meanwhile, the film casts George Ibrahim, a Palestinian-Israeli known for his man-and-puppet children's show *Sami and Susu*, broadcast by the state-controlled one TV channel, on its Arabic program, from 1974-1986. Arabic radio and TV broadcastings have supplied work for Palestinians and Arab-Jews but have been viewed as state propaganda, pacifying the natives. In *Divine Intervention,* George Ibrahim's popular Sami character, a kind of a cute Arab on state TV, is the object of an iconoclastic vengeance wrought by Suleiman's children.

Creative casting or role reversals for some actors can serve to disavow a dubious cinematic past. For the Mizarhi actor Yossef Shiloach, whose success thrived on playing both evil Arabs and buffoonish Mizrahis, the partial jettisoning of this regrettable history paralleled the actor's involvement in leftist Mizrahi circles that sought to assert a different vision of peace. In alternative films such as Moshe Mizrahi's films, Shiloach did portray complex Sephardic characters already during the 1970s, but he explicitly took a position against stereotyping around the time he joined the Mizrahi Front activist group in the second half of the 1980s. He protested the National Theater HaBima's adaptation of Ephraim Kishon's Orientalist play/film *Sallah*. (In contrast to the 1964 film that predictably cast an Ashkenazi-Sabra actor, Topol, to play the paradigmatically stereotypical Mizrahi, the 1988 HaBima version cast Ze'ev Revah, a Moroccan Mizrahi actor and Bourekas filmmaker, a casting that hardly altered the narrative's Orientalist vision.) During that period, Shiloach searched for an alternative path, but he also continued to act in films embedded in hegemonic discourse. Shiloach played in Yizhak Halutzi's *Braids* (1989), a non-stereotypical yet ideologically charged film depicting the heroism of the Zionist underground in Iraq, a film produced in the very same year Shiloach participated in the historical meeting between Mizrahim/Arab-Jews and Palestinians in Toledo, Spain. (A key Toledo organizer was the alternative filmmaker Simone Bitton.) In fact, Shiloach continued to play "the Arab" or the "Muslim" in Hollywood films such as *Rambo III, Not Without my Daughter, Night Terrors* (1993), and *Chain of Command* (1994), which featured highly problematic representations of the Middle East. Such contradictions, I may add, reveal the ways that Israeli and American Orientalist representations have been deeply intertwined not only ideologically but also institutionally. Negotiating between contradictory positions, performers are inevitably caught up in the web of casting politics emblematic of a powerful institutional apparatus.

With the growing visibility of Mizrahi cultural activism in the 1990s, there has been a surge in narratives set within enclosed Mizrahi neighborhood spaces, which employ virtually all-Mizrahi casts, as in the case of Yamin Messika's *Love Victim* (1994) and *The Vineyard of Hope* (1997) and Benny Torati's *Yonanam* (1987) and *Desperado Square* (2001). Involved in Mizrahi activism long before directing films, both Messika and Torati approached casting as part of a larger movement to consciously accentuate a symbolic return of the Mizrahim to their Arab and Middle Eastern culture. Torati's *Desperado Square* predominantly casts Mizrahim players to perform in a Mizrahi narrative. Here Shiloach plays the role of Israel Hahodi, whose name combines his first name "Israel" with his nickname "the Indian", an index of his country of origin but also a reference to his beloved Hindi music/cinema—a virtual embodiment of Bollywood culture. *Desperado Square* also creates a certain dissonance by casting an Ashkenazi actress, Yona Elian, for the female protagonist role, and the Palestinian Mohammad Bakri for the male protagonist role. The presence of Yona Elian, a 1970s star of the Bourekas melo-drama, forms part of a broader intertextual dialogue with the fading Bourekas genre. Yet, Elian's screen persona "passed" for Mizrahi, given the memory of her role as the heroine of George Ovadia's melodramas (especially *Nurit*, 1972). The casting of the Palestinian Bakri as the Mizrahi protagonist, meanwhile, inverts ear-lier heroic-nationalist filmic paradigms, where Mizrahim played Arab antagonists within a casting politics that denied subjectivity both to the Arab character and the Arab-Jewish actor.

The casting of Bakri in Yehuda Ne'eman's *Nuzhat al-Fuad* (2007) is similarly intriguing. The film strings together contemporary Tel Aviv stories with layered allusions to *A Thousand and One Nights*. Bakri plays two contemporary figures, a Palestinian patient and an Iraqi-Jewish writer, along with the historical figure of the Caliph of Baghdad, Harun Al-Rashid. Bakri, who has often performed the role of the dignified Palestinian in a series of Israeli, Palestinian, and international productions, here lends his poised screen aura to the Mizrahi characters.[13] Casting Bakri as Mizrahi or Arab-Jew incorporates and assimilates Bakri's established role as the dignified Palestinian in the Palestinian film wave since the 1980s, but here it is appropriated and re-signified. The "return of the repressed" is now not the absent Palestinian of the heroic-nationalist genre but the repressed Arab-Jew whose Arabness is accentuated precisely through the blurring of the boundaries between the screened (Arab) "body" of the Mizrahi and that of the Palestinian. This incorporation of the Palestinian actor/body forms part of a larger tendency to deny Arabness to the Arab-Jew. Bakri's character enacts the role of a returning brother after years of disappearance from the town, a return that melodramatically resonates with the film's closure. At the same time, *Desperado Square*'s provocative casting is not without its allegorical limits and representational dilemmas, as the corporeal interface between the Palestinian and the Arab-Jew blurs their different positionings within the state of Israel, while also narratively keeping the explicit figure of the Palestinian away from Mizrahi space.

My critique of casting hierarchies in the book formed part of a broader discussion of the politics of representation, probing the East/West relations in narrative, genre, discourse, and institutional politics, along with the specifically cinematic elements. Unlike novels, cinematic narratives require concrete choices involving complexion and facial characteristics. Appearance and description in the cinema are grounded in the concrete and the specific; phrases such as "menacing looks" or "seductive eyes" have to be translated into the shape, color, and physiognomy of a particular performer. In contrast to written texts, the voice in the cinema too raises the problem of embodiment. The voice, not unlike the body and face, is inevitably specific: it is gendered, classed, and raced; it has a grain, an accent, an intonation, a timbre, a pronunciation, and even a vocal manner, all of which may remain "inaudible" in a text. The performer's voice, furthermore, has to be mediated via a specific language. It was, we may recall, the Iraqi Arye Elias's Arabic accent, looks, and body language that prevented him from playing Shakespearian roles (in Hebrew), despite playing such roles in Baghdad. At the same time, it was also Elias's Iraqiness that has made him a desired screen presence for the emergent Mizrahi cinema, especially given the melancholy realization of the slow disappearance of the older generation Iraqis, Moroccans, Egyptians, or Yemenis who actually lived in the Arab world.

Audio-visual narrative forces the filmmaker to take a stance. Cinematic production necessitates a selection of actors in a casting process that inevitably locates face and body within concepts of gender, race, class, and nation. Indeed, as noted in the book, in Western iconography, Christ was gradually remodeled as Aryan, deemed more appropriate for the supreme being as seen by a white normative ethos. The de-Semitization of the Jewish body becomes more evident in a visual medium such as the cinema, than it does in a verbal medium such as the novel. Thus, the break with such imagery becomes especially meaningful within a national and social space where Arab looks and Arabic language tend to signify an imminent danger that triggers the policing machine.

Recent films have also explored the Zionist project of the Hebrew revival, from the realm of the sacred to the mundane, seen in Nurit Aviv's documentary *Sacred Language, Spoken Language* (2008). Her *From Language to Language* (2004), meanwhile, engages the consequences of the forced cultural-linguistic conversion into Hebrew of a heteroglossic space. The film interviews artists for whom Hebrew is not their mother tongue, reflecting on their complex relationship to Hebrew, living in-between languages. Accented Hebrew on the screen signified newcomers, but it would be misleading to think that all accents and non-Hebrew languages occupied the same status in the eyes and ears of the dominant culture. Yiddish, Russian, German, English, Ladino, Arabic, Turkish, or Farsi possessed very different coefficients of cultural capital (Bourdieu). Arabic is itself caught within a fraught citizenship. Iraqi, Moroccan, or Yemeni Arabic dialects or accents in Hebrew are associated with the safe zone of Jewishness, while a Palestinian Arabic accent in Hebrew remains explosively charged. On the screen, beginning with the anti-occupation films of the 1980s, gradually Palestinian Arabic has come to possess a less negative presence, yet still occupies a highly anxious narrative slot.

Over the past two decades, Israeli films have come to accentuate the multiplicity of languages in Israel, with some films even eclipsing the national language, Hebrew, in order to reflect a new immigrant social milieu. Already TV films like Ram Levi's *Bread* (1987) staged performances in Moroccan Arabic, and Arabic is significantly present in Shmuel Hasfari and Hanna Azouly-Hasfari's *Sh'hur* and Ronit Elkabetz and Shlomi Elkabetz's *The Seven Days* (2008). A substantial part of the dialogue in *The Band's Visit* takes place in English, which disqualified the film for the Academy Award nomination in the foreign film category, while a few snippets of Arabic dialogue are performed by Palestinian and Mizrahi actors mimicking the Egyptian dialect. Dover Koshashvili's *Late Marriage* (2001) is primarily spoken in Georgian, while Leonid Gorovets's *Coffee with Lemon* (1994) and Arik Kaplun's *Yana's Friends* (1999) feature dialogue in Russian. Vietnamese is crucial in Duki Dror's documentary *The Journey of Vaan Nguyen* (2005), which tells the story of "the boat people," Vietnamese refugees who arrived in Israel in the late 1970s, but who now want to return to Vietnam, while their children, who feel Israeli, face an identity conflict. Radu Mihaileanu's *Live and Become* (2005) and Dan Wolman's *Foreign Sister* (2004), or documentaries such as Dastao Damato's *Black Music* (2005) and David Davro's *Sisay* (2005), incorporate Amharic. Filipino is spoken by a "foreign worker" character in Etgar Keret's *Jelly Fish* (2007); French in Amos Gitai's *Disengagement* (2007); and English in David Ofek and Yossi Madmony's *The Barbecue People* (2003) and in Ra'anan Alexandrowicz's *James' Journey to Jerusalem* (2003).

Representing Israel as a multilingual space, beyond the Hebrew/Arabic split, places the country within a globalized world of increasingly fluid identities. Hebrew in contemporary Israeli cinema tends to break away from earlier cinematic monoculturalist realism, even moving beyond a strict Jewish nationalism to represent a more extensive social fabric including Mizrahim, Ethiopians, Russians, Georgians, and a variety of "foreign workers," along with Arab/Palestinians. Arabic is increasingly spoken alongside Hebrew; and the Hebrew spoken by Palestinian characters/actors is hardly given an accent (e.g., Eytan Fox's *The Bubble*, 2006). Corrective representation of Israeli polyglossia becomes a vital element in the shaping of a new cinematic realism. In sum, whereas early Zionist cinema was embedded in the mission of "Hebrew Language Revival" redeemed away from the Diaspora Babel, contemporary Israeli cinema features a polyglossia no longer haunted by national linguistic anxiety. From the place of a secure core national-idiom, Israeli cinema is opening its ears to its surrounding linguistic diversity, though it is still overshadowed by the East/West civilizational clash. Not coincidentally, Ne'eman's *Nuzhat al-Fuad* (2007) has Arabic enunciated only in the fantasy sequences, allegorizing the repressed existence and the denied legitimacy of a language only possible in the state of dreams and memories—a linguistic unconscious, often nightmarish, reflected upon in Samir's *Forget Baghdad* (2003).

A younger generation of Mizrahi filmmakers has come to focus on Arabic as the link to a vanishing past. In documentaries such as Rami Kimchi's *Cinema Egypt* (2001), Sigalit Banai's *Mama Faiza* (2002), Duki Dror's *Café Noah* (1996), and *Taqasim* (1999), Arabic functions as both metonym and metaphor for a world prior to the transformation of the Arab-Jew into an Israeli.

Addressing the Intertext

In methodological terms, *Israeli Cinema* was concerned with the fraught politics of national, colonial, social, and ethnic representation. The book pursued a materialist post-structuralist methodology designed to highlight issues of representation, while also investigating the question of the "real" and "realism." Weaving together textual, intertextual, and contextual analyses, the book looked at the unconscious allegories, tropes, and narrative structures as much as at the discourses and institutional politics informing the film text. Yet, *Israeli Cinema* was often read, including by scholars and activists who enthusiastically embraced the book, as a critique of the negative stereotyping of the East endemic in Israeli culture. While examining the image of the Arabs, Palestinians, and Mizrahim, the book also pointed to the pitfalls of a positive/negative stereotype approach by offering a relational reading of the image within broader discursive trends and narrative movements. The image of Arabs, Palestinians, or Mizrahim was not simply negative, as it often split into good and bad, a co-implicated and co-dependent bifurcation. Literary or filmic texts often reserved a slot for the good Sephradi/Mizrahi character, who indicted the backwardness of his or her community and applauded Euro-Israeli redemptive modernity, indirectly warding off charges of intentional discriminatory policies. Hebrew/Israeli fiction, similarly, deployed the positive image of the "Arab" (a category also standing in for "Palestinian") to make a case for the inevitable march of Zionist progress. Within this narrative space, "the good Arab" is granted a temporary residence, as it were, even as the story unfolds within his or her indigenous terrain, and even while the dispossession of Palestinians is taking place. Even the foundational Zionist narrative, Herzl's 1902 futuristic novel *Altneuland,* which details the two-decade metamorphosis of a miserable turn-of-the-century Palestine into a wonderfully civilized oasis of scientific progress and humanist tolerance, already relied on "the good Arab" (Reschid Bey and his wife Fatma) as witness to the advantages of Zionism's Manifest Destiny. The fragile project of occupying an Eastern site to implant Zionism's Western utopia perhaps even required the expressed approval of the vanishing Arab.

Israeli Cinema thus argued that a character-centered analysis could not fully account for the narrative's "political unconscious" (Fredric Jameson). Instead, the book deployed a different methodological grid, one made possible by the linguistic, the poststructuralist, and the cultural "turn." In *Unthinking Eurocentrism*

(1994), Robert Stam and I subsequently developed a fuller theoretical analysis of these issues. A "mimetic" and "stereotypes-and-distortions" approach, we argued, entailed a number of dangers, such as essentialism, ahistoricism, and an exaggerated emphasis on "realism" and "authenticity," along with a privileging of plot and character at the expense of film language, discursive formation, and institutional politics. Such a multi-dimensional textual analysis seems all the more pertinent to the concerns of a contemporary Israeli cinema that is trying to shatter decades of stereotyping and offer ambivalent postmodern spaces for its stories and characters. Eytan Fox's *Walk on Water* (2004), for example, portrays a Mossad-Israeli protagonist, who gradually comes to opt out of the killing machine, revealing the "feminine" side of the macho Israeli. *The Bubble*, although it ends with a suicide bombing, does not rehearse the stereotype of the "terrorist." Instead, the film portrays a sympathetic Palestinian man, involved in a gay relationship with a progressive and sensitive Israeli man, but where the relationship is doomed to fail. After the killing of his beloved sister by the military, the Palestinian carries out the fateful act that also kills his Israeli lover. Such narratives seem to work against the grain of previously established stereotypes, as they simultaneously relay a narrative of historically equal partners in tragedy. Yet to what extent do such films move beyond the fixed ethnic, gender, sexual, and national stereotypes? Can they still be read along national-allegorical, or has that allegory become hopelessly fragmented and fraught?

Israeli Cinema also explored what came to be called the "intersectionality" (Kimberlé Crenshaw) of diverse axes of social stratification, precisely those elements that fissure any nation-state and throw into question monolithically nationalist ethnographies and historiographies. Rather than separate gender from nation and race, *Israeli Cinema* deployed gender critique as part of an analysis of a masculinist national imaginary, seen for example in the visualized rescue tropes of "virgin land" and "making the desert bloom;" in the heroic de-Semitization of the Euro-Israeli Sabra; in the "feminization" of the Diaspora Semitic Jew; in the exoticization of Middle Eastern women; and in the idealized images of Western "women's equality" contrasted with Eastern patriarchy—a dichotomy legitimizing the dispossession of Palestinians and marginalization of Arab-Jews or Mizrahim. This intersectionality can be seen for example in the discussion of Mizrahi representation through multiple prisms—class, gender, ethnicity, nationalism, colonialism, and Third World—rather than through the single prism of class.

My approach partly reflected a dialogue with the indispensable work of the sociologist Shlomo Swirski, whose study of Mizrahim was premised on a Marxist class-based analysis. My project, in contrast, stressed the importance of also addressing the question of Eurocentrism and of Zionist discourse as significant to the Mizrahi question. Mizrahi culture and Arab-Jewish identity, in my view, were as relevant to the debate about power as class. Central to my project were the historical and discursive links between the representation of the Mizrahim

Yes
a\icm le
in
Morob lo

and the Palestinians. Dismantling the Eurocentric approach to the Mizrahim, my work tried to go beyond the nationalist narrative. It critiqued the "erasure of the hyphen" that rendered the concept of "Arab-Jew" oxymoronic, tracing the dislocation of Arab-Jews not simply to their moment of arrival in Israel but also earlier, to the advent of colonialism and later Zionism in Arab-Muslim spaces. Given the conflictual pressures of Zionism, on the one hand, and Arab-nationalism, on the other, the Arab-Jewish/Mizrahi question could not be simply "contained" within the geography of Israel. My work, in this sense, has attempted to outline the contours of a Mizrahi epistemology, one that would transcend Zionist teleology and the narrow disciplinary framework that regards the Mizrahi question as "inside" and the Arab/Palestinian question as "outside." The Mizrahi, in my view, forms an in-between figure, at once inside and outside, "in" in terms of privileged citizenship within the Jewish state, in contrast to the Palestinian citizens of Israel, but hardly "of" the hegemonic national culture.

My hope was also to bring poststructuralism to bear on the study of Zionism by speaking of Zionism not merely as an ideology, but also as a discourse and as a "master narrative" (Jameson) or a "metanarrative" (Lyotard)—concepts that by now have become commonplace in texts that came to be called in the 1990s "post-Zionism." In retrospect, *Israeli Cinema* can also be seen as part of a larger intellectual movement within literary, film, and cultural studies—the poststructuralist-inflected scholarship that came later to be called "postcolonial." To begin with, although the book's title called attention to the subject of "Israel," it did not adopt the hegemonic Israeli-Zionist approach to the topic. This feature was disconcerting for some readers because, at the time, the tacit assumption was that such a work would "naturally" be celebratory of the official story. But my project was premised on interrogating the nationalist teleology informing fields such as history, literature, sociology, anthropology, art history, and so on. It tried to question the metanarrative of modernization, progress, and enlightenment as purely libratory forces. These contradictions and paradoxes continue to inform contemporary debates, evident in an official regime that is fond of oxymorons: "present-absentees," "unrecognized villages", and "Jewish democracy." Indeed, modern Israel has demodernized contemporary Palestine, for example, which has had its potential nation-state apparatus undermined, its infrastructure destroyed, its educational system compromised, its population living in a virtual prison under the gaze of a state-produced panopticon of surveillance and hyper-regulation.

Israeli Cinema looked at the gaps, fissures, and crevices along the East/West fault line. In that sense, it formed part of what was to become an ongoing critique of Eurocentric epistemology in general—worked out more systematically in my co-authored (with Robert Stam) work *Unthinking Eurocentrism*—and of the assumptions undergirding hegemonic writings on Jewish history and culture, more specifically. Rather than a signifier of a natural geographical division or an essentialist cultural opposition, the "East/West" in the subtitle referred to a concept mobilized by Eurocentric discourse. The question of syncretic space between East and West is raised already in the book's introduction. Indeed, I have insisted throughout my work on this historical syncretism of Jewish culture(s) within multiple spaces, while also suggesting that the nation-state boundaries of Israel do not correspond to a simplistic East/West cultural geography. *Israeli Cinema* viewed Jewish Israel through the lens of anti-colonial discourse, as articulated by writers such as Césaire and Fanon, while also attempting to draw out the implications of the critique of Orientalism *à la* Said not only for Palestine and Palestinians, but also for the production of Israeli culture and for the representation of Mizrahi/Arab-Jews. Through the figure of the "Arab-Jew," my work has challenged the facile East/West schism, whereby Israel and Judaism were coterminous with "the West," while all that was Muslim and Arab fell under the sign of "the East." At times, the book was misread (both by supporters and detractors) as an argument for the very East/West dichotomy that I hoped to undo, unfortunately quite pervasive in the discursive realm of "Israel" and "the Arab/Muslim world." Far from suggesting any essentialist content for "the East" and "the West," *Israeli Cinema* highlighted instead the intersection of power and representation in the spatial imaginary.

Over the past decade, as we shall see subsequently, the discourse of postcolonial "hybridity" has traveled from English into Hebrew. While "hybridity" has been an invaluable instrument for cultural analysis in transcending the racial purity myth central to colonial discourse as well as in challenging a Third Worldist discourse that projected "the Nation" as culturally homogenous, it is also always-already power-laden. "Hybridity" has become a catchall term, often void of any serious probing of its different modalities. In a copy/paste approach to Anglophone postcolonial discourse, the postcolonial in its Hebrew translation offers an undifferentiated valorization of "hybridity." But, how can we think through the relation between a postcolonial discourse that reads resistance into hybridities, on the one hand, and the current apartheid-like and literally fenced-in reality of Israel/Palestine, on the other? One thinks of the cruel hybridity imposed, for example, on Palestinian workers on construction sites of the Separation Wall, where the linguistic frontiers of Hebrew and Arabic are indeed traversed, but where Palestinians are obliged to build the very wall that tears their lives apart. Simone Bitton's documentary *The Wall* (2004) captures the daily absurdities generated by the Wall, while Danae Elon's autobiographical documentary *Another Road Home* (2005) zooms into the contradictions of Palestinian-Israeli domesticity. Elon's quest for the Palestinian man who had been her caregiver, Mahmoud "Musa" Obeidallah, for whom she had deep affection, but also about whom she knew very little, ends up with a corrective and therapeutic voyage to get to know him now as a Palestinian. Revisiting the premise that made it natural for him to iron her army uniform, Elon dissects the distorted nature of intimacy typically inhabiting classed-colonial situations. Such filmic moments encapsulate the aporias of hybridity discourse, provoking the question of what is gained when such asymmetries are bracketed or even elided and encoded as resistant. The postcolonial Israeli discourse lacks an in-depth engagement with the English-language postcolonial debate that a decade earlier probed the potentially depoliticizing effects of "hybridity." Notions of "oppression" and "resistance" nowadays are too easily dismissed as binarist simplifications, irrelevant in a new all-embracing space where the colonizer and the colonized perform mutual mimicry. Passing off "hybridity" as always already "resistant" appears to sanctify the *fait accompli* of colonial violence.

In the present Israel/Palestine world of social segregation and the Separation Wall, national and ethnic belonging continue to be defined by East-versus-West geographical reductionism and essentialist civilizational clashes. The project of the re-territorialization of the Jews and their settlement in Palestine/Eretz Israel has overshadowed a polyphonic narrative of Jewish experiences and possibilities. In *Israeli Cinema*, I was making some first steps in moving from a discourse of "the Jewish Diaspora" toward more diasporic perspectives. *Israeli Cinema* questioned the very premises of the earlier denigration of the Diaspora Jew in Zionist texts, while also posing questions about the Zionist reading of the Bible. Herzl's *Altneuland*, for example, revisits the Biblical Exodus, but unlike Freud's *Moses*, it enlists Exodus in the service of a territorial tale of a reunited and a uniformed Jewish Identity. In the chapter entitled "Passover," the first supper provides a pretext for relating the miraculous conversion of old into new, pronounced by the born-again Zionist character:

> First we shall finish our Seder after the manner of our forefathers, and then we shall let the new era tell you how it was born. Once more there was an Egypt, and again a happy exodus—under twentieth-century conditions . . . and with modern equipment. It could not have been otherwise. The age of machinery had to come first. The great nations had to grow mature enough for a colonial policy . . . We had to become new men, and yet remain loyal to our ancient race.[14]

Performed for approving Christian Europeans, this didactic allegory has the rejected and emasculated Jew who mimics "Europe" confidently joining the West but this time in the East. Herzl's desire for a modern repetition of the Biblical Exodus contains a double movement—not simply *out* of "Egypt" but also *into* "Canaan," the grounded Eastern topos paradoxically of his Western utopia. Both the inward and outward movements, however, potentially disrupt the axioms of this utopia. Known in Hebrew as *Yetziat Mitzrayim* or the "departure from Egypt," Exodus also entails "entering Egypt," as Genesis suggests that the Pharaoh initially welcomed Joseph's family. The Egyptian shelter could equally have inspired a narrative of the homing, as it were, of the displaced in Egypt. The Biblical Exodus, furthermore, manifests a teleological movement towards the Promised Land in which the escape from slavery is coupled with the conquest of Canaan, thus becoming a contested site between Zionist versus Palestinian readings.

Two decades prior to engaging with Freud's *Moses*, Edward Said participated in a related debate over the inscription of the Biblical Exodus as a paradigmatic liberation narrative. In his review of Michael Walzer's *Exodus and Revolution*, Said asked:

> How can one exit Egypt for an already inhabited promised land, take that land over, exclude the natives from moral concern . . . kill or drive them out, and call the whole thing "liberation"?[15]

Within this "exodus politics," imagining a Canaanite perspective on the Israelite conquest, as Said does, subverts the reading of Exodus as simply a revolutionary utopia. It is instructive to compare what might be called Said's "Canaanite" critique with the views pressed by the actual Canaanite (or *Cna'anim*) intellectual movement that began prior to the establishment of Israel, a movement that leaves traces in texts by Amos Kenan, A.B. Yehoshua, and Amos Oz, as well as in the personal cinema. Grounded in the anti-exilic Zionist rupture with diasporic Judaism, the *Cna'anim* envisioned a harmonious future for all the inhabitants of the contested land to be guaranteed through a return to a Canaanite past. The *Cna'anim* sought to revive the ancient, pre-Judaic Hebraic culture, along with Canaanite, Assyrian, and other non-Monotheist myths and rituals. In contradistinction to the Judaic culture presumably corrupted by millennial exilic wandering, the *Cna'anim* believed in the teaching of Hebrew culture even to Palestinians. Thus, while drawing a romanticized genealogy that traced back to vanished civilizations, the *Cna'anim*'s archeological cultural project also filtered out the Arabized stratum of Palestine. Whereas the *Cna'anim*'s archeological "dig" into pre-biblical Hebraic origins reveals a Zionist anxiety about their own diasporic antecedents, Said's Canaanite reading uncovers the colonial substratum of Zionist versions of the Exodus narrative.

Israeli Cinema critiqued the nationalist reading of the Bible and the obsessive negation of the Diaspora, which was at times accompanied by a romanticized image of "the Arab" as pre-exilic Jewish figure. The Sabra was celebrated, in an idiosyncratic version of the Freudian *familienroman* (family romance), as the native Jewish son more worthy than his non-native progenitors. The Sabra, as a kind of *sui generis* being, was born out of nature, "from the sea"—to use the words of a foundational Israeli novel, Moshe Shamir's *Bemo Yadav* (See discussions of "Oded the Wanderer," "Sabra," and "Rebels Against the Light.") Personal cinema, although revisiting the Sabra myth, continued to evoke the menacing heteroglossia of the Diaspora (see the "Seeds of Disillusionment" section.) Arguing for a more polyphonic diasporic perspective, *Israeli Cinema* sought to view the Zionist notion of "normality" (in fact, a mimicking of European nationalist discourses) and the "return to history" (the Eurocentric Hegelian vision) through the silences and repressions it provoked. The goal was to unpack, within a kind of critique later associated with whiteness studies, the unspoken normativity of Sabraness and Euro-Israeliness that had come to subsume all Jewish cultures. In the context of Israel, Ashkenaziness has been synonymous with whiteness, although the term Asknenazi is historically associated with the Diaspora Jew. Over the years, diverse Israeli scholars have deconstructed Sabra whiteness (Yerach Gover, Smadar Lavie, Sami Chetrit, Irit Rogoff, Henriette Dahan-Kalev, Yosefa Lushitzky, Sharon Rotbard, and Raz Yosef), and some, in addition, have reclaimed Jewish Ashkenazi identity from nationalist Israeli conceptualization (Daniel Boyarin, Amnon Raz-Krakotzkin, Sarah Khinski, and Jonathan Boyarin). Critiques of the Zionist negation of exile and the Massada myth, more specifically, were peformed in writings by Amnon Raz-Krakotzkin and Yael Zrubavel, respectively.[16]

More than merely portraying Sabra protagonists as anti-heroes or destabilizing their normative (hetero)masculinity, some recent films have deconstructed foundational readings of the Bible through a nationalist grid. Avi Mughrabi's film *Avenge but One of My Two Eyes* (2005) examines the heroic figure of Samson as a kind of a fanatic suicide bomber *avant la lettre*, while documentaries, such as Udi Aloni's *Local Angel* (2002) and Asher de Bentolila Tlalim's *Exile* (2003), reflect on the virtue of diasporic Jewishness. Michal Aviad's *For My Children* (2002) registers the quotidian uneasiness, estrangement, and anxiety around endemic violence, asking a question usually associated with the Jewish diasporic experience: "Is it time to go?" Rachel Leah Jones' *Ashkenaz* (2008), meanwhile, serves up a probing analysis of the contradictions of Ashkenaziness as it has functioned within Israel. Rather than a celebratory exercise in Yiddishkeit nostalgia, *Ashkenaz* paints a refreshingly complex portrait of Ashkenazi identity as seen not only through the eyes of Ashkenazim themselves but also through the eyes of Mizrahim and Palestinians, in an audaciously lucid gaze at the ironic twists of history. This re-examination of the Diaspora Jew and the Sabra, including by Sabras themselves, offers a daring critique of the Diaspora/Sabra binary. Articulated within postnationalist paradigms, such texts or films offer a de-territorialization of the Jewish re-territorialization project.

Palestinians-in-Israel: Cinematic Citizenship in the Liminal Zone

When *Israeli Cinema* was first published, there was a dearth of revisionist critical work addressing Zionist discourse and Israeli culture. Since the 1990s, Israeli scholars have adopted increasingly critical perspectives, while Israeli cultural production has engaged more audacious themes and histories. In the cinema, the release of a number of historically revisionist films on Israel/Palestine points to the emergence of the "polyphonic" cinema for which I had hoped. Although my discussion ended with the films of the mid-1980s, a contemporary rereading of the book helps us appreciate the multiple transformations that have taken place. Today an impressive corpus of new work offers alternative perspectives on the history of Israel and Palestine. Cinema, in this sense, can write the history not only of the winners but also of the dominated.

Any discussion of the interrelationship of politics and cinema in this context must begin with the very definition of Israeli cinema, paying special attention to the complex place occupied by Palestinian citizens of Israel, born and raised within the borders of the Jewish state. As already suggested at the beginning of the book, the question of naming is itself highly contentious and political. At the time, however, I felt that the title "Israeli Cinema" was appropriate since it pointed to a film culture that, for the most part, saw itself firmly grounded within the Zionist ethos. My subtitle, "East/West and the Politics of Representation," meanwhile, pointed to the project's critical reading of that culture's Eurocentric imaginary. Over the past decades, the emergence of "post-Zionist" thought within certain milieux in Jewish Israel, as well as the visible demand for equality and rights by a younger generation of Palestinian citizens of Israel, has resulted in cultural practices that challenge monolithic boundaries of belonging. The following discussion of recent Israeli and Palestinian films echoes the contemporary debate over the conceptualization of Israel itself as "the state of all its citizens," in this case viewing Israeli cinema as the cinema of all of Israel's citizens. Within such a perspective, Palestinian filmmakers and visual artists raised within Israel (Michel Khleifi, Elia Suleiman, Hana Elias, Nizar Hassan, Ibtisam Mara'ana, Hany Abu-Assad, Ali Nassar, Muhammad Bakri, Tawfik Abu Wael, Ula Tabari, Sharif Waked, and Ahlam Shibli) clearly merit discussion not only under the rubric of Palestinian cinema, but also in the context of writing about cinema produced *in* and *around* Israel, or in the liminal zone *between* Israel and Palestine.

The densely interwoven relation of Israel and Palestine, as well as of the transnational traffic of media images, sounds, and peoples, then begs us to broaden the discussion of "national cinema" generally, and of "Israeli cinema" more specifically, beyond films produced or directed by individuals from a single ethnicity/nation within demarcated borders. When my book was originally published, some Israeli reviewers questioned, even mocked, my decision to scrutinize co-productions (*Rebels Against the Light*) or even foreign productions (*Exodus*) since they were not "Israeli films." Apart from the fact that some of the co-productions were directed by Israelis (even if recent immigrants) and that foreign productions involved Israeli crews or actors, shot on location in Israel, and so forth, their narrative movement replicated the official metanarrative. These quibbles, more importantly, only reveal the ideological and ethnic drift of a supposedly normative Israeliness and the nationalist imaginary of a purist definition of what constitutes Hebrew-Israeli identity and culture.

How, for example, should we place the work of Simone Bitton, a native of Morocco, who moved with her family to Israel at the age of 11, then left Israel in 1976 to study film and cinematography at the Institut des Hautes Etudes Cinematographiques in Paris? Bitton has since been based in France, but a glance at her filmography reveals her multiple affiliations. Her documentaries about the Arab world, such as her film about the disappeared Moroccan leader Mehdi Ben Barka, *Ben Barka: The Moroccan Equation* (2002), or her documentaries on Egyptian singers and musicians Muhammad Abdul Wahab, Farid al-Atrash, and Umm Kulthum, are inseparable from her own history of dislocation. Although usually made for French TV and shot largely in Egypt, the films were also broadcast on Israeli Arabic TV and consumed avidly by Mizrahim. At the same time, her films on Israel/Palestine—*Mahmoud Darwish: As the Land is the Language* (1998), the Palestinian-Israeli politician Azmi Bishara (*Citizen Bishara*, 2001), *Palestine: The Story of a Land* (1993), *The Bombing* (1999), and *The Wall*—form another vital aspect of her affiliations. Bitton's work on Israel and Palestine must be situated in relation to her work on cultural production in the Arab world. It would be misleading, therefore, to simply identify her work as "Israeli," just as it would be misleading to completely overlook its Israeli dimension, including in its strong challenge to Zionist orthodoxy. Her work does not fall into an either/or paradigm, whence the necessity of reading it as situated in the interstitial spaces of Morocco, Israel, Palestine, and France.

More recently, diasporic Arab filmmakers have also explored the leaky cultural boundaries between Israel and the Arab world in films such as the reflexive documentary *Forget Baghdad*, by the Iraqi-Swiss filmmaker Samir. While technically a Swiss film, it was partly filmed in Israel, and treats multiple dislocations, not only on a Swiss-Iraqi axis, but also, and more centrally, on an Iraqi-Israeli axis, as well as the Iraqi-American and Iraqi-French axes. Organized largely around the life stories of Iraqi-Israeli writers (Shimon Ballas, Sami Michael, Samir Naqqash, and Mousa Houri), mostly former members of the Communist Party, *Forget Baghdad* reopens a lost chapter of Middle Eastern history. "What does it mean to be an enemy of your own past?" asks the filmmaker. Within an aesthetic of multilayered fragmentation, the film tells a cross-border tale of a religious minority in Iraq becoming an ethnic minority in Israel: Jews in Iraq and Iraqis in Israel. The film also delves into the painful yet humorous stories of the younger generation represented by Samir himself (whose family also had to flee Iraq) and by the trajectory of another interviewee (the author of this text) cross-cutting between the Iraqi homes in Switzerland and Israel.[17] *Forget Baghdad* deploys a rich array of archival materials—British, Iraqi, and Israeli newsreels, Hollywood features (*Son of the Sheik* [1926], *Exodus*, and Schwarzenegger's *True Lies*), Israeli Bourekas comedies (*Sallah*), and Egyptian musical-comedies involving Muslims, Jews, and Christians (Helmy Rafla's *Fatma, Marica and Rachelle*, 1949).

"Israel," in my usage, stands less for cultural-nationalist content than for a state where Palestinians also live and struggle for representation. Films made by Palestinians are also partially about Israel. Writing about Palestinian filmmakers, including also those in the occupied West Bank or Gaza, as well as those in the Diaspora raise equally vexed questions. At this point of history, "Palestine" and "Israel" are co-implicated and must be discussed relationally. In the aftermath of a colonial-settler project, the scattering of dispossessed Palestinians, multiple dislocations, and the ongoing occupation, the question of a "right of return" has been contested, even though sometimes treated as "off the table" in peace negotiations. And while in the following I will largely touch on the work of Palestinian filmmakers who grew up *fil-dakhel* (i.e., inside, or within the boundaries of the state of Israel, and subjected to military rule until 1966), the discussion of Palestine-within-Israel inevitably traverses state borders. Indeed, these contradictions often provide the themes of the films themselves. The point here is that the boundaries of Israel and Palestine, which on one level would seem to constitute an irreconcilable wall-like division, are often subverted and interrogated by very complex filmic and cultural negotiations. In some ways, it is virtually impossible to speak of Israeli cinema without "Palestine," just as it is virtually impossible to speak of Palestinian cinema without "Israel." "Palestine" and "Israel" as imagined in the cinema are not merely national place markers, but constitute an intellectual space of conflictual and interdependent utopias and dystopias.

The boundaries between "Israel Cinema" and "Palestinian cinema," then, are clear only to the extent that we endow each one with an overarching nationalist teleology. The label "Palestinian cinema" is assumed not only by diasporic Palestinians, but also by filmmakers born and raised within the state of Israel. Yet the boundaries are complicated not only when one examines biography, ideology, and citizenship, but also when the use of the Hebrew language and Israeli cultural references, along with Israeli production contexts and institutional sponsorship and reception, are taken into consideration. Rashid Masharawi, a filmmaker from Gaza who grew up in the Shati refugee camp, began his career while working on the sets of Israeli films. For his film *The Shelter* (1989), which revolved around workers from Gaza in Israel, obliged to spend their nights illegally locked down in makeshift shelters on an Israeli construction site, Masharawi cast the Palestinian-Israeli actor Mohammad Bakri as the protagonist. Bakri, who began his career in Haifa Theatre and in films such as Costa Gavras' *Hanna K.*, has acted in numerous Israeli films screened in Israeli film festivals and film societies.[18] To cite another pertinent example, Elia Suleiman's *Chronicle of a Disappearance* (1996) was partly funded by the Israeli Fund For Quality Films, viewed by the filmmaker himself as part of "a civil rights fight."[19] His later film, *Divine Intervention* (2002), provoked opposition to its submission for the entry as the Foreign-Language Oscar, since Palestine was not a country.[20] Collaborative work between Jewish-Israeli and Palestinian filmmakers has especially posed a challenge to fixed categorizations, for example, between Elia Suleiman (a citizen of Israel) and Amos Gitai in *War and Peace in Vesoul* (1997), who also shared a spotlight at the Cannes Film Festival; or *On the Edge of Peace* (1998) co-produced by the Palestinian Daoud Kuttab and the

Israelis Ilan Ziv and Amit Breur; or between the Jewish Israeli Eyal Sivan, who has been living in France and now the U.K., and the Palestinian Michel Khleifi (also a citizen of Israel) who has been living in Belgium, on *Route 181* (2004). How would such collaborations, especially when performed within shared political perspectives, fit into any schematic opposition between Israeli and Palestinian cinema?

The relationship between biography and geography are further complicated when a Palestinian filmmaker from Israel makes a film about the West Bank. The plots of films by Hany Abu-Assad (who is from Nazareth and has been living in Holland), such as *Rana's Wedding* (2002) and *Paradise Now* (2005) revolve largely around the West Bank; the former shot on location in East Jerusalem, Ramallah, and at checkpoints in-between, looking at the quotidian details of the conflict as a young woman faces roadblocks, soldiers, and stone throwers on the way to her lover, while the latter tells a comic-tragic tale of two Palestinian men preparing for a suicide mission inside Israel. Mohammad Bakri's *Jenin Jenin* (2002), a documentary about the 2002 Israeli takeover of the Jenin camps and its tragic aftermath of rubble and massacre, provoked anger in Israel. (Bakri was also denounced when one of his relatives was associated with a suicide bombing.) After years of being feted in Israel as the beloved Arab, he metamorphosed into a traitor, a *persona non-grata*, a veritable "enemy of the people." His subsequent documentary, *Since You Left* (2005), which details the efforts in the Israeli legislature to have legal actions taken against Bakri, investigates the hurdles and limitations involved in living as an "Arab Israeli" by reflecting on his Kafkaesque downward spiral. As a Palestinian citizen of Israel, Bakri's personal saga in some ways recalls the absurd existence endured by the protagonist of Emile Habiby's novel *The Secret Life of Saeed: The Pessoptimist*, which Bakri in fact adapted for the stage and performed in both Arabic and Hebrew both in Israel and in the West Bank. If Habiby's novel is framed within the epistolary genre as a letter to a creature from outer space, Bakri's film is framed as an audio-visual letter to his dead mentor, Habiby, to whom he recounts the fantastic tragic-comic tale of his own life.

The boundaries between "inside" and "outside," then, are permeated by ambiguity. Palestinian cinema filmed, produced, or even subsidized by Israeli institutions, allegorizes the paradoxes of Palestinian-Israeli citizenship. Caught between Israelization projects and seen from the dominant perspective as "the enemy from within," the Palestinian citizens of the state of Israel have been taking an active role in their self-representation. Most visible within recent years are such organizations as Adalah and such figures as ex-Knesset member Azmi Bishara, who has been arguing for Israel as a "state of its citizens." (As we have seen, Bishara was the subject of Simone Bitton's *Citizen Bishara*). Inside and outside Israel/Palestine, Palestinian scholars have been critically examining identity formations of Palestinians within Israel (for example, work by Nahla Abdo, Nur Masalha, Nadim Rouhana, As'ad Ganim, Marwan Bishara, Rohda Kanane, Ibtissam Ibrahim, Isis Nusair, Samera Esmeir, Bashir Abu Manneh, Suheir Daoud, Leena Meari, and Ahmad Sa'di).

Palestinians within Israel have been revisiting images, sometimes disseminated even by diasporic Palestinian and Arab intellectuals, which have branded them "traitors" and "collaborators." Emile Habiby's words inscribed on his tombstone provide one answer to such narratives: "Remained in Haifa." In Bakri's *Since You Left*, a visit to Habiby's tombstone triggers a confessional monologue that becomes a dialogue with Habiby's legacy. (A member of the communist party and a member of the Knesset, Habiby was also the subject of Dalia Karpel's documentary *I Stayed in Haifa*, 1997). In his monologue/dialogue with Habiby in *Since you Left*, Bakri recalls their shared travels outside of Israel/Palestine. In Cypress, Bakri reminds his deceased interlocutor of an incident where a taxi driver asked where they were from, and they answered that they were Palestinians. The driver continues to insist on a more precise answer, since Palestinians are dispersed in many countries, but he roars with laughter when they say "Israel." The distraction generated by his astonishment at this absurdity results in a car accident. What is being negotiated in such conversations, then, is the variable perspective on those who remained in what became Israel, i.e., the Palestinian "inside" Israel. While for exiled authors on the "outside"—for example Ghassan Kanafani in his 1970 novella "Returning to Haifa"—the "inside" is in allegorical terms hopelessly lost to Zionism, for Habiby and Bakri, "remaining" in Haifa can be seen as constituting an "inside" version of *sumud*, a term usually associated with the West Bank. (Indeed, one of the characters in *The Pessoptimist* is named "*Baqiyya*," or she who has stayed, in contrast to the woman "outside," named "Yuaad," or to be returned.) Palestinian fictions in Israel or *fil-dakhel*, in other words, have explored the paradoxes of Palestinian existence within Israel; their implied addressees are also Palestinians on the outside.

Over the past two decades, a new cinema, taking both documentary and fiction form, has focused on Palestinians within Israel, living as veritable exiles on their own land. Michel Khleifi's *Wedding in Galilee* was one of the first major Palestinian features to highlight the plight of Palestinians within Israel. The allegorical strategies hinge on the ritual of the wedding, overdetermined with meaning due to its implicit linking of families, histories, and genealogies, but here exacerbated by the Israeli/Palestinian conflict. The wedding is infiltrated by the Israeli military because the bridegroom's father, the Mukhtar, is required to get a permit from the governor to continue the festivities until nightfall. His invitation to the governor and his staff brings to the surface latent tensions not only between Israel and Palestine, but also between diverse ideological and generational forces within the Palestinian community. The camera oscillates between diverse perspectives, contrasting the attitudes of the young radicals born under Israeli occupation with those of the older, "patient" generation.

In films such as *Wedding in Galilee*, the loss of Palestine is represented through images of emasculation and loss of virility, as the son becomes impotent as a result of his filial resentments at his father's accommodating conduct.[21] While one may object to the film's masculinist preference for female (over male) nudity, and at times for Orientalist imagery, female characters do nonetheless exercise a vital presence in the story, privileged as nurturers of the collective memory. (The film was made around the time that children and women became major participants in the first Intifada.)[22] At the same time, although *Wedding in Galilee* alludes to the differences and tensions within the Palestinian community, it also asserts a common struggle against the occupation, along with a common history and cultural identity indigenous to the land. Images of Palestinian lives on the screen thus challenge the Israeli denial of Palestinian existence, whether through the physical elimination of Palestinian villages or through the verbal-ideological obfuscation implicit in terms like "nomads." In this sense, the camera's painstaking, affectionate scrutiny of rural ceremonies and rituals makes less an anthropological than a simple political point: "We are here, and we exist." The fluid movement from character to character and the embroidering of diverse discourses and languages (daily slang, proverbs, popular rhymes, sloganeering speeches, and hallucinatory poetic monologs) display the nation's textured complexity. Even more, the film associates earth, crops, trees, vegetation, and abundance of food with Palestinians—in contradistinction to the Zionist narrative of pioneers "making the desert bloom," while simultaneously celebrating the fusion of Muslim and Christian Palestinian customs—in contradistinction to an official discourse that devalues Palestinian national identity by speaking of the "non-Jewish minorities." The narrative structure thus reinforces national legitimization. By focusing on a Palestinian ritual circumscribed by Israeli power, the film subverts the media trope of Arabs besieging Israel and Palestinians disrupting Israeli routines.[23] A tale with Palestinians at the center and Israelis as "visitors" inverts a master-narrative that favors the land's "original," that is, Jewish, inhabitants over its present-day Arab "guests." In Palestinian eyes, Israel represents just one more invasive foreign power arriving in the wake of the Ottomans and the British. *Wedding in Galilee*, like Khleifi's earlier documentary *Fertile Memories* (1980), suggests that Palestinian memory is not only alive, but also capable of engendering new beginnings.[24]

Films such as *Wedding in Galilee, The Mountain* (1992), *The Olive Harvest* (2003), *Since You Left*, and Ibtisam Mara'ana's *Paradise Lost* (2003) craft images of Palestine in Israel. A great number of the filmmakers—Michel Khleifi, Elia Suleiman, Hanna Elias, Hany Abu-Assad, and Ula Tabari—have left, working on Palestine-in-Israel outside, in Brussels, Paris, New York, Amsterdam, or Los Angeles, thus making it necessary to address the issue of multiple dislocations, beyond a strict national geography and within diasporic, exilic, and transnational perspectives. Suleiman's early films, *Homage by Assassination* (1991) and *Introduction to the End of an Argument* (1990, co-directed with the Lebanese-Canadian Jayce Salloum), were made when the filmmaker was based in New York, while later films, *Chronicle of a Disappearance* and *Divine Intervention*, were produced after Suleiman had relocated to Paris, but both retain their relation to Nazareth as a key frame of reference. Making diasporic films on the Israel/Palestine axis accentuates a paradoxical situation of multiple insides and outsides. Moving in between spaces can be said to be at the core of this cinema, both in terms of the narrative and in terms of the process of production. The films and artwork of Palestinians, whether of those born in exile (Mai Masri, Mona Hatoum, Emily Jacir, and Annmarie Jacir), or of those growing up under Israeli occupation in the West Bank and Gaza (Rashid Mashrawi and Sobhi al-Zobaidi), or of those raised in Israel (Michel Khleifi, Elia Suleiman, Hany Abu-Assad, Hana Elias, and Sharif Waked), are themselves embedded in an artistic *modus operandi* implicated in the intricacies of fragmented lives dating back to 1948. Indeed such recent work has shifted the emphasis from earlier macro-narratives of national liberation, re-envisioning "the nation" as a dappled multiplicity of trajectories. While most Third Worldist films assumed the fundamental coherence of national identity, with the expulsion of the colonial intruder fully completing the process of national becoming, diasporic films call attention to the fault-lines of gender, class, ethnicity, religion, partition, migration, and exile. Many of the films explore the complex identities wrought by exile—from one's own geography, from one's own history, from one's own body—with the assistance of innovative narrative strategies.

Homage by Assassination, for example, chronicles Suleiman's claustrophobic experience in New York during the Persian Gulf war, foregrounding multiple failures of communication: a radio announcer's aborted efforts to reach the filmmaker by phone; the filmmaker's failed attempts to talk to his family in Nazareth; his impotent look at old family photographs; despairing answering-machine jokes about the Palestinian situation. The glorious dream of nationhood is here reframed as a Palestinian flag on a TV monitor, the land as a map on a wall, and the return *(Aawda)* as the "return" key on a computer keyboard. At one point, Suleiman receives a fax from a friend, who narrates her history as an Arab-Jew, her multiple identifications during the bombing of Iraq and the Scud attacks on Israel, and the story of her family's displacement from Iraq, through Israel/Palestine, and then on to the United States.[25] The communications media become the imperfect means by which dislocated people retain their national imaginary, while also creating new diasporic spaces of belonging, including in countries (the United States, Britain) whose foreign policies have helped create their fragmented lives. Like Mona Hatoum's *Measures of Distance* (1988), *Homage by Assassination* invokes the diverse spatialities and temporalities marking the exile experience. A shot of two clocks, in New York and in Nazareth, points to the double spatio-temporality lived by the diasporic subject, a temporal doubleness underlined by an intertitle saying that the filmmaker's mother, due to the Scud attacks, is adjusting her gas mask at that very moment. The friend's letter similarly stresses the fractured space-time of being in the United States while identifying with relatives in both Iraq and Israel.

A certain linguistic sleight of hand is also crucial for Palestinian filmmakers within Israel. The schism between Hebrew and Arabic is emphasized, while also negotiating other languages depending on exilic trajectories. Yet, language is not a mere vehicle to register the reality of exile; it becomes part of the aesthetic/cinematic space. *Homage by Assassination* plays with a strategic refusal to translate the Arabic when the director (in person) types out Arab proverbs on a computer screen, without providing any translation, echoing Hatoum's *Measures of Distance*, where recorded conversations between the filmmaker and her mother or Arabic handwritten letters are shown—all without subtitles. Such diasporic media artists thus cunningly provoke non-Arab spectators by simulating the same alienation experienced by a displaced person, invoking, through inversion, the asymmetry in cultural exchange between exiles and their "host" communities. At the same time, they catalyze a sense of belongingness for the minoritarian-speech community, a strategy especially suggestive in the case of diasporic filmmakers, who often wind up in the First World precisely because colonial/imperial power has turned them into displaced persons. Rather than evoking a longed-for ancestral home, *Homage by Assassination,* like *Measures of Distance,* affirms the process of recreating identity in the liminal space of diaspora, where dense sound/image layering makes it possible to capture the fluid, multiple identities of the dislocated subject.

Independence, Nakba and the Visual Archive

When I completed *Israeli Cinema,* the bulk of Israeli films, and documentary cinema in particular, relayed the official Israeli view of history. Today, in contrast, one finds a documentary cinema that has both researched the existing archive and created a new aural/visual archive, actively intervening in the debate over the representation of history. At the same time, cinema/media studies have gradually gained a more legitimate place within academia. Yet a subliminal prejudice against the visual, *per se*, perhaps explains the refusal to see such film work as fundamentally historiographical and the reluctance to view photographic and cinematic documents as a vital part of the archive and the reassessment of history. Revisionist documentaries address historical quandaries, foregrounding issues and insights unavailable through conventional written historiography. In the case of Israel, this critical cinema has gradually come to haunt the Zionist metanarrative, and, in the process, has redefined the parameters of legitimate history as well as the format of legitimate historiography.[26]

Contemporary Israeli cinema exists against a backdrop in which revisionist Israeli historians, in the wake of Palestinian scholars, have helped debunk the founding myths surrounding the creation of the state of Israel. Posing irreverent questions, revisionist documentary cinema too has been preoccupied with memory and history, as each film sheds new light on these foundational narratives. In the vein of revisionist historiography, the emergent revisionist cinema has highlighted the misrepresentation, distortion, and manipulation of "historical truth."

Demonstrating the repercussions of historical representation for national identity, often the cinematic space becomes a meeting point between antithetical historical perspectives. By foregrounding issues, stories, and insights usually rendered invisible, the oral interviews and audio-visual archival material come to constitute an interdisciplinary cinematic project, at once oral history and critical ethnography.[27] Such documentaries could also be seen as on a continuum with books such as Sarah Graham-Brown's *Palestinians and Their Society 1880-1946: A Photographic Essay*, Walid Khalidi's *Before their Diaspora: A Photographic History of the Palestinians*, and *All That Remains: The Palestinian Villages Occupied and Depopulated by Israel in 1948*, Elias Sanbar's *Les Palestiniens: La Photographie D'une Terre Et De Son Peuple De 1839 a Nos Jours*, and Issam Nassar's *Photographing Jerusalem: The Image of the City in Nineteenth Century Photography*.[28] Taken together, this raiding of the colonial archive unearths a hidden past and shapes a visual cultural archive.[29] Revisionist documentaries have accessed a wide intertext of both still and moving images, capturing pieces of Palestine in a recuperative project that demonstrates the existence of an inhabited land now disappeared but surviving as celluloid Palestine.

Simone Bitton's historical documentary, *Palestine: the Story of a Land*, draws on visual evidence—period photographs, archival film clips, textual documents, illustrative map graphics, interviews, and on-location shooting. The film's montage of pre-existing visual material is narrated within a chronological order, divided into two parts: part one covers 1880–1950, while part two covers 1950–1991. The imaging of Palestine takes place through the history of the medium itself, through the referencing of the photographic travelogues of "the Orient" and the "Holy Land" by nineteenth-century photographers such as Maxime Du Camp and Felix Bonfils, as well as of the early cinematography of the Lumière Brothers, especially of Jaffa and Jerusalem. The film also interweaves the work of indigenous photographers, such as Khalil Raad, one of the first Jerusalem Palestinians to open a studio, working from 1890 till 1948. Whether taken by travelers or indigenous camerapersons, the images of Palestine in Bitton's film function on one level as backdrop illustration subordinated to the voiceover; but on another level, they form the core argument, as the visual documentation of agricultural landscapes and urban spaces, as well as public events and private scenes—all offer evidence of a vital Palestine that contradicts the idea of an "empty land."

Palestine: Story of a Land opens with nineteenth-century photographs of Palestine "as it was then," calling attention to the Palestine of the archive. The spectator is introduced first to panoramic images of vistas of towns and cities such as Tiberias, Haifa, Nazareth, Jerusalem, and Nablus, followed by quotidian scenes from Palestine, including a boy sorting grain, a family in front of a house, women sipping tea, and brick cutters at work. From the outset, the archival footage permits a certain intimacy with life in Palestine, while the montage and the voiceover undermine the earlier Zionist romanticization of pastoral wandering shepherds and Bedouin nomads (see my discussion in the first two chapters).[30] The film's mobilization of the visual archive comes to contradict the Orientalist imaginary of Palestine and Palestinians by fusing archival moving images of a bustling urban world with a voiceover narration that undermines the modernization discourse of a backward and rural Palestine, pronouncing it ". . . a society much like that of Cairo, Damascus or Beirut, an Arab city much like any other." While the film deploys familiar archival images, their sequencing scrambles the official Israeli syntagma. The foundational narrative of "the establishment of the state of Israel" introduces the viewer to archival footage of the 1947 U.N. vote on Resolution 181 followed by shots of Hora dancing in Tel Aviv's streets, which then segues into Arab attack and siege. *Palestine: the Story of a Land*, in contrast, uses U.N. footage documenting the diverse efforts (including by Arab and Pakistani representatives) *before* the vote, warning of the disastrous consequences of partition for generations to come. The renowned image of the U.N. vote is followed in Bitton's film not by Hora dancing, but instead by Palestinians in flight, thereby defamiliarizing the paradigmatic sequencing and historicizing the origins of the so-called "refugee problem."

This project of unearthing a largely submerged history has gained momentum over the years. Zionist texts, diaries, memoirs, state documents, and museological projects are revisited, as in films such as Dalia Karpel's *The Diaries of Yossef Nachmani* (2005) and *Route 181: Fragments of a Journey in Palestine-Israel*. A collaboration between Israeli filmmaker Eyal Sivan and Palestinian-from-Israel Michel Khleifi, *Route 181*, is a six-hour documentary "road movie," which chronicles a journey along the partition line proposed in the U.N.'s 1947 Partition Plan (U.N. General Assembly Resolution 181). Tracing the 181 line is revealed to be a doomed quest, disoriented by the contradictions of proliferating maps and facts on the ground. Divided into three chapters—beginning from the South, through the Center, and up to the North—the film moves back and forth between the present and the past, exploring the traces of a suppressed past in the words and memories— and even the body language—of interviewees who directly or indirectly lived the events that led to the creation of the state of Israel. Traveling along the roads that would have been closest to this imaginary line, the filmmakers interview the people they encounter along the way—Palestinians, Ashkenazis, Mizrahis, and so forth. For the most part, Khleifi interviews the Palestinians in Arabic, while Sivan interviews Jews in Hebrew; the filmmakers' "insider" identities encourage self-revelation, whether by Israelis or Palestinians recounting '48. In this sense, the film constitutes a kind of oral history project, often counter-staging Israeli and Palestinian perspectives on 1948.

The film's multi-track capacity allows it to stage, as it were, mutually exclusive and overlapping perspectives on history, here in terms of debates emanating from what Zionists call the "War of Independence" and what Palestinians call the "*Nakba*." *Route 181* not only explores the devastating consequences of partition; it also highlights the paradoxes and fissures between the official history as preserved in museums, maps, memorials, or songs and the invisible history of Palestine, one at times quite literally submerged. A traveling shot of the ruins of a Palestinian village stands in sharp contrast to the contemplative gaze at a recently planted forest. The spectator is made aware of the ironies of memory—Israeli homages to the ancient ruins of the Biblical Land that simultaneously repress the more recent ruins of "abandoned" Palestinian villages. *Route 181* introduces the spectator to such diverse characters as Palestinians in Israel who recall their 1948 experience of losing land, home, village, or neighborhood; Arab-Jews nostalgic for Morocco or Tunisia, hinting at their regret of moving to Israel; war veterans of the Palmach forces voicing the official War of Independence discourse. At times, the simple process of interviewing Jewish-Israeli participants in the 1948 war exposes the lacunae of dominant historiography. In some cases, elderly veterans speak confidently to the camera, assuming the filmmaker to be a safe interlocutor, "one of us," to whom one can relate heroic tales about outwitting Palestinians. Such interviews undergo a dramatic turn when the interviewee suddenly realizes that the filmmakers share neither the celebratory attitude toward the official recounting nor the unofficial "wink-wink" confessions of trickery.

Route 181 has the Israeli 1948 fighters recount the military actions that provoked Palestinian flight and dispersal. During one of the interviews in "the North" chapter, a war veteran speaks of "Operation Broom." The marked Euro-Israeliness, in terms of appearance and language, of one of the filmmakers, Sivan, allows for a safe zone of confessional discourse. Gradually, Sivan makes the interviewee aware that the war veteran's "heroic" action of forcibly removing a civilian population could be viewed in a rather different light, perhaps even as a war crime. Feigning naiveté, Sivan asks about the choice of the word "broom," virtually forcing the interviewee to acknowledge having committed what from another angle would seen as an example of "ethnic cleansing," while defamiliarizing these events for those spectators raised on the taken-for-granted vocabulary of the hegemonic historical narrative.[31] At that moment, the status of the interview shifts, and the interviewee ceases to be a willing participant who passes on heroic tales from father to sons. Rather, the '48 war veteran becomes suspicious and asks the filmmakers for their authorization to film, vehemently shifting from familial and soldierly camaraderie to the policing apparatus of the state. Dialogism here has both utopian and dystopian aspects. In *cinéma vérité*-like style, the film makes palpable the contested narration of history. This "*J'Accuse*" from two filmmakers (Israeli and Palestinian), working in concert, anatomizes the ongoing denials and repressions inevitably haunting every peace initiative. Such re-enactment of history allows for a journey into the archive that sometimes reveals glaring contradictions.

In *Route 181,* the '48 war veterans administer local museums whose exhibits carefully orchestrate a detailed audio-visual tale of heroic settlement against be-sieging Arabs. Yet the veterans' admissions of the use of political tricks and military force acknowledge the status of their guided tours as a calculated effort to "manage" the historical narrative. The critique of this pioneer and war veteran generation now forms a key feature of Israeli films that demystify the founding nationalistic catechism. Revisionist films about 1948 can thus be seen as existing in dialogue with a broad revisionist trend within Israeli cinema. Yehuda Ne'eman's 1981 documentary *The Seamen's Strike: Ya, Brechen*, for example, debunks a key founding father figure—Prime minister Ben Gurion—by recounting his brutal crushing of the 1951 Seamen' strike. The film delves into the archive to offer up what would later be called a "revisionist" history. The subtitle, "Ya, Brechen," refers to Ben Gurion's order to break the strike (in Yiddish "Yes, to Break")—an order that defined the centralized Mapai regime for years to come, but which also brought to the surface the contradictions of socialist Zionism, willing to break both a strike and bones. Rather than base his analysis on previous historical findings, Ne'eman researched the archives himself, thereby bypassing the Establishment template usually employed for assessing the past. A fecund demonstration of the historiographical vocation of cinema, *The Seamen's Strike* cites diverse archival materials—textual and audio-visual—and deploys them as evidence to undercut the official Ben Gurionist rhetoric.[32]

In some revisionist films, deconstruction also accompanies reconstruction. *Route 181* mediates the memory of Palestine before dispersal, enabling the recollection of the details formerly composing a coherent Palestinian existence. Both Palestinian and alternative Israeli films, then, have attempted to confront the rampant denial of the Palestinian *Nakba*. While some films have focused on the framing of historical "fact," others have dealt with the ongoing repercussions of that history in contemporary life. Ra'anan Alexandrowicz's *The Inner Tour* (2001), for example, does not present intellectual arguments concerning the "truth" and "veracity" of the 1948 events. Instead, it displays the broken voices and bodies of Palestinians who experienced the catastrophe, still weathering the aftermath of these traumas of forced evacuation of land, home, and community. Indeed the title "Inner Tour" evokes a literal journey to "the inside" of Palestine (i.e., in Israel), but it also underlies a voyage to the interior emotional terrain of a forcefully dislocated people. For the Palestinian from the West Bank the land is at once familiar and foreign, and here the viewers see Israel through Palestinian eyes. Tourism masks a voyage to the primal sites of the catastrophe—the ruins of houses and villages— compelling even the most skeptical spectator to confront the living memory of the *Nakba*.[33]

Critical films about 1948, whether by Israelis or Palestinians, depict contemporary Israel as a conflictual and multilayered space that contains a repressed Palestine within it. Films dealing specifically with Palestinian citizens of Israel constantly highlight the question of this absent-presence. The pre-state Pioneer films, which spoke of an empty land even when the camera captured the indigenous inhabitants in the background, unwittingly revealed this paradox (See Chapter 1). Contemporary critical Israeli and Palestinian films, meanwhile, defy the tropes of emptiness as well as the official denial of acts of transfer, while also granting legitimacy to voices usually unheard within the Israeli context. Rachel Leah Jones' *500 Dunam On the Moon* (2002), for example, examines the structural ironies inherent in the Israeli artist colony "Ein Hod," founded by Marcel Janco (of the Dada movement) and largely inhabited by Israeli liberals—an exotic magnet for tourist pilgrims. Built on top of the former Palestinian village of 'Ayn Hawd, the Israeli Ein Hod was constructed out of the 1948 remains of an "abandoned Palestinian village" (in official Hebrew discourse). 'Ayn Hawd's indigenous inhabitants have scattered, but some of the original families live in the new town "'Ayn Hawd al-Jadida" (Arabic for new 'Ayn Hawd)—one of the "unrecognized" villages, whose residents, under Israeli law, are classified as "present absentees." Disparities between pronunciation of Hebrew and Arabic names play into the subtleties of defining who and what is "new," since the inhabitants of the new 'Ayn Hawd were the Palestinians of the "old" village, prior to its Israelization. Embedded within the official Zionist narrative is a historical erasure of the indigenous inhabitants. Even the remains of the Arab village are incorporated literally into the residential domains of Jewish spaces, with the arches remodeled into an airy living room, or with the remains of the Mosque integrated into a spacious restaurant, modeled on Café Voltaire in Zurich.

Architectural fusion has thus involved an appropriation within a kind of old/new aesthetic, where the residues of an "Arab house" become the stepping-stone for constructing "authentic" expansions in an indigenous style. Palestinian workers from the displaced families are permitted entrance to a place once their own, at the price of silence. Capturing this process from the perspective of the remaining Palestinian villagers, living on the outskirts of their old home, Jones' film puts the "present absentees" back, as it were, on the map. *500 Dunam on the Moon* narrates the memory of a place in which an exiled population lives adjacent to the community that exiled it, in geographical proximity but in cultural, economic, political, and legal distance.[34] Within the film, the pictorial setting of the region does not encourage pastoral nostalgia; rather it highlights a palimpsestic history of silence. The much glorified ("hod" of the Hebrew) hybrid architectural style that melds "East" and "West" has literally covered the remainders of Palestinian houses. The celebrated Ein Hod has given the term "artists' colony" an ironic twist.

Revisionist cinema forms a significant component of a changing Jewish-Israeli ideological landscape. Documentaries by such filmmakers as Yehuda Ne'eman (*Seamen's Strike*), Simone Bitton (*Palestine: The Story of a Land*), Michal Aviad (*Ramleh*, 2001), David Benchetrit (*Through the Veil of Exile*, 1992, *Kaddim Wind*, 2002), David Belhassen and Asher Hemias (*Ringworm Children*, 2003), Eli Hamo and Sami Chetrit's (*The Black Panthers [in Israel] Speak*, 2003), Eyal Sivan

(*Izkor: Slaves of Memory*, 1991, *Route 181*), Danae Elon (*Another Road Home*), Eran Torbiner (*Matzpen*, 2004), Avi Mograbi (*August*, 2002, *Avenge But One of My Two Eyes*, 2006), and Amos Gitai (*House*, 1981, or *News from Home/News from House*, 2006), attempt to write an alternative history in a way that links past and present. Activist organizations, meanwhile, have made a parallel attempt to shape public debate by zooming in on contemporary aggressions. The Israeli Human Rights organization B'Tselem has deployed media documentation as court evidence to facilitate investigations against violators. B'Tselem has placed cameras in the hands of Palestinians who have recorded settlers' abuses, images that have become a significant source of information for local and international media, its footage broadcast in major media networks.[35] To take another example, the activist group Zochrot, whose Hebrew name indicates "remembering," (in the feminine plural). has disrupted the official Israeli collective memory by inscribing the narrative of Palestinian existence onto the landscape. Zochrot has worked to remind Israelis of the *Nakba* by including trips to destroyed Palestinian villages, and hanging signs in Arabic and Hebrew over them, identifying these sites according to their pre-1948 Arabic names. Artists Without Walls, an *ad hoc* group of Israeli and Palestinian artists/activists, meanwhile, was formed in 2004 at the height of the construction of the Wall, deploying diverse forms of cultural activism to dismantle it and produce an alternative Israel/Palestine space. Such performative gestures unearth the subterranean history of these sites, removing them from the comfort zone of Israeli oblivion.

This remembrance of the *Nakba* within Israel itself makes such films even more controversial than the anti-occupation films set in the West Bank, especially when they are made by Palestinian citizens of Israel—such as Mohammad Bakri's *1948* (1998) and Nizar Hassan's *Egteyah* (2003) and *Istiqlal* (1994). The documentary *Istiqlal* (Arabic for independence) explores the dilemmas Israel's "Independence Day" poses to Palestinian citizens of Israel, chronicling responses to the Israeli flags and the "Tzfira," the national siren sound that requires citizens to stand in homage on Independence Day. Whether due to economic realities, political ambitions, or simply survival anxiety, Palestinians perform the ritual of respect in the Jewish public sphere, but the film undercuts the celebratory nature of the day in Israel by seeing it through the lens of the ongoing humiliation of Palestinians. The title "Istiqlal" alludes to the film's theme of Israel's independence but also provokes questions about Palestinian lack of independence. The year "1948"—a foundational moment both for Israel and Palestine—is registered in revisionist cinema not merely as a past moment, but one that is lived everyday within the boundaries of Israel. Within an ironic gaze, Elia Suleiman's *Chronicle of a Disappearance* stages the quotidian nightly presence of the Israeli flag on the TV screen accompanied by the national anthem, Hatikva (the Hope), marking the end of the broadcast day,[36] only to reveal Palestinian viewers (Suleiman's parents) sound asleep, a scene evocative of Emile Habiby's words: ". . . I've disappeared. But I'm not dead."[37]

In some films, the very moment of celebrating or commemorating 1948 becomes the theme of the film. Avi Mograbi's *Happy Birthday, Mr. Mograbi* (1999) interweaves stories about his commissions to make fiftieth anniversary films about both Israeli independence and the Palestinian *Nakba*. On the one hand, Mograbi's TV producer commissions a film about the celebrations of Israel's fiftieth anniversary, but his concept of theme shifts and oscillates according to news reports. On the other hand, a Palestinian producer from the Palestinian Authority asks Mograbi to help in the production of a film about the *Nakba*, by filming locations that used to be Palestinian and became Jewish following 1948. In a sardonic tone and within a diary-like video journal, *Happy Birthday, Mr. Mograbi* stages a counterpoint between two clashing film projects. Shots of ruins of Palestinian villages, for example, take over the film, disrupting both projects, turning the initial optimism of the project into a nightmarish vision. *Happy Birthday, Mr. Mograbi* ends with street celebrations of Israel's Independence Day and with the parallel commemoration of the *Nakba* in the Occupied Territories. As fireworks light up the sky, Palestinian protesters are shot dead by Israeli soldiers; and the interrupted semi-digressive filmic narrative ends but never concludes.

Juliano Mer-Khamis' documentary *Arna's Children* (2003), meanwhile, creates its own archive. Made over a period of ten years, Mer-Khamis chronicles the activism of his mother, Arna, a former Israeli Palmach fighter who married a Palestinian and who ultimately rejected the Zionist legacy. Arna was the founder of a theatre project for children in Jenin on the West Bank, for which she was awarded the alternative Nobel peace prize. As the documentary's protagonist, Arna mediates between the spectatorial worlds of Israelis and Palestinians. Although Arna's looks, body language, speaking intonation, and generally confident authority places her squarely within Euro-Israeli Palmach generation, she has also "crossed the lines," now identifying with the very people she had fought against in 1948. While her Palmach generation borrowed music, food, and even *Kaffiyas*, in an instance of cultural appropriation combined with military camouflage, Arna, to borrow from the American frontier discourse, can be said to have "gone native." She wraps a *Kaffiya* around her head to protest the military closure of Jenin at a checkpoint. The *Kaffiya* further shifts signification from an emblem of solidarity with Palestinian struggle to an emblem of a struggle of a diseased body, when the viewer learns that it covers a head rendered bald by chemotherapy. Arna's son, the filmmaker Juliano Mer-Khamis, a well-known actor, traces the evolution of his mother's theatre project, but in the process also prods the spectator to reflect on his own in-between-ness. The filmmaker's own story as a son of a mixed-couple, fluent in both Arabic and Hebrew, figures in the film to illustrate the broader politics of border crossing.

In the film, years after his mother's death and now post-Jenin, Juliano Mer-Khamis revisits the destroyed theater. The filmmaker sees again the children first filmed in the late 1980s, now grown-ups at the dawn of the twenty-first century. Mer-Khamis's voiceover narration guides the viewers, introducing the characters and anchoring the back-and-forth between the present tense and the past tense. *Arna's Children* incorporates older footage of the children readying themselves for the show in the same space where the filmmaker now stands. Such a return to the space of past hopefulness coaxes the spectator into contradictory identifications, both with the children's suffering as well as with the suffering they inflicted later with their attacks in Israel. In a kind of a double-voiced narrative, the film shows a suicide bombing in Israel and a massive Israeli tank patrolling the narrow streets. While recognizing the suffering on the Israeli side, the film's politics of focalization demonstrate a commitment to an overall anti-occupation stance, a cinematic strategy reminiscent of Pontecorvo's *The Battle of Algiers* (1966). *Arna's Children* paints a disheartening picture of the occupation, where violence, death, and hopelessness, along with determination and struggle, relentlessly haunt the waking lives of Palestinians, many of whom mourn the friends and relatives who have not survived. Far from being a sensationalist psychologist drama about the making of a terrorist, the film prods the spectator to identify with children whose dreams of normality in the midst of violence have taken them into the pre-scripted end of a tragedy. Refugee camp children are not simply performing theatrical pieces but are also sharing their everyday life dramas under occupation. During rehearsals, they end up re-visiting shocking incidents of the previous day. The spectator witnesses their visible paralysis in the face of yet another bulldozing of their houses, as they absurdly find literal shelter in the theater. In this version of a Boalian "theatre of the oppressed," the stage is transformed into a cathartic space; to potentially act they must theatrically re-enact. *Arna's Children* recounts a voyage to the interior of an injured Palestinian collective through the eyes of its children. Childhood becomes the site of both infuriating impasse and resilient hope.

In contrast to documentaries such as Justine Shapiro and B.Z. Goldberg's *Promises* (2003), *Arna's Children* does not perform a "balanced" delineation of both Israeli and Palestinian perspectives. Palestinian children are not represented as occupying a parallel space within a tragedy of equal proportions; the Palestinian children act as both metonymy and metaphor for a story of ongoing occupation and besieged existence, where expanding fences, walls, and borders bite into land, house, and home. At the center of the images of encirclement are Palestinian children, in contrast to the earlier Palestinian Wave cinema (see Chapter 5), where focalization was mediated either through besieged Israeli liberal/leftists or reluctant soldiers—a practice that persists till today in films such as Ari Folman's "animated documentary" *Waltz with Bashir* (2008). *Arna's Children* interweaves past scenes of children joyfully participating in theatrical rehearsals with scenes of the same boys seven years later, shown as leaders of the Al-Aqsa brigades or in posters hailing them as martyrs. In one conversation, the adolescents recount their first encounter with Arna and Juliano, revealing their initial suspicions that Arna and her son might be Israeli agents. Only by working together, the Palestinians admit, did they learn to develop trust and love—to the point of regarding Arna and Juliano as virtual family members. In a later sequence, the spectator learns that two of the boys, best friends, killed four Israeli women in Hadera before they were shot to death. What was a hopeful story of creativity amidst violence at the beginning of the film, reaches a depressing note of renewed violence at the conclusion of the film, suggesting a classic violence-begets-violence structure.[38]

Critical documentaries, then, explore the imaging and imagining of the con- tested geography of "Palestine" and "Israel" in the wake of Western imperial expansion into what came to be called "the Middle East" as well as in the light of conflicting national desires. Some films begin with the moment when the desire to visualize the Holy Land encounters the scientific invention of mimetic tech- nologies, pointing to the historical role of visual culture in the competing claims for Palestine and Israel. Rather than take for granted such notions as "seeing is believing" and "images do not lie," such reflexive films critically re-assemble and re-sequence the standard forms of montage. The figuring of landscape, architec- ture, maps, archeological sites, and agricultural and urban spaces has itself come to constitute a kind of a visual archive that both documents the past and serves as "evidence" for specific historical narratives. In the context of partition and dis- placement, audio-visual mediation has occupied center-stage in the battle over representation, defining national identity and communal belonging. Throughout, revisionist cinema reflects on this question of "mediation" within what might be called a social semiotics of geography.

Iconographies of Spatial Anxiety

Maps, borders, checkpoints, and the Wall have now become signature icons of the Israeli/Arab conflict. In early heroic-nationalist films, didactic maps and ar- rows signified a state under siege, relaying frontier-like images of encirclement. Contemporary cinema, meanwhile, has subverted the David and Goliath trope, revamping the visual representation of the conflict. Alternative films reverse the paradigmatic point of view of the Hebrew pioneer or the Israeli soldier, along with the tropes of siege and encirclement. Rashid Masharawi confines the spectator, in *The Shelter*, to a claustrophobic tin hut where a Gazan worker in Israel must hide each night, and in *Curfew* (1993), to the home of the Abu Raji family, observ- ing twenty-four hours in their everyday life. This out-of-the-ordinary quotidian- ness comes to allegorize the ordinary besieged Palestinian existence under mili- tary rule. Numerous documentary, fiction, or non-linear films—Eran Riklis's *The*

Syrian Bride (2004), *Divine Intervention, The Wall, Route 181*, Amos Gitai's *Free Zone* (2006), and Michal Rovner's *Border* (1997)—represent spatial frictions, whether in relation to the West Bank, Gaza, Lebanon, or Syria. Within these cinematic projects, images of borders obscure the blueprint of the old/new "Promised Land" as narrated within the modern nation-state project; spatial anxiety is no longer unidirectional. In *Route 181*, for example, the filmmakers search for an elusive partition line, a kind of mirage lacking any concrete form on the land, and which yet impacts lives in the most direct and material way. The partition map lies on the car's dashboard and is reflected in the window, as though the real and its shadow orient the film's quest for the map's referents, only to gradually reveal the absurdity of partition lines written in the shifting sands of conflicting political imaginaries. An elderly Palestinian whose house was divided from his orchard as a result of the partition line recounts how, at night, after the U.N. officials' departure, he literally repainted the white line, thus reuniting his land and house, while ironically expanding the Israeli territory. Drawing the literal line in the sand triggers in the film a series of dialectics between absence and presence, visibility and invisibility, since, as in the case of Native Americans and Chicanos, it was not simply a case of Palestinians crossing the border but of borders crossing them.

While borders would seem to offer firm ground for spatial orientation, recent cinema, then, has denaturalized these very borders. In some instances, border images provoke an ironic philosophical reflection on the very idea of border, while in others they interrogate historical partition in the wake of Israel's continually expanding borders. Michal Rovner's *Border* offers an ironic postmodernist glance at borders, while *Route 181* gives a sarcastic gloss on a political process that has generated an absurd existence generated by an absurd partition.[39] *Route 181* portrays an intricate web of a multiply partitioned Israel/Palestine. In one sequence, the spectator accompanies the stretching of a barbed wire across a field, viewing the implementation of zoning in "real time" and in "real space." The film also calls attention to the industrial production of the border, to zoning in its very materiality. The camera follows the manufacturing of barbed wire, detailing of the diversity of fences, some potentially lethal. A metaphor and a metonym of war, the barbed wire fence, the object of the cinematic gaze, is simultaneously an image in search of its own iconoclasm. Simone Bitton's *The Wall* also explores the partitioning of land in the wake of the construction of Israel's gigantic wall, part of an attempt to claim more land for Israel. The Wall divides homes from their neighboring fields, sending Palestinians to checkpoints miles away just to cultivate their land, or compelling them to sneak through cracks in the wall to go to work. In another vein, Catherine Yass' *Wall* (2005) focuses almost entirely on the Wall itself—an architectural construct that blocks the view of the buildings behind it, an omnipresent vertical obstacle that testifies to the injury done not only to the people but also to the land. While such films focus on the present, their portrait of the Wall reverberates with the history of the mutilation of the land.

Borders are not always demarcated by fences and walls, however, and at times are visually indiscernible. Films concerning Palestinian citizens of Israel have high-lighted a forgotten Palestine within Israel. After the end of the military rule in 1966, the invisible walls of ghettoization and segregation have continued to guide a policy of separate (but hardly equal) lives of Palestinians "on the inside." Borders, in this sense, reflect mental maps of belonging, setting boundaries between "us" and "them." Existing in the limbo between recognition and denial, the plight of Israel's Bedouin in the Negev (or Naqab in Arabic) desert has also been registered on the screen. In Ori Kleiner's documentary *Recognized* (2007), the Bedouins are "recognized" when they serve in the military, but not recognized as having a right to the land. Constantly mounting restrictions make planting, herding, and building houses, schools, clinics, and roads extremely difficult. Eschewing any overarching historical narrative, this quietly eloquent documentary laconically observes the situation of Bedouins, some fluent in Hebrew, who served in the military and see themselves as Israelis. The film opens with officials tearing down the tent of the protesting Bedouin Nuri. The camera exposes the bureaucratic production of ruins created in the present. As the film progresses, the image is retroactively re-signified as an iterative shot—the demolition ritually takes place once a month, at the consequence of an arsenal of petty laws and decrees. Different shots throughout the film allow for a glimpse into the dissonances in the Israeli narrative of progress: a long shot, both in distance and duration, lingers on a Bedouin toddler reaching for a leaky, rusty outdoor water tap. One village, Wadi Naam, borders on the toxic chemical industrial site of Ramat Hovav. The camera gazes at the flies feasting on a decaying dog carcass lying adjacent to the state's local electric power station, on a Bedouin village denied access to electricity. The camera dwells on one of the families in a tent, as they watch TV—an Arabic channel—continuing to consume its entertainment from a surviving TV monitor attached to a generator that requires manual cranking to breathe life into the screen. Combining *vérité* style interviews with slow-take visual lyricism, the film's long shots offer a melancholy-ironic look at an existence where the desert landscape, despite its beauty, offers no refuge. The desert is a dystopic space, not one of nomadic freedom, but rather one of state control and indigenous imprisonment. Here the topos of the morbid desert, far from the Promethean narrative of making the desert bloom, is associated with the state's reckless (and wrecking) agencies.

The iconography of Palestine and Israel is dominated by images of the land. In Zionist cinema, the barren desert allegorizes the absence and the future presence of the land's true heirs—the Jewish people. In Palestinian representations, meanwhile, the land is imaged not as barren but as fertile and productive. As early as Tawfik Saleh's *The Dupes* (1972), based on Ghassan Kanafani's 1963 novella *Men in the Sun*, Palestinian dispossession from the land is detailed through flashback memories of rural life before partition. In the opening sequence, Abu Qais, a middle-aged refugee, hoping to relocate to Kuwait for a better life for his family, crosses the desert to Iraq, and ultimately collapses in the shade of palm trees on the Tigris. But in his delirious state, the land that appears in his nostalgic mind is that of the fertile fields in Palestine. The recurrent figure of the destitute *fallah* (peasant) thus underlines the immensity of dislocation for a people now rendered—to amend a slogan—as a people without a land, and a land without its people. Abu Qais confesses to a fellow Palestinian: "I am a peasant as my father was a peasant," lamenting having to invent a new life in exile, Kuwait—a destination he tragically does not reach. In the heat of the sun, the *fallah*, smuggled inside a tanker, perishes on the Iraqi-Kuwaiti desert border. In contrast to Israeli representations of 1948, the desert in Palestinian narratives, then, is not located in Palestine but elsewhere. The narrative framing of *The Dupes*, beginning and ending with two deserts, the latter as a direct result of the *Nakba*. Rather than the Promethean narrative of bringing modernity to Palestine, Palestinians themselves are imaged as being thrown into a desert in what for them was a process of demodernization.

Exilic Palestinian fiction depicts a land imbued with color, aroma, and texture. In almost Proustian tones, the memory of things past in Youssry Nasrallah's film *Bab al-Shams* (2004) (based on Elias Khoury's novel) is made tangible in images of oranges and grapes. In a scene in Patrick Bürge's *Al-Sabbar* (2000), a refugee from the Ain-Al-Hilwah camp in Lebanon repeatedly insists that Palestinian pomegranates will always be "the best." In films made in exile, nostalgia for the land figures more centrally than in films made "inside," that is, by Palestinians exiled, as it were, within the state of Israel. Yet even "inside," life before the *Nakba* is recalled nostalgically in the interviews with internally dislocated Palestinians in films such as *Route 181* and *500 Dunam on the Moon*, from al-Shajara in the Galilee in the former film, and from 'Ayn Hawd in the latter. Depicting olive trees uprooted in favor of transplanted non-native vegetation, such as Eucalyptuses or cypresses, critical Israeli and Palestinian films make the silences and crevices of the land speak. Such films clash with the Zionist Genesis narrative of creation out of nothingness. The desire to create by decree a "Switzerland of the Middle East" is hardly an innocuous cosmetic project, but rather an act of ecological violence. The visual clash of discrepant forms of vegetation calls attention to an official attempt to obscure the organic traces of Palestinian presence, striving to contain, erase, or bury a rooted past. Cinema, then, becomes a site for reconfiguring the face of the land.

The Zionist version of the colonial-settler creationist narrative is also articulated in relation to the very land invoked by the original Biblical creation story. Hebrew fiction and cinema depicts the old-new land as dominated by emblems of technology and modernity of ploughs and tractors, celebrating a civilization created *ex-nihilo*. Even in films about the "*Olim*" [immigrants] from Arab/Muslim countries, the image of vegetation as a signifier of order and of a fruitful and productive pioneering enterprise plays a central role in asserting authority over the land. In Arie Lahola's *Tent City* (1961),the new immigrant ("ole hadash"), an Iraqi boy, initially says: "I didn't see order, I didn't see trees," praising his new adoptive country, implicitly indicting both his Arab country of origin and Palestine. The tent city is transformed thanks to the guiding hand of the state agency, assuming the parental role for disoriented immigrants. As a product of technologically-driven modernity, this order was already portrayed in Herzl's *Altneuland*, where the members of the New Society "laid roads, dug canals, built houses, cleared stones from the fields that were to be plowed with electric plows, planted trees"[40] toward a horticultural aesthetic deemed modern and civilized. Zionism's Prospero Complex can be said to offer a modern version of miraculous deeds.

Tropes of miracles have been resurrected, this time within an ironic sensibility, in some recent films. Elia Suleiman's highly reflexive *Divine Intervention* intermingles the grave realities of fragmented Palestinian lives with the vigorous realm of the imaginary, which comes to haunt, boomerang-like, the Israelis. The film relays two parallel narratives: one focusing on the ailing father of the filmmaker/main character ("E.S.") and taking place in Nazareth (in Israel) and the second focusing on the challenges of cross-border love between two Palestinians, a citizen of Israel ("E.S.") and a resident of Ramallah (the West Bank) and taking place largely in the vicinity of the checkpoint. As a quintessential mechanism of the occupation, the checkpoint frustrates the lovers' desire, as it also allows them—and the spectators—to witness a sadistic military panopticon, while triggering, finally, a series of tragicomic encounters and confrontations.

Generically hybrid, the film is at once hyperrealist and magical realist, an aesthetic anticipated already in the bifurcated prelude. The first shot captures a panoramic view of Nazareth followed by the title "Divine Intervention," seemingly anchoring the image in the realm of the scripture. A Santa Claus figure appears from a distance, chased by a group of children; his fleeing, as the gifts fall off his bag, disturbs the postcard-like shot of Nazareth. He passes through cactus plants, often the vegetative traces of destroyed Palestinian villages, seeking shelter in the ruins of a house. He leans against a column, as the viewer realizes that this Santa Claus has been stabbed in the chest. The first part of the prelude concludes with the title "Nazareth" superimposed on the deserted house, along with a barely visible stabbed Santa. This ironically exalted allegory gives way to a different generic space of the quotidian. The father of E.S. drives through the narrow lanes of Nazareth, responding to neighborly greetings with a faint smile or a waved hand, accompanied by muttered curses. Suleiman's film opens then with Nazareth as a tale of two cities: one dwelling in the phantasmatic realm of Christian symbolism and the other existing in the Palestine/Israel materiality of the everyday. *Divine Intervention* crafts a meeting ground for these two parallel discursive universes. The film's Nazareth offers a window into a claustrophobic no-exit existence, conveyed through a hyperrealist portrayal of repetitive quotidian actions: the father opening his mail, a neighbor sweeping her backyard, two old men sitting on the roof glaring at the street without exchanging a word or a glance, and neighbors fighting over trivia. This comic vision of the mundane resonates, however, with a colonial theater of the absurd; the confined space exists within a hostile Israeli surrounding that continues to reduce the space of Palestine within Israel. Suleiman's Nazareth is far from a site of national resistance *a la The Battle of Algiers*, a film cited in his and Jayce Salloum's earlier film collage *Introduction to the End of an Argument*.[41] At the same time, Suleiman's Nazareth departs sharply from both Israeli modernization narratives with regards to Palestine and the Christian romantic imaginary of the Holy Land.

The film's playful irreverence must be viewed in relation to the long tradition of visual portraiture of the Holy Land in paintings, photography, and cinema, dating back to the first shot-on-location story of Christ, *From the Manger to the Cross* (1912).[42] It is instructive to compare Suleiman's diary-like imaging of Christian-Palestine within Israel with that of Pier Paolo Pasolini's travelogue-diary *Seeking Locations in Palestine for the Gospel According to St. Matthew* (1964), which documents the filmmaker's crushing disenchantment with the Holy Land's scenery. Pasolini had sought a majestic "Biblical, archaic world," but instead was "struck by the poverty and humility of this place," and by "its smallness, its bareness, its lack of scenery." For Pasolini, Palestinian towns and villages, such as Nazareth, are wretched, while Biblical sites, such as Mount Tabor or the Sea of Galilee, are disappointingly measly. The Jordan River seems like "a poor, humble, desperate little stream," quite in contrast to the scenery of his native Italy but also in contrast to the painterly visualization of the Biblical Land. Pasolini also documents the modern building springing up around Nazareth, a landscape "contaminated by modernity," as "these houses could be seen in Rome or Switzerland." Although Pasolini contrasts Arab archaism with Israeli modernity, this archaic exceeds *his* Holy Land imaginary, fully grounded in the language of orientalist travel narratives: "their faces are pagan, pre-Christian, indifferent, cheerful, animal-like . . . Christianity has left no trace on the local faces." Pasolini concludes: "I think I have completely transformed my idea of sacred places. Rather than adapt places, I must adapt myself." As a result, he comes to the realization that he will not be filming his adaptation of Matthew's gospel in the Holy Land after all. Pasolini's film was recently revisited within a posthumous dialogue in Ayreen Anastas's *Pasolini Pa* Palestine* (2005), which attempts to repeat the Italian filmmaker's voyage. In *Pasolini Pa* Palestine*, Pasolini's script becomes a guiding map to a contemporary landscape, unraveling the tensions between his vision of the past and present-day Palestine/Israel—both of Pasolini and Anastas's times; and thus exploring the very premises separating the imaginary and the real.

Whereas Pasolini's narrative of disillusionment unfolds in the name of the sacred, *Divine Intervention* conducts an aesthetic quarrel with the epic-scale grandeur of Christian imaginary of Palestine/Israel. Nazareth becomes a stage on which an absurdist play is enacted, as in Habiby's *The Secret Life of Saeed: The Pessoptimist*, whose generically oxymoronic Arabic title melds the chronicle with the surreal conundrum. *Divine Intervention: A Chronicle of Love and Pain,* like Suleiman's earlier *Chronicle of a Disappearance* performed an end run around the dichotomies associated with both Christian and Zionist narratives about Palestine; it is neither backward and desolate nor pastoral and archaic. Nazareth is at once a local and global town, provincial and transnational. The iterative shots of tourists unloaded from air-conditioned buses to consume Holy Land souvenirs are filmed repeatedly from the same long-shot angle, suggesting a kind of nothing-happens-here; yet the stasis of Nazareth's ghetto extends to the global tourist scene in its own vacuous chase after bottled holiness. In Suleiman's *Chronicle of a Disappearance,* Christian pilgrims to the Sea of Galilee address the camera in *vérité* style interviews about "the miracle," but the film undercuts their verbal ecstasy, revealing contemporary Jesus-like walkers on water—water-skiers. Tourists participate in a well-established travel literature tradition that captures in writing or on camera Holy Land sites, editing out as it were indigenous Palestine. Suleiman and Jayce Salloum's earlier film, *Introduction to the End of an Argument* also jujitsu-like incorporated archival black-and-white Kodak travelogue footage, as well as contemporary televisual tourist ads, for example, of American-Jewish "birthright trips" to Massada.[43] The Biblical-land mania of tourists, whether Christian or Jewish, renders the indigenous population invisible, but itself is dissected under the filmic return of the orientalist gaze.

Miracles do take place in Suleiman's work, but they are attributed to the autonomous kingdom of art. Although the title "Divine Intervention" alludes to a religious discourse of miraculous victory, thanks to "*yadun ilahiyya*" (the godly hand), the film makes a literal-minded reading of the title impossible. Miracles happen in the unexpected realm of the tragic political reality that begs for divine intervention. The surreally quotidian aspect is accentuated through a literalization of the film's title within a Middle Eastern version of magic realism. Within the film's ironic yet melancholic gaze and within a pess-optimistic tone—to evoke Habiby's novel—a "Divine Intervention" for Palestine is made possible through a digital version of *Deus ex Machina.* In one sequence, E.S. is driving his car while eating an apricot. He throws the pit from the car window, hitting an Israeli tank, which explodes, and E.S. continues calmly on his way. At another point, a balloon bearing Arafat's image soars over the checkpoint, in the face of bewildered soldiers, miraculously making it possible for the lovers to enter Jerusalem in the ensuing confusion. In another sequence, the soldiers, practicing firing on *Kaffiya* targets, are soon overcome by a female Palestinian Ninja, a reversal of the David/Goliath trope common to the Israeli heroic war films. The enchanting Palestinian ninja guarantees an imaginary digital triumph over the otherwise invincible soldiers, choreographed to march, kick, jump, and pull their guns in harmonic unison. In "Divine Intervention," the crescent and star-tipped darts that appear in the Palestinian Ninja scene are dispatched as totems marshaled against the occupation—all within the generic frame of a surreal comedy. Drawing on elements from American and Arab popular cultures, the film alludes to the action and kung fu movie genres, along with video game iconography. The Ninja sequence also conjures up images of Palestinian resistant culture: the *Kaffiya*, stones, the flag, the dart's Islamic crescent, the bullets collected around the ninja's head like Christ's crown of thorns. Richly evocative, the Palestinian Ninja sequence subverts the colonial narrative, while also revisiting the genre of anticolonial and Palestinian militant cinemas. Heroism is placed in quotation marks, mediated through cinematic magic. Miraculously, the Ninja emerges out of nowhere, from the dust, and manages to overcome the Israeli military and allowing free movement.

Indeed, checkpoints have come to constitute a topos in recent Palestinian and Israeli films of diverse genres. Numerous films (Yoav Shamir's *Checkpoint* [2003] and Annemarie Jacir's *Like Twenty Impossibles* [2003], *The Syrian Bride, Rana's Wedding, The Bubble, Route 181, The Wall,* and *Divine Intervention,* to name only a few) visually inscribe the continuous fragmentation of Palestine through shifting borders of roadblocks, checkpoints, fences, and walls. The checkpoint, in many films a site of spectacular violence, makes it possible to foreground quotidian dehumanization, pithily encapsulating the daily indignities borne by Palestinians. The checkpoint forms a metaphor and metonymy for structural violence even if no spectacular bloodshed unfolds on the screen. In other words, even when no grand epic media event is registered, the films look at the hyper-regulation of movement as a daily nightmare, a death by a thousand cuts. The checkpoint topos makes visible the usually invisible abuse by a technocratic maze of exhausting, frustrating hurdles and long lines. Bifurcating the land, the checkpoint interrupts the mundane activities of attending school or university, going to work, farming one's land, visiting relatives or friends, holding weddings or funerals, reuniting with family members, seeking medical care, and so forth. When denied passage in emergency cases, checkpoints can be an indirect cause of death, including of babies born at the checkpoint (a scene staged by *The Bubble.*) Permits and visas arbitrarily regulate life; traveling for the purpose of acquiring documents can be denied for insufficient or expired documentation. In a Sisyphean loop, crossing a checkpoint can never guarantee a roundtrip; in sum, petty harassments engender slow-motion suffocation. In sum, the checkpoint forms a condensed image of the total lack of indigenous sovereignty.

As a site where issues of health, education, economy, sovereignty, human rights, and psychology all intersect, the checkpoint can also become the site of the sol-diers' power trip (staged in *Divine Intervention*). The cinematic checkpoint offers exemplary vignettes or, better, a synecdoche, where one story stands in for many stories. The vignettes tend to highlight the sadism entailed in controlling peo-ple's movement, exposing the state's invasion of the very intimacy of life through biopower, whereby bodies are surveyed by a penalizing panopticon. Subjected to "discipline and punish," the checkpoint also becomes a topos for the banality of evil. Indeed, the makers of *Route 181* confront a checkpoint soldier interested in philosophical conversation with Hanna Arendt's dictum. Such films do not focus on *Nakba*-scale dispossession, but on the violence of asymmetrical legalism, images of a past macro-*Nakba* give way to tales of ongoing micro-*nakbas*. The evidence of administrative violence not only appears on the individual level of a story but also in the cumulative effect of many stories, embedded in state regulations and military practices themselves. The 1948 expulsion continues by bureaucratic means, through a web of measures designed to harass, intimidate, and ultimately drive Palestinians away (hence the Palestinian idea of "*sumud*"). As a well-designed panopticon, the occupation's curfews, walls, checkpoints, and unpredictable roadblocks have turned Palestine into an archipelago of prisons. Preempting as it were the guards' power to discipline and punish Palestinian bodies, Sharif Waked's non-narrative video, *Chic Point* (2005), takes the logic of the inspected "Arab" body on display to its absurd extreme—the fashion runway. On the mock-runway, Palestinian male models flaunt fashionably cut shirts, designed to render visible the usually invisible parts of the body—the waste or belly—demonstrating the absence of a bomb. The anxiety-ridden checkpoint body is transformed into the entertaining runway body; altered clothing redeems it from the terrorist sign, granting it free movement. In a satirical look at the infiltration of the Palestinian (male) body, *Chic Point* resignifies the Palestinian body associated with threat to the safety zone of consumerist desire and pleasure.

Israeli and Palestinian bodies on the screen have themselves come to allegorize contested national boundaries. As a gendering project, Zionist culture aimed to transform the feminized Diaspora Jew into a masculine man (see the discussion of concepts of "*gever*," man, "*gvura*," and "heroism" in Chapter 2). Internalizing the anti-Semitic description of the weak and non-muscular Jew, the language of nation-building venerated (hetero)masculinity while inscribing a process of redemption from emasculation.[44] Not unlike colonial narratives, Zionist fiction, furthermore, reverberated with sexualized dissonances in texts at once heteronormative and homoerotic. Homoeroticism and homophobia commingled promiscuously in the same narrative space. Recent films and scholarship have revisited the fetish of Israeli (hetero)masculinity. Ariella Azoulay's *A Sign from Heaven* (1999) deconstructs the gendered public/private dichotomies, linking diverse episodes of media-covered violence, Rabin's assassination by Yigal Amir, Carmella Buhbut's killing of her abusive husband, and the target assassination of the Palestinian "Engineer" Yehiya Ayash by Israeli security forces. Recent artistic and scholarly projects have also subverted Israeli (hetero)masculinity, queering its militaristic zones. Israeli military films, as Raz Yosef demonstrates, exhibit the sexuality of militarism even when the films do not thematize sexual relations.[45]

A growing number of films have blurred the boundaries separating the Israeli and Palestinian bodies on screen. Transgressing the sexual/national divide, such films have centered on heterosexual desire, as in *Silences of the Lamb* and *Hamsin* (see the last chapter). Based on the Sami Michael novel, the Lina and Slava Chaplin film *Trumpet in the Wadi* (2001) features an impossible love story between a Christian Palestinian and a new Jewish immigrant from Russia. Michel Khleifi's documentary *Mixed Marriage in the Promised Land* (1995), showcases heterosexual couples who transgressed the Jewish/Arab taboo. Until recently, there had been only rare examples of films depicting Israeli and Palestinian desiring male bodies, such as Amos Guttman's *Drifting* (1983), with its fleeting moment of sex between a Mizrahi Israeli and a Palestinian man under duress.[46] Some recent films, such as Elle Flanders' documentary *Zero Degrees of Separation* (2005) and Eytan Fox's feature *The Bubble*, violated the twin taboos against Palestinian/Israeli love and gay lovemaking. These charged representations register a discursive and activist shift within Israel, at a time when groups such as Women in Black, QUIT (Queers Undermining Israeli Terrorism), Aswat, and Black Laundry make links between sexuality and nationality.[47] The Gay Day Parade in Jerusalem, in this period, became the subject of a heated debate, seen by some as challenging the dominant Israeli macho ethos, and by others as covertly staging a Zionist nationalist agenda. As with women and gender, issues of gays and queerness have provoked the question of whether a progressive discourse on one level, i.e., gender and sexuality, can be recuperated so as to buttress a colonial-nationalist project, or, conversely, deployed to promote the democratization of Israel.

The Arab-Jew and the Inscription of Memory

Recent years have seen a renaissance of Mizrahi and/or Arab-Jewish cultural prac-tices related to identity and belonging. These practices too must be seen against the backdrop of contested histories and terminologies. The identity crisis provoked by the rupture of Jews from their largely Arab/Muslim countries is reflected in a terminological crisis in which no single term seems to fully represent a coherent entity. The very proliferation of terms suggests the enormous difficulties of grap-pling with the complexities of this identity. To name a few: "Sephardim," "Jews of Islam," "Arab-Jews," "Jewish-Arabs," "Middle Eastern Jews," "Asian and African Jews," "Non-European Jews," "Third World Jews," "Levantine Jews," "Bnei Edot Ha-Mizrah" (descendents of the Eastern communities), "Blacks," "Mizrahim" (Easterners), or "Iraqi-Jews," "Moroccan Jews," "Iranian-Jews," "Kurdish-Jews," "Turkish Jews," "Palestinian Jews," and so-forth. Each term raises questions about the implicit discursive politics that both generated the terms and made them catchwords at specific conjunctures. Each term encodes a historical, geographical, and political point-of-view. Prior to their arrival in Israel, Jews in Iraq, for exam-ple, regarded themselves as Jews but within a diacritical identity that played off and depended on a relation to other communities. Within a transregional space that extended from the Atlantic through the Mediterranean to the Indian Ocean, Jews retained a Jewishness that was culturally and socially interwoven into Islamic civilization. Shaped by Arab-Muslim culture, more specifically, they also helped shape that culture, in a dialogical process that generated their Judeo-Arab identity. The proliferating hyphens, in this sense, highlight a complexly embedded identity that must be articulated in relation to multiple communities and geographies.

The rise of Zionism and Arab nationalism, along with the implementation of partitions as a colonial solution for regional conflicts, inevitably impacted the identity designations of Jews in the Arab Muslim world. Arabness came to signify a national identity, requiring a realignment of Ottoman definitions. Their religion (Judaism) rapidly became a national marker in the international arena, conflicting with their Arab civilizational belonging. They have come to occupy an ambivalent position *vis-à-vis* both Zionism and Arab nationalism. The explosive political situation subsequent to the partition of Palestine and the establishment of the state of Israel produced a new context, rendering their existence in Arab countries virtually impossible. Upon arrival in Israel, Arab-Jews entered a new linguistic/discursive paradigm, shaped by geo-political (the Israel/Arab conflict), legal (Israeli citizenship), and cultural (East versus West) forces. The normative term became "Israeli," not merely a signifier of a new passport, but also an indicator of a new cultural and ideological formation.

Whereas Jewishness in Arab/Muslim spaces formed part of a constellation of co-existing and complexly stratified ethnicities and religions, Jewishness in Israel was now the assumed cultural/political "dominant." Arabness became the marginalized category, while the religion of Arab-Jews, for the first time in their history, came to be affiliated with the dominant state power and attuned to the very basis of national belonging. Their cultural Arabness, meanwhile, was transformed into an embarrassing excess, a marker of ethnic, even racial, otherness. If in the Arab world, it was their Jewishness (associated now with Zionism) that was subjected to surveillance, in Israel, it was their affiliation with an Arab cultural geography that was similarly disciplined and punished. The processes of spatial rupture and cultural displacement, in this sense, have impacted and shifted the identity labels. Each term, then, gives expression to a different historical moment, geographical space, and ideological perspective. Each calls attention to a different dimension of a complex socio-historical and spatial trajectory, foregrounding specific aspects of communal affiliation. Each suggests a frame that illuminates only partial aspects of overlapping itineraries shaped within the movement across borders. Each addresses specific and even contradictory dynamics between and within different world zones.

Another aspect of this terminological problematic is how to verbally convey the unprecedented movement across borders of West Asian/North African Jews in the wake of the partition of Palestine. Nationalist paradigms cannot capture the ambivalence of this historical movement, particularly for Arab-Jews. Given the idiosyncratic situation of a community trapped between two nationalisms—Arab and Jewish—each term used to designate the displacement seems problematic.

Terms such as "Aliya" (ascendancy), "*yetzia*" (exit), "exodus," "expulsion," "im-migration," "emigration," "exile," "refugees," "ex-patriots," and "population-exchange" do not seem adequate. In the case of the Palestinians, forced into a mass exodus, the term "refugee" is appropriate since they never wanted to leave Palestine and have steadfastly nourished the desire to return. In the case of Arab-Jews, the question of will, desire, and agency remains highly ambiguous. It is not only a matter of legal definition of citizenship that is at stake, but also mental maps of belonging within the context of rival nationalisms. Did Arab-Jews want to stay? Did they want to leave? If so, did they want to leave for Israel or elsewhere? Did they exercise free will in deciding to leave? Once in Israel, did they want to go elsewhere, or go back to their countries of origin? Were they able to do so? And did they regret the impossibility of returning? Different answers to these questions imply distinct assumptions about agency, memory, and space.

The official term "Aliya"(ascent), meanwhile, is multiply misleading. It suggests a commitment to Zionism, when, in fact, the majority of Jews—and certainly Jews within the Levant—were hardly Zionists in the modern nationalist sense of the word. Zionist discourse normalizes the telos of a Jewish nation-state; any move toward its borders is represented as the ultimate Jewish act. When the actual departure of Arab-Jews is represented on the screen, it is usually narrated as an act of devotion. In the controversial TV series produced for Israel's fiftieth anniversary, *Tkuma*, images of Yemeni Jews arriving at the camps set up by the Jewish Agency are juxtaposed with a voice-over that reductively speaks of persecution and Messianic will.[48] The Yemeni Jews are represented as voluntarily crossing the desert and sacrificing their lives to get to the Promised Land, which the film implicitly equates with the state of Israel. Zionist writings often naturalize the inevitability of this destination while erasing the diverse Zionist tactics to actively dislodge these communities, including false wrappings of the nation-state with the "coming of the Messiah." This Aliya metanarrative at times is axiomatically assumed even within revisionist films, as when David Belhassen and Asher Hemias's documentary *The Ringworm Children* begins its arrival story with a voice-over that describes "the wave of massive Aliya knocking on the gates of the land."

Critical films, such as David Benchetrit's epic scale documentary *Kaddim Wind: Moroccan Chronicles* (2002), rewrite the foundational Aliya discourse. The film begins with the Moroccan national anthem on the sound track, thereby acousti-cally counteracting the assumption that Moroccan Jews by definition belonged to Israel. Through the archival footage of departing vehicles, we glimpse the moment of rupture for Moroccan Jews, narrated with an almost dirge-like elegy. The tes-timonial interviews with diverse Moroccan-Israelis address their confused reasons for moving to Israel, which for the most part do not reflect a Zionist desire, as well as their initial traumatic encounters with the Ashkenazi-dominated Israeli appara-tus. Whether through archival material or contemporary interviews, the film, in a kind of a double movement, interweaves nostalgic memories of the Moroccan past with the shock of arrival in Israel. Deconstructing the metanarrative of modernization, revisionist cinema fills in an important representational gap—the challenge of being at once of the larger Middle East and living within the boundaries of Israel. Instead of constituting merely a euphoric beginning of modern Jewish life, here Israel constitutes a topos of loss, including the loss of Jewishness as lived and known before the arrival of Zionism in the region.

Critical Mizrahi work has called attention to the chasm between official discourse and the actual experiences of Middle Eastern Jews, both in terms of the before and the after of their arrival in Israel. (Here I use Mizrahi less in the sense of origins and more in the sense of conveying a critical perspective.) Revisionist films do not view Arab-Muslim spaces through the prism of pogroms and the Holocaust; instead, they interrogate the dominant paradigms. Some even go as far as to articulate the latent "what ifs" of history, expressing a forbidden desire for a lost Arab homeland. A few documentaries capture moments where interviewees express regret over their destination to and in Israel, or reveal, however unrealistically, a desire to return. An unofficial chronicle of Moroccan Jews, *Kaddim Wind* orchestrates a polyphonic conversation with a variety of interviewees from the Moroccan-Israeli political spectrum, including politicians, activists, writers, scholars, and religious leaders, such as Erez Bitton, Reuven Abergel, Shlomo Ben Ami, Arieh Der'i, Sami Shalom Chetrit, and Ovad Aboutbul, who arrived in Israel at a young age. Diverse in terms of class, status, occupation, and residency, as well as in terms of ideological perspectives, they all recount a traumatic first encounter with Israel and an ongoing struggle for equality. A deep nostalgia for Morocco is often expressed, and at times, even moving toward a beyond-the-pale potential affiliation with Palestinians and Palestine. One sequence, shot in the moshav town Mevasseret Zion, near Jerusalem, follows homeless families and squatters protesting discriminatory policies in land and housing. They report having asked for asylum from Yasser Arafat's Palestinian Authority in Jericho. Benny Torati's *Barzent Roofs* (1994), meanwhile, documents a southern Tel Aviv tent "settlement" camp protesting housing policies and angrily promising an "Intifada" (using the Arabic word in Hebrew) worse than the Palestinian Intifada. (That one-and-a-half-year-long protest, like many, was completely crushed.) In these instances, "Palestine" signifies crossing the outer limits of a licensed imaginary; it points to an emotional exhaustion point, to the failure to contain Mizrahi anger and a refusal to be "bad children," and to evoke Golda Meir's 1970s condescending phrase about the Black Panthers.

The Mizrahi/Palestinian nexus is explored in Nizar Hassan and Danae Elon's documentary *Cut* (2000), which recounts the 1950s settlement of the Palestinian village 'Agur with largely Kurdish Jews from Iraq and Turkey. The residents describe the reasons for their departure for Israel: "It was not Zionism; it was religion, and therefore we kissed the earth." When Hassan asks if they wish to return, they respond that their Iraqi departure document stated "*Roha bala Rag'a*" (in Arabic, "leaving without returning"). In fact, the Laissez-Passer issued by the Iraqi monarchy stated: "*La yasmah lihamilihi bil'awda ila al-Iraq batatan*," or the (document) holder is not permitted to return definitively. Yet, the interviewee's rendering of the Laissez-Passer's idiom as a colloquial expression, "*roha bala raj'a*," actually a curse, echoes the morbid sentiment around departure. At the same time, one of the residents admits with visible emotion: "To return would have been the greatest pleasure of my life . . . but to live there, I wouldn't want it. Can't even think of it. . . . It's impossible to leave. To visit, I did visit. My uncle who converted to Islam became the Sheikh of the village. . . . I visited the grave of my father." Throughout, the film captures an existence caught between the anxieties of the Israeli/Palestinian conflict, on the one hand, and Arab spaces of nostalgia, on the other. On the soundtrack the contemporary moment is largely evoked by the Iraqi music of Ilham Al Madfai, who emerged onto the music scene almost two decades after the departure of Iraqi Jews. Syncretizing traditional Iraqi songs with jazz and salsa, the film's non-diegetic music invokes Iraq in the past and present tenses. The soundtrack registers multiple dislocations and exoduses from Iraq (Al Madfai has been residing in Jordan), producing diverse Iraqi diasporic syncretisms. At the same time, Israel/Palestine is evoked through the recurrent sounds and images of military helicopters. Under the shadow of the conflict, the residents recall their desperate struggle to survive in Israel: hunger, joblessness, crowded shacks, lack of electricity, protests and clashes with police, along with fatal confrontation with "*mistanenim*" / "*fida'iyun*." Symptomatically, they oscillate between Hebrew and Arabic when they refer to the Palestinians who crossed back across the borders, whom the Israelis called "infiltrators" and the Palestinians, "men of sacrifice" or "freedom fighters"—an instability having to do with the anxiety of either Israeli or Palestinian addressees.

Partly narrated in Arabic, using Arabic text in the prelude and deploying Arabic subtitles throughout, *Cut* attempts to mediate the story of Arab-Jews for Palestinians in Israel. The filmmakers, furthermore, incorporate their own presence into the story, addressing the residents' anxiety concerning the filming. Hassan challenges the interviewees when they use the Hebrew pronunciation "'Agur" (pronounced with a hard "g") to refer to their moshav, reminding them that prior to filming they consistently used the Arabic name "'agur" (pronounced with a soft "g"). The presence of non-Mizrahi filmmakers, it could be argued, provokes Mizrahim to become self-aware and relay the official discourse, virtually performing docile citizenship. Numerous anti-occupation films use the hostile dark faces of Mizrahim to represent the oppressive nature of occupation. Their aggressivity toward the interrogative camera and their hand covering the lens tend to underline the Euro-Israeli image of Mizrahi fanaticism or even fascism. Yet, without idealizing Mizrahim—or any community, for that matter—what such representations do not acknowledge is the underlying Mizrahi class/ethnic hostility to the privileged Euro-Israeli filmmaker, whose camera, car, and body-language communicate an assumed authority or entitlement over the space. Such tensions go unmarked in such anti-occupation documentaries as Amos Gitai's *Field Diary* (1982), where the soldier-filmmaker friction is framed as merely about the occupation, between the enlightened camera and the (dark) forces that shut its view. *Cut*, in contrast, reflexively narrates a triangular encounter between a Euro-Israeli filmmaker (Elon) and a Palestinian filmmaker (Hassan), on the one hand, and Arab-Jews, on the other. It calls attention to the process—from the suspicion with which the filmmakers are greeted to their bonding with some of the interviewees. The film itself relays an edifying story of building trust—of hopeful possibilities and anxious impossibilities. Thus, while subjectivizing the Mizrahim, *Cut* ends with an appreciation of the limits of trust in the war zone. The concluding acknowledgement—"This film would not have been possible without the love and the trust of 'Agur's residents"—is cut short by the aggressive acoustic and visual presence of the military helicopters.

The interviews with Arab-Jews in *Route 181*, similarly, reveal an intricate relationship to Israel/Palestine on the part of individuals entangled in a war situation but also imbued with memories of life in the Arab world. In the "North" chapter, the filmmakers interview North Africans, who speak of a Moroccan or Tunisian past, which would seem out-of-place given their fraught situation near the Lebanese border. A Tunisian woman, who lost a son in a war, expresses a longing for her former life in Tunisia, thus illuminating the Arab/Jewish interfaces that were much more likely before 1948. The Iraqi-Jews in Samir's *Forget Baghdad*, similarly, some of whom were communists in Iraq and never actually intended to move to Israel, shed light on the circumstances that dislocated them, asserting that Israel would not have been their preferred destination had there been other options. Indeed, the writer Samir Naqqash stubbornly continued to write his novels in Arabic even after moving to Israel, crafting a heteroglossic array of Iraqi ethnic, religious, and regional dialects, while Sami Michael and Shimon Ballas shifted to Hebrew, but continued to write about Iraq or about Iraqis in Israel. Set in Iraq, the protagonists of Michael's *A Handful of Fog* are communists who belong to diverse ethnicities and religions. Ballas's *Outcast*, meanwhile, recounts the case of a Jewish-Iraqi scholar who stayed in Baghdad after the Jewish community's departure and converted to Islam.[49] The treatment of the Arab-Jew in literature and cinema thus offers the reader/spectator an imaginary voyage into the past, prior to the severing of the Arab-Jewish body, and hints at the possibility of reclaiming the Arab Jew for a reconfigured future. "Arab" and "Jew" are revealed to be contingent signifiers rather than essential categories. Home and homelessness, meanwhile, do not coincide neatly with the boundaries of the nation-state or with official documents of citizenship. The figure of the Arab Jew, in this sense, transcends past fixities and blurs contemporary boundaries.

Above and beyond the initial rupture, whether contested, mourned, or celebrated, recent displacements represent an end to an era that elicits potential allegorical readings of the earlier displacement. The representation of recent dislocation poses a retroactive question of whether Jews could, should, or would have remained in the Arabic/Muslim world. Against the backdrop of the "return from exile" operation, which brought elderly Iraqi Jews to Israel following the outbreak of the Iraq War, Inigo Gilmore's *The Last Jews of Babylon* (2003) tells the story of 85-year-old Ezra Levy's journey from Iraq to Israel. In Baghdad, where he feels at home in his spacious house, he longs for his family and for his lost love Daisy, whom he last saw more than 50 years ago, with the departure of the majority Jewish population. The cross-border move that began with the excitement of reunification ends with an elderly man alone in his narrow living quarter, visibly depressed. In one sequence, Ezra visits an Israeli school, where he answers (in English) rather prejudicial questions about Iraq. A sense of alienation emerges even with the Iraqi-Israelis, the decades of separation lived in different worlds having created a gap that seems unbridgeable. Through Ezra's unique perspective, the spectator reflects on the measure and the degree of the acculturation of his old Iraqi acquaintances in Israel. Whereas he had lived as a Jewish minority in a Muslim space, Ezra begins to live as an Iraqi minority in a Jewish state. In Israel, his joyful moments are visible in Palestinian spaces; in a Jaffah café or at a Palestinian wedding, dancing to Arab music. While the film revolves around the theme of *Aliya*, it does not replicate the Aliya discourse, performing neither the rescue of the Baghdadi Jew, nor the happy end of a homecoming among fellow Jews, even, for that matter, with fellow Iraqi Jews.

Such narratives of rupture diverge from the more paradigmatic films on the same theme. In *Sallah Shabbati*, we may recall, the spectator was first introduced to the Oriental Jew, Sallah, when he and his family descend from the airplane, landing in Israel. He comes from the Levant, but within the film's Eurocentric imaginary mapping, he comes from nowhere: first, in the literal sense, since his place of origin remains unknown; and second, in the metaphorical sense, since Asian and African geographies are suggested to amount to nothing of substance. While the protagonist's Levantine essence forms the dynamic center of the narrative, his Levantine geography is crucially invisible. Sallah's physical presence in Israel only embodies that geography's absence and highlights the process of erasure. Within Zionist discourse, Jews from West Asia/North Africa arrive from obscure corners of the globe to Israel, the Promised Land, to which they have always already been destined. Mizrahim are thus claimed as part of a continuous Jewish history/geography whose alpha and omega is the Land of Israel. While superimposing a nationalist discourse on the messianic idea of Jewish revival, Zionist ideologues, especially in the wake of the physical transfer of Palestinians to Arab countries, sought the transfer of Jews from Arab/Muslim countries to Palestine. However, for the displaced Jews, physical dislocation was to be accompanied by a metamorphosis. The establishment, in a contemporary retelling of the biblical Exodus from Egypt, called for "the death of the desert generation," in order to facilitate their birth as the New Jews-Israelis, embodied by the Sabra generation.

The question of continuity and discontinuity is central, therefore, to the Zionist vision of the nation-state. Yet, one could argue that by provoking the geographical dispersal of Middle Eastern/Arab-Jews, by placing them in a new situation "on the ground," by attempting to reshape their identity as simply "Israeli," by disdaining and trying to uproot their Arabness, and by racializing them and discriminating against them as a group—the Zionist project of the in-gathering of exiles itself provoked a dislocation that resulted in traumatic ruptures and exilic identity-formations. The Israeli establishment obliged Arab-Jews to redefine themselves in relation to new ideological paradigms and polarities, thus provoking the aporias of an identity constituted out of its own ruins. The Jews within Islam had thought of themselves as Jews, but that Jewishness was interwoven within a larger Judeo-Islamic cultural geography. Under pressure from Zionism, on the one hand, and Arab nationalism, on the other, that set of affiliations gradually changed, resulting in a transformed cultural semantics.

The Mizrahi Cinema of Displacement

In a roundabout way, the Mizrahim as "imagined community"(Benedict Anderson) constitute, at least in part, a Zionist invention. The Mizrahi identity is, then, on one level, one of Zionism's unintended consequences, one that marks a certain departure from previous Jewish cultural geographies. Yet, the delegitimization of Middle Eastern culture has also resulted in a new identity formation, shaped out of the shards of a non-European past, which brought together a massive encounter among Arab, Iranian, Turkish, Kurdish, Berber, Indian, Georgian, and Ethiopian cultures. From Jews of such diverse regions as the Maghreb and Yemen has emerged a new overarching umbrella identity, what began to be called in the late 1980s "the Mizrahim." The term "Mizrahim," I have suggested elsewhere, condenses a number of connotations: it celebrates the Jewish past in the Eastern world; it affirms the pan-Oriental communities developed in Israel itself; and it invokes a future of revived cohabitation with the Arab Muslim East. All these emergent collective definitions arose, as often occurs, in diacritical contrast with a newly encountered hegemonic group, in this case the Ashkenazim of Israel. Indeed, the cultural productions of the decade following the publication of *Israeli Cinema* authorize us to speak of an emergent Mizrahi culture, including an emergent Mizrahi cinema.

Critical Mizrahi cultural practices—including by non-Mizrahim but from a decidedly Mizrahi perspective—not only revisit hegemonic narratives of the Sephardi/Ashkenazi ethnic tension, but also confront core questions of identity and historical memory. Mizrahi films have given voice to a different perspective, closer to that developed in critical scholarship, which has denaturalized the view of the terms "Jew" and "Arab" as mutually exclusive and inimical identities. Instead, the Arab-versus-Jew binary opposition is re-presented within the hyphenated space of the "Arab-Jew." No longer an uncanny figure, the Arab-Jew here is a speaking voice and body that must be reckoned with. Many of these films deal with linguistic quandaries, especially concerning the relationship between Arabic and Hebrew as well as between Mizrahi culture and the Middle East. Numerous autobiographical films write, voice, and "image" what was earlier marginalized and de-legitimized. If within Zionist discourse the Arab-Jew was delinked from Arab history to be claimed as part of "the (Jewish) Nation," recent cultural practices re-link Mizrahim to Arabic and Middle Eastern cultural geography. They negotiate the imposed dilemma of choosing between Jewishness and Arabness in a geopolitical context that has perpetuated the equation between Arabness, Middle Easternness, and Islam, on the one hand, and between Jewishness, Europeanness and Westernness, on the other.

Whereas orientalist ethnographic cinema has often conveyed a folkloristic and miserablist picture of Jews in the Muslim world, revisionist Arab-Jewish/Mizrahi cultural practices have undermined these exotic tropes and rescue narratives. The penchant for conjuring up urban spaces belonging to the Arab-Jewish past—Baghdad, Tunis, Alexandria, Beirut, Aleppo, Tangier, and Algiers—can be read in relation to the homogenizing narrative of the universal Jewish ghetto, as well as in relation to the rural reductionism of the Middle East as a whole. A number of historical documentaries, auto/biographical films, memoirs, novels, visual productions, and performance pieces recall, often against the grain of Zionist ideology, a presumably "alien" and "distant" geography. Despite occasional traces of self-exoticization, Mizrahi cultural practices have begun to embark on introspective voyages into a multifaceted "East." It is not that the Mizrahi/Euro-Israeli axis is eliminated, as much as it sidestepped, pushed to the periphery of the narrative, informing it as an assumed backdrop. Such a representational move can be considered a form of a conceptual return to a pre-Israel world of wider horizons, a geocultural domain stretched from the Indian Ocean to the Mediterranean and the Atlantic, where Jews traveled and exchanged ideas under the aegis of a largely Muslim world.[50] The rather anomalous nature of "the departure" and "the entry" has generated narratives preoccupied with dislocation and the inscription of memory. The cross-border imaginary can be found even in films made by non-Mizrahi or non-Jewish filmmakers, such as Samir's *Forget Baghdad*, Suleiman's *Homage by Assassination*, Inigo Gilmore's *The Last Jews of Babylon*, and Florence Straus's *Between Two Notes*, all of which chronicle life in the in-between of hostile political camps.

Recent Mizrahi cultural practices invoke Arabic or Middle Eastern culture as inhabiting the present-day Mizrahi body, liminally figuring life on the edge of the intimate and the distant, of home and exile, state citizenship, and cultural belonging. The question of the Arabic language—a mother tongue for Arab-Jews but also Israel's enemy language—has thus become a metonym and metaphor for the displacement. Arabic, in this context, is not merely a language but a trope that evokes the dilemmas of continuity and discontinuity between past and present where one's previous homeland has become the enemy of the current one. In contrast to Mizrahi literature, where Hebrew occasionally stands in for Arabic, and where Arabic phrases are sometimes written in Hebrew script, cinema as a multi-track medium has made it possible for Arabic to neighbor and intersect with Hebrew—both written and spoken. The celluloid inscription of Arabic, along with Mizrahi accented Hebrew, relocates the Mizrahim within cultural contexts and historical moments that transcend nation-state boundaries. Unlike literary texts, films allow for the literal registry of the multiplicity of dialects in Israel and the diversity of Mizrahi and non-Ashkenazi accents in Hebrew (inflected not only by Arabic but also by other tongues, such as Turkish, Farsi, Ladino, Georgian, and Amharic). Mizrahi cinema, in this sense, tends to deploy a multi-accentual soundtrack. The broken Hebrew of the older generation and the broken Arabic of the younger generation no longer signifies inferiority, but rather a culturally dense fault-line existence. (At times, a single sentence features multiple languages, rendered comprehensible with the help of subtitles). Eschewing the generic "mark of the plural," Mizrahi cinema thus orchestrates the variety of Mizrahi voices, invoking multiple geographies and diverse classes. Mizrahi subaltern proletarians, without access to upwardly mobile institutional spaces, gain access to a space of representation. Repressed memories, whether of Muslim spaces or of the immediate aftermath of the arrival to Israel, are reenacted and documented, generating a new Mizrahi testimonial cinema. In a vital audio-visual revisionist project, critical cinema revisits the literal polyglossia that informs the intricate social-cultural space of Israel/Palestine.

The Mizrahi project of reclaiming "Arabness" and "Easternness," whatever its political implications, has cumulatively redefined the cultural parameters of an Israel that is no longer merely a prolongation of Europe, "in" but not "of" the Middle East. Over the past decade, Mizrahi literature and cinema of the second and third generation have been engaging the departure from the Arab world and the move to Israel, whether in semi-autobiographical fiction or in autobiographical documentaries. Duki Dror's *My Fantasia* (2001) traces the story of the filmmaker's family in Iraq and Israel using the family's Hanukia menorah workshop as a backdrop for probing conversations. Rami Kimchi's *Cinema Egypt* cites Egyptian cinema to rekindle memories of a lost Egyptian past that, nonetheless, continues to survive in present-day Israel. Interviewing his mother about her life in Egypt and in Israel, Kimchi screens her one of her favorite Egyptian films *Leila the Village Girl* (1941), directed by the Jewish-Egyptian Togo Mizrahi, and starring the Jewish-Egyptian movie star, Leila Mourad. These autobiographical documentaries go down film's memory lane, as it were, in order to paint a cosmopolitan portrait of Egypt. (Other films, meanwhile, recount literal return journeys. In Duki Dror's *Taqasim*, the Egyptian Israeli musicians visit their old Cairo neighborhood and friends, while in Asher de Bentolila Tlalim's *Exile*, the filmmaker returns to

Morocco to the family's house in Tangier. Return, whether literal or symbolic, has become a common motif, within a process of reflection triggered by the search for "roots.")

Documentaries such as Eyal Halfon's *Chalrie Baghdad* (2003) and Duki Dror's *Taqasim* and *Café Noah* are devoted to the music of the dislocated generation, specifically the story of Arab-Jewish musicians who ended up in a country that disdained their Arabic music, denying them access to funding and public outlets. While *Taqasim* follows the voyage of the musician Felix Mizrahi to Cairo where he grew up, *Café Noah* tells the story of the consumption of Arabic music in Israel by Arab-Jews throughout the 1950s and 1960s. Other films, meanwhile, shed light on Arab-Jewish writers and Mizrahi literature, delving into the linguistic rupture for writers whose mother tongue was Arabic. David Benchetrit's documentary, *Samir* (1997), focuses on the Iraqi-Israeli writer Sami Michael, who, along with other writers such as Shimon Ballas, made a conscious decision to shift from writing in Arabic to writing in Hebrew, while Samir Naqqash, as we have seen, continued to write in Arabic. The homage to Sami Michael attempts to recuperate the place of the Arab-Jewish/Mizrahi writer within the Hebrew literary canon.

The surge in memoirs and personal essays, in autobiographical and diary documentaries, and in the performing and visual arts' incorporation of familial memorabilia must all be seen as part of a desire to reconfigure a conflictual Mizrahi identity.[51] Films such as Simone Bitton's *Yoredet*, Yochi Dadon-Spigel's *Gifted* (2000), Serge Ankri's *Mama's Couscous* (1994), Sini Bar David's *The South—Alice Never Lived Here* (1998), David Benchetrit's *Kaddim Wind*, Rami Kimchi's *Cinema Egypt* and *Father Language* (2006), Sigalit Banai's *Mama Faiza,* Duki Dror's *My Fantasia,* Sarit Haymian's *Gole Sangam* (2007) "out," as it were, the formerly closeted Arab, Iranian, Sephardi, or syncretic Mizrahi cultures, which had been rejected and therefore confined to the private sphere of home. Even mundane activities, such as cooking, singing, and dancing, form part of an effort to recuperate rejected home culture associated with "the enemy" across the border. Such films explore, often through a cross-generational encounter, the fault line between the Arabic/Middle-Eastern world of the parents' generation and that of their now adult children shaped by new Israeli cultural paradigms. *Mama Faiza*, for example, follows the case of Faiza Rushdi, an Egyptian-Jewish singer, who continues to sing in Arabic in Israel, accompanied by Arab-Jewish musicians. This story is filtered through the daughter, the actress Yaffa Tusia Cohen, who is shown not only in her everyday life but also on stage, where she offers a wrenching theatrical version of their intergenerational relationship.

Mizrahi narratives dissect the pain of dislocation that had been kept until recently in the shadows of an Euro-Israeli facade. Sini Bar David's *The South* offers an introspective voyage through the story of the dislocations of the filmmaker's grandmother, who reflects on a communal history that spans cross-border movements between Turkey, Greece, and Bulgaria after World War II and Nazi deportations, ending in Israel, in a south Tel Aviv neighborhood bordering on the mixed Jewish/Arab city of Jaffa. In the slum, in the morbid vicinity of Tel Kabir's Forensic Institute, the grandmother lives a confined existence, echoed by both Bar-David's own childhood experiences and those of the present-day younger generation. Slow-motion sequences at the beginning and the end portray a young girl playing hopscotch and jumping rope in an empty street full of shuttered storefronts. A no-exit situation is also portrayed in films made by non-Israeli Arab-Jews; for example, in Mary Halawani's *I Miss the Sun*, which tells the story of the filmmaker's Egyptian-Jewish grandmother, chronicling the exodus from sunny Egypt in 1956 to grim Brooklyn, where the Passover ritual of commemorating the Biblical Exodus clashes with the grandmother's deep sense of loss and of missing Egypt. Nostalgia and claustrophobia are intimately linked in Arab-Jewish exilic narratives.

Other films have addressed not only the dislocation to Israel but also the subsequent emigration *from* Israel. Amit Goren's *66 Was a Good Year for Tourism* (1992) reflects on the fragmented identity of a family, given disagreements about this emigration, especially between the Egyptian Israeli father, content in the United States, and the Ashkenazi Israeli mother, who resents their departure from Israel. Yael Bitton's *The Rabbi's 12 Children* (2007), meanwhile, chronicles the dispersal of the filmmaker's family from Morocco to Israel, and then to Switzerland and the United States. From the interviews and the domestic ambience, there emerges a portrait of their disparate trajectories that elicit a comparative reading of the siblings as a social microcosm. The stark class contrast, manifested not only in economics but also in vocabulary, expressiveness, confidence, and body language, between family members living in Israel and those in Switzerland and the United States, becomes a social document and a celluloid allegory for the "descent" of Arab-Jews into Israel. Rather than a telos, Israel here is only one station, however crucial, in the fragmented story of Jewish-Moroccan diaspora.

For Mizrahim, the Israeli experience has not been conducive to success. Many families who led prosperous lives in Egypt, Iran, Iraq, Morocco, or Tunisia encountered a social crisis in Israel. In a short period, the identity of Middle Eastern Jews was fractured, their life possibilities diminished, their hopes deferred. In the Mizrahi cinema of displacement, thus, the question of memory is embedded in a sense of geographical dislocation, of loss without gain. What may be termed Mizrahi displacement cinema relays a skeptical or ambivalent relation to the official account, disrupting its totalizing coherence through a paradoxical poetics of exile in the Promised Land. In many ways, such cultural practices, in tandem with sociopolitical struggle, point to a dystopian take on the utopian project of the "ingathering of Exiles." Euro-Israeli ideologues promoted the myth of the melting pot in the wake of mass *Aliya* in the 1950s and 1960s, but cultural mixing did not take place exactly in the ways foreseen and imagined by the dominant Euro-Israeli institutions. In the working class neighborhoods, Mizrahim of Arab or Turkish or Iranian origin acquired new multiplicities, the product of a new historical encounter of cultures. They quickly learned slang and recipes from other "Oriental" countries. While they experienced delegitimization by Euro-Israel, they were also only marginally connected to an Arab world that knew little of their new existence. In Mizrahi neighborhoods in the 50s and 60s, the radio dial was turned to Arab music. They continued to listen to Umm Kulthum and Nazim al-Ghazali, and, in the age of television, especially since the 1970s, when Mizrahim *en masse* began purchasing TV sets, they viewed Arabic programs and films from within cramped living rooms.

Hybrid identities cannot be reduced to a fixed recipe; rather, they form a changing repertory of cultural modalities. Occupying contradictory social and discursive spaces, the Mizrahi identity, like all identities, is dynamic and mobile, less an achieved synthesis than an unstable constellation of discourses. Mizrahi popular culture has clearly manifested a vibrant dialogue with Arab, Turkish, Greek, Indian, and Iranian popular cultures. Despite the separation from the Arab world, Mizrahi culture has been nourished through the enthusiastic consumption of Egyptian, Jordanian, and Lebanese television programs, films, and music video performances that have ruptured the Euro-Israeli public sphere in a kind of subliminal transgression of forbidden reminiscences. In fact, some Mizrahi music is produced in collaboration with (Israeli) Palestinians, as is the case with the musicians working with Yair Dalal. The Moroccan-Israeli musical group Sfatayim was one of the first to travel back to Morocco to produce a music video sung in Moroccan Arabic against the scenery of the cities and villages that Moroccan Jews have left behind, just as Israeli-born Iraqi singers, such as Ya'aqub Nishawi, sing old and contemporary Iraqi music. This yearning for a symbolic return "to the Diaspora" results in an ironic reversal of the conventional narrative of "next year in Jerusalem," as well as a reversal of the Biblical expression that substitutes "Babylon" for "Zion": "By the waters of Zion, where we sat down, and there we wept, when we remembered Babylon."

Over the past decade, critical Mizrahi voices have become more audible in the public sphere. The "periphery" has come to occupy center stage, whether in social documentaries such as Benny Torati's *Barzent Roofs*, Rino Tzror Doron Tsabari's *Underdogs: A War Movie* (1996), Amit Goren's *6 Open, 21 Closed* (1994), or in autobiographical quest and personal diary films, Duki Dror's *My Fantasia*, Ronen Amar's *My Family's Pizza* (2003), and Assaf Basson's *Maktub Aleik: A Voice Without a Face* (2005), or in fictional allegories such as Meital Abikasis's *White Walls* (2005), Benny Zada's *Hamara* (1999), and Aya Somech's *Questions of a Dead Worker* (2002). The documentary series *A Sea of Tears* (1999), directed by Ron Kahlili, founder of the Mizrahi TV Channel, Briza, reclaims the place of the hybrid Mizrahi music produced in Israel by the younger generation of the immigrants' children.[52] Recounting the history of Mizrahi music, the series links the emergence of music to a broader sociopolitical context, addressing the institutional discrimination practiced by Israeli radio and TV. One of the interviewees, the singer Nissim Sarrousi, recalls one of the most visible public encounters between Euro-Israel and Sephardic Israel on the only state-controlled TV channel. In an interview that took place in 1974, the host of the "Tandu" show, Yaron London, insulted the music, the voice, the singing, the dress, the looks, and even the shoes of the singer Sarousi—a traumatic moment engraved in the Mizrahi consciousness as a humiliation for all Mizrahim. In *A Sea of Tears*, Sarrousi recounts his visceral response to this interview, which was to immediately leave Israel for France. Narrated by the activist Tikva Levi, *A Sea of Tears* offers an embrace of the rejected singers, in an act of legitimation of Mizrahi music and, allegorically, of the Mizrahi identity.

Such a retrospective look links present-day Mizrahi investments in the past to earlier manifestations of cross-border affinities, already found not only in the cinema (George Ovadia's films, which, unlike most Bourekas films, dedicated less narrative space to ethnic tensions), but also in music (The Natural Alternative and *Sfatayim*), literature (Gavriel Ben Simhon, Erez Bitton, and Shelly Elkayam), magazines and newspapers (*HaPaamon*, *Iton Aher*, *Hapatish*, and *Hila News*), socio-political spaces (Kivun Hadash, documented in the Eli Hamo's *New Direction*, 1989), and movements throughout the 1980s and early 1990s (East for Peace, The Oriental Front, and Perspectives Judeo-arabes), which dealt not only with political issues but also with their cultural dimension.[53] Like Mizrahi music, George Ovadia's Bourekas cinema was often marginalized and publicly excoriated as "vulgar." In fiction films, several Mizrahi filmmakers, most notably Yamin Messika and Benny Torati, have revisited Bourekas cinema in homage to a genre that offered—whatever its limitations—second-generation Mizrahim a space for identity-formation. In the wake of Ovadia's work, Torati's *Desperado Square* cleanses the genre, as it were, of its ethnic conflict, centering on a Mizrahi "periphery" oblivious to Euro-Israel. The film's ambiguous temporality renders the Mizrahi neighborhood strangely timeless. Anachronistically interweaving visual references to both past and present, the film creates a sense of an enclosed Mizrahi space, somewhere in the south Tel Aviv area, as though even in the digital age time stands still for the Mizrahim of the "hood," rather like a town that time forgot. While the neighborhood evokes a bygone era spanning the 1950s to the 1970s, hegemonic Israel, which looms in the background via a shot of the Ayalon highway and the Azrieli towers, is seen to have architecturally entered the world of global capitalism, even while as it has continued to underdevelop Mizrahi Israel. But rather than produce a sense of miserablist claustrophobia, *Desperado Square,* not unlike Spike Lee's *Crooklyn* (1994), evokes the down-to-earth sensuous pleasures of hood life.

Reflexively, *Desperado Square* dialogues not only with Bourekas cinemas but also with Indian, Turkish, Iranian, Arab, Italian, and American cinema. The invention of Mizrahi culture in Israel takes places against the backdrop of an internalized self-rejection, where Greek music and Turkish cinema, however, marginalized, were for a long time seen as somewhat more legitimate than Arabic music and cinema (a topic addressed in Chapter 3). The film dialogues explicitly with the popular Indian film *Sangam* (1964), stringing together seemingly different worlds. The cinematic paradise gratifies the at once ludic and melancholy imaginary, which revolves around the hood, but also strives toward an "elsewhere." In *Desperado Square*, this multi-layered intertext is shaped through reflexive evocations, allusions, and quotations of Raj Kapoor's Bollywood film *Sangam*, through dialogues, monologues, music, and film-within-the-film. The parallel and intersecting narratives between *Desperado Square* and *Sangam*, which revolve around a triangle love and sacrifice between two men and a woman, however, end differently. *Sangam* concludes with the tragic suicide of the protagonist, while *Desperado Square* culminates with the Bourekas-like melodramatic unification of the couple. In this film about cinematic nostalgia and escapist spectatorship, the *mise-en-abyme* has the film's protagonist watch an Indian film, itself also watched by the spectators of *Desperado Square*. The film embraces an imaginary Mizrahiness that, despite its confined hood zone, is also interwoven into a wider "Oriental" geography that includes the "local" Arab. Casting the Palestinian Bakri to play the role of the Mizrahi, as suggested earlier, inverts the casting practices of the heroic nationalist films wherein the Mizrahi played the Arab enemy, but more importantly, it reclaims an explicit Arab identity, denigrated and denied to the Arab-Jew. The quotations from *Sangam*, especially in the decades following the arrival to Israel, express nostalgia for a cultural geography, for genre aesthetics, and for the gregarious collectivity of movie-going.

Denied and rejected, a sense of "Easternness," as suggested earlier, was shaped by the consumption of films, music, radio, and later TV programs from a variety of countries, including Egypt, Lebanon, and Jordan. Spectatorship on the margins of both Israel and the Arab world in a sense actively shaped an emerging new syncretic identity—the Mizrahim. The movie-theater and television, as spaces of social formation, generated a new collective memory specific to the Mizrahi experience in Israel. In a kind of recuperative discourse, Mizrahi intellectuals/ artists/ activists have come to express a *mea culpa* about years of self-rejection, denial, and internalization of the condemnations of their popular culture. In an aesthetic jujitsu, recent Mizrahi films have revisited the very signs of Levantine primitiveness— magic, folklore, and superstition. Shmuel Hasfari and Hana Azoulay-Hasfari's *Sh'hur* (the title is the Arabic word for magic in its Moroccan pronunciation) on one level reinforces Mizrahi stereotypes but, at the same time it appropriates magic and insanity, mobilizing them against the emblems of Establishment modernity— Television.[54] *Desperado Square,* similarly, resignifies superstition, specifically the urgency to respond to dreams of visits from the dead. One of the sons dreams that his dead father asks him to reopen their defunct theater; and the film ends with the carrying out of that dream-wish. The Hebrew title corresponds to the centrality of dream—"the square of dreams." The melodramatic genre, in other words, is endorsed shamelessly, as though taunting the critics who condemned the "vulgar" Bourekas genre in the name of "quality cinema." Ran Tal's *George Ovadia: Merchant of Feelings* (1992) explicitly revisits the genre, rendering homage to a leading Bourekas melodrama director —the Iraqi-Iranian-Israeli George Ovadia).[55] The reclaiming of the melodrama in Benny Torati's *Desperado Square* or in Messika's *Desperate Steps* can thus be seen as a way to assert Mizrahi popular taste whereby narrative and music serve to establish a confident voice from "the other Israel."

Despite the reunion of the couple at the end of the film, *Desperado Square* eschews the Bourekas cinema intra-Jewish mixed-marriage trope. Rather than a desire for integration, films like *Desperado Square* manifest a withdrawal into a world devoid of Ashkenazi characters, as though the fictive romance with "the East" would be disrupted by an overpowering iconic Euro-Israeli presence. Mixed marriage ending in divorce comes to allegorize the fraught Ashkenazi-Mizrahi relationship. At the height of the Bourekas genre's popularity, when mixed-marriage allegorically resolved the narrative's ethnic conflict, Sami Michael's first novel *All Men are Equal—But Some Are More* crafted mixed-marriage as a site of pathological formation, reminiscent, I would suggest, of themes from Frantz Fanon's "The Black Man and the White Woman" in *Black Skin, White Masks*. Over the years, the Ashkenazi/Mizrahi mixed-marriage trope has returned, but not necessarily within the same sensibility or ideology. Set during the first Gulf War, the David Ofek's film *Home* (1994), for example, offers a bemused look at an Iraqi-Israeli family in a middle class Iraqi town, Ramat Gan, trying to spot its old Baghdadi house from the TV images of Baghdad under attack. Iraq is abstracted, a dim reminiscence from the older generation's fading memory; the family house remains in an Iraq that is clearly not home. The film ends with a pan to the filmmaker's future family—his Euro-Israeli wife and children. The Iraqiness is subsumed into a transcendent ethnicity discourse, and in the vein of standup Mizrahi comedy, pokes fun at its own identity, at times in a self-Orientalizing fashion. The film's ending asserts a postmodern Israel, beyond the old Ashkenazi/Mizrahi tensions, where "Iraqiness" becomes just one element in an ultimately coherent and integrated Israeli identity. Within such representational practices, we find a tendency to highlight fluid multicultural identities, where the pre-Israeli past is indeed fixed back in the past, a quaint background for a new Israeli culture.

Despite shared leitmotifs, the Mizrahi cultural movement is thus not at all monolithic, given the undergirding political rifts around the historical Middle-Eastern Jewish relation to Zionism and the place of Mizrahim vis-à-vis the state. The distinct narratives and genres also relay different sensibilities, investments, and negotiations vis-à-vis the hegemonic Euro-Israeli culture, on the one hand, and the marginalized Arab culture, on the other. While some films assume a nationalist framing of Mizrahi dislocation or belonging, others (for example, Simone Bitton's

Yoredet, Eli Hamo's *New Direction*, Benny Zada's *Hamara: A Place Near Life* [1999], David Benchetrit's *Kaddim Wind*, and Eli Hamo and Sami Chetrit's *The Black Panthers [in Israel] Speak*) cast doubt on the Zionist masternarrative.

Revisionist Cultural Practice

If diasporic Palestinian cultural practices explore the shock of departure from Palestine, Israeli Mizrahi practices address the shock of entry to Israel. Many Mizrahi films, whether explicitly or implicitly, have as their reference point the traumatic period of arrival in Israel. The past two decades have brought a significant increase in documentaries that challenge Orientalist representations and inscribe an alternative Mizrahi perspective. Critical Mizrahi cinema (even, at times, when not made by Mizrahim) is embedded in a long sociopolitical struggle. The past two decades have seen a surge in revisionist accounts of history, explicitly tackling discriminatory state and Establishment policies and practices during the period of the "*Ma'abarot*" (transit camps), including the controversial subjects of the Kidnapped Yemeni and Mizrahi Babies and the Ringworm Children. Archival footage and historical research are central to what can be called a revisionist Mizrahi cinema. Here "Mizrahi" stands less for the origins of the makers than for a sociopolitically critical perspective.

Ayelet Heller's *Unpromised Land* (1992), for example, follows the story of Yemeni Jews, who during the Ottoman period settled in the Sea of Galilee area and cultivated the land, largely as part of a messianic vision of the "promised land." Yet in 1914, the land became "unpromised," when a group of Ashkenazi pioneers, the well-known founders of Kvutzat Kinneret, took their land away, leading to the Yeminis' dislocation. One of the elder Yemenis weeps as he recalls the disrespect and the humiliation, countering the kibbutz' claim of an exclusively Ashkenazi "development," denying Yemini labor. The camera follows the Yemeni descendants mourning their loss and confronting the Kibbutzniks who have erased their presence from the official history, now conveyed by tour guides, which glorifies the (European) founding fathers. While rewriting this history, the film frames the ethnic division of labor within the Jewish settlement without relating it to the question of Palestine. The socialist Zionist ideal of "Hebrew Work" was partly realized in the form of the exploitation and discrimination of Yemeni workers, called "Jews in the form of Arabs," a concept crucial to the colonization of Palestine. Films such as Tali Shemesh's *White Gold/Black Labor* (2004), meanwhile, examine continued labor discrimination in the contemporary era, in this case, in a development town in the South, revealing the persistence of an ethnic division of labor within Jewish Israel.

Some documentaries perform historical research, uncovering erased moments in the repressed history of Arab-Jews' arrival to Israel. Some films deal with the still buried story of the kidnapping of Yemeni and Mizrahi babies from the late 1940s to the early 1960s. Disoriented by the new reality in Israel, Yemenis, as well as Jews from other Arab and Muslim countries, fell prey to the state's welfare institutions, which provided babies for adoption largely in Israel and in the United States while telling the biological parents that their babies had died. Over several decades the government has ignored or silenced Mizrahi demands for investigation. Kidnappings were at least in part a result of a belief in the mission of Western Science and Progress, operating on a continuum with the reigning academic discourses of the time. In this intersection of race, gender, and class, the displaced Jews from Muslim countries became victims of the logic of Progress, bearing the marks of its pathologies on their bodies. In 1986, "Mabat Sheni," a TV program on the subject denied and downplayed the historical veracity of the accusations, producing Orientalist narratives about neglectful children-breeding parents. Documentaries such as Tzipi Talmor's *Down a One Way Road* (1997) and Uri Rozenwax's *Fact* (Chanel 2, 1996)[56] raise questions about this still unresolved episode. The topic is also dramatized in Yamin Messika's fictional film, *The Vineyard of Hope*, about an American woman who comes to a south Tel Aviv neighborhood in search of her biological parents only to find out that she was never willingly given for adoption, that she is one of the kidnapped Yemeni babies.[57]

The investigative testimonial documentary *Ringworm Children*, by David Belhassen and Asher Hemias, opens up another suppressed chapter—the case of the X-ray radiation, said to be a treatment for ringworm, administered to approximately 100,000 children, primarily from North Africa, in the early 1950s. The radiation resulted in high rates of mortality for children and fatal or chronic diseases for the survivors, including excruciating headaches, infertility, epilepsy, amnesia, Alzheimer's, psychosis, cancer, and sexual dysfunction, along with aesthetic and psychological scars. According to the officials, the medical establishment was concerned with severe danger to public health posed by ringworm, but was unaware of the grave consequences of the treatment itself. A minor skin or scalp problem, which used to be treated in their home countries with vinegar, was "treated" in Israel with X-ray radiation doses surpassing 35,000 times the maximum recommended, this in an era, as the film shows, when the dangers of radiation were already known to the medical community. At times, children without any manifestation of a ringworm problem also received the X-rays, causing the deaths of several family members. Thousands of the children died shortly thereafter, while thousands of others perished as a result of cancers and other disorders, and others are still dying up to the present.

As with other charges against the state apparatus, the official response is to claim that the calamity was unintentional. The film argues, in contrast, that the X-rays formed part of an experiment to test the effects of large radiation doses on humans. The program was apparently funded by American sponsors who supplied outmoded X-ray machines and made large payments to an Israeli government that could not have otherwise afforded the treatment/experiment. Whereas such experiments were no longer legal within the United States, they were still possible in Israel. A key official facilitator of the experiment, director general of the Israeli Health Ministry, Dr. Chaim Sheba, according to the film, had opposed the "bringing" of North Africans to Israel on the basis of their supposedly contagious diseases as a threat to public health. After their arrival, Dr. Sheba's rhetoric continued in the same vein; he spoke of the war against ringworm as an "epidemic extermination." The film includes archival footage, interviews with government officials, survivors' testimonials, and written texts, all orchestrated to demonstrate the logic of racism. *Ringworm Children's* examination of the Israeli-U.S. scientific institutional links evokes other documentaries on eugenics, such as *La Operacion* (1982), which details the experimentation with birth control pills and forced sterilization on women in Puerto Rico. In the case of the ringworm children, it was the vulnerable "Third World" of Israel that was made available for medical experiments. The argument made throughout is that the children were deliberately poisoned, within an institutional racism that disregarded non-European lives, all carried out by the "Division for Social Medicine," a euphemism for eugenics.

Revisionist documentaries contribute, then, to the Mizrahi testimonial narrative. As with the documentaries about the kidnappings, some of the interviews with the ringworm survivors take place at the trauma site, for example in Sha'ar *Aliya* (The Gate of *Aliya*) near the Haifa port. The film recalls the event from the point of view of the children, now adults, their bodies ravaged by time. The interviewees, addressing their testimonials to the camera, speak of their experiences, including having their head forcibly "scalped," being "plucked like chicken," and being "tied like sacrifice," before being placed under a heavy machine without anti-radiation protection and left alone for the duration of the radiation. They confess their resentment at their parents for permitting such an action, only to realize that, on the radiation day, the parents had been told that the students were being taken on a school trip. The non-diegetic music of Shlomo Bar and "The Natural Alternative"—a syncretic East/West musical ensemble associated both with protest and with recovering the Eastern dimension—underlines the larger historical and social pain. As with the kidnappings, the ringworm case has been suppressed for decades. The film tracks down the administrative processes that usually lead to the rejection of cases for "lack of proof," but in the Ringworm case, in 1995, after a long struggle led by a few Mizrahi Knesset members, the Knesset passed a law mandating government compensation for the victims. (The "Ringworm Law," however, did not include any admission of governmental wrongdoing.) The film intercuts scenes of official defenders of the government with the interviewees, in shots showing them both as individuals and as a collective. As the children of the 1950s continue to suffer and die, the film's investigation reveals the extent to which information about such cases has been buried. This documentary, it is implied, has only begun to scratch the surface, highlighting the urgent need for more revisionist Mizrahi histories.

In many ways, such films denaturalize and disrupt the discourse of *Aliya* and the teleological narrative of the Jewish nation-state. While it has been common in official political discourse as well as in artistic and scholarly practice to separate the Mizrahi question from the Palestinian question, and even sometimes to posit them as simply in conflict (e.g., by stressing the eternal persecution of Jews in the Arab world, or the putative ingrained tendency of Mizrahi to hate Arabs), such hegemonic narratives have been increasingly challenged. Directed by the Jewish-Moroccan filmmaker, David Benchetrit, the documentary *Through the Veil of Exile* follows three Palestinian women as they narrate their experiences under Israeli occupation in Gaza and the West Bank. But, in this instance, the exile of Palestinians and their dispossession comes to illuminate the subject position of the filmmaker himself, whose exile as a Moroccan Jew in Israel is allegorically displaced through the Palestinian narrative. In *Kaddim Wind*, as we have seen, Benchitrit narrates the nightmarish Moroccan experience in Israel as beginning already in Morocco, with the lure of Zion/ism. The archival footage that shows vehicles transferring Moroccan Jews to waiting boats revisits moments of traumatic separation. The sense of uprootedness is thus visually performed at the very overture of this epic documentary. The acoustic presence of the Moroccan national anthem on the soundtrack, meanwhile, stages the very question of living in between nation-states and the sense of a return to a taboo belonging in Morocco.

Mizrahi cultural practices revisit the traumatic moment of entry into Israel that redefined a new collective identity born on the ruins of a hasty departure from one geography and a disturbed entrance into another. It is perhaps not a coincidence that, time and again, Mizrahim have returned to this primal scene—the moment of landing in the Holy Land, only to be sprayed by government agents with the disinfectant DDT. Already in 1974, Sami Michael's novel *All Men are Equal—But Some Are More* registered that paradigmatic moment of arrival when the protagonist's father, full of dreamy hope, is met with DDT. Literary fiction legitimated an experience that formerly had only been part of oral narratives, discussed in Mizrahi homes and neighborhoods. Three decades later, a new literature and cinema has emerged centering on the shocking moment of arrival, but this time actively shaping the visual and oral archive.

Revisionist Mizrahi Cinema has invariably depicted the impact of this history on the lives of Mizrahim. While some of the films form part of a broader intellectual project critiquing Euro-Israeli historiography, others take this history and the struggle on the "periphery" as a backdrop for captivating dramas or autobiographies of the protagonists of Mizrahi struggle, as in such films as Amit Goren's *6 Open, 21 Closed*, David Ofek's *No. 17* (2003), Nissim Mossek's *Have You Heard About the Black Panthers?* (2002) and *Who is Mordechai Vanunu?* (2004), and David Fisher's

Buried But Alive (1996). Nissim Mossek's *Who is Mordechai Vanunu?*, for example, tells the story of the Moroccan-Israeli nuclear whistle-blower who was recently released after 18 years in solitary confinement, in a context where Vanunu had been vilified as the enemy of the people. Told against the backdrop of the Black Panther rebellion of the 1970s, *Buried But Alive*, for its part, narrates the story of Mazal Sa'il, wife of Dani Sa'il, an "*aguna*" who fights the rabbinical establishment in a convoluted case involving a Black Panther who vanished, or was perhaps made to "disappear." Although Dani Sa'il declared his intention to return to the "enemy country" of Iraq in the late 1970s, his whereabouts and trajectory have yet to be revealed. Caught in the gears of the rabbinical state apparati, Mazal Sa'il has lived in legal limbo for about 20 years.[58] Also, in Nissim Mossek's *Have You Heard About the Black Panthers?* "the Black Panthers' past looms against the present, with Mossek incorporating his own 1973 footage of Jerusalem's Musrara neighborhood and of the young rebels from his earlier documentary *Have You Heard About the Panthers, Mr. Moshe?*" The quoted film becomes a steppingstone for a contemporary journey for the older Black Panthers—notably Charlie Bitton, Sa'adia Martziano, and Kokhavi Shemesh—who remained on the political scene even after the dissolution of the movement. In a kind of Black Panther road movie, the film travels across the country in search of other former members. Many members still live in poverty; some continue in the same activist path, while others have found solace in religious mysticism, as in the case of 'Amram Cohen, who relocated to the ancient city of Safad. The spectator comes to reflect on the passage of time—their language, discourses, and faces that no longer correspond to the iconic images of the young Panthers. Providing the narrative's organizational principle, the journey thus metaphorizes the long road travelled since the heydays of Sephardi rebellion.

Eli Hamo and Sami Chetrit's *The Black Panthers (in Israel) Speak*, meanwhile, pays homage to the egalitarian vision of the Black Panthers, elucidating the radicalization of the Mizrahi struggle. The film offers a sociopolitical analysis through interviews with leaders of the movement—Charlie Bitton, Sa'adia Martziano, Kochavi Shemesh, Reuven Abergil, and also including Haim Hanegbi of the leftist Matzpen group.[59] Seeing themselves as the children of earlier protests, and especially of the 1959 Wadi Salib rebellion, they address some of the movement's better-known symbolic actions, such as removing milk bottles from the rich Ashkenazi neighborhood and distributing them to the residents of the Mizrahi working class neighborhood in Jerusalem. For the Ashkenazim, they left a provocative flyer: "We're taking your milk today in order to give it to people in need. We assume this milk was for your cats and dogs." And to the Mizrahim, the milk arrived with the message: "We managed to get milk for you today, but don't get used to it. If you'll join us, we'll do a lot more together." The film also examines the movement's relation to the Palestinian struggle, reminding viewers that the Black Panthers met with the PLO leaders already in 1972 and recognized them as the leaders of the

Palestinian people, in a period when Golda Meir used to say that there was no such thing as the Palestinian people. In line with subsequent Mizrahi leftist movements, which have emphasized the interdependency of Palestinian and Mizrahi issues, the film offers a retrospective prism that simultaneously engages the present. Lamenting the Shas Party's destructive impact on the radical Mizrahi struggle,[60] the film addresses the negative role of diverse Sephardi/Mizrahi establishment-dominated organizations, while offering an ideological analysis of the emergence of anti-racist struggle in Israel.

Past decades have witnessed a multi-dimensional revisionist project of public pedagogy by organizations such as Hila, Kedma, Andalus, and the Alternative Information Center. Documentaries such as Simone Bitton's *Yoredet* and Yochi Dadon-Spigel's *Gifted* focus especially on the role of the centralized educational system, and specifically on the boarding school education track whose purpose was to inject young generation Mizrahim with Euro-Israeli "values." The assimilationist institution of the boarding school separated Mizrahi children from their parents, community, and home culture. Staging a reunion among a few 1978 graduates, *Gifted* presents conflicting perspectives on the experience. While some see boarding school as a steppingstone for success, others, such as activist Tikva Levi, regard it as a "meat grinder," which produces a shocking encounter between impoverished Mizrahim and the children of Jerusalem's elite. The activism of alternative educational organizations such as Hila and Kedma, for Levi, provided an antidote against a racist educational system that provoked shame, self-hatred, and identity crises in Mizrahi pupils. Artists too have participated in this process of curricular critique. Meir Gal's artwork "9 out of 400" challenged the state-determined school curriculum through a photo showing the artist holding the 9 pages devoted to the Jews of Islam from a 400-page book on Jewish History. The textual proportions, hanging literally in the face of the viewer, provide dramatic visual evidence of pedagogical marginalization.

The period since the mid-1990s has witnessed a notable increase in cultural activism. New films and media venues include local cable TV and a channel, Briza, devoted to Mizrahi social concerns and cultural issues.[61] The creation of diverse public spaces for the screening of critical films has in itself further facilitated collective narration and reassessment of Mizrahi struggle and history. Co-curated by Moshe Behar, Tikva Levi, and Osnat Trabelsi, the film series "From a Dark Angle" (2003-4) in the privileged space of the Tel Aviv Cinematheque featured some of the revisionist films discussed earlier, and thus redefined the cinemateque space both in terms of themes and of audience. The screening of *Ringworm Children*, for instance, gathered the survivors of that unfortunate episode, allowing for a cathartic experience and an activist debate that transformed a Cinematheque site seldom frequented by working class Mizrahim.[62] Another key festival, combining films, exhibition, and conference, entitled "Mother Tongue" (2002), highlighted the intricate question of language for Mizrahim, exploring the linguistic discontinuities generated by colonial education in the countries of origin and by the dislocation to Israel. The film festival program, organized by Sigal Morad Eshed, featured films that looked at familial biographies characterized by cultural fragmentation and linguistic discontinuity, between Hebrew and Arabic as well as with other languages, such as French, Farsi, and Ladino. The exhibit, curated by Tal Be Zvi, included visual work by Pinchas Cohen Gan, Meir Gal, Yaacob Ronen Morad, Miriam Cabessa, Dafna Shalom, Adi Nes, Yigal Nizri, Khen Shish, Eli Fatal, Tal Matzliah, and David Adika.

The emerging field of critical Arab-Jewish/Sephardi/Mizrahi writing, meanwhile, challenged the canon of Jewish, Hebrew, and Israel studies. Eschewing Eurocentric frames of reference, intellectuals have anatomized the complexities of the Mizrahi identity and cultural production. To mention just a few key texts, Sami Chetrit's *100 Years of Mizrahi Writing*, a three-volume anthology, redraws the contours of the canon of modern Hebrew literature by calling attention to a wealth of texts written over the past century, Ammiel Alcalay's edited volume *Keys to the Garden: New Israeli Writing*, an assemblage of poems, short stories, novel excerpts, and interviews, also relays a multifaceted spectrum of Israeli writing, while his *After Jews and Arabs: Remaking Levantine Culture* delves into such writings against the backdrop of the wider geographical and historical frame of the Mediterranean. Yerach Gover's *Zionism: The Limits of Moral Discourse in Israeli Hebrew Fiction*, for its part, foregrounds insurgent Hebrew literature by Mizrahi writers; Gil Hochberg's *In Spite of Partition: Jews, Arabs, and the Limits of Separatist Imagination* explores the signifiers "Arab" and "Jew" in contemporary Jewish and Arab literatures. Smadar Lavie's work centers on Mizrahi and Palestinian writers working between Hebrew and Arabic as Third World authors. Zvi Ben-Dor addresses the charged Israeli context for the speaking and teaching of Arabic for Arab-Jews. Ruth Tsoffar analyzes the Mizrahi body through tropes of hunger, eating, and feeding in Mizrahi poetry. Yigal Nizri's introduction and edited volume *Eastern Appearance: A Present that Stirs the Thickets of its Arab Past* probes issues of identity in terms of looks, body, and language. Several scholars have examined the representation of the Mizrahi identity on screen, specifically, Yaron Shemer, whose dissertation explores identity and place in contemporary Mizrahi cinema, and Shoshana Madmoni-Gerber, whose dissertation examines the media rhetoric on the episode of the Kidnapped Yemeni children.[63] No longer invisible, critical scholarship on Arab-Jews/Mizrahim, in general, has come to form a transdisciplinary field that might be termed "Mizrahi studies."

These variegated texts and cultural practices allow elisions and ambivalences to emerge in full force. Against this backdrop, revisionist Mizrahi cinema has interrogated the doxa of official History, posing questions about the "what ifs" and the haunting silences of history. The potency of such work ultimately lies in the poetics of dissonance that facilitate a reading of Arab-Jewish/Mizrahi narratives beyond the boundaries of Israel, accentuating multi-directional regional connectivities. Whether in cinema, literature, or the visual arts, Arab-Jews narrate their memory of their Arab past, reinscribing the hyphen, as it were, between Jews and Arabs, and at times, between the Jew and the Muslim. Political geographies and state borders, in sum, do not always coincide with imaginary geographies, whence the existence of "internal émigrés," nostalgics, and rebels—that is, groups of people who share the same passport but whose relationship to the nation-state is conflictual and ambivalent. Within a situation where the state created the nation, the educational and social apparatus was mobilized to enforce an adherence to narrowly defined notions of Jewishness and Arabness. Yet despite the efforts to transform Middle Eastern/Arab-Jews into Israeli Jews, Mizrahi Israeliness remains complex, ambivalent, and contingent, and now expressed in a new sense of cultural politics.

Translation, Reception, and Traveling Postcolonialism

Israeli Cinema was translated and published in Hebrew in 1991. The oft-noted gap between English and Hebrew as academic languages, at the time, was especially pertinent for a book like this one that assumed and elaborated a theoretical framework that melded the critique of Eurocentric, colonialist, and racist discourses with postmodernist, poststructuralist, and feminist vocabularies and methodologies. The challenge was to translate a discursive apparatus and a critical language that did not exist at the time in Hebrew. Inevitably, the text provoked a sense of defamiliarization with what on the surface was a familiar subject matter for the Hebrew reader. The very terminology also produced a feeling of estrangement. The book addressed the problem of naming for a contested geography ("Israel" and/or "Palestine") and for events ("independence war" or "catastrophe"). Even the deployment of the relatively neutral term "1948 war" created a sense of distance toward the axioms of Israeli scholarship, at least at the time.

Already before the translation into Hebrew, the book's arguments provoked passionate responses within and around Israel. The early attacks on *Israeli Cinema* and on "deviant" intellectuals generally at the time came largely from Euro-Israelis positioned on what was seen in Israel as the left. The book struck a nerve because it questioned the aura of left progressiveness, especially given the liberal-left's historical, cultural, and familial embeddedness in the Establishment. The Israeli Peace Camp generally addressed its criticism only toward that establishment, but not in dialogue with its subalterns. Its narratives often depicted peacenik protagonists besieged by both the Establishment and its subalterns (a depiction analyzed in the last two chapters of *Israeli Cinema*). This reading challenged a taken-for-granted sense of entitlement, including even entitlement to critique the official national his/story. (The politics of representation at the time, in line with this entitlement, were such that panels revolving around the book in presumably progressive spaces did not include Mizrahis and Palestinians). The book generated *ad hominem* attacks from some quarters and passionate defenses from others. Israeli reviewers tried to disqualify my work, suggesting that I could not write knowledgeably since I no longer lived in Israel, or claiming that I would never have been granted a Ph.D. in Israel. (This last charge was probably true at the time, although not for the reasons cited but rather for reasons of discrimination and ideology.)

Engaging with diverse writers on colonial discourse, including with Edward Said's critique of Orientalism, my work examined the politics of representation in Zionist historiographical discourse and Israeli cultural practices. The sometimes-hostile reception of *Israeli Cinema* was partly due, one suspects, to its association with Said's work. For example, Yigal Bursztyn, a liberal-leftist Tel Aviv University professor and filmmaker, contrasted Said and myself, as presumably inauthentic products of the Western academe, with Fanon as an authentic Third Worlder, even though Fanon too was also educated in the Western academe. The review article "The Bad Ashkenazis Are Riding Again," whose title gives off a certain scent of offended narcissism, wrapped its critique in ersatz anti-colonialism. The author compared our supposedly naive admiration for the western "intellectual apparatus" to that of the "miserable nigger, the victim of colonization, who licks his lips in excitement at the gold buttons and colorful glass beads offered by the cunning white merchant."[64] This besmirching of our "authenticity" as "spokespersons for the Third World" appealed, ironically, to the old trope of colonized "mimic men," while projecting the East/West dichotomy onto intellectuals whose biographies and analyses clearly refused that dichotomy.[65]

In the heated debate over the book and in interviews, I insisted on the concept of the "Arab-Jew," as well as on the word "racism" rather the then more prevalent psychologizing "prejudice" or the weakly sociological "discrimination." Subsequently, the alternative newspaper *Hapatish* published a full issue on the question of racism toward Mizrahim. Earlier, in 1988, on the basis of the English manuscript of the book and related articles in Hebrew, Knesset member Haim Hanegbi (the Progressive List Party) had tried to get support withdrawn from the government-subsidized National Theater Habima for staging the stereotypical play, *Sallah*, for the 40th anniversary of the state of Israel. The book was also well received in some critical circles in Israel, especially by Mizrahim and Palestinians. Within Jewish Israel, the book's reception revealed a major schism between Mizrahi activist/intellectual milieu (which also included Ashkenazim) and that of Ashkenazi journalists and academics, and thus exposed the very social fissures that the book itself had probed. *Israeli Cinema* was published in Hebrew by an alternative independent press, *Breirot*, founded by the American-Israeli feminist Barbara Swirski and the Argentinian-Israeli sociologist Shlomo Swirski, among a minority of Euro-Israeli scholar-activists to participate in Mizrahi struggles. The divided responses to *Israeli Cinema* mirrored the ideological contradictions both within Israel itself and within its academic satellites abroad, demonstrating the living gaps of perceptions, experiences, and perspectives between dominant Israel (including academia) and the worlds of the marginalized and the excluded. Not coincidentally, much of the critical work about Israel had to be first published in English (or other languages), whereby it could first find a more sympathetic readership outside of Israel.

Over the years, as more critical perspectives have become common in academic circles, *Israeli Cinema* has been adopted as a textbook and has even been embraced by a new generation of scholars.[66] Yet despite or even because of the impact of the work of critical scholars generally, the process of delegitimization of this kind of critical work continues not only in Israel but also in some quarters in the United States. The enforcing of a very restrictive notion of Zionist correctness often has devastating consequences. In the United States, curating any cultural events devoted to Palestinian issues usually triggers vocal complaints about "balance." (Needless to say, the call for "balance" is almost always unilateral and non-reciprocal; pro-Israeli events are not seen as needing to be "balanced" by a pro-Palestinian presence or standpoint.) At the same time, the I. B. Taurus republication of *Israeli Cinema* encounters a highly modified academic landscape, at least in terms of cracks in the hegemony of official Israeli discourse in the United States, even while the literal landscape of Palestine / Israel has been redesigned for the worse through walls, bulldozing, settlements, and militarization. Yet voices seldom heard earlier are now more audible.[67] In the United States, many intellectuals and scholars have become more vocally critical of Israeli policies. And that is precisely why the academe, and especially the field of "Middle Eastern studies," has been subjected to ideological patrols, supposedly in the name of "diversity of opinion," but really in the name of precluding any *prise de position* critical of Israeli occupation or overly sympathetic to the Palestinians. Meanwhile, 9/11 has had a surprisingly paradoxical effect. On the one hand, it radicalized the militaristic American right, thus enabling an indiscriminate "War on Terror," which has not only destabilized the Middle East but also threatened foundational American institutions and civil liberties. At the same time, 9/11 generated more interest in the Arab/Muslim world, often summed up in the misformulated query "Why Do They Hate Us?," providing "an opening" for Middle Eastern studies and for Middle East scholars in non-Middle Eastern studies departments.

The republication of *Israeli Cinema* in English, two decades after its original publication, meanwhile, comes in the wake of a new engagement, in Hebrew, with Anglophone postcolonial studies. This literature enters Israeli intellectual space at a time when academic discourse is not about colonialism but rather about postcoloniality. While post-Zionist texts have been attacked by the mainstream academia in Israel, the notion of post-Zionism brings with it myriad paradoxes and ironic twists, especially when examined *vis-à-vis* the emergence of multicultural and postcolonial studies in the Anglo-American academy. In contrast to the situation elsewhere, Israeli intellectuals did not engage the key anti-colonialist writings of Césaire, Fanon, and Cabral, which for decades remained untranslated into Hebrew—even at the height of the major debates over anti-colonialism. As a result, the 1990s postcolonial theory that arrived from the Anglo-American academy entered a certain post-Zionist-postcolonial discourse in Israel, where the "colonial" itself had hardly been thought through in any depth.

Postcolonial theory was thus introduced to the Hebrew reader in an out-of-sequence manner, within an intellectual and political vacuum, not only in relation to the large corpus of postcolonial work, but more importantly in relation to anti-colonial history and writings. In Israel, the anti-colonial texts by DuBois, C.L.R. James, Cabral, Césaire, Senghor, Retamar, Dorfman, Rodinson, and perhaps most importantly Fanon, were either only recently translated or never translated into Hebrew. Symptomatically, Albert Memmi's books on Jewish-related questions were translated in the 1960s and 1970s, but not his classic anti-colonialist texts. In his preface to the recent (1999) Hebrew translation of his 1982 book *Racism*, Memmi writes

> We cannot boast of having created morality and simultaneously dominate another people. For this reason I always regretted that no Israeli publisher agreed to publish any of my writing on these issues, and especially the Portrait of the Colonized . . . I am waiting hopefully for [it] also . . . [to] be published in Hebrew. It will mean that the Israeli public will see itself finally as deserving to cope with the difficulties of its national existence.[68]

Memmi's *The Colonizer and the Colonized*, as noted earlier, was published in Hebrew in 2005, around the same time as Fanon's *The Wretched of the Earth* (2006), and subsequent to Fanon's *Black Skin, White Masks* (2003) and Said's *Orientalism* (2000). *The Wretched of the Earth* arrives, in other words, in an anachronistic context, where the postcolonial came *before* the anti-colonial. The relatively late essays by Homi Bhabha came into Hebrew existence not only before Said's seminal *Orientalism*, but also before the work of the very figure referenced by both Said and Bhabha as a significant influence and interlocutor, i.e., Fanon himself. For some Israeli postcolonials who discover and ventriloquize Fanon only via Bhabha, the intellectual "jump" into the "post" gives the impression of a faddish recycling of Anglo-American academic trends without a thoroughgoing engagement of the historical trajectories that shaped those trends.

In the Anglo-American context, as well as that of what used to be called the "Third World," the terrain for both anti-colonialist and post-colonialist discourse had been prepared, on the Left, by a long series of struggles around civil rights, decolonization, Third Worldism, Black Power, and anti-imperialism. In Israel, intellectuals lived these moments in a sharply discrepant manner. With a few exceptions, such as the Matzpen group and the left wing of the Mizrahi Black Panthers, Israeli intellectuals did not engage in the debates about decolonization, Black Power, and Third Worldism. Thus, the arrival of the "postcolonial" in the Anglo-American academy in the late 1980s, unlike its subsequent arrival in Israel, formed part of a clearer and more coherent trajectory. In the United States academe, postcolonial discourse emerged *after* black studies, Latino studies, Native American studies, and Asian-American studies had already challenged the Western canon and in the wake of substantial institutional reforms and corrective measures like affirmative action—themselves the result of various anti-racist and anti-imperialist revolts dating back to the 1960s and 1970s. Yet, just when *The Wretched of the Earth* was stimulating activism on many campuses around the world, Israeli students were living the euphoria of the victory in the '67 war, with little engagement with Palestinian or anti-colonial historical perspectives.

In the Anglo-American academy, postcolonial theory emerged out of the anti-colonialist moment and Third Worldist perspective; that is, at least partly, what makes it "post." Post-Zionist-postcolonial writing in Israel, in contrast, comes out of an academic context often untouched by the history of anti-colonialist debates. Thus we find a "post" without its past. In the Third World, anti-colonial nationalism gave way to some "course corrections" and a measure of disillusionment, partially due to the return of neo-colonialism and due to the abuses taking place in the name of the Revolution. This disillusionment with the aftermath of decolonization, which provides the affective backdrop for postcolonial theory, had no equivalent in the Israeli context. Outside of Israel, the question of exactly when the "post" in the "post-colonial" begins already provoked a debate in English.[69] But in Israel, it was not anti-Zionist discourse that gave way to post-Zionist discourse, but rather Zionist discourse that gave way to post-Zionist discourse. To argue for moving beyond "the colonial," as suggested by postcolonial theory, within a nation-state and within an academic space hardly touched, historically, by the Third-Worldist perspective requires that we ask the question of the (anti)colonial with even more vigor.

As the cultural field became more adaptive to poststructuralist currents, even the Hebrew lexicon changed. The English subtitle of my book, "East/West and the Politics of Representation," which in the early 1990s could only be rendered as "History and Ideology," could now be translated with a phrase like "the politics of representation," a phrase no longer seen as indigestible or strange to Hebrew ears. In Israel, the kind of arguments that made *Israeli Cinema* controversial were subsequently absorbed into critical discourses and have become a taken-for-granted presence within the critical intellectual field. Courses and panels now discuss Israeli and Palestinian cinema and culture within what were once taboo paradigms.

When *Israeli Cinema* first appeared in Hebrew, film, media, and cultural studies were hardly recognized as legitimate fields of inquiry within academic spaces in Israel. Much of the academic work on Zionism and Israel as well as in Jewish studies at the time did not reference or dialogue with the critiques of Orientalism and colonial discourse. Despite the limitations discussed earlier, dramatic changes in the discursive environment have occurred since then. The recent republication of *Israeli Cinema* in Hebrew and the current English republication must be seen in relation to newly translated work in the fields of multicultural studies and postcolonial theory. The republication places the book in a new light, both in relation to the book's initial reception and in relation to the newly translated theoretical literature into Hebrew. A new generation of scholars in such diverse fields as anthropology, history, sociology, literary criticism, and media studies, moreover, has further elaborated on the arguments and analytical frameworks outlined in earlier work.

The last decade, more specifically, has witnessed a substantial modification in the realm of film, literary, and cultural studies scholarship concerned with Israel. Research on Israeli cinema/media had become a vital field of study characterized by a deeper investigation of the relation between film/media cultural practices and national identity (including work by Yehuda Ne'eman, Nurit Gertz, Moshe Zimmerman, Haim Bresheeth, Eli Avraham, Orly Lubin, Yosefa Lushitzky, Nitzan Ben Shaul, Livia Alexander, George Khleifi, Raz Yosef, Yaron Shemer, Dorit Naaman, Tasha Oren, Ariel Schweitzer, and Shoshana Madmoni-Gerber). On the whole, the collaborative effort to fight for the institutional recognition of cinema as a legitimate art form, as well as for cinema studies as a legitimate academic field, has made considerable strides. The scholarly work on cinema has contributed to the shaping of a new understanding that cuts through the literary-elite prejudices toward the cinema and toward media scholarship. The emergence of cinema/media/cultural studies in Israel has been accompanied by the questioning of the false dichotomies of "high" versus "low" arts, which has calibrated prestige, controlling access to the "heights" of Israeli/Hebrew culture.[70]

Israeli and Palestinian cinemas, meanwhile, have also become a much more visible presence on the world stage. A Palestinian-made film, *Paradise Now*, was nominated for the Best Foreign Language Film Award at the 78th Annual Academy Awards in 2006, while Israeli/Palestinian films have been exhibited in major U.S. commercial venues, and the number of festivals focusing on Israeli, Palestinian, Arab, or Middle Eastern cinemas has mushroomed. Israeli and Palestinian films are screened at popular venues such as The San Francisco Film Festival, the Los Angeles Film Festival, The New York Film Festival, and the Tribeca Film Festival, not to mention in ongoing activist cultural events such as those promoted by Alwan, ArteEast, Human Rights Watch Film festival, Women Make Movies, and The Other Israel Film Festival in New York. Hardly limited to U.S. cities, this enthusiastic reception occurred in cities throughout the world; and critical films by Israeli and Palestinian-from-Israel filmmakers, despite the normalization anxiety, have sometimes been screened at Arab festivals, such as Carthage. But more importantly, the kind of films discussed here have forged a vital polyphonic space for representation and debate that one could only have hoped for in 1986, when the manuscript was completed.

Today, both the critique of Orientalism and the dialogue with postcolonial studies have come to inform writings (in diverse languages) on Zionist discourse and Israeli culture. Scholarly writings about Israel (including my *Israeli Cinema* and *Forbidden Reminiscences*) have been translated into Arabic. Israel and the work of Israeli scholars have come to form a legitimate object of critical study for Arab writers. Meanwhile, a new interest in cultural studies has emerged in Middle Eastern studies in general. Scholars are now pursuing issues having to do with cultural politics, within which the cinema is seen as a multifaceted phenomenon shaped by diverse formations, such as the state apparatus, cultural codes, colonial, national and religious ideologies, and transnational flows of images and sounds. The study of Israel, Palestine, and the Middle East within the framework of cultural studies has been gaining momentum in diverse locations.[71] In this sense, the cultural studies approach and the intersecting fields of inquiry informing *Israeli Cinema: East/West and the Politics of Representation* have found a more receptive intellectual place today than when originally published.

Notes

Transliterations from the Hebrew and Arabic do not necessarily correspond to academic associations' norms, rather often replicating common journalistic uses especially with regards to names of organizations or terms for policies. Similarly, transliterations of authors and filmmakers' names as well as of films and books' titles follow the transliterations of publishing houses and distribution companies.

(Publications in Hebrew and Arabic are indicated by asterisks.)

Introduction

1. See Edward Said, *Orientalism.*
2. My definition here draws on Albert Memmi's definition of racism in his *Dominated Man*, p. 156.
3. See Tzvetan Todorov, *The Conquest of America.*
4. See Robert Stam and Louise Spence, "Colonialism, Racism, and Representation," *Screen* 24:2 (March–April 1983): 2–20.
5. See Walter Benjamin, *Understanding Brecht.*
6. See Christian Metz, *Langage et cinéma*, pp. 160–165.
7. See Jacques Derrida, "Edmond Jabès and the Question of the Book," in *Writing and Difference*, pp. 64–78. See also Georges Steiner, "Our Homeland, the Text," *Salmagundi* 66 (Winter–Spring 1985): 4–25.
8. See Fredric Jameson, *The Political Unconscious.*
9. See Lucien Goldmann, *Essays on Method in the Sociology of Literature.*
10. See Fredric Jameson, "Third World Literature in the Era of Multinational Capitalism," *Social Text* 15 (Fall 1986): 65–88. See also the critique of the Jameson article by Aijaz Ahmad, "Jameson's Rhetoric of Otherness and the National Allegory," *Social Text* 17 (Fall 1987):3–25.
11. Ismail Xavier, "Allegories of Underdevelopment: From the 'Aesthetics of Hunger' to the 'Aesthetics of Garbage'" (Ph.D. dissertation, New York University, 1982).
12. Ora Gloria Jacob-Arzooni, *The Israeli Film: Social and Cultural Influences, 1912–1973*, p. 22.
13. Ibid., pp. 23, 25.
14. *Yehuda Har'el, "Thirty Years of the Israeli Film," in *Cinema from Its Beginning to the Present* (Tel Aviv: Yavne, 1956), pp. 229–230.
15. *Nathan Gross, "The Israeli Film, 1905–1948," *Kolnoa* 1 (1974): 93–103; *idem, "The Second Five Years of Israeli Cinema, 1953–1958," *Kolnoa* 5 (April–May 1975): 61–74. *Arye Agmon, "The Zionist Cinema and the Israeli Film," *Musag* 11 (1976). * Renen Schorr, "Israeli Cinema—Israeli History," *Skira Hodshit*, May 1984.

1. Beginnings in the Yishuv: Promised Land and Civilizing Mission

1. Talila Ben Zakai, "When *Rachel* was pornography," *Maariv*, 2 June 1978.
2. The material concerning Axelrod's work is based on my interviews with the filmmaker, May–June 1986.
3. *Amram Klein, "The First Silent Picture-Show," *Kolnoa* 5 (April–May 1975 [Israeli Film Institute, Tel Aviv]): 75; my translation. Subsequent translations from Hebrew sources are mine unless otherwise indicated.
4. *Avigdor Hameiri, "Chaplin the Artist," *HaAretz*, 1 February 1927.
5. *Klein, "The First Silent Picture-Show," p. 76.
6. *Avraham Adar, "Theaters, Bands, Actors, and Directors," in *The First Twenty Years*, ed. A. B. Yoffe, pp. 51–52.
7. *Klein, "The First Silent Picture-Show," p. 78.
8. *Yehoash Hirschberg, "Music in Little Tel Aviv," in *The First Twenty Years*, ed. Yoffe, p. 110.
9. Rosenberg's film is available at the Rad Archive in Jerusalem. Weiss' film was sent to a laboratory abroad by the Jewish National Fund, but was lost during World War I.
10. *Renen Schorr, "And Axelrod Was There," *BaMahane*, no. 24 (May 1985).
11. *Ibid., p. 23.
12. For a detailed article on Ben-Dov, see *Menahem Levin, "Ya'acov Ben-Dov and the Beginning of the Jewish Silent Film Industry in Eretz Israel, 1921–1924," *Kathedra* 38 (December 1985): 127–135.
13. *Ya'acov Davidon, *Fated Love*, p. 227. According to Davidon, the filmmaker of *The Life of the Jews in Eretz Israel* remained anonymous probably because it was assigned to a foreign cameraperson who came to Palestine specifically to make the film and subsequently returned home. From Davidon's accounts, however, we may conclude that *The Life of the Jews in Eretz Israel* which he saw in Russia is in fact Moshe Rosenberg's *The First Film of Palestine, 1911*.
14. *L. Be'eri, "In Palestine No One Faints," *At*, May 1978: 56.
15. *Davidon, *Fated Love*, pp. 214–215.
16. Interview with Nathan Axelrod, 20 June 1986.
17. Quoted by David Geffen, "Palestine on Film," *Jerusalem Post*, 4 July 1983.
18. *Schorr, "And Axelrod Was There," p. 24.
19. *Nathan Gross, "The Second Five Years of Israeli Cinema," *Kolnoa* (April–May 1975): 69.
20. *Adar, "Theaters, Bands, Actors, and Directors," p. 96.
21. Interview with Axelrod, 20 June 1986.
22. *Nathan Gross, "In the Time of Nathan," *Hotam*, 17 April 1981, p. 14.
23. *Hayeem Halachmi, "Memories of Hayeem Halachmi," *HaAretz*, 10 January 1964.
24. *Quoted by L. Be'eri, "The First Star," *LaIsha* 1218 (August 10, 1978): 23.
25. *Amos Elon, *The Israelis*, p. 171.
26. See *Tamar Gozansky, *Formation of Capitalism in Palestine*.
27. See *Yossef Meir, *The Zionist Movement and the Jews of Yemen*; *Niza Droyan, *And Not with a Magic Carpet*; *idem, *The Pioneers of Aliya from Yemen* (Jerusalem: Zalman Shazar Center, 1982).

28. Karl Marx, *Surveys from Exile*, ed. David Fernbach (London: Pelican Books, 1973), p. 320.
29. See *Aharon David Gordon, *The Nation and Work*.
30. *Tzvi Lieberman, *Oded the Wanderer* (Tel Aviv: Yehoshua Chechik, 1930), p. 50.
31. Quoted in Said, *Orientalism*, p. 306.
32. *Lieberman, *Oded the Wanderer*, p. 38.
33. *Ibid., p. 68.
34. *Seber Flotzker, "The Career of *Sabra*," *Kolnoa* 2 (Summer 1974): 72.
35. *Ibid.
36. *Ibid., p. 73.
37. *Ibid.
38. *Be'eri, "In Palestine No One Faints," p. 91.
39. *Flotzker, "The Career of *Sabra*," p. 73.
40. After Alexander Ford was dismissed in 1963 on political and anti-Semitic grounds, he emigrated to Israel. Later he left the country and lived abroad, remaining somewhat connected to Israel, where he directed an Israeli-German co-production, *The Life of Yanush Korchuk*, in 1973.
41. *See Amnon Rubinstein, *To Be Free People*, p. 103.
42. See *Dov Ber Borochov, *Class Struggle and the Jewish Nation*.
43. See Maxime Rodinson, *Israel: A Colonial-Settler State?*
44. The Sheik was played by Pesakh Bar-Adon, the other Arab character by R. Davidov.
45. Karl Wittfogel, *Oriental Despotism: A Comparative Study of Total Powers* (New Haven: Yale, 1957).
46. Rodinson, *Israel: A Colonial-Settler State*, p. 81.
47. Ibid., pp. 81–82.
48. Female participants in the Palmach (Hebrew initials for "Strike Forces," the most mythified military organization before the establishment of the state, closely linked to the Labor kibbutzim) and in the Israeli Defense Forces were familiar with arms.
49. Quoted by Said, *Orientalism*, p. 106.
50. This view ignores the possibility of corrupt pro-Zionist Arab leaders such as King Feisal. In his agreement with Chaim Weizmann, Feisal was ready to give virtually all of Palestine to the Zionists in return for Jewish diplomatic, financial, and technical support for the future great Arab state that he would lead, thus sacrificing the part to the whole, in line with traditional dynastic policy. But he never received support from the Arab masses for such demands, and was obliged to follow the majority of the people.
51. *Sabra*'s director, Alexander Ford, it has to be pointed out, did not speak Hebrew.
52. *Ya'acov Rabi, "Herzliya Gymnasium as a Cultural Center of Young Tel Aviv," in *The First Twenty Years*, ed. Yoffe, p. 241.
53. Eric A. Goldman, *Visions, Images, and Dreams: Yiddish Film Past and Present*, p. 61.
54. *Hirschberg, "Music in Little Tel Aviv," p. 110.
55. *Avraham Matalon, *The Hebrew Pronunciation in Its Struggle*, pp. 157–158.
56. *Ze'ev Vladimir Jabotinsy, *The Hebrew Accent*, pp. 4–9.
57. *Arye Elias, "A Drop of Bitter Taste at the Mouth," *Apirion* 2 (Winter 1983/1984): 59.
58. See Pierre Bourdieu, *Distinction: A Social Critique of the Judgment of Taste*.

59. *Elias, "A Drop of Bitter Taste at the Mouth," p. 59.
60. The refusal is ironic on other levels as well; first, because Shakespearean language in English is characterized by heteroglossia and muliplicity of class, ethnic, and regional accents; second, because Shakespeare is played in a variety of forms of English—British, American, Irish; third, because the imposition of prejudicial intra-Hebrew hierarchies reflects little understanding of the dynamics of Shakespearean language which carnivalizes such categories.
61. Such binary opposition between East and West, as Edward Said suggests in *Orientalism*, formed part of a general current within nineteenth-century ideology concerning the biological bases of racial inequality. Thus the racial classifications found in Cuvier's *Le Règne animal*, Gobineau's *Essai sur l'inégalité des races humaines*, and Robert Knox's *The Races of Man* were absorbed into Orientalism.
62. It is for this very reason that extremist religious Jews have rejected Zionism; the Return, in their tradition, meant waiting for the Messiah. Thus, they rejected the secular, mundane use of a "divine language delivered by God," reserving it for the Millennium, and preserving its ancient Biblical forms exclusively for sacred activities.

2. Post-1948: The Heroic-Nationalist Genre

1. Nathan Axelrod's *On the Ruins* (*Me'al haHoravot*, 1936) and Herbert Kline's *My Father's House* (*Beit Avi*, 1947) were among the few narratives produced before the establishment of the state.
2. Originally Peter Frey was assigned to direct the film, but he was replaced, due to disagreements with the producers, by Dickinson. Based on a court decision Frey was credited as one of the producers.
3. See Sabri Jiryis, *The Arabs in Israel*.
4. In *Sword in the Desert*, the Jewish lovers' kiss that concludes the film still suggests the Western link through a background image of a church accompanied with choir-style music and church bells.
5. *Ze'ev Vardi, *Who Runs in the Lanes* (Tel Aviv: M. Mizrahi Publishers, 1974), p. 110; *Sarig On, *Danideen in the Hijacked Airplane* (Tel Aviv: M. Mizrahi Publishers, 1972), p. 59.
6. Maxime Rodinson, *The Arabs*, p. 99.
7. A filmic treatment of the Egyptian anti-colonialism which occasionally engendered sympathy for the Axis during World War II is Youssef Chahine's *Alexandria Why?* (*Iskandariya Leh?*, 1979). A reflexive film about an aspiring Egyptian filmmaker who entertains Hollywood dreams, *Alexandria Why?* offers an Egyptian perspective on Western political conflicts and cultural products. A subplot involves a decadent Egyptian aristocrat murdering British soldiers (the film emphasizes their oppression as lower class) as a contribution to the anti-colonial effort, as well as the petit-bourgeois officers (an allusion to the Free Officer Movement that led the 1952 revolution) who entertain themselves with the idea of murdering King Farouk (who advanced British interests in Egypt) and attempt to contact the Germans; all soon form part of the parodic juxtapositions of an Egyptian theater play, documentary footage, and staged material. In the theatrical sketch, for example, each European colonial power is reduced to a stereotypical cultural emblem: Hitler's moustache, Churchill's cigar, a French chef, an Italian pizza. In a reversal

of traditional representation, it is now the Third World colonized who caricature the colonizer. As representatives of the Allied and the Axis powers chaotically pursue each other across the stage (as well as across the space of mixed documentary and staged material), all mumbling their own idioms, the Egyptian characters remain seated, spectators of an alien imperialist war on their own land. Irrationality, a feature insistently projected by the West onto Arabs and their language, here boomerangs against the Europeans. The Egyptians hold quietly a sign in Arabic: "From here no one passes"—an evocation of the Egyptian anti-colonialist slogan: "Egypt for the Egyptians"—which is completely disregarded by the rapidly changing ethnocentric European colonizers, whether Allies or Axis. The autobiographical film about the forties ends by mocking the power that substituted European colonial power after World War II, the United States, seen from a seventies perspective. Upon arriving in the national home of musicals, the protagonist encounters the Statue of Liberty transformed into a vulgar prostitute toothlessly laughing.

Another subplot of *Alexandria Why?* treats Egyptian Jews, portraying them in a completely positive light, as connected to the Socialists fighting for an equal and just Egyptian society, forced to evacuate Egypt fearing the Nazis' arrival, and thus immigrating to Palestine/Israel. Here the film performs an interesting point-of-view structuring whereby the Egyptian Jew views the clashes between Israelis and Palestinians together with Arabs from the Arab point of view; realizing that the rights of one people are obtained at the expense of another people, he returns to Egypt. The film, thus, emphasizes its dichotomy between Arab Jews and European Jews, finally reinforced at the end of the film through the protagonist's arrival in the United States and his encounter with Ashkenazi religious Jews, Hassidim, implicitly suggesting the distance between his Jewish-Egyptian friends (with whom he shares a similar culture) and European Jews. Such a representation, however, is quite uncommon within Arab fiction, and the film was banned by several Arab countries, even though it was approved by Palestinian organizations.

8. *Yehoshafat Harkabi, "The Israeli-Arab Conflict in High-School," in *The Israeli-Arab Conflict and Its Meaning within Education*, ed. Yitzhak Ben-Yossef (Tel Aviv: Center for Teachers Federation and Pedagogic Council, 1970), p. 14.

9. See *Shmuel Moreh, "The Image of Israeli in Arab Literature since the Establishment of the State," in *The Arab-Israeli Conflict Reflected by Arab Literature* (Jerusalem: Lecture Publications by Van Lear Institute, no. 12); *Shimon Ballas, *Arab Literature under the Shadow of War.*

10. Ballas, *Arab Literature*, pp. 27–28.

11. *Moreh, "The Image of Israeli," p. 29.

12. See *Adir Cohen, *An Ugly Face in the Mirror;* Fouzi el-Asmar, *Through the Hebrew Looking-Glass.*

13. *See also Rubinstein, *To Be Free People*, p. 105.

14. The schizophrenia of being Arab-Jews in Israel took humorous form throughout the shootings of *Hill 24 Doesn't Answer.* In the sequence of Jewish evacuation of the old city of Jerusalem, a Sephardi extra, forgetting his role as a Jordanian soldier, ran to kiss Seffer haTorah (a traditional ritual to kiss a big Torah book when carried in public). The entire scene employing some six hundred extras had to be shot over again (*Variety*, 2 November 1955).

15. Edward W. Said, *The Question of Palestine*, pp. 60–68.
16. For a collection of negative images of Arabs in American popular culture, see Laurence Michalak, "Cruel and Unusual," *ADC Issues* 19 (January 1984). See also Jack Shaheen, *The TV Arab*.
17. Vincent Canby, "Terror over the Super Bowl," *New York Times*, 1 April 1977.
18. Leon Uris, *The Haj* (Garden City, N.Y.: Doubleday and Company, 1984), pp. 545–546.
19. *Rubinstein, *To Be Free People*, p. 127.
20. *Emile Habiby, *alWaqae' alGhareeba fi Ikhtifa'a Sa'eed Abi alNakhs alMutasha'il* (Haifa: Manshurat Arabesque Matba'at alItihad, 1974).
21. For a broader discussion see Otave Manoni, *Prospero and Caliban: The Psychology of Colonialism* (New York: Praeger, 1956), an analysis refuted by Frantz Fanon, *Black Skin, White Masks*, leading ultimately to an anti-colonialist version of *The Tempest* (*Une Tempête*) by Aimé Césaire (Paris: Seuil, 1969).
22. *Eliezer Smoli, *The Sons of the First Rain* (Tel Aviv: Sifriyat Tevat Noah, n.d.), p. 172.
23. Said, *Orientalism*, p. 307.
24. For further discussion on the subject see Tom Engelhardt, "Ambush at Kamikaze Pass," *Bulletin of Concerned Asian Scholars* 3:1 (Winter–Spring 1971); and Robert Stam and Louise Spence, "Colonialism, Racism, and Representation," *Screen* 24:2 (March–April 1983): 2–20.
25. *Gershon Shaked, *No Other Place*, p. 72.
26. See *A. N. Polak, "The Origins of Palestinian Arabs," *Molad* (November 1967): 298.
27. *Elon, *The Israelis*, p. 168.
28. Said, *The Question of Palestine*, p. 62.
29. *Elon, *The Israelis*, p. 168.
30. Said, *Orientalism*, p. 177.
31. See *Shlomo Swirski, *Campus, Society and State*.
32. * "Did the Shooting of *Is Tel Aviv Burning?* Begin?" *Davar*, 17 August 1967.
33. *Emanuel Bar-Kadma, "Assaf Requires a Governmental Investigation Committee," *Yedioth Ahronoth*, 21 January 1968.
34. New items in *South African Jewish Times* (Johannesburg), 15 September 1967.
35. For discussion of language-power relationships, see Ella Shohat and Robert Stam, "The Cinema after Babel: Language, Difference, Power," *Screen* 26:3 (May–August 1985): 35–58.
36. Such phenomena have been taking place even in Hollywood's more progressive, liberal films as in Costa Gavras' *Hanna K.* For a discussion of linguistic colonialism in *Hanna K.*, see Richard Porton and Ella Shohat, "The Trouble with Hanna," *Film Quarterly* 38:2 (Winter 1984–1985): 54.

3. The Representation of Sephardim/Mizrahim

1. For a critical discussion of Israel's hegemonic discourse concerning Sephardim, see Ella Shohat, "Sephardim in Israel," *Social Text* 19–20 (Fall 1988).
2. See Anouar Abdel-Malek, *La Pensée politique arabe contemporaine*.

3. *Arye Gelblum, *HaAretz*, 22 April 1949.
4. *David Ben-Gurion, *Eternal Israel* (Tel Aviv: Ayanot, 1964), p. 34.
5. Quoted in Sammy Smooha, *Israel: Pluralism and Conflict*, p. 88.
6. Abba Eban, *Voice of Israel* (New York: 1957), as quoted in Smooha, *Israel*, pp. 76, 88.
7. Quoted in Smooha, *Israel*, pp. 88–89.
8. Quoted in Tom Segev, *1949: The First Israelis*, pp. 156–157.
9. *Amnon Dankner, "I have No Sister," *HaAretz*, 18 February 1983.
10. Quoted in David K. Shipler, *Arab and Jew* (New York: Times Books, 1986), p. 241.
11. Dr. Dvora and Rabbi Menachem Hacohen, *One People: The Story of the Eastern Jews*, introduction by Abba Eban, pp. 6–9.
12. See Shmuel N. Eisenstadt, *The Absorption of Immigrants* (London: Routledge and Kegan Paul, 1954); idem, *Modernization: Protest and Change* (Englewood Cliffs, N.J.: Prentice Hall, 1966).
13. *See Shlomo Swirski, *Orientals and Ashkenazim in Israel*, pp. 53–54.
14. Shlomo Swirski, "Oriental Jews in Israel," *Dissent* 31:1 (Winter 1984): 84.
15. *Shaul Shiran, Interview with Boaz Davidson, *Kolnoa* 15–16 (Fall–Winter 1978): 23.
16. Seven films were made in the series, which describes the sexual adventures of three adolescents (Yiftah Katzur, Jonathan Segal, and Tzahi Noi) during the late fifties. The films, a kind of Israeli version of *American Graffiti*, use the same male actors but employ different women characters/actresses, as the fetishized objects, for each film. *Lemon Popsicle* (*Eskimo Limon*, 1978) was the title of the first film in the series.
17. Avraham Hefner is considered to be one of the early personal filmmakers, but filmmaker and film critic *Nissim Dayan ("Second Step in the Journey of the Vanguard," *Kolnoa* 14 [Summer 1977]) defined *Aunt Klara* as a "gefilte-fish" film as well.
18. Davidson's first film, *Snail* (*Shablul*, 1970), was well received and regarded by critics as the work of a filmmaker with potential. Davidson's move to direct "bourekas" films was, therefore, regarded as a "profit-oriented" move.
19. Shiran, Interview with Davidson, p. 23.
20. In 1960 there was laid the basis for the tax-return policy of the Ministry of Commerce and Industry. The tax return—a retroactive governmental subsidy—for each bought ticket began at a rate of 30 percent, and a large amount of the tax return was given as an advance allowance with a low interest on the eve of shooting.
21. *Nissim Dayan, "From Bourekas to the Ghetto Culture," *Kolnoa* 11 (Fall 1976): 54.
22. *Ibid.
23. Distributed abroad as *Kazablan*. I prefer the transliteration *Casablan* in order to keep the allusion to Casablanca, the protagonist's Moroccan city of origin.
24. *Yael Okansky, "Israeli Cinema Is Not a Cinema of Creators: A Conversation with Eli Tavor," *Kolnoa* 6/7 (Summer 1975): 58.
25. *Yael Okansky, "I Am Tired of Making Films for Film Critics: An Interview with Boaz Davidson," *Kolnoa* 6/7 (Summer 1975): 55.
26. *Nahum Menahem, *Ethnic Tensions and Discrimination in Israel*, pp. 61–62.
27. Revah's films, such as *Today Only* and *Papa Leon* (1982), show a different image of the Sephardi father than *Sallah Shabbati* or *Fortuna*. The "patriarchal" father, is, in many

ways, powerless against his children. He is also loving and warm, despite his hardships. A similar situation is shown in Fred Steinhardt's *Salomonico* with its hard-working Sephardi protagonists.

28. See *Yehuda Ne'eman, "Zero Degree in Cinema," *Kolnoa* 5 (September 1979): 23.

29. See Swirski, "Oriental Jews in Israel."

30. Based on data from the Ministry of Commerce and Industry.

31. Yaron London, Israeli Television Interview with Chaim Topol and Ephraim Kishon, broadcast on Israeli Independence Day, 1983.

32. *News item in various dailies on 13 April 1966.

33. *News item, *HaAretz*, 9 June 1966.

34. *Y. H. Biltzki, "Another Opinion on *Sallah Shabbati*," *Al haMishmar*, 30 July 1964.

35. *Nehama Ganoth, "The People Chose—an Elite Film," *Al haMishmar*, 1964. See *Sallah Shabbati* file in Jerusalem Film Archives.

36. *Ibid. "Back when we came" is a typical sentence once heard in Israel from veterans in bureaucratic and managing positions as well as from politicians proudly recalling their hard work and great deeds, such as drying the swamps and working in forestation; it is used by the bureaucrat in *Sallah Shabbati* as well. Such phrases often had the role of justifying the speakers' high status in the present.

37. *Ganoth, "The People Chose."

38. *Jerusalem Post*, 5 June 1964. See *Sallah Shabbati* file in Jerusalem Film Archives.

39. *Biltzki, "Another Opinion on *Sallah Shabbati*."

40. *Ibid.

41. The first film version, produced and directed by Golan in 1969, was called *Tevye the Milkman* (*Tuvya haKholev*), with Shmuel Rodenski in the lead.

42. Advertisement quoting Juditii Crist (*Herald Tribune*): "More than a touch of Tevye and the delightful score echoes *Fiddler on the Roof*."

43. *Yossef Sharik, "The Hero Who Matured," *HaAretz*, 5 November 1970.

44. Leslie Fiedler, in *To the Gentiles*, interestingly refers to Sallah's character as a "kind of Oriental Jewish Old Black Joe."

45. The term "Working Eretz Israel" refers basically to the Zionist and Socialist world view largely under the auspices of the Labor Party—an ideology of a powerful milieu that dictated the values and patterns of behavior of the "Israeli." These different parties, as discussed in Chapter 1, regarded "Hebrew work" as a necessary condition of the realization of the return to Zion; work as a moral obligation of the new Jews in Zion—unlike their ghetto ancestors.

46. *Sharik, "The Hero Who Matured."

47. Oriental immigrants played an important role in the large-scale projects for the development of the agricultural infrastructure initiated by the government in order to relieve rampant unemployment throughout the fifties. The projects included drainage works, soil improvement, and forestation. The Orientals provided most of the necessary wage labor. In forestation, for example, they constituted 75 percent of all workers. In agricultural areas, as well as in others, wages were very low, and in many cases the workers were given, as Swirski shows in "Oriental Jews in Israel," unemployment compensation rather than regular salaries.

48. *An interview with Topol, *Davar*, 5 June 1964.

49. This notion was so widespread that it reverberated through a children's rhyme— "LeMa'an hamoledet/asara banim laledet/ulekabel begaon/et pras Ben-Gurion" ("For the country/to give birth to ten children/and to proudly receive/Ben-Gurion's prize").

50. In some communities such as Iraq, the dowry is not simply a matter of gender roles, but more flexible, depending on the economic situation of the bride and groom; it is paid sometimes by the bride's family and sometimes by the groom's.

51. It should be noted that many Third World films have struggled to destroy these myths. For example, in the Senegalese film by Osmane Sembene, *La Noire de...* (1966), we see the Senegalese maid working in the kitchen, while through her we hear salon conversation between the French about her laziness and the laziness of all Blacks.

52. *Such prejudices are still expressed officially. For example, the former Chief of Staff, Mordechai Gur, said that it would take years before Orientals could be entrusted with top military posts, because given their "special" (i.e., backward) mentality, they would not know how to operate a sophisticated Western organizational and technological machine (*Al haMishmar*, 10 May 1978).

53. *Swirski, *Orientals and Ashkenazim in Israel*, p. 54.

54. *Ibid., p. 54.

55. These distinctions are strongly emphasized in *Sami Michael's novel *All Men are Equal-But Some are More*—whose title echoes another satire on oppressive pseudo-Socialism, Orwell's *Animal Farm*—where Michael underlines the contrasting treatment given to Ashkenazi *olim* versus Sephardim. The latter, for example, although dressed in suits, are sprayed with DDT as if they needed decontamination, unlike the Europeans. While the small group of Ashkenazim are transferred out of the *ma'abara*, the Sephardim remain there.

56. *Davar* is a Histadrut mouthpiece traditionally reflecting a Labor viewpoint; prior to the defeat of the Labor Party in 1977, it also expressed the government viewpoint on most issues.

57. *Ze'ev Rav-Nof, "Bona Fortuna—Mazal Tov!" *Davar*, 14 September 1966.

58. *Immanuel Bar-Kadma, "The Sold Bride from Dimona," *Yedioth Ahronoth*, n.d. See *Fortuna* file in Jerusalem Film Archive.

59. *Mibad el Bad," broadcast in "Shidurei Israel," 11 September 1966.

60. *Broadcast in Galei Tzahal, transcription from the radio in *Fortuna* file in Jerusalem Film Archives, n.d.

61. *Alex, "Beautiful Fortuna," *LaMathil*, 20 September 1966.

62. *Meshulam Ad, "We Are Called Fortuna," *Davar*, 25 November 1966.

63. *News item, "Objecting to the Screening of *Fortuna*," *BaMa'aracha*, 8 July 1966.

64. *Ibid.

65. The Israeli army has been referred to in official discourse as a "melting pot" for different ethnic communities; the army is also seen as having the role of educating for "Zionist-democratic values" in a new society.

66. *Fortuna*, with its relatively daring shots, as in the Ein Gedi sequence, gained a good deal of publicity for sensationalism. No Israeli film before had shown so much nudity.

67. The North African character Margo, played by Gila Almagor, appears in several of Golan's films from the sixties: *Eldorado* (1963), *Fortuna* (1966); in *My Margo* (1969) the leading role was played by Levana Finkelstein.

68. A more recent film, Rephael Revivo's *A Forced Testimony* (*Edut meOnes*, 1983), produced by Golan-Globus, features two rapes of Ashkenazi women by tough Sephardi men, although ethnicity is only an implicit issue in this "realistic film."

69. Interestingly, Pierre Brasseur, who plays the role of Fortuna's father, also played in Clair's films. On the subject of French colonial fantasies about Algerian women, see Malek Alloula, *The Colonial Harem.*

70. *For a discussion of images of Sephardim in Hebrew short stories, see Lev Hakak, *Inferiors and Superiors.*

71. The juxtaposition of "Sephardic" and "orthodoxy," as the Algerian-French-Jewish philosopher Shmuel Trigano points out, is somewhat oxymoronic. (See *Apirion* 2 [Winter 1983–1984]: 30–31.)

72. For more in-depth interest in the subject, see *Shlomo Swirski and Menahem Shoshan, *Development Towns toward a Different Tomorrow.*

73. *Maariv*, 14 September 1966, quoted in Hakak, *Inferiors and Superiors*, p. 16.

74. During the late fifties and mid-sixties, in the wake of the 1956 "Suez" war, which allied Great Britain, France, and Israel against Egypt, there appeared a noticeable pro-French attitude in Israel, reflected not only in popular music (previously a Russian domain) but also in a number of Franco-Israeli coproductions.

75. As Swirski points out in "Oriental Jews in Israel," there is a clear pattern of ethnic segregation in the large towns and cities: Ashkenazim live mainly in the northern and "better" neighborhoods, while Orientals are mainly concentrated in the southern ones.

76. *Bar-Kadma, "The Sold Bride from Dimona."

77. Not unlike *Zorba, the Greek* (1964), which was successfully distributed in Israel, *Fortuna* features, along with the Sirtaki, a village idiot.

78. For an in-depth examination of the subject, see *Gabriel Ben-Simhon, "Theatrical Elements in the Daily Life of the North African Jewish Community," in *The Legacy of Jews of Spain and the Orient.*

79. Youssef Chahine's *Alexandria Why?* (1979) offers a parallel representation of Egyptian culture, especially through a diversity of languages spoken within a cosmopolitan atmosphere. Both films, which were produced in the seventies about the forties, are autobiographical, depicting growing up in the Middle East against the background of national struggles against colonialism.

80. Sephardi poetry is deeply embedded in Arabic poetry.

81. Quoted in *Nurit Gertz, "Mizrahi Returns to the East," *Yedioth Ahronoth*, n.d. Jerusalem Film Archive.

82. "State on the Way," the retroactive historiographic Zionist naming of the period before the establishment of the state, in which Jewish organizations were functioning, in many ways, like a state.

83. Casting in Haim Shiran's *Pillar of Salt*, meanwhile, suggests an ironic historical parallel, since Ashkenazi actors are cast in the roles of French colonizers and Sephardi in the roles of Tunisian Jews and Arabs.

84. *Azriel Kaufmann, "Cinema of the Street: An Interview with Nissim Dayan," *Kolnoa* 74 (March 1974): 71.

85. *Ibid.

86. The anger expressed toward the Histadrut implicitly has to do with its role as a major center of economic power that benefits, in many ways, the interest of the elite, despite, paradoxically, its Socialist ideology.
87. This tradition, inflected especially by Russian folk music/dance, is the heritage since the Second Aliya (from Russia), those who became the major ideologues of "Israeli culture."
88. In this period, there occurred large-scale immigration from the Soviet Union, and the Soviet immigrants were given preferential treatment, thus angering Sephardim, who over decades in Israel had never enjoyed similar governmental largesse. References to this bitterness can be seen as well in Bourekas films such as *Salomonico*, also from 1973.

4. Personal Cinema and the Politics of Allegory

1. The Exodus story, for example, as Michael Walzer points out in *Exodus and Revolution*, has been a key source for generation after generation of religious and political revolutionaries.
2. Perlov's government-assigned documentaries from the early sixties, such as *In Jerusalem* (*BiYrushalayim*, 1963), *Elderly House* (*Beit Zkenim*, 1963), and *Tel-Katzir* (1964), were not understood by the bureaucrats, who, at times, decided not to use them on the grounds that they did not fulfill their purposes. See *David Perlov on "Politics in Cinema," an interview by Liora Ktziri and Levi Zini, *Prosa* 51–53 (February 1982): 37–38.
3. Although the film was basically made in 1968, due to various problems with investors it was exhibited only in 1972.
4. See *Kolnoa* 14 (Summer 1977): 63.
5. See *Meir Schnitzer, "The State of Israeli Cinema, Part One," *Hadashot*, 15 September 1985, and "The State of Israeli Cinema, Part Two," *Hadashot*, 20 September 1985.
6. The bankruptcy of George Ovadia, for example, was partly due to the changing of policies.
7. Renen Schorr, "The Cinematic Experience: The Sabra Reflection in Uri Zohar's Films," *Kolnoa* 15/16 (Fall–Winter 1978): 35.
8. *Ibid.
9. The film was dramatically changed from the script.
10. *Program notes for *Hole in the Moon*, edited by Amikam Gurevitch, and published with the assistance of the American Israeli Paper Mills (1965).
11. Ibid.
12. *Interview in *Maariv*, "The More I Shoot, the Less I Understand." In *Hole in the Moon* file in the Israeli Film Institute, n.d.
13. Program notes published by the Israeli Film Institute. In *Hole in the Moon* file in the Israeli Film Institute.
14. Ibid.
15. The title *Hole in the Moon* is also a citation from an old song sung in the Hebrew/Israeli youth movement. The French musician Michel Colombieu's arrangement of the song is a leitmotif throughout the film. See *Raphael Bashan, "Indeed I Have Public Anxiety," *Yedioth Ahronoth*, n.d., in *Hole in the Moon* file in the Israeli Film Institute.

16. In *Take Off* Fellini's influence is quite dominant. There are even explicit references to Italian cinema through Uri Zohar's parodic monologue on cinema, expressed in a kind of Italianized "esperanto."
17. *Conversation with Nahman Ingber, Yigal Bursztyn, Avraham Hefner, Yitzhak Yeshurun, Yehuda Ne'eman, Micha Shagrir, Irma and Uri Klein, "We Simply Were in the Army Together," *Kolnoa*, Summer 1981, p. 9.
18. *Ibid., p. 10.
19. The film is based on Yitzhak Ben-Ner's novel of the same title. Ben-Ner, who also belongs to the "state generation," has a more realistic style than most of the makers of personal films.
20. See, for example, *"We Simply Were in the Army Together."
21. Oded Kotler won the "Best Actor" award at the Cannes Film Festival for his role in *Three Days and a Child.*
22. *Schorr, "The Cinematic Experience."
23. See Paul de Man, *Allegories of Reading.*
24. It must be pointed out that "bourekas" films are at times reflexive as well, but their self-referentiality is parodic, unlike that of most personal cinema. In Kishon's *Arvinka*, the protagonist pretends to film a bank robbery to divert police attention from his actual bank robbery, resulting in generous police assistance for the "shooting." In Golan's *999 Aliza Mizrahi* we see a poster advertising Golan's previous film (*Fortuna*) and a couple use as their alibi to the police that they had gone to see *Fortuna*. In Kishon's *The Policeman Azulay*, the schlemiel policeman, Azulay, watches on television the heroic deeds of an American private-eye detective, and gradually projects himself, à la Buster Keaton, as an English-speaking private-eye hero, able to easily defeat the criminals—in "real life" his oppressive boss—and rescue the woman—in "real life," his beloved, a young prostitute. In another sequence, Azulay visits a crowded movie theater and inadvertently turns it into a battlefield when he suspects that a viewer who entered the theater with a package in his hand is a terrorist carrying a bomb. (Israeli movie theaters in the early seventies were occasionally the targets of Palestinian bombs.) Revah's film *He Who Steals from a Thief Is Not Guilty* alludes to figures in the Israeli film industry (a policeman is named after the filmmaker Boaz Davidson); to the archetypical "gefilte-fish" film anti-hero, Kuni Lemel, by having the "bourekas" schlemiel crook, Sasson, who runs for his life, dress up as the schlemiel Hassid Kuni Lemel; and to Indian popular cinema by his dressing up as a Maharishi singing in Indian "Ichikdana," a song synonymous in Israel with Indian cinema, viewed in Israel by the same audience which views "bourekas" cinema. The song is taken from Raj Kapoor's popular film *Mr. 420* (*Shri 420*, 1955). Raj Kapoor, like Revah, stars in his films, and in the case of *Mr. 420* he also plays a little crook. *He Who Steals from a Thief Is Not Guilty* also has its protagonist mistakenly escape to the screen tests for an American production of a film about Entebbe (Revah's film was directed after the Entebbe operation, which provided the subject for three fiction films at the time). Sasson has to dress like Idi Amin for the shooting; he superimposes his stereotypically Oriental tastes onto the African leader, telling his servant: "I love bourekas in the morning." Here, Revah, impersonating the ultimate negative image of the Black (or Sephardi) embodied by Idi Amin, states his love for bourekas in a double, ambiguously voiced reference to both the pastry and the film genre. His expression of love is offered within the framework of a Hollywoodean film-within-the-film, itself framed by Revah's "bourekas" film.

25. *Yossef Sharik, "To Be Rootless," *HaAretz*, 31 December 1978.
26. *"We Simply Were in the Army Together," p. 11.
27. Avi Cohen's *The Real Game* (1980) also attempts to deal with both a political scandal and a personal crisis.
28. *Till the End of the Night* offers a similar lamentation for past idealism versus present materialism not only via the characterization of father versus son but also via casting; Yossef Millo as the father and Assaf Dayan as the son had already been cast in similar roles in the heroic-nationalist *He Walked through the Fields*. The very repetition in casting, yet within different genres, calls attention to the contrast between the clarity of outlook in the past and the disorientation in the present.
29. *Gloves* is based on Dan Tzalka's novel of the same title.
30. Harold Clurman, introduction to Clifford Odets, *Six Plays* (New York: Grove Press, 1979), p. x.

5. The Return of the Repressed: The Palestinian Wave in Recent Israeli Cinema

1. *Nurit Gertz, *Amos Oz*, pp. 45–46.
2. Ram Levi had already filmed a short docudrama, *I Am Ahmed* (*Ani Ahmed*, 1966), which revolves around the difficulties of an Israeli-Palestinian high school graduate who must work in construction. The film was censored, the censors claiming it distorts reality. In recent years it has enjoyed a certain revival and has been shown in cinematheques.
3. S. Yizhar's story has been part of high school matriculation exams (programmed by the Ministry of Education and Culture); it provoked angry reactions only when it was shown on the small screen. The explanation might lie in the effect of images versus that of written words.
4. *Nira Gal, "Hot Film," *HaOlam haZe*, October 1982.
5. *Joan Borstein, *Jerusalem Post* (International Edition), 11–12 November 1983.
6. *Razi Gotterman, "Israel Consulate in New York Banishes the Israeli Film Festival Because of Screening of *Hamsin*," *Maariv*, 12 April 1983.
7. "The Council for Criticism Censored a Film That Badly Hurt IDF," *HaAretz*, 4 December 1983.
8. *Dafna Barak, "We Live like Drugged People," *Hotam*, 8 July 1983.
9. *Eyal Halfon, "Movie, Movie," *HaIr*, 22 February 1985.
10. Marsha Pomerantz, "Preoccupation," *Jerusalem Post*, 22 November 1985.
11. *Thiya Adar, "Twenty Million Dollars in Four Weeks," *Yedioth Ahronoth*, 18 April 1986.
12. *Ibid.
13. *Meir Shnitzer, "Making a Movie about How to Make a Movie," *Hadashot*, 25 February 1985.
14. Pomerantz, "Preoccupation." According to Nissim Dayan, Costa-Gavras' assistant on *Hanna K.*, a Nazareth Palestinian and a member of the Communist Party, when asked to work on *A Very Narrow Bridge*, refused, suggesting that he would work on it if the Arab female lead were played by a Jewish actress.
15. *Idit Na'aman, "Free in Jail," *Yedioth Ahronoth*, 21 September 1984.

16. Quoted in *Itzick Yosha, "Torn from all Directions," *Hadashot*, 27 November 1985.
17. Quoted in *Meir Shnitzer, "Barabash," *Hadashot*, 26 September 1984.
18. Quoted in *Brurya Avidan-Brir, "With Each Slap I Understood the Arab Problem," *LaIsha*, 17 September 1984, p. 98.
19. Quoted in *Dalya Karpel, "Palestinian Tragedy," *Hair*, 6 June 1986, p. 32.
20. *Moshava* are agricultural settlements/villages established by Zionist settlers.
21. Thomas L. Friedman, "Ricochets," *New York Times*, 11 June 1986.
22. *Beyond the Walls* cast non-professional actors, such as Ramzi Asman and Ezra Rephael, including ex-prisoners, such as Eliezer Albla and Shlomo Nir. Released from the prison around the time of the filming, Nir was also employed as a consultant, and contributed to the authenticity of the prison scenes. See Idit Neman, "Free from Prison," *Yediot Ahronot*, September 21, 1984; and Ilan Shaoul, "The Dark Guts of the State," *Yediot Ahronot*, January 13, 1984.
23. Ne'eman's real-life political stances, it should be pointed out, have tended to be to the left of the ideological position implied by his film.
24. See, for example, *Meir Shnitzer, "Where Fell *A Very Narrow Bridge*," *Hadashot*, 6 December 1985.
25. *Mordechai Bar-On, *Peace Now: The Portrait of a Movement* (Tel Aviv: HaKibbutz haMeuchad, 1985), pp. 89–90.
26. The research was directed by Harriet Arnone and Amiel Alcalay and was partially supported by a Ford Foundation grant.
27. *Nahman Ingber, "An Optimist Thing: Making Movies," *Hair*, 7 September 1984, p. 23.
28. *Amir Rotem, "A Good Arab is an Arab in a Movie," *Davar*, 6 December 1984.

Postscript

1. The reader will note that some of the chapter titles and subheadings in this republication have been changed from the specific film titles of the original publication to broader themes in order to facilitate the central issues at stake for the non-film reader.
2. Over the past two decades, a vast field of cinema/media studies concerning Israel and Palestine has come to the forefront in numerous publications in diverse journals and languages. To mention only a few books specifically dedicated to the subject: Nurith Gertz, Orly Lubin, Yehuda Ne'eman, eds., *Fictive Looks—On Israeli Cinema* (Tel Aviv: The Open University, 1998, Hebrew); Yosefa Loshitzky, *Identity Politics on the Israeli Screen* (Austin: University of Texas Press, 2002); Raz Yosef, *Beyond Flesh: Queer Masculinities and Nationalism in Israeli Cinema* (New Jersey: Rutgers University Press, 2004); Nurit Gertz and George Khleifi, *Landscape in Mist: Space and Memory in Palestinian Cinema* (Tel Aviv: Am Oved & the Open University, 2005, Hebrew).
3. For an elaborate account of the role of archeology, see Nadia Abu El-Haj's *Facts on the Ground: Archeological Practice and Territorial Self-Fashioning in Israeli Society* (Chicago: University of Chicago Press, 2001).
4. I continued to elaborate on such analogies between Jews and blacks, and anti-Semitism and Racism, in "Post-Fanon and the Colonial: A Situational Diagnosis," included in Shohat's *Taboo Memories, Diasporic Voices* (Durham: Duke University Press, 2006),

and on the analogies between the Zionist and American settler discourses in "Staging the Quincentenary: The Middle East and the Americas," *Third Text* No. 21 (Winter 1992–93), or in "Taboo Memories, Diasporic Visions: Columbus, Palestine, and Arab-Jews" (1997, republished in *Taboo Memories, Diasporic Voices*.)

5. I explicitly spoke of "placing Zionism on the psychoanalyst's couch" in an interview with Dalia Karpel, *Ha'ir* No. 472, 10 October 1989.

6. Sephardim in Israel: Zionism from the Standpoint of its Jewish Victims," *Social Text* No. 19/20 (Autumn 1988) (also in *Dangerous Liaisons: Gender, Nation, and Postcolonial Perspectives*, co-edited by A. McClintock, A. Mufti & E. Shohat (Minneapolis: University of Minnesota Press, 1997); "Rethinking Jews and Muslims," *Middle East Report* (September-October 1992); "The Narrative of the Nation and the Discourse of Modernization: the Case of the Mizrahim," *Critique* 10 (Spring 1997); "Taboo Memories, Diasporic Visions: Columbus, Palestine, and Arab-Jews;" "The Invention of the Mizrahim," *Journal of Palestine Studies*, No. 1 (Autumn 1999); "Rupture and Return: Zionist Discourse and the Study of Arab-Jews," *Social Text* 75 21, No. 2 (Spring 2003) (also in Shohat's *Taboo Memories, Diasporic Voices* (Durham: Duke University Press, 2006)).

7. The phrase "Rejecting the Arab Jew" alludes to the title of a recent article, "Rejecting the Arab Jew: On Language," by Philologos, in *The Forward* (January 30, 2008) (http://www.forward.com/articles/12561/). See also David Shasha's critique of the rejection: "Rejecting the 'Arab Jew:' Philologos and David Shasha" (February 16, 2008) (http://www.kedma.co.il/index.php?id=1740&t=pages).

8. Relationality has been central to my discussion of identity formation, e.g., "Ethnicities-in-Relation: Toward a Multi-Cultural Reading of American Cinema," in Lester Friedman, ed., *Unspeakable Images: Ethnicity and the American Cinema* (Champaign, IL: University of Illinois Press, 1991); "Columbus, Palestine, and Arab Jews: Toward A Relational Approach to Community Identity," in Keith Ansell Pearson, Benita Parry & Judith Squires, eds., *Cultural Readings of Imperialism* (London: Lawrence & Wishart in association with New Formations, 1997); "The Shaping of Mizrahi Studies: A Relational Approach," *Israeli Studies Forum: An Interdisciplinary Journal* 17, No. 2 (Spring 2002); and throughout *Unthinking Eurocentrism* (co-authored with Robert Stam) (New York: Routledge Press, 1994).

9. Several other authors have also explored the question of Arab-Jews within a cross-border perspective, for example: Ammiel Alcalay, *After Jews and Arabs: Remaking Levantine Culture* (Minneapolis: University of Minnesota Press, 1992); Gil Anidjar, *The Jew, the Arab: A History of the Enemy* (Stanford: Stanford University Press, 2003); Moshe Behar, "Palestine, Arabized Jews and the Elusive Consequences of Jewish and Arab National Formations," in *Nationalism and Ethnic Politics* 13, No. 4 (October 2007); Joel Beinin, *The Dispersion of Egyptian Jewry: Culture, Politics, and the Formation of a Modern Diaspora* (Berkeley: University of California Press, 1998); Zvi Ben-Dor, "Invisible Exile: Iraqi Jews in Israel," *Journal of the Interdisciplinary Crossroads* 3, No. 1 (April 2006); Sami Chetrit, *The Mizrahi Struggle in Israel: 1948–2003* (Tel-Aviv: Am Oved Publishers, 2004; Hebrew; forthcoming in English from Routledge Press); Yerach Gover, *Zionism: The Limits of a Moral Discourse* (Minneapolis: University of Minnesota Press, 1994); Gil Hochberg, *In Spite of Partition: Jews, Arabs, and the Limits of Separatist Imagination* (Princeton: Princeton University Press, 2007); Smadar Lavie, "Blowups in

the Borderzones: Third World Israeli Authors' Gropings for Home," *New Formations* 18 (1992) and Smadar Lavie and Ted Swedenberg's "Introduction," in Lavie and Swedenberg, eds., *Displacement, Diaspora, and the Geographies of Identity* (Durham: Duke University Press, 1996); Joseph Massad, "Zionism's Internal Others: Israel and the Mizrahim," in *The Persistence of the Palestinian Question* (Routledge, 2006); Yigal Nizri, ed., *Eastern Appearance: A Present that Stirs in the Thickets of Its Arab Past* (Tel Aviv: Babel Publishing House, 2004); and Ruth Tsoffar, *The Stains of Culture: An Ethno-Reading of Karaite Jewish Women* (Detroit: Wayne State University Press, 2006).

10. I continued to explore this topic in "The Struggle Over Representation: Casting, Coalitions, and the Politics of Identification" in Román De La Campa, E. Ann Kaplan, Michael Sprinker. eds., *Late Imperial Culture* (London: Verso, 1995); and "Stereotype, Realism, and the Struggle Over Representation," in *Unthinking Eurocentrism* (co-authored with Robert Stam) (New York: Routledge Press, 1994).

11. Despite my noting of this irony, the University of Texas Press doubled the irony by reproducing this error, when a caption identified Bakri as Tzadok and vice versa.

12. The Palestinian and Arab–Jewish encounter on the Lebanese border is narrated differently in Yousry Nasrallah's film adaptation (2004) of Elias Khoury's novel *Gate of the Sun* (Humphrey Davies, trans., NY: Archipelago Books, 2006), recounting post 1948 events of Palestinians crossing back the border to see their families in the Galilee, and an Arab–Jewish character longing for Lebanon.

13. Bakri performed in films directed by Jewish Israelis such as Eran Riklis's *Cup Final* and Uri Barabash's *Beyond the Walls*; by Palestinians such as Michel Khleifi's *The Tale of Three Jewels* (1994), Ali Nassar's *The Milky Way* (1997), and Rashid Masharawi's *Haifa* (1995); as well as Constantin Costa-Gavras' *Hanna K.* (1983) and Saverio Costanzo's *Private* (2004).

14. Theodor Herzl, *Altneuland* (1902), trans. from German by Lotta Levensohn (Princeton, NJ: Marcus Weiner Publishers, 2000), p. 190.

15. Edward Said, "Michael Walzer's *Exodus and Revolution:* A Canaanite Reading," Grand Street 5, No. 2 (Winter 1986), p. 90.

16. Amnon Raz-Krakotzkin, "Exile Within Sovereignty," (Hebrew) *Theory and Criticism* 4–5 (1993), and *Exil et souveraineté. Judaïsme, sionisme et pensée binationale* (Paris: La fabrique, 2007); and Yael Zrubavel, *Recovered Roots: Collective Memory and the Making of Israeli National Tradition* (The University of Chicago Press, 1995).

17. For further analysis, see Ruth Tsoffar, "*Forget Baghdad:* Jews and Arabs—the Iraqi Connection," in Gonul Donmez–Colin, ed., *The Cinema of North Africa and the Middle East* (London: Wallflower Press, 2007).

18. Costa-Gavras made one of the first Hollywood films sympathetic to Palestinians (*Hanna K.*, 1983), although limited by a liberal and in some ways orientalist perspective (see, Richard Porton and Ella Shohat, "The Trouble with Hanna," *Film Quarterly* 38, No. 2 (Winter 1984–1985).

19. Steve Erickson, "A Breakdown of Communication: Elia Suleiman Talks About 'Divine Intervention,'" *IndieWire*, http://www.indiewire.com/people/people_030115elia .html. See also Richard Porton's interview with Elia Suleiman, "Notes from the Palestinian Diaspora," *Cineaste* 28, no. 3 (22 June 2003).

20. Kareem Fahim, "Stateless Cinema: Palestinian Film and Oscar Eligibility" *The Village Voice* (21 January 2003), http://www.villagevoice.com/film/0304,fahim2,41328,20 .html.

21. Similarly in Kanafani's *Men in the Sun* and in the adaptation, *The Dupes*, the 1948 defeat is metaphorized by the castration of the character Abu al-Khaizran due to a bomb.

22. For a discussion of the gendering of Palestine in political discourse, especially of the language of the communiqués issued by the Palestinian Liberation Organization (PLO) depicting Intifada as "the Palestinian wedding," see: Joseph Massad, "Conceiving the Masculine: Gender and Palestinian Nationalism," *The Middle East Journal* 49, No. 3 (Summer 1995); and Massad's *The Persistence of the Palestinian Question* (London: Routledge, 2006).

23. Produced before the first Intifada, *Wedding in Galilee* was one of the first features length films to transcend the a Manichaean schema of "peaceloving Israelis" versus "violence-prone Arabs," while also avoiding a reverse tale of "good Palestinians" versus "evil Israelis." As in Gillo Pontecorvo's *The Battle of Algiers* (1966), Khleifi humanizes the individual military members, but highlights instead the oppressive nature of colonial rule.

24. In one visibly allegorical sequence, Palestinian and Israelis together coax a mare out of a field that the Israelis have mined, evoking a vision of a communal future. A pastoral epilogue depicting the Mukhtar's child running in the fields underlines a desire for harmony in a bloodstained land, as if closing the circle opened at the beginning of the film, where the voices of Palestinian children at play dissolve into the roar of Israeli jets. Coming after the soldier's evacuation of the village, this epilogue affirms a desire for liberation. Palestinian and Israeli national cultures thus suffuse each other's memories and tales, but, from a Palestinian perspective, a dialogical future will be made possible only by an end to the occupation. The analysis here of *Wedding in Galilee* is taken from my articles "Wedding in Galilee," *Middle East Report* 154 (September–October 1988); and from "Anomalies of the National: Representing Israel/Palestine," *Wide Angle* 11, No. 3 (July 1989).

25. The friend in question is myself, reading in voiceover a text based on a piece written during the Gulf War, Shohat, "Dislocated Identities: Reflections of an Arab-Jew," *Movement Research: Performance Journal* 5 (Fall–Winter 1992).

26. Yehuda Ne'eman has been a key figure in the formation of the field of cinema studies in Israel. As the chair of the Film & TV department at Tel Aviv University, he transformed what was a semi-vocational film school into an academic curriculum offering a required course, "Introduction to Israeli Cinema, " which formed a new generation of filmmakers and film scholars.

27. In Israel, Sivan launched a new journal *South Cinema Notebooks*, dedicated to cinema and politics, published in conjunction with Sapir College Film Studies Program, whose alternative direction had been initiated under the directorship of Haim Bresheeth, Dean of the School of Media, Film and Cultural Studies.

28. Sarah Graham-Brown, *Palestinians and Their Society 1880–1946: A Photographic Essay* (London: Quartet Books, 1980); Walid Khalidi, *Before their Diaspora: A Photographic History of the Palestinians* (Washington D.C.: Institute for Palestine Studies, 1984); Walid Khalidi, ed., *All That Remains: The Palestinian Villages Occupied and Depopulated by Israel in 1948* (Washington, D.C.: Institute for Palestine Studies, 1992); Elias Sanbar, *Les Palestiniens : La Photographie D'une Terre Et De Son Peuple De 1839 a Nos Jours* (Paris: Hazan 2004); Issam Nassar, *Photographing Jerusalem: The Image of the City in Nineteenth Century Photography* (Boulder, CO: East European Monographs, Distributed by Columbia University, 1997). For archival work on early Jewish photographers and filmmakers in Palestine, see: Amy Kronish, Edith Falk, Paula Weiman-Kelman,

eds., *The Nathan Axelrod Collection*, vol. 1 (Wiltshire: Flicks Books, 1994); Hillel Tryster, *Israel Before Israel: Silent Cinema in the Holy Land* (Jerusalem: Steven Spielberg Jewish Film Archive, 1995); Guy Raz, *Photographers of Eretz Israel from the Beginning of Photography Until Today*) (Tel Aviv: Map & Hakibbutz Hameuchad, 2003; Hebrew); and *The Nathan Axelrod Collection*, an extensive listing of films by Axelrod.

29. Work by Palestinian photographers include: Farouk Mardam-Bey et. al., *Palestine: Postcards from the Collection of Ezzedine Kalak* (Cairo: Arab Graphic Center, n.d.) and Raffi Safieh, *Hanna Safieh, A Man and his Camera: Photographs of Palestine 1927–1967* (Raffi Safieh, 1999).

30. Smadar Lavie's work developed a major critique of Israel's policies and discourses of the Bedouins, including in *The Poetics of Military Occupation: Mzeina Allegories of Bedouin Identity Under Israeli and Egyptian Rule* (Berkeley: University of California Press, 1990).

31. On the basis of official documents and on Palestinian and Israeli memoirs, in *The Ethnic Cleaning of Palestine*, Israeli historian Ilan Pappe challenges the myth of a "voluntary transfer" of hundreds of thousands of Palestinians who left their homes to make way for invading Arab armies, instead showing that Palestinians were the victims of a calculated project of ethnic cleansing. (Oxford: One World Publications, 2006).

32. Demystification in Ne'eman's work was also combined with an empathetic representation of Palestinians hardly registered on the Israeli screen at the time, with the notable exception of Ram Levi's documentary, *I am Ahmed* (1966). Ne'eman's 1970s TV documentary *Acco* is a tale of two cities-the Arab and the Jewish. Combining cinéma vérité and neorealism, the film moves back-and-forth between two spaces in a visual contrast reminiscent of the Fanonian description of the divided city of Algiers.

33. Recent publications have focused on the contemporary memory of the Nakba in cultural practices, for example: Lila Abu-Lughod and Ahmad H. Sa'di, eds., *Nakba: Palestine, 1948, and the Claims of Memory* (NY: Columbia University Press, 2007) and Hamid Dabashi, ed., *Dreams of a Nation: On Palestinian Cinema* (London: Verso, 2006). One essay in Abu-Lughod's and Sa'di's book, in particular, by Haim Bresheeth's "The Continuity of Trauma and Struggle: Recent Cinematic Representations of the Nakba," addresses the *Nakba* in the cinema. See also, Bresheeth and Haifa Hammami, eds., of "The Conflict and Contemporary Visual Culture in Palestine & Israel" in *Third Text* 80–81 (May/July 2006).

34. On Ein Hod / 'Ayn Hawd, see Susan Slyomovics's *The Object of Memory: Arab and Jew Narrate the Palestinian Village* (Philadelphia: University of Pennsylvania Press, 1998).

35. Online visual activism by Israelis has taken place on diverse websites, such as Oznik, edited by Oz Shelach, http://oznik.com/index.html.

36. Suleiman explained the negative reactions to *Chronicle of a Disappearance* at the Carthage Film Festival: "They misunderstood the irony of the use of the Israeli flag in the final scene and accused me of being a Zionist collaborator." Steve Erickson, "A Breakdown of Communication: Elia Suleiman Talks About 'Divine Intervention,'" *IndieWire*, http://www.indiewire.com/people/people_030115elia.html.

37. Quote from Emile Habiby, *The Secret Life of Saeed: The Pessoptimist*, trans. Sama K. Jayyusi and Trevor LeGassik (Gloucestershire: Arris Books, 2002), p. 3.

38. The film's project was further elaborated on the Internet—"Arna's Active Memorial Site"—showing the impact of the occupation on Palestinian lives. (http://www.arna.info/Arna/).

39. For a different take on Rovner's work, see Irit Roggof's *Terra Infirma: Geography's Visual Culture* (London and New York: Routledge, 2000) and on the surveillance of land, Eyal Weizman, *Hollow Land: Israel's Architecture of Occupation* (London: Verso, 2007). See also: Rafi Segal and Eyal Weizman, eds., *A Civilian Occupation: The Politics of Israeli Architecture* (Verso: London, 2003); Sharon Rotbard, 'Ir Levana, 'Ir Shehora (*White City, Black City*) (Tel Aviv: Babel Publishing House, 2005); and Mark Levine, *Overthrowing Geography: Jaffa, Tel Aviv, and the Struggle for Palestine, 1880–1948* (Berkeley: University of California Press, 2005).

40. Theodore Herzl, *Altneuland* (Old New Land), 1902. Trans. Lotta Levensohn (Princeton, NJ: Markus Wiener, 1997), p. 226.

41. The first Palestinian cinema unit, established by Fatah, documented Palestinian life with a militancy reminiscent of a certain anti-colonial and Third Worldist cinema, in film such as *Zionist Aggression* (1972), *Zionist Terror* (1973), *Why do we plant flowers? Why do we bear Arms?* (1974), *A Counter Siege* (1978) and *The Homeland of Barbed Wire* (1980). The 1980s witnessed the emergence of a new Palestinian cinema—of a kind that I elsewhere characterized as "Post-Third Worldist"—which engaged a broader range of issues and styles, initiated by Michel Khleifi, Mai Masri, Rashid Masharawi, and Elia Suleiman. Writings on the Israeli/Arab conflict in Arab and Palestinian cinemas have included: Viola Shafik, *Arab Cinema: History and Cultural Identity* (Cairo: American University in Cairo Press, 1998); Viola Shafik "Cinema in Palestine," in O. Leaman, ed., *Companion Encyclopedia of Middle Eastern and North African Film* (London: Routledge, 2001); Bashar Ibrahim, *al-Sinima al-Falastiniayya al-Jadida* (New Palestinian Cinema) (Arabic) (2003); *al-Sinima al-Falastiniyya fi al-Qarn al-'Ashrin 1935–2001* (Palestinian Cinema in the Twentieth Century 1935–2001) (Arabic) (Damascus: the National Organization for Cinema, the Syrian Ministry of Culture, 2001); Rasha Salti, ed., *Insights Into Syrian Cinema: Essays & Conversations With Contemporary Filmmakers* (Rattapallax press, 2006); and Hamid Dabashi, ed., *Dreams of a Nation: On Palestinian Cinema* (London: Verso, 2006), especially, Joseph Massad's "The Weapon of Culture: Cinema in the Palestinian Liberation Struggle."

42. The filming of Sidney Olcott's *From the Manger to the Cross* had already demonstrated the anxiety of Westerner travelers with regards to the Arab character of the Holy Land. Despite the help of their Palestinian "faithful guide," Ameen Zaroun, Gene Gauntier, the film's screenwriter, recounted the crew's difficulties during the filming in the Via Dolorosa, Jerusalem. Conjuring up images of ominous encirclement, she described the crew's trepidation as a "mob of angry Arabs and Turks muttered threats" and "demanded Baksheesh;" with the on-location "greedy Arabs" evoked as the modern-day equivalents of the "greedy Jews" in the film.

43. For a critical discussion of contemporary tourism and consumerism, especially Israeli visits to predominantly Palestinian locales inside Israel, see Rebecca L. Stein's *Itineraries in Conflict: Israelis, Palestinians, and the Political Lives of Tourism.* (Durham, NC: Duke University Press, 2008).

44. My discussion here is drawn from my essays "Master Narrative/Counter Readings," Robert Sklar & Charles Musser, eds., *Resisting Images: Essays on Cinema and History* (Philadelphia: Temple University Press, 1990); "Making the Silences Speak," Barbara Swirski & Marilyn Safir, eds., *Calling the Equality Bluff: Women in Israel* (Oxford: Pergamon Press, 1991); and "Gender and the Culture of Empire," *Quarterly*

Review of Film & Video, 131:1–2 (Spring 1991) and in *Taboo Memories, Diasporic Voices*. See also Simona Sharoni, *Gender and the Israeli-Palestinian Conflict, The Politics of Women's Resistance* (Syracuse: Syracuse University Press, 1995); Nira Yuval Davis, *Gender and Nation* (Thousand Oaks, CA: Sage Publications Inc., 1997); and Joseph Massad, "Conceiving the Masculine: Gender and Palestinian Nationalism," in *The Persistence of the Palestinian Question* (London: Routledge, 2006).

45. Raz Yosef, *Beyond Flesh: Queer Masculinities and Nationalism in Israeli Cinema* (New Jersey: Rutgers University Press, 2004). Recent visual art in Israel has centralized this issue, whether in the artwork of Adi Nes or in films such as *Yossi and Jagger* (2003). Within this perspective, Zionism is a sexual project, in the punning words of Daniel Boyarin, a "return to Phallistine, not to Palestine." See, "Outing Freud's Zionism, or, the Bitextuality of the Diaspora Jew," in Cindy Patton and Benigno Sanchez-Eppler, eds., *Queer Diasporas* (Durham: Duke University Press, 2000).

46. I briefly touched on Guttman's problematic representation of (Mizrahi) Israeli/ Palestinian gay sex, see in a review article, *Film Quarterly* 40, No. 3 (April 1987).

47. See, for example, Yael Ben-Zvi, "Zionist Lesbianism and Transsexual Transgression: Two Representations of Queer Israel," *Middle East Report* (Spring 1998).

48. On the production of *Tkuma*, see Eric Saranovitz's *Negotiating History in an Era of Globalization: The Production of Narratives of a Nation's Past in the Israeli Media*, Ph.D. Dissertation, New York University, 2006.

49. In the realm of film and music, Salima Mourad Pasha, an Iraqi-Jewish singer, and Leila Mourad, an Egyptian musical film star, both converted to Islam and stayed in Iraq and Egypt respectively.

50. For an account of travel in the region, from the Mediterranean to the Indian Ocean, see Amitav Ghosh, *In an Antique Land* (New York: Knopf, 1992).

51. One exhibition was dedicated to diaries written by Mizrahi women, curated by Shula Keshet at the Ami Steinitz's Gallery—Contemporary Art, 2000.

52. Both Ron Kahlili and Shosh Gabay conceived the series, narrated by Tikva Levi.

53. For an account of the Mizrahi struggle, see Sami Chetrit, "Mizrahi Politics in Israel: Between Integration and Alternative," *Journal of Palestine Studies* 29, No. 4. (Autumn, 2000); and *The Mizrahi Struggle in Israel: 1948–2003* (Tel-Aviv: Am Oved Publishers, 2004) (Hebrew).

54. The film, directed by Shmuel Hasfari and written by Azoulay-Hasfari, provoked a passionate debate among Mizrahim: some saw it as continued stereotyping while others saw it as an assertion of Moroccan culture.

55. The recuperation of the melodrama in the cinema also appears at a moment when te-lenovelas, especially from Latin America, are consumed in Israel via Israeli or Jordanian broadcast. For an account of Latin American telanovelas in Israel, see Tomas Lopez, "Telenovelas and the Israeli Television Market," *Television & New Media* 8, No. 3 (2007).

56. The research for the documentaries was prepared by Shoshana Madmoni-Gerber.

57. The screenplay was written by Yirmi Kadosh, Messika's longtime collaborator, and by Mizrahi activist Ilana Sugbeker.

58. After the completion of the film, some testimony suggested that Sa'il was buried in Baghdad in the early 1980s, although no witness claimed to have seen his body, and thus

the full story of a person considered a traitor by the Shabak remains unknown. The film-maker also traveled with Mazal Sa'il to Amsterdam to meet a newly-arrived Baghdadi Jew who was able to testify and thus release her from the status of 'aguna. http://www.itu.org.il/Index.asp?ArticleID=4924& CategoryID=762& Page=1.

59. While Haim Hanegbi at the time was not active in the Black Panthers, he did participate in the 1989 Toledo meeting between Palestinians and Mizrahi intellectuals. In his speech, he brought up his Sephardi Hebronite background, at a time when some critical intellectuals were claiming their identity as Palestinian Jews to delegitimize the settlers' claim on the old city of Hebron (or al-Khalil in Arabic), supposedly in the name of the indigenous Hebronite Jewish inhabitants.

60. Eli Hamo has documented Mizrahi activism going back to the 1980s with Bimat Kivun Hadash in south Tel Aviv. Some of this filmic record can be found on the Kedma website established by Sami Chetrit, and dedicated to leftist Mizrahi perspectives. In conjunction with *The Black Panthers (in Israel) Speak*, Sami Chetrit and Eli Bareket organized an event dedicated to "30 Years to the Black Panthers," in cooperation with Shatil and TZAH—Students for Social Justice at the Hebrew University.

61. Briza, part of the satellite station YES, was founded by Ron Kahlili in the late 1990s.

62. Osnat Trabelsi also produced some of the revisionist films about both Mizrahi and Palestinian issues.

63. Sami Chetrit, ed., *One Hundred Years of Mizrahi Writing: An Anthology* (Tel Aviv: Kedem Publishing, 1988; Hebrew); Ammiel Alcalay, *Keys to the Garden: New Israeli Writing* (San Francisco: City Lights Publishers, 1996) and *After Jews and Arabs*; Yerach Gover's *Zionism: The Limits of Moral Discourse in Israeli Hebrew Fiction*; Gil Hochberg, *In Spite of Partition*; Smadar Lavie, "Blowups in the Borderzones: Third World Israeli Authors' Gropings for Home;" Zvi Ben Dor, "Eyb, Heshumah, Infajrat Qunbula: Towards a History of Mizrahim and Arabic," in Yigal Nizri, ed., *Eastern Appearance* (Hebrew) and in Oznik, http://www.oznik.com/toward-a-history-of-mizrahim-and-arabic.html; Ruth Tsoffar, "'A Land that Devours its People': Mizrahi Writing from the Gut," *Body & Society* 12, No. 2, (2006); Yigal Nizri, ed., *Eastern Appearance*; Yaron Shemer, "Identity, Place, and Subversion in Contemporary Mizrahi Cinema," Ph.D. Dissertation, University of Texas, Austin, 2005; Shoshana Madmoni-Gerber, "Media Construction of Public Sphere and the Discourse of Conflict: A Case Study of the Kidnapped Yemenite Babies Affair in Israel," Ph.D. Dissertation, University of Massachusetts at Amherst, 2003, forthcoming from Palgrave McMillan Press.

64. Yigal Bursztyn, "The Bad Ashkenazis Are Riding Again," *Maariv*, 7 February 1992.

65. In a phenomenon examined by "whiteness studies" in the United States and elsewhere, Israelis who participate in what might be called "normative Ashkenaziness" are sometimes surprised that this perspective is not universally shared. In a 1992 primetime talk show on Israeli national TV (then the only TV channel, and like radio stations, owned by the government), the host challenged my contention that Israel was racist toward the Mizrahim by appealing to the audience. After asking how many in the audience were Mizrahim—roughly half raised their hand—he asked, in a rather imprecise and skewed way: "Do you think the Ashkenazim are trying to screw you?" He was very surprised when the audience shouted back: "Yes! Yes!" (The moment is captured in Samir's documentary *Forget Baghdad*).

66. Yehuda Ne'eman, then the chair of the Film Department at Tel Aviv University was the first to assign it as a required text in his "Introduction to Israeli Cinema" course. In 2005 *Israeli Cinema* was republished in Hebrew by The Open University of Israel, with a preface by Ne'eman, and the Hebrew translation edited by Yigal Nizri. The republication was initiated by Nurit Gertz, in conjunction with a course designed around the book, entitled "East / West in the Cinema." The Arabic translation, *Alcinema Alesraeliya*, meanwhile, was translated from English by Mahmoud Ali (Cairo: Sawt wa sura, 2000). The Arabic Translation of chapters from *Israeli Cinema in Adab wa-Naqad* (Literature and Criticism) was by Ahmad Yusuf: "Muqadama," (Introduction,) # 172, Dec. 1999; "Al-Falastiniyun wa-yahud al-sharq" (chapters 1 and 3) # 173, January 2000; "Al-Cinima al-Israiliyya ba'ad 1948" (chapter 2) # 175, March 2000. My second book in Hebrew, *Forbidden Reminiscences* (Zikhronot Asurim), was published by Bimat Kedem LeSifrut Publishing, with the Alternative Information Center (2001), and in Arabic, *Thakariat Mamnua*, with a preface by Ismail Dabaj (Damascus: Dar Kan'an, 2004).

67. See, for example, Jimmy Carter's *Palestine: Peace Not Apartheid* (New York: Simon and Schuster, 2006) and John Mearsheimer and Stephen Walt's *The Israel Lobby and U.S. Foreign Policy* (New York: Farrar, Straus and Giroux, 2007).

68. Albert Memmi's books appeared in Hebrew in the following order: *Pillar of Salt* (Tel Aviv: Am Oved, 1960), *Jews and Arabs* (Tel Aviv: Sifriat HaPoalim, 1975), *The Liberation of the Jew* (Tel Aviv: Am Oved, 1976) and *Racism* (Jerusalem: Karmel, 1999.) Memmi's book *The Colonizer and The Colonized* has also been published (Jerusalem: Karmel & Van Lear, 2005.)

69. My argument here in based on my essays "Notes on the 'Post-colonial'" *Social Text* No. 31–32 (1992); and "The 'Postcolonial' in Translation: Reading Edward Said between English and Hebrew," in *Taboo Memories, Diasporic Voices* (Durham: Duke University Press, 2006); and the "Postscript" to the Hebrew translation of Frantz Fanon's *The Wretched of The Earth*," (Tel Aviv: Babel Publishing House, 2006; Hebrew).

70. Cinema has often been marginalized, especially in a context where Judaic culture has privileged "the word" over "the image," where the taboo on "graven images" has raised anxieties about the legitimacy and even the possibility of representation.

71. As evidence, see for example Rebecca L. Stein and Ted Swedenburg. eds, *Palestine, Israel, and the Politics of Popular Culture* (Durham: Duke University Press, 2005), or the emergence of the new journal *Middle East Journal of Culture and Communication*, as well as the growing number of panels addressing these issues at the Middle East Studies Association.

Selected Bibliography

(Publications in Hebrew and Arabic are indicated by asterisks.)

Abdel-Malek, Anouar. *La Pensée politique arabe contemporaine.* Paris: Le Seuil, 1970.

Abu-Lughod, Ibrahim A., ed. *The Transformation of Palestine.* Evanston: Northwestern University Press, 1971.

*Ahad, Ha'Am. *On a Crossroads.* Tel Aviv: Dvir, 1947.

Ahmad, Aijaz. "Jameson's Rhetoric of Otherness and the 'National Allegory.'" *Social Text* 17 (Fall 1987): 3–25.

Alloula, Malek. *The Colonial Harem.* Translated by Myrna Godzich and Wlad Godzich. Minneapolis: University of Minnesota Press, 1986.

Alter, Robert. *The Art of Biblical Narrative.* New York: Basic Books, 1981.

Amin, Samir, Giovanni Arrighi, André Gunder Frank, and Immanuel Wallerstein, eds. *Dynamics of Global Crisis.* New York: Monthly Review Press, 1982.

Arendt, Hannah. *The Jew as Pariah: Jewish Identity and Politics in the Modern Age.* New York: Grove Press, 1978.

el-Asmar, Fouzi. *Through the Hebrew Looking-Glass.* London: Zed Press, 1986.

Auerbach, Erich. *Mimesis: The Representation of Reality in Western Literature.* Translated by Willard Trask. Princeton: Princeton University Press, 1953.

Bakhtin, Mikhail M. *Rabelais and His World.* Translated by Helene Iswolsky. Cambridge: M.I.T. Press, 1968.

Bakhtin, Mikhail M., and Pavel Medvedev Nikolaevich. *The Formal Method in Literary Scholarship: A Critical Introduction to Sociological Poetics.* Translated by Albert J. Wehrle. Baltimore: Johns Hopkins University Press, 1978.

*Ballas, Shimon. *Arab Literature under the Shadow of War.* Tel Aviv: Am Oved Publishers, 1978.

Barthes, Roland. *Image, Music, Text.* Translated by Stephen Heath. New York: Hill and Wang, 1980.

———. *Mythologies.* Translated by Annette Lavers. New York: Hill and Wang, 1972.

———. *S/Z.* Translated by Richard Miller. Hill and Wang, 1974.

Benjamin, Walter. *Illuminations.* Translated by Hannah Arendt. London: Fontana Books, 1973.

———. *Understanding Brecht.* London: New Left Books, 1973.

*Ben-Simhom, Gabriel. "Theatrical Elements in the Daily Life of the North African Jewish Community." In *The Legacy of Jews of Spain and the Orient*. Jerusalem: Magnes, 1982.

*Ber Borochov, Dov. *Class Struggle and the Jewish Nation*. Jerusalem: Ber Borochov Book Publications, 1928.

Boulanger, Pierre, *Le Cinéma colonial*. Paris: Seghers, 1974.

Bourdieu, Pierre. *Distinction: A Social Critique of the Judgment of Taste*. Translated by Richard Nice. Cambridge: Harvard University Press, 1984.

Brecht, Bertold. *Brecht on Theater*. Translated by John Willett. New York: Hill and Wang, 1964.

Brooks, Peter. *The Melodramatic Imagination*. New York: Columbia University Press, 1985.

Buber, Martin, *I and Thou*. Translated by Ronald Gregor Smith. New York: Scribner's, 1957.

_____. *Israel and Palestine: The History of an Idea*. Translated by Stanley Goodman. London: East and West Library, 1952.

*Calderon, Nissim. *In a Political Context: Pour Essays on Writers*. Tel Aviv: HaKibbutz haMeuchad, 1980.

Césaire, Aimé. *Discourse on Colonialism*. Translated by Joan Pinkham. New York: Monthly Review Press, 1972.

Chomsky, Noam. *Peace in the Middle East? Reflections on Justice and Nationhood*. New York: Pantheon Books, 1974.

*Cohen, Adir. *An Ugly Face in the Mirror*. Tel Aviv: Reshafim Publishers, 1985.

Cohen, Sarah Blacher, ed. *From Hester Street to Hollywood*. Bloomington: Indiana University Press, 1986.

Critical Inquiry 12:1 (Autumn 1985). Special issue on "'Race,' Writing, and Difference."

Cuddihy, John Murray. *The Ordeal of Civility*. Boston: Beacon Press, 1974.

Daniel, Norman. *Islam and the West: The Making of an Image*. Edinburgh: Edinburgh University Press, 1966.

*Davidon, Ya'acov. *Fated Love*. Tel Aviv: Zmora-Bitan, 1983.

Davies, Miranda, ed. *Third World Second Sex*. London: Zed Press, 1983.

de Man, Paul. *Allegories of Reading*. New Haven: Yale University Press, 1979.

Derrida, Jacques. *Writing and Difference*. Translated by Alan Bass. Chicago: University of Chicago Press, 1978.

Deutscher, Isaac. *The Non-Jewish Jew*. Oxford: Oxford University Press, 1986.

Dorfman, Ariel. *The Empire's Old Clothes*. New York: Pantheon, 1983.

*Droyan, Niza. *And Not with a Magic Carpet*. Jerusalem: Ben Tzvi Institute for Research into the Communities of Israel in the East, 1982.

Eagleton, Terry. *Criticism and Ideology*. London: Verso, 1978.

_____. *Marxism and Literary Criticism*. Berkeley: University of California Press, 1976.

*Elisar, Eliyahu. *To Live with Jews*. Jerusalem: Markus, 1981.

*Elon, Amos. *The Isrealis*. Jerusalem: Adam, 1981.

Engelhardt, Tom. "Ambush at Kamikaze Pass." *Bulletin of Concerned Asian Scholars* 3:1 (Winter–Spring 1971).

Enzensberger, Hans Magnus. *The Consciousness Industry*. New York: Seabury Press, 1974.

Erens, Patricia. *The Jew in American Cinema*. Bloomington: Indiana University Press, 1984.

Fanon, Frantz. *Black Skin, White Masks.* Translated by Charles Lam Markmann. New York: Grove Press, 1967.

———. *A Dying Colonialism.* Translated by Haakon Chevalier. New York: Grove Press, 1967.

———. *The Wretched of the Earth.* Translated by Constance Farrington. New York: Grove Press, 1979.

Fernea, Elizabeth Warnock, ed. *Women and the Family in the Middle East: New Voices of Change.* Austin: University of Texas Press, 1985.

Feuerlicht, Roberta Strauss. *The Fate of the Jews.* New York: Times Books, 1983.

Fletcher, Angus. *Allegory—the Theory of a Symbolic Mode.* Ithaca: Cornell University Press, 1971.

*Flotzker, Seber. "The Career of *Sabra*." *Kolnoa* 2 (Summer 1974).

Foucault, Michel. *Discipline and Punish.* Translated by Alan Sheridan. New York: Vintage Books, 1979.

———. *The Order of Things: An Archeology of the Human Sciences.* New York: Random House, 1970.

Friar, Ralph E., and Natasha A. Friar. *The Only Good Indian: The Hollywood Gospel.* New York: Drama Book Specialists, 1972.

Friedman, Lester D. *Hollywood's Image of the Jew.* New York: Frederick Ungar Publishing, 1982.

Genette, Gérard. *Figures of Literary Discourse.* Translated by Alan Sheridan. New York: Columbia University Press, 1982.

———. *Narrative Discourse: an Essay in Method.* Translated by Jane E. Lewin. Ithaca: Cornell University Press, 1980.

*Gertz, Nurit. *Amos Oz.* Tel Aviv: Sifriat Poalim, 1980.

Gilman, Sander L. *Difference and Pathology: Stereotypes of Sexuality, Race, and Madness.* Ithaca: Cornell University Press, 1985.

———. *Jewish Self-Hatred.* Baltimore: Johns Hopkins University Press, 1986.

Goldberg, Judith N. *Laughter through Tears: The Yiddish Cinema.* Rutherford. N.J.: Fairleigh Dickinson University Press, 1982.

Goldman, Eric A. *Visions, Images, and Dreams: Yiddish Film Past and Present.* Ann Arbor: UMI Research Press, 1983.

Goldmann, Lucien. *Essays on Method in the Sociology of Literature.* Translated by William Q. Boelhower. St. Louis: Telos Press, 1980.

*Gordon, Aharon David. *The Nation and Work.* Jerusalem: HaSifria haTzionit, 1954.

*Gozansky, Tamar. *Formation of Capitalism in Palestine.* Haifa: Mifalim Universitaim Ie'Hotza'a la'Or, 1986.

Gramsci, Antonio. *Prison Notebooks.* Translated by Quintin Hoare and Geoffrey Nowell Smith. New York: International Publishers, 1983.

———. *Selections from Political Writings, 1910–1920.* Translated by John Mathews. New York: International Publishers, 1977.

Greimas, Julien. *Sémantique structurale.* Paris: Larousse, 1966.

Hacohen, Dr. Dvora and Rabbi Menahem. *One People: The Story of the Eastern Jews.* Introduction by Abba Eban. New York: Adama Books, 1986.

*Hakak, Lev. *Inferiors and Superiors.* Jerusalem: Kiryat Seffer, 1981.

Harlow, Barbara. *Resistance Literature*. New York and London: Methuen, 1987.

Hennebelle, Guy, and Janine Euvrard, eds. *Israel Palestine: que peut le cinéma?* A special issue of *L'Afrique Littéraire et Artistique* 47 (Summer 1978).

*Herzl, Binyameen Ze'ev. *The State of the Jews.* Jerusalem: HaSifriya haTzionit. 1973.

*Hess, Moshe. *Rome and Jerusalem*. Tel Aviv: Hevrat Omanut, 1938.

hooks, bell. *Feminist Theory: From Margin to Center*. Boston: South End Press, 1984.

Insdorf, Annette. *Indelible Shadows: Film and the Holocaust*. New York: Random House, 1983.

*Jabotinsky, Ze'ev Vladimir. *Hebrew State—the Solution of the Question of Jews*. Tel Aviv: T. Kop Publishing House, 1937.

*_____. *The Hebrew Accent*. Tel Aviv: haSefifer, 1930.

Jacob-Arzooni, Ora Gloria. *The Israeli Film: Social and Cultural Influences, 1912–1973*. New York: Garland Publishing, 1983.

Jameson, Fredric. *Marxism and Form: Twentieth-Century Dialectical Theories of Literature*. Princeton: Princeton University Press, 1971.

_____. *The Political Unconscious: Narrative as a Socially Symbolic Art*. Ithaca: Cornell University Press, 1981.

_____. "Third World Literature in the Era of Multinational Capitalism." *Social Text* 15 (Fall 1986): 65–88.

JanMohamed, Abdul. *Manichean Aesthetics*. Amherst: University of Massachusetts Press, 1983.

Jiryis, Sabri. *The Arabs in Israel*. Translated by Inea Bushnaq. New York: Monthly Review Press, 1976.

*Katz, Elihu, and Michael Gurevitz. *The Culture of Leisure in Israel*. Tel Aviv: Am Oved, 1973.

*Kaznelson, Berl. *Zionism as a Realization Movement*. Tel Aviv: HaMishmeret haTze'ira, 1945.

Kettle, Arnold. *An Introduction to the English Novel*, vols. 1 and 2. New York: Harper Torchbooks, 1960.

*Klausner, Margot. *The Dream Industry*. Herzliya: Herzliya Studios Publishing, 1974.

Kuhn, Annette. *Women's Pictures: Feminism and Cinema*. London: Routledge and Kegan Paul, 1982.

Leyda, Jay. *Kino: A History of the Russian and Soviet Film*. New York: Collier Books, 1973.

Lukács, George. *The Theory of the Novel: A Historico-Philosophical Essay on the Forms of Great Epic Literature*. Translated by Anna Bostock. Cambridge: MIT Press, 1975.

Manuel, Frank E., and Fritzie P. Manuel. *Utopian Thought in the Western World*. Cambridge: Harvard/Belknap, 1979.

*Matalon, Avraham. *The Hebrew Pronunciation in Its Struggle*. Tel Aviv: Hadar Publishing House, 1979.

Mattelart, Armand, and Seth Siegelaub, eds. *Communication and Class Struggle*. 2 vols. New York: International General, and Bagnolet, France: International Mass Media Research Center, 1983.

Maynard, Richard A. *Africa on Film: Myth and Reality*. Rochelle Park, N.J.: Hayden Book Company, 1974.

*Meir, Yossef. *The Zionist Movement and the Jews of Yemen*. Tel Aviv: Afrikim, 1983.

Memmi, Albert. *The Colonizer and the Colonized.* Boston: Beacon Press, 1967.

———. *Dominated Man.* Boston: Beacon Press, 1968.

———. *La Libération du juif.* Paris: Editions Gallimard, 1966.

*Menahem, Nahum. *Ethnic Tensions and Discrimination in Israel.* Ramat Gan: Rubin Advertisement, 1983.

Metz, Christian. *The Imaginary Signifier.* Translated by Celia Britton, Annwyl Williams, Ben Brewster, and Alfred Guzzetti. Bloomington: Indiana University Press, 1982.

———. *Langage et cinemá.* Paris: Librarie Larousse, 1971.

Michalak, Laurence. "Cruel and Unusual." A special issue of *ADC Issues* 19 (January 1984).

Niv, Yeshayahu. *The Bible and the Image: The History of Photography in the Holy Land, 1839–1899.* Philadelphia: University of Pennsylvania Press, 1985.

*Okansky, Yael. "Israeli Cinema Is Not a Cinema of Creators: A Conversation with Eli Tavor." *Kolnoa* 6/7 (Summer 1975).

Pinsker, Judah Leon. *Auto-Emancipation.* Jerusalem: HaHistadrut HaTzionit, 1952.

Poliakov, Leon. *The History of Anti-Semitism: From Mohammed to the Marranos.* Translated by Richard Howard. New York: Vanguard, 1973.

Rodinson, Maxime. *The Arabs.* Chicago: University of Chicago Press, 1981.

———. *Cult, Ghetto, and State.* London: Al Saqi Books, 1983.

———. *Israel: A Colonial-Settler State?* Translated by David Thorstad. New York: Monad Press, 1973.

———. *Israel and the Arabs.* New York: Penguin Books, 1982.

*Rubenstein, Amnon. *To Be Free People.* Tel Aviv: Schocken, 1977.

Said, Edward W. *Orientalism.* New York: Vintage, 1978.

———. "Orientalism Reconsidered." *Cultural Critique* 1 (1985).

———. *The Question of Palestine.* New York: Vintage, 1979.

———. *The World, the Text, and the Critic.* Cambridge: Harvard University Press, 1983.

Sayigh, Rosemary. *Palestinians: From Peasants to Revolutionaries.* London: Zed Press, 1979.

Scholem, Gershom G. *The Messianic Idea in Judaism and Other Essays on Jewish Spirituality.* New York: Schocken Books, 1971.

Screen Reader 1: Cinema/Ideology/Politics. London: Society for Education in Film and Television, 1977.

*Segev, Tom. *1949: The First Israelis.* Jerusalem: Domino Publications, 1984. Translation, New York: Free Press, 1986.

Shaheen, Jack. *The TV Arab.* Bowling Green, Ohio: Bowling Green State University Popular Press, 1984.

*Shaked, Gershon. *No Other Place.* Tel Aviv: Ha'Kibbutz Ha'Meuchad, 1983.

———. *Wave after Wave in Hebrew Literature.* Jerusalem: Keter Publishing House, 1985.

*Shavit, Ya'acov. *From Hebrew to Canaanite.* Jerusalem: Domino Press, 1984.

Shiblak, Abbas. *The Lure of Zion.* London: Al Saqi Books, 1986.

Shohat, Ella. "Sephardim in Israel." *Social Text* 19–20 (Spring–Summer 1988).

Shohat, Ella, and Robert Stam. "The Cinema after Babel: Language, Difference, Power." *Screen* 26:3 (May–August 1985): 35–58.

Sloterdijk, Peter. *Critique of Cynical Reason.* Minneapolis: University of Minnesota Press, 1987.

Smith, Barbara. *Towards a Black Feminist Criticism.* Trumansburg, N.Y.: Out and Out Books, 1977.

Smooha, Sammy. *Israel: Pluralism and Conflict.* Berkeley: University of California Press, 1978.

Snitow, Ann, Christine Stansell, and Sharon Thompson, eds. *Powers of Desire.* New York: Monthly Review Press, 1983.

*Stal, Avraham. *Ethnic Tensions and the People of Israel.* Tel Aviv: Am Oved, 1979.

Stam, Robert. *Reflexivity in Film and Literature: From Don Quixote to Jean Luc Godard.* Ann Arbor: UMI Press, 1985.

Stam, Robert, and Louise Spence. "Colonialism, Racism, and Representation." *Screen* 24:2 (March–April 1983): 2–20.

Steiner, George. *After Babel.* Oxford: Oxford University Press, 1978.

———. "Our Homeland, the Text." *Salmagundi* 66 (Winter–Spring 1985): 4–25.

Swirski, Barbara. *Daughters of Eve, Daughters of Lilith: On Women in Israel.* Givatayim: Second Sex Publishing House, 1984.

*Swirski, Shlomo. *Campus, Society, and State.* Jerusalem: Mifras Publishing House, 1982.

———. "Oriental Jews in Israel." *Dissent* 31:1 (Winter 1984).

*———. *Orientals and Ashkenazim in Israel.* Haifa: Makhbarot leMehkar u'le-Vikoret, 1981.

*Swirski, Shlomo, and Menahem Shushan. *Development Towns toward a Different Tomorrow.* Haifa: Yated, 1985.

Todorov, Tzvetan. *The Conquest of America.* Translated by Richard Howard. New York: Harper and Row, 1984.

Trachtenberg, Joshua. *The Devil and the Jews: The Medieval Conception of the Jew and Its Relation to Modern Anti-Semitism.* New York: Harper, 1943.

Uspensky, Boris. *A Poetics of Composition.* Berkeley: University of California Press, 1973.

Walzer, Michael. *Exodus and Revolution.* New York: Basic Books, 1985.

Weinstock, Nathan. *Zionism: False Messiash.* London: Iuk Links, 1979.

White, Hayden. *Metahistory: The Historical Imagination in Nineteenth Century Europe.* Baltimore: Johns Hopkins, 1973.

Williams, Raymond. *Marxism and Literature.* Oxford: Oxford University Press, 1977.

Xavier, Ismail. "Allegories of Underdevelopment: From the 'Aesthetics of Hunger' to the 'Aesthetics of Garbage.'" Ph.D. dissertation, New York University, 1982.

*Yoffe, A. B., ed. *The First Twenty Years.* Tel Aviv: Keren Tel Aviv leSifrut veOmanut and Hotza'at haKibbutz haMeuchad, 1980.

Name Index

General Index

tensions with the national, 276
See also: Eurocentrism; Orientalism
Critical Israeli cinema
  Arab-Jews in, 250, 301, 307, 319
  borders and checkpoint(s) in, 216, 260,
    274, 285, 287, 288, 294–295
  as the cinema of "all of Israel's citizens,"
    271
  as critical ethnography, 279
  dialogism in, 82, 281
  documentary as revisionist history in,
    202
  dystopic space in, 289
  masculinity in, 85, 270, 295
  as oral history, 279–280
  polyphonic, 203, 247, 253, 268–270,
    324
  representation of Palestine in, 253
  Zionist tropes in, 8
Cultural studies, 251, 266, 323–325
  Cinema studies, 324
  Gender critique in, 265
  Middle Eastern and, 31, 38, 69, 92,
    116, 132, 136, 140, 150, 152, 188,
    304, 261, 303–304
  relational approach to, 254

Diaspora/Diasporic
  Arab-, 306–307, 310, 312, 315,
    318–319, 324
  Arab-Jewish-, 50, 126, 249, 252, 261,
    265, 266, 296, 304, 306, 318
  European-, 20
  Feminized diasporic Jew, 254, 270
  films, 276–278
  Jewish-, 1–2, 5–7, 15–19, 24–32,
    69–70, 229–230, 236, 251, 255, 257,
    265–266
  as menacing heteroglossia, 188, 269
  Palestinian filmmakers in the, 230, 271,
    273, 277
  perspective(s), 253, 268
  rejection of the Diaspora Jew, 26, 31–32,
    36, 102, 186, 253, 268, 270, 295
  syncretism and, 2, 267, 300

and the Zionist "negation of exile," 253,
  270
Ethnic studies
  Asian-American studies, 323
  Black Studies, 323
  Jewish studies, 323
  Latino Studies, 323
  Native American studies, 323
  whiteness studies, 270
Eurocentrism
  Barbarism and, 54, 96
  as "civilizing mission," 13, 40, 253
  critique of, 250
  Enlightenment and, 2, 28, 34, 38, 69,
    71, 76, 81, 88, 92, 102, 188, 266
  epistemology of, 255, 266
  Meta-narrative of, 299
  Modernization and, 36, 108, 126, 251,
    254, 256, 266, 280, 290, 292, 299
  "ordeals of civility," 188–189
  Oriental Jews (Mizrahim) and, 5,
    68–70, 101, 105, 109, 124–125,
    134–135, 139–140, 153–154, 188,
    241–243, 245, 247
  Primitivism and, 2, 5, 68, 70, 101, 105,
    109, 124–125, 135, 139–140, 143,
    188, 241–247
  Progress and, 16, 23, 28, 36, 47, 69,
    107–108, 117, 168, 176, 253, 264,
    266, 289, 313
  Savagery and, 34, 254
  under/development and, 69, 94,
    108–109, 113, 124, 140–142
  universality/universalism and, 182, 185,
    216
  Zionist discourse and, 39, 50, 177,
    251–252, 254, 255–256, 265, 270,
    298, 302–304, 323
Exotic/Exoticism
  Arabs as, 45, 59, 67–68, 82, 85, 89, 234
  Bedouin as, 33, 34, 93–94, 289
  Folklore and, 66, 107, 110, 114, 116,
    122, 159, 310
  food and, 71

ועש עגי לו ר למ סבכ ני בכסב מ
ואני בכל אני נה לא לר א בכ אני ו
לו ניה ראי למ